BLESSED
HOPE

Daily Inspirations for
Your Spiritual Growth

KENDALL T. KERRIGAN SR.

WESTBOW
PRESS®
A DIVISION OF THOMAS NELSON
& ZONDERVAN

WestBow Press books may be ordered through booksellers or by contacting:

WestBow Press
A Division of Thomas Nelson & Zondervan
1663 Liberty Drive
Bloomington, IN 47403
www.westbowpress.com
844-714-3454

Scripture quotations are taken from the New King James Version. Copyright © 1982 by Thomas Nelson, Inc. Used by permission. All rights reserved.

ISBN: 979-8-3850-3409-3 (sc)
ISBN: 979-8-3850-3410-9 (e)

Library of Congress Control Number: 2024919950

Print information available on the last page.

WestBow Press rev. date: 10/24/2024

Dear Reader,

Jesus Christ is our only blessed hope, the Savior who offers a promise of eternal life to all who believe in Him and repent of their sins. Through His sacrifice on the cross, Jesus bridged the gap between humanity and God, providing a way for us to be forgiven and reconciled with our Creator. By turning away from sin and placing our faith in Him, we are granted the assurance of everlasting life—a life filled with His peace, joy, and presence forever. Jesus is not just a hope for the future but a present reality that transforms our lives, giving us the strength to live for Him each day.

Here is an example of a sinners prayer that you could pray to the Father with a contrite heart.

Heavenly Father,

I humbly confess that I am a sinner in need of Your grace and mercy. I believe that Your Son, Jesus Christ, died on the cross for my sins and rose again on the third day in fulfillment of the scriptures, defeating death and offering me the gift of eternal life. I ask for Your forgiveness, Lord, for all the wrongs I have done and the ways I have strayed from Your path.

From this day forward, I surrender my life to You. I am Yours, Lord. Please guide me, strengthen me, and help me to follow You each and every day. Fill me with Your Holy Spirit so that I may live a life that is pleasing to You, reflecting Your love and grace to those around me.

In Jesus' name, I pray.
Amen.

Rest assured in Christ Jesus!

Kendall T. Kerrigan Sr.
Pastor Calvary Chapel Pompano Beach

MORNING DEVOTION

Scripture: Proverbs 3:5-6
"Trust in the Lord with all your heart, and lean not on your own understanding; In all your ways acknowledge Him, And He shall direct your paths."

Reflection: As you begin your day, consider the profound wisdom in these verses. Life often presents us with situations that can be confusing and overwhelming. Our natural inclination is to rely on our own understanding and instincts. However, Proverbs 3:5-6 invites us to a deeper level of trust—one that involves surrendering our plans and worries to God. Trusting in the Lord with all your heart means giving Him your fears, uncertainties, and the areas of life you can't control. It's about acknowledging that His wisdom surpasses ours and that His plans for us are good.

Prayer: Heavenly Father, as I start this day, help me to trust You with all my heart. I surrender my plans and my worries to You. Guide my steps and give me the wisdom to follow Your path. Help me to lean not on my own understanding but to seek Your guidance in every decision I make. May Your presence be with me throughout the day, and may I bring glory to Your name in all I do. Amen.

Meditative Thought: Take a moment to write down any worries or decisions that are on your mind. Pray over each one, asking God for His guidance and trusting that He will make your path straight.

Scripture: Proverbs 3:5-6
"Trust in the Lord with all your heart, and lean not on your own understanding; In all your ways acknowledge Him, And He shall direct your paths."

Reflection: As the day draws to a close, reflect on how you trusted in the Lord today. Were there moments when you leaned on your own understanding rather than seeking God's guidance? Were there situations where you felt the peace that comes from submitting to Him? God's promise is clear: when we trust Him completely and acknowledge Him in all our ways, He will guide us. This evening, take comfort in knowing that God is in control and that He is faithful to lead you.

Prayer: Dear Lord, thank You for being with me throughout this day. I confess that there were moments when I relied on my own understanding instead of seeking Your wisdom. Forgive me and help me to trust You more fully. As I rest tonight, I submit my heart and my plans to You. Guide me and give me peace, knowing that You are making my path straight. Thank You for Your constant love and faithfulness. In Jesus' name, Amen.

Meditative Thought: Before you go to bed, take a few minutes to reflect on your day. Write down any instances where you felt God's guidance or where you struggled to trust Him. Offer these reflections to God in prayer, asking for greater trust and reliance on Him for tomorrow.

Scripture: Ephesians 6:11-12

"Put on the whole armor of God, that you may be able to stand against the wiles of the devil. For we do not wrestle against flesh and blood, but against principalities, against powers, against the rulers of the darkness of this age, against spiritual *hosts* of wickedness in the heavenly *places*."

Reflection: As you prepare for the day ahead, remember that we are engaged in a spiritual battle. The struggles you face are not merely physical or emotional; they are spiritual. Ephesians 6:11-16 reminds us to equip ourselves with the full armor of God. Each piece of this armor represents a crucial aspect of our faith and protection. The belt of truth holds everything together, the breastplate of righteousness protects our hearts, and the gospel of peace readies us to move forward with confidence. The shield of faith is our defense against the enemy's attacks. Begin your day by consciously putting on this armor, standing firm in God's strength and truth.

Prayer: Lord, as I start this day, help me to put on Your full armor. Equip me with truth, righteousness, peace, and faith. Protect me from the schemes of the enemy and give me the strength to stand firm in You. Help me to recognize the spiritual battles around me and to trust in Your power and protection. May I walk in Your victory today and always. In Jesus' name, Amen.

Meditative Thought: Visualize yourself putting on each piece of God's armor as you get ready for the day. Pray specifically for truth, righteousness, peace, and faith to guide and protect you in every situation you encounter.

Scripture: Ephesians 6:11-12
"Put on the whole armor of God, that you may be able to stand against the wiles of the devil. For we do not wrestle against flesh and blood, but against principalities, against powers, against the rulers of the darkness of this age, against spiritual *hosts* of wickedness in the heavenly *places*."

Reflection: As you wind down from your day, reflect on the spiritual battles you faced. Were there moments when you felt the attacks of the enemy? How did the armor of God help you to stand firm? The belt of truth, breastplate of righteousness, gospel of peace, and shield of faith are not just morning preparations but constant protections. By keeping them in place, you can extinguish the flaming arrows of doubt, fear, and temptation. This evening, thank God for His armor and for the strength He gave you to stand your ground.

Prayer: Heavenly Father, thank You for Your protection and strength throughout this day. Thank You for the armor You provide to withstand the enemy's attacks. Forgive me for any moments I relied on my own strength instead of Yours. Help me to remain vigilant and steadfast in Your truth, righteousness, peace, and faith. As I rest tonight, renew my spirit and prepare me for the battles of tomorrow. In Jesus' name, Amen.

Meditative Thought: Reflect on your day and identify moments where you felt spiritually challenged. Journal about how you applied each piece of God's armor and where you can improve. Pray for God's continued protection and guidance as you rest and for the upcoming day.

Scripture: Psalm 23:1-3

"The Lord *is* my shepherd; I shall not want. He makes me to lie down in green pastures; He leads me beside the still waters. He restores my soul; He leads me in the paths of righteousness for His name's sake. Yea, though I walk through the valley of the shadow of death, I will fear no evil; For You *are* with me; Your rod and Your staff, they comfort me."

Reflection: As you begin your day, take a moment to reflect on the profound assurance found in these verses. The imagery of the Lord as our shepherd is powerful and comforting. A shepherd is attentive, caring, and protective of his sheep. Similarly, God provides for us, ensuring that we lack nothing essential for our well-being.

Imagine starting your day in "green pastures" and beside "quiet waters." This speaks of peace, rest, and provision. No matter what challenges or tasks lie ahead, you can trust that God will guide you and refresh your soul. His guidance is always towards what is best for you, aligned with His perfect will and for His glory.

Prayer: Heavenly Father, thank You for being my Shepherd. As I start this day, help me to trust in Your provision and guidance. Lead me beside the quiet waters and refresh my soul with Your presence. Guide me along the right paths for Your name's sake. May everything I do today reflect Your love and faithfulness. Amen.

Meditative Thought: "The Lord is my shepherd; I lack nothing." Let this assurance carry you through your day, knowing that God is with you, providing and guiding every step of the way.

Scripture: Psalm 23:1-3
"The Lord *is* my shepherd; I shall not want. He makes me to lie down in green pastures; He leads me beside the still waters. He restores my soul; He leads me in the paths of righteousness for His name's sake. Yea, though I walk through the valley of the shadow of death, I will fear no evil; For You *are* with me; Your rod and Your staff, they comfort me."

Reflection: As the day comes to a close, reflect on the comforting promise that even in the darkest valleys, God is with you. There may have been moments today that were challenging or difficult, but the presence of God provides comfort and courage. His "rod and staff" symbolize His protection and guidance, ensuring you are never alone.

The imagery of a table prepared in the presence of enemies speaks of God's provision and blessing, even in the midst of adversity. Being anointed with oil signifies being chosen and blessed, while the overflowing cup represents abundance. As you end your day, remember that God's goodness and love are with you constantly, and His promise of eternal dwelling with Him offers peace and hope.

Prayer: Dear Lord, thank You for being with me throughout this day, especially during the difficult moments. Your presence is my comfort and strength. As I rest tonight, I am grateful for Your protection and provision. May Your goodness and love continue to follow me all the days of my life. Help me to rest in the assurance of Your eternal promise. Amen.

Meditative Thought: "Surely your goodness and love will follow me all the days of my life." Let this promise give you peace and comfort as you rest, knowing that God's love and goodness are with you always.

JANUARY 4

MORNING DEVOTION

Scripture: 1 Peter 5:6-7
"Therefore, humble yourselves under the mighty hand of God, that He may exalt you in due time, casting all your care upon Him, for He cares for you."

Reflection: As you begin your day, consider the call to humility and trust in these verses. Humbling ourselves under God's mighty hand means recognizing His sovereignty and our dependence on Him. It's an act of faith to surrender our plans, ambitions, and worries to God, trusting that He will lift us up at the right time.

Starting the day with this attitude can transform your perspective. Instead of carrying the weight of your anxieties, you can cast them onto God, who cares deeply for you. This act of casting your anxiety is a deliberate choice to trust God's care and provision. It's an acknowledgment that He is in control, and His timing is perfect.

Prayer: Heavenly Father, as I start this day, I choose to humble myself under Your mighty hand. I trust that You will lift me up in due time. I cast all my anxieties and worries onto You, knowing that You care for me deeply. Help me to walk in humility and trust throughout this day. Amen.

Meditative Thought: "Cast all your anxiety on him because he cares for you." Let this assurance guide your thoughts and actions today, freeing you from worry and filling you with peace.

Scripture: 1 Peter 5:6-7
"Therefore humble yourselves under the mighty hand of God, that He may exalt you in due time, casting all your care upon Him, for He cares for you."

Reflection: As the day draws to a close, reflect on how these verses have shaped your day. Did you find moments to humble yourself under God's mighty hand? Were you able to cast your anxieties onto Him? Evening is a good time to assess and realign your heart with God's word.

Humility involves recognizing where we've tried to control outcomes instead of trusting God. It's about admitting our need for His guidance and strength. Casting your anxieties on Him can bring a profound sense of relief, knowing that God cares deeply for you and is attentive to your needs. Trust that He has been with you throughout the day, lifting you up in His perfect timing.

Prayer: Lord, as I end this day, I come before You with a humble heart. I acknowledge the times I tried to handle things on my own and thank You for being with me through every moment. I cast my remaining anxieties and concerns onto You, trusting in Your care and provision. Thank You for lifting me up and sustaining me. Amen.

Meditative Thought: "Humble yourselves under God's mighty hand." As you rest tonight, let go of any lingering worries, and trust in God's loving care and perfect timing for your life.

Scripture: Isaiah 49:13

"Shout for joy, you heavens; rejoice, you earth; burst into song, you mountains! For the Lord comforts his people and will have compassion on his afflicted ones."

Reflection: As you begin your day, let the words of Isaiah 49:13 inspire you to start with a heart full of joy and gratitude. The heavens, earth, and mountains are called to rejoice and burst into song because of the Lord's comfort and compassion. These natural elements, often seen as silent witnesses to God's majesty, are personified to illustrate the depth of His love and care for us.

Consider the comfort and compassion God extends to His people. Whatever challenges you may face today, remember that the Lord is with you, ready to offer His comfort. His compassion is not just a distant, abstract idea but a tangible reality that can transform your day. Begin with praise and thanksgiving, knowing that God's presence goes before you.

Prayer: Heavenly Father, I join the heavens, earth, and mountains in shouting for joy and bursting into song this morning. Thank You for Your boundless comfort and compassion. As I face today's challenges, remind me of Your presence and fill my heart with joy and gratitude. Amen.

Meditative Thought: "For the Lord comforts his people and will have compassion on his afflicted ones." Let this truth be the foundation of your day, filling you with peace and joy.

Scripture: Isaiah 49:13

"Shout for joy, you heavens; rejoice, you earth; burst into song, you mountains! For the Lord comforts his people and will have compassion on his afflicted ones."

Reflection: As the day comes to a close, take time to reflect on how you have experienced God's comfort and compassion. This verse reminds us of the grandeur of creation rejoicing in God's goodness. Despite any struggles or afflictions, you faced today, God's promise of comfort remains steadfast.

Think back on moments where you felt God's presence and compassion. Perhaps it was a kind word from a friend, a moment of peace in prayer, or a small but significant blessing. As you prepare for rest, let the knowledge of God's unfailing compassion soothe any remaining anxieties or burdens. End your day with gratitude and peace, knowing that you are deeply loved and cared for.

Prayer: Lord, I thank You for Your comfort and compassion throughout this day. Even in moments of difficulty, You have been with me. As I rest tonight, help me to release any lingering worries and find peace in Your presence. Fill my heart with gratitude for Your unending love and care. Amen.

Meditative Thought: "Shout for joy, you heavens; rejoice, you earth; burst into song, you mountains!" Let the echo of creation's praise fill your heart as you rest, confident in God's compassionate care.

JANUARY 6

MORNING DEVOTION

Scripture: Hebrews 13:5-6
"Keep your lives free from the love of money and be content with what you have, because God has said, 'Never will I leave you; never will I forsake you.' So, we say with confidence, 'The Lord is my helper; I will not be afraid. What can mere mortals do to me?'"

Reflection: As you start your day, reflect on the powerful promise in these verses. The call to keep our lives free from the love of money and to be content with what we have is a challenge in today's materialistic world. However, the reason for this contentment is profound: God's constant presence. He has promised never to leave or forsake us.

This assurance allows us to face the day with confidence and courage. We don't need to fear because the Lord is our helper. Whatever challenges or uncertainties lie ahead, remember that God's presence is with you, providing strength and support. His help is greater than any fear or obstacle.

Prayer: Heavenly Father, as I begin this day, help me to keep my life free from the love of money and to be content with what I have. Thank You for Your promise to never leave me or forsake me. Fill me with confidence and courage, knowing that You are my helper. I will not be afraid, for You are with me. Amen.

Meditative Thought: "The Lord is my helper; I will not be afraid." Let this assurance guide your actions and thoughts today, giving you confidence and peace.

Scripture: Hebrews 13:5-6
"Keep your lives free from the love of money and be content with what you have, because God has said, 'Never will I leave you; never will I forsake you.' So we say with confidence, 'The Lord is my helper; I will not be afraid. What can mere mortals do to me?'"

Reflection: As the day comes to an end, reflect on how these verses have impacted your day. Did you find moments where you practiced contentment? Were you aware of God's presence and help throughout the day? The promise that God will never leave or forsake us is a source of profound comfort and peace.

Consider any moments of fear or anxiety you faced today. How did the knowledge of God's constant presence influence your response? As you prepare for rest, let go of any lingering worries or fears, and rest in the assurance that God is your helper. His presence is a constant source of strength, and His promises are unchanging.

Prayer: Lord, I thank You for Your unwavering presence and help throughout this day. As I rest tonight, I release any fears or anxieties into Your hands. Help me to find contentment in Your provision and to trust in Your promise that You will never leave or forsake me. Fill me with peace and confidence as I sleep, knowing that You are always with me. Amen.

Meditative Thought: "Never will I leave you; never will I forsake you." As you rest, let this promise be a source of peace and assurance, knowing that God's presence surrounds you always.

JANUARY 7

MORNING DEVOTION

Scripture: 1 Thessalonians 2:16-17
"Forbidding us to speak to the Gentiles that they might be saved, to fill up their sins always: for the wrath is come upon them to the uttermost. But we, brethren, being taken from you for a short time in presence, not in heart, endeavored the more abundantly to see your face with great desire."

Reflection: Good morning! As we start this new day, let us consider the commitment and love Paul had for the Thessalonian believers. Despite being forcibly separated from them, his heart remained connected to theirs, and he longed to see them face to face. This passage highlights the challenges and oppositions we may face in spreading the Gospel, but it also underscores the power of our spiritual bonds.

Paul's dedication, even amidst obstacles, encourages us to persevere in our own faith journeys. There will be times when we encounter resistance or when circumstances keep us apart from those we care about. Yet, through prayer and persistent efforts, we can continue to support and uplift each other.

Prayer: Heavenly Father, thank You for the gift of community and the bonds we share with our fellow believers. Help us to remain steadfast in our faith, even when faced with opposition. Grant us the perseverance to continue sharing Your love and message of salvation. As we go through this day, remind us of the importance of staying connected with those we love and supporting each other in our faith journeys. In Jesus' name, we pray. Amen.

Meditative Thought: Reflect on the people in your life who strengthen your faith. Take a moment to pray for them and consider how you can support and encourage them today, even if you are physically apart.

Scripture: 1 Thessalonians 2:16-17
"Forbidding us to speak to the Gentiles that they might be saved, to fill up their sins always: for the wrath is come upon them to the uttermost. But we, brethren, being taken from you for a short time in presence, not in heart, endeavored the more abundantly to see your face with great desire."

Reflection: Good evening! As the day winds down, let us reflect on Paul's unwavering dedication to the Thessalonian believers. Though physical separation was imposed on him, his heart and thoughts never wavered in their connection to the Thessalonians. This passage serves as a poignant reminder of the enduring strength of spiritual bonds.

Even when circumstances keep us apart from our loved ones or fellow believers, our spiritual connection remains intact.

Prayer: Dear Lord, thank You for the relationships and connections we have through You. As we prepare for rest tonight, we lift up those from whom we are separated, asking for Your protection and guidance over them. Help us always to strive to encourage and support one another, regardless of the physical distance. May our hearts remain united in Your love, and may we find ways to stay connected and uplift each other. In Jesus' name, we pray. Amen.

Meditative Thought: As you settle down for the night, think of those who are far from you. Offer a prayer for their well-being and consider reaching out to them tomorrow to share your love and encouragement.

JANUARY 8

MORNING DEVOTION

Scripture: Psalm 91:1-2
"He who dwells in the secret place of the Most High shall abide under the shadow of the Almighty. I will say of the Lord, 'He is my refuge and my fortress; my God, in Him I will trust.'"

Reflection: Good morning! As we rise to greet this new day, let us reflect on the profound assurance found in Psalm 91:1-2. This passage invites us to dwell in the secret place of the Most High, where we can find true rest and protection. By abiding under the shadow of the Almighty, we are shielded from life's storms and challenges.

The imagery of God as our refuge and fortress reminds us of His unwavering strength and protection. No matter what we face today, we can trust in God's promise to be our safe haven. Let us start this day with a heart full of trust, knowing that God is with us, guiding and protecting us through every moment.

Prayer: Heavenly Father, thank You for being our refuge and fortress. As we begin this day, help us to dwell in Your presence and trust in Your protection. Guide us through the challenges we may face and remind us of Your constant love and care. Let our hearts be filled with peace and confidence, knowing that we are safe under Your shadow. In Jesus' name, we pray. Amen.

Meditative Thought: Take a few moments this morning to breathe deeply and imagine yourself resting in God's protective embrace. Let this image fill you with peace and strength as you go about your day.

Scripture: Psalm 91:1-2

"He who dwells in the secret place of the Most High shall abide under the shadow of the Almighty. I will say of the Lord, 'He is my refuge and my fortress; my God, in Him I will trust.'"

Reflection: Good evening! As the day draws to a close, let us find comfort in the words of Psalm 91:1-2. Reflecting on our day, we recognize the moments where God's presence and protection were evident, whether in times of joy or challenges. Dwelling in the secret place of the Most High offers us a sanctuary of peace, no matter what we have encountered today.

The assurance that God is our refuge and fortress allows us to rest securely. As we prepare for rest, let us cast our worries and fears upon Him, trusting in His divine protection and care. Remember that in every situation, we are under the shadow of the Almighty, safe and secure in His love.

Prayer: Dear Lord, thank You for Your constant protection and for being our refuge and fortress. As we settle down for the night, we place our trust in You and rest in the knowledge of Your care. Help us to release our worries and find peace in Your presence. May we wake refreshed and ready to dwell in Your secret place once more. In Jesus' name, we pray. Amen.

Meditative Thought: As you lie down to sleep, envision yourself under the shadow of the Almighty, enveloped in His love and protection. Let this thought bring you peace and comfort, knowing that you are safe in His care.

JANUARY 9

MORNING DEVOTION

Scripture: Acts 4:12
"Nor is there salvation in any other, for there is no other name under heaven given among men by which we must be saved."

Reflection: Good morning! As we begin this new day, let us meditate on the powerful truth found in Acts 4:12. This verse reminds us of the exclusivity and sufficiency of Jesus Christ as our Savior. There is no other name, no other way, by which we can be saved. This truth is a cornerstone of our faith, providing us with assurance and clarity in a world full of uncertainty and competing voices.

The message of salvation through Jesus alone is both a comfort and a call to action. It comforts us because we know our salvation is secure in Christ, not dependent on our efforts or other means. It calls us to share this truth with others, to be witnesses of the transformative power of Jesus' name. As we go about our day, let this truth fill us with confidence and purpose.

Prayer: Heavenly Father, thank You for the gift of salvation through Your Son, Jesus Christ. Help us to remember that there is no other name under heaven by which we can be saved. Fill our hearts with gratitude and our minds with the assurance of this truth. Empower us to share this message with others, that they too may come to know the saving power of Jesus. In His name, we pray. Amen.

Meditative Thought: Take a moment to reflect on the significance of Jesus' name in your life. How has knowing Him as your Savior impacted you? Let this thought guide you as you interact with others today, sharing the love and truth of Christ.

Scripture: Acts 4:12
"Nor is there salvation in any other, for there is no other name under heaven given among men by which we must be saved."

Reflection: Good evening! As the day comes to a close, let us revisit the profound declaration in Acts 4:12. Throughout the day, we may have encountered various challenges, distractions, and opportunities. This verse brings us back to the core of our faith: the singular, saving power of Jesus Christ. Reflecting on this truth brings us peace and refocuses our hearts on what truly matters.

The exclusivity of salvation in Jesus is a profound gift. It assures us that our relationship with God is secured through Christ, not through our own merits or any other means. As we prepare to rest, let this assurance calm our minds and hearts. We can rest knowing that our salvation is firm and unshakeable, grounded in the powerful name of Jesus.

Prayer: Dear Lord, thank You for the unchanging truth that salvation is found in no other name but Jesus. As we reflect on this day, we are grateful for the assurance and peace this brings. Help us to rest tonight with the confidence that our salvation is secure in You. Strengthen our faith and prepare us to share this truth with others. In Jesus' name, we pray. Amen.

Meditative Thought: As you settle down for the night, contemplate the power and significance of Jesus' name. Let this thought bring you peace and security, knowing that your salvation is firmly anchored in Him. Rest in this assurance, and let it prepare you for a new day of living out your faith.

JANUARY 10

MORNING DEVOTION

Scripture: Isaiah 1:18
"Come now, and let us reason together," says the Lord, "Though your sins are like scarlet, they shall be as white as snow; though they are red like crimson, they shall be as wool."

Reflection: Good morning! As we start this new day, let us reflect on the invitation extended to us by the Lord in Isaiah 1:18. God beckons us to come and reason with Him, to engage in dialogue and reconciliation. Despite our sins staining us like scarlet or crimson, God offers us forgiveness and restoration. This verse reminds us of the transformative power of God's grace.

No matter how deeply we may have fallen, no sin is beyond the reach of God's mercy. His forgiveness is not just about erasing our sins but about transforming us completely, making us as pure as snow and as white as wool. Let this truth fill you with hope and gratitude as you embark on this new day.

Prayer: Heavenly Father, thank You for Your boundless mercy and grace. As we come before You this morning, we acknowledge our sins and shortcomings. Yet, we are filled with hope knowing that Your forgiveness is available to us. Help us to embrace Your offer of reconciliation and restoration. May Your grace transform us from within, making us new creations in You. In Jesus' name, we pray. Amen.

Meditative Thought: Take a moment to visualize yourself standing before God, with all your sins represented as scarlet or crimson stains. Now, envision God's cleansing and transforming touch, washing away those stains until you are as pure as snow. Let this image remind you of God's unfailing love and the power of His forgiveness.

Scripture: Isaiah 1:18

"Come now, and let us reason together," says the Lord, "Though your sins are like scarlet, they shall be as white as snow; though they are red like crimson, they shall be as wool."

Reflection: Good evening! As we conclude this day, let us reflect once again on the promise of forgiveness and restoration found in Isaiah 1:18. God's invitation to reason with Him is not limited to the morning but extends throughout the day and into the evening. No matter how the day has unfolded, God's grace remains available to us.

This verse reminds us that our sins, no matter how deep or how scarlet they may be, can be washed away by the blood of Jesus. As we prepare for rest, let us surrender our burdens and mistakes to God, knowing that He can make us clean and whole once again. May His promise of transformation bring peace to our hearts as we sleep.

Prayer: Dear Lord, as we come to the end of this day, we thank You for Your faithfulness and grace. We acknowledge our sins and failures, and we lay them before You, trusting in Your promise of forgiveness and restoration. Wash us clean, Lord, and renew our spirits as we sleep. May Your peace guard our hearts and minds throughout the night. In Jesus' name, we pray. Amen.

Meditative Thought: Before you sleep, take a few moments to reflect on the forgiveness and restoration God offers you. Allow yourself to release any guilt or shame you may be carrying and surrender it to God's cleansing love. Rest in the assurance that you are forgiven and made new in Christ.

JANUARY 11

MORNING DEVOTION

Scripture: James 1:12
"Blessed is the one who perseveres under trial because, having stood the test, that person will receive the crown of life that the Lord has promised to those who love him."

Reflection: Good morning! As we begin this day, let us meditate on the words of James 1:12. This verse reminds us of the blessings that come to those who endure trials with perseverance. In the midst of life's challenges and difficulties, our faith is tested. Yet, as we remain steadfast in our love for the Lord, we are promised the crown of life.

Trials and hardships are inevitable parts of life, but they also present opportunities for growth and refinement. Each trial we face is an opportunity to deepen our faith and trust in God's faithfulness. Let us approach this day with courage and resilience, knowing that our perseverance will ultimately lead to the fulfillment of God's promises in our lives.

Prayer: Heavenly Father, thank You for Your promise of blessings to those who persevere under trial. As we face the challenges of this day, grant us the strength and courage to endure with faith and patience. Help us to keep our eyes fixed on You, knowing that You are faithful to fulfill Your promises. May our love for You deepen as we trust in Your provision and guidance. In Jesus' name, we pray. Amen.

Meditative Thought: Consider a trial or challenge you are currently facing. How can you approach it with perseverance and faith, knowing that God is with you? Reflect on the ways God has helped you overcome trials in the past and draw strength from those experiences as you face today's challenges.

Scripture: James 1:12
"Blessed is the one who perseveres under trial because, having stood the test, that person will receive the crown of life that the Lord has promised to those who love him."

Reflection: Good evening! As we reflect on the events of this day, let us hold onto the promise of blessing found in James 1:12. Despite the trials and challenges we may have encountered, we are reminded that those who persevere under trial are blessed. Through our endurance, we demonstrate our love for the Lord and our trust in His promises.

Evening is a time for reflection and introspection. Let us consider the ways in which we have persevered today, even in the face of difficulty. Take comfort in the knowledge that your perseverance is not in vain; it is leading you closer to the fulfillment of God's promises in your life. May this assurance bring you peace as you rest tonight.

Prayer: Dear Lord, as we come to the close of this day, we thank You for Your faithfulness and the strength You have given us to persevere under trial. We acknowledge that our endurance is only possible through Your grace and power at work within us. Help us to rest tonight with the assurance that You are with us, guiding us through every trial we face. In Jesus' name, we pray. Amen.

Meditative Thought: Before you sleep, take a moment to thank God for His faithfulness in helping you persevere through today's trials. Reflect on one specific way you experienced His strength and presence. Let this reflection fill you with gratitude and confidence as you entrust tomorrow's challenges into God's hands.

JANUARY 12

MORNING DEVOTION

Scripture: Matthew 11:28
"Come to me, all you who are weary and burdened, and I will give you rest."

Reflection: Good morning! As we begin this day, let us reflect on the comforting invitation extended to us by Jesus in Matthew 11:28. In the midst of our weariness and burdens, Jesus offers us rest. This rest is not just physical but also spiritual and emotional—a deep, soul-rest that comes from surrendering our worries and cares to Him.

Life can often feel overwhelming, and we may find ourselves carrying heavy burdens of stress, anxiety, or responsibilities. Yet, Jesus reminds us that we don't have to bear these burdens alone. He invites us to come to Him, to lay down our burdens at His feet, and to find rest and refreshment in His presence. Let us accept His invitation today and experience the peace that only He can give.

Prayer: Gracious Lord, thank You for Your invitation to come to You and find rest. As we face the challenges of this day, we confess our weariness and burdens to You. We ask for Your strength to sustain us and Your peace to fill us. Help us to trust in Your promise of rest and to find comfort in Your presence. In Jesus' name, we pray. Amen.

Meditative Thought: Consider the burdens you are carrying today—whether they be physical, emotional, or spiritual. Visualize yourself surrendering these burdens to Jesus and allowing Him to carry them for you. Reflect on how this act of surrender brings you a sense of peace and rest as you begin your day.

Scripture: Matthew 11:28
"Come to me, all you who are weary and burdened, and I will give you rest."

Reflection: Good evening! As the day comes to a close, let us revisit the comforting words of Jesus in Matthew 11:28. Throughout the day, we may have encountered moments of weariness and burdens, both physical and emotional. Yet, Jesus assures us that in Him, we can find rest.

As we prepare for rest tonight, let us release the burdens we have carried throughout the day into Jesus' hands. Let us trust that He will provide the rest and refreshment our souls need. In His presence, we find peace that surpasses understanding, and in His embrace, we find solace for our weary hearts. May His promise of rest bring us comfort and assurance as we sleep tonight.

Prayer: Heavenly Father, we thank You for the rest and refreshment You offer us through Your Son, Jesus Christ. As we end this day, we surrender our weariness and burdens to You. We trust that You will give us the rest we need to face tomorrow with renewed strength and courage. May Your peace fill our hearts as we sleep, knowing that You are always with us. In Jesus' name, we pray. Amen.

Meditative Thought: Before you sleep, take a moment to reflect on the rest and refreshment you have found in Jesus today. How has His presence brought you comfort and peace amidst life's challenges? Allow these reflections to fill you with gratitude and trust as you rest in His care tonight.

Scripture: John 11:35
"Jesus wept."

Reflection: Good morning! As we begin this new day, let us reflect on the profound simplicity of John 11:35. In just two words, this verse encapsulates the depth of Jesus' humanity and compassion. Despite knowing that He would soon raise Lazarus from the dead, Jesus wept alongside Mary and Martha, sharing in their grief and pain.

Jesus' tears remind us of His empathy and understanding of the human experience. He doesn't stand aloof from our suffering but enters into it with us, offering His comfort and presence. As we face the challenges and uncertainties of this day, let us remember that Jesus understands our struggles intimately. He weeps with us in our sorrows and rejoices with us in our joys.

Prayer: Compassionate Lord, thank You for Your empathy and understanding. As we begin this day, we bring before You our joys and sorrows, knowing that You share in both. Help us to find comfort in Your presence and strength in Your compassion. May Your tears remind us of Your deep love for us and Your unwavering commitment to walk alongside us in every season of life. In Your name, we pray. Amen.

Meditative Thought: Take a moment to reflect on a situation in your life that brings you sorrow or grief. Imagine Jesus standing beside you, His eyes filled with tears, His heart breaking with yours. Allow His presence to bring you comfort and assurance, knowing that He understands and cares for you deeply.

Scripture: John 11:35
"Jesus wept."

Reflection: Good evening! As we come to the end of this day, let us once again reflect on the significance of Jesus' tears in John 11:35. In the midst of our busy lives and hectic schedules, it's easy to overlook the profound truth contained in these two words. Jesus, the Son of God, wept.

His tears remind us that our emotions are not foreign to Him. He understands the depth of our pain, the weight of our sorrows, and the intensity of our joys. He enters into our experiences with us, offering His comfort and compassion. As we prepare for rest tonight, let us find solace in the knowledge that Jesus walks with us through every trial and triumph.

Prayer: Loving Savior, as we end this day, we thank You for Your presence and compassion. We bring before You our joys and sorrows, our triumphs and trials. Help us to release our burdens into Your care and to find rest in Your embrace. May Your tears remind us of Your deep love for us and Your unwavering commitment to walk alongside us always. In Your name, we pray. Amen.

Meditative Thought: Before you sleep, visualize Jesus standing before you, His eyes filled with tears, His heart full of love for you. Reflect on the ways He has entered into your experiences today, sharing in your joys and sorrows. Allow His presence to bring you peace and comfort as you rest in Him tonight.

JANUARY 14

MORNING DEVOTION

Scripture: John 1:29
"The next day John saw Jesus coming toward him and said, 'Look, the Lamb of God, who takes away the sin of the world!'" - John 1:29

Reflection: Good morning! As we begin this new day, let us reflect on the powerful proclamation made by John the Baptist in John 1:29. John's declaration points to the central mission of Jesus—to be the Lamb of God who takes away the sin of the world. In this statement, we find the essence of Jesus' identity and purpose.

The imagery of Jesus as the Lamb of God is rich with meaning. It harkens back to the sacrificial system of the Old Testament, where lambs were offered as atonement for sin. Jesus, the perfect and spotless Lamb, offered Himself as the ultimate sacrifice for our sins, making a way for reconciliation with God. As we go about this day, let us remember the profound significance of Jesus' sacrifice and the freedom it brings us from sin.

Prayer: Heavenly Father, we thank You for sending Your Son, Jesus Christ, to be the Lamb of God who takes away the sin of the world. As we begin this day, we reflect on the magnitude of His sacrifice and the freedom it brings us. Help us to live in the light of this truth, embracing the forgiveness and redemption offered to us through Jesus. May His sacrifice inspire us to walk in righteousness and love. In His name, we pray. Amen.

Meditative Thought: Consider the weight of your sins and burdens. Visualize Jesus, the Lamb of God, taking them upon Himself and offering Himself as the perfect sacrifice for your sins. Allow this image to fill you with gratitude and awe as you start your day, knowing that through Jesus, you are forgiven and set free.

Scripture: John 1:29
"The next day John saw Jesus coming toward him and said, 'Look, the Lamb of God, who takes away the sin of the world!'"

Reflection: Good evening! As we conclude this day, let us once again reflect on the profound truth revealed in John 1:29. John the Baptist's declaration of Jesus as the Lamb of God reminds us of the sacrificial love that Jesus demonstrated for us on the cross. His sacrifice has the power to take away the sin of the world and bring us into reconciliation with God.

As we prepare for rest tonight, let us ponder the significance of Jesus' sacrifice for our lives. His death on the cross was not just a historical event but a personal demonstration of His love for each one of us. Through His sacrifice, we find forgiveness, redemption, and the hope of eternal life. May we rest tonight in the assurance of His love and the freedom He has secured for us.

Prayer: Gracious Lord, as we come to the end of this day, we thank You for the sacrifice of Your Son, Jesus Christ, who is the Lamb of God. We are grateful for His atoning sacrifice, which takes away our sins and brings us into communion with You. As we rest tonight, may Your love and grace surround us, filling us with peace and gratitude. In Jesus' name, we pray. Amen.

Meditative Thought: Before you sleep, take a moment to reflect on the love and sacrifice of Jesus, the Lamb of God. Consider the ways His sacrifice has impacted your life and transformed your relationship with God. Allow His love to wash over you and bring you peace as you rest in Him tonight.

Scripture: Luke 9:62
"Jesus replied, 'No one who puts a hand to the plow and looks back is fit for service in the kingdom of God.'"

Reflection: Good morning! As we embark on this new day, let us reflect on the challenging words of Jesus in Luke 9:62. This verse reminds us of the importance of wholehearted commitment and dedication in our journey of faith. Just as a farmer who plows a field must focus on what lies ahead and not look back, so too must we fix our eyes on Jesus and the call He has placed on our lives.

It can be easy to become distracted or discouraged by the past—by mistakes, failures, or missed opportunities. However, dwelling on the past can hinder our progress and effectiveness in serving God's kingdom. Jesus calls us to press forward with faith and determination, trusting in His grace to guide us and His strength to sustain us.

Prayer: Heavenly Father, as we begin this day, we confess that sometimes we are prone to looking back instead of pressing forward in faith. Help us to fix our eyes on Jesus, the author and perfecter of our faith, and to trust in Your guidance and provision for the journey ahead. Give us the strength and courage to serve You faithfully, without hesitation or regret. In Jesus' name, we pray. Amen.

Meditative Thought: Reflect on any areas of your life where you may be tempted to look back instead of moving forward in faith. Ask God to help you release any regrets, fears, or distractions that are hindering your progress. Visualize yourself pressing forward with determination, trusting in God's guidance and provision every step of the way.

Scripture: Luke 9:62
"Jesus replied, 'No one who puts a hand to the plow and looks back is fit for service in the kingdom of God.'"

Reflection: Good evening! As we bring this day to a close, let us once again reflect on the sobering words of Jesus in Luke 9:62. This verse serves as a reminder of the importance of wholehearted commitment and focus in our walk with God. Just as a farmer must keep his eyes fixed ahead while plowing a field, so too must we keep our eyes fixed on Jesus and His kingdom.

Looking back can hinder our progress and effectiveness in serving God's purposes. Whether it be dwelling on past mistakes or challenges that lie ahead. Tonight, let us surrender any tendencies to look back to God, trusting in His grace to cover our past and His guidance to lead us forward.

Prayer: Gracious God, as we conclude this day, we thank You for Your guidance and presence in our lives. Forgive us for the times when we have been tempted to look back instead of pressing forward in faith. Help us to trust in Your leading and provision for the journey ahead, knowing that You are always with us. Grant us the courage and strength to serve You faithfully, without hesitation or regret. In Jesus' name, we pray. Amen.

Meditative Thought: Before you sleep, take a moment to surrender any regrets, fears, or distractions from the past to God. Visualize yourself placing them at the foot of the cross, allowing God's grace to cover them completely. As you release the past, embrace the hope and freedom that comes from pressing forward in faith, knowing that God is with you every step of the way.

Scripture: Genesis 3:9
"But the Lord God called to the man, 'Where are you?'"

Reflection: Good morning! As we start this new day, let us

reflect on the profound question posed by God in Genesis 3:9. After Adam and Eve had eaten from the forbidden tree and hid from God, He called out to them, asking, "Where are you?" This question goes beyond physical location; it speaks to the state of their hearts and their relationship with God.

In our own lives, God continues to ask us this question: "Where are you?" He longs for us to be in close fellowship with Him, but sin and disobedience can lead us to hide from His presence. This morning, let us examine our hearts and consider our own spiritual posture. Are we drawing near to God, or are we hiding from Him? Let us respond to His call, seeking His presence and surrendering our hearts to Him anew.

Prayer: Heavenly Father, as we begin this day, we acknowledge that there are times when we hide from Your presence due to sin and disobedience. Forgive us for our shortcomings and draw us near to You once again. Help us to respond to Your call with open hearts, seeking Your presence and guidance in all that we do. May our lives be a reflection of Your grace and love. In Jesus' name, we pray. Amen.

Meditative Thought: Take a moment to reflect on your spiritual journey. Are there areas where you have been hiding from God? What steps can you take today to draw nearer to Him and cultivate a deeper relationship with Him?

Scripture: Genesis 3:9
"But the Lord God called to the man, 'Where are you?'"

Reflection: Good evening! As we bring this day to a close, let us once again reflect on the poignant question posed by God in Genesis 3:9. After Adam and Eve had sinned and hidden themselves from His presence, God called out to them, asking, "Where are you?" This question reveals God's desire for intimacy and relationship with His creation.

Throughout the day, we may have encountered moments of spiritual distance or disobedience in our own lives. Yet, even in those moments, God continues to call out to us, longing for us to return to Him. Tonight, let us take time to examine our hearts and respond to God's call. Let us confess any areas of sin or disobedience, surrendering them to God and seeking His forgiveness and grace.

Prayer: Gracious Lord, as we conclude this day, we thank You for Your relentless pursuit of us, even when we stray from Your presence. Forgive us for the times when we have hidden from You due to sin and disobedience. Help us to respond to Your call with humility and repentance, surrendering our hearts to You once again. May Your presence fill us with peace and assurance as we rest tonight. In Jesus' name, we pray. Amen.

Meditative Thought: Before you sleep, take a moment to reflect on God's unwavering love and grace. Consider His call to you, asking, "Where are you?" Allow this question to prompt introspection and confession, surrendering any areas of sin or disobedience to Him. Rest in the assurance of His forgiveness and presence as you sleep tonight.

Scripture: Deuteronomy 26:11
"Then you and the Levites and the foreigners residing among you shall rejoice in all the good things the Lord your God has given to you and your household."

Reflection: Good morning! As we begin this new day, let us reflect on the call to rejoice found in Deuteronomy 26:11. This verse instructs the Israelites, along with the Levites and foreigners among them, to rejoice in all the good things that the Lord has given them and their households. It is a reminder to express gratitude and celebrate God's blessings together as a community.

In our own lives, it's easy to become focused on the challenges and struggles we face, overlooking the many blessings and provisions that God has bestowed upon us. This morning, let us cultivate a spirit of gratitude and rejoicing, recognizing the abundant goodness of God in our lives. Let us rejoice not only in our blessings but also in the opportunity to share in the joy of others within our community.

Prayer: Heavenly Father, we thank You for the abundance of blessings You have poured out upon us and our households. As we begin this day, help us to cultivate hearts of gratitude and rejoicing. May we recognize Your goodness in every aspect of our lives and share in the joy of our community. Open our eyes to the blessings around us, and fill our hearts with thanksgiving. In Jesus' name, we pray. Amen.

Meditative Thought: Take a moment to reflect on the blessings God has bestowed upon you and your household. Consider the ways He has provided for you, protected you, and shown His love to you. Allow these reflections to fill you with gratitude and joy as you start your day, and look for opportunities to share that joy with others.

Scripture: Deuteronomy 26:11
"Then you and the Levites and the foreigners residing among you shall rejoice in all the good things the Lord your God has given to you and your household."

Reflection: Good evening! As we come to the end of this day, let us once again reflect on the call to rejoice found in Deuteronomy 26:11. This verse reminds us of the importance of celebrating God's blessings and expressing gratitude for His goodness in our lives. It is a reminder that joy is not meant to be experienced in isolation but shared within our community.

As you reflect on the events of today, consider the ways in which God has blessed you and your household. Take a moment to give thanks for His provisions, protections, and the moments of joy He has granted you.

Prayer: Gracious God, as we conclude this day, we thank You for the abundance of blessings You have bestowed upon us and our households. We rejoice in Your goodness and express gratitude for Your provision and protection. Help us to share this joy with others within our community, spreading the light of Your love to those around us. May our hearts overflow with thanksgiving as we rest tonight. In Jesus' name, we pray. Amen.

Meditative Thought: Before you sleep, take a moment to recount the blessings and joys you experienced today. Reflect on the ways God has shown His goodness to you and your household. Allow these reflections to fill you with gratitude and joy, and offer a prayer of thanks to God for His abundant blessings in your life.

JANUARY 18

MORNING DEVOTION

Scripture: Psalm 29:2
"Ascribe to the Lord the glory due his name; worship the Lord in the splendor of his holiness."

Reflection: Good morning! As we begin this new day, let us meditate on the words of Psalm 29:2. This verse calls us to ascribe glory to the Lord and worship Him in the splendor of His holiness. It reminds us of the greatness and majesty of God and invites us to respond in awe and reverence.

In the busyness of life, it's easy to lose sight of the holiness and glory of God. Yet, in moments of worship and reflection, we are reminded of His greatness and goodness. This morning, let us set aside time to worship the Lord, acknowledging His sovereignty over our lives and the world around us. May our worship be a reflection of the splendor of His holiness.

Prayer: Heavenly Father, we come before You this morning to worship and adore You. You are worthy of all glory and honor, and we ascribe to You the praise due Your name. Help us to recognize Your holiness and greatness afresh today. May our worship be pleasing to You, and may it draw us closer to Your presence. In Jesus' name, we pray. Amen.

Meditative Thought: Take a moment to reflect on the holiness and greatness of God. Consider His attributes—His love, mercy, power, and faithfulness. How does contemplating His holiness inspire you to worship Him more fully? Allow these thoughts to guide your heart as you begin your day.

Scripture: Psalm 29:2
"Ascribe to the Lord the glory due his name; worship the Lord in the splendor of his holiness."

Reflection: Good evening! As we bring this day to a close, let us once again reflect on the words of Psalm 29:2. This verse reminds us of the importance of worshiping the Lord and acknowledging His holiness. Even in the midst of our daily activities, it is essential to pause and offer Him the praise and adoration He deserves.

As you prepare for rest tonight, take a moment to reflect on the ways you have worshiped the Lord throughout the day. Have you acknowledged His presence and sovereignty in your thoughts and actions? Have you ascribed to Him the glory due His name? Let this verse prompt you to offer a prayer of worship and gratitude to God before you sleep.

Prayer: Gracious God, as we conclude this day, we thank You for the opportunity to worship and adore You. You are holy and deserving of all glory and honor. Forgive us for the times when we have neglected to acknowledge Your greatness and majesty. Tonight, we offer You our worship and praise, knowing that You are worthy of it all. In Jesus' name, we pray. Amen.

Meditative Thought: Before you sleep, take a moment to offer a prayer of worship and gratitude to God. Reflect on His holiness and greatness, and thank Him for His presence and provision throughout the day. Let your heart be filled with awe and reverence as you rest in His love and care tonight.

Scripture: Psalm 90:12
"Teach us to number our days, that we may gain a heart of wisdom."

Reflection: In this verse, we are invited to contemplate the brevity and preciousness of our lives. Time is a gift from God, and each day is an opportunity to grow in wisdom and live in alignment with His will. When we recognize the finite nature of our time on earth, we are compelled to prioritize what truly matters—deepening our relationship with God and serving others with love and compassion.

Prayer: Heavenly Father, teach us to value each moment you have given us on this earth. Help us to use our time wisely, seeking first your kingdom and righteousness. Grant us the wisdom to discern your will and the courage to follow it faithfully. May our lives be a reflection of your love and grace, shining brightly in a world filled with darkness. Amen.

Meditative Thought: As you begin your day, take a moment to reflect on the gift of time. How will you choose to invest it today? Will you prioritize activities that nourish your soul and draw you closer to God? Allow Psalm 90:12 to guide your thoughts and actions, reminding you of the importance of living with intention and purpose.

Scripture: Psalm 90:12
"Teach us to number our days, that we may gain a heart of wisdom."

Reflection: As the day draws to a close, let us reflect on how we have spent our time. Have we used each moment wisely, or have we allowed distractions to lead us astray? Psalm 90:12 reminds us of the importance of cultivating a heart of wisdom, which comes from recognizing the fleeting nature of life and seeking God's guidance in all that we do.

Prayer: Lord, as we come to the end of another day, we thank you for the time you have given us. Forgive us for the moments we have wasted, and help us to make the most of the opportunities you provide. Grant us wisdom as we reflect on our actions and choices, and guide us in the paths of righteousness. May we rest tonight knowing that you are faithful, and your mercies are new every morning. Amen.

Meditative Thought: Take a few moments to review your day with honesty and humility. Are there areas where you could have used your time more wisely? What lessons have you learned that you can carry forward into tomorrow? Allow Psalm 90:12 to shape your reflections, inspiring you to live each day with purpose and intention, guided by the wisdom of God.

JANUARY 20

MORNING DEVOTION

Scripture: Psalm 51:2
"Wash away all my iniquity and cleanse me from my sin."

Reflection: In this verse, we find a plea for cleansing and renewal. The psalmist acknowledges their need for God's forgiveness and asks for purification from their sins. As we begin our day, it's essential to recognize our own shortcomings and to come before God with humility, seeking His mercy and grace. Just as the psalmist seeks cleansing, we too can approach God with honesty, knowing that He is ready to forgive and restore us.

Prayer: Heavenly Father, we come before you with contrite hearts, acknowledging our need for your forgiveness. Wash away our sins and cleanse us from all unrighteousness. Help us to let go of the burdens of guilt and shame, knowing that you offer us redemption and restoration through your Son, Jesus Christ. Grant us the strength to walk in your ways today, empowered by your love and grace. Amen.

Meditative Thought: As you start your day, reflect on the power of God's forgiveness. How does it feel to know that you are cleansed and made new through His mercy? Allow Psalm 51:2 to remind you of the freedom found in surrendering your sins to God and experiencing His transforming love.

Scripture: Psalm 51:2
"Wash away all my iniquity and cleanse me from my sin."

Reflection: As the day comes to a close, let us reflect on our actions and attitudes. Have we fallen short of God's standards? Have we harbored thoughts or engaged in behaviors that do not honor Him? Psalm 51:2 invites us to come before God once again, acknowledging our need for cleansing and renewal. Just as in the morning, we can approach Him with humility and repentance, confident in His willingness to forgive and restore us.

Prayer: Lord, as we prepare to rest tonight, we confess our sins before you. Wash away all traces of iniquity from our hearts and minds. Help us to surrender ourselves fully to your cleansing power, knowing that you are faithful and just to forgive us. Grant us peaceful sleep tonight, knowing that we are forgiven and loved by you. Amen.

Meditative Thought: Take a few moments to review your day in the light of God's mercy and grace. Are there areas where you need His cleansing touch? How can you surrender more fully to His transforming work in your life? Allow Psalm 51:2 to guide your reflections and renew your commitment to living a life that honors God in all things.

JANUARY 21

MORNING DEVOTION

Scripture: John 3:16
"For God so loved the world that he gave his one and only Son, that whoever believes in him shall not perish but have eternal life."

Reflection: As we begin our day, John 3:16 reminds us of the profound love God has for each of us. The gift of Jesus Christ is a testament to the lengths to which God will go to save us and bring us into eternal life. This divine love is not just a distant theological concept but a daily reality that can transform our lives. Knowing that we are deeply loved and valued by our Creator can give us the strength and confidence to face the challenges of the day. Let this truth sink in and shape how you view yourself and others. God's love is the foundation of our faith and the reason we can live with hope and joy.

Prayer: Heavenly Father, thank you for your incredible love that you demonstrated by giving your only Son for us. Help us to grasp the depth of this love and let it fill our hearts with gratitude and joy. As we go about our day, may we reflect your love to those around us, showing kindness, compassion, and grace. Empower us to live in a way that honors you and spreads your love to a world in need. Amen.

Meditative Thought: As you begin your day, meditate on the fact that you are deeply loved by God. How can this knowledge influence your actions, decisions, and interactions today? Consider ways you can share this love with others, bringing hope and light into their lives.

Scripture: John 3:16
"For God so loved the world that he gave his one and only Son, that whoever believes in him shall not perish but have eternal life."

Reflection: As the day draws to a close, John 3:16 provides a comforting reminder of God's eternal love and the promise of everlasting life through faith in Jesus Christ. Reflecting on this verse can help us find peace and assurance, even if the day has been filled with challenges or failures. God's love is unchanging and steadfast, offering us hope and rest. We can end the day knowing that our ultimate destiny is secure in Him. This verse invites us to rest in the knowledge that God's love for us is greater than any mistake or shortcoming.

Prayer: Lord, as we end this day, we thank you for your boundless love and the gift of eternal life through your Son, Jesus Christ. Forgive us for the times we have fallen short today, and cleanse our hearts and minds. Help us to rest in your love and to wake up refreshed and ready to serve you anew. Thank you for the assurance that comes from believing in you. May we continually grow in our faith and understanding of your love. Amen.

Meditative Thought: Before you sleep, meditate on the depth of God's love for you. How has this love manifested in your life today? Allow the assurance of His eternal promise to bring you peace and rest. Reflect on how you can deepen your faith and trust in His love in the days to come.

Scripture: Psalm 119:89
"Forever, O LORD, thy word is settled in heaven."

Reflection: As we start our day, Psalm 119:89 reminds us of the eternal and unchanging nature of God's Word. In a world that is often chaotic and unpredictable, the stability and reliability of God's Word provide us with a solid foundation. Knowing that His Word is forever settled in heaven gives us confidence and peace, allowing us to face the day's challenges with assurance. God's promises are steadfast, and His teachings are timeless. Let this truth guide our thoughts and actions today, grounding us in His eternal wisdom.

Prayer: Heavenly Father, thank You for Your Word, which is forever settled in heaven. As we embark on this new day, help us to anchor our hearts and minds in Your eternal truths. Guide us in our decisions and interactions, that we may reflect Your love and wisdom. Fill us with peace and confidence, knowing that Your Word remains unchanged and trustworthy. May our lives be a testimony to Your faithfulness and grace. Amen.

Meditative Thought: As you begin your day, meditate on the constancy of God's Word. How does the unchanging nature of His promises provide you with stability and confidence? Consider how you can apply the truths of Scripture in your daily activities, allowing them to shape your actions and attitudes.

Scripture: Psalm 119:89
"Forever, O LORD, thy word is settled in heaven."

Reflection: As the day comes to a close, Psalm 119:89 invites us to reflect on the enduring nature of God's Word. Throughout the day, we have encountered various situations and challenges, but God's Word has remained our constant guide and source of strength. This verse reassures us that, despite the uncertainties we may face, God's promises are unchanging and His guidance is ever-present. As we review our day, we can find peace and rest in the knowledge that God's Word is firmly established and will continue to be our foundation.

Prayer: Lord, as we end this day, we thank You for the steadfastness of Your Word. Throughout the day's ups and downs, Your Word has been a source of comfort and guidance. Forgive us for any moments when we have strayed from Your teachings. Help us to rest tonight with the assurance that Your Word is forever settled in heaven. Renew our strength and prepare us for tomorrow, that we may continue to live in accordance with Your will. Amen.

Meditative Thought: Before you sleep, take a moment to meditate on the enduring nature of God's Word. How did Scripture guide and support you today? Reflect on the stability and peace that comes from trusting in God's unchanging promises. Let this assurance fill you with peace as you rest, knowing that His Word is a firm foundation for your life.

Scripture: Psalm 34:18
"The Lord is near to those who have a broken heart, and saves such as have a contrite spirit."

Reflection: As we begin our day, Psalm 34:18 offers a comforting reminder of God's closeness to us, especially in times of heartache and sorrow. Life can be filled with challenges and moments of deep emotional pain, but this verse assures us that God is near to us in those times. He sees our brokenness and draws close to provide comfort and healing. Starting our day with this knowledge helps us face the day with hope, knowing that no matter what we encounter, God is with us, ready to heal our broken hearts and lift our spirits.

Prayer: Heavenly Father, thank You for Your promise to be near to those who have a broken heart. As we start this day, we ask for Your presence to fill us with hope and strength. Comfort us in our times of sorrow and give us the courage to face the challenges ahead. Help us to lean on Your love and grace, trusting that You are always near, ready to heal and save. May we carry this assurance with us throughout the day, bringing Your light to others who may also be hurting. Amen.

Meditative Thought: As you begin your day, reflect on the nearness of God in your moments of brokenness. How can this assurance of His presence bring you comfort and strength? Consider how you can be a source of God's love and comfort to those around you today, showing compassion and understanding to those who are hurting.

Scripture: Psalm 34:18
"The Lord is near to those who have a broken heart and saves such as have a contrite spirit."

Reflection: As the day draws to a close, Psalm 34:18 invites us to reflect on God's comforting presence throughout our day. No matter what we have faced, whether moments of joy or times of sorrow, God has been near, especially in our brokenness. This verse reassures us that He not only sees our pain but also offers salvation and healing to those with a contrite spirit. As we prepare to rest, we can find peace in knowing that God's presence is a constant source of comfort and strength, guiding us through our darkest moments.

Prayer: Lord, as we end this day, we thank You for Your unwavering presence and comfort. You have been near to us in our moments of brokenness, providing healing and hope. We ask for Your continued presence as we rest, bringing peace to our hearts and minds. Help us to release our burdens to You and trust in Your saving grace. May we wake refreshed, knowing that You are always near, ready to heal and restore. Amen.

Meditative Thought: Before you sleep, take a moment to meditate on God's nearness in your times of brokenness. Reflect on how He has comforted and sustained you throughout the day. Allow the assurance of His presence to bring you peace as you rest, knowing that He is always close, ready to heal and save. Consider how you can trust Him more deeply with your heart and the hearts of those around you.

Scripture: Revelation 22:14
"Blessed are those who do His commandments, that they may have the right to the tree of life and may enter through the gates into the city."

Reflection: As we start our day, Revelation 22:14 offers a vision of the ultimate blessing for those who follow God's commandments. This verse promises us access to the tree of life and entrance into the holy city, symbolizing eternal life and communion with God. Our daily actions and choices matter deeply in God's eyes, and living in obedience to His Word leads to profound spiritual blessings. This verse encourages us to begin our day with a commitment to follow God's ways, seeking His guidance and strength to live a life that honors Him.

Prayer: Heavenly Father, thank You for the promise of blessing for those who follow Your commandments. As we start this new day, we ask for Your guidance and strength to walk in obedience to Your Word. Help us to make choices that honor You and reflect Your love. Fill our hearts with the desire to follow Your will, and grant us the courage to live out our faith boldly. May our lives be a testimony to Your goodness and grace, leading others to know the blessings of following You. Amen.

Meditative Thought: As you begin your day, reflect on the promise of eternal life and the blessing of obedience to God's commandments. How can you live out His Word in your daily actions and decisions? Consider ways to align your choices with His will, seeking to honor Him in all that you do.

Scripture: Revelation 22:14
"Blessed are those who do His commandments, that they may have the right to the tree of life, and may enter through the gates into the city."

Reflection: As the day comes to an end, Revelation 22:14 reminds us of the eternal blessings that await those who faithfully follow God's commandments. Reflecting on our day, we can assess how we lived according to His Word and where we might seek His forgiveness and strength to do better. This verse reassures us of the ultimate reward for our obedience—a place in God's eternal kingdom. It encourages us to remain steadfast in our faith, knowing that our efforts to live righteously are not in vain but are part of our journey toward eternal life with God.

Prayer: Lord, as we conclude this day, we thank You for Your Word and the promise of eternal blessings for those who follow Your commandments. Forgive us for any moments when we failed to live according to Your will, and grant us the strength to do better tomorrow. Help us to end this day with a heart full of gratitude for Your grace and a renewed commitment to walk in obedience to Your Word. May we rest in the assurance of Your promises, looking forward to the eternal life You have prepared for us. Amen.

Meditative Thought: Before you sleep, meditate on the eternal blessings promised to those who follow God's commandments. Reflect on how you lived out His Word today and where you can grow in obedience. Allow the assurance of His promises to bring you peace and rest, knowing that your faithfulness leads to eternal life with God. Consider how you can continue to align your life with His will, seeking to honor Him in all things.

JANUARY 25

MORNING DEVOTION

Scripture: 1 John 5:1
"Whoever believes that Jesus is the Christ is born of God, and everyone who loves Him who begot also loves him who is begotten of Him."

Reflection: As we begin our day, 1 John 5:1 reminds us of the fundamental truth of our faith: belief in Jesus as the Christ signifies our rebirth as children of God. This profound transformation not only redefines our identity but also calls us to a life of love. Loving God naturally extends to loving others who are also born of Him. This morning, let us focus on living out this love in our actions and interactions, reflecting the divine love that has been lavished upon us. By embracing this truth, we can face the day with a renewed sense of purpose and unity with our fellow believers.

Prayer: Heavenly Father, thank You for the gift of faith in Jesus Christ and the new birth it brings. Help us to live out this truth today by loving others as You have loved us. Fill our hearts with Your love and let it overflow in our actions and words. May we reflect Your grace and kindness to everyone we encounter, and strengthen our bond with our fellow believers. Guide us in our journey today, keeping our hearts aligned with Your will. Amen.

Meditative Thought: As you start your day, meditate on the fact that believing in Jesus makes you a child of God. How does this identity shape your view of yourself and others? Consider practical ways you can express love to those around you today, reflecting the divine love you have received.

Scripture: 1 John 5:1
"Whoever believes that Jesus is the Christ is born of God, and everyone who loves Him who begot also loves him who is begotten of Him."

Reflection: As the day comes to a close, 1 John 5:1 invites us to reflect on how our belief in Jesus and our identity as children of God have influenced our actions today. Have we lived out the love that comes from being born of God? This verse reminds us that our faith is intrinsically linked to our love for others, especially those who share our faith. As we review our day, let's consider how we have shown love and how we can grow in this aspect. Ending the day with this reflection helps us to realign ourselves with God's will and prepare for a new day of faithful living.

Prayer: Lord, as we end this day, we thank You for the new birth we have in Jesus Christ. We reflect on the ways we have shown love to others today and ask for Your forgiveness for any moments we have fallen short. Help us to grow in our love for others, especially our fellow believers. Fill our hearts with Your love and help us to extend it more fully. As we rest tonight, renew our spirits and prepare us for another day of living out our faith. Thank You for Your constant presence and guidance. Amen.

Meditative Thought: Before you sleep, take a moment to meditate on the love you have experienced and expressed today. How has your belief in Jesus influenced your interactions? Reflect on ways to deepen your love for others, aligning more closely with your identity as a child of God. Let this reflection bring you peace and prepare you for a new day of faithful living.

Scripture: 2 Peter 1:18
"And we heard this voice which came from heaven when we were with Him on the holy mountain."

Reflection: As we start our day, 2 Peter 1:18 invites us to remember the profound moments of divine revelation in our lives. Peter recalls hearing God's voice on the holy mountain, a moment of undeniable divine presence and affirmation of Jesus' divinity. This verse encourages us to seek and cherish our encounters with God, whether they come through prayer, Scripture, or moments of deep spiritual insight. Beginning our day with an openness to hear God's voice can transform our ordinary experiences into holy moments where we feel His presence and guidance.

Prayer: Heavenly Father, thank You for the moments when You make Your presence known to us. As we start this day, open our hearts and minds to hear Your voice. Help us to be attentive to Your guidance and to recognize Your hand at work in our lives. May our experiences today be filled with the awareness of Your divine presence, and may we carry that sense of holiness into everything we do. Strengthen our faith and deepen our relationship with You. In Jesus' name, we pray. Amen.

Meditative Thought: As you begin your day, reflect on moments when you have felt God's presence and heard His voice. How can you cultivate a greater awareness of His presence today? Consider starting a journal to record these divine encounters, helping you to remember and cherish them.

Scripture: 2 Peter 1:18
"And we heard this voice which came from heaven when we were with Him on the holy mountain."

Reflection: As the day draws to a close, 2 Peter 1:18 encourages us to reflect on our day and recognize moments when God might have spoken to us. Just as Peter recalled hearing God's voice on the holy mountain, we too can find sacred moments in our everyday lives. Reflecting on these encounters helps us to appreciate God's ongoing work in our lives and strengthens our faith. Tonight, let us look back and thank God for His presence and guidance throughout the day, recognizing that each day holds opportunities to experience His voice and His touch.

Prayer: Lord, as we end this day, we thank You for Your presence and guidance. Help us to see and remember the moments today when You were near and spoke to our hearts. We are grateful for the ways You reveal Yourself to us, and we ask for Your continued guidance and presence in our lives. As we rest, fill us with peace and a deeper sense of Your love. Prepare us for a new day where we can continue to seek and hear Your voice. In Jesus' name, we pray. Amen.

Meditative Thought: Before you sleep, take a moment to meditate on the ways God might have spoken to you today. How did you sense His presence and guidance? Reflect on how you can stay attuned to His voice and carry the awareness of His presence into tomorrow. Consider sharing your experiences with a trusted friend or in a faith community, strengthening one another through shared testimonies of God's work.

JANUARY 27

MORNING DEVOTION

Scripture: James 4:7
"Therefore, submit to God. Resist the devil and he will flee from you."

Reflection: As we start our day, James 4:7 offers a clear directive: submit to God and resist the devil. This verse reminds us of the importance of placing ourselves under God's authority and seeking His will in all we do. By submitting to God, we align our hearts and minds with His purpose, drawing on His strength to stand firm against the temptations and challenges we face. Starting the day with this mindset empowers us to navigate our daily lives with a sense of purpose and protection, knowing that as we resist the devil, he will flee from us.

Prayer: Heavenly Father, as we begin this day, we submit ourselves to Your authority and seek to follow Your will. Help us to resist the temptations and challenges that come our way, knowing that Your strength is sufficient for us. Guide our actions and thoughts, and protect us from the schemes of the enemy. Fill us with Your Spirit, that we may walk in obedience and faithfulness to You. Thank You for the promise that as we resist the devil, he will flee from us. In Jesus' name, we pray. Amen.

Meditative Thought: As you start your day, reflect on what it means to submit to God fully. How can you align your actions and thoughts with His will? Consider practical ways to resist temptation and seek God's strength, knowing that His power is greater than any challenge you may face.

Scripture: James 4:7
"Therefore, submit to God. Resist the devil and he will flee from you."

Reflection: As the day comes to a close, James 4:7 encourages us to reflect on how we have submitted to God and resisted the devil throughout the day. This verse calls us to assess our actions and thoughts, recognizing moments when we stood firm in our faith and times when we might have struggled. By submitting to God, we invite His guidance and strength into our lives, enabling us to resist the devil's schemes. Reflecting on this at the end of the day helps us to learn and grow, preparing us to face tomorrow with renewed commitment and faith.

Prayer: Lord, as we conclude this day, we thank You for Your guidance and strength. We acknowledge the moments when we were able to submit to Your will and resist the devil, and we ask for forgiveness for any times we fell short. Help us to learn from today's experiences and grow in our faith. Fill us with Your peace as we rest, and prepare our hearts for a new day where we can continue to walk in obedience to You. Thank You for the promise of Your protection and the assurance that the devil will flee when we resist him. In Jesus' name, we pray. Amen.

Meditative Thought: Before you sleep, take a moment to meditate on your day. How did you submit to God and resist the devil? Reflect on the strength and guidance God provided, and consider areas where you can grow in your submission and resistance. Let this reflection bring you peace and prepare you for tomorrow, trusting in God's ongoing presence and protection.

Scripture: Hebrews 11:1
"Now faith is the substance of things hoped for, the evidence of things not seen."

Reflection: As we begin our day, Hebrews 11:1 offers a profound definition of faith. Faith is not just a vague hope; it is the very substance and assurance of what we hope for, even when we cannot see it. This assurance gives us confidence to face the uncertainties and challenges of the day ahead. Faith anchors us in God's promises and fuels our hope, reminding us that our trust in Him is well-placed. This morning, let us embrace the assurance that comes from our faith, knowing that God is faithful to fulfill His promises, even when we cannot yet see the outcome.

Prayer: Heavenly Father, thank You for the gift of faith that gives substance to our hopes and assurance to our hearts. As we start this day, help us to live by faith, trusting in Your promises even when we cannot see the outcome. Strengthen our faith and remind us of Your constant presence and faithfulness. Guide our steps and help us to face today's challenges with confidence, knowing that our faith in You is well-placed. In Jesus' name, we pray. Amen.

Meditative Thought: As you start your day, reflect on the substance of your faith. How does your faith give you confidence and hope? Consider the promises of God that you hold onto and how they can guide your actions and decisions today.

Scripture: Hebrews 11:1
"Now faith is the substance of things hoped for, the evidence of things not seen."

Reflection: As the day draws to a close, Hebrews 11:1 encourages us to reflect on the role faith has played throughout our day. Faith is the foundation of our hope and the evidence of what we do not see. This evening, we can look back and consider how our faith has sustained us and provided assurance in the unseen. Reflecting on our day through the lens of faith helps us to recognize God's presence and work in our lives, even in the moments when outcomes were uncertain. This reflection strengthens our trust and prepares us for the days ahead.

Prayer: Lord, as we end this day, we thank You for the faith that sustains us and gives substance to our hopes. Help us to reflect on how our faith has guided and strengthened us today. Thank You for Your constant presence and the assurance that comes from trusting in You. As we rest tonight, renew our faith and give us peace, knowing that You are always at work, even when we cannot see it. Prepare our hearts for tomorrow, that we may continue to walk by faith and not by sight. In Jesus' name, we pray. Amen.

Meditative Thought: Before you sleep, take a moment to meditate on how your faith has been the substance of your hope today. Reflect on moments when you trusted in God's promises and felt His assurance. Let this reflection deepen your faith and bring you peace as you rest, knowing that God is faithful, and His promises are sure.

JANUARY 29

MORNING DEVOTION

Scripture: 2 Timothy 2:15
"Be diligent to present yourself approved to God, a worker who does not need to be ashamed, rightly dividing the word of truth."

Reflection: As we begin our day, 2 Timothy 2:15 calls us to diligence in our spiritual lives. Being diligent means putting in effort and care in studying God's Word and living out its truths. This verse reminds us that our goal is to be approved by God, a worker who rightly understands and applies His Word. Starting our day with this commitment sets a tone of purpose and dedication, encouraging us to seek God's approval above all else. As we encounter various situations today, let us strive to rightly divide the word of truth, applying God's wisdom in all our actions and decisions.

Prayer: Heavenly Father, thank You for the guidance and wisdom found in Your Word. As we begin this day, help us to be diligent in our study and application of Scripture. Give us the discernment to rightly divide the word of truth and the courage to live it out in our daily lives. May our efforts be pleasing to You, and may we grow closer to You through our commitment to Your Word. Guide us in all our actions and decisions today, that we may reflect Your truth and love. In Jesus' name, we pray. Amen.

Meditative Thought: As you start your day, consider how you can be diligent in studying and applying God's Word. What steps can you take to deepen your understanding of Scripture? Reflect on how you can live out biblical truths in your interactions and decisions today.

Scripture: 2 Timothy 2:15
"Be diligent to present yourself approved to God, a worker who does not need to be ashamed, rightly dividing the word of truth."

Reflection: As the day draws to a close, 2 Timothy 2:15 invites us to reflect on our diligence in studying and living out God's Word. Did we approach our tasks and interactions with the goal of being approved by God? Did we seek to rightly understand and apply His truths? Reflecting on these questions helps us assess our spiritual growth and commitment. Ending the day with this reflection encourages us to strive for greater diligence and faithfulness in our walk with God, preparing us for continuous growth.

Prayer: Lord, as we end this day, we thank You for Your Word and the guidance it provides. Help us to reflect on how we have been diligent in our study and application of Scripture today. Forgive us for any shortcomings and strengthen our resolve to seek Your approval in all that we do. Give us wisdom and understanding as we continue to rightly divide the word of truth. May our lives be a reflection of Your love and truth. As we rest tonight, renew our spirits and prepare us for another day of faithful living. In Jesus' name, we pray. Amen.

Meditative Thought: Before you sleep, take a moment to meditate on your diligence in studying and applying God's Word today. How can you improve in your understanding and application of Scripture? Reflect on the areas where you sought God's approval and consider ways to deepen your commitment to His truth. Let this reflection bring you peace and prepare you for continued spiritual growth.

JANUARY 30

MORNING DEVOTION

Scripture: Ephesians 2:10
"For we are His workmanship, created in Christ Jesus for good works, which God prepared beforehand that we should walk in them."

Reflection: As we start our day, Ephesians 2:10 reminds us of our identity and purpose in Christ. We are God's workmanship, uniquely created for good works that He has already prepared for us. This truth instills a sense of purpose and direction, encouraging us to live out our faith through actions that reflect God's love and grace. Today, let us embrace the opportunities to do good, knowing that each act of kindness and service is part of God's divine plan. Being aware of our role in His workmanship helps us to approach our day with intention and gratitude.

Prayer: Heavenly Father, thank You for creating us as Your workmanship and for preparing good works for us to walk in. As we begin this day, open our eyes to the opportunities to serve and love others in Your name. Guide our steps and fill our hearts with Your love, so that we may reflect Your grace in all we do. Help us to remember our identity in Christ and to live out our purpose with joy and gratitude. In Jesus' name, we pray. Amen.

Meditative Thought: As you start your day, reflect on the fact that you are God's workmanship, created with a unique purpose. How can you walk in the good works God has prepared for you today? Consider ways to actively seek opportunities to serve and love others, living out your faith in tangible ways.

Scripture: Ephesians 2:10
"For we are His workmanship, created in Christ Jesus for good works, which God prepared beforehand that we should walk in them."

Reflection: As the day draws to a close, Ephesians 2:10 encourages us to reflect on how we have lived out our identity as God's workmanship. Have we recognized and embraced the good works He prepared for us? Reflecting on this helps us to see where we have succeeded and where we might improve. It also reminds us of God's ongoing work in our lives, shaping and guiding us for His purposes. Ending the day with this reflection allows us to thank God for His guidance and to seek His strength for continuing to walk in His plans.

Prayer: Lord, as we end this day, we thank You for the privilege of being Your workmanship, created for good works in Christ Jesus. Help us to reflect on how we have walked in the good works You prepared for us today. Forgive us for any missed opportunities and guide us to be more attentive to Your leading. Thank You for Your constant presence and for shaping us according to Your purposes. As we rest tonight, renew our hearts and minds, preparing us for another day of serving You. In Jesus' name, we pray. Amen.

Meditative Thought: Before you sleep, take a moment to meditate on how you lived out your identity as God's workmanship today. Reflect on the good works you embraced and any opportunities you might have missed. Let this reflection deepen your understanding of God's purpose for your life and prepare you to walk more faithfully in His plans tomorrow.

JANUARY 31

MORNING DEVOTION

Scripture: John 16:27
"For the Father Himself loves you, because you have loved Me, and have believed that I came forth from God."

Reflection: As we begin our day, John 16:27 offers a profound assurance of God's love. Jesus tells us that the Father Himself loves us because we love Jesus and believe in His divine origin. This affirmation is a source of immense comfort and strength. Knowing that we are loved by God the Father because of our faith in Jesus Christ gives us a sense of security and purpose. As we step into our day, let's carry this truth in our hearts, letting it shape our interactions and decisions. Embracing God's love empowers us to face the day with confidence and joy.

Prayer: Heavenly Father, thank You for the incredible love You have for us. As we start this day, help us to remember and embrace this truth. Strengthen our faith and deepen our love for Jesus. May Your love fill our hearts and guide our actions today. Let us reflect Your love in all that we do, bringing glory to Your name. In Jesus' name, we pray. Amen.

Meditative Thought: As you begin your day, meditate on the fact that God the Father loves you because you love Jesus and believe in Him. How does this assurance of divine love influence your attitude and actions today? Let this thought bring you peace and purpose as you go about your day.

Scripture: John 16:27
"For the Father Himself loves you, because you have loved Me, and have believed that I came forth from God."

Reflection: As the day comes to a close, John 16:27 invites us to reflect on the love of God that has been with us throughout the day. We are reminded that God the Father loves us deeply because of our love for Jesus and our belief in His divine mission. Reflecting on this truth can bring a sense of peace and gratitude. As we review our day, we can see the ways God's love has been present and active in our lives, guiding us and giving us strength. This reflection helps us to end the day with a heart full of thankfulness and a renewed sense of God's unwavering love.

Prayer: Lord, as we end this day, we thank You for Your love that has surrounded and sustained us. We are grateful for the assurance that You love us because we love Jesus and believe in Him. Help us to reflect on the moments today when we experienced Your love and guidance. Forgive us for any shortcomings and draw us closer to You. As we rest tonight, fill our hearts with peace and gratitude, and prepare us for another day of living in Your love. In Jesus' name, we pray. Amen.

Meditative Thought: Before you sleep, take a moment to meditate on the love God has for you because of your love for Jesus and your belief in Him. Reflect on how this divine love has been evident in your day. Let this reflection fill you with peace and gratitude, preparing your heart for a restful night and a new day in God's love.

Scripture: John 17:10
"And all Mine are Yours, and Yours are Mine, and I am glorified in them."

Reflection: As we start our day, John 17:10 reminds us of the profound unity between Jesus and the Father and our inclusion in this divine relationship. Jesus speaks of the mutual belonging between Him and the Father, and how He is glorified in us, His followers. This verse encourages us to reflect on our identity and purpose as believers. We belong to God, and through our lives, Jesus is glorified. As we begin our day, let's focus on how we can live in a way that honors and glorifies Jesus, knowing that our actions reflect our divine connection.

Prayer: Heavenly Father, thank You for the incredible truth that we belong to You and that Jesus is glorified in us. As we start this day, help us to live in a way that reflects this divine relationship. May our words and actions honor You and bring glory to Jesus. Fill us with Your Spirit and guide us in all that we do, that our lives may be a testament to Your love and grace. In Jesus' name, we pray. Amen.

Meditative Thought: As you begin your day, meditate on the fact that you belong to God and that Jesus is glorified in you. How can you live today in a way that reflects this truth? Consider the ways your actions and words can honor and glorify Jesus throughout the day.

Scripture: John 17:10
"And all Mine are Yours, and Yours are Mine, and I am glorified in them."

Reflection: As the day comes to a close, John 17:10 invites us to reflect on how we have lived out our divine relationship. Jesus' words remind us of the deep connection we have with Him and the Father, and the call to glorify Him in our lives. Reflecting on our day, we can consider the moments where we have succeeded in bringing glory to Jesus and areas where we might improve. This reflection helps us to end the day with a heart of gratitude and a desire for continuous growth in our faith journey.

Prayer: Lord, as we conclude this day, we thank You for the privilege of belonging to You and the opportunity to glorify Jesus through our lives. Help us to reflect on our actions and words today and see where we have honored You and where we need Your forgiveness and guidance. Fill us with Your peace and renew our commitment to live for Your glory. As we rest tonight, prepare our hearts for another day of serving You. In Jesus' name, we pray. Amen.

Meditative Thought: Before you sleep, take a moment to meditate on how you have lived out your identity as one who belongs to God and brings glory to Jesus. Reflect on the ways you succeeded and areas where you can grow. Let this reflection deepen your commitment to God.

FEBRUARY 2

MORNING DEVOTION

Scripture: Matthew 23:11
"But he who is greatest among you shall be your servant."

Reflection: As we begin our day, Matthew 23:11 challenges us to rethink greatness and leadership. In the world's eyes, greatness often means power and prestige, but Jesus turns this concept upside down. True greatness, according to Jesus, is found in serving others. As we go about our day, let us embrace this call to servanthood. Whether it's in our workplaces, homes, or communities, we can find ways to serve and uplift others. By doing so, we reflect the heart of Christ and fulfill our purpose as His followers.

Prayer: Heavenly Father, thank You for teaching us that true greatness is found in serving others. As we start this day, open our eyes to the opportunities around us to serve. Fill our hearts with humility and compassion, and guide our actions so that we may uplift and support those we encounter. Help us to reflect Your love and grace in all that we do. In Jesus' name, we pray. Amen.

Meditative Thought: As you start your day, meditate on the ways you can serve others in your daily life. How can you reflect the heart of Christ in your actions and interactions today? Consider practical steps you can take to embrace servanthood and make a positive impact on those around you.

Scripture: Matthew 23:11
"But he who is greatest among you shall be your servant."

Reflection: As the day draws to a close, Matthew 23:11 invites us to reflect on our actions and attitudes throughout the day. Have we embraced the call to servanthood that Jesus describes? Reflecting on our day, we can see the moments where we have served others and the times we might have missed opportunities to do so. Ending the day with this reflection helps us to grow in humility and commitment to living out the teachings of Jesus. It also encourages us to seek God's guidance and strength to serve more faithfully in the future.

Prayer: Lord, as we conclude this day, we thank You for the opportunities we had to serve others. Help us to reflect on our actions with honesty and humility. Forgive us for the times we missed chances to serve and guide us to be more attentive and compassionate. Fill our hearts with a greater desire to serve and honor You through our actions. As we rest tonight, renew our spirits and prepare us for another day of living out Your call to servanthood. In Jesus' name, we pray. Amen.

Meditative Thought: Before you sleep, take a moment to meditate on how you have embraced the call to servanthood today. Reflect on the ways you served others and the opportunities you may have missed. Let this reflection deepen your commitment to living out Jesus' teachings and prepare you to serve more faithfully tomorrow.

FEBRUARY 3

MORNING DEVOTION

Scripture: Psalm 91:1
"He who dwells in the secret place of the Most High shall abide under the shadow of the Almighty."

Reflection: As we begin our day, Psalm 91:1 offers us a profound promise of divine protection and intimacy with God. To dwell in the secret place of the Most High means to live in close fellowship with God, seeking His presence and guidance continually. This morning, let's focus on cultivating our relationship with God, finding our refuge and strength in Him. By starting our day in His presence, we can face whatever comes with confidence, knowing that we are under the shadow of the Almighty.

Prayer: Heavenly Father, thank You for the promise of Your protection and presence. As we start this day, help us to dwell in Your secret place, seeking Your guidance and strength. Let us find refuge under Your shadow and walk with confidence, knowing that You are with us. Fill our hearts with peace and our minds with Your wisdom. Guide us in all our actions and decisions today. In Jesus' name, we pray. Amen.

Meditative Thought: As you start your day, meditate on what it means to dwell in the secret place of the Most High. How can you seek God's presence and guidance more intentionally today? Reflect on the assurance and peace that come from abiding under the shadow of the Almighty.

Scripture: Psalm 91:1
"He who dwells in the secret place of the Most High shall abide under the shadow of the Almighty."

Reflection: As the day comes to a close, Psalm 91:1 invites us to reflect on how we have experienced God's presence and protection throughout the day. Dwelling in the secret place of the Most High means that we have sought His presence and relied on His strength. Reflecting on our day, we can see the moments when we felt His guidance and protection. This reflection helps us to end the day with a heart full of gratitude and a deeper awareness of God's constant care.

Prayer: Lord, as we conclude this day, we thank You for Your protection and presence. Help us to reflect on how we have sought and experienced Your guidance today. Forgive us for any moments we failed to seek Your presence and draw us closer to You. As we rest tonight, let us find peace under Your shadow and renew our spirits for tomorrow. Thank You for being our refuge and strength. In Jesus' name, we pray. Amen.

Meditative Thought: Before you sleep, take a moment to meditate on how you have dwelt in the secret place of the Most High today. Reflect on the times you felt God's presence and guidance. Let this reflection deepen your sense of peace and gratitude as you rest under the shadow of the Almighty.

FEBRUARY 4

MORNING DEVOTION

Scripture: 1 Samuel 17:37
"Moreover, David said, 'The Lord, who delivered me from the paw of the lion and from the paw of the bear, He will deliver me from the hand of this Philistine.' And Saul said to David, 'Go, and the Lord be with you!'"

Reflection: As we begin our day, 1 Samuel 17:37 reminds us of God's faithfulness and the courage that comes from trusting in Him. David's confidence in facing Goliath stemmed from his past experiences of God's deliverance. Remembering how God has helped us in the past can strengthen our faith and give us the courage to face today's challenges. Like David, we can trust that the same God who delivered us before will be with us and deliver us again. As we start this day, let's step forward with confidence and faith, knowing that God is with us and will help us overcome any obstacles.

Prayer: Heavenly Father, thank You for Your faithfulness and for the many ways You have delivered us in the past. As we start this day, help us to remember Your past faithfulness and trust You with today's challenges. Give us the courage and strength to face whatever comes our way, knowing that You are with us. Help us to rely on Your power and not our own. Guide us and protect us throughout this day. In Jesus' name, we pray. Amen.

Meditative Thought: As you start your day, reflect on the times God has delivered you from difficult situations in the past. How does remembering His faithfulness give you courage and confidence to face today's challenges? Trust in God's presence and power as you move forward.

Scripture: 1 Samuel 17:37
"Moreover, David said, 'The Lord, who delivered me from the paw of the lion and from the paw of the bear, He will deliver me from the hand of this Philistine.' And Saul said to David, 'Go, and the Lord be with you!'"

Reflection: As the day comes to a close, 1 Samuel 17:37 invites us to reflect on how God has been with us throughout the day. Just as David trusted in God's deliverance, we too can see how God has helped us face our own "giants" today. Reflecting on the challenges we encountered and how God provided for us strengthens our faith and deepens our gratitude. This reflection helps us to end the day with a heart full of thankfulness and trust in God's continued faithfulness.

Prayer: Lord, as we conclude this day, we thank You for Your presence and faithfulness. Help us to reflect on how You have been with us and delivered us from today's challenges. Forgive us for any moments of doubt and strengthen our faith. As we rest tonight, fill our hearts with peace and gratitude. Prepare us for tomorrow, that we may continue to trust in Your deliverance and guidance. Thank You for being our protector and provider. In Jesus' name, we pray. Amen.

Meditative Thought: Before you sleep, take a moment to meditate on how God has been with you today and the ways He has delivered you from challenges. Reflect on His faithfulness and let this reflection deepen your trust and gratitude. Rest in the assurance of God's continued presence and care.

FEBRUARY 5

MORNING DEVOTION

Scripture: Psalm 23:6
"Surely goodness and mercy shall follow me All the days of my life; And I will dwell in the house of the Lord Forever."

Reflection: As we begin our day, Psalm 23:6 fills our hearts with assurance and hope. The psalmist declares with confidence that goodness and mercy will follow him all the days of his life. This promise reminds us of God's steadfast love and faithfulness, which accompany us each step of the way. As we face the uncertainties and challenges of the day ahead, let us hold onto this truth. With God by our side, we can walk in confidence, knowing that His goodness and mercy will never leave us. And ultimately, we have the hope of dwelling in His presence forever.

Prayer: Gracious God, thank You for Your goodness and mercy that accompany us every day. As we begin this day, help us to trust in Your unfailing love and faithfulness. May Your presence fill us with confidence and hope, knowing that You are with us through every moment. Guide our steps and lead us in Your ways. Help us to dwell in Your house both now and forevermore. In Jesus' name, we pray. Amen.

Meditative Thought: Reflect on the assurance of God's goodness and mercy that accompanies you each day. How does this truth impact your outlook and attitude as you face the challenges ahead? Take a moment to dwell on the hope of eternal fellowship with God.

Scripture: Psalm 23:6
"Surely goodness and mercy shall follow me All the days of my life; And I will dwell in the house of the Lord Forever."

Reflection: As the day draws to a close, Psalm 23:6 invites us to reflect on the goodness and mercy of God that have accompanied us throughout the day. Despite the challenges and uncertainties, we can testify to God's faithfulness in providing for our needs and guiding our steps. As we reflect on His goodness, we are reminded of His promise of eternal fellowship with Him. Tonight, let us rest in the assurance of God's unfailing love, knowing that we are surrounded by His goodness and mercy both now and forevermore.

Prayer: Heavenly Father, we thank You for Your goodness and mercy that have followed us throughout this day. As we conclude this evening, we are grateful for Your faithfulness in guiding and providing for us. May Your presence bring us peace and rest as we prepare for the night. Help us to trust in Your promise of eternal fellowship with You. Keep us safe under Your care, now and forever. In Jesus' name, we pray. Amen.

Meditative Thought: Take a moment to reflect on the goodness and mercy of God that you experienced today. How did His presence sustain you through the day? As you prepare for rest, dwell on the hope of eternal fellowship with Him in His house.

Scripture: 1 Peter 1:15
"But as He who called you is holy, you also be holy in all your conduct,"

Reflection: As we begin our day, 1 Peter 1:15 calls us to a life of holiness. Just as God, who called us, is holy, we are called to reflect His holiness in all aspects of our lives. Holiness isn't just about avoiding sin, but it's about living in a way that honors God and reflects His character. This morning, let's commit ourselves to pursuing holiness in our thoughts, words, and actions. As we go about our day, may everything we do be guided by our desire to honor God and live in accordance with His will.

Prayer: Heavenly Father, thank You for calling us to a life of holiness. As we begin this day, help us to understand what it means to be holy as You are holy. Give us the strength and wisdom to live in a way that reflects Your character and brings glory to Your name. May Your Spirit guide us in all our conduct today, leading us closer to You. In Jesus' name, we pray. Amen.

Meditative Thought: Take a moment to reflect on what holiness means to you. How can you strive for holiness in your thoughts, words, and actions today? Consider the areas of your life where you can grow in holiness and ask God for His guidance and strength.

Scripture: 1 Peter 1:15
"But as He who called you is holy, you also be holy in all your conduct,"

Reflection: As the day comes to a close, let's reflect on 1 Peter 1:15 and our pursuit of holiness. Did we strive to live in a way that honored God and reflected His character throughout the day? Reflecting on our conduct allows us to assess our actions and attitudes, recognizing areas where we fell short and moments where we honored God. As we acknowledge our shortcomings, let's also seek God's forgiveness and ask for His strength to continue pursuing holiness in our lives.

Prayer: Lord, as we end this day, we thank You for Your call to holiness. Forgive us for the times when we failed to live up to Your standard. Strengthen us to walk in holiness, honoring You in all that we do. May Your Spirit convict and guide us, leading us closer to You. Help us to reflect on our day with honesty and humility, seeking Your grace and mercy. In Jesus' name, we pray. Amen.

Meditative Thought: Take a moment to reflect on your conduct throughout the day. In what ways did you reflect God's holiness, and in what areas did you fall short? How can you grow in holiness as you continue your journey with God? Surrender any shortcomings to Him and ask for His help to live more fully in His holiness.

FEBRUARY 7

MORNING DEVOTION

Scripture: Galatians 6:9
"And let us not grow weary while doing good, for in due season we shall reap if we do not lose heart."

Reflection: As we begin our day, Galatians 6:9 encourages us to persevere in doing good. It's easy to become weary in our efforts to live according to God's principles, especially when we face challenges or opposition. However, this verse reminds us to remain steadfast and persistent. Our labor in serving God and others is not in vain. Just as a farmer patiently tends to his crops, trusting in the promise of a harvest, we can trust that God will bring about blessings and rewards in due time. So let's press on with faith and determination, knowing that our efforts are not futile.

Prayer: Heavenly Father, thank You for the reminder to not grow weary in doing good. Strengthen us, Lord, when we feel discouraged or tired. Help us to keep our eyes fixed on You and to persevere in living out Your will. May Your Spirit empower us to continue doing good, trusting in Your promises of blessings and rewards. Give us the grace to stay faithful and steadfast, even in the face of challenges. In Jesus' name, we pray. Amen.

Meditative Thought: Consider the areas in your life where you might be feeling weary or discouraged. How can you draw strength from God's promises in Galatians 6:9? Reflect on the hope and assurance that come from trusting in God's faithfulness, even when circumstances seem difficult.

Scripture: Galatians 6:9
"And let us not grow weary while doing good, for in due season we shall reap if we do not lose heart."

Reflection: As the day comes to a close, let's reflect on Galatians 6:9 and the encouragement it brings. Did we remain steadfast in doing good throughout the day, or did we grow weary and lose heart? Reflecting on our attitudes and actions allows us to assess our perseverance in living out God's will. Even when we face setbacks or challenges, let's remember the promise of a harvest in due season if we do not lose heart. As we surrender any weariness or discouragement to God tonight, let's trust in His faithfulness to bring about blessings and rewards according to His perfect timing.

Prayer: Lord, as we end this day, we thank You for Your faithfulness and the promise of a harvest in due season. Forgive us for the times when we grew weary or lost heart in doing good. Renew our strength, Lord, and help us to persevere in living according to Your will. May Your Spirit fill us with hope and assurance, knowing that our labor in You is not in vain. Grant us a restful night's sleep, and may we wake up refreshed to continue serving You tomorrow. In Jesus' name, we pray. Amen.

Meditative Thought: Before you sleep, reflect on the ways you remained steadfast in doing good today, and also on the moments when you felt weary or discouraged. Surrender any weariness to God, trusting in His promise of a harvest in due season. Let His assurance bring you peace and rest tonight.

FEBRUARY 8

MORNING DEVOTION

Scripture: Jonah 2:10
"So, the Lord spoke to the fish, and it vomited Jonah onto dry land."

Reflection: As we begin our day, Jonah 2:10 reminds us of God's faithfulness and mercy. Despite Jonah's disobedience and rebellion, God hears his cry for help from the belly of the great fish. In His mercy, God commands the fish to release Jonah onto dry land. This verse teaches us that even in our darkest moments, when we feel trapped or overwhelmed by our circumstances, God is there, ready to rescue us when we call out to Him. Today, let's remember that no situation is too dire for God to intervene. Let's trust in His faithfulness and mercy as we face the challenges of the day.

Prayer: Heavenly Father, thank You for Your faithfulness and mercy, even when we stray from Your will. As we begin this day, help us to remember that You are always near, ready to rescue us when we call upon Your name. Give us the courage to trust in Your provision and guidance, knowing that You are sovereign over every circumstance. Help us to surrender our fears and worries to You, and to walk in faith, knowing that You are with us. In Jesus' name, we pray. Amen.

Meditative Thought: Reflect on a time when you felt overwhelmed or trapped by your circumstances. How did God intervene and rescue you? Consider His faithfulness and mercy in your life, and let it strengthen your trust in Him as you face the challenges of today.

Scripture: Jonah 2:10
"So, the Lord spoke to the fish, and it vomited Jonah onto dry land."

Reflection: As the day comes to a close, let's reflect on Jonah 2:10 and God's faithfulness to rescue His people. Despite Jonah's disobedience, God hears his cry for help and commands the fish to release him onto dry land. This verse reminds us that God is always ready to rescue us from our troubles when we call upon Him. As we reflect on the events of today, let's remember the times when God intervened in our lives, bringing us through difficult situations. Let's give thanks for His faithfulness and mercy, and trust in His continued provision and guidance.

Prayer: Lord, as we end this day, we thank You for Your faithfulness and mercy in our lives. Thank You for being our rescuer in times of trouble and for always hearing our cries for help. Help us to trust in Your provision and guidance, knowing that You are sovereign over every circumstance. Give us peace as we rest tonight, knowing that You are watching over us. Renew our strength for the day ahead, that we may continue to walk in faith and obedience to Your will. In Jesus' name, we pray. Amen.

Meditative Thought: Before you sleep, reflect on the ways God has intervened and rescued you from difficult situations in the past. How does His faithfulness in Jonah's story parallel His faithfulness in your life? Let His past interventions strengthen your trust in Him for the future.

Scripture: Isaiah 46:9

"For I am God, and there is no other; I am God, and there is none like Me,"

Reflection: As we begin our day, Isaiah 46:9 reminds us of the uniqueness and supremacy of God. He declares that there is no other God besides Him, and there is none like Him. This truth calls us to acknowledge God's sovereignty and to worship Him alone. In a world filled with distractions and competing voices, let's take a

moment to reflect on the incomparable nature of God. He is the Creator of the universe, the Alpha and Omega, the one who holds all things together by His power. There is no one who can compare to His greatness, His love, and His faithfulness. As we start our day, let's anchor our hearts in the truth that God alone is worthy of our worship and adoration.

Prayer: Heavenly Father, we thank You for Your greatness and Your unmatched power. Help us to recognize Your sovereignty in our lives and to worship You with all our hearts. May we never be swayed by the distractions of this world, but may our focus always remain on You. Thank You for being our God, the one who is like no other. In Jesus' name, we pray. Amen.

Meditative Thought: Take a moment to meditate on the incomparable nature of God. Reflect on His attributes—His power, His love, His faithfulness—and consider how they impact your life. How does knowing that God is like no other shape your perspective and attitudes as you begin your day?

Scripture: Isaiah 46:9

"For I am God, and there is no other; I am God, and there is none like Me,"

Reflection: As the day comes to a close, let's reflect on the truth of Isaiah 46:9 once again. God declares that He is unmatched in His greatness and power. There is no one like Him, and there is no other God besides Him. This reminder prompts us to reflect on our response to God's uniqueness. Have we truly worshiped Him as the one true God today? Have we acknowledged His sovereignty in every aspect of our lives? Let's take this opportunity to reaffirm our commitment to worship and serve God alone, recognizing His unmatched worthiness.

Prayer: Lord, as we conclude this day, we thank You for the reminder of Your uniqueness and supremacy. Forgive us for the times when we have failed to worship You as the one true God. Help us to recommit ourselves to You, acknowledging Your sovereignty in our lives. May our hearts be filled with awe and reverence for You, the God like no other. In Jesus' name, we pray. Amen.

Meditative Thought: Reflect on your day and consider whether you have truly worshiped God as the one true God. Have there been moments when other things or people have taken priority in your life? How can you recommit yourself to acknowledging God's uniqueness and supremacy in all areas of your life?

FEBRUARY 10

MORNING DEVOTION

Scripture: Proverbs 20:27
"The spirit of a man is the lamp of the Lord, Searching all the inner depths of his heart."

Reflection: As we start our day, Proverbs 20:27 reminds us that our spirit is the lamp of the Lord, illuminating the innermost parts of our heart. God uses our conscience and inner thoughts to guide us, reveal our true motives, and help us grow in righteousness. This morning, let's invite God's light to shine into every corner of our lives. By allowing His Spirit to search us, we can identify areas that need repentance, growth, and alignment with His will. As we go through our day, may we be attentive to His gentle guidance and correction.

Prayer: Heavenly Father, thank You for Your Spirit that searches and knows the depths of our hearts. As we begin this day, we invite You to shine Your light into every part of our lives. Reveal to us anything that is not in alignment with Your will, and give us the grace to make the necessary changes. Help us to walk in Your truth and reflect Your light to those around us. Guide our thoughts, words, and actions today. In Jesus' name, we pray. Amen.

Meditative Thought: Reflect on how God's Spirit works within you to guide and correct. Consider the areas of your life that may need His light and truth. How can you be more attentive to His guidance throughout the day? Allow His presence to search and know your heart, leading you in the way everlasting.

Scripture: Proverbs 20:27
"The spirit of a man is the lamp of the Lord, Searching all the inner depths of his heart."

Reflection: As the day comes to a close, Proverbs 20:27 invites us to reflect on how God has been at work within us throughout the day. The Lord uses our spirit as a lamp to search the inner depths of our hearts, revealing our true selves. Reflecting on our thoughts, actions, and motives today, we can see how God has been guiding and shaping us. This evening, let's take time to acknowledge His work within us, confess any shortcomings, and thank Him for His ongoing transformation in our lives.

Prayer: Lord, as we end this day, we thank You for Your Spirit that searches our hearts and guides us in Your truth. Forgive us for any thoughts, words, or actions that were not pleasing to You. Help us to learn from today's experiences and grow in our walk with You. Thank You for Your patience and grace as You work within us. As we rest tonight, renew our spirits and prepare us for a new day of following Your guidance. In Jesus' name, we pray. Amen.

Meditative Thought: Before you sleep, take a moment to reflect on how God has searched your heart today. What has He revealed to you about your thoughts, actions, and motives? How can you respond to His guidance and allow His light to transform you further? Rest in the assurance of His love and ongoing work within you.

Scripture: Genesis 6:8
"But Noah found grace in the eyes of the Lord."

Reflection: As we start our day, Genesis 6:8 reminds us of the incredible gift of God's grace. Noah lived in a time of great wickedness, yet he found favor with God. This was not due to his own merit but because of God's grace. This morning, we can take comfort in knowing that God's grace is available to us as well. No matter the circumstances around us or the challenges we face, God's grace is sufficient. Let us strive to live righteously and seek His favor, trusting that His grace will guide and sustain us through the day.

Prayer: Heavenly Father, thank You for Your amazing grace that is always available to us. As we begin this day, help us to seek Your favor and live in a way that honors You. Give us the strength to stand firm in our faith amidst the challenges of this world. Guide our thoughts, words, and actions so that they reflect Your love and righteousness. Thank You for Your unending grace. In Jesus' name, we pray. Amen.

Meditative Thought: Consider the ways in which you can seek and reflect God's grace today. How can you stand firm in your faith and be a light in a world that often goes against God's ways? Let the thought of God's grace being with you guide your actions and decisions throughout the day.

Scripture: Genesis 6:8
"But Noah found grace in the eyes of the Lord."

Reflection: As we conclude our day, Genesis 6:8 invites us to reflect on the grace that Noah found in the eyes of the Lord. Throughout the day, we may have encountered various challenges and temptations, but through it all, God's grace has been with us. Like Noah, we are called to live righteously in a world that often strays from God's ways. This evening, let us take time to thank God for His grace that has guided and sustained us. Let's reflect on how we have lived today and seek His continued favor and guidance for tomorrow.

Prayer: Lord, as we end this day, we thank You for Your abundant grace that has been with us. Forgive us for any moments where we may have strayed from Your will. Help us to continue seeking Your favor and living in a way that honors You. Thank You for sustaining us and guiding us through the challenges we faced today. As we rest tonight, renew our spirits and prepare us for a new day. In Jesus' name, we pray. Amen.

Meditative Thought: Reflect on how God's grace has been present in your life today. How have you experienced His guidance and favor? Consider ways you can continue to seek and reflect His grace in the days to come. Let this reflection bring you peace and a renewed commitment to living righteously.

FEBRUARY 12

MORNING DEVOTION

Scripture: 1 Kings 18:21
"And Elijah came to all the people, and said, 'How long will you falter between two opinions? If the Lord is God, follow Him; but if Baal, follow him.' But the people answered him not a word."

Reflection: As we start our day, 1 Kings 18:21 challenges us to examine our commitment to God. Elijah confronted the people of Israel, who were wavering between worshiping God and following Baal. This verse calls us to make a clear and decisive choice about whom we will serve. In our daily lives, we often face decisions that test our faith and allegiance. Today, let us resolve to follow the Lord wholeheartedly, without hesitation or compromise. Let us acknowledge Him as the true God and live in a way that reflects our commitment to Him.

Prayer: Heavenly Father, thank You for reminding us of the importance of our commitment to You. As we begin this day, help us to make a decisive choice to follow You wholeheartedly. Remove any wavering or hesitation from our hearts. Give us the courage and strength to stand firm in our faith, regardless of the challenges we face. May our actions and decisions today reflect our dedication to You. In Jesus' name, we pray. Amen.

Meditative Thought: Reflect on areas in your life where you may be faltering between two opinions. What steps can you take to reaffirm your commitment to God today? Consider how you can live out your faith boldly and without compromise.

Scripture: 1 Kings 18:21
"And Elijah came to all the people, and said, 'How long will you falter between two opinions? If the Lord is God, follow Him; but if Baal, follow him.' But the people answered him not a word."

Reflection: As we conclude our day, 1 Kings 18:21 invites us to reflect on our commitment to God throughout the day. Elijah's question to the people of Israel challenges us to consider whether we have been steadfast in our faith or if we have wavered. This evening, let us take a moment to examine our actions and decisions. Have we followed God wholeheartedly, or have we allowed other influences to distract us? Let's reaffirm our commitment to God, acknowledging Him as the true and living God, and seek His strength to remain steadfast in our faith.

Prayer: Lord, as we end this day, we thank You for Your constant presence and guidance. Forgive us for any moments where we may have faltered in our commitment to You. Help us to reflect on our day with honesty and humility. Strengthen our resolve to follow You wholeheartedly, and guide us in living out our faith with courage and conviction. As we rest tonight, renew our spirits and prepare us for a new day of serving You. In Jesus' name, we pray. Amen.

Meditative Thought: Before you sleep, reflect on your commitment to God throughout the day. Were there moments when you wavered or hesitated? How can you strengthen your resolve to follow God more faithfully? Let this reflection guide you as you seek to deepen your relationship with Him.

Scripture: John 2:5
"His mother said to the servants, 'Whatever He says to you, do it.'"

Reflection: As we begin our day, John 2:5 provides us with a powerful reminder of the importance of obedience to Jesus. Mary's instruction to the servants at the wedding in Cana is simple yet profound: "Whatever He says to you, do it." This call to obedience is just as relevant for us today as it was for those servants. Each day, Jesus speaks to us through His Word, His Spirit, and our circumstances. Our task is to listen and obey. Starting today with a heart ready to follow Jesus' guidance can transform our lives and bring about God's purposes in ways we might not expect.

Prayer: Heavenly Father, thank You for Your Word and the guidance it provides. Help us today to have ears that listen and hearts that are quick to obey whatever Jesus tells us. Give us the courage and strength to follow His directions, even when we do not fully understand. May our obedience lead to Your will being done in our lives and the lives of those around us. In Jesus' name, we pray. Amen.

Meditative Thought: Take a moment to reflect on how you can be more attentive to Jesus' voice today. What specific steps can you take to ensure that you are ready to obey His guidance? Consider how obedience to Him can bring transformation and blessing into your life and the lives of others.

Scripture: John 2:5
"His mother said to the servants, 'Whatever He says to you, do it.'"

Reflection: As we conclude our day, let us reflect on the events at the wedding in Cana and the obedience of the servants who followed Mary's instruction. Their willingness to do whatever Jesus said led to the miraculous transformation of water into wine. This evening, consider how you responded to Jesus' guidance today. Did you listen and obey His voice? Reflect on the moments where you felt His leading and how you responded. Let this be a time of honest assessment and renewed commitment to follow His instructions more faithfully.

Prayer: Lord, as we end this day, we thank You for Your presence and guidance. Forgive us for any moments where we may have failed to listen or obey Your voice. Help us to learn from these experiences and grow in our ability to follow You faithfully. May we be like the servants at Cana, ready to do whatever You say, trusting that Your plans are good. As we rest tonight, renew our hearts and minds, preparing us for another day of walking in obedience to You. In Jesus' name, we pray. Amen.

Meditative Thought: Reflect on your day and how you responded to Jesus' guidance. Were there moments when you hesitated or ignored His leading? How can you improve your attentiveness and obedience to Him? Let this reflection strengthen your commitment to follow Jesus more closely tomorrow.

MORNING DEVOTION

Scripture: Luke 1:46-47
"And Mary said: 'My soul magnifies the Lord, and my spirit has rejoiced in God my Savior.'"

Reflection: As we begin our day, let us join Mary in her song of praise. Her response to the incredible news of bearing the Messiah was one of profound worship and joy. "My soul magnifies the Lord, and my spirit has rejoiced in God my Savior." Mary's humility and gratitude are inspiring. She recognized God's greatness and rejoiced in His salvation. Today, let's start with a heart full of praise, acknowledging God's work in our lives. Regardless of our circumstances, we can choose to magnify the Lord and rejoice in Him, our Savior.

Prayer: Heavenly Father, thank You for the example of Mary, who magnified and rejoiced in You despite the challenges she faced. As we begin this day, help us to have a heart of worship and gratitude. May our souls magnify You, and may our spirits rejoice in Your salvation. Guide our thoughts, words, and actions today so that they reflect Your love and grace. In Jesus' name, we pray. Amen.

Meditative Thought: Consider the ways in which you can magnify the Lord today. Reflect on His goodness and the blessings in your life. How can you express your gratitude and joy in God your Savior throughout the day?

FEBRUARY 14

EVENING DEVOTION

Scripture: Luke 1:46-47
"And Mary said: 'My soul magnifies the Lord, and my spirit has rejoiced in God my Savior.'"

Reflection: As we close our day, we return to Mary's beautiful declaration of praise. Reflecting on the day's events, let us consider how we have magnified the Lord and rejoiced in Him. Have our actions, thoughts, and words reflected a heart that rejoices in God our Savior? Mary's song is a reminder to consistently recognize and celebrate God's presence and work in our lives. This evening, let us quiet our hearts and express our gratitude for His faithfulness and love.

Prayer: Lord, as this day comes to an end, we thank You for Your constant presence and guidance. Forgive us for any moments where we may have failed to magnify You or rejoice in Your salvation. Help us to learn from today's experiences and grow in our ability to praise You continually. As we rest tonight, fill our hearts with Your peace and joy, and prepare us for a new day of glorifying You. In Jesus' name, we pray. Amen.

Meditative Thought: Before you sleep, reflect on how you have magnified the Lord today. In what ways have you rejoiced in God your Savior? Consider how you can carry this spirit of praise and gratitude into tomorrow, continually magnifying the Lord in all you do.

Scripture: 1 Timothy 6:6
"Now godliness with contentment is great gain."

Reflection: As we start our day, 1 Timothy 6:6 offers us a powerful reminder about the true source of gain in life: godliness with contentment. In a world that often pushes us to seek more—more wealth, more success, more possessions—Paul's words call us to a different path. Godliness, living a life that reflects God's values and His love, combined with contentment, brings true and lasting gain. This morning, let's focus on cultivating godliness and practicing contentment, trusting that in these, we will find true fulfillment and peace.

Prayer: Heavenly Father, thank You for reminding us that true gain comes from living a godly life with contentment. Help us today to seek after godliness and to be content with what You have provided. Guard our hearts against the temptations of greed and dissatisfaction. Fill us with Your peace and joy as we walk in Your ways. May our lives reflect Your love and grace to those around us. In Jesus' name, we pray. Amen.

Meditative Thought: Reflect on what it means to combine godliness with contentment. How can you practice contentment in your current circumstances? Consider ways to cultivate a deeper sense of godliness and gratitude throughout your day.

Scripture: 1 Timothy 6:6
"Now godliness with contentment is great gain."

Reflection: As we conclude our day, 1 Timothy 6:6 encourages us to reflect on the concepts of godliness and contentment. Have we sought to live in a way that honors God today? Have we found contentment in the blessings He has provided, regardless of our circumstances? True gain comes not from worldly achievements but from a heart aligned with God's will and at peace with His provisions. This evening, let us evaluate our day through the lens of godliness and contentment and seek God's help to grow in these areas.

Prayer: Lord, as we end this day, we thank You for Your guidance and provision. Forgive us for any moments where we may have lacked contentment or strayed from godliness. Help us to learn and grow from today's experiences. Fill our hearts with a deeper sense of Your presence and peace. As we rest tonight, renew our commitment to living a godly life and finding contentment in You. In Jesus' name, we pray. Amen.

Meditative Thought: Reflect on your day and consider how you have demonstrated godliness and contentment. Were there moments of struggle or dissatisfaction? How can you cultivate a greater sense of peace and godliness in your daily life? Let this reflection guide you as you seek to grow closer to God and live out His principles.

Scripture: James 2:23
"And the Scripture was fulfilled which says, 'Abraham believed God, and it was accounted to him for righteousness.' And he was called the friend of God."

Reflection: As we begin our day, James 2:23 reminds us of the profound relationship between faith and righteousness. Abraham's belief in God was credited to him as righteousness, and he was called a friend of God. This morning, let's reflect on the depth of Abraham's faith and how it pleased God. His trust in God was not passive; it was active and demonstrated through obedience. Today, let us strive to live out our faith actively, trusting God's promises and aligning our actions with His will. By doing so, we, too, can deepen our relationship with God and be counted as His friends.

Prayer: Heavenly Father, thank You for the example of Abraham's faith and how it was counted as righteousness. As we start this day, help us to trust You wholeheartedly and demonstrate our faith through our actions. Guide us in making decisions that align with Your will and bring glory to Your name. Strengthen our relationship with You, so we may be known as Your friends. In Jesus' name, we pray. Amen.

Meditative Thought: Reflect on the nature of your faith. How can you demonstrate your belief in God through your actions today? Consider ways to deepen your relationship with God and trust Him more fully.

Scripture: James 2:23

"And the Scripture was fulfilled which says, 'Abraham believed God, and it was accounted to him for righteousness.' And he was called the friend of God."

Reflection: As we end our day, let's revisit the faith of Abraham as described in James 2:23. Abraham's belief in God and his actions reflecting that belief led to him being called God's friend. This evening, let's reflect on how our faith has been manifested throughout the day. Have our actions aligned with our belief in God? True faith is active and evident in how we live. Let's take this time to assess our day, seek forgiveness where we've fallen short, and commit to growing in our faith and obedience to God.

Prayer: Lord, as we conclude this day, we thank You for Your faithfulness and guidance. Forgive us for any moments where our actions did not reflect our belief in You. Help us to grow in our faith, making it active and visible in our daily lives. May we strive to be called Your friends, just as Abraham was. As we rest tonight, renew our hearts and minds, preparing us to walk faithfully with You tomorrow. In Jesus' name, we pray. Amen.

Meditative Thought: Consider how your faith has influenced your actions today. Were there moments where you demonstrated trust in God? Reflect on ways to deepen your faith and let it guide your daily actions, striving to be a true friend of God.

FEBRUARY 17

MORNING DEVOTION

Scripture: Proverbs 17:27
"He who has knowledge spares his words, and a man of understanding is of a calm spirit."

Reflection: As we begin our day, Proverbs 17:27 provides us with a powerful lesson on the virtues of knowledge and understanding. In a world full of noise and constant communication, this verse reminds us of the value of speaking wisely and maintaining a calm spirit. True knowledge isn't just about knowing many things but knowing when and how to speak. A person of understanding cultivates a calm and composed demeanor. Today, let us strive to be mindful of our words, using them thoughtfully, and seek to maintain a peaceful spirit in all our interactions.

Prayer: Heavenly Father, thank You for Your wisdom that guides us. As we start this day, help us to be mindful of our words and to speak with knowledge and wisdom. Grant us a calm spirit, so that we may reflect Your peace in our interactions with others. Guide our thoughts and actions so that they align with Your will. May we be a source of calm and wisdom to those around us today. In Jesus' name, we pray. Amen.

Meditative Thought: Reflect on the power of your words. How can you use your speech to bring wisdom and calm to your day? Consider the impact of maintaining a calm spirit in your interactions with others and the difference it can make.

Scripture: Proverbs 17:27
"He who has knowledge spares his words, And a man of understanding is of a calm spirit."

Reflection: As we end our day, Proverbs 17:27 invites us to reflect on how we used our words and maintained our spirit throughout the day. Did we speak with knowledge and wisdom, choosing our words carefully? Did we maintain a calm and understanding demeanor in our interactions? This evening, let us take a moment to evaluate our day. Let's seek God's guidance to grow in these virtues, recognizing the importance of thoughtful speech and a peaceful spirit.

Prayer: Lord, as we conclude this day, we thank You for the moments of wisdom and calm You provided. Forgive us for any times we may have spoken hastily or lacked a calm spirit. Help us to learn from today and grow in our ability to speak with knowledge and maintain a peaceful demeanor. Fill us with Your peace as we rest tonight, and prepare us to walk in Your wisdom tomorrow. In Jesus' name, we pray. Amen.

Meditative Thought: Reflect on your day and how you used your words. Were there moments when you could have spoken less or chosen your words more wisely? How did you maintain or lose your calm spirit? Consider ways to cultivate these virtues more deeply in your life.

FEBRUARY 18

MORNING DEVOTION

Scripture: Revelation 21:4
"And God will wipe away every tear from their eyes; there shall be no more death, nor sorrow, nor crying. There shall be no more pain, for the former things have passed away."

Reflection: As we begin our day, Revelation 21:4 offers us a glimpse of the ultimate hope and comfort that we have in God. This verse reminds us that there will come a time when God will wipe away every tear, and all forms of suffering—death, sorrow, crying, and pain—will be no more. The former things will pass away, making way for a new reality where we will experience eternal joy and peace. Today, let this promise fill our hearts with hope and encourage us to face our challenges with the assurance that God's perfect plan is unfolding.

Prayer: Heavenly Father, thank You for the promise of a future where there will be no more pain, sorrow, or death. As we start this day, help us to hold on to this hope and find comfort in Your unfailing love. Strengthen us to face the challenges of today with courage and faith, knowing that You are with us and that You have a perfect plan for our future. Fill our hearts with Your peace and joy. In Jesus' name, we pray. Amen.

Meditative Thought: Reflect on the promise of God wiping away every tear and removing all pain. How does this hope impact your perspective on the challenges you face today? Consider how you can share this message of hope and comfort with others.

Scripture: Revelation 21:4
"And God will wipe away every tear from their eyes; there shall be no more death, nor sorrow, nor crying. There shall be no more pain, for the former things have passed away."

Reflection: As we end our day, Revelation 21:4 provides us with a powerful reminder of God's ultimate promise. Reflecting on this verse, we are reminded that all the pain, sorrow, and suffering of this world are temporary. God has promised a future where He will personally comfort us, and all the former things will pass away. This evening, let us take comfort in knowing that our current trials are fleeting compared to the eternal joy and peace that await us. Let this promise renew our strength and fill us with hope as we rest tonight.

Prayer: Lord, as we conclude this day, we thank You for the assurance of a future without pain, sorrow, or death. Help us to find peace in Your promises and to trust in Your perfect plan. As we rest tonight, comfort our hearts and minds with the hope of Your eternal kingdom. Renew our strength and prepare us to face a new day with faith and courage. Thank You for Your love and the promise of a better future. In Jesus' name, we pray. Amen.

Meditative Thought: Before you sleep, reflect on the temporary nature of our present struggles in light of God's eternal promise. How does this perspective change your outlook on today's challenges? Consider how you can live in a way that reflects this hope and brings comfort to those around you.

Scripture: 1 Corinthians 13:4
"Love suffers long and is kind; love does not envy; love does not parade itself, is not puffed up."

Reflection: As we begin our day, let's reflect on the profound nature of love as described in 1 Corinthians 13:4. Love, as defined here, is patient and kind. It is not envious or boastful, nor does it seek attention or elevate itself above others. This kind of love, modeled after God's own love for us, calls us to a higher standard of living and interacting with one another. Today, let's strive to embody this love in all our relationships, showing patience, kindness, humility, and selflessness to those around us.

Prayer: Heavenly Father, thank You for the gift of love, which You have generously poured out upon us. As we embark on this new day, help us to live out the qualities of love described in Your Word. Teach us to be patient and kind, to resist envy and pride, and to show genuine care and concern for others. Fill our hearts with Your love so that we may be vessels of Your grace and mercy to those around us. In Jesus' name, we pray. Amen.

Meditative Thought: Consider the ways in which you can demonstrate love to others today. How can you practice patience, kindness, humility, and selflessness in your interactions? Reflect on the impact of embodying these qualities in your relationships.

Scripture: 1 Corinthians 13:4
"Love suffers long and is kind; love does not envy; love does not parade itself, is not puffed up."

Reflection: As we conclude our day, let's reflect on the characteristics of love outlined in 1 Corinthians 13:4. Love, as described here, is enduring and compassionate. It does not harbor jealousy or arrogance, nor does it seek to draw attention to itself. This evening, let's examine our interactions and attitudes throughout the day. Have we lived in accordance with the love described in this passage? Have we shown patience, kindness, and humility to those around us? Let's take this time to seek forgiveness for any shortcomings and ask God to fill us afresh with His love, empowering us to love others more fully tomorrow.

Prayer: Lord, as we come to the close of this day, we thank You for Your perfect love that never fails. Forgive us for the times when we fell short of embodying Your love in our actions and attitudes. Fill us with Your Spirit tonight, Lord, and renew within us a deep sense of love for others. Help us to grow in patience, kindness, and humility, reflecting Your love to the world around us. May Your love be evident in all we do. In Jesus' name, we pray. Amen.

Meditative Thought: Reflect on your day and consider how well you demonstrated love to others. Were there moments when you struggled to embody the qualities of love described in this passage? How can you grow in love and become more like Christ in your relationships?

Scripture: Jude 1:25
"To God our Savior, Who alone is wise, Be glory and majesty, Dominion and power, Both now and forever. Amen."

Reflection: As we begin our day, let's reflect on the powerful words of praise found in Jude 1:25. This verse directs our attention to God, our Savior, who alone is wise. It acknowledges His glory, majesty, dominion, and power, both now and forever. In the midst of our daily activities and responsibilities, it's important to pause and offer praise to the One who is worthy of all honor and adoration. Today, let's make it a priority to glorify God in all that we do, recognizing His sovereignty over every aspect of our lives.

Prayer: Heavenly Father, we come before You with hearts full of praise and adoration. You alone are worthy of all glory, majesty, dominion, and power. As we embark on this new day, help us to live in a way that brings honor to Your name. May Your wisdom guide our decisions, and Your strength empower us to fulfill Your purposes. We acknowledge Your sovereignty over our lives and commit to glorifying You in all that we do. In Jesus' name, we pray. Amen.

Meditative Thought: Reflect on the attributes of God mentioned in Jude 1:25—His wisdom, glory, majesty, dominion, and power. How can you acknowledge and honor these attributes in your daily life? Consider ways to live in alignment with God's sovereignty and bring glory to His name throughout your day.

Scripture: Jude 1:25
"To God our Savior, Who alone is wise, Be glory and majesty, Dominion and power, Both now and forever. Amen."

Reflection: As we conclude our day, let's return to the words of praise found in Jude 1:25. This verse serves as a beautiful reminder of God's eternal attributes and His sovereignty over all things. As we reflect on the events of the day, let's take a moment to offer Him glory and honor for His wisdom, majesty, dominion, and power. Despite the challenges we may have faced, we can find comfort and strength in knowing that God reigns both now and forever. Let's rest in His unfailing love and trust in His perfect plan for our lives.

Prayer: Lord, we thank You for Your unchanging nature and Your eternal attributes. Tonight, we offer You praise and honor for Your wisdom, glory, majesty, dominion, and power. As we prepare to rest, we find comfort in Your sovereignty over all things. Grant us peaceful sleep and renew our strength for the day ahead. May Your name be exalted in our lives, both now and forevermore. In Jesus' name, we pray. Amen.

Meditative Thought: Reflect on the ways in which you have witnessed God's wisdom, majesty, dominion, and power throughout your day. How can you continue to acknowledge and honor these attributes in your life? Take a moment to express gratitude to God for His presence and provision.

Scripture: 1 John 5:2
"By this we know that we love the children of God, when we love God and keep His commandments."

Reflection: As we begin our day, let's reflect on the connection between our love for God and our love for His children as described in 1 John 5:2. This verse reminds us that our love for others is a reflection of our love for God and our obedience to His commandments. Loving our brothers and sisters in Christ is not merely an option but an essential expression of our relationship with God. Today, let's ask ourselves: Are we demonstrating our love for God by loving and caring for His children? Let's seek opportunities to extend love, kindness, and compassion to those around us, knowing that in doing so, we honor God.

Prayer: Heavenly Father, thank You for the gift of love, both for You and for Your children. Help us to love others as You have loved us, with selflessness and compassion. May our actions today be a reflection of our love for You and our desire to obey Your commandments. Guide us to reach out to those in need and to show kindness to everyone we encounter. May our love for Your children bring glory to Your name. In Jesus' name, we pray. Amen.

Meditative Thought: Consider your interactions with others yesterday. How did you demonstrate love for God's children? Were there moments when you could have shown more compassion or kindness? Reflect on how you can be more intentional in expressing love to those around you today.

Scripture: 1 John 5:2
"By this we know that we love the children of God, when we love God and keep His commandments."

Reflection: As we conclude our day, let's revisit the truth presented in 1 John 5:2. Loving the children of God is intimately connected to our love for God and our obedience to His commandments. Tonight, let's reflect on our actions and attitudes throughout the day. Have we demonstrated love for God by loving and caring for His children? Have we obeyed His commandments in our interactions with others? Let's take this time to seek forgiveness for any shortcomings and to ask God to fill us afresh with His love, empowering us to love others more fully tomorrow.

Prayer: Lord, as we come before You at the end of this day, we confess any moments when we failed to love Your children as You have commanded. Forgive us, Lord, and fill us with Your love anew. Help us to live out our love for You by loving and caring for those around us. Grant us opportunities to show kindness, compassion, and grace to everyone we encounter. May our actions bring honor to Your name and draw others closer to You. In Jesus' name, we pray. Amen.

Meditative Thought: Reflect on the ways in which you demonstrated love for God's children today. Were there moments when you could have shown more compassion or understanding? Consider how you can actively love others tomorrow, seeking to obey God's commandments and reflect His love in all you do.

Scripture: Deuteronomy 10:22
"Your fathers went down to Egypt with seventy persons, and now the Lord your God has made you as the stars of heaven in multitude."

Reflection: As we begin our day, let's reflect on the faithfulness of God as demonstrated in Deuteronomy 10:22. This verse recounts the journey of the Israelites from Egypt, where they started as a small group of seventy persons. Yet, through God's providence and blessing, they multiplied and became as numerous as the stars in the sky. Today, let's remember that our God is a faithful and promise-keeping God. Just as He fulfilled His promises to the Israelites, He will also fulfill His promises to us. Let's start this day with gratitude for His faithfulness and trust in His plans for our lives.

Prayer: Gracious God, we thank You for Your faithfulness throughout history and in our lives today. As we embark on this new day, help us to trust in Your promises and provision. May we remember Your faithfulness in times past and rely on Your guidance for the future. Thank You for making us part of Your grand plan and for the blessings You have bestowed upon us. Strengthen our faith, Lord, and help us to walk in obedience to Your will. In Jesus' name, we pray. Amen.

Meditative Thought: Reflect on the faithfulness of God in your life. How has He fulfilled His promises to you in the past? Consider the ways in which He has blessed you and brought you to where you are today. Let this reflection inspire confidence in His continued faithfulness and provision.

Scripture: Deuteronomy 10:22

"Your fathers went down to Egypt with seventy persons, and now the Lord your God has made you as the stars of heaven in multitude."

Reflection: As we conclude our day, let's meditate on the transformation described in Deuteronomy 10:22. The small group of seventy persons that entered Egypt grew into a multitude as numerous as the stars of heaven, all by the hand of God. This evening, let's consider the ways in which God has multiplied blessings in our lives. Even in times of difficulty or uncertainty, He remains faithful to His promises. Let's rest tonight in the assurance that God's plans for us are good, and He will continue to guide and provide for us in the days to come.

Prayer: Heavenly Father, we are grateful for Your faithfulness and provision in our lives. As we end this day, we thank You for the blessings You have multiplied and for Your steadfast love that never fails. Help us, Lord, to trust in Your promises and to walk in obedience to Your will. May we rest tonight knowing that You are with us, guiding us and providing for us each step of the way. Renew our strength for tomorrow, Lord, and fill us with hope for the future. In Jesus' name, we pray. Amen.

Meditative Thought: Reflect on the ways in which God has multiplied blessings in your life. How have you seen His faithfulness demonstrated recently? Consider the areas in which you need to trust Him more fully and surrender to His plans.

FEBRUARY 23

MORNING DEVOTION

Scripture: Philippians 4:13
"I can do all things through Christ who strengthens me."

Reflection: As we begin our day, let's meditate on the empowering words of Philippians 4:13. This verse reminds us that through Christ, we have the strength to overcome any challenge or obstacle that comes our way. It's a declaration of confidence and faith in God's power working within us. As we face the tasks and responsibilities of the day ahead, let's remember that we are not alone. Christ is with us, empowering us to accomplish all that He has called us to do. With His strength, we can face any situation with courage and perseverance.

Prayer: Heavenly Father, thank You for the promise of Your strength that enables us to face each day with confidence and courage. As we embark on this new day, we surrender ourselves to Your will and Your power at work within us. Strengthen us, Lord, for the tasks ahead, and help us to rely fully on Your provision and guidance. May Your presence be evident in all that we do today. In Jesus' name, we pray. Amen.

Meditative Thought: Reflect on the challenges you anticipate facing today. How can you approach them with the confidence that comes from knowing Christ strengthens you? Consider how you can lean on His power and guidance in every situation you encounter throughout the day.

Scripture: Philippians 4:13
"I can do all things through Christ who strengthens me."

Reflection: As we come to the close of this day, let's reflect on the truth of Philippians 4:13. This verse serves as a reminder that our strength and abilities are not limited to our own efforts but are empowered by Christ who strengthens us. As we look back on the events of the day, let's acknowledge the ways in which His strength sustained us and enabled us to persevere through challenges. Whatever successes or setbacks we encountered, let's give thanks for His faithfulness and provision. Let's rest tonight in the assurance that with Christ, we can face whatever tomorrow may bring.

Prayer: Gracious God, we thank You for Your strength that sustains us through every trial and triumph. As we conclude this day, we offer You our gratitude for Your faithfulness and provision. Help us to trust in Your power at work within us and to rely fully on Your strength for each new day. Renew our minds and hearts tonight, Lord, as we rest in Your presence. May Your peace fill us as we sleep, knowing that You are with us always. In Jesus' name, we pray. Amen.

Meditative Thought: Reflect on the ways in which Christ's strength sustained you throughout the day. How did you experience His power working within you? Consider how you can continue to rely on His strength in the days ahead, facing each challenge with confidence and trust in His provision.

FEBRUARY 24

MORNING DEVOTION

Scripture: Psalm 30:5
"For His anger is but for a moment, His favor is for life; Weeping may endure for a night, But joy comes in the morning."

Reflection: As we begin our day, let's reflect on the comforting words of Psalm 30:5. This verse reminds us that though we may experience moments of hardship and sorrow, God's favor and joy are enduring. Even in the darkest of nights, His light will shine, bringing hope and renewal. Let's take comfort in the assurance that God's love and mercy far outweigh any temporary trials we may face. As we journey through this day, let's hold fast to the promise of joy that comes in the morning, trusting in God's faithfulness to bring beauty from our ashes.

Prayer: Gracious Father, we thank You for Your unfailing love and faithfulness. As we begin this day, we find comfort in Your promise that joy comes in the morning. Help us to trust in Your timing and to remain steadfast in hope, even in the midst of trials. May Your presence be our source of strength and courage today, knowing that Your favor rests upon us for life. Grant us grace to endure any weeping that may come our way, knowing that Your joy will dawn upon us. In Jesus' name, we pray. Amen.

Meditative Thought: Consider a difficult time you've experienced in the past. How did God's joy eventually replace your sorrow? Reflect on His faithfulness in bringing you through that season, and find encouragement knowing that He will do the same in any current struggles you face.

Scripture: Psalm 30:5
"For His anger is but for a moment, His favor is for life; Weeping may endure for a night, But joy comes in the morning."

Reflection: As we come to the close of this day, let's meditate on the hopeful promise found in Psalm 30:5. This verse reminds us that though we may experience seasons of weeping and sorrow, joy awaits us in the morning. Even in our darkest moments, God's favor and love remain constant. Let's take comfort in the assurance that our trials are temporary, but His joy is everlasting. As we prepare to rest tonight, let's entrust our cares and burdens to Him, knowing that He will bring beauty from our ashes and turn our mourning into dancing.

Prayer: Heavenly Father, as we conclude this day, we thank You for Your steadfast love and faithfulness. Thank You for the promise that joy comes in the morning. As we rest tonight, may Your peace surround us, and may Your joy fill our hearts. Help us to release any burdens or worries we carry, knowing that You are in control. Grant us restful sleep and renew our strength for the day ahead. We trust in Your unfailing love, Lord, and eagerly anticipate the joy that You will bring. In Jesus' name, we pray. Amen.

Meditative Thought: Reflect on the joy that awaits you in the morning. How does this promise bring you comfort and hope as you prepare for rest tonight? Surrender any burdens or worries to God, trusting in His ability to bring joy and renewal in the days ahead.

Scripture: Psalm 3:3
"But You, O Lord, are a shield for me, My glory and the One who lifts up my head."

Reflection: As we begin our day, let's meditate on the comforting words of Psalm 3:3. In times of trouble and distress, the psalmist finds solace in the Lord as his shield, glory, and the lifter of his head. This verse reminds us that God is our protector, our source of honor, and the One who lifts us up when we are downcast. Whatever challenges or uncertainties we may face today, let's take comfort in knowing that the Lord is with us, surrounding us with His love and strength. Let's trust in His unfailing protection and allow Him to lift our heads in confidence and hope.

Prayer: Heavenly Father, we thank You for being our shield and our source of strength. As we begin this day, we place our trust in You, knowing that You are our protector and our glory. Lift up our heads, Lord, and fill us with confidence and courage to face whatever lies ahead. May Your presence go before us, guiding us in Your ways and surrounding us with Your love. Help us to rest in Your care, knowing that You are always with us. In Jesus' name, we pray. Amen.

Meditative Thought: Consider a time when you felt discouraged or downtrodden. How did God lift you up and restore your hope? Reflect on His faithfulness in being your shield and your source of strength. As you face the challenges of today, trust in His promise to lift your head and fill you with confidence.

Scripture: Psalm 3:3
"But You, O Lord, are a shield for me, My glory and the One who lifts up my head."

Reflection: As we come to the close of this day, let's reflect on the reassuring words of Psalm 3:3. Even in the midst of trials and difficulties, the psalmist finds refuge in the Lord as his shield, glory, and the One who lifts up his head. This evening, let's take comfort in the presence of God as our protector and source of honor. As we lay our heads down to rest, let's surrender any worries or fears to Him, trusting in His unfailing love and provision. May His presence bring us peace and assurance as we sleep, knowing that He watches over us and lifts us up in His grace.

Prayer: Gracious God, we thank You for being our shield and our glory. As we conclude this day, we surrender our cares and concerns to You, knowing that You are the One who lifts up our heads. Grant us peaceful sleep tonight, Lord, and surround us with Your loving presence. Protect us through the night, and may we awaken refreshed and renewed, ready to face a new day in Your strength. Thank You for Your faithfulness, Lord. In Jesus' name, we pray. Amen.

Meditative Thought: Reflect on the ways in which God has been your shield and the lifter of your head throughout this day. How did His presence bring you comfort and assurance? As you prepare for rest, trust in His continued care and provision, knowing that He watches over you through the night.

Scripture: Daniel 4:34
"And at the end of the time I, Nebuchadnezzar, lifted my eyes to heaven, and my understanding returned to me; and I blessed the Most High and praised and honored Him who lives forever: For His dominion is an everlasting dominion, And His kingdom is from generation to generation."

Reflection: As we begin our day, let's meditate on the profound words of Nebuchadnezzar in Daniel 4:34. After experiencing a period of madness, Nebuchadnezzar humbly acknowledges the sovereignty and eternal nature of God's dominion and kingdom. This verse serves as a reminder that God's reign is unchanging and everlasting, extending from generation to generation. As we face the uncertainties of life, let's take comfort in knowing that God's rule is constant and unwavering. Let's start this day with reverence and praise for the Most High, acknowledging His eternal dominion over all things.

Prayer: Heavenly Father, we bless Your name and praise You for Your eternal dominion and kingdom. As we embark on this new day, help us to remember that You are the sovereign ruler over all creation. May Your will be done on earth as it is in heaven. Grant us wisdom and discernment to live according to Your purposes, trusting in Your unfailing guidance. May Your name be honored and glorified in all that we do. In Jesus' name, we pray. Amen.

Meditative Thought: Reflect on the eternal nature of God's dominion and kingdom. How does this truth bring you comfort and assurance as you face the challenges of today? Consider how you can live in alignment with God's sovereign rule, trusting in His wisdom and providence.

Scripture: Daniel 4:34
"And at the end of the time I, Nebuchadnezzar, lifted my eyes to heaven, and my understanding returned to me; and I blessed the Most High and praised and honored Him who lives forever: For His dominion is an everlasting dominion, And His kingdom is from generation to generation."

Reflection: As we come to the close of this day, let's reflect on the profound declaration of Nebuchadnezzar in Daniel 4:34. After experiencing a period of madness, Nebuchadnezzar acknowledges the eternal dominion and kingdom of God. This evening, let's join him in blessing and praising the Most High, recognizing His unchanging sovereignty over all generations. As we prepare for rest, let's surrender any worries or anxieties to God, trusting in His eternal rule and provision. May His kingdom reign in our hearts and minds, bringing peace and assurance through the night.

Prayer: Gracious God, we bless Your name and praise You for Your eternal dominion and kingdom. As we conclude this day, we lift our hearts in worship and adoration to You. Thank You for Your unchanging sovereignty and steadfast love. As we rest tonight, may Your kingdom come and Your will be done in our lives. Grant us peaceful sleep and renewal for the day ahead. May Your name be exalted forever and ever. In Jesus' name, we pray. Amen.

Meditative Thought: Reflect on the eternal nature of God's dominion and kingdom. How does this truth bring you comfort and assurance as you prepare for rest tonight? Surrender any concerns or fears to Him, trusting in His unchanging sovereignty and provision.

Scripture: Romans 8:1
"There is therefore now no condemnation to those who are in Christ Jesus, who do not walk according to the flesh, but according to the Spirit."

Reflection: As we begin our day, let's meditate on the liberating truth found in Romans 8:1. This verse reminds us that through Christ Jesus, there is no condemnation for those who walk according to the Spirit. It is a powerful declaration of God's grace and mercy, offering freedom from the guilt and shame of sin. Today, let's remember that we are forgiven and accepted by God because of Christ's sacrifice on our behalf. Let's strive to live in obedience to His Spirit, walking in righteousness and holiness, and embracing the abundant life He has promised us.

Prayer: Heavenly Father, we thank You for the freedom we have in Christ Jesus. Thank You for the forgiveness of sin and the assurance of Your love and acceptance. Help us to walk according to Your Spirit today, avoiding the ways of the flesh. Fill us with Your wisdom and strength, that we may live in obedience to Your will and bring glory to Your name. May Your grace and mercy guide us through this day. In Jesus' name, we pray. Amen.

Meditative Thought: Consider the freedom you have in Christ Jesus. How does the absence of condemnation impact your daily life and choices? Reflect on ways you can walk more closely with the Spirit today, embracing the abundant life He offers.

Scripture: Romans 8:1
"There is therefore now no condemnation to those who are in Christ Jesus, who do not walk according to the flesh, but according to the Spirit."

Reflection: As we come to the close of this day, let's reflect on the reassuring truth of Romans 8:1. Through Christ Jesus, there is no condemnation for those who walk according to the Spirit. This evening, let's take comfort in the freedom we have from the guilt and shame of sin. Let's confess any shortcomings or failures to God, knowing that His grace covers all our sins. As we prepare for rest, let's surrender ourselves anew to the leading of the Holy Spirit, seeking to walk in obedience and righteousness.

Prayer: Gracious Father, we thank You for the assurance of Your love and forgiveness through Christ Jesus. As we conclude this day, we confess any ways in which we have fallen short of Your glory. Thank You for Your abundant grace that covers our sins. Fill us afresh with Your Spirit tonight, Lord, and help us to walk in obedience to Your will. Grant us peaceful rest and assurance of Your presence through the night. In Jesus' name, we pray. Amen.

Meditative Thought: Reflect on the freedom you have from condemnation through Christ Jesus. How does this truth impact your mindset as you prepare for rest tonight? Surrender any guilt or shame to God, trusting in His grace to cover all your sins.

FEBRUARY 28

MORNING DEVOTION

Scripture: Philippians 4:5
"Let your gentleness be known to all men. The Lord is at hand."

Reflection: As we begin our day, let's reflect on the exhortation found in Philippians 4:5. This verse encourages us to let our gentleness be known to all people. It's a reminder to interact with others in a spirit of kindness, patience, and humility, reflecting the character of Christ. As we go about our tasks and encounters today, let's strive to demonstrate gentleness in our words and actions, showing grace and compassion to those around us. And let's remember the comforting truth that the Lord is near, guiding and sustaining us in every moment.

Prayer: Gracious Father, help us to embody gentleness in all our interactions today. May Your Spirit empower us to respond to others with kindness and compassion, reflecting Your love to the world around us. Thank You for the assurance that You are near, guiding and comforting us in every situation. Grant us the wisdom to walk in Your ways and the humility to extend grace to others. In Jesus' name, we pray. Amen.

Meditative Thought: Consider how you can demonstrate gentleness in your interactions today. How might your words and actions reflect the kindness and compassion of Christ? Reflect on the impact of gentleness in building relationships and fostering unity in your community.

Scripture: Philippians 4:5
"Let your gentleness be known to all men. The Lord is at hand."

Reflection: As we come to the close of this day, let's reflect on the call to gentleness found in Philippians 4:5. This evening, let's consider how well we lived out this exhortation in our interactions with others. Did we respond with kindness and patience, reflecting the character of Christ? And let's take comfort in the reminder that the Lord is near, ever-present to guide and sustain us. As we prepare for rest, let's surrender any burdens or concerns to Him, trusting in His loving care.

Prayer: Heavenly Father, forgive us for any moments today when we failed to demonstrate gentleness in our interactions with others. Grant us Your Spirit's help to respond with kindness and patience, reflecting Your love to the world around us. Thank You for Your nearness, Lord, and for Your faithful presence in every moment. As we rest tonight, may Your peace fill our hearts, knowing that You are with us always. In Jesus' name, we pray. Amen.

Meditative Thought: Reflect on your interactions today. Were there moments when you could have responded with more gentleness? How might you cultivate a spirit of gentleness in your relationships going forward? Surrender any areas of struggle to God, asking for His strength to walk in His ways.

Scripture: Colossians 3:16
"Let the word of Christ dwell in you richly in all wisdom, teaching and admonishing one another in psalms and hymns and spiritual songs, singing with grace in your hearts to the Lord."

Reflection: As we begin our day, let's reflect on the instruction given in Colossians 3:16. This verse encourages us to let the word of Christ dwell in us richly, guiding us in wisdom and understanding. It reminds us of the importance of engaging with Scripture and allowing its truth to permeate every aspect of our lives. Today, let's commit to immersing ourselves in God's Word, seeking His guidance and direction in all that we do. Let's also encourage one another through songs of praise and worship, lifting our hearts in gratitude to the Lord.

Prayer: Heavenly Father, we thank You for the gift of Your Word, which guides us in wisdom and understanding. Help us to let the word of Christ dwell in us richly today, transforming our hearts and minds according to Your will. Grant us the grace to encourage and uplift one another through songs of praise and worship. May Your Spirit work in us, teaching and admonishing us as we engage with Scripture and seek Your guidance. In Jesus' name, we pray. Amen.

Meditative Thought: Consider how you can let the word of Christ dwell in you richly today. How might you engage with Scripture in a deeper way, allowing its truth to shape your thoughts and actions? Reflect on the impact of worship and praise in fostering a heart of gratitude and joy.

Scripture: Colossians 3:16

"Let the word of Christ dwell in you richly in all wisdom, teaching and admonishing one another in psalms and hymns and spiritual songs, singing with grace in your hearts to the Lord."

Reflection: As we come to the close of this day, let's reflect on the exhortation found in Colossians 3:16. Did we allow the word of Christ to dwell in us richly, guiding us in wisdom and understanding? Let's take a moment to consider our engagement with Scripture and our willingness to be transformed by its truth. And let's also reflect on the ways we encouraged and uplifted others through songs of praise and worship, singing with grace in our hearts to the Lord. As we prepare for rest, let's commit ourselves anew to letting God's Word dwell richly in us each day.

Prayer: Gracious Father, as we conclude this day, we thank You for the guidance and wisdom found in Your Word. Forgive us for any moments when we neglected to let the word of Christ dwell in us richly. Renew our commitment to engaging with Scripture and allowing its truth to shape our lives. Thank You for the opportunity to encourage and uplift one another through songs of praise and worship. As we rest tonight, may Your Word continue to dwell in us richly, transforming us into the image of Christ. In Jesus' name, we pray. Amen.

Meditative Thought: Reflect on your engagement with Scripture and worship today. How did these practices impact your relationship with God and others? Consider how you can cultivate a deeper connection with God's Word and worship in the days ahead.

MARCH 1

MORNING DEVOTION

Scripture: 1 Timothy 4:12
"Let no one despise your youth, but be an example to the believers in word, in conduct, in love, in spirit, in faith, in purity."

Reflection: As we start our day, let's reflect on the exhortation Paul gives to Timothy in 1 Timothy 4:12. Despite his youth, Timothy is encouraged to set an example for other believers in every aspect of his life. This verse challenges us, regardless of our age, to lead by example in our words, actions, love, spirit, faith, and purity. Today, let's strive to live out these qualities, influencing those around us positively. Our conduct should reflect the character of Christ, inspiring others to grow in their faith and relationship with God.

Prayer: Heavenly Father, thank You for the opportunity to be an example to those around us. Help us to embody Your love, spirit, faith, and purity in all that we do today. Guide our words and actions so that they may reflect Your character and bring glory to Your name. Strengthen us to lead by example, showing others what it means to follow You wholeheartedly. In Jesus' name, we pray. Amen.

Meditative Thought: Consider how you can be an example to others today in your words, conduct, love, spirit, faith, and purity. Reflect on specific actions you can take to demonstrate the character of Christ to those around you.

Scripture: 1 Timothy 4:12
"Let no one despise your youth, but be an example to the believers in word, in conduct, in love, in spirit, in faith, in purity."

Reflection: As we conclude our day, let's revisit the powerful message of 1 Timothy 4:12. Reflect on how you demonstrated being an example to others in your words, actions, love, spirit, faith, and purity. Did your conduct today reflect the character of Christ? This evening, take time to acknowledge both your successes and areas for improvement. Remember that being an example is a continual journey of growth and transformation in Christ. Let's ask God for the strength and wisdom to keep striving to be a positive influence on those around us.

Prayer: Gracious God, thank You for Your guidance and presence throughout this day. As we reflect on our actions and words, we ask for Your forgiveness for any shortcomings. Help us to continually grow in love, spirit, faith, and purity. Empower us to be better examples to others, leading them closer to You. Grant us restful sleep and renew our strength for the day ahead. In Jesus' name, we pray. Amen.

Meditative Thought: Reflect on your day and how you set an example in various areas of your life. Consider the impact of your actions and words on others. As you rest, think about how you can improve and continue to grow in Christ's likeness.

MARCH 2

MORNING DEVOTION

Scripture: John 16:33b
"In the world you will have tribulation; but be of good cheer, I have overcome the world."

Reflection: As we begin our day, let's take comfort in the words of Jesus from John 16:33b. He acknowledges that we will face tribulation in this world, but He also assures us of His victory over the world. This promise is a source of hope and encouragement for us as we navigate the challenges and uncertainties of life. Today, let's hold on to the truth that Jesus has overcome the world. No matter what difficulties we encounter, we can face them with confidence and joy, knowing that our Savior has already secured the ultimate victory.

Prayer: Heavenly Father, thank You for the assurance of victory through Jesus Christ. As we face the challenges of this day, help us to remember that Jesus has overcome the world. Fill our hearts with peace and joy, even in the midst of tribulation. Strengthen our faith and give us the courage to face whatever comes our way. May we live as overcomers, reflecting the hope and victory we have in Christ. In Jesus' name, we pray. Amen.

Meditative Thought: Reflect on the challenges you may face today. How can the knowledge that Jesus has overcome the world influence your perspective and response to these challenges? Consider how you can live with confidence and joy, trusting in His victory.

Scripture: John 16:33b
"In the world you will have tribulation; but be of good cheer, I have overcome the world."

Reflection: As we come to the end of our day, let's reflect on the comforting words of Jesus in John 16:33b. We may have faced various trials and difficulties today, but we can find peace and joy in the knowledge that Jesus has overcome the world. His victory gives us hope and strength, even in the midst of tribulation. Let's take this time to surrender our worries and burdens to Him, trusting in His power and love. As we rest tonight, may His peace fill our hearts and minds, reminding us that we are more than conquerors through Him.

Prayer: Gracious Lord, thank You for Your victory over the world and the assurance it brings us. As we reflect on the challenges of this day, we surrender our worries and burdens to You. Fill us with Your peace and joy, knowing that You have already overcome every obstacle we face. Help us to rest in Your love and power tonight, renewing our strength for tomorrow. May Your presence comfort and sustain us always. In Jesus' name, we pray. Amen.

Meditative Thought: As the day comes to a close, let your heart find peace in the words of Jesus. No matter the struggles you face, remember that Christ has already triumphed over every challenge. His victory is your assurance of strength and hope in the midst of trials. Rest tonight in the knowledge that you are held by the One who has conquered all.

Scripture: Hebrews 13:5

"Let your conduct be without covetousness; be content with such things as you have. For He Himself has said, 'I will never leave you nor forsake you.'"

Reflection: As we start our day, let's focus on the powerful message in Hebrews 13:5. This verse calls us to live a life free from covetousness, encouraging us to be content with what we have. The reason for our contentment is grounded in the promise of God's unfailing presence: "I will never leave you nor forsake you." In a world that constantly pushes us to desire more, this assurance reminds us that our true satisfaction comes from God's presence in our lives. Today, let's choose contentment, knowing that God is with us and He provides all we need.

Prayer: Heavenly Father, thank You for Your promise that You will never leave us nor forsake us. Help us to live contentedly, free from the desire for more worldly possessions. Remind us throughout the day of Your constant presence and provision. Guide our actions and thoughts, and help us to find satisfaction in You alone. May we walk in Your peace and joy, knowing that You are always with us. In Jesus' name, we pray. Amen.

Meditative Thought: Consider the things you have and the areas of your life where you can practice contentment today. Reflect on the promise that God will never leave you nor forsake you. How does this assurance impact your attitude towards your possessions and desires?

Scripture: Hebrews 13:5

"Let your conduct be without covetousness; be content with such things as you have. For He Himself has said, 'I will never leave you nor forsake you.'"

Reflection: As we conclude our day, let's revisit the comforting truth in Hebrews 13:5. Reflect on how you practiced contentment today. Did you find peace in God's promise of His unfailing presence? This evening, let's examine our hearts for any traces of covetousness or discontent and surrender them to God. The assurance that He will never leave us nor forsake us is a powerful reminder of His constant love and care. As we prepare for rest, let's embrace the peace that comes from trusting in His presence and provision.

Prayer: Gracious Lord, thank You for Your steadfast promise to never leave us nor forsake us. As we reflect on this day, we surrender any discontent or covetousness in our hearts. Fill us with Your peace and contentment, knowing that Your presence is our greatest treasure. Help us to rest in the assurance of Your love and care. Renew our strength and fill us with Your joy as we trust in Your unfailing promises. In Jesus' name, we pray. Amen.

Meditative Thought: Reflect on your day and how you experienced God's presence. Did you find contentment in what you have? Consider how the promise of God's constant presence can bring you peace as you rest tonight. Trust in His provision and let go of any worries or desires for more.

Scripture: Romans 15:4
"For whatever things were written before were written for our learning, that we through the patience and comfort of the Scriptures might have hope."

Reflection: As we begin our day, let's reflect on the wisdom of Romans 15:4. This verse reminds us that the Scriptures were written for our learning, offering us patience, comfort, and hope. Each morning is a new opportunity to delve into God's Word, drawing strength and encouragement from its timeless truths. Today, let's commit to spending time in the Scriptures, allowing their wisdom to guide us, comfort us, and instill in us a deep, abiding hope. The Bible is not just a historical document; it is a living source of divine instruction and inspiration meant to shape our lives and fortify our spirits.

Prayer: Heavenly Father, thank You for the gift of Your Word, which provides us with patience, comfort, and hope. As we start this day, help us to seek wisdom and guidance in the Scriptures. May Your Word dwell richly in our hearts, guiding our actions and thoughts. Grant us the patience to endure challenges and the comfort that comes from Your promises. Fill us with hope that comes from knowing You are always with us. In Jesus' name, we pray. Amen.

Meditative Thought: Consider how you can incorporate Scripture into your daily routine today. Reflect on the promise that the Scriptures bring patience, comfort, and hope. How can this truth influence your approach to the day's tasks and challenges?

Scripture: Romans 15:4
"For whatever things were written before were written for our learning, that we through the patience and comfort of the Scriptures might have hope."

Reflection: As we end our day, let's revisit the profound message of Romans 15:4. Reflect on the role of Scripture in your life today. Did you find patience and comfort through its words? The Bible is our constant source of hope, guiding us through life's ups and downs. This evening, let's thank God for His Word and the lessons it teaches us. Let's also seek His forgiveness for moments when we may have neglected its wisdom. As we prepare for rest, let's immerse ourselves in the hope that Scripture provides, trusting in God's everlasting promises.

Prayer: Gracious Lord, thank You for Your Word that guides, comforts, and gives us hope. As we reflect on this day, we are grateful for the lessons and encouragement found in Scripture. Forgive us for any times we overlooked its wisdom. Help us to carry the patience and comfort of Your Word into our rest tonight and into the new day tomorrow. Fill our hearts with hope as we trust in Your promises. In Jesus' name, we pray. Amen.

Meditative Thought: Reflect on how the Scriptures provided you with patience, comfort, and hope today. How did God's Word influence your interactions and decisions? As you rest tonight, meditate on the enduring hope that comes from His promises and let it fill your heart with peace.

Scripture: Proverbs 1:5
"A wise man will hear and increase learning, and a man of understanding will attain wise counsel."

Reflection: As we begin our day, let's meditate on the wisdom of Proverbs 1:5. This verse encourages us to be active listeners and continuous learners. A wise person is always open to gaining more knowledge and understanding. In our busy lives, it's easy to think we know enough or to be resistant to new ideas and correction. However, true wisdom comes from a humble heart that seeks to grow and learn. Today, let's approach each situation with a teachable spirit, eager to listen and gain wisdom. Seek out opportunities to learn from others, whether through conversations, experiences, or Scripture.

Prayer: Heavenly Father, thank You for the gift of wisdom and understanding. As we embark on this day, help us to have open hearts and minds, ready to hear and increase our learning. Grant us the humility to seek wise counsel and the discernment to recognize it. Guide our steps and fill us with a desire to grow in knowledge and understanding according to Your will. In Jesus' name, we pray. Amen.

Meditative Thought: Consider how you can be an active listener and learner today. Reflect on the importance of seeking wise counsel and the humility required to grow in understanding. How can you approach your interactions and tasks with a teachable spirit?

Scripture: Proverbs 1:5
"A wise man will hear and increase learning, and a man of understanding will attain wise counsel."

Reflection: As we end our day, let's revisit the counsel of Proverbs 1:5. Reflect on the moments today where you actively listened and sought to increase your learning. Did you approach situations with a teachable spirit? Were there opportunities to seek or provide wise counsel? This verse reminds us of the ongoing journey of gaining wisdom and understanding. As we wind down, let's thank God for the knowledge we gained today and ask for continued growth in wisdom. Let's commit to being lifelong learners, always open to God's guidance and the insights of others.

Prayer: Gracious God, thank You for the opportunities to learn and grow today. We are grateful for the wisdom and understanding You provide. Forgive us for any moments of pride or resistance to learning. Help us to continually seek Your counsel and the guidance of wise individuals. As we rest tonight, fill our hearts with peace and a desire to grow in knowledge and wisdom. In Jesus' name, we pray. Amen.

Meditative Thought: Reflect on your day and how you approached learning and listening. Did you seek wise counsel and embrace opportunities for growth? As you prepare for rest, consider how you can maintain a teachable spirit and a commitment to increasing your understanding in the days to come.

MARCH 6

MORNING DEVOTION

Scripture: 2 Timothy 2:15
"Be diligent to present yourself approved to God, a worker who does not need to be ashamed, rightly dividing the word of truth."

Reflection: As we start our day, let's focus on the exhortation found in 2 Timothy 2:15. This verse calls us to be diligent in our efforts to understand and apply God's Word. It emphasizes the importance of studying Scripture carefully and correctly, ensuring that we handle the word of truth with accuracy. Our goal is to present ourselves approved to God, unashamed of our work. Today, let's commit to deepening our understanding of the Bible, allowing its truths to guide our thoughts and actions. This diligence in study will not only enhance our personal spiritual growth but also equip us to share God's Word effectively with others.

Prayer: Heavenly Father, thank You for the gift of Your Word. As we begin this day, grant us the diligence to study and understand Scripture deeply. Help us to rightly divide the word of truth, applying its teachings accurately in our lives. May our efforts be pleasing to You, and may we be unashamed workers in Your kingdom. Guide us in our studies and interactions, allowing Your Word to shape our thoughts, words, and actions. In Jesus' name, we pray. Amen.

Meditative Thought: Reflect on how you can incorporate diligent study of Scripture into your daily routine. Consider specific ways to deepen your understanding and application of God's Word. How can this commitment impact your day and your interactions with others?

Scripture: 2 Timothy 2:15
"Be diligent to present yourself approved to God, a worker who does not need to be ashamed, rightly dividing the word of truth."

Reflection: As we conclude our day, let's revisit the charge in 2 Timothy 2:15. Reflect on how you approached the study and application of God's Word today. Were you diligent in seeking understanding and rightly dividing the word of truth? This verse reminds us of the importance of being dedicated students of Scripture, striving to live in a way that is approved by God. As we end our day, let's evaluate our efforts and seek God's guidance for continual growth in our understanding and application of His Word.

Prayer: Gracious Lord, thank You for guiding us through this day. As we reflect on our efforts to study and apply Your Word, we seek Your forgiveness for any shortcomings and ask for Your help in becoming more diligent. Strengthen our resolve to be workers who rightly divide the word of truth and live according to Your teachings. Fill us with a desire to continually grow in our understanding of Scripture. As we rest tonight, let Your Word dwell richly in our hearts, shaping us to be more like Christ. In Jesus' name, we pray. Amen.

Meditative Thought: Reflect on your day and how you engaged with God's Word. Did you approach Scripture with diligence and a desire to rightly understand and apply it? Consider ways to improve your study habits and deepen your relationship with God through His Word as you prepare for rest.

Scripture: Matthew 14:31
"And immediately Jesus stretched out His hand and caught him, and said to him, 'O you of little faith, why did you doubt?'"

Reflection: As we begin our day, let's reflect on the moment when Peter walked on water towards Jesus and then started to sink due to doubt. In Matthew 14:31, we see Jesus' immediate response: He stretched out His hand and caught Peter. This act of rescue is a powerful reminder of Jesus' readiness to save us whenever we falter. Despite our moments of doubt and fear, Jesus is always there, extending His hand to lift us up. Today, let's focus on strengthening our faith, trusting in Jesus' unwavering presence and support. Whatever challenges we face, let's remember that He is ready to catch us when we call out to Him.

Prayer: Heavenly Father, thank You for Your constant presence and willingness to rescue us in times of doubt. As we start this day, help us to strengthen our faith and trust in You. Remind us that You are always there, ready to catch us when we falter. Fill us with courage and confidence to face today's challenges, knowing that Your hand is always extended towards us. In Jesus' name, we pray. Amen.

Meditative Thought: Reflect on moments in your life when you have felt doubt or fear. How can you rely more on Jesus' presence and trust in His readiness to catch you? Consider starting each task today with a conscious reminder of His unwavering support.

Scripture: Matthew 14:31
"And immediately Jesus stretched out His hand and caught him, and said to him, 'O you of little faith, why did you doubt?'"

Reflection: As we end our day, let's revisit the comforting scene in Matthew 14:31. Reflect on the times today when you experienced doubt or fear. How did you respond? Did you reach out to Jesus, trusting in His ability to rescue you? This verse serves as a reminder that Jesus is always near, ready to extend His hand and lift us out of our struggles. As we prepare for rest, let's take a moment to thank Him for His constant support and reflect on how we can cultivate greater faith. Let's commit to letting go of our doubts and embracing the assurance of His presence in our lives.

Prayer: Gracious Lord, thank You for being our ever-present help in times of need. As we reflect on this day, we acknowledge the moments of doubt and fear we experienced. Forgive us for our lack of faith and strengthen our trust in You. Thank You for always being ready to catch us when we fall. Help us to rest in the assurance of Your presence and wake up with renewed faith and confidence. In Jesus' name, we pray. Amen.

Meditative Thought: Consider the events of the day and how Jesus' presence impacted your experiences. Reflect on moments of doubt and how you can grow in faith. As you prepare for rest, meditate on the assurance that Jesus is always ready to extend His hand to you, providing support and strength.

Scripture: Isaiah 41:10
"Fear not, for I am with you; Be not dismayed, for I am your God. I will strengthen you, Yes, I will help you, I will uphold you with My righteous right hand."

Reflection: As we start our day, let's focus on the comforting promise found in Isaiah 41:10. This verse reassures us that we need not fear or be dismayed because God is with us. He promises to strengthen, help, and uphold us with His righteous right hand. Today, whatever challenges or uncertainties we may face, we can trust that God's presence and power are with us. His promise to support and strengthen us is unwavering. Let this truth fill your heart with peace and confidence as you go about your day, knowing that the Almighty God is by your side.

Prayer: Heavenly Father, thank You for the assurance that You are always with us. As we begin this day, help us to trust in Your promise to strengthen, help, and uphold us. Remove any fear or dismay from our hearts and fill us with Your peace and confidence. Guide our steps and help us to lean on Your strength in every situation we encounter. Thank You for being our ever-present help and support. In Jesus' name, we pray. Amen.

Meditative Thought: Reflect on the areas of your life where you need God's strength and support today. How can you consciously remind yourself of His promise to be with you and uphold you? Carry this assurance with you throughout the day, letting it influence your thoughts and actions.

Scripture: Isaiah 41:10
"Fear not, for I am with you; Be not dismayed, for I am your God. I will strengthen you, Yes, I will help you, I will uphold you with My righteous right hand."

Reflection: As we conclude our day, let's reflect on the powerful promise of Isaiah 41:10. Consider how God's presence and strength supported you today. Were there moments of fear or dismay where you felt God's comforting presence? This verse reminds us that God is always with us, ready to strengthen, help, and uphold us. As we prepare for rest, let's thank God for His faithfulness throughout the day and trust in His continued support for tomorrow. Rest in the assurance that God's righteous right hand will continue to uphold you.

Prayer: Gracious God, thank You for Your constant presence and support throughout this day. As we reflect on the day's events, we are grateful for the strength and help You provided. Forgive us for any moments of fear or doubt and help us to grow in our trust in You. As we rest tonight, fill us with Your peace and reassurance. Renew our strength for tomorrow and remind us of Your promise to uphold us with Your righteous right hand. In Jesus' name, we pray. Amen.

Meditative Thought: Consider the ways God has strengthened and upheld you today. Reflect on His promise to always be with you and to help you. As you rest tonight, meditate on His unwavering presence and let His peace fill your heart, preparing you for a new day with renewed confidence in His support.

Scripture: Romans 1:17
"For in it the righteousness of God is revealed from faith to faith; as it is written, 'The just shall live by faith.'"

Reflection: As we begin our day, let's reflect on the powerful truth in Romans 1:17. This verse reveals that God's righteousness is manifested through faith, and it emphasizes that those who are righteous will live by faith. Starting our day with this mindset encourages us to trust in God's promises and live out our faith in every situation. Our faith journey is progressive—growing and deepening from one level to another. Today, let's commit to living by faith, trusting that God's righteousness is working in and through us. Let this faith guide our actions, decisions, and interactions throughout the day.

Prayer: Heavenly Father, thank You for revealing Your righteousness through faith. As we start this day, help us to live by faith, trusting in Your promises and guidance. Strengthen our faith and help it to grow deeper as we encounter different experiences today. Let Your righteousness be evident in our lives as we seek to honor You in all that we do. In Jesus' name, we pray. Amen.

Meditative Thought: Reflect on the areas of your life where you need to exercise greater faith. How can you live out your faith more fully today? Consider the progression of your faith journey and seek opportunities to deepen your trust in God.

Scripture: Romans 1:17
"For in it the righteousness of God is revealed from faith to faith; as it is written, 'The just shall live by faith.'"

Reflection: As we conclude our day, let's revisit Romans 1:17 and reflect on how we lived out our faith today. Did we trust in God's promises and let faith guide our actions? This verse reminds us that living by faith is a continuous journey, growing from one stage to the next. As we wind down, let's thank God for the moments where our faith was strengthened and seek His forgiveness for times we may have faltered. Let's commit to continuing our faith journey with renewed determination, knowing that God's righteousness is revealed through our steadfast trust in Him.

Prayer: Gracious Lord, thank You for guiding us through this day. As we reflect on our actions and decisions, we seek Your forgiveness for any moments where our faith wavered. Thank You for the times when our faith was strengthened, and Your righteousness was revealed. Help us to continue growing in our faith, moving from strength to strength. As we rest tonight, fill us with peace and the assurance that You are with us on this journey. In Jesus' name, we pray. Amen.

Meditative Thought: Consider how you exercised faith today. Reflect on the progression of your faith and how it has grown. As you prepare for rest, meditate on the continuous journey of living by faith and trust in God's ongoing work in your life.

Scripture: 1 Timothy 6:12

"Fight the good fight of faith, lay hold on eternal life, to which you were also called and have confessed the good confession in the presence of many witnesses."

Reflection: As we begin our day, let's meditate on the call to "fight the good fight of faith" in 1 Timothy 6:12. This verse reminds us that our faith journey is an active and ongoing battle. We are called to persistently strive towards living a life that reflects our commitment to Christ. By laying hold on eternal life, we focus on the hope and promise of our salvation. Today, let's approach our tasks and interactions with the mindset of a spiritual warrior, ready to stand firm in our faith. Let's remember our calling and the confession we have made before others, using it as motivation to stay true to our faith amidst any challenges we may face.

Prayer: Heavenly Father, thank You for the call to fight the good fight of faith. As we start this day, grant us the strength and determination to live out our faith boldly. Help us to focus on the hope of eternal life and to remain steadfast in our commitment to You. Guide our actions and words so that they reflect our faith in You. Empower us to overcome any challenges we encounter with grace and confidence in Your promises. In Jesus' name, we pray. Amen.

Meditative Thought: Reflect on the areas in your life where you need to actively fight the good fight of faith. How can you remind yourself of your calling and the hope of eternal life throughout the day? Consider the impact of your faith on those around you and strive to live as a witness to God's goodness.

Scripture: 1 Timothy 6:12
"Fight the good fight of faith, lay hold on eternal life, to which you were also called and have confessed the good confession in the presence of many witnesses."

Reflection: As we end our day, let's revisit the exhortation in 1 Timothy 6:12. Reflect on the moments where you actively engaged in the fight of faith today. Were there challenges or temptations that you faced with the strength of your faith? This verse encourages us to hold tightly to the promise of eternal life and to remember the confession we have made before others. As we prepare for rest, let's thank God for the strength He provided and seek His guidance for areas where we can improve. Let's commit to continuing the good fight with renewed vigor tomorrow, always focusing on the eternal reward.

Prayer: Gracious Lord, thank You for guiding us through this day and for the strength to fight the good fight of faith. As we reflect on today's events, we ask for Your forgiveness for any moments of weakness and thank You for the victories we experienced. Help us to hold firmly to the hope of eternal life and to live out our faith with boldness and integrity. As we rest tonight, renew our spirit and prepare us for the challenges of tomorrow. Thank You for Your unwavering presence and support. In Jesus' name, we pray. Amen.

Meditative Thought: Reflect on how you engaged in the good fight of faith today. Consider any challenges you faced and how your faith influenced your responses. As you prepare for rest, meditate on the eternal life promised to you and how it can inspire you to live out your faith more fully each day.

MARCH 11

MORNING DEVOTION

Scripture: Matthew 24:35
"Heaven and earth will pass away, but My words will by no means pass away."

Reflection: As we begin our day, let's reflect on the enduring truth of Matthew 24:35. In a world of uncertainty and change, God's Word stands firm and unchanging. This verse assures us that even as everything else fades away, the words of Jesus remain steadfast and eternal. Today, let's find comfort and stability in the unchanging promises of Scripture. Let's allow God's Word to guide our thoughts, decisions, and actions, knowing that it is a reliable anchor for our souls. As we face the challenges and uncertainties of the day, let's cling to the eternal truths found in God's Word and find strength in its unwavering reliability.

Prayer: Faithful Father, thank You for the assurance that Your Word endures forever. As we embark on this new day, help us to anchor our hearts and minds in Your unchanging truth. Grant us wisdom to understand and apply Your Word to our lives. May it be a lamp to our feet and a light to our path. In moments of uncertainty, remind us of Your steadfast promises, and may they fill us with hope and courage. In Jesus' name, we pray. Amen.

Meditative Thought: Consider the unchanging nature of God's Word in contrast to the ever-changing world around you. How can you rely more fully on Scripture as your foundation and guide today? Reflect on a specific promise from God's Word that brings you comfort and strength.

Scripture: Matthew 24:35
"Heaven and earth will pass away, but My words will by no means pass away."

Reflection: As we conclude our day, let's meditate on the eternal truth of Matthew 24:35. Reflect on the ways God's Word has sustained you throughout the day. Even as the world around us shifts and changes, God's promises remain constant and unwavering. Take a moment to thank God for the stability and comfort His Word provides. As you prepare for rest, entrust your cares and concerns to the One whose words endure forever. Find peace in the assurance that His promises are trustworthy and His love for you is steadfast.

Prayer: Eternal God, we praise You for the unchanging nature of Your Word. Thank You for sustaining us throughout this day with Your promises and truths. As we prepare for rest, we place our trust in You, knowing that Your words will never pass away. Grant us peaceful sleep and renew our strength for the day ahead. May Your presence continue to guide and sustain us, now and always. In Jesus' name, we pray. Amen.

Meditative Thought: Reflect on the ways God's Word has impacted your day and brought you peace and strength. How can you continue to rely on His promises in the days to come? Allow His eternal truth to fill your heart with confidence and assurance as you rest tonight.

Scripture: Hebrews 4:12
"For the word of God is living and powerful, and sharper than any two-edged sword, piercing even to the division of soul and spirit, and of joints and marrow, and is a discerner of the thoughts and intents of the heart."

Reflection: As we embark on a new day, let's contemplate the profound truth of Hebrews 4:12. This verse describes the Word of God as living and powerful, capable of penetrating to the deepest recesses of our being. Just as a sharp sword can divide bone and marrow, God's Word discerns our innermost thoughts and desires. Today, let's approach Scripture with reverence and humility, recognizing its transformative power in our lives. Let's invite God's Word to penetrate our hearts, revealing areas where we need His grace and guidance. As we meditate on Scripture, may it shape our thoughts, words, and actions, leading us closer to Him.

Prayer: Heavenly Father, thank You for the gift of Your living and powerful Word. As we begin this day, we humbly acknowledge its ability to pierce through our defenses and reveal the condition of our hearts. Grant us a deeper understanding and appreciation for Scripture, and help us to apply its truths to our lives. May Your Word guide and transform us, shaping us into vessels of Your love and grace. In Jesus' name, we pray. Amen.

Meditative Thought: Reflect on the power of God's Word to penetrate the depths of your soul. How can you approach Scripture with greater reverence and openness today? Consider specific areas of your life where you need God's guidance and invite His Word to illuminate your path.

Scripture: Hebrews 4:12

"For the word of God is living and powerful, and sharper than any two-edged sword, piercing even to the division of soul and spirit, and of joints and marrow, and is a discerner of the thoughts and intents of the heart."

Reflection: As we conclude our day, let's reflect on the transformative power of God's Word described in Hebrews 4:12. Consider how Scripture has impacted your thoughts, attitudes, and actions throughout the day. Just as a sharp sword divides bone and marrow, God's Word penetrates to the very core of our being, revealing our true intentions and desires. Take a moment to thank God for His Word and its ability to bring about conviction, correction, and renewal in our lives. As you prepare for rest, commit to allowing Scripture to continue its transformative work in you, yielding to its guidance and wisdom.

Prayer: Gracious God, we thank You for Your living and powerful Word, which shapes and transforms us from the inside out. As we reflect on this day, we acknowledge its impact on our hearts and minds. Forgive us for any resistance to Your truth and grant us a greater openness to Your Word. May we surrender to its leading and allow it to shape us into vessels of Your love and grace. Prepare our hearts for rest, Lord, and may Your Word continue to dwell richly within us. In Jesus' name, we pray. Amen.

Meditative Thought: Consider how Scripture has influenced your thoughts and actions today. Are there areas where you sensed conviction or guidance through God's Word? How can you continue to yield to its transformative power in the days ahead? Allow God's Word to dwell richly in your heart as you prepare for rest.

MARCH 13

MORNING DEVOTION

Scripture: John 14:1
"Let not your heart be troubled; you believe in God, believe also in Me."

Reflection: As we begin our day, let's meditate on the comforting words of Jesus in John 14:1. In the midst of life's uncertainties and challenges, Jesus offers a powerful exhortation: "Let not your heart be troubled." He invites us to place our trust not only in God but also in Himself. This assurance reminds us that even in the face of adversity, we can find peace and security in our faith. Today, let's choose to anchor our hearts in the unwavering promises of God and Jesus Christ. As we face the day ahead, may this verse serve as a reminder to entrust our worries and anxieties to the One who holds us in His loving care.

Prayer: Heavenly Father, we thank You for the reassurance found in Your Word. As we start this day, help us to release our fears and anxieties into Your hands. Grant us the faith to trust not only in You but also in Your Son, Jesus Christ. Fill our hearts with Your peace that surpasses all understanding, guarding us from the troubles of this world. May our trust in You deepen as we navigate the challenges of today. In Jesus' name, we pray. Amen.

Meditative Thought: Reflect on the areas of your life where you may be feeling troubled or anxious. How can you actively trust in God and Jesus Christ in those moments? Consider specific ways you can surrender your worries to Him throughout the day, finding peace in His presence.

Scripture: John 14:1
"Let not your heart be troubled; you believe in God, believe also in Me."

Reflection: As we conclude our day, let's reflect on the comforting words of Jesus in John 14:1. Consider the moments today where you felt troubled or anxious. How did you respond to those feelings? Jesus invites us to trust in Him, just as we trust in God. As you prepare for rest, take comfort in knowing that Jesus is with you, offering peace and security in the midst of life's challenges. Let go of any lingering worries and uncertainties, surrendering them to the loving care of Jesus Christ. Allow His presence to bring calm to your heart and assurance to your soul.

Prayer: Gracious Lord, we thank You for Your presence with us throughout this day. As we reflect on Your words in John 14:1, we are reminded of Your call to trust in You. Forgive us for the times when we allowed fear and anxiety to overshadow our faith. Tonight, we surrender our worries and troubles into Your hands, trusting in Your provision and care. Grant us restful sleep, knowing that You are watching over us. May Your peace fill our hearts and minds as we sleep, preparing us for the day ahead. In Jesus' name, we pray. Amen.

Meditative Thought: Consider the ways Jesus' presence brought peace to your heart today. How can you cultivate a deeper trust in Him moving forward? As you prepare for rest, meditate on His promise to be with you always, allowing His peace to settle over you.

MARCH 14

MORNING DEVOTION

Scripture: Psalm 55:22
"Cast your burden on the Lord, And He shall sustain you; He shall never permit the righteous to be moved."

Reflection: As we begin our day, let's reflect on the comforting words of Psalm 55:22. This verse reminds us of the incredible invitation God extends to us: to cast our burdens upon Him. In the midst of life's challenges and uncertainties, we are assured that God will sustain us. He promises to uphold the righteous and prevent them from being shaken. Today, let's take a moment to release our worries, fears, and anxieties into God's hands. Let's trust in His faithfulness and provision, knowing that He is always near to support and strengthen us.

Prayer: Gracious God, we come before You with grateful hearts, acknowledging Your promise to sustain us. As we start this day, we cast our burdens upon You, trusting in Your unfailing love and care. Help us to release any worries or anxieties that weigh heavily on our hearts, knowing that You are able to bear them. Strengthen us, Lord, and uphold us by Your righteous right hand. May Your presence bring peace and stability to our hearts as we navigate the day ahead. In Jesus' name, we pray. Amen.

Meditative Thought: Consider the burdens you are carrying today. How can you actively release them into God's hands and trust in His provision? Reflect on times in the past when God has sustained you through difficult circumstances. Allow those memories to bolster your faith as you face new challenges today.

Scripture: Psalm 55:22
"Cast your burden on the Lord, And He shall sustain you; He shall never permit the righteous to be moved."

Reflection: As we conclude our day, let's revisit the comforting words of Psalm 55:22. Reflect on the ways God has sustained you throughout the day, upholding you in His righteous grip. Even in moments of trial or uncertainty, His presence has been a constant source of strength and stability. Take a moment to thank God for His faithfulness in carrying your burdens and preventing you from being moved. As you prepare for rest, entrust your cares once again into His capable hands, knowing that He will watch over you through the night.

Prayer: Heavenly Father, we thank You for Your sustaining presence throughout this day. As we reflect on Your promise in Psalm 55:22, we are reminded of Your faithfulness to uphold the righteous. Tonight, we cast our burdens upon You once again, knowing that You are able to bear them. Grant us peaceful rest, Lord, knowing that You watch over us and protect us through the night. May Your unfailing love surround us as we sleep, preparing us for the new mercies of tomorrow. In Jesus' name, we pray. Amen.

Meditative Thought: Consider the ways God has sustained you today and prevented you from being moved. How can you continue to trust in His provision and care as you rest tonight? Surrender your worries and anxieties into His hands once again, finding peace in His presence as you sleep.

MARCH 15

MORNING DEVOTION

Scripture: Romans 8:18
"For I consider that the sufferings of this present time are not worthy to be compared with the glory which shall be revealed in us."

Reflection: As we begin our day, let's meditate on the powerful words of Romans 8:18. This verse reminds us that no matter what trials or hardships we may face in this present time, they pale in comparison to the glorious future that awaits us in Christ. In the midst of life's challenges, it can be easy to lose sight of this eternal perspective. But as followers of Jesus, we are called to fix our eyes not on our temporary circumstances but on the promise of future glory. Today, let's approach each moment with hope and anticipation, knowing that God is working all things together for our ultimate good and His glory.

Prayer: Heavenly Father, we thank You for the assurance of future glory that You have given us through Your Son, Jesus Christ. As we face the challenges of this day, help us to keep our eyes fixed on the eternal hope that awaits us. Grant us strength and perseverance to endure the sufferings of this present time, knowing that they are temporary and fleeting. Fill us with Your peace and joy as we trust in Your promises and walk in faith. In Jesus' name, we pray. Amen.

Meditative Thought: Reflect on the sufferings or challenges you may be facing in this present time. How does the promise of future glory in Christ give you hope and perspective? Consider how you can maintain an eternal mindset throughout the day, focusing on the ultimate victory that awaits you as a follower of Jesus.

Scripture: Romans 8:18
"For I consider that the sufferings of this present time are not worthy to be compared with the glory which shall be revealed in us."

Reflection: As we conclude our day, let's reflect on the truth of Romans 8:18. Despite the trials and sufferings we may have experienced throughout the day, they are nothing compared to the glorious future that awaits us in Christ. Take a moment to thank God for His faithfulness and provision, even in the midst of difficulties. As you prepare for rest, entrust your worries and burdens to Him, knowing that He is working all things together for your ultimate good. May the promise of future glory fill your heart with peace and hope as you sleep tonight.

Prayer: Gracious Lord, we thank You for the reminder that the sufferings of this present time are temporary and fleeting. As we reflect on the events of this day, we acknowledge Your faithfulness in carrying us through every trial and hardship. Tonight, we surrender our worries and burdens into Your hands, trusting in Your promise of future glory. Grant us restful sleep, knowing that You are watching over us and working all things together for our good. May Your peace fill our hearts and minds as we sleep, preparing us for the new mercies of tomorrow. In Jesus' name, we pray. Amen.

Meditative Thought: Consider the ways God has sustained you through the sufferings of this present time. How can you maintain a perspective of hope and anticipation for the future glory that awaits you? Surrender any lingering worries or burdens to God as you prepare for rest, trusting in His faithfulness to carry you through.

Scripture: Galatians 6:1

"Brethren, if a man is overtaken in any trespass, you who are spiritual restore such a one in a spirit of gentleness, considering yourself lest you also be tempted."

Reflection: As we begin our day, let's reflect on the compassionate instruction given in Galatians 6:1. This verse reminds us of our responsibility to care for and restore those who have stumbled in their faith. Rather than judging or condemning them, we are called to gently help them back onto the right path. However, this task requires humility and self-awareness, as we must also guard ourselves against temptation. Today, let's cultivate a spirit of compassion and gentleness towards others, offering support and encouragement to those in need. Let's also remain vigilant against the snares of sin, relying on God's strength to keep us steadfast in our own walk with Him.

Prayer: Heavenly Father, we thank You for Your compassion and mercy towards us, even when we stumble in our faith. As we start this day, help us to extend that same compassion to others who may be struggling. Grant us wisdom and discernment to gently restore them, bearing their burdens with love and understanding. Protect us from the lure of temptation, Lord, and strengthen us to walk in obedience to Your Word. May Your grace abound in our interactions today, bringing healing and restoration to those in need. In Jesus' name, we pray. Amen.

Meditative Thought: Reflect on a time when someone extended grace and restoration to you during a moment of weakness. How can you emulate that same spirit of gentleness and compassion towards others today? Consider specific ways you can offer support and encouragement to those who may be struggling in their faith.

Scripture: Galatians 6:1
"Brethren, if a man is overtaken in any trespass, you who are spiritual restore such a one in a spirit of gentleness, considering yourself lest you also be tempted."

Reflection: As we conclude our day, let's reflect on the admonition given in Galatians 6:1. Consider the interactions you had today and whether there were opportunities to extend grace and restoration to those in need. If you encountered someone who was struggling in their faith, did you respond with gentleness and compassion, or did you judge them harshly? As you reflect on your actions, ask God to reveal areas where you may have fallen short and to help you grow in compassion and humility. Remember that none of us are immune to temptation, and let's commit to supporting one another with love and understanding on our journey of faith.

Prayer: Gracious Lord, as we reflect on the events of this day, we acknowledge our need for Your grace and mercy. Forgive us for the times when we failed to extend that same grace and restoration to others who were struggling. Teach us to walk in humility and compassion, bearing one another's burdens with gentleness and love. Protect us from the temptation to judge or condemn, and help us to be instruments of Your healing and restoration. May Your Spirit guide us as we seek to live out Your love in our interactions with others. In Jesus' name, we pray. Amen.

Meditative Thought: Consider any interactions today where you may have missed an opportunity to extend grace and restoration to someone in need. How can you grow in compassion and humility moving forward? Pray for God's guidance and strength to walk in His love and to support others on their journey of faith.

Scripture: 2 Corinthians 5:17
"Therefore, if anyone is in Christ, he is a new creation; old things have passed away; behold, all things have become new."

Reflection: As we begin our day, let's meditate on the transformative truth of 2 Corinthians 5:17. This verse reminds us that when we place our faith in Christ, we are made new. The old ways of living, the past mistakes, and the burdens of sin are washed away, replaced by the promise of a fresh start and a renewed purpose in Christ. Today, let's embrace the reality of our new identity in Christ, walking in the freedom and joy that comes from being children of God. Let's allow His transforming power to work in us, shaping us into vessels of His love and grace.

Prayer: Heavenly Father, we thank You for the promise of new life in Christ. As we start this day, help us to embrace our identity as new creations, freed from the bondage of sin and death. Renew our minds and hearts, Lord, and empower us to live in accordance with Your will. May Your Spirit guide us in every decision and action, leading us closer to You and to the abundant life You have promised. Fill us with gratitude for Your transforming grace, and may we shine brightly as reflections of Your love in the world. In Jesus' name, we pray. Amen.

Meditative Thought: Consider the ways God has transformed your life since you placed your faith in Christ. How have old habits and patterns of thinking been replaced by new attitudes and perspectives? Reflect on the areas of your life where you still need His transformative work, and invite Him to continue making you into a new creation.

Scripture: 2 Corinthians 5:17
"Therefore, if anyone is in Christ, he is a new creation; old things have passed away; behold, all things have become new."

Reflection: As we conclude our day, let's reflect on the truth of 2 Corinthians 5:17. Consider the ways God has worked in your life today, renewing your mind and transforming your heart. Even in moments of struggle or weakness, His grace has been sufficient to sustain you and to make all things new. Take a moment to thank God for His faithfulness and for the promise of ongoing transformation in your life. As you prepare for rest, surrender any burdens or struggles to Him, trusting that He will continue His good work in you.

Prayer: Gracious God, we thank You for the promise of new life in Christ and for the ongoing work of transformation in our lives. As we reflect on this day, we acknowledge Your faithfulness in making all things new. Tonight, we surrender our worries and cares into Your hands, knowing that You are able to bring beauty from ashes and to restore what is broken. Renew our strength as we sleep, Lord, and continue to mold us into vessels of Your grace and love. May Your peace fill our hearts as we rest, knowing that You are always at work in us. In Jesus' name, we pray. Amen.

Meditative Thought: Reflect on the ways God has made all things new in your life recently. How have you experienced His transformative power in your attitudes, relationships, or circumstances? Pray for His continued work of renewal in your life, trusting that He who began a good work in you will bring it to completion.

Scripture: Ephesians 5:1-2
"Therefore, be imitators of God as dear children. And walk in love, as Christ also has loved us and given Himself for us, an offering and a sacrifice to God for a sweet-smelling aroma."

Reflection: As we begin our day, let's reflect on the exhortation given in Ephesians 5:1-2. These verses call us to imitate God and to walk in love, following the example of Christ who sacrificed Himself for us. As children of God, we are called to reflect His character and embody His love in all that we do. Today, let's strive to live in a manner that honors God, treating others with kindness, compassion, and grace. Let's look for opportunities to sacrificially love those around us, just as Christ loved us. May our lives be a sweet-smelling offering to God, bringing glory to His name.

Prayer: Heavenly Father, we thank You for the example of sacrificial love set forth by Your Son, Jesus Christ. As we start this day, help us to imitate Your character and to walk in love towards others. Fill us with Your Spirit, Lord, empowering us to extend grace and compassion to those around us. Show us how we can sacrificially love others as Christ loved us, offering ourselves as living sacrifices for Your glory. May our lives be a fragrant offering to You, bringing honor and praise to Your name. In Jesus' name, we pray. Amen.

Meditative Thought: Consider how you can imitate God's love in your interactions with others today. Are there areas where you can sacrificially serve and love those around you, following the example of Christ? Reflect on specific ways you can demonstrate love and kindness to others, seeking to embody the character of God in your daily life.

Scripture: Ephesians 5:1-2
"Therefore, be imitators of God as dear children. And walk in love, as Christ also has loved us and given Himself for us, an offering and a sacrifice to God for a sweet-smelling aroma."

Reflection: As we conclude our day, let's reflect on the call to imitate God's love given in Ephesians 5:1-2. Consider the ways you lived out this exhortation today. Did you strive to walk in love, treating others with kindness, compassion, and grace? Were there moments where you sacrificially served others, following the example of Christ's selfless love? Take a moment to thank God for the opportunities He provided to reflect His character and to be a blessing to others. As you prepare for rest, commit to continuing to imitate God's love in your thoughts, words, and actions, bringing glory to His name.

Prayer: Gracious Lord, as we reflect on this day, we thank You for the opportunities You provided to imitate Your love and to walk in kindness towards others. Forgive us for the times when we fell short of reflecting Your character. Renew our hearts, Lord, and empower us to continue walking in love, following the example of Christ. As we rest tonight, may Your Spirit fill us with Your peace and grace, preparing us for the new mercies of tomorrow. May our lives continue to be a sweet-smelling offering to You, bringing glory and honor to Your name. In Jesus' name, we pray. Amen.

Meditative Thought: Reflect on a specific moment today where you demonstrated Christ-like love to someone else. How did it feel to be an imitator of God's love in that moment? Pray for God's strength and guidance to continue walking in love tomorrow, seeking to reflect His character in all that you do.

MARCH 19

MORNING DEVOTION

Scripture: Psalm 119:9
"How can a young man cleanse his way? By taking heed according to Your word."

Reflection: As we begin our day, let's reflect on the wisdom found in Psalm 119:9. This verse highlights the importance of aligning our lives with God's Word for guidance and cleansing. In a world filled with distractions and temptations, it can be easy to lose our way. However, God's Word serves as a lamp to our feet and a light to our path, showing us the way we should go. Today, let's commit to taking heed to God's Word, allowing it to shape our thoughts, words, and actions. As we immerse ourselves in Scripture, may it cleanse and renew our hearts, guiding us on the path of righteousness.

Prayer: Heavenly Father, we thank You for the gift of Your Word, which serves as a guide and light for our lives. As we start this day, help us to take heed to Your Word, aligning our thoughts, words, and actions with Your will. Cleanse us from every impurity and sin, Lord, and renew our hearts and minds by Your Spirit. Give us a hunger and thirst for Your Word, that we may grow in wisdom and understanding. May Your Word be a lamp to our feet and a light to our path, guiding us in righteousness and truth. In Jesus' name, we pray. Amen.

Meditative Thought: Reflect on the ways you can prioritize God's Word in your life today. Are there specific passages or themes you feel led to study or meditate on? Consider how immersing yourself in Scripture can bring cleansing and renewal to your heart and mind, guiding you in the path of righteousness.

Scripture: Psalm 119:9
"How can a young man cleanse his way? By taking heed according to Your word."

Reflection: As we conclude our day, let's reflect on the truth of Psalm 119:9. Consider the ways you took heed to God's Word throughout the day. Did you prioritize time for prayer and Bible study, allowing God's Word to guide and cleanse your way? Or did distractions and busyness crowd out the opportunity to immerse yourself in Scripture? Take a moment to confess any shortcomings to God and ask for His forgiveness and grace. As you prepare for rest, commit to prioritizing God's Word in your life tomorrow, allowing it to continue shaping and renewing your heart.

Prayer: Gracious Lord, as we reflect on this day, we acknowledge our need for Your Word to guide and cleanse our way. Forgive us for the times when we neglected to prioritize time in Your Word, allowing distractions to take precedence. Renew our commitment to taking heed to Your Word, Lord, and help us to make it a priority in our lives. As we rest tonight, may Your Spirit continue to work in us, shaping us into vessels of Your love and truth. Prepare our hearts for the new mercies of tomorrow, as we seek to walk in obedience to Your will. In Jesus' name, we pray. Amen.

Meditative Thought: Consider how you can create space for God's Word in your daily routine tomorrow. Are there adjustments you need to make to prioritize Bible study and prayer? Reflect on the impact immersing yourself in Scripture can have on your spiritual growth and relationship with God.

Scripture: 2 Timothy 3:16-17
"All Scripture is given by inspiration of God, and is profitable for doc-trine, for reproof, for correction, for instruction in righteousness, that the man of God may be complete, thoroughly equipped for every good work."

Reflection: As we begin our day, let's meditate on the profound truth found in 2 Timothy 3:16-17. These verses affirm the divine inspiration and authority of Scripture, emphasizing its purpose in equipping us for every good work. The Word of God is not merely a collection of ancient writings; it is living and active, capable of shaping our beliefs, correcting our behavior, and guiding us in the ways of righteousness. Today, let's approach Scripture with reverence and humility, recognizing its trans-formative power in our lives.

Prayer: Heavenly Father, we thank You for the gift of Your inspired Word. As we start this day, help us to approach Scripture with reverence and humility, recognizing its authority in our lives. Open our hearts and minds to receive Your Word, Lord, and allow it to shape our beliefs, correct our behavior, and guide us in righteousness. May Your Word be a lamp to our feet and a light to our path, equipping us for every good work You have prepared for us. Grant us wisdom and understanding as we study Your Word today, Lord, and may it bear fruit in our lives for Your glory. In Jesus' name, we pray. Amen.

Meditative Thought: Consider the ways Scripture has impacted your life and guided you in the past. How can you prioritize time in God's Word today, allowing it to shape your beliefs and actions? Reflect on specific passages or themes you feel led to study, asking God to speak to you through His Word and to equip you for every good work.

Scripture: 2 Timothy 3:16-17
"All Scripture is given by inspiration of God, and is profitable for doctrine, for reproof, for correction, for instruction in righteousness, that the man of God may be complete, thoroughly equipped for every good work."

Reflection: As we conclude our day, let's reflect on the timeless truth of 2 Timothy 3:16-17. Consider the ways Scripture has spoken to you and guided you throughout the day. Did you prioritize time in God's Word, allowing it to shape your beliefs and actions? Take a moment to thank God for His inspired Word and for the transformative work it is doing in your life. As you prepare for rest, commit to continuing to prioritize Scripture in your life, recognizing its authority and power to equip you for every good work.

Prayer: Gracious Lord, as we reflect on this day, we thank You for the gift of Your inspired Word. Forgive us for the times when we neglected to prioritize time in Scripture, Lord, and renew our commitment to studying Your Word faithfully. Thank You for the ways Your Word has spoken to us and guided us throughout the day, Lord. As we rest tonight, may Your Spirit continue to work in us, shaping us into vessels of Your love and truth. Prepare our hearts to receive Your Word afresh tomorrow, Lord, and may it continue to equip us for every good work You have prepared for us. In Jesus' name, we pray. Amen.

Meditative Thought: Reflect on a specific way Scripture spoke to you or guided you today. How did it impact your beliefs or actions? Consider how you can continue to prioritize time in God's Word tomorrow, allowing it to shape and equip you for the work God has called you to.

MARCH 21

MORNING DEVOTION

Scripture: Joshua 1:9
"Have I not commanded you? Be strong and of good courage; do not be afraid, nor be dismayed, for the Lord your God is with you wherever you go."

Reflection: As we embark on a new day, let's meditate on the encouraging words of Joshua 1:9. This verse captures God's command to Joshua as he prepared to lead the Israelites into the Promised Land. Similarly, God calls us to be strong and courageous in the face of challenges and uncertainties, knowing that He is always with us. Whatever obstacles or fears we may encounter today, we can take comfort in the presence and promises of our faithful God. Let's approach this day with confidence, trusting in His strength and guidance to lead us through every situation.

Prayer: Heavenly Father, we thank You for Your promise to be with us wherever we go. As we start this day, help us to embrace the courage and strength that come from knowing You are by our side. May we not be afraid or dismayed by the challenges ahead, but rather trust in Your unfailing presence and provision. Grant us wisdom and discernment, Lord, to navigate this day with confidence and grace. May Your Spirit guide and empower us, enabling us to walk in obedience to Your will. In Jesus' name, we pray. Amen.

Meditative Thought: Reflect on a situation where you need to be courageous today. How does knowing that God is with you give you strength and confidence? Consider specific ways you can trust in His presence and promises as you face challenges and uncertainties throughout the day.

Scripture: Joshua 1:9
"Have I not commanded you? Be strong and of good courage; do not be afraid, nor be dismayed, for the Lord your God is with you wherever you go."

Reflection: As we conclude this day, let's reflect on the reassuring words of Joshua 1:9. Consider the ways God's presence and strength have sustained you throughout the day, enabling you to face challenges with courage and confidence. Take a moment to thank God for His faithfulness and for the peace that comes from knowing He is always with us. As you prepare for rest, entrust any worries or fears to Him, trusting that He will continue to guide and protect you wherever you go.

Prayer: Gracious Lord, as we reflect on this day, we thank You for Your constant presence and strength. Thank You for being our source of courage and confidence in the face of challenges. As we rest tonight, we entrust our cares and concerns to You, knowing that You are always with us. Grant us peaceful sleep, Lord, as we place our trust in Your unfailing love and care. May Your Spirit continue to work in us, shaping us into vessels of Your grace and truth. In Jesus' name, we pray. Amen.

Meditative Thought: Think about a moment today when you felt God's presence and strength guiding you. How did His assurance give you peace and courage? Reflect on how you can continue to rely on His presence and promises in the days ahead, trusting that He will never leave you nor forsake you.

MARCH 22

MORNING DEVOTION

Scripture: Philippians 1:6b
"He who has begun a good work in you will complete it until the day of Jesus Christ."

Reflection: As we begin this new day, let's meditate on the assurance found in Philippians 1:6b. This verse reminds us that God, who initiated a good work in us, will bring it to completion. Whatever challenges or uncertainties we may face today, we can take comfort in the fact that God is at work within us, shaping us according to His purposes. As we journey through this day, let's trust in His faithfulness and sovereignty, knowing that He is committed to perfecting His work in our lives. Let's approach each moment with confidence, knowing that God is actively working for our good and His glory.

Prayer: Heavenly Father, we thank You for the assurance that You are at work within us, shaping us according to Your purposes. As we start this day, help us to trust in Your faithfulness and sovereignty, knowing that You will bring to completion the good work You have begun in us. Grant us confidence and peace, Lord, as we navigate the challenges and opportunities of this day, knowing that You are with us every step of the way. May Your Spirit guide and empower us to live according to Your will, bringing glory to Your name. In Jesus' name, we pray. Amen.

Meditative Thought: Reflect on a recent experience where you sensed God at work in your life. How did His presence and guidance bring you comfort and assurance? Consider the areas of your life where you still need His transformative work, and surrender them to His care, trusting that He will bring His work to completion.

Scripture: Philippians 1:6b
"He who has begun a good work in you will complete it until the day of Jesus Christ."

Reflection: As we conclude this day, let's reflect on the truth of Philippians 1:6b. Consider the ways God has been at work in your life today, shaping you according to His purposes. Take a moment to thank Him for His faithfulness and for the progress He is making in your life, even in the midst of challenges and uncertainties. As you prepare for rest, entrust yourself anew to His care, knowing that He who began a good work in you will bring it to completion. May His assurance bring you peace and comfort as you sleep, trusting in His unfailing love and commitment to perfecting His work in you.

Prayer: Gracious Lord, as we reflect on this day, we thank You for the progress You are making in our lives, even in the midst of challenges and uncertainties. Thank You for the assurance that You will bring to completion the good work You have begun in us. As we rest tonight, we entrust ourselves anew to Your care, knowing that You are faithful to fulfill Your promises. Grant us peaceful sleep, Lord, as we place our trust in Your unfailing love and commitment to perfecting Your work in us. In Jesus' name, we pray. Amen.

Meditative Thought: Think about a specific area of your life where you have seen God at work recently. How has His faithfulness and guidance encouraged you? Reflect on how you can continue to surrender yourself to His care, trusting that He will bring His work to completion in your life.

MARCH 23

MORNING DEVOTION

Scripture: Hebrews 4:16
"Let us therefore come boldly to the throne of grace, that we may obtain mercy and find grace to help in time of need."

Reflection: As we begin our day, let's meditate on the invitation extended to us in Hebrews 4:16. This verse encourages us to approach the throne of grace with confidence, knowing that we will find mercy and grace to help in our time of need. Regardless of what challenges or uncertainties we may face today, we can take comfort in the fact that we serve a God who is full of compassion and ready to extend His grace to us. Let's approach this day with boldness, knowing that we can bring our cares and concerns before the throne of grace and receive the help and strength we need to overcome every obstacle.

Prayer: Heavenly Father, we thank You for the privilege of coming boldly to Your throne of grace. As we start this day, help us to approach You with confidence, knowing that You are eager to extend Your mercy and grace to us. Grant us the strength and wisdom we need to navigate the challenges and opportunities of this day, Lord. May Your Spirit guide and empower us, enabling us to walk in obedience to Your will. Thank You for Your faithfulness and compassion, Lord, and for the assurance that You are always there to help us in our time of need. In Jesus' name, we pray. Amen.

Meditative Thought: Reflect on a specific area of need in your life today. How does the promise of God's grace and mercy encourage you to face this need with boldness? Take a moment to surrender this need to God, trusting that He will provide the help and strength you need to overcome it.

Scripture: Hebrews 4:16
"Let us therefore come boldly to the throne of grace, that we may obtain mercy and find grace to help in time of need."

Reflection: As we conclude this day, let's reflect on the assurance found in Hebrews 4:16. Consider the ways God's grace and mercy sustained you throughout the day, providing the help and strength you needed in your time of need. Take a moment to thank Him for His faithfulness and for the privilege of coming boldly to His throne of grace. As you prepare for rest, entrust any cares or concerns to Him, knowing that He is eager to extend His grace and help to you. May His presence bring you peace and comfort as you sleep, trusting in His unfailing love and provision.

Prayer: Gracious Lord, as we reflect on this day, we thank You for Your abundant grace and mercy in our lives. Thank You for the help and strength You provided in our time of need, Lord. As we rest tonight, we entrust our cares and concerns to You, knowing that You are eager to extend Your grace and help to us. Grant us peaceful sleep, Lord, as we place our trust in Your unfailing love and care. May Your Spirit continue to work in us, shaping us into vessels of Your grace and truth. In Jesus' name, we pray. Amen.

Meditative Thought: Think about a specific moment today when you experienced God's grace and help in your time of need. How did His presence sustain you? Reflect on how you can continue to rely on His grace and mercy in the days ahead, knowing that He is always there to help you in your time of need.

MARCH 24

MORNING DEVOTION

Scripture: Acts 5:29
"But Peter and the other apostles answered and said: 'We ought to obey God rather than men.'"

Reflection: As we embark on a new day, let's reflect on the bold declaration of Peter and the apostles in Acts 5:29. Despite facing pressure and opposition from human authorities, they remained steadfast in their commitment to obeying God above all else. This verse challenges us to examine our own priorities and allegiances. Are we willing to stand firm in our faith and obedience to God, even when it goes against the expectations or demands of others? As we navigate the challenges and decisions of this day, let's resolve to prioritize pleasing God above all else, trusting in His wisdom and guidance.

Prayer: Heavenly Father, we thank You for the example of courage and obedience demonstrated by Peter and the apostles. As we start this day, help us to have the same boldness to obey You above all else, regardless of the pressures or opposition we may face. Give us wisdom and discernment, Lord, to discern Your will and follow it faithfully. Strengthen us, Lord, to stand firm in our faith, even when it goes against the expectations or demands of others. May our obedience bring glory to Your name and further Your kingdom here on earth. In Jesus' name, we pray. Amen.

Meditative Thought: Reflect on a time when you faced pressure to compromise your faith or values. How did you respond? Consider how you can cultivate a deeper commitment to obeying God above all else in every aspect of your life, trusting in His guidance and provision.

Scripture: Acts 5:29
"But Peter and the other apostles answered and said: 'We ought to obey God rather than men.'"

Reflection: As we conclude this day, let's reflect on the profound truth of Acts 5:29. Consider the ways you lived out this principle today, prioritizing obedience to God above all else. Did you face any challenges or opportunities to stand firm in your faith? Take a moment to thank God for His strength and guidance, enabling you to remain faithful to Him. As you prepare for rest, entrust any decisions or uncertainties to God, renewing your commitment to obeying Him above the expectations of others.

Prayer: Gracious Lord, as we reflect on this day, we thank You for Your faithfulness and strength, enabling us to obey You above all else. Forgive us for the times when we faltered or compromised our faith, Lord, and renew our commitment to following You wholeheartedly. As we rest tonight, we entrust any decisions or uncertainties to You, knowing that You are faithful to guide and provide for us. Grant us peaceful sleep, Lord, as we place our trust in Your unfailing love and care. In Jesus' name, we pray. Amen.

Meditative Thought: Think about a specific moment today when you prioritized obedience to God above the expectations of others. How did it impact your day? Reflect on how you can continue to cultivate a heart that is fully committed to obeying God in every aspect of your life, trusting in His wisdom and guidance.

MORNING DEVOTION

Scripture: 1 John 1:9
"If we confess our sins, He is faithful and just to forgive us our sins and to cleanse us from all unrighteousness."

Reflection: As we begin a new day, let's meditate on the promise of forgiveness and cleansing found in 1 John 1:9. This verse reminds us that when we confess our sins to God, He is faithful and just to forgive us and cleanse us from all unrighteousness. It's a beautiful invitation to come before God with honesty and humility, knowing that He stands ready to extend His mercy and grace to us. Today, let's take a moment to examine our hearts and confess any sins or shortcomings to God. As we do so, may we experience the freedom and restoration that comes from His forgiveness and cleansing.

Prayer: Heavenly Father, we thank You for Your promise of forgiveness and cleansing found in 1 John 1:9. As we start this day, help us to come before You with honesty and humility, confessing our sins and shortcomings. Thank You for Your faithfulness and justice, Lord, to forgive us and cleanse us from all unrighteousness. May Your Spirit convict us of any areas where we have strayed from Your will, Lord, and empower us to walk in obedience to You. Grant us a fresh sense of Your presence and peace as we experience the freedom that comes from Your forgiveness. In Jesus' name, we pray. Amen.

Meditative Thought: Reflect on a specific sin or area of your life where you need God's forgiveness and cleansing today. Take a moment to confess it to Him, acknowledging His faithfulness and justice to forgive and cleanse you. Allow His grace to wash over you, bringing freedom and restoration to your soul.

Scripture: 1 John 1:9
"If we confess our sins, He is faithful and just to forgive us our sins and to cleanse us from all unrighteousness."

Reflection: As we conclude this day, let's reflect on the promise of forgiveness and cleansing found in 1 John 1:9. Take a moment to thank God for His faithfulness and justice to forgive us when we confess our sins to Him. Consider the ways His forgiveness and cleansing have impacted your life today, bringing freedom and restoration to your soul. As you prepare for rest, surrender any lingering guilt or shame to God, trusting in His grace to cover you and His love to restore you.

Prayer: Gracious Lord, as we reflect on this day, we thank You for Your faithfulness to forgive us when we confess our sins to You. Thank You for the cleansing and restoration You bring to our lives through Your grace. As we prepare for rest tonight, we surrender any lingering guilt or shame to You, trusting in Your love to cover us and Your grace to restore us. Grant us peaceful sleep, Lord, as we rest in the assurance of Your forgiveness and cleansing. In Jesus' name, we pray. Amen.

Meditative Thought: Think about how God's forgiveness and cleansing have impacted your day today. Reflect on any areas where you still need His grace and restoration, and surrender them to Him in prayer. Allow His love to wash over you, bringing peace and assurance as you rest in His forgiveness.

MARCH 26

MORNING DEVOTION

Scripture: Revelation 3:20-21
"Behold, I stand at the door and knock. If anyone hears My voice and opens the door, I will come in to him and dine with him, and he with Me. To him who overcomes I will grant to sit with Me on My throne, as I also overcame and sat down with My Father on His throne."

Reflection: As we begin this new day, let's meditate on the invitation of Jesus in Revelation 3:20. He stands at the door of our hearts, gently knocking, waiting for us to invite Him in. What a beautiful picture of His desire for intimate fellowship with us! Today, let's be attentive to His voice and open the door of our hearts to Him. And as we journey through this day, let's keep in mind the promise of Revelation 3:21 – that to those who overcome, Jesus offers the incredible privilege of sitting with Him on His throne. Let's live today in light of this glorious promise.

Prayer: Heavenly Father, we thank You for the invitation of Jesus to dine with Him and enjoy intimate fellowship. As we start this day, help us to open the door of our hearts to Him, welcoming Him into every aspect of our lives. May we experience the richness of His presence and the joy of communion with Him today. Give us the strength and perseverance, Lord, to overcome every obstacle in our path, knowing that You have promised to grant us the privilege of sitting with You on Your throne. May Your Spirit empower us to live in victory, bringing glory to Your name. In Jesus' name, we pray. Amen.

Meditative Thought: Reflect on your willingness to open the door of your heart to Jesus today. Are there areas of your life where you have kept Him at a distance? Consider the joy and intimacy that come from dining with Him and the privilege of sitting with Him on His throne.

Scripture: Revelation 3:20-21
"Behold, I stand at the door and knock. If anyone hears My voice and opens the door, I will come in to him and dine with him, and he with Me. To him who overcomes I will grant to sit with Me on My throne, as I also overcame and sat down with My Father on His throne."

Reflection: As we conclude this day, let's reflect on the invitation and promise of Jesus in Revelation 3:20-21. Consider the moments today when you opened the door of your heart to Him, inviting Him into your life and circumstances. How did His presence and fellowship enrich your day? Take a moment to thank Him for the joy of communion with Him and for the promise of sitting with Him on His throne. And as you prepare for rest, surrender any burdens or worries to Him, trusting in His faithfulness to guide and sustain you.

Prayer: Gracious Lord, as we reflect on this day, we thank You for the joy of communion with You and for the promise of sitting with You on Your throne. Thank You for the moments today when we opened the door of our hearts to You, experiencing Your presence and fellowship. As we prepare for rest tonight, we surrender any burdens or worries to You, trusting in Your faithfulness to guide and sustain us. Grant us peaceful sleep, Lord, as we rest in the assurance of Your love and promise. In Jesus' name, we pray. Amen.

Meditative Thought: Think about the moments today when you experienced the presence and fellowship of Jesus. How did His presence impact your day? Reflect on how you can continue to cultivate intimacy with Him in the days ahead, opening the door of your heart to Him and seeking His guidance and companionship in all things.

MORNING DEVOTION

Scripture: 1 Peter 4:19
"Therefore let those who suffer according to the will of God commit their souls to Him in doing good, as to a faithful Creator."

Reflection: As we embark on a new day, let's reflect on the encouragement found in 1 Peter 4:19. This verse reminds us that even in times of suffering, we can trust in the faithfulness of God as our Creator. When we face challenges that are aligned with His will, we are called to commit our souls to Him, trusting that He is faithful to sustain us. Today, let's approach each moment with a sense of surrender and trust, knowing that God is with us and that He is working all things together for our good. As we seek to do good and honor Him in our actions, may we find comfort and strength in His unfailing love and faithfulness.

Prayer: Heavenly Father, we thank You for Your faithfulness as our Creator. As we start this day, help us to trust in Your sovereignty and goodness, even in the midst of suffering. Give us the strength to commit our souls to You, knowing that You are faithful to sustain us and work all things together for our good. May Your Spirit empower us to do good and honor You in all that we do today, Lord. Grant us Your peace and presence as we navigate the challenges and opportunities of this day. In Jesus' name, we pray. Amen.

Meditative Thought: Reflect on a time when you faced suffering or challenges that aligned with God's will. How did you experience His faithfulness and sustenance during that time? Consider how you can trust Him more fully in the challenges you face today, committing your soul to His care and relying on His faithful provision.

Scripture: 1 Peter 4:19
"Therefore let those who suffer according to the will of God commit their souls to Him in doing good, as to a faithful Creator."

Reflection: As we conclude this day, let's reflect on the assurance of God's faithfulness as our Creator, as mentioned in 1 Peter 4:19. Consider the ways His faithfulness sustained you throughout this day, especially in moments of suffering or challenge. Take a moment to commit your soul afresh to Him, trusting in His faithful provision and care. And as you seek to do good and honor Him in your actions, may you find peace and rest in His unfailing love.

Prayer: Gracious Lord, as we reflect on this day, we thank You for Your faithfulness as our Creator. Thank You for sustaining us and guiding us through the challenges we faced today. As we prepare for rest tonight, we commit our souls afresh to You, trusting in Your faithful provision and care. Grant us peaceful sleep, Lord, as we rest in the assurance of Your love and faithfulness. May Your Spirit continue to work in us, shaping us into vessels of Your grace and truth. In Jesus' name, we pray. Amen.

Meditative Thought: Think about the ways you experienced God's faithfulness today, especially in moments of suffering or challenge. How did His presence sustain you? Reflect on how you can continue to trust Him more fully in the days ahead, committing your soul to His care and relying on His faithful provision.

MARCH 28

MORNING DEVOTION

Scripture: Deuteronomy 32:4
"He is the Rock, His work is perfect; For all His ways are justice, A God of truth and without injustice; Righteous and upright is He."

Reflection: As we begin a new day, let's meditate on the attributes of God described in Deuteronomy 32:4. He is the Rock, a firm foundation upon which we can build our lives. His work is perfect, without flaw or error. In all His ways, He exemplifies justice, truth, righteousness, and uprightness. What a comfort it is to serve a God whose character is unchanging and whose ways are always just and true! Today, let's rest in the assurance that God is sovereign over all things, and His purposes will prevail. As we face the challenges and uncertainties of this day, may we find strength and confidence in the unchanging character of our God.

Prayer: Heavenly Father, we thank You for Your unchanging character and perfect ways. As we start this day, help us to anchor our lives on the firm foundation of Your truth. Thank You for Your justice, truth, righteousness, and uprightness, Lord. May we find peace and confidence in Your sovereignty over all things. Grant us the wisdom and discernment to walk in Your ways, Lord, and to trust in Your perfect plan for our lives. May Your Spirit guide and empower us as we navigate the challenges of this day. In Jesus' name, we pray. Amen.

Meditative Thought: Reflect on the attributes of God described in Deuteronomy 32:4. How do these attributes bring you comfort and assurance as you face the day ahead? Consider how you can anchor your life more firmly on the unchanging character of God, trusting in His sovereignty and perfect plan for your life.

Scripture: Deuteronomy 32:4
"He is the Rock, His work is perfect; For all His ways are justice, A God of truth and without injustice; Righteous and upright is He."

Reflection: As we conclude this day, let's reflect on the unchanging character of God described in Deuteronomy 32:4. He is the Rock, our firm foundation in the midst of life's uncertainties. His work is perfect, and His ways are just, true, righteous, and upright. Take a moment to thank God for His faithfulness and sovereignty over all things. Consider the ways His perfect plan unfolded in your life today, even in moments of challenge or difficulty. As you prepare for rest, entrust any concerns or burdens to the God who is always just and true.

Prayer: Gracious Lord, as we reflect on this day, we thank You for Your unchanging character and perfect ways. Thank You for being our firm foundation and for guiding us with Your justice and truth. As we prepare for rest tonight, we entrust any concerns or burdens to You, knowing that You are always righteous and upright in Your dealings with us. Grant us peaceful sleep, Lord, as we rest in the assurance of Your faithfulness and sovereignty. May Your Spirit continue to work in us, shaping us into vessels of Your grace and truth. In Jesus' name, we pray. Amen.

Meditative Thought: Think about the ways you experienced God's faithfulness and sovereignty today. How did His perfect plan unfold in your life? Reflect on how you can continue to trust in His unchanging character, anchoring your life on the firm foundation of His truth and righteousness.

Scripture: John 14:1
"Let not your heart be troubled; you believe in God, believe also in Me."

Reflection: As we begin this new day, let's reflect on the comforting words of Jesus in John 14:1. In the midst of life's uncertainties and challenges, He encourages us not to let our hearts be troubled. Instead, He invites us to place our trust and confidence in Him. Just as we believe in God, Jesus calls us to also believe in Him. Today, let's take these words to heart and choose to trust in the unchanging character and promises of Jesus. Let's surrender our anxieties and worries to Him, knowing that He is always faithful and that He holds us securely in His hands.

Prayer: Heavenly Father, we thank You for the comforting words of Jesus in John 14:1. As we start this day, help us to trust in You and in Your Son, Jesus Christ. Strengthen our faith, Lord, and help us not to let our hearts be troubled by the challenges and uncertainties of life. May we find peace and confidence in Your unchanging character and promises. Guide us, Lord, and lead us in Your ways as we navigate this day. In Jesus' name, we pray. Amen.

Meditative Thought: Reflect on the areas of your life where you may be feeling anxious or troubled. How can you apply the words of Jesus in John 14:1 to these situations? Take a moment to surrender your worries to Him and choose to trust in His faithfulness and sovereignty.

Scripture: John 14:1
"Let not your heart be troubled; you believe in God, believe also in Me."

Reflection: As we conclude this day, let's reflect on the reassuring words of Jesus in John 14:1. He encourages us once again not to let our hearts be troubled but to place our trust in Him just as we trust in God. Take a moment to consider how you experienced the peace and presence of Jesus throughout this day. Despite any challenges or difficulties, He has been with you, offering comfort and assurance. As you prepare for rest, choose to release any remaining anxieties or worries to Him, knowing that He holds you securely in His love.

Prayer: Gracious Lord, as we reflect on this day, we thank You for Your constant presence and reassurance in our lives. Thank You for the peace and comfort You provide, even in the midst of life's challenges. As we prepare for rest tonight, we release any remaining anxieties or worries to You, trusting in Your faithfulness and love. Grant us peaceful sleep, Lord, as we rest in the assurance of Your care and provision. May Your Spirit continue to work in us, shaping us into vessels of Your peace and grace. In Jesus' name, we pray. Amen.

Meditative Thought: Think about the ways you experienced the presence and reassurance of Jesus throughout this day. How did His words in John 14:1 bring you comfort and peace? Reflect on how you can continue to trust in Him, even in the midst of life's uncertainties, as you prepare for rest.

MORNING DEVOTION

Scripture: Proverbs 3:13-14
"Happy is the man who finds wisdom, And the man who gains understanding; For her proceeds are better than the profits of silver, And her gain than fine gold."

Reflection: As we begin this new day, let's reflect on the value of wisdom as described in Proverbs 3:13-14. The writer tells us that happiness is found in discovering wisdom and gaining understanding. Unlike material wealth, which can be fleeting, the benefits of wisdom are enduring and surpass even the most precious treasures. Today, let's seek after wisdom with diligence and humility, recognizing its importance in every aspect of our lives. Let's ask God to grant us wisdom and understanding as we navigate the challenges and opportunities of this day, knowing that true happiness is found in aligning our lives with His wisdom.

Prayer: Heavenly Father, we thank You for the wisdom and understanding You offer us through Your Word. As we start this day, help us to seek after wisdom with diligence and humility. Grant us the discernment to make wise decisions and the understanding to apply Your principles to our lives. May we find true happiness in aligning our lives with Your wisdom, Lord. Guide us, teach us, and lead us in Your ways, that we may live according to Your will. In Jesus' name, we pray. Amen.

Meditative Thought: Reflect on the value you place on wisdom in your life. How does seeking wisdom compare to seeking material wealth or success? Consider how you can prioritize seeking wisdom in your decisions and actions today, trusting in its enduring benefits.

Scripture: Proverbs 3:13-14
"Happy is the man who finds wisdom, And the man who gains understanding; For her proceeds are better than the profits of silver, And her gain than fine gold."

Reflection: As we conclude this day, let's reflect on the wisdom and understanding described in Proverbs 3:13-14. Take a moment to consider the ways you encountered wisdom throughout this day – perhaps through Scripture, wise counsel, or personal reflection. Reflect on how embracing wisdom has enriched your life and brought you happiness. And as you prepare for rest, ask God to continue granting you wisdom and understanding, knowing that they are more valuable than any material wealth. May you find peace and contentment in aligning your life with God's wisdom, trusting in His guidance for tomorrow and the days ahead.

Prayer: Gracious Lord, as we reflect on this day, we thank You for the wisdom and understanding You have provided us. Thank You for the happiness and fulfillment we experience when we align our lives with Your wisdom. As we prepare for rest tonight, we ask You to continue granting us wisdom and understanding, Lord. May we seek after Your wisdom above all else, trusting in its enduring benefits. Grant us peaceful sleep, Lord, as we rest in Your wisdom and care. In Jesus' name, we pray. Amen.

Meditative Thought: Think about the ways you encountered wisdom throughout this day. How did embracing wisdom enrich your life and bring you happiness? Reflect on how you can continue seeking wisdom in the days ahead, trusting in its enduring benefits and prioritizing its pursuit in your life.

MARCH 31

MORNING DEVOTION

Scripture: Acts 1:8
"But you shall receive power when the Holy Spirit has come upon you; and you shall be witnesses to Me in Jerusalem, and in all Judea and Samaria, and to the end of the earth."

Reflection: As we embark on a new day, let's reflect on the promise of power and purpose found in Acts 1:8. Jesus assures His disciples that they will receive power when the Holy Spirit comes upon them. This power is not merely for personal gain but for a specific purpose – to be witnesses to Jesus, spreading His message from their local community to the ends of the earth. Today, let's ask God to fill us afresh with His Holy Spirit, empowering us to live as bold witnesses for Christ in our spheres of influence. May we be mindful of the opportunities to share the love and truth of Jesus with those around us, knowing that His Spirit equips and empowers us for this divine task.

Prayer: Heavenly Father, we thank You for the promise of power and purpose found in Acts 1:8. As we start this day, fill us afresh with Your Holy Spirit, Lord. Empower us to be bold witnesses for Christ in our communities and beyond. Help us to recognize the opportunities to share Your love and truth with those around us, Lord. May Your Spirit guide and equip us for this divine task. Use us, Lord, to spread the message of Jesus to the ends of the earth. In Jesus' name, we pray. Amen.

Meditative Thought: Consider the ways you can be a witness for Christ in your daily life, from your local community to the ends of the earth. Reflect on the power of the Holy Spirit within you, empowering you to fulfill this purpose. Ask God to open your eyes to opportunities to share His love and truth with those around you today.

Scripture: Acts 1:8
"But you shall receive power when the Holy Spirit has come upon you; and you shall be witnesses to Me in Jerusalem, and in all Judea and Samaria, and to the end of the earth."

Reflection: As we conclude this day, let's reflect on the promise of power and purpose found in Acts 1:8. Take a moment to consider the opportunities you had today to be a witness for Christ – whether through your words, actions, or attitudes. Reflect on how the Holy Spirit empowered you to fulfill this purpose and spread the message of Jesus to those around you. And as you prepare for rest, ask God to continue filling you with His Spirit, guiding and empowering you to be a bold witness for Christ in the days ahead. May you rest in the assurance that His Spirit equips and empowers you for this divine task.

Prayer: Gracious Lord, as we reflect on this day, we thank You for the promise of power and purpose found in Acts 1:8. Thank You for empowering us to be witnesses for Christ in our communities and beyond. As we prepare for rest tonight, fill us anew with Your Holy Spirit, Lord. Guide and empower us to continue spreading the message of Jesus in the days ahead. May Your Spirit go before us, preparing hearts to receive Your love and truth. Grant us peaceful sleep, Lord, as we rest in Your Spirit's empowering presence. In Jesus' name, we pray. Amen.

Meditative Thought: Think about the ways the Holy Spirit empowered you to be a witness for Christ today. Reflect on how you can continue fulfilling this purpose in the days ahead, trusting in His guidance and empowerment. Surrender any fears or hesitations to God, knowing that His Spirit equips you for this divine task.

Scripture: Romans 12:2
"And do not be conformed to this world, but be transformed by the renewing of your mind, that you may prove what is that good and acceptable and perfect will of God."

Reflection: As we begin this new day, let's focus on the transformative power of renewing our minds as described in Romans 12:2. The Apostle Paul instructs us not to conform to the patterns and values of this world but to be transformed by the renewal of our minds. This transformation allows us to discern and follow God's good, acceptable, and perfect will. Today, let's commit to renewing our minds through prayer, meditation on God's Word, and seeking His guidance in every decision we make. By doing so, we align ourselves with His divine purpose and reflect His love and truth in our daily lives.

Prayer: Heavenly Father, as we start this day, help us not to conform to the ways of this world but to be transformed by the renewal of our minds. Fill us with Your Holy Spirit, guiding our thoughts and actions according to Your will. Grant us discernment to understand what is good, acceptable, and perfect in Your eyes. May we reflect Your love and truth in all that we do today. In Jesus' name, we pray. Amen.

Meditative Thought: Consider the areas of your life where you may be conforming to the patterns of this world. How can you actively renew your mind today? Spend a few moments in prayer, asking God to guide your thoughts and actions, transforming you to better reflect His will.

Scripture: Romans 12:2
"And do not be conformed to this world, but be transformed by the renewing of your mind, that you may prove what is that good and acceptable and perfect will of God."

Reflection: As we conclude this day, let's reflect on the impact of renewing our minds as described in Romans 12:2. Consider the moments today when you resisted conforming to worldly patterns and instead sought transformation through God's Word and Spirit. Reflect on how this renewal allowed you to better understand and follow God's will. As you prepare for rest, ask God to continue this transformative work in you, enabling you to discern and live out His perfect will. May you find peace in knowing that God is continually renewing and transforming you into His likeness.

Prayer: Gracious Lord, as we reflect on this day, we thank You for the transformative power of Your Word and Spirit. Thank You for guiding us away from the patterns of this world and renewing our minds. As we prepare for rest tonight, continue Your transformative work in us. Help us to discern and live out Your good, acceptable, and perfect will. Grant us peaceful sleep, knowing that You are continually at work within us. In Jesus' name, we pray. Amen.

Meditative Thought: Think about the ways you experienced transformation through the renewal of your mind today. How did this impact your decisions and actions? Reflect on how you can continue this process of renewal, trusting God to guide and transform you according to His perfect will.

APRIL 2

MORNING DEVOTION

Scripture: Colossians 3:1-2
"If then you were raised with Christ, seek those things which are above, where Christ is, sitting at the right hand of God. Set your mind on things above, not on things on the earth."

Reflection: As we begin this new day, let us focus on the heavenly perspective Paul encourages in Colossians 3:1-2. Being raised with Christ signifies our new life in Him, and this calls us to seek the things that are above, where Christ is seated at the right hand of God. Our minds should be set on the eternal, not the temporal. Today, let us consciously direct our thoughts and actions towards what is above – values and virtues that reflect the character of Christ. By doing so, we align ourselves with His purposes and find true fulfillment.

Prayer: Heavenly Father, as we start this day, help us to seek the things that are above. Remind us constantly of our identity in Christ and the new life we have in Him. Guide our thoughts and actions to reflect Your heavenly values. Let us prioritize what is eternal over what is fleeting. In all we do today, may we bring glory to Your name. In Jesus' name, we pray. Amen.

Meditative Thought: Consider the difference between earthly concerns and heavenly priorities. Reflect on how you can align your thoughts and actions today with the eternal values of God's kingdom. Ask God to help you maintain a heavenly perspective throughout the day.

Scripture: Colossians 3:1-2
"If then you were raised with Christ, seek those things which are above, where Christ is, sitting at the right hand of God. Set your mind on things above, not on things on the earth."

Reflection: As we close this day, let's reflect on how we sought after the things above, as Paul instructs in Colossians 3:1-2. Think about the moments when your thoughts and actions were aligned with heavenly values, reflecting the character of Christ. Where did you find joy and fulfillment in focusing on the eternal rather than the temporal? As you prepare for rest, thank God for the opportunities to live out your new life in Christ today and ask Him to continue transforming your mind to focus on His purposes.

Prayer: Gracious Lord, as we reflect on this day, we thank You for the opportunity to seek the things that are above. Thank You for guiding our thoughts and actions towards heavenly values. As we prepare for rest, help us to continue setting our minds on the eternal. Transform us daily to reflect more of Christ in all we do. Grant us peaceful sleep, knowing that we are secure in Your love and purposes. In Jesus' name, we pray. Amen.

Meditative Thought: Reflect on the moments today when you focused on heavenly priorities. How did it affect your decisions and interactions? Consider how you can continue to cultivate a heavenly perspective in your life, trusting God to guide and transform you each day.

Scripture: James 4:4

"Adulterers and adulteresses! Do you not know that friendship with the world is enmity with God? Whoever therefore wants to be a friend of the world makes himself an enemy of God."

Reflection: As we start this day, let's reflect on the strong words of James 4:4. James warns us about the dangers of aligning ourselves too closely with the world's values and priorities. Friendship with the world often means adopting attitudes and behaviors that are contrary to God's will. This scripture challenges us to evaluate our loyalties and where we place our trust. Are we more influenced by the world or by God? Today, let's commit to seeking God's guidance in our decisions and actions, striving to be faithful to Him in all we do.

Prayer: Heavenly Father, as we begin this day, we ask for Your wisdom and discernment. Help us to see clearly where we may be too closely aligned with the world's values. Guide us to seek Your will in every aspect of our lives. Strengthen our resolve to live in a way that honors You, rejecting what draws us away from Your love and truth. Help us to be faithful to You, Lord, in all our thoughts, words, and actions today. In Jesus' name, we pray. Amen.

Meditative Thought: Consider the influences in your life that may be pulling you away from God. Reflect on how you can prioritize your relationship with Him over the pressures and values of the world. Ask God to help you remain faithful to His ways today.

Scripture: James 4:4
"Adulterers and adulteresses! Do you not know that friendship with the world is enmity with God? Whoever therefore wants to be a friend of the world makes himself an enemy of God."

Reflection: As we end this day, let's take a moment to reflect on James 4:4 and its implications for our lives. Think about the choices and interactions you had today. Were there moments when you felt the pull of worldly values over God's truth? How did you respond? This verse calls us to a higher allegiance – one that places God above all else. As you prepare for rest, consider the ways you can deepen your commitment to God and distance yourself from worldly influences that lead you away from Him.

Prayer: Gracious Lord, as we reflect on this day, we ask for Your forgiveness for the times we allowed worldly influences to guide our actions. We desire to be faithful to You and Your ways. Help us to recognize and resist the pull of the world that leads us away from You. Fill us with Your Spirit, guiding us to live in a way that honors You. As we rest tonight, renew our commitment to follow You wholeheartedly. In Jesus' name, we pray. Amen.

Meditative Thought: Reflect on the day and identify any moments where worldly influences overshadowed your faithfulness to God. Think about steps you can take to strengthen your relationship with God and diminish the influence of the world. Trust in God's guidance to help you live faithfully for Him each day.

APRIL 4

MORNING DEVOTION

Scripture: 1 Corinthians 15:58
"Therefore, my beloved brethren, be steadfast, immovable, always abounding in the work of the Lord, knowing that your labor is not in vain in the Lord."

Reflection: As we begin this new day, let's take to heart Paul's exhortation in 1 Corinthians 15:58. This verse encourages us to be steadfast and immovable in our faith, constantly abounding in the work of the Lord. The assurance that our labor is not in vain provides great motivation to persevere. Today, let's commit to being unwavering in our dedication to God's work, whether through acts of kindness, sharing the Gospel, or serving others. Our efforts, grounded in faith, have eternal significance.

Prayer: Heavenly Father, as we start this day, help us to be steadfast and immovable in our faith. Empower us to abound in Your work, knowing that our labor in You is not in vain. Fill us with Your Spirit, guiding us to make choices that honor You. May our efforts today reflect Your love and truth, bringing glory to Your name. In Jesus' name, we pray. Amen.

Meditative Thought: Consider the tasks and interactions you have ahead today. Reflect on how you can approach each one with a steadfast heart, dedicated to abounding in the work of the Lord. Trust that every effort made in faith and service to God has lasting value.

Scripture: 1 Corinthians 15:58
"Therefore, my beloved brethren, be steadfast, immovable, always abounding in the work of the Lord, knowing that your labor is not in vain in the Lord."

Reflection: As we end this day, let's reflect on how we lived out the encouragement found in 1 Corinthians 15:58. Think about the moments when you were steadfast and immovable in your faith and how you abounded in the work of the Lord. Consider the challenges you faced and how you relied on God's strength to persevere. As you prepare for rest, take comfort in the knowledge that your labor in the Lord is not in vain. Each act of faithfulness contributes to His eternal purposes.

Prayer: Gracious Lord, as we reflect on this day, we thank You for the strength to remain steadfast and immovable in our faith. Thank You for the opportunities to abound in Your work. Help us to rest in the assurance that our labor in You is not in vain. Refresh our spirits as we sleep, and prepare us to serve You anew tomorrow. In Jesus' name, we pray. Amen.

Meditative Thought: Think back on your day and identify specific instances where you were able to serve and honor God through your actions. Reflect on the eternal significance of your efforts, no matter how small they may seem. Rest in the assurance that God values and uses your faithfulness for His purposes.

MORNING DEVOTION

Scripture: Galatians 6:7-8

"Do not be deceived, God is not mocked; for whatever a man sows, that he will also reap. For he who sows to his flesh will of the flesh reap corruption, but he who sows to the Spirit will of the Spirit reap everlasting life."

Reflection: As we start this new day, let's ponder the profound truth in Galatians 6:7-8. These verses remind us of the spiritual principle of sowing and reaping. Our actions and choices have consequences, and we are encouraged to sow to the Spirit rather than to the flesh. This means living according to the Spirit's guidance and pursuing what is pleasing to God. Today, let's be mindful of what we are sowing through our thoughts, words, and actions, aiming to sow seeds that lead to everlasting life and bring glory to God.

Prayer: Heavenly Father, as we begin this day, help us to sow to the Spirit and not to the flesh. Guide our thoughts, words, and actions to align with Your will. Remind us of the eternal significance of our choices and give us the strength to live in a way that pleases You. May our lives be a reflection of Your love and truth. In Jesus' name, we pray. Amen.

Meditative Thought: Consider what it means to sow to the Spirit today. Reflect on the choices you have before you and how you can honor God through them. Trust that as you sow seeds of righteousness, you will reap the rewards of everlasting life and spiritual growth.

Scripture: Galatians 6:7-8
"Do not be deceived, God is not mocked; for whatever a man sows, that he will also reap. For he who sows to his flesh will of the flesh reap corruption, but he who sows to the Spirit will of the Spirit reap everlasting life."

Reflection: As we conclude this day, let's reflect on how we have sown to the Spirit. Were there moments when we chose to follow the Spirit's guidance over the desires of the flesh? Think about the actions you took today and the seeds you planted through your behavior. The assurance that sowing to the Spirit reaps everlasting life encourages us to continue striving for spiritual growth. Let us ask God for forgiveness where we fell short and strength to sow better seeds tomorrow.

Prayer: Gracious Lord, as we reflect on this day, we thank You for Your guidance and patience. Forgive us for the times we sowed to the flesh rather than to the Spirit. Strengthen our resolve to live according to Your will. Help us to learn from today's experiences and to be more mindful of our actions. May we continually sow seeds that lead to everlasting life. In Jesus' name, we pray. Amen.

Meditative Thought: Think back on the day and identify moments when you sowed to the Spirit. Consider how these actions contributed to your spiritual growth. As you rest, commit to sowing even more faithfully to the Spirit in the days to come, trusting God to bring forth a bountiful harvest of righteousness.

MORNING DEVOTION

Scripture: Psalm 34:14
"Depart from evil and do good; Seek peace and pursue it."

Reflection: As we begin this day, let us reflect on the wisdom of Psalm 34:14. This verse calls us to actively turn away from evil and commit ourselves to doing good. It also encourages us to seek and pursue peace in all areas of our lives. This pursuit requires intentionality and effort. Today, let us focus on the choices we make, ensuring they align with God's desire for us to live righteous and peaceful lives. By doing so, we reflect His love and grace to those around us.

Prayer: Heavenly Father, as we start this new day, help us to turn away from all forms of evil. Guide us to do good in every situation we encounter. Fill our hearts with a desire for peace and give us the courage to pursue it actively. May our actions today reflect Your goodness and bring glory to Your name. In Jesus' name, we pray. Amen.

Meditative Thought: Consider the areas in your life where you need to depart from evil and seek to do good. Reflect on how you can actively pursue peace in your interactions and decisions today. Ask God for the strength and wisdom to follow His path.

Scripture: Psalm 34:14
"Depart from evil and do good; Seek peace and pursue it."

Reflection: As we end this day, let us look back and reflect on our actions and choices. Were there moments when we turned away from evil and did good? Did we actively seek and pursue peace in our interactions and decisions? Psalm 34:14 reminds us that living a righteous life requires continuous effort and mindfulness. As we prepare for rest, let us commit to making these choices again tomorrow, trusting in God's guidance and strength.

Prayer: Gracious Lord, as we reflect on this day, we thank You for Your guidance. Forgive us for any moments when we failed to turn away from evil or pursue peace. Help us to learn from these experiences and to strive for goodness and peace in all that we do. Renew our spirits as we rest, and prepare us to live more faithfully tomorrow. In Jesus' name, we pray. Amen.

Meditative Thought: Reflect on your day and identify moments when you chose to do good and seek peace. Consider how these actions impacted your relationships and inner peace. As you rest, ask God to help you continue to pursue righteousness and peace in the days to come.

Scripture: Revelation 21:4
"And God will wipe away every tear from their eyes; there shall be no more death, nor sorrow, nor crying. There shall be no more pain, for the former things have passed away."

Reflection: As we greet the new day, let's find hope and comfort in Revelation 21:4. This verse speaks of a future where God Himself will wipe away every tear, and there will be no more death, sorrow, crying, or pain. The promise of a new heaven and a new earth offers us a glimpse of the ultimate restoration and peace that God has planned for His people. Today, let this hope fill your heart and give you strength. Whatever challenges you face, remember that God's final victory over all suffering and pain is assured.

Prayer: Heavenly Father, as we start this day, we thank You for the promise of a future free from pain and sorrow. Help us to live with this hope in our hearts, finding comfort and strength in Your promises. Guide us today to be a source of hope and peace to others, reflecting Your love in all we do. In Jesus' name, we pray. Amen.

Meditative Thought: Reflect on the promise of a future without pain and sorrow. Let this vision of God's ultimate restoration give you hope and encouragement. Carry this hope with you throughout the day, letting it influence your thoughts, actions, and interactions with others.

Scripture: Revelation 21:4
"And God will wipe away every tear from their eyes; there shall be no more death, nor sorrow, nor crying. There shall be no more pain, for the former things have passed away."

Reflection: As we conclude the day, let's reflect on the comforting promise of Revelation 21:4. This verse assures us that a time is coming when God will personally wipe away every tear, and all forms of suffering will be eliminated. In the quiet of the evening, let this promise bring you peace. Consider the struggles and sorrows of the day and place them in God's hands, trusting in His ultimate plan for restoration and joy.

Prayer: Gracious Lord, as we end this day, we thank You for the promise of a future without pain and sorrow. Help us to rest in the assurance that You will wipe away every tear and bring an end to all suffering. Give us peace as we sleep, and renew our strength for tomorrow. May we always find comfort in Your unfailing love. In Jesus' name, we pray. Amen.

Meditative Thought: Before you sleep, take a moment to visualize the promise of a world free from pain and sorrow. Let the peace of this vision calm your mind and heart. Trust in God's ultimate plan and find rest in His loving care, knowing that He will make all things new.

APRIL 8

MORNING DEVOTION

Scripture: Isaiah 40:31
"But those who wait on the Lord shall renew their strength; They shall mount up with wings like eagles, they shall run and not be weary, They shall walk and not faint."

Reflection: As we rise to greet the new day, Isaiah 40:31 provides us with a powerful promise of strength and endurance. Waiting on the Lord means placing our trust and hope in Him, knowing that He will provide for us in His perfect timing. When we do this, God promises to renew our strength. We will soar like eagles, run without growing weary, and walk without fainting. This morning, let us commit to waiting on the Lord, trusting in His strength to carry us through whatever lies ahead.

Prayer: Heavenly Father, as we begin this day, we place our hope and trust in You. Renew our strength and fill us with Your power. Help us to soar above our challenges and to run the race set before us without growing weary. Guide our steps so that we may walk without fainting. Thank You for Your promise of renewed strength. In Jesus' name, we pray. Amen.

Meditative Thought: Consider what it means to wait on the Lord today. Reflect on areas in your life where you need to place your trust in God and rely on His strength. Visualize yourself soaring like an eagle, running with endurance, and walking with steadfastness, all empowered by God's grace.

Scripture: Isaiah 40:31
"But those who wait on the Lord shall renew their strength; They shall mount up with wings like eagles, they shall run and not be weary, They shall walk and not faint."

Reflection: As we end this day, let's reflect on how God has renewed our strength. Waiting on the Lord throughout the day, we may have experienced His power in moments of challenge and fatigue. Isaiah 40:31 reminds us that in God, we find the strength to rise above our circumstances. As we prepare to rest, let us thank Him for His faithfulness and for renewing our strength when we needed it most.

Prayer: Gracious Lord, we thank You for being with us throughout this day. Thank You for renewing our strength and helping us to overcome challenges. As we rest tonight, we ask for Your continued presence and peace. Renew us once more so that we may wake up refreshed and ready to serve You. Help us to always wait on You and trust in Your unfailing strength. In Jesus' name, we pray. Amen.

Meditative Thought: Reflect on how God has renewed your strength today. Think about moments when you felt His presence and power uplifting you. As you rest, embrace the peace that comes from waiting on the Lord and trust that He will continue to renew your strength each day.

MORNING DEVOTION

Scripture: Romans 14:7-8
"For none of us lives to himself, and no one dies to himself. For if we live, we live to the Lord; and if we die, we die to the Lord. Therefore, whether we live or die, we are the Lord's."

Reflection: As we start this new day, Romans 14:7-8 reminds us of a profound truth: our lives belong to the Lord. Every action, thought, and decision should be viewed through the lens of living for God. We are not isolated beings; our lives have meaning and purpose because we are connected to Christ. Today, let us strive to live in a way that honors Him, recognizing that our existence is deeply entwined with His divine plan.

Prayer: Heavenly Father, thank You for the gift of life and the assurance that we belong to You. As we begin this day, help us to live with the awareness that our lives are not our own but are dedicated to Your glory. Guide our thoughts, words, and actions so that they reflect Your love and purpose. Strengthen us to live faithfully for You in all that we do. In Jesus' name, we pray. Amen.

Meditative Thought: Consider how your life is a reflection of your relationship with the Lord. Think about how you can live today in a way that honors Him. Remember, every moment is an opportunity to live for Christ and demonstrate His love and grace to others.

Scripture: Romans 14:7-8

"For none of us lives to himself, and no one dies to himself. For if we live, we live to the Lord; and if we die, we die to the Lord. Therefore, whether we live or die, we are the Lord's."

Reflection: As the day comes to a close, reflect on how Romans 14:7-8 has manifested in your life today. Have you lived in a way that acknowledges that you belong to the Lord? Our daily actions, though sometimes small, contribute to a life lived for God. Whether in joy or in struggle, we are the Lord's. This evening, let us reaffirm our commitment to living for Him, trusting in His guidance and grace.

Prayer: Gracious Lord, as we end this day, we thank You for the reminder that our lives are in Your hands. Forgive us for the moments when we may have lived for ourselves instead of for You. Help us to rest in the knowledge that we are Yours, and renew our commitment to living for You each day. Give us peace and strength as we prepare for tomorrow. In Jesus' name, we pray. Amen.

Meditative Thought: Reflect on your day and identify moments when you felt connected to God's purpose for your life. Consider how you can continue to live with the awareness that you belong to the Lord. As you rest, thank God for His presence and guidance, and seek His strength to live faithfully for Him each day.

APRIL 10

MORNING DEVOTION

Scripture: Proverbs 22:1
"A good name is to be chosen rather than great riches, Loving favor rather than silver and gold."

Reflection: As we start our day, Proverbs 22:1 reminds us of the value of a good reputation and loving favor. In a world that often measures success by wealth and material possessions, this verse challenges us to prioritize integrity and the respect of others. A good name reflects our character and the way we treat others. Today, let us strive to act with honesty, kindness, and integrity in all our interactions, valuing the priceless treasure of a good name.

Prayer: Heavenly Father, thank You for the wisdom of Your Word. As we begin this day, help us to value a good name and loving favor above material wealth. Guide our actions so that we may reflect Your love and integrity in all we do. Grant us the strength to choose what is right and to honor You in every aspect of our lives. In Jesus' name, we pray. Amen.

Meditative Thought: Consider how your actions today can build and maintain a good name. Reflect on the importance of integrity and the impact it has on your relationships and witness. Let your desire for a good reputation guide your thoughts and deeds throughout the day.

Scripture: Proverbs 22:1
"A good name is to be chosen rather than great riches, Loving favor rather than silver and gold."

Reflection: As we conclude the day, let's reflect on the wisdom of Proverbs 22:1. Think about how you conducted yourself today and the ways in which you either upheld or compromised your integrity. A good name is built through consistent actions of honesty and kindness. This evening, let us examine our hearts and seek God's guidance to maintain a reputation that honors Him.

Prayer: Gracious Lord, we thank You for guiding us through this day. Help us to reflect on our actions and to seek forgiveness where we have fallen short. Teach us to value a good name and loving favor above all else. May our lives be a testament to Your love and integrity. Renew our strength and grant us peace as we rest. In Jesus' name, we pray. Amen.

Meditative Thought: Reflect on the events of the day and how they have contributed to your reputation. Consider ways in which you can further cultivate a good name and loving favor. As you rest, ask God to continue shaping your character to reflect His love and truth.

APRIL 11

MORNING DEVOTION

Scripture: Philippians 2:13
"For it is God who works in you both to will and to do for His good pleasure."

Reflection: As we begin our day, let's meditate on the truth of Philippians 2:13. This verse reminds us that God is actively at work within us, shaping our desires and empowering us to carry out His purposes. We are not left to navigate life's challenges on our own; rather, we can trust that God is leading and guiding us every step of the way. Today, let's surrender our will to His and allow Him to work in us for His good pleasure.

Prayer: Heavenly Father, thank You for Your presence and power at work within us. Help us to yield our will to Yours and to be sensitive to Your leading throughout this day. Guide our thoughts, words, and actions so that they align with Your good pleasure. Strengthen us to walk in obedience and trust in Your unfailing guidance. In Jesus' name, we pray. Amen.

Meditative Thought: Reflect on the ways in which you have sensed God working in your life recently. Consider the desires He has placed in your heart and the opportunities He has presented for you to serve Him. As you go about your day, remain open to His leading and trust that He is working in you for His good purposes.

Scripture: Philippians 2:13
"For it is God who works in you both to will and to do for His good pleasure."

Reflection: As we conclude the day, let's reflect on the truth of Philippians 2:13. God is continually at work within us, shaping our desires and empowering us to carry out His will. Even in moments of fatigue or uncertainty, we can find strength and confidence in knowing that God is working in us for His good pleasure. Let's entrust our lives to His care and rest in the assurance that He is faithfully leading us.

Prayer: Gracious Lord, we thank You for Your constant presence and guidance in our lives. As we reflect on this day, we acknowledge Your hand at work within us. Help us to surrender our will to Yours and to trust in Your perfect plan for our lives. Grant us restful sleep tonight, knowing that You are working in us for Your good pleasure. In Jesus' name, we pray. Amen.

Meditative Thought: Consider the events of the day and how you have sensed God's presence and leading. Reflect on any moments when you felt His prompting or guidance. As you prepare for rest, thank God for His faithfulness and trust that He will continue to work in you for His good purposes.

MORNING DEVOTION

Scripture: Psalm 31:24
"Be of good courage, And He shall strengthen your heart, all you who hope in the Lord."

Reflection: As the morning sun rises, let Psalm 31:24 be a beacon of encouragement for your day. In times of uncertainty or difficulty, God calls us to be of good courage. He promises to strengthen our hearts as we place our hope in Him. Today, let's face whatever challenges come our way with confidence, knowing that God is with us, empowering us to overcome.

Prayer: Heavenly Father, thank You for the assurance that You strengthen the hearts of those who hope in You. As we begin this day, fill us with courage and confidence in Your unfailing love and power. Help us to face the challenges ahead with faith, knowing that You are with us every step of the way. Strengthen us, Lord, and guide us in Your truth. In Jesus' name, we pray. Amen.

Meditative Thought: Reflect on the challenges you may face today and the areas where you need courage. Visualize God strengthening your heart and empowering you to overcome. Carry this image with you throughout the day, knowing that He is with you, giving you the courage to face whatever comes your way.

Scripture: Psalm 31:24
"Be of good courage, And He shall strengthen your heart, all you who hope in the Lord."

Reflection: As the day draws to a close, let Psalm 31:24 remind you of God's faithfulness. Take a moment to reflect on the courage you displayed today, knowing that it was God who strengthened your heart. Whether the day brought victories or challenges, God was with you, upholding you with His grace. As you rest tonight, place your hope firmly in the Lord, trusting in His strength for tomorrow.

Prayer: Gracious God, as we come to the end of this day, we thank You for Your faithfulness and strength. Help us to continue placing our hope in You, knowing that You are the source of our courage and resilience. Grant us peaceful rest tonight, Lord, and renew our strength for the day ahead. May we wake up tomorrow with hearts full of courage and hope in You. In Jesus' name, we pray. Amen.

Meditative Thought: Reflect on the ways God strengthened your heart today. Think about moments when you felt His presence and courage rising within you. As you prepare for rest, thank God for His faithfulness and trust that He will continue to strengthen you as you hope in Him.

Scripture: Hebrews 13:16
"But do not forget to do good and to share, for with such sacrifices God is well pleased."

Reflection: As the morning dawns, let Hebrews 13:16 guide your thoughts. In a world filled with distractions and busyness, it's easy to overlook opportunities to do good and share with others. Yet, God calls us to live differently. He delights in acts of kindness and generosity. Today, let's open our hearts to the needs of those around us and seek opportunities to bless others, knowing that such sacrifices are pleasing to God.

Prayer: Heavenly Father, open our eyes to the needs of those around us. Help us not to overlook opportunities to do good and share with others. May our actions today bring joy to Your heart and honor Your name. Give us hearts of compassion and generosity, Lord, that we may reflect Your love to a world in need. In Jesus' name, we pray. Amen.

Meditative Thought: Consider the ways you can do good and share with others today. Reflect on the impact small acts of kindness and generosity can have on those around you. As you go about your day, be mindful of opportunities to bless others and bring joy to God's heart through your actions.

Scripture: Hebrews 13:16
"But do not forget to do good and to share, for with such sacrifices God is well pleased."

Reflection: As the day comes to a close, reflect on Hebrews 13:16. Consider the ways you lived out this verse today. Did you seize opportunities to do good and share with others? Take a moment to thank God for His provision and guidance throughout the day. Remember, even the smallest acts of kindness are pleasing to Him.

Prayer: Gracious God, as we reflect on this day, we thank You for Your goodness and provision. Forgive us for any missed opportunities to do good and share with others. Help us to be more attentive to Your leading, Lord, and to respond with generosity and compassion. May our lives continually bring joy to Your heart. In Jesus' name, we pray. Amen.

Meditative Thought: Think about one moment today where you did good or shared with someone. How did it feel? Consider how you can incorporate more acts of kindness and generosity into your daily life. As you prepare for rest, ask God to continue guiding you in ways that please Him and bless others.

Scripture: 2 Corinthians 7:1

"Therefore, having these promises, beloved, let us cleanse ourselves from all filthiness of the flesh and spirit, perfecting holiness in the fear of God."

Reflection: As the morning unfolds, meditate on 2 Corinthians 7:1. This verse urges us to cleanse ourselves from all impurities, both physical and spiritual, and to pursue holiness in reverence for God. We are reminded of the promises of God, which inspire us to live lives marked by purity and devotion to Him. Today, let us commit to aligning our thoughts, words, and actions with God's standard of holiness, motivated by our love and reverence for Him.

Prayer: Heavenly Father, thank You for the promises You have given us. Help us to cleanse ourselves from all impurities and to pursue holiness with reverence for You. Grant us the strength and wisdom to resist temptation and to live lives that honor You in every way. May our pursuit of holiness be a testament to Your grace and love at work within us. In Jesus' name, we pray. Amen.

Meditative Thought: Consider areas in your life where you need to cleanse yourself from impurities. Reflect on the promises of God that inspire you to pursue holiness. How can you perfect holiness in the fear of God today? Allow these thoughts to guide your actions as you navigate the day ahead.

Scripture: 2 Corinthians 7:1
"Therefore, having these promises, beloved, let us cleanse ourselves from all filthiness of the flesh and spirit, perfecting holiness in the fear of God."

Reflection: As the day comes to a close, reflect on 2 Corinthians 7:1. Consider how you lived out the call to cleanse yourself from impurities and pursue holiness in reverence for God. Did you align your thoughts, words, and actions with His standard of holiness? Take a moment to thank God for His grace that empowers you to live a life marked by purity and devotion to Him.

Prayer: Gracious Lord, as we reflect on this day, we thank You for Your faithfulness and grace. Forgive us for any moments when we fell short of pursuing holiness in reverence for You. Strengthen us, Lord, to continue cleansing ourselves from impurities and perfecting holiness in our lives. May our pursuit of holiness bring glory to Your name. In Jesus' name, we pray. Amen.

Meditative Thought: Think about one area where you struggled to maintain holiness today. Ask God for forgiveness and guidance in overcoming this challenge. Reflect on the grace He has shown you and the strength He provides to pursue holiness. As you prepare for rest, entrust yourself to His care, knowing that He is faithful to complete the work He has begun in you.

APRIL 15

MORNING DEVOTION

Scripture: Jeremiah 29:12-13
"Then you will call upon Me and go and pray to Me, and I will listen to you. And you will seek Me and find Me, when you search for Me with all your heart."

Reflection: As the morning breaks, let the words of Jeremiah 29:12-13 inspire you. God promises to listen when we call upon Him in prayer and seek Him with all our hearts. This assurance invites us into a deeper relationship with Him, where we can experience His presence and guidance. Today, let's approach God in prayer with sincerity and earnestness, knowing that He eagerly awaits our communion with Him.

Prayer: Heavenly Father, thank You for the promise that You listen to us when we call upon You and seek You with all our hearts. Help us to approach You in prayer today with sincerity and earnestness. May our hearts be open to Your leading and our minds attentive to Your voice. Guide us, Lord, as we seek to walk in Your ways. In Jesus' name, we pray. Amen.

Meditative Thought: Consider the sincerity of your prayers. Are you truly seeking God with all your heart? Reflect on the times when you have experienced His presence and guidance in response to your prayers. How can you deepen your relationship with Him through prayer today?

Scripture: Jeremiah 29:12-13
"Then you will call upon Me and go and pray to Me, and I will listen to you. 13 And you will seek Me and find Me, when you search for Me with all your heart."

Reflection: As the day draws to a close, reflect on Jeremiah 29:12-13. Have you called upon God in prayer today, seeking Him with all your heart? Take a moment to consider the times when you have experienced His presence and answered prayers. Remember that God eagerly listens to those who seek Him sincerely. As you prepare for rest, entrust yourself into His care, knowing that He is faithful to be found by those who earnestly seek Him.

Prayer: Gracious God, as we reflect on this day, we thank You for the assurance that You listen to us when we call upon You and seek You with all our hearts. Forgive us for the times when we have not pursued You wholeheartedly. Help us to deepen our relationship with You, Lord, through sincere prayer and earnest seeking. May Your presence fill our hearts as we rest tonight. In Jesus' name, we pray. Amen.

Meditative Thought: Think about the ways you sought God with all your heart today. Reflect on any moments when you experienced His presence or guidance. As you prepare for rest, commit to seeking Him earnestly each day, knowing that He is faithful to be found by those who diligently seek Him.

Scripture: 1 Peter 3:8-9
"Finally, all of you be of one mind, having compassion for one another; love as brothers, be tenderhearted, be courteous; 9 not returning evil for evil or reviling for reviling, but on the contrary blessing, knowing that you were called to this, that you may inherit a blessing."

Reflection: As the morning begins, let's reflect on the wisdom of 1 Peter 3:8-9. This passage calls us to unity, compassion, brotherly love, tenderness, and courtesy. Moreover, it challenges us to respond to evil with blessing, knowing that we are called to inherit blessings ourselves. Today, let's strive to embody these virtues in our interactions with others, trusting that God's grace empowers us to live as beacons of love and peace in a world often marked by strife.

Prayer: Heavenly Father, help us to live out the virtues outlined in 1 Peter 3:8-9. Grant us unity, compassion, brotherly love, tenderness, and courtesy in our relationships. Fill us with Your grace and strength so that we may respond to evil with blessing, following the example of Your Son, Jesus Christ. May our lives reflect Your love and bring glory to Your name. In Jesus' name, we pray. Amen.

Meditative Thought: Consider the ways you can embody unity, compassion, love, tenderness, and courtesy in your interactions today. Reflect on any opportunities to respond to evil with blessing. As you go about your day, invite God to guide your words and actions, allowing His grace to flow through you to those around you.

Scripture: 1 Peter 3:8-9
"Finally, all of you be of one mind, having compassion for one another; love as brothers, be tenderhearted, be courteous; 9 not returning evil for evil or reviling for reviling, but on the contrary blessing, knowing that you were called to this, that you may inherit a blessing."

Reflection: As the day comes to a close, let's reflect on 1 Peter 3:8-9 once again. Did you strive to embody unity, compassion, love, tenderness, and courtesy in your interactions today? Were you able to resist the temptation to return evil for evil or reviling for reviling, instead choosing to bless others? Take a moment to thank God for His grace that enabled you to live out these virtues and ask for His continued guidance in walking in love and peace.

Prayer: Gracious God, we thank You for the wisdom and guidance found in Your Word. Forgive us for any shortcomings in living out the virtues outlined in 1 Peter 3:8-9 today. Strengthen us, Lord, to continue walking in unity, compassion, love, tenderness, and courtesy. Help us to respond to evil with blessing, trusting in Your promise of inheritance. May Your love continue to shape our hearts and lives. In Jesus' name, we pray. Amen.

Meditative Thought: Reflect on the moments when you were able to embody unity, compassion, love, tenderness, and courtesy today. Consider any instances where you chose to bless others instead of returning evil. How did these actions impact your relationships and bring glory to God? As you prepare for rest, surrender any remaining concerns to God, trusting in His provision and guidance for tomorrow.

Scripture: Matthew 6:31-34

"Therefore, do not worry, saying, 'What shall we eat?' or 'What shall we drink?' or 'What shall we wear?' For after all these things the Gentiles seek. For your heavenly Father knows that you need all these things. But seek first the kingdom of God and His righteousness, and all these things shall be added to you. Therefore, do not worry about tomorrow, for tomorrow will worry about its own things. Sufficient for the day is its own trouble."

Reflection: As the morning unfolds, let's meditate on the comforting words of Matthew 6:31-34. Jesus encourages us not to worry about our material needs but to trust in our heavenly Father, who knows what we need even before we ask. Instead of being consumed by concerns about the future, Jesus invites us to seek first the kingdom of God and His righteousness. Today, let's focus on living in alignment with God's purposes, trusting Him to provide for our needs as we seek His will above all else.

Prayer: Heavenly Father, we thank You for Your provision and care for us. Forgive us for the times when we allow worry to overshadow our trust in You. Help us to seek Your kingdom and righteousness above all else, knowing that You will provide for our needs. Grant us peace and contentment in Your presence today, Lord, as we surrender our concerns to You. In Jesus' name, we pray. Amen.

Meditative Thought: Consider the worries and concerns you may be carrying today. How can you actively seek God's kingdom and righteousness in the midst of these worries? Reflect on the ways God has provided for you in the past and trust Him to do the same today. As you go about your day, focus on living in alignment with God's will, knowing that He is faithful to provide for all your needs.

Scripture: Matthew 6:31-34

"Therefore, do not worry, saying, 'What shall we eat?' or 'What shall we drink?' or 'What shall we wear?' For after all these things the Gentiles seek. For your heavenly Father knows that you need all these things. But seek first the kingdom of God and His righteousness, and all these things shall be added to you. Therefore, do not worry about tomorrow, for tomorrow will worry about its own things. Sufficient for the day is its own trouble."

Reflection: As the day comes to a close, let's reflect on the wisdom of Matthew 6:31-34 once again. Did you trust God to provide for your needs today, or did worries about the future consume your thoughts? Take a moment to acknowledge God's faithfulness in providing for you throughout the day. As you prepare for rest, surrender any remaining worries about tomorrow to God, trusting in His provision and care.

Prayer: Gracious Father, as we reflect on this day, we thank You for Your faithfulness and provision. Forgive us for the times when we allowed worry to overshadow our trust in You. Help us to continue seeking Your kingdom and righteousness above all else, knowing that You will provide for our needs. Grant us peaceful rest tonight, Lord, as we entrust our worries to You. In Jesus' name, we pray. Amen.

Meditative Thought: Think about the worries and concerns you carried throughout the day. Surrender them to God in prayer, trusting in His provision and care for you. Reflect on the peace that comes from seeking God's kingdom and righteousness above all else. As you prepare for rest, trust in God's promise that He will provide for all your needs according to His riches in glory.

APRIL 18

MORNING DEVOTION

Scripture: Amos 3:3
"Can two walk together, unless they are agreed?"

Reflection: As the morning begins, ponder on the profound simplicity of Amos 3:3. This verse presents a compelling question about the nature of harmony and unity. It prompts us to reflect on the importance of agreement and alignment in relationships, particularly in our walk with God. Just as two people cannot walk together unless they agree on the direction, so too must we be in agreement with God's will and purpose to walk closely with Him. Today, let's consider our alignment with God's plans and seek to deepen our agreement with Him in every aspect of our lives.

Prayer: Heavenly Father, help us to align our hearts and minds with Your will and purpose. Grant us the wisdom to discern Your plans and the willingness to walk in agreement with You. May our relationship with You be marked by unity and harmony, as we strive to follow Your lead in all things. In Jesus' name, we pray. Amen.

Meditative Thought: Consider the areas in your life where you may be out of alignment with God's will. Reflect on how you can actively seek agreement with Him in those areas. As you go about your day, invite God to guide your steps and help you walk closely with Him in unity and harmony.

Scripture: Amos 3:3
"Can two walk together, unless they are agreed?"

Reflection: As the day comes to a close, let's reflect on the question posed in Amos 3:3. Did you walk in agreement with God today, or were there moments of discord and misalignment? Take a moment to acknowledge any areas where you may have strayed from His will and purpose. As you seek to deepen your relationship with God, ask Him to help you align your heart and mind more closely with His, so that you may walk together in unity and harmony.

Prayer: Lord, we confess that there are times when we stray from Your will and purpose. Forgive us for any moments of discord and misalignment in our walk with You. Help us to realign our hearts and minds with Your plans, so that we may walk together in unity and harmony. Grant us the strength and wisdom to follow Your lead faithfully. In Jesus' name, we pray. Amen.

Meditative Thought: Think about the moments today when you felt closest to God. Reflect on the areas where you may have experienced discord in your relationship with Him. How can you seek greater agreement with God in those areas? As you prepare for rest, commit to walking more closely with Him in the days to come.

Scripture: Nahum 1:17
"The Lord is good, A stronghold in the day of trouble; And He knows those who trust in Him."

Reflection: As the morning light dawns, let the words of Nahum 1:17 remind you of God's goodness and faithfulness. In times of trouble, God is our stronghold, our refuge, and our source of strength. He knows those who trust in Him intimately and cares for them deeply. Today, let us take comfort in knowing that God is with us, even in the midst of life's storms. May we trust in His goodness and find refuge in His unfailing love.

Prayer: Gracious God, we thank You for Your goodness and faithfulness. In times of trouble, You are our stronghold and refuge. Help us to trust in You wholeheartedly, knowing that You care for us deeply. Strengthen us with Your presence and fill us with Your peace. May we find our security in You alone. In Jesus' name, we pray. Amen.

Meditative Thought: Reflect on a time when you felt God's presence and strength in the midst of trouble. Consider how His faithfulness has sustained you in difficult times. As you go about your day, rest in the assurance that God is with you, and trust in His goodness to see you through every trial.

Scripture: Nahum 1:17
"The Lord is good, A stronghold in the day of trouble; And He knows those who trust in Him."

Reflection: As the day draws to a close, let us reflect on the comforting words of Nahum 1:17. Despite the challenges we may face, God remains good and steadfast. He is our stronghold in times of trouble, offering us refuge and strength. Moreover, He knows us intimately and cares for us deeply. Tonight, let us find peace in His presence and rest securely in His unfailing love.

Prayer: Heavenly Father, we thank You for being our stronghold and refuge in times of trouble. As we reflect on this day, we are grateful for Your faithfulness and goodness. Help us to trust in You more deeply and find rest in Your unfailing love. May Your presence fill us with peace as we prepare for rest tonight. In Jesus' name, we pray. Amen.

Meditative Thought: Think about the ways God has shown Himself to be your stronghold and refuge throughout the day. Consider the moments when you felt His presence and strength. As you surrender to His care tonight, trust in His goodness to sustain you and find comfort in knowing that He knows and cares for you intimately.

APRIL 20

MORNING DEVOTION

Scripture: Jeremiah 29:11
"For I know the thoughts that I think toward you, says the Lord, thoughts of peace and not of evil, to give you a future and a hope."

Reflection: As the morning sun rises, let the promise of Jeremiah 29:11 fill your heart with hope and assurance. God's plans for us are filled with peace and goodness, and He desires to give us a future filled with hope. Even in times of uncertainty, we can trust that God has a purpose and a plan for our lives. Today, let us rest in the knowledge that God is working all things together for our good, and may this assurance give us courage to face the day ahead with confidence.

Prayer: Heavenly Father, thank You for the promise of Jeremiah 29:11. Help us to trust in Your plans for our lives, knowing that they are filled with peace and hope. Give us the courage to embrace each moment of this day, knowing that You are with us every step of the way. May Your presence fill us with peace and assurance as we journey forward. In Jesus' name, we pray. Amen.

Meditative Thought: Reflect on the assurance that God's plans for you are filled with peace and hope. Consider any areas of your life where you may be feeling uncertain or anxious, and surrender them to God, trusting in His goodness and faithfulness. As you go about your day, remember that God is working all things together for your good, and let this truth fill you with courage and confidence.

Scripture: Jeremiah 29:11
"For I know the thoughts that I think toward you, says the Lord, thoughts of peace and not of evil, to give you a future and a hope."

Reflection: As the day comes to a close, let us reflect on the promise of Jeremiah 29:11. God's thoughts toward us are filled with peace and goodness, and He desires to give us a future filled with hope. Even as we face challenges and uncertainties, we can trust that God is working all things together for our good. Tonight, let us find rest in the knowledge that our heavenly Father holds our future in His hands, and may His promise of peace and hope bring comfort to our hearts as we prepare for rest.

Prayer: Lord, as we reflect on the promise of Jeremiah 29:11, we are grateful for Your faithfulness and goodness toward us. Thank You for the assurance that You hold our future in Your hands and that Your plans for us are filled with hope. As we surrender this day to You, may Your peace fill our hearts and minds, and may we rest securely in Your love. In Jesus' name, we pray. Amen.

Meditative Thought: Think about the ways God has shown His faithfulness and goodness to you throughout this day. Reflect on any moments where you experienced His peace and hope, even in the midst of challenges. As you prepare for rest, trust in God's promise to give you a future filled with hope, and let His peace guard your heart and mind.

Scripture: Luke 23:44-47

"Now it was about the sixth hour, and there was darkness over all the earth until the ninth hour. Then the sun was darkened, and the veil of the temple was torn in two. And when Jesus had cried out with a loud voice, He said, "Father, 'into Your hands I commit My spirit.'" Having said this, He breathed His last. So, when the centurion saw what had happened, he glorified God, saying, "Certainly this was a righteous Man!"

Reflection: As you begin your day, meditate on the profound events described in Luke 23:44-47. Reflect on the darkness that covered the land and the tearing of the temple veil, symbolic of the access to God made possible through Jesus' sacrifice. Consider the centurion's response to witnessing Jesus' death, acknowledging Him as a righteous man. Let this passage remind you of the immense love and sacrifice of Jesus, who willingly gave His life for you. As you face the challenges of the day ahead, may you find strength and courage in the knowledge of Christ's victory over sin and death.

Prayer: Lord Jesus, thank You for Your sacrificial love demonstrated on the cross. Help us to grasp the depth of Your sacrifice and to live our lives in gratitude and obedience to You. As we face the challenges of this day, may Your victory over sin and death empower us to walk in faith and righteousness. May Your Holy Spirit guide and strengthen us, and may we bring glory to Your name in all that we do. Amen.

Meditative Thought: Consider the significance of Jesus' death on the cross for your life. Reflect on the love and sacrifice He demonstrated for you, and ponder how His victory over sin and death impacts your daily life. As you go about your day, carry with you the assurance of Christ's presence and the hope of His redemption.

Scripture: Luke 23:44-47
"Now it was about the sixth hour, and there was darkness over all the earth until the ninth hour. Then the sun was darkened, and the veil of the temple was torn in two. And when Jesus had cried out with a loud voice, He said, "Father, 'into Your hands I commit My spirit.'" Having said this, He breathed His last. So, when the centurion saw what had happened, he glorified God, saying, "Certainly this was a righteous Man!""

Reflection: As the day comes to a close, reflect on the events described in Luke 23:44-47. Contemplate the darkness that covered the earth and the tearing of the temple veil, signifying the fulfillment of God's plan of redemption through Jesus Christ. Consider the centurion's acknowledgment of Jesus as a righteous man and the impact His death had on those who witnessed it. Let this passage deepen your gratitude for Jesus' sacrifice and renew your commitment to follow Him wholeheartedly. As you prepare for rest, may you find peace in the assurance of Christ's victory over sin and death.

Prayer: Gracious Lord, as we reflect on the events of Jesus' death, we are humbled by the magnitude of Your love for us. Thank You for the sacrifice You made on the cross to redeem us from sin and death. Help us to live in gratitude for Your grace and to walk in obedience to Your will. As we rest tonight, may Your peace fill our hearts, and may we find comfort in Your presence. Amen.

Meditative Thought: Consider how Jesus' sacrifice on the cross impacts your life. Reflect on the significance of His death for your salvation and the hope it brings for eternity. As you prepare for rest, surrender any burdens or worries to the Lord, and find peace in His presence.

Scripture: Isaiah 9:6-7
"For unto us a Child is born, Unto us a Son is given; And the government will be upon His shoulder. And His name will be called Wonderful, Counselor, Mighty God, Everlasting Father, Prince of Peace. Of the increase of His government and peace There will be no end, Upon the throne of David and over His kingdom, To order it and establish it with judgment and justice From that time forward, even forever. The zeal of the Lord of hosts will perform this."

Reflection: As you begin your day, reflect on the prophetic words of Isaiah 9:6-7. This passage speaks of the coming of a Child who will bring hope, peace, and eternal reign. Jesus Christ, the Son of God, fulfills this prophecy. He is the Wonderful Counselor, Mighty God, Everlasting Father, and Prince of Peace. Today, as you face the challenges and uncertainties of life, remember that Jesus is with you. Let this truth fill you with hope and confidence as you navigate the day ahead.

Prayer: Heavenly Father, we thank You for the gift of Your Son, Jesus Christ, who brings hope and peace to our lives. Help us to fix our eyes on Him and to trust in His sovereign reign. May His presence fill us with courage and strength as we face the challenges of this day. Guide us by Your Spirit, and lead us in the path of righteousness. In Jesus' name, we pray. Amen.

Meditative Thought: Consider the names given to Jesus in Isaiah 9:6: Wonderful Counselor, Mighty God, Everlasting Father, Prince of Peace. Reflect on what each of these names means to you personally and how they reflect Jesus' character and role in your life. As you go about your day, meditate on the truth that Jesus is with you, reigning in power and bringing peace that surpasses all understanding.

Scripture: Isaiah 9:6-7
"For unto us a Child is born, Unto us a Son is given; And the government will be upon His shoulder. And His name will be called Wonderful, Counselor, Mighty God, Everlasting Father, Prince of Peace. 7 Of the increase of His government and peace There will be no end, Upon the throne of David and over His kingdom, To order it and establish it with judgment and justice From that time forward, even forever. The zeal of the Lord of hosts will perform this."

Reflection: As the day comes to a close, ponder once again the profound words of Isaiah 9:6-7. Reflect on the significance of Jesus Christ, the Child born to us and the Son given to us. He reigns with authority and brings everlasting peace to those who trust in Him. As you prepare for rest, take comfort in the promise that His government and peace will have no end. Let the truth of His eternal reign fill you with hope and assurance, knowing that He is with you always.

Prayer: Gracious God, as we reflect on the words of Isaiah 9:6-7, we are reminded of Your faithfulness and sovereignty. Thank You for sending Your Son, Jesus Christ, to be our Wonderful Counselor, Mighty God, Everlasting Father, and Prince of Peace. May His eternal reign bring comfort and peace to our hearts tonight. Help us to trust in Your promises and to rest securely in Your love. In Jesus' name, we pray. Amen.

Meditative Thought: Consider the promise of Jesus' eternal reign and peace in Isaiah 9:6-7. Reflect on how this truth brings comfort and assurance to your life, especially in times of uncertainty or difficulty. As you prepare for rest, surrender any worries or fears to the Lord and find peace in His presence.

Scripture: Zephaniah 3:17

"The Lord your God in your midst, The Mighty One, will save; He will rejoice over you with gladness, He will quiet you with His love, He will rejoice over you with singing."

Reflection: As you begin your day, meditate on the beautiful words of Zephaniah 3:17. This verse reminds us of God's presence in our midst, His power to save, and His overwhelming love for us. Consider the imagery of God rejoicing over you with gladness and singing, and let it fill you with awe and gratitude. No matter what challenges you may face today, know that God is with you, ready to save and to quiet your fears with His love. May this truth bring you comfort and confidence as you step into the day ahead.

Prayer: Heavenly Father, thank You for Your constant presence in our lives. We are grateful for Your power to save and Your unfailing love for us. As we begin this day, help us to trust in Your promises and to rest in Your love. Quiet our hearts with Your presence, and fill us with Your peace that surpasses all understanding. May we walk in the assurance of Your love and rejoice in Your salvation. Amen.

Meditative Thought: Reflect on the image of God rejoicing over you with gladness and singing. Consider the depth of His love for you and how it brings you comfort and assurance. As you go about your day, carry with you the knowledge that God is with you, ready to save and to quiet your fears with His love.

Scripture: Zephaniah 3:17
"The Lord your God in your midst, The Mighty One, will save; He will rejoice over you with gladness, He will quiet you with His love, He will rejoice over you with singing."

Reflection: As the day draws to a close, reflect on the comforting words of Zephaniah 3:17. Consider how God has been with you throughout the day, rejoicing over you with gladness and quieting you with His love. Take a moment to thank Him for His presence, His saving power, and His overwhelming love for you. As you prepare for rest, may you find peace in the knowledge that God is with you, rejoicing over you with singing.

Prayer: Gracious God, we thank You for Your constant presence in our lives. Thank You for rejoicing over us with gladness and quieting us with Your love. As we prepare for rest tonight, may Your presence fill us with peace and assurance. Help us to trust in Your saving power and to rest securely in Your love. May we find comfort in knowing that You are with us always. Amen.

Meditative Thought: Reflect on the ways God has shown His love for you throughout the day. Consider the moments when you felt His presence and His peace quieting your heart. As you surrender to His love tonight, may you find rest in His presence and rejoice in His salvation.

Scripture: Jeremiah 17:7-8

"Blessed is the man who trusts in the Lord, and whose hope is the Lord. For he shall be like a tree planted by the waters, Which spreads out its roots by the river, And will not fear when heat comes; But its leaf will be green, And will not be anxious in the year of drought, Nor will cease from yielding fruit.

Reflection: As you begin your day, meditate on the profound truth of Jeremiah 17:7-8. This passage paints a vivid picture of the blessings that come from trusting in the Lord. Like a tree planted by the waters, those who put their hope and trust in God are deeply rooted and nourished by His presence. Even in times of difficulty and trial, they remain steadfast, bearing fruit and flourishing. Reflect on your own trust in the Lord and consider how you can deepen your reliance on Him today. May the assurance of His faithfulness fill you with confidence and peace as you face the challenges ahead.

Prayer: Heavenly Father, we thank You for the promise of blessing and abundance found in trusting in You. Help us to place our hope fully in You, knowing that You are faithful and steadfast. As we navigate the day ahead, may Your presence sustain us like the waters sustain a tree by the river. Grant us the strength and courage to remain steadfast in our trust in You, even when faced with difficulties. In Jesus' name, we pray. Amen.

Meditative Thought: Reflect on the imagery of the tree planted by the waters in Jeremiah 17:7-8. Consider how your trust in the Lord can deepen your spiritual roots and sustain you through all seasons of life. As you go about your day, let the assurance of God's faithfulness and provision fill you with confidence and peace.

Scripture: Jeremiah 17:7-8

"Blessed is the man who trusts in the Lord, and whose hope is the Lord. For he shall be like a tree planted by the waters, Which spreads out its roots by the river, And will not fear when heat comes; But its leaf will be green, And will not be anxious in the year of drought, Nor will cease from yielding fruit.

Reflection: As the day comes to a close, reflect on the comforting words of Jeremiah 17:7-8. Consider how your trust in the Lord has sustained you throughout the day, like a tree planted by the waters. Even in the midst of challenges and uncertainties, you have remained steadfast, drawing strength and nourishment from God's presence. Take a moment to thank Him for His faithfulness and provision in your life. As you prepare for rest, may you find peace in knowing that God is with you, and may His promise of blessing and abundance fill you with hope for the days ahead.

Prayer: Gracious God, we thank You for Your faithfulness and provision in our lives. Thank You for sustaining us like a tree planted by the waters, even in times of difficulty and trial. As we rest tonight, may Your presence continue to sustain us, and may Your peace fill our hearts. Help us to trust in You more deeply each day, knowing that You are faithful to fulfill Your promises. In Jesus' name, we pray. Amen.

Meditative Thought: Reflect on how your trust in the Lord has sustained you throughout the day. Consider the ways He has provided for you and brought you peace in the midst of challenges. As you surrender to His presence tonight, may you find rest in His faithfulness and provision.

Scripture: John 15:10-11

"If you keep My commandments, you will abide in My love, just as I have kept My Father's commandments and abide in His love. These things I have spoken to you, that My joy may remain in you, and that your joy may be full."

Reflection: As you begin your day, reflect on the words of Jesus in John 15:10-11. Jesus invites us to abide in His love by keeping His commandments, just as He abides in the love of the Father by keeping His commandments. This mutual abiding is the foundation of true joy. Consider what it means to keep Jesus' commandments—not merely as a duty but out of love for Him. As you seek to obey Him in all things, may His joy fill your heart and overflow into your day, bringing you a deep and lasting sense of fulfillment and contentment.

Prayer: Gracious Lord, thank You for the invitation to abide in Your love by keeping Your commandments. Help us to obey You out of love, knowing that Your commands are for our good and lead to true joy. Fill us with Your joy today, Lord, that our hearts may be full and our lives may overflow with gratitude and praise. In Your precious name, we pray. Amen.

Meditative Thought: Consider how you can abide in Jesus' love by keeping His commandments today. Reflect on specific areas of your life where you can align your actions with His teachings. As you surrender to His will, may His joy fill your heart and sustain you throughout the day.

Scripture: John 15:10-11
"If you keep My commandments, you will abide in My love, just as I have kept My Father's commandments and abide in His love. These things I have spoken to you, that My joy may remain in you, and that your joy may be full."

Reflection: As the day draws to a close, reflect on the promise of joy found in Jesus' words in John 15:10-11. Jesus desires for His joy to remain in us and for our joy to be full. Consider the ways in which you have experienced His joy today—perhaps through moments of obedience, fellowship with Him, or witnessing His work in your life. Take time to thank Him for these moments and ask Him to continue filling you with His joy as you rest tonight. May His joy sustain you through every trial and triumph, reminding you of His abiding love for you.

Prayer: Heavenly Father, we thank You for the joy that comes from abiding in Your love and keeping Your commandments. As we reflect on the day that has passed, we are grateful for the moments of joy You have graciously given us. May Your joy remain in us tonight, Lord, and may it overflow into every aspect of our lives. Fill us with Your peace as we rest, knowing that Your love surrounds us always. In Jesus' name, we pray. Amen.

Meditative Thought: Reflect on the moments of joy you have experienced today and thank God for His faithfulness in bringing them to you. As you prepare for rest, surrender any worries or burdens to Him and allow His joy to fill your heart, knowing that He is with you always.

Scripture: Psalm 19:7-8
"The law of the Lord is perfect, converting the soul; The testimony of the Lord is sure, making wise the simple; 8 The statutes of the Lord are right, rejoicing the heart; The commandment of the Lord is pure, enlightening the eyes."

Reflection: As you begin your day, ponder the profound truth of Psalm 19:7-8. This passage extols the virtues of God's Word—the law, testimony, statutes, and commandment of the Lord. Reflect on how God's Word has the power to transform hearts, impart wisdom, bring joy, and illuminate minds. Consider your own relationship with Scripture. Are you allowing it to penetrate your soul, making you wise and rejoicing your heart? Take a moment to commit yourself anew to the study and application of God's Word, knowing that it holds the keys to a life of true fulfillment and enlightenment.

Prayer: Heavenly Father, we thank You for the gift of Your Word. Help us to approach it with reverence and eagerness, recognizing its power to transform our lives. May Your Word penetrate our hearts, making us wise, rejoicing our souls, and enlightening our minds. Grant us the discipline and desire to study Your Word diligently, that we may grow in our understanding of You and Your will for our lives. In Jesus' name, we pray. Amen.

Meditative Thought: Consider the ways in which God's Word has impacted your life. Reflect on specific verses or passages that have brought you wisdom, joy, or enlightenment. As you go about your day, meditate on the transformative power of Scripture and seek to apply its principles to every aspect of your life.

Scripture: Psalm 19:7-8
"The law of the Lord is perfect, converting the soul; The testimony of the Lord is sure, making wise the simple; The statutes of the Lord are right, rejoicing the heart; The commandment of the Lord is pure, enlightening the eyes."

Reflection: As the day comes to a close, reflect on the beauty and power of Psalm 19:7-8. Consider how God's Word has been a guiding light throughout your day, illuminating your path and bringing joy to your heart. Take a moment to thank God for the wisdom, joy, and enlightenment He has provided through His Word. As you prepare for rest, commit yourself anew to the study and application of Scripture, knowing that it holds the key to a life of true fulfillment and purpose.

Prayer: Gracious God, we thank You for the gift of Your Word, which is a lamp to our feet and a light to our path. As we reflect on the day that has passed, we are grateful for the wisdom, joy, and enlightenment Your Word has brought us. Help us to treasure Your Word in our hearts and to apply its principles to our lives each day. May we find comfort and guidance in Your Word as we rest tonight, knowing that You are always with us. In Jesus' name, we pray. Amen.

Meditative Thought: Reflect on the ways in which God's Word has illuminated your life today. Consider specific moments when Scripture has brought you wisdom, joy, or enlightenment. As you prepare for rest, meditate on the truth that God's Word is perfect and pure, and allow it to guide your thoughts and actions even in your dreams.

APRIL 27

MORNING DEVOTION

Scripture: Revelation 1:18
"I am He who lives, and was dead, and behold, I am alive forevermore. Amen. And I have the keys of Hades and of Death."

Reflection: As you begin your day, meditate on the powerful words of Revelation 1:18. These words were spoken by Jesus Himself, asserting His victory over death and declaring His eternal sovereignty. Reflect on the significance of Jesus being the one who lives, who conquered death, and who holds the keys of Hades and Death. Consider the implications of this truth for your own life. Because Jesus lives, you can face each day with confidence, knowing that He has overcome every obstacle, including death itself. Let this assurance fill you with hope and courage as you step into the day ahead.

Prayer: Lord Jesus, we thank You for Your victory over death and for the assurance that You are alive forevermore. Help us to live each day in the light of Your resurrection, knowing that You hold the keys to Hades and Death. Give us confidence in Your sovereignty and strength to face whatever challenges may come our way. May Your victory be our source of hope and courage as we go forth into this new day. Amen.

Meditative Thought: Reflect on the implications of Jesus' victory over death for your own life. Consider how His resurrection gives you hope and courage to face each day with confidence. As you go about your day, meditate on the truth that Jesus is alive forevermore, and allow this reality to shape your thoughts and actions.

Scripture: Revelation 1:18
"I am He who lives, and was dead, and behold, I am alive forevermore. Amen. And I have the keys of Hades and of Death."

Reflection: As the day comes to a close, reflect on the profound truth of Revelation 1:18. Jesus declares Himself to be the one who lives, who was once dead, but who is now alive forevermore. Contemplate the significance of His resurrection and the assurance it brings of His eternal sovereignty. As you prepare for rest, take comfort in the fact that Jesus holds the keys of Hades and Death. No power in heaven or on earth can stand against Him. Surrender any fears or worries to Him, knowing that He has already overcome them all.

Prayer: Lord Jesus, we thank You for Your victory over death and for the assurance that You are alive forevermore. As we prepare for rest tonight, we entrust ourselves into Your hands, knowing that You hold the keys of Hades and Death. May Your presence fill our hearts with peace and security, and may we rest securely in Your sovereignty. Amen.

Meditative Thought: Reflect on the security you have in Jesus' victory over death. Consider how His resurrection gives you peace and assurance, even in the face of uncertainty. As you surrender to His sovereignty tonight, may you find rest in His eternal presence.

MORNING DEVOTION

Scripture: James 3:17-18
"But the wisdom that is from above is first pure, then peaceable, gentle, willing to yield, full of mercy and good fruits, without partiality and without hypocrisy. Now the fruit of righteousness is sown in peace by those who make peace."

Reflection: As you start your day, reflect on the qualities of wisdom described in James 3:17-18. True wisdom, which comes from above, is characterized by purity, peace, gentleness, humility, mercy, and sincerity. Consider how you can embody these qualities in your interactions with others today. Strive to be a peacemaker, sowing seeds of righteousness and fostering harmony in your relationships. As you seek to cultivate wisdom in your life, may you experience the fruit of righteousness and the blessings of peace that come from walking in God's ways.

Prayer: Heavenly Father, we thank You for the wisdom that comes from above, which brings purity, peace, and righteousness. Help us to embody these qualities in our lives, particularly in our interactions with others. Grant us the humility to seek peace and the courage to sow seeds of righteousness in all that we do. May Your wisdom guide our steps today, Lord, and may we be instruments of Your peace in the world. Amen.

Meditative Thought: Consider how you can cultivate the wisdom described in James 3:17-18 in your own life. Reflect on specific situations where you can demonstrate purity, peace, gentleness, and mercy. As you go about your day, strive to be a peacemaker, seeking harmony and righteousness in all your relationships.

Scripture: James 3:17-18
"But the wisdom that is from above is first pure, then peaceable, gentle, willing to yield, full of mercy and good fruits, without partiality and without hypocrisy. Now the fruit of righteousness is sown in peace by those who make peace."

Reflection: As the day comes to a close, reflect on the qualities of wisdom outlined in James 3:17-18. Consider how well you have embodied these characteristics in your interactions and decisions throughout the day. Take a moment to acknowledge any areas where you may have fallen short and ask God for His forgiveness and guidance. Remember that true wisdom leads to righteousness and peace, and commit yourself anew to pursuing these virtues in your life. As you seek to sow seeds of peace and righteousness, may you experience the abundant fruitfulness that comes from walking in God's wisdom.

Prayer: Gracious God, we confess that we often fall short of embodying Your wisdom in our lives. Forgive us for any lack of purity, peace, or humility, and help us to grow in these virtues day by day. Grant us Your strength and guidance as we seek to sow seeds of peace and righteousness in our relationships and communities. May Your wisdom continue to shape our hearts and minds, leading us into paths of righteousness and peace. Amen.

Meditative Thought: Reflect on the ways in which you have demonstrated or lacked the wisdom described in James 3:17-18 throughout the day. Ask God to reveal areas where you can grow and improve in embodying His wisdom. As you prepare for rest, commit yourself to seeking peace and righteousness in all your interactions and decisions, trusting in God's guidance and grace to lead you forward.

APRIL 29

MORNING DEVOTION

Scripture: Isaiah 61:10
"I will greatly rejoice in the Lord, My soul shall be joyful in my God; For He has clothed me with the garments of salvation, He has covered me with the robe of righteousness, As a bridegroom decks himself with ornaments, And as a bride adorns herself with her jewels."

Reflection: As you begin your day, meditate on the words of Isaiah 61:10 and rejoice in the Lord. This passage expresses the profound joy and gratitude of the prophet Isaiah for the salvation and righteousness that God has bestowed upon him. Reflect on the imagery of being clothed with the garments of salvation and covered with the robe of righteousness. Consider the immense privilege and blessing it is to be counted among the redeemed of the Lord. Allow this truth to fill you with gratitude and joy as you embark on the day ahead, knowing that you are clothed in the righteousness of Christ.

Prayer: Heavenly Father, we thank You for the salvation and righteousness that You have graciously provided for us through Your Son, Jesus Christ. As we start this day, may our hearts overflow with joy and gratitude for the incredible gift of salvation. Help us to live in the reality of our identity as Your redeemed children, clothed in the righteousness of Christ. May our lives reflect the beauty and splendor of Your grace as we walk in obedience and love. Amen.

Meditative Thought: Reflect on the significance of being clothed with the garments of salvation and covered with the robe of righteousness. Consider how this truth shapes your identity and perspective as a follower of Christ. As you go about your day, let the reality of your salvation fill you with joy and confidence, knowing that you belong to God and are dearly loved by Him.

Scripture: Isaiah 61:10
"I will greatly rejoice in the Lord, My soul shall be joyful in my God; For He has clothed me with the garments of salvation, He has covered me with the robe of righteousness, As a bridegroom decks himself with ornaments, And as a bride adorns herself with her jewels."

Reflection: As the day draws to a close, reflect on the words of Isaiah 61:10 and the profound joy that comes from being clothed in the garments of salvation and covered with the robe of righteousness. Take a moment to thank God for His faithfulness in providing for your spiritual needs and for the assurance of salvation that you have in Christ. Consider the imagery of a bridegroom and bride adorning themselves for a wedding. As you prepare for rest, let the truth of your identity as a beloved child of God bring you peace and comfort, knowing that you are secure in His love.

Prayer: Gracious Lord, we thank You for the privilege of being clothed in the garments of salvation and covered with the robe of righteousness. As we reflect on this truth tonight, may our hearts overflow with gratitude and joy for Your unfailing love and faithfulness. Help us to rest in the assurance of Your salvation, knowing that You have clothed us with Your righteousness. May Your peace guard our hearts and minds as we sleep, and may we wake up tomorrow with renewed strength and hope in You. Amen.

Meditative Thought: Reflect on the imagery of being clothed with the garments of salvation and covered with the robe of righteousness. Consider how this truth brings you comfort and assurance in your relationship with God. As you prepare for rest, allow the reality of your salvation to fill you with peace and gratitude, knowing that you are deeply loved and cherished by your Heavenly Father.

APRIL 30

MORNING DEVOTION

Scripture: Proverbs 23:12
"Apply your heart to instruction, And your ears to words of knowledge."

Reflection: As you begin your day, meditate on the wisdom of Proverbs 23:12. This verse encourages us to be attentive to instruction and eager to learn from the words of knowledge. Reflect on the importance of cultivating a teachable heart, one that is open to receiving guidance and wisdom from God and others. Consider how you can apply this principle in your life today. Are there areas where you need to humble yourself and be receptive to correction or guidance? Take time to seek God's wisdom through prayer and His Word, and commit yourself to being a lifelong learner in the school of wisdom.

Prayer: Heavenly Father, we thank You for the gift of wisdom that You offer us through Your Word and through the counsel of others. Help us to be attentive to instruction and eager to learn from the words of knowledge that You provide. Give us teachable hearts, Lord, that are open to Your guidance and correction. May we apply ourselves diligently to the pursuit of wisdom, knowing that it leads to a life of blessing and fulfillment. Amen.

Meditative Thought: Reflect on the state of your heart and your willingness to receive instruction and guidance from God and others. Ask yourself if there are areas in your life where you need to be more teachable and receptive to wisdom. As you go about your day, be intentional about seeking God's guidance and being attentive to the lessons He wants to teach you.

Scripture: Proverbs 23:12
"Apply your heart to instruction, And your ears to words of knowledge."

Reflection: As the day comes to a close, reflect on the wisdom of Proverbs 23:12. Consider how well you have applied your heart to instruction and your ears to words of knowledge throughout the day. Take a moment to evaluate your receptiveness to guidance and correction from God and others. Are there areas where you have been resistant or stubborn? Confess any pride or self-reliance to God, and ask Him to help you cultivate a more teachable spirit. Commit yourself anew to the pursuit of wisdom and the diligent application of God's truths in your life.

Prayer: Gracious Lord, as we reflect on the day that has passed, we confess that we often fall short of applying our hearts to instruction and our ears to words of knowledge. Forgive us for our pride and stubbornness, Lord, and help us to cultivate hearts that are open to Your guidance and correction. Give us a hunger for Your wisdom, and help us to apply it diligently in our lives. May we grow in knowledge and understanding, and may Your Word shape every aspect of our being. Amen.

Meditative Thought: Consider how well you have applied your heart to instruction and your ears to words of knowledge throughout the day. Reflect on any areas where you have been resistant or stubborn, and ask God to help you cultivate a more teachable spirit. As you prepare for rest, commit yourself anew to the pursuit of wisdom and the diligent application of God's truths in your life.

Scripture: Malachi 1:11
"For from the rising of the sun, even to its going down, My name shall be great among the Gentiles; in every place incense shall be offered to My name, and a pure offering; for My name shall be great among the nations," says the Lord of hosts."

Reflection: As you begin your day, consider the powerful declaration in Malachi 1:11. From sunrise to sunset, God's name is to be revered and exalted among all nations. This verse reminds us that God's greatness and glory are not confined to one people or place but are to be acknowledged universally. Reflect on how you can contribute to making God's name great in your own life and community today. Whether through your words, actions, or attitudes, aim to honor God and make His name known.

Prayer: Lord Almighty, we praise Your great name this morning. As the sun rises, we are reminded of Your majesty and the call to honor You in all that we do. Help us to live in a way that glorifies Your name and makes Your greatness known to those around us. Give us opportunities to share Your love and truth with others, and may our lives be a pure offering to You. Amen.

Meditative Thought: Ponder how you can make God's name great today. Think about specific actions you can take to reflect His glory and love to those you encounter. Let this thought guide your intentions and interactions throughout the day.

MAY 1

EVENING DEVOTION

Scripture: Malachi 1:11
"For from the rising of the sun, even to its going down, My name shall be great among the Gentiles; in every place incense shall be offered to My name, and a pure offering; for My name shall be great among the nations," says the Lord of hosts."

Reflection: As the day ends, reflect on how you have lived out the truth of Malachi 1:11. Have you contributed to making God's name great through your actions and words? Consider the moments where you succeeded and the times you fell short. Thank God for His presence throughout your day and ask for His help in areas where you need growth. Remember that our worship and reverence for God should extend from morning till night.

Prayer: Heavenly Father, as the sun sets, we reflect on Your greatness and our desire to honor You in all we do. We thank You for Your presence with us today and for the opportunities to make Your name known. Forgive us for the moments we fell short, and guide us to live more fully for You tomorrow. May our lives be a continuous offering of praise, bringing glory to Your name from sunrise to sunset. Amen.

Meditative Thought: Think about how you can continually offer your life as a pure and pleasing offering to God. Reflect on specific areas where you can improve in honoring His name and plan for how you can better glorify Him in the coming days. Let this reflection prepare your heart for restful sleep and a renewed commitment to God.

Scripture: John 14:23
"Jesus answered and said to him, 'If anyone loves Me, he will keep My word; and My Father will love him, and We will come to him and make Our home with him.'"

Reflection: As you start your day, reflect on the profound promise in John 14:23. Jesus assures us that loving Him and keeping His word results in an extraordinary relationship with God. It's not merely about obedience, but about welcoming God's presence into your life. This morning, think about what it means to keep Jesus' word. How can you live out His teachings in your daily activities? Consider the incredible blessing of God making His home with you, providing guidance, comfort, and strength throughout your day.

Prayer: Heavenly Father, as I begin this day, I commit to loving You and keeping Your word. Thank You for the promise of Your presence in my life. Help me to walk in obedience to Your teachings and to reflect Your love to those around me. Fill my heart with Your wisdom and guide my actions today. May Your presence be evident in all that I do. Amen.

Meditative Thought: Ponder the concept of God making His home with you. Let this thought influence your behavior and decisions today. Carry the awareness of His presence with you, knowing that He is with you, guiding and loving you through every moment.

Scripture: John 14:23
"Jesus answered and said to him, 'If anyone loves Me, he will keep My word; and My Father will love him, and We will come to him and make Our home with him.'"

Reflection: As the day draws to a close, take a moment to reflect on how you experienced God's presence. Did you keep Jesus' word in your actions and interactions? Jesus' promise that He and the Father will make their home with you is a reminder of the intimate relationship you can have with God. Reflect on the love and guidance He provided throughout your day. Acknowledge where you might have fallen short and be encouraged by His continual presence and love.

Prayer: Dear Lord, as I end this day, I thank You for Your constant presence with me. Forgive me for any moments when I failed to keep Your word. Thank You for Your love and the promise that You make Your home with those who love You. Help me to rest in Your presence tonight and to wake up tomorrow with a renewed commitment to follow Your teachings. Amen.

Meditative Thought: Before you sleep, meditate on the promise of God's presence in your life. Imagine God making His home with you, filling your space with His peace and love. Let this thought bring you comfort and prepare you for a restful night, secure in the knowledge that you are deeply loved and never alone.

MAY 3

MORNING DEVOTION

Scripture: Psalm 93:1-2
"The Lord reigns, He is clothed with majesty; The Lord is clothed, He has girded Himself with strength. Surely the world is established, so that it cannot be moved. Your throne is established from of old; You are from everlasting."

Reflection: As the new day begins, let us reflect on the majesty and eternal reign of the Lord. Psalm 93:1-2 reminds us of God's sovereign power and the unchanging nature of His rule. The Lord is described as being clothed with majesty and strength, establishing the world firmly. His throne has been established from ancient times, signifying His eternal presence and authority. As you go about your day, let this truth be a foundation for your thoughts and actions. Remember that no matter what challenges you face, God's reign is secure and everlasting.

Prayer: Heavenly Father, as I start this day, I acknowledge Your majesty and strength. Thank You for being my everlasting King and for establishing the world with Your power. Help me to trust in Your sovereignty and to find peace in Your unchanging nature. Guide my steps today and remind me of Your presence in every situation. In Jesus' name, Amen.

Meditative Thought: Meditate on the image of the Lord clothed in majesty and strength. Let this vision inspire confidence and peace as you navigate through the day, knowing that the same powerful God is with you.

Scripture: Psalm 93:1-2
"The Lord reigns, He is clothed with majesty; The Lord is clothed, He has girded Himself with strength. Surely the world is established, so that it cannot be moved. Your throne is established from of old; You are from everlasting."

Reflection: As the day ends, take a moment to reflect on God's enduring reign. Psalm 93:1-2 speaks of His majesty and strength, emphasizing that His throne is eternal. Think back on your day and recognize where you saw evidence of God's established order and strength in your life. Even when the world feels chaotic, God's throne remains unshaken, and His rule is everlasting. Let this assurance bring you comfort and peace as you prepare to rest.

Prayer: Lord, as I conclude this day, I thank You for Your steadfast reign and eternal presence. Your majesty and strength have guided me, and Your eternal throne has been my foundation. Help me to rest in the assurance of Your unchanging nature. Forgive me for any moments of doubt or fear, and fill me with Your peace tonight. In Jesus' name, Amen.

Meditative Thought: Before you sleep, meditate on the stability and security that comes from God's eternal reign. Let the knowledge that His throne is established and unmovable bring you peace and rest, knowing that you are held in His mighty hands.

Scripture: Proverbs 8:34-35
"Blessed is the man who listens to me, watching daily at my gates, Waiting at the posts of my doors. For whoever finds me finds life, and obtains favor from the Lord."

Reflection: As we begin this day, let us focus on the wisdom found in Proverbs 8:34-35. These verses remind us of the blessings that come from listening to God's wisdom. By watching daily at His gates and waiting at the posts of His doors, we position ourselves to receive His guidance and favor. To seek wisdom daily is to seek God's will in every aspect of our lives. When we find His wisdom, we find life and obtain His favor. Start your day by committing to seek God's wisdom in your decisions, conversations, and actions.

Prayer: Heavenly Father, thank You for the gift of a new day. Help me to listen to Your wisdom and to watch daily at Your gates. Guide me in my decisions and actions so that I may walk in Your favor. Grant me the patience to wait at the posts of Your doors, seeking Your guidance in all that I do. Fill me with Your life-giving wisdom today. In Jesus' name, Amen.

Meditative Thought: Take a moment to envision yourself at the gates of God's wisdom, eagerly waiting for His guidance. Let this image inspire a day of intentional listening and seeking His direction in every situation.

Scripture: Proverbs 8:34-35
"Blessed is the man who listens to me, watching daily at my gates, Waiting at the posts of my doors. For whoever finds me finds life, and obtains favor from the Lord."

Reflection: As the day draws to a close, reflect on how you have sought and applied God's wisdom throughout the day. Proverbs 8:34-35 encourages us to continually listen and wait for God's guidance. Consider the moments when you watched daily at His gates and how His wisdom influenced your choices. Acknowledge the life and favor you have received from the Lord as a result. Even in moments of uncertainty or difficulty, trusting in God's wisdom brings peace and assurance.

Prayer: Lord, I thank You for guiding me through this day with Your wisdom. Forgive me for any times I failed to listen or seek Your guidance. Help me to continue watching daily at Your gates and waiting at the posts of Your doors. As I rest tonight, fill me with Your peace and prepare my heart to seek Your wisdom again tomorrow. Thank You for the life and favor You bestow upon me. In Jesus' name, Amen.

Meditative Thought: Before you sleep, meditate on the blessings of listening to and waiting for God's wisdom. Reflect on how His guidance has shaped your day and brought you life and favor. Rest in the assurance that His wisdom will continue to guide you.

MAY 5

MORNING DEVOTION

Scripture: Psalm 51:1-2
"Have mercy upon me, O God, According to Your lovingkindness; According to the multitude of Your tender mercies, Blot out my transgressions. Wash me thoroughly from my iniquity, And cleanse me from my sin."

Reflection: As we start the day, let us reflect on the mercy and lovingkindness of God. Psalm 51:1-2 is a heartfelt plea for forgiveness and cleansing. We often carry the weight of our sins and transgressions, but this scripture reminds us that God is abundant in mercy. He is willing to blot out our transgressions and wash us clean. Begin your day by acknowledging any sins you need to confess and seek God's forgiveness. Embrace the new day with a clean heart and a renewed spirit, knowing that His mercy is greater than any of our shortcomings.

Prayer: Heavenly Father, I come before You this morning, seeking Your mercy and lovingkindness. Forgive me for my transgressions and wash me thoroughly from my iniquity. Cleanse me from my sins and renew my spirit. Help me to walk in Your ways today, reflecting Your love and mercy to others. Thank You for Your endless grace and forgiveness. In Jesus' name, Amen.

Meditative Thought: Take a moment to breathe deeply and meditate on God's mercy. Visualize His tender mercies washing over you, cleansing you from all sin, and renewing your heart. Let this sense of divine forgiveness set the tone for your day.

Scripture: Psalm 51:1-2
"Have mercy upon me, O God, According to Your lovingkindness; According to the multitude of Your tender mercies, Blot out my transgressions. Wash me thoroughly from my iniquity, And cleanse me from my sin."

Reflection: As the day comes to an end, reflect on the mercy and grace that have carried you through. Psalm 51:1-2 invites us to seek God's forgiveness and cleansing continually. Examine your day and recognize moments where you fell short or sinned. Offer these moments to God, asking for His mercy to blot out your transgressions. Let His lovingkindness wash over you, cleansing you from all iniquity. Embrace the peace that comes from being forgiven and rest in the assurance of His unending mercy.

Prayer: Lord, as I close this day, I ask for Your mercy upon me. Forgive my sins and wash me clean from my iniquities. Thank You for Your lovingkindness and the multitude of Your tender mercies. Help me to learn from today's shortcomings and grow closer to You. Grant me a peaceful night's rest, renewed by Your forgiveness and grace. In Jesus' name, Amen.

Meditative Thought: Before you sleep, meditate on the lovingkindness and mercy of God. Envision His tender mercies blotting out your transgressions and cleansing you thoroughly. Let this assurance of divine forgiveness bring you peace and rest.

MAY 6

MORNING DEVOTION

Scripture: Deuteronomy 29:29
"The secret things belong to the Lord our God, but those things which are revealed belong to us and to our children forever, that we may do all the words of this law."

Reflection: As we begin the day, let us reflect on the mystery and revelation of God. Deuteronomy 29:29 reminds us that while some things are known only to God, He has revealed enough to guide our lives. Today, focus on what God has revealed to you through His Word and through the Holy Spirit. Trust that He holds the mysteries of life in His hands and that His revelations are sufficient for our daily walk. Embrace the knowledge and wisdom He has given, and let it direct your actions and decisions today.

Prayer: Heavenly Father, I thank You for the wisdom and knowledge You have revealed to us through Your Word. As I start this day, help me to embrace Your guidance and live according to Your teachings. Grant me the humility to accept that some things are known only to You and the faith to trust in Your divine plan. May Your revealed truths light my path and direct my steps today. In Jesus' name, Amen.

Meditative Thought: Take a moment to meditate on the balance between the known and the unknown. Consider the peace that comes from trusting God with the mysteries of life while focusing on the clear guidance He has provided. Let this trust and clarity give you strength and direction for the day ahead.

Scripture: Deuteronomy 29:29
"The secret things belong to the Lord our God, but those things which are revealed belong to us and to our children forever, that we may do all the words of this law."

Reflection: As the day concludes, reflect on the day's experiences and the divine truths that have guided you. Deuteronomy 29:29 highlights the importance of living by the revelations God has given us while trusting Him with the unknown. Consider how God's Word has been a lamp to your feet today. Have there been moments when you trusted in His revealed will, or times when the mysteries of life seemed overwhelming? Rest in the assurance that God's revelations are sufficient for your journey and that He holds all secrets in His loving care.

Prayer: Lord, I come to You at the end of this day, grateful for the revelations You have provided through Your Word. Thank You for guiding me and for the peace that comes from trusting in Your divine plan. Help me to remember that while some things are known only to You, You have given us all we need to live according to Your will. Grant me restful sleep, and let Your truths continue to shape my heart and mind. In Jesus' name, Amen.

Meditative Thought: As you prepare for sleep, meditate on the balance of God's mysteries and revelations. Reflect on how His revealed truths have guided you today and trust Him with the unknown. Let this contemplation bring you peace and assurance as you rest.

Scripture: John 13:7-8
"Jesus answered and said to him, 'What I am doing you do not understand now, but you will know after this.' Peter said to Him, 'You shall never wash my feet!' Jesus answered him, 'If I do not wash you, you have no part with Me.'"

Reflection: As we begin this day, let us reflect on the humility and servant leadership of Jesus. In John 13:7-8, Jesus teaches a profound lesson about understanding and acceptance. Peter, not fully grasping the significance of Jesus washing his feet, initially resists. However, Jesus explains that although Peter may not understand now, the meaning will become clear later. This reminds us that we might not always understand God's actions in our lives immediately. Today, trust in His divine wisdom and purpose, knowing that in time, His plans will be revealed and understood.

Prayer: Dear Lord, as I start this day, I acknowledge that there are many things I do not yet understand about Your plans for me. Help me to trust in Your wisdom and accept Your guidance, even when it doesn't make sense to me. Give me a heart of humility and willingness to be led by You. Thank You for Your patience and love, and help me to walk in faith today. In Jesus' name, Amen.

Meditative Thought: Spend a few moments meditating on the idea of trust and acceptance. Think about areas in your life where you may not fully understand God's plan. Allow His peace to fill your heart, reassuring you that understanding will come in His perfect timing.

Scripture: John 13:7-8

"Jesus answered and said to him, 'What I am doing you do not understand now, but you will know after this.' Peter said to Him, 'You shall never wash my feet!' Jesus answered him, 'If I do not wash you, you have no part with Me.'"

Reflection: As we close the day, let's look back on how God has been at work in our lives. In John 13:7-8, Jesus reminds us that understanding often comes after the fact. Reflect on the day's events and consider moments where God's actions or guidance might not have been clear. Trust that in time, His purposes will be revealed. Jesus' act of washing the disciples' feet was a symbol of spiritual cleansing and humility. Let's end this day with a heart open to God's ongoing work in us, even if we don't fully comprehend it now.

Prayer: Heavenly Father, I thank You for being with me throughout this day. There are still things I do not understand, but I trust in Your wisdom and timing. Help me to embrace Your actions in my life with faith and humility. Cleanse my heart and mind from doubts and fears, and fill me with Your peace. As I rest tonight, may Your presence be with me, guiding and teaching me. In Jesus' name, Amen.

Meditative Thought: Before you sleep, meditate on the idea of divine timing and trust. Recall moments from today where you had to lean on faith rather than understanding. Let this meditation bring you peace, knowing that God's plans for you are good and His understanding surpasses all.

MAY 8

MORNING DEVOTION

Scripture: Revelation 19:5
"Then a voice came from the throne, saying, 'Praise our God, all you His servants and those who fear Him, both small and great!'"

Reflection: As we begin this day, let us focus on the call to worship and praise our God, as mentioned in Revelation 19:5. This verse reminds us that all of God's servants, regardless of their status, are called to praise Him. No matter where we find ourselves in life, our primary purpose is to glorify God. Today, let us consciously make an effort to start our day with praise and thanksgiving, acknowledging God's greatness and goodness in our lives.

Prayer: Heavenly Father, as I begin this day, I come before You with a heart full of praise. Thank You for Your goodness, Your mercy, and Your love that knows no bounds. Help me to remember that my ultimate purpose is to glorify You in everything I do. Guide my steps today, and may my actions and words reflect Your glory. In Jesus' name, Amen.

Meditative Thought: Spend a few moments reflecting on the greatness of God. Consider His many blessings and acts of mercy in your life. Allow your heart to overflow with gratitude and praise, setting a tone of worship for the day ahead.

Scripture: Revelation 19:5
"Then a voice came from the throne, saying, 'Praise our God, all you His servants and those who fear Him, both small and great!'"

Reflection: As we conclude this day, let's reflect on our responses to God's call to praise Him. Revelation 19:5 encourages all of His servants, regardless of their status, to offer praise. Think back on your day and consider the moments when you felt God's presence and goodness. Did you respond with praise? Tonight, let us reaffirm our commitment to worship God continually, recognizing His hand in both the small and great aspects of our lives.

Prayer: Dear Lord, as this day ends, I thank You for Your constant presence and guidance. Forgive me for the times I may have overlooked Your blessings or failed to give You praise. Help me to be more mindful of Your works in my life and to respond with gratitude and worship. Thank You for the gift of this day and for the assurance that You are always with me. In Jesus' name, Amen.

Meditative Thought: Before you rest, meditate on the many ways God has blessed you today. Let your heart be filled with praise and thanksgiving. Remember that praising God is not confined to moments of worship but is a continuous response to His love and grace.

MORNING DEVOTION

Scripture: Mark 1:35
"Now in the morning, having risen a long while before daylight, He went out and departed to a solitary place; and there He prayed."

Reflection: Jesus sets a powerful example for us by rising early in the morning to pray. Before the busyness of the day began, He sought solitude and communion with His Father. This act underscores the importance of starting our day with prayer and quiet time with God. It's a reminder that connecting with God first thing in the morning helps us align our hearts and minds with His will, providing us with the strength and clarity needed to face the day's challenges.

Prayer: Heavenly Father, I thank You for the gift of a new day. As I follow the example of Jesus, help me to prioritize time with You in the morning. Quiet my mind and open my heart to hear Your voice. Guide me in Your wisdom and strength throughout this day. May my thoughts, words, and actions reflect Your love and grace. In Jesus' name, Amen.

Meditative Thought: Spend a few moments in silence, focusing on the presence of God. Reflect on the peace and guidance that comes from starting your day in prayer. Let this peaceful moment set the tone for the rest of your day.

Scripture: Mark 1:35
"Now in the morning, having risen a long while before daylight, He went out and departed to a solitary place; and there He prayed."

Reflection: As we end the day, let us reflect on the example Jesus set for us. Even amidst His busy ministry, He prioritized time alone with God. Think back on your day and consider the moments when you sought God's presence. Were there times when you felt His guidance or missed opportunities to connect with Him? As we prepare for rest, let us commit to seeking God diligently, just as Jesus did, and remember the importance of consistent and intentional prayer.

Prayer: Dear Lord, as I conclude this day, I thank You for Your presence and guidance. Forgive me for the moments I did not seek You today. Help me to follow Jesus' example and make time for You, even in the midst of busyness. May Your peace fill my heart as I rest tonight. Renew my spirit and prepare me for a new day. In Jesus' name, Amen.

Meditative Thought: Reflect on the solitude Jesus sought in the early morning. Consider how you can incorporate similar moments of quiet and prayer into your routine. Allow the peace of God to wash over you, bringing calm and rest to your soul as you prepare for sleep.

Scripture: 1 John 5:4-5

"For whatever is born of God overcomes the world. And this is the victory that has overcome the world—our faith. Who is he who overcomes the world, but he who believes that Jesus is the Son of God?"

Reflection: As we begin this new day, let us remember the profound truth of our faith: through Jesus Christ, we are overcomers. The challenges and trials we face today are opportunities to demonstrate our victory in Him. Our faith is not just a belief but a powerful force that enables us to overcome the world's difficulties. Believing in Jesus as the Son of God equips us with the strength and courage needed to face any situation.

Prayer: Heavenly Father, I thank You for the gift of faith and the victory that comes through Jesus Christ. As I step into this new day, help me to remember that I am an overcomer through You. Strengthen my faith and guide my steps. May my actions and decisions reflect the victory I have in Jesus. Fill me with courage and confidence to face whatever comes my way today. In Jesus' name, Amen.

Meditative Thought: Take a few moments to visualize the challenges you might face today. Picture yourself overcoming them through the strength and victory you have in Jesus. Let this vision of triumph fill you with confidence and peace as you go about your day.

Scripture: 1 John 5:4-5
"For whatever is born of God overcomes the world. And this is the victory that has overcome the world—our faith. Who is he who overcomes the world, but he who believes that Jesus is the Son of God?"

Reflection: As the day comes to an end, reflect on how your faith helped you navigate through today's challenges. Did you face difficulties with the confidence that comes from being an overcomer in Christ? Remember, our faith is the victory that has already overcome the world. Let us find comfort in knowing that believing in Jesus as the Son of God gives us the strength to conquer any obstacle.

Prayer: Dear Lord, thank You for being with me throughout this day. I am grateful for the strength and victory I have in You. As I reflect on today, I ask for Your forgiveness for any moments of doubt. Help me to grow stronger in my faith and to always remember that I am an overcomer through You. Give me rest tonight and renew my spirit for tomorrow. In Jesus' name, Amen.

Meditative Thought: In the quiet of the evening, reflect on the victories, big and small, that you experienced today through your faith. Let gratitude fill your heart as you meditate on the overcoming power of belief in Jesus. Allow this reflection to bring you peace and assurance as you prepare to rest.

Scripture: Acts 2:37-39
"Now when they heard this, they were cut to the heart, and said to Peter and the rest of the apostles, 'Men and brethren, what shall we do?' Then Peter said to them, 'Repent, and let every one of you be baptized in the name of Jesus Christ for the remission of sins; and you shall receive the gift of the Holy Spirit. For the promise is to you and to your children, and to all who are afar off, as many as the Lord our God will call.'"

Reflection: As we begin this new day, let's reflect on the transformative power of the gospel message. Peter's words in Acts 2:37-39 remind us that the call to repentance and baptism is not just for the early believers but for us as well. This promise extends to us and our children, ensuring that through repentance and faith in Jesus Christ, we receive forgiveness and the gift of the Holy Spirit. This morning, let's embrace this promise and allow it to guide our actions and thoughts throughout the day.

Prayer: Heavenly Father, thank You for the gift of repentance, forgiveness, and the Holy Spirit. As I start this day, help me to live in the light of Your promise. Guide my steps and let my actions reflect the transformation You have brought into my life. Fill me with Your Spirit and empower me to be a witness of Your love and grace to those around me. In Jesus' name, Amen.

Meditative Thought: Spend a few moments in quiet reflection, considering the gift of the Holy Spirit in your life. Think about how this promise impacts your daily walk and relationships. Let this awareness fill you with gratitude and purpose as you move through your day.

Scripture: Acts 2:37-39
"Now when they heard this, they were cut to the heart, and said to Peter and the rest of the apostles, 'Men and brethren, what shall we do?' Then Peter said to them, 'Repent, and let every one of you be baptized in the name of Jesus Christ for the remission of sins; and you shall receive the gift of the Holy Spirit. For the promise is to you and to your children, and to all who are afar off, as many as the Lord our God will call.'"

Reflection: As the day draws to a close, let's take time to reflect on the message of repentance and the promise of the Holy Spirit. How have we responded to God's call today? Have we embraced His forgiveness and sought to live by the guidance of the Holy Spirit? This evening, let's re-affirm our commitment to God and His promises. Remember that His call to repentance and the gift of the Holy Spirit is a daily invitation to draw closer to Him.

Prayer: Dear Lord, thank You for Your faithfulness and the promise of Your Spirit. As I reflect on this day, I seek Your forgiveness for any short-comings and ask for Your strength to grow in faith. Thank You for the gift of the Holy Spirit, who guides and empowers me. Help me to rest in Your presence tonight and wake up refreshed and ready to serve You. In Jesus' name, Amen.

Meditative Thought: In the stillness of the evening, meditate on the presence of the Holy Spirit in your life. Reflect on how His guidance has been evident today and how you can be more open to His leading tomorrow. Let this time of reflection bring peace to your heart and mind as you prepare for rest.

MAY 12

MORNING DEVOTION

Scripture: Titus 3:9-11

"But avoid foolish disputes, genealogies, contentions, and strivings about the law; for they are unprofitable and useless. Reject a divisive man after the first and second admonition, knowing that such a person is warped and sinning, being self-condemned."

Reflection: As we start this day, let's consider Paul's counsel to Titus regarding the importance of avoiding pointless arguments and divisive people. Engaging in unproductive debates can drain our energy and distract us from what truly matters. Instead, let's focus our efforts on pursuits that honor God and build up others. Let's pray for discernment to recognize when to walk away from unfruitful discussions and when to engage with love and grace.

Prayer: Heavenly Father, help me to be wise in my interactions today. Grant me discernment to recognize conversations that are unprofitable and lead to division. Guide me in speaking words of grace and love, even in difficult situations. May my words and actions reflect Your truth and bring honor to Your name. In Jesus' name, Amen.

Meditative Thought: Reflect on the conversations you've had recently. Were there any that were unfruitful or divisive? Ask God to help you navigate future interactions with wisdom and grace.

Scripture: Titus 3:9-11
"But avoid foolish disputes, genealogies, contentions, and strivings about the law; for they are unprofitable and useless. Reject a divisive man after the first and second admonition, knowing that such a person is warped and sinning, being self-condemned."

Reflection: As we conclude this day, let's reflect on Paul's exhortation to Titus about dealing with divisive individuals. Sometimes, despite our best efforts, conflicts arise, and certain people prove unyielding in their contentious ways. In such cases, we're encouraged to lovingly distance ourselves after providing opportunities for correction. Let's pray for wisdom and strength to navigate relationships wisely, seeking unity where possible, and peace where necessary.

Prayer: Lord, as I reflect on this day, I bring before You any interactions that were challenging or divisive. Grant me a heart of wisdom to discern when to engage and when to step back. Help me to pursue peace and unity, even in the face of disagreement. Guide me in extending grace to those who may be contentious. In Your name, I pray, Amen.

Meditative Thought: Consider any relationships or situations where you've encountered divisiveness. Ask God to grant you wisdom and grace as you seek to navigate these dynamics with love and humility.

Scripture: James 3:17-18
"But the wisdom that is from above is first pure, then peaceable, gentle, willing to yield, full of mercy and good fruits, without partiality and without hypocrisy. Now the fruit of righteousness is sown in peace by those who make peace."

Reflection: As we embark on this new day, let's reflect on the qualities of heavenly wisdom described by James. True wisdom is not just about knowledge or intellect; it's about living in a way that reflects God's character. It leads to peace, gentleness, and humility, bearing the fruit of righteousness. Let's ask God to fill us with His wisdom so that we may be peacemakers, spreading His love and grace wherever we go.

Prayer: Heavenly Father, grant me Your wisdom today. Help me to embody the qualities described in Your Word: purity, peace, gentleness, and mercy. May Your wisdom guide my thoughts, words, and actions, leading me to sow seeds of peace and righteousness in all my interactions. Use me as an instrument of Your peace in the world. In Jesus' name, Amen.

Meditative Thought: Think about a situation where you can apply the wisdom described in James 3:17-18 today. How can you bring peace and gentleness into that situation? Take a moment to envision the positive impact your actions could have.

Scripture: James 3:17-18
"But the wisdom that is from above is first pure, then peaceable, gentle, willing to yield, full of mercy and good fruits, without partiality and without hypocrisy. Now the fruit of righteousness is sown in peace by those who make peace."

Reflection: As the day comes to a close, let's reflect on how we've lived out God's wisdom. Have we been agents of peace, showing gentleness and mercy to those around us? Reflecting on James' words, let's assess our interactions and attitudes, acknowledging where we fell short and seeking God's forgiveness and guidance for improvement.

Prayer: Lord, as I reflect on this day, I confess any moments where I failed to live out Your wisdom. Forgive me for times of impurity, conflict, or hypocrisy. Help me to sow seeds of peace and righteousness in all my relationships. Fill me anew with Your Spirit, that I may bear the fruit of Your wisdom in abundance. In Jesus' name, Amen.

Meditative Thought: Think about a specific interaction or situation from today where you struggled to exhibit God's wisdom. Ask God to show you how you can approach similar situations differently in the future, with His wisdom guiding your actions.

Scripture: James 3:17-18
"But the wisdom that is from above is first pure, then peaceable, gentle, willing to yield, full of mercy and good fruits, without partiality and without hypocrisy. Now the fruit of righteousness is sown in peace by those who make peace."

Reflection: As we embark on this new day, let's reflect on the qualities of heavenly wisdom described by James. True wisdom is not just about knowledge or intellect; it's about living in a way that reflects God's character. It leads to peace, gentleness, and humility, bearing the fruit of righteousness. Let's ask God to fill us with His wisdom so that we may be peacemakers, spreading His love and grace wherever we go.

Prayer: Heavenly Father, grant me Your wisdom today. Help me to embody the qualities described in Your Word: purity, peace, gentleness, and mercy. May Your wisdom guide my thoughts, words, and actions, leading me to sow seeds of peace and righteousness in all my interactions. Use me as an instrument of Your peace in the world. In Jesus' name, Amen.

Meditative Thought: Think about a situation where you can apply the wisdom described in James 3:17-18 today. How can you bring peace and gentleness into that situation? Take a moment to envision the positive impact your actions could have.

Scripture: James 3:17-18
"But the wisdom that is from above is first pure, then peaceable, gentle, willing to yield, full of mercy and good fruits, without partiality and without hypocrisy. Now the fruit of righteousness is sown in peace by those who make peace."

Reflection: As the day comes to a close, let's reflect on how we've lived out God's wisdom. Have we been agents of peace, showing gentleness and mercy to those around us? Reflecting on James' words, let's assess our interactions and attitudes, acknowledging where we fell short and seeking God's forgiveness and guidance for improvement.

Prayer: Lord, as I reflect on this day, I confess any moments where I failed to live out Your wisdom. Forgive me for times of impurity, conflict, or hypocrisy. Help me to sow seeds of peace and righteousness in all my relationships. Fill me anew with Your Spirit, that I may bear the fruit of Your wisdom in abundance. In Jesus' name, Amen.

Meditative Thought: Think about a specific interaction or situation from today where you struggled to exhibit God's wisdom. Ask God to show you how you can approach similar situations differently in the future, with His wisdom guiding your actions.

MAY 15

MORNING DEVOTION

Scripture: Proverbs 6:6-8
"Go to the ant, you sluggard! Consider her ways and be wise, which, having no captain, overseer, or ruler, provides her supplies in the summer, and gathers her food in the harvest."

Reflection: As we start our day, Proverbs 6:6-8 calls us to consider the diligence of the ant. Despite its small size, the ant is wise and hardworking, preparing for the future without needing external motivation. This scripture encourages us to be proactive, disciplined, and industrious in our tasks, taking personal responsibility for our lives and work. Today, let's strive to emulate the ant's diligence and foresight, recognizing that our efforts, no matter how small they seem, contribute to our future well-being and God's greater plan.

Prayer: Heavenly Father, thank You for the wisdom found in Your Word. Help me to learn from the ant's diligence and industriousness. Grant me the strength and discipline to be proactive in my responsibilities today. May my efforts be pleasing to You and fruitful in Your kingdom. Guide my actions and decisions, and help me to work with integrity and foresight. In Jesus' name, Amen.

Meditative Thought: Think about your tasks and responsibilities for today. How can you approach them with the diligence and foresight of the ant? Visualize yourself working steadily and purposefully, contributing to your future and God's plan.

Scripture: Proverbs 6:6-8
"Go to the ant, you sluggard! Consider her ways and be wise, which, having no captain, overseer, or ruler, provides her supplies in the summer, and gathers her food in the harvest."

Reflection: As we wind down and reflect on our day, let's revisit the wisdom of Proverbs 6:6-8. The ant's example challenges us to reflect on our productivity and efforts. Did we approach our tasks with diligence and wisdom, or did we rely on external motivation? The ant's self-motivation and foresight remind us that we are responsible for our work and preparation. Let's evaluate our actions today and seek ways to improve our diligence and foresight in the days to come.

Prayer: Lord, as I reflect on my day, I ask for Your guidance and forgiveness where I have fallen short. Help me to learn from the ant's diligence and apply that wisdom to my life. Strengthen my resolve to be proactive and disciplined in my responsibilities. May I work with a heart full of integrity and foresight, honoring You in all that I do. Thank You for Your grace and the lessons You teach me through Your Word. In Jesus' name, Amen.

Meditative Thought: Think about a specific area of your life where you can improve your diligence and preparation. How can you take personal responsibility and initiative in this area, following the ant's example? Commit to making small, consistent efforts to be more proactive and wise.

MAY 16

MORNING DEVOTION

Scripture: 1 Kings 18:38-39
"Then the fire of the Lord fell and consumed the burnt sacrifice, and the wood and the stones and the dust, and it licked up the water that was in the trench. Now when all the people saw it, they fell on their faces; and they said, 'The Lord, He is God! The Lord, He is God!'"

Reflection: As we begin our day, let's reflect on the powerful demonstration of God's might on Mount Carmel. Elijah's bold faith and the consuming fire from heaven remind us of God's sovereignty and power. In our daily lives, we may face challenges and situations that seem insurmountable, much like the prophets of Baal facing Elijah. But just as God answered with fire, He can demonstrate His power in our lives today. Trust in His ability to make Himself known, and step out in faith, knowing that He is capable of great and miraculous things.

Prayer: Heavenly Father, thank You for Your mighty power and Your faithfulness. As I begin this day, I ask for a heart full of faith like Elijah's. Help me to trust in Your power and sovereignty in every situation I face today. May my life be a testament to Your greatness and glory. Strengthen me to step out in boldness, knowing that You are with me. In Jesus' name, Amen.

Meditative Thought: Contemplate on a situation where you need God's intervention today. Imagine His consuming fire bringing clarity, resolution, and demonstrating His power. Hold onto the assurance that "The Lord, He is God!" in every circumstance you face.

Scripture: 1 Kings 18:38-39
"Then the fire of the Lord fell and consumed the burnt sacrifice, and the wood and the stones and the dust, and it licked up the water that was in the trench. Now when all the people saw it, they fell on their faces; and they said, 'The Lord, He is God! The Lord, He is God!'"

Reflection: As we conclude our day, let's reflect on how God revealed Himself to the people of Israel through the fire on Mount Carmel. Think back on your day and recognize the moments where God's presence was evident. Whether through answered prayers, small blessings, or moments of peace, God's hand is at work in our lives. Just as the Israelites proclaimed "The Lord, He is God!" we too should acknowledge His presence and power in our lives. Let this be a time to thank Him for His faithfulness and to reaffirm our trust in His sovereignty.

Prayer: Lord, thank You for being present in my life today. As I reflect on this day, I see Your hand at work in so many ways. Forgive me for the times I failed to recognize Your presence. I acknowledge that You are God, and I trust in Your power and sovereignty. Help me to carry this awareness into tomorrow, living in a way that honors You and proclaims Your greatness. In Jesus' name, Amen.

Meditative Thought: Think back on a moment today where you felt God's presence or saw His hand at work. Hold onto that moment and let it remind you that "The Lord, He is God!" in every aspect of your life. Carry this recognition into your evening, resting in His sovereignty.

Scripture: 1 Samuel 17:37
"Moreover, David said, 'The Lord, who delivered me from the paw of the lion and from the paw of the bear, He will deliver me from the hand of this Philistine.' And Saul said to David, 'Go, and the Lord be with you!'"

Reflection: As we start this new day, let's reflect on David's unwavering faith. Despite the overwhelming challenge before him, David remembered how God had delivered him from previous dangers. He drew strength and confidence from his past experiences with God's faithfulness. As we face today's challenges, let's remember the times God has delivered us and trust in His continued faithfulness. No matter how daunting the obstacles may seem, we can have confidence that the same God who helped us before will help us again.

Prayer: Heavenly Father, thank You for Your faithfulness and for the many times You have delivered me from difficult situations. As I face the challenges of today, help me to remember Your past faithfulness and to trust that You will deliver me again. Give me the courage and confidence that David had, and let me face today's battles with a heart full of faith in You. In Jesus' name, Amen.

Meditative Thought: Recall a specific instance where God has delivered you in the past. Meditate on that memory, allowing it to strengthen your faith and confidence as you face today's challenges. Trust that the same God who delivered you then will be with you now.

Scripture: 1 Samuel 17:37
"Moreover, David said, 'The Lord, who delivered me from the paw of the lion and from the paw of the bear, He will deliver me from the hand of this Philistine.' And Saul said to David, 'Go, and the Lord be with you!'"

Reflection: As the day comes to a close, let's reflect on the courage and faith of David. He faced Goliath with confidence because he remembered God's previous deliverances. Think back on your day—were there moments when you felt overwhelmed? How did God help you through them? By reflecting on these moments, we strengthen our faith and prepare our hearts to trust Him more deeply in the future. David's story is a powerful reminder that God is always with us, ready to deliver and support us.

Prayer: Lord, thank You for being with me throughout this day. As I reflect on the challenges I faced, I see Your hand guiding and delivering me. Forgive me for the times I doubted or feared. Help me to remember Your faithfulness and to trust in You more deeply each day. As I rest tonight, fill my heart with peace and assurance that You are always with me, ready to deliver and support me. In Jesus' name, Amen.

Meditative Thought: Reflect on a challenge you faced today and how God helped you through it. Let this reflection fill you with gratitude and strengthen your faith. Rest in the assurance that the God who delivered you today will be with you tomorrow, ready to deliver and support you again.

Scripture: Luke 2:14
"Glory to God in the highest, And on earth peace, goodwill toward men!"

Reflection: As the day begins, let us reflect on the angelic proclamation made on the night of Jesus' birth. "Glory to God in the highest" reminds us that our primary purpose is to glorify God in everything we do. The angels also spoke of peace and goodwill toward men. This peace is not just the absence of conflict, but a deep, abiding peace that comes from knowing Jesus Christ. As we start our day, let us seek to glorify God in our actions, thoughts, and words, and let His peace guide us in our interactions with others.

Prayer: Heavenly Father, I praise You for Your glory and for the peace that You offer through Jesus Christ. As I begin this day, help me to live in a way that glorifies You. Fill my heart with Your peace and let it overflow into my interactions with others. May Your goodwill be evident in my life, and may I be a reflection of Your love and grace to those around me. In Jesus' name, Amen.

Meditative Thought: As you go through your day, continuously bring to mind the words "Glory to God in the highest, and on earth peace, goodwill toward men." Let this proclamation shape your actions and interactions, guiding you to glorify God and promote peace and goodwill in all you do.

Scripture: Luke 2:14
"Glory to God in the highest, And on earth peace, goodwill toward men!"

Reflection: As the day comes to a close, let us revisit the angelic message and reflect on how we have lived out these words today. Have we glorified God in our thoughts, words, and actions? Have we been bearers of His peace and goodwill? The peace that the angels declared is a peace that surpasses understanding, given to us through Jesus. As we wind down, let's consider how we can further embody this peace and goodwill in our lives.

Prayer: Lord, thank You for the day You have given me and for the opportunities to glorify You and spread Your peace. Forgive me for the moments I fell short and did not live out Your will. Help me to rest in Your peace tonight, knowing that Your goodwill is toward me. Fill my heart with Your love and grace, and prepare me to start fresh tomorrow, ready to glorify You in all I do. In Jesus' name, Amen.

Meditative Thought: Before you sleep, meditate on the peace and goodwill that God offers through Jesus Christ. Reflect on how you experienced and shared His peace today, and how you can continue to do so tomorrow. Rest in the assurance of His love and grace, and let His peace fill your heart and mind.

MORNING DEVOTION

Scripture: Matthew 28:19-20
"Go therefore and make disciples of all the nations, baptizing them in the name of the Father and of the Son and of the Holy Spirit, teaching them to observe all things that I have commanded you; and lo, I am with you always, even to the end of the age."

Reflection: As we begin our day, we are reminded of the Great Commission given to us by Jesus. These verses call us to actively share the Gospel and make disciples of all nations. It's a call to action that transcends our comfort zones and challenges us to spread the love and teachings of Jesus. The promise that Jesus is with us always, even to the end of the age, gives us the confidence and strength we need to fulfill this mission. Let's start our day with the mindset of being ambassadors for Christ, ready to share His love and truth with those we encounter.

Prayer: Heavenly Father, thank You for the privilege of being Your disciple. As I begin this day, help me to carry out the Great Commission with boldness and love. Fill me with Your Spirit, so I may speak and act in ways that bring others closer to You. Remind me constantly of Your presence with me, giving me courage and strength. Use me today to make a difference in someone's life for Your kingdom. In Jesus' name, Amen.

Meditative Thought: Throughout the day, keep the Great Commission in your heart and mind. Consider every interaction as an opportunity to share God's love and message. Remember that you are never alone in this mission; Jesus is with you always.

Scripture: Matthew 28:19-20
"Go therefore and make disciples of all the nations, baptizing them in the name of the Father and of the Son and of the Holy Spirit, teaching them to observe all things that I have commanded you; and lo, I am with you always, even to the end of the age."

Reflection: As the day comes to an end, reflect on how you lived out the Great Commission today. Did you seize opportunities to share Christ's love and teachings? These verses remind us of our ongoing mission and the assurance of Jesus' constant presence. Whether today was filled with successes or challenges, take comfort in knowing that Jesus is with you always, guiding and supporting you in your efforts to make disciples.

Prayer: Lord Jesus, thank You for being with me today and for giving me the strength to fulfill Your Great Commission. I am grateful for the opportunities to share Your love and teachings, and I ask for forgiveness for any missed opportunities or moments of hesitation. As I rest tonight, renew my spirit and prepare me for another day of service to Your kingdom. Help me to continually grow as Your disciple and to lead others to You with grace and love. In Your precious name, Amen.

Meditative Thought: Before you sleep, meditate on the promise of Jesus' constant presence. Reflect on how His guidance and support were evident throughout your day, and rest in the assurance that He will continue to be with you in all your endeavors for His kingdom.

Scripture: Jude 1:3-4
"Beloved, while I was very diligent to write to you concerning our common salvation, I found it necessary to write to you exhorting you to contend earnestly for the faith which was once for all delivered to the saints. For certain men have crept in unnoticed, who long ago were marked out for this condemnation, ungodly men, who turn the grace of our God into lewdness and deny the only Lord God and our Lord Jesus Christ."

Reflection: As we begin this day, Jude's exhortation to "contend earnestly for the faith" calls us to be vigilant and proactive in defending the truth of the Gospel. In a world where ungodly influences and false teachings can easily infiltrate, it is crucial to hold fast to the faith that has been handed down to us. This morning, reflect on the importance of safeguarding your faith against compromise and distortion. Remember that our salvation is a precious gift, and we are called to protect and uphold the truth with diligence and love.

Prayer: Heavenly Father, thank You for the gift of salvation and the faith delivered to us through Your Word. As I start this day, help me to be vigilant and steadfast in my faith. Give me the wisdom to discern truth from falsehood and the courage to stand firm against anything that seeks to distort or undermine Your Gospel. Fill me with Your Spirit, so I may contend earnestly for the faith with grace and love. In Jesus' name, Amen.

Meditative Thought: As you go through your day, keep in mind the call to protect and defend your faith. Be mindful of the influences around you and stay rooted in the truth of God's Word. Let your actions and words reflect a commitment to upholding the Gospel with integrity and love.

Scripture: Jude 1:3-4
"Beloved, while I was very diligent to write to you concerning our common salvation, I found it necessary to write to you exhorting you to contend earnestly for the faith which was once for all delivered to the saints. For certain men have crept in unnoticed, who long ago were marked out for this condemnation, ungodly men, who turn the grace of our God into lewdness and deny the only Lord God and our Lord Jesus Christ."

Reflection: As the day winds down, take time to reflect on how you have contended for the faith today. Did you stand firm in the truth and reject ungodly influences? Jude's words remind us that there are always challenges to our faith, but through God's strength, we can overcome them. Consider the ways in which you encountered and responded to these challenges. How did you protect the integrity of your faith and the truth of the Gospel?

Prayer: Lord Jesus, thank You for guiding me through this day and for giving me the strength to stand firm in my faith. Forgive me for any moments where I may have faltered or failed to defend Your truth. As I rest tonight, renew my commitment to contend earnestly for the faith. Help me to be ever vigilant and discerning, and to reflect Your grace and truth in all that I do. Strengthen my resolve to uphold Your Gospel in the face of any opposition. In Your holy name, Amen.

Meditative Thought: Before you sleep, meditate on the importance of guarding your faith. Reflect on the moments when you stood firm and the areas where you can improve. Trust in God's guidance and strength as you continue to contend for the faith, knowing that He is with you always.

MAY 21

MORNING DEVOTION

Scripture: Daniel 7:27
"Then the kingdom and dominion, and the greatness of the kingdoms under the whole heaven, shall be given to the people, the saints of the Most High. His kingdom is an everlasting kingdom, and all dominions shall serve and obey Him."

Reflection: As we begin this new day, let us ponder the incredible promise found in Daniel 7:27. This verse speaks of a future where God's kingdom is established, and His saints—His people—are given dominion. This is a powerful reminder that no matter the challenges or difficulties we face today, there is a greater plan and a glorious future ahead. God's kingdom is everlasting, and His authority is supreme. As His saints, we are called to live in the light of this truth, knowing that our efforts and faithfulness are part of His eternal plan.

Prayer: Heavenly Father, thank You for the promise of Your everlasting kingdom. As I begin this day, help me to live with the assurance that You are in control and that Your kingdom will ultimately prevail. Strengthen my faith and give me the courage to face today's challenges, knowing that I am part of Your eternal plan. Guide my actions and words to reflect Your glory and honor Your name. In Jesus' name, Amen.

Meditative Thought: Throughout the day, remind yourself of the eternal kingdom of God. Let this truth bring you peace and purpose, knowing that you are part of something far greater than any temporary challenge. Seek to reflect God's kingdom values in all that you do.

Scripture: Daniel 7:27
"Then the kingdom and dominion, and the greatness of the kingdoms under the whole heaven, shall be given to the people, the saints of the Most High. His kingdom is an everlasting kingdom, and all dominions shall serve and obey Him."

Reflection: As the day comes to an end, take time to reflect on the hope and assurance we have in God's everlasting kingdom. Consider the ways you experienced His presence and guidance today. How did the promise of His eternal dominion influence your actions and decisions? Remember, despite any challenges or setbacks, God's plan is moving forward, and His kingdom will prevail. This eternal perspective can provide comfort and strength as we rest and prepare for a new day.

Prayer: Lord God, thank You for being with me throughout this day. As I reflect on Your everlasting kingdom, I am reminded of Your faithfulness and power. Forgive me for any moments where I may have lost sight of Your eternal plan. Help me to rest in the assurance that Your kingdom is everlasting, and Your dominion is supreme. Renew my spirit and prepare me for the challenges and opportunities of tomorrow. May I continue to serve and obey You in all things. In Jesus' name, Amen.

Meditative Thought: Before you sleep, meditate on the greatness and eternal nature of God's kingdom. Let this truth fill you with peace and hope, knowing that you are part of God's divine plan. Rest in His promise and wake up ready to serve Him with renewed strength and purpose.

Scripture: Isaiah 53:4-5

"Surely He has borne our griefs and carried our sorrows; Yet we esteemed Him stricken, smitten by God, and afflicted. But He was wounded for our transgressions, He was bruised for our iniquities; The chastisement for our peace was upon Him, and by His stripes we are healed."

Reflection: As we start this day, let's reflect on the profound sacrifice of Jesus Christ. These verses from Isaiah remind us that He took on our griefs and sorrows, bore our transgressions, and suffered for our iniquities. His wounds bring us healing and peace. This morning, let's remember the depth of Christ's love for us and His willingness to endure suffering on our behalf. This understanding should inspire us to live lives of gratitude and dedication to Him.

Prayer: Heavenly Father, thank You for sending Your Son, Jesus, to bear my griefs and sorrows. I am humbled by the immense love demonstrated through His suffering and sacrifice. Help me to start this day with a heart full of gratitude and a desire to live in a way that honors His sacrifice. Guide my actions and words to reflect Your love and grace. Strengthen me to walk in the peace and healing that Christ has provided. In Jesus' name, Amen.

Meditative Thought: Throughout today, keep in mind the healing and peace that come from Jesus' sacrifice. Let this awareness guide your interactions and decisions, knowing that you are deeply loved and eternally healed by His stripes.

Scripture: Isaiah 53:4-5
"Surely He has borne our griefs and carried our sorrows; Yet we esteemed Him stricken, smitten by God, and afflicted. But He was wounded for our transgressions, He was bruised for our iniquities; The chastisement for our peace was upon Him, and by His stripes we are healed."

Reflection: As the day draws to a close, take a moment to reflect on the sacrifices of Jesus Christ. Consider how His suffering and wounds have brought healing and peace into your life. Reflect on how this truth has impacted your day and how you responded to challenges and opportunities. Recognize the ways you have experienced His grace and mercy.

Prayer: Lord Jesus, thank You for carrying my sorrows and bearing my griefs. Thank You for the wounds You endured for my transgressions and iniquities. As I reflect on today, I am grateful for Your healing and peace that sustain me. Forgive me for the moments I may have forgotten Your sacrifice. Help me to rest tonight with a heart full of gratitude and a mind focused on Your love. May Your peace guard my heart and mind as I sleep. In Your precious name, Amen.

Meditative Thought: Before you sleep, meditate on the healing and peace that come from Jesus' sacrifice. Let this truth fill you with gratitude and rest, knowing that you are deeply loved and cared for by the Savior. Rest in the assurance of His love and wake up ready to live in His grace and truth.

MAY 23

MORNING DEVOTION

Scripture: Psalm 145:9
"The Lord is good to all, and His tender mercies are over all His works."

Reflection: As we begin this new day, let's reflect on the boundless goodness and mercy of God. Psalm 145:9 reminds us that God's goodness extends to everyone and His tender mercies cover all His creation. This is a powerful reminder that no matter what we face today, we are surrounded by God's loving-kindness. His goodness is not limited by our circumstances, and His mercy is always available to us.

Prayer: Dear Heavenly Father, I thank You for Your unending goodness and tender mercies that are new every morning. As I start this day, help me to recognize Your goodness in all things and to see Your mercies in every moment. Let Your love guide my actions and thoughts today. Help me to be a reflection of Your goodness to those around me. In Jesus' name, Amen.

Meditative Thought: Throughout today, focus on the goodness and mercy of God. Let this awareness fill your heart with gratitude and inspire you to extend kindness and mercy to others.

Scripture: Psalm 145:9
"The Lord is good to all, and His tender mercies are over all His works."

Reflection: As we end the day, take a moment to reflect on God's goodness and mercy that have been present throughout your day. Despite any challenges or difficulties, God's tender mercies have been with you. Reflect on the ways you have experienced His goodness and how it has shaped your day. Recognize the moments of grace, provision, and kindness that have come from His hand.

Prayer: Gracious God, thank You for Your goodness and mercy that have been with me throughout this day. As I reflect on the events of today, I am grateful for Your presence and the ways You have shown Your love and care. Forgive me for any moments when I may have overlooked Your goodness. Help me to rest tonight with a heart full of gratitude and peace. Let Your mercies continue to renew me as I sleep, and may I wake up ready to experience Your goodness again tomorrow. In Jesus' name, Amen.

Meditative Thought: Before you sleep, meditate on the goodness and tender mercies of the Lord. Let this truth bring you peace and rest, knowing that God's love surrounds you and His mercies are new every morning.

MAY 24

MORNING DEVOTION

Scripture: John 4:13-14
"Jesus answered and said to her, 'Whoever drinks of this water will thirst again, but whoever drinks of the water that I shall give him will never thirst. But the water that I shall give him will become in him a fountain of water springing up into everlasting life.'"

Reflection: As we begin this day, let's reflect on the living water that Jesus offers. Unlike physical water that quenches our thirst temporarily, the living water He gives satisfies our deepest spiritual needs permanently. This living water becomes a wellspring within us, leading to everlasting life. As we go about our day, let's remember to draw from this spiritual source, allowing it to nourish and refresh our souls continually.

Prayer: Heavenly Father, thank You for the living water that You offer through Jesus Christ. As I start this day, I ask that You fill me with Your Spirit and help me to draw from this well of eternal life. Let Your presence be a constant source of refreshment and strength for me. Help me to carry Your living water to others, so they too may experience Your love and grace. In Jesus' name, Amen.

Meditative Thought: Throughout the day, remind yourself that you have access to the living water Jesus provides. Let this awareness sustain you, knowing that His life-giving presence is with you always.

Scripture: John 4:13-14
"Jesus answered and said to her, 'Whoever drinks of this water will thirst again, but whoever drinks of the water that I shall give him will never thirst. But the water that I shall give him will become in him a fountain of water springing up into everlasting life.'"

Reflection: As the day comes to a close, take a moment to reflect on how the living water of Christ has sustained you. Consider the moments when you felt His refreshing presence and how His Spirit has guided you. Despite any challenges or fatigue, His living water remains a source of continual renewal. Reflect on the promise that this living water will lead to everlasting life, giving you hope and strength for tomorrow.

Prayer: Gracious Lord, thank You for the living water that has sustained me throughout this day. As I prepare to rest, I am grateful for Your constant presence and the refreshment You provide to my soul. Help me to rest in the assurance of Your promise of everlasting life. Renew my spirit tonight, and let Your living water continue to flow within me, bringing peace and rest. In Jesus' name, Amen.

Meditative Thought: As you prepare for sleep, meditate on the promise of the living water that Jesus offers. Let this truth bring you peace and comfort, knowing that His presence is an eternal source of life and renewal.

MORNING DEVOTION

Scripture: John 4:26
"Jesus said to her, "I who speak to you am He.""

Reflection: As we begin this day, let's reflect on the encounter between Jesus and the Samaritan woman at the well. In verse 26, Jesus reveals Himself as the Messiah to her. This revelation is not just for her but for all of us. Jesus is the fulfillment of God's promises, the Savior of the world. As we embark on this day, let's remember that Jesus is not just a historical figure or a wise teacher; He is the Son of God, the one who offers us eternal life and salvation.

Prayer: Lord Jesus, thank You for revealing Yourself to us as the Messiah, the Savior of the world. As I start this day, help me to recognize Your presence and Your guidance in every aspect of my life. Open my heart to receive Your truth and Your love. May I live today in the light of Your revelation, sharing Your message of hope and salvation with others. In Your holy name, Amen.

Meditative Thought: Reflect on the significance of Jesus revealing Himself as the Messiah. Let His identity as the Savior of the world shape your perspective and guide your actions throughout the day.

Scripture: John 4:26
"Jesus said to her, "I who speak to you am He."

Reflection: As the day comes to a close, let's reflect on the profound truth of Jesus' revelation to the Samaritan woman. He declared Himself to be the Messiah, the one whom they had been waiting for. This revelation transformed her life and the lives of many others who encountered Jesus. As we end this day, let's reaffirm our faith in Jesus as the Son of God, the Savior of the world. Let's thank Him for His presence in our lives and for the hope and salvation He offers to all who believe in Him.

Prayer: Gracious Savior, as I reflect on the events of this day, I am reminded of Your revelation to the Samaritan woman. Thank You for declaring Yourself to be the Messiah, the one who brings salvation and eternal life. Help me to trust in You more deeply and to share Your message of hope with others. As I rest tonight, may Your presence bring me peace and assurance. In Your precious name, Amen.

Meditative Thought: Consider how Jesus' revelation as the Messiah impacts your life. Allow this truth to fill you with gratitude and confidence in His saving grace as you prepare for rest.

MAY 26

MORNING DEVOTION

Scripture: 1 Corinthians 2:9

"But as it is written: 'Eye has not seen, nor ear heard, nor have entered into the heart of man the things which God has prepared for those who love Him.'"

Reflection: As we begin this day, let's reflect on the profound promise contained in this verse. It reminds us that the blessings God has in store for us are beyond our imagination. Our human senses cannot fully grasp the extent of His goodness and the wonders He has prepared for those who love Him. This encourages us to trust in His plans for our lives, even when we can't see the outcome. As we go about our day, let's remember that God's blessings are abundant and await us as we walk in love and obedience to Him.

Prayer: Heavenly Father, thank You for the promise of the blessings You have prepared for those who love You. Help me to trust in Your plans, knowing that they are far greater than anything I can imagine. Guide me today to walk in Your love and obedience, so I may experience the fullness of Your blessings in my life. Open my heart to receive Your goodness and to share it with others. In Jesus' name, Amen.

Meditative Thought: Consider the vastness of God's blessings that await those who love Him. Allow this truth to inspire you to trust in His plans and to walk in obedience and love throughout the day.

Scripture: 1 Corinthians 2:9
"But as it is written: 'Eye has not seen, nor ear heard, nor have entered into the heart of man the things which God has prepared for those who love Him.'"

Reflection: As the day comes to a close, let's reflect on the promise of God's abundant blessings for those who love Him. Even as we reflect on the events of today, we can't fully comprehend the extent of what God has in store for us. This should fill us with anticipation and gratitude as we rest tonight. Let's thank God for His faithfulness and for the assurance that His plans for us are filled with goodness beyond our understanding. May this truth bring us peace and comfort as we prepare for rest.

Prayer: Gracious Lord, as I reflect on Your promise of abundant blessings, I am in awe of Your goodness. Thank You for Your faithfulness and for the assurance that You have wonderful plans for my life. Help me to rest tonight in the confidence of Your promises and to wake up tomorrow with renewed faith and anticipation. May Your love and blessings overflow in my life as I continue to walk in obedience to You. In Jesus' name, Amen.

Meditative Thought: As you prepare for sleep, meditate on the promise of God's abundant blessings for those who love Him. Allow this truth to fill you with gratitude and anticipation for what He has in store for you.

Scripture: Galatians 5:1
"Stand fast therefore in the liberty by which Christ has made us free, and do not be entangled again with a yoke of bondage."

Reflection: As we begin this day, let's reflect on the freedom we have in Christ. Paul urges the Galatians, and us, to stand firm in the liberty that comes from being set free by Christ. This freedom isn't just from the bondage of sin but also from the burdensome yoke of legalism and religious rituals. As we go about our day, let's remember that our identity and worth are found in Christ alone, not in any set of rules or regulations. Let's live in the freedom He has provided, rejoicing in His grace and walking confidently in His truth.

Prayer: Lord Jesus, thank You for the freedom I have in You. Help me to stand firm in this liberty and to resist the temptation to return to bondage. May I live today in the fullness of Your grace, free from the burden of legalism and self-reliance. Guide me by Your Spirit to walk in obedience to Your word, trusting in Your unfailing love and grace. In Your name, Amen.

Meditative Thought: Consider the areas in your life where you may still feel entangled by legalism or worldly expectations. Ask God to help you fully embrace the freedom He offers and to walk confidently in His truth throughout the day.

Scripture: Galatians 5:1
"Stand fast therefore in the liberty by which Christ has made us free, and do not be entangled again with a yoke of bondage."

Reflection: As the day comes to a close, let's reflect on our response to the freedom we have in Christ. Paul's exhortation to the Galatians is just as relevant to us today. Have we remained steadfast in our liberty, or have we allowed ourselves to become entangled again in the yoke of bondage? Take a moment to examine your heart and ask God to reveal any areas where you may have drifted away from His truth. Surrender those areas to Him and recommit yourself to living in the freedom He has provided.

Prayer: Heavenly Father, as I reflect on this day, I confess any areas where I have allowed myself to become entangled in bondage. Thank You for Your unfailing love and grace that sets me free. Help me to stand firm in this liberty and to live in obedience to Your word. May I continually rely on Your strength and guidance as I walk in Your truth. In Jesus' name, Amen.

Meditative Thought: Think about the freedom you have in Christ and how you can more fully embrace it in every aspect of your life. Ask God to empower you to live as a free child of God, liberated from the chains of sin and legalism.

MORNING DEVOTION

Scripture: Ephesians 3:20-21

"Now to Him who is able to do exceedingly abundantly above all that we ask or think, according to the power that works in us, to Him be glory in the church by Christ Jesus to all generations, forever and ever. Amen."

Reflection: As we begin this day, let's meditate on the limitless power of God at work within us. Paul's words remind us that God is not only able but also willing to do far more than we could ever imagine or request. This power is not external but resides within us through the Holy Spirit. Let's approach this day with confidence, knowing that the same power that raised Christ from the dead is working in us. Let's trust God to accomplish His purposes in and through us, bringing glory to His name.

Prayer: Heavenly Father, I thank You for Your unlimited power at work within me. Help me to fully grasp the depth of Your love and the extent of Your ability to accomplish great things through me. As I face the challenges of this day, may I rely on Your strength and trust in Your promises. Let Your power be evident in my life, bringing glory to Your name. In Jesus' name, Amen.

Meditative Thought: Consider the vastness of God's power and His willingness to work in and through you. Reflect on how you can surrender more fully to His plans and trust Him to exceed your expectations in every aspect of your life.

Scripture: Ephesians 3:20-21
"Now to Him who is able to do exceedingly abundantly above all that we ask or think, according to the power that works in us, to Him be glory in the church by Christ Jesus to all generations, forever and ever. Amen."

Reflection: As the day draws to a close, let's reflect on the power and glory of God that we have experienced throughout the day. Despite any challenges or setbacks, His power has been at work within us, enabling us to overcome and accomplish more than we could have imagined. Let's take a moment to praise God for His faithfulness and to acknowledge His sovereignty over every aspect of our lives. May His name be glorified in the church and in our lives for all generations to come.

Prayer: Gracious Father, as I reflect on this day, I am in awe of Your mighty power and Your unwavering faithfulness. Thank You for the ways You have worked in and through me, exceeding my expectations and accomplishing Your purposes. May Your name be glorified in my life and in Your church, both now and forevermore. Help me to rest in Your promises and to trust in Your provision as I prepare for rest tonight. In Jesus' name, Amen.

Meditative Thought: Think about the ways God has demonstrated His power and faithfulness in your life today. Consider how you can continue to surrender to His will and trust Him to work exceedingly abundantly in the days to come.

Scripture: Ephesians 5:15-16

"See then that you walk circumspectly, not as fools but as wise, redeeming the time, because the days are evil."

Reflection: As we begin this day, let's reflect on the importance of walking wisely in a world filled with distractions and temptations. Paul urges us to be intentional about how we live, making the most of every opportunity. This requires us to be vigilant and discerning, carefully considering our actions and choices. Let's ask God for wisdom and guidance as we navigate the challenges of today, trusting Him to help us redeem the time and live in a manner that honors Him.

Prayer: Heavenly Father, grant me the wisdom to walk circumspectly in a world that often leads astray. Help me to discern Your will and make choices that honor You. May I be intentional about how I use my time, seeking opportunities to glorify You and serve others. Guide my steps today, Lord, and help me to remain steadfast in Your truth. In Jesus' name, Amen.

Meditative Thought: Consider how you can walk wisely and redeem the time today. Reflect on areas of your life where you may need to be more intentional or discerning. Ask God to help you make the most of every opportunity He presents.

Scripture: Ephesians 5:15-16
"See then that you walk circumspectly, not as fools but as wise, redeeming the time, because the days are evil."

Reflection: As the day comes to a close, let's reflect on how we have used our time wisely and with purpose. Paul's words remind us of the importance of being intentional in our actions and choices, especially in a world filled with evil and distractions. Take a moment to evaluate your day and consider if there were moments where you could have been more discerning or proactive. Ask God for forgiveness for any shortcomings and invite His guidance for the days ahead.

Prayer: Lord, as I reflect on this day, I acknowledge that I am often prone to distractions and foolish choices. Forgive me for the times when I have not walked circumspectly or redeemed the time as You have called me to do. Grant me the wisdom and discernment to make better choices tomorrow. Help me to remain steadfast in Your truth and to use my time in ways that honor You. In Jesus' name, Amen.

Meditative Thought: Think about how you can improve your use of time and be more intentional in your actions and choices. Ask God to help you walk circumspectly and redeem the time for His glory.

Scripture: Philippians 3:7
"But what things were gain to me, these I have counted loss for Christ."

Reflection: As we begin this day, let's reflect on the profound truth expressed by the apostle Paul. He recognized that all the achievements and accolades he once prized were nothing compared to knowing Christ. Paul willingly let go of his past accomplishments and treasures, considering them as loss for the sake of Christ. Let's examine our own lives and ask ourselves what we are holding onto that might be hindering our relationship with Jesus. May we, like Paul, be willing to surrender everything for the surpassing worth of knowing Christ.

Prayer: Lord Jesus, help me to recognize and let go of anything that comes between me and a deeper relationship with You. Give me the courage to count all earthly gains as loss compared to the surpassing greatness of knowing You. May my heart's desire be to know You more intimately and to live fully surrendered to Your will. In Your precious name, Amen.

Meditative Thought: Consider what things in your life you might need to let go of in order to pursue a deeper relationship with Christ. Reflect on the value of knowing Him above all else and ask God to help you prioritize Him in every aspect of your life.

Scripture: Philippians 3:7
"But what things were gain to me, these I have counted loss for Christ."

Reflection: As the day draws to a close, let's reflect on our willingness to let go of earthly gains for the sake of Christ. Paul's example challenges us to examine our own priorities and attachments. Are there things we are holding onto that are hindering our relationship with Jesus? Take a moment to surrender these things to Him and reaffirm your commitment to prioritize Him above all else. May we find true joy and fulfillment in knowing and serving Christ with our whole hearts.

Prayer: Heavenly Father, thank You for the reminder that knowing Christ is of surpassing worth. Help me to continually evaluate my priorities and let go of anything that hinders my relationship with You. Grant me the grace to count all earthly gains as loss compared to the privilege of knowing Your Son. May my life be a reflection of Your love and grace to the world. In Jesus' name, Amen.

Meditative Thought: Reflect on any attachments or priorities that may be hindering your relationship with Christ. Surrender them to Him and reaffirm your commitment to prioritize knowing and serving Him above all else.

Scripture: 1 Thessalonians 5:16-18
"Rejoice always, pray without ceasing, in everything give thanks; for this is the will of God in Christ Jesus for you."

Reflection: As we begin this day, let's meditate on these powerful words from the apostle Paul. He encourages us to cultivate a lifestyle of joy, prayer, and gratitude. Regardless of our circumstances, we are called to rejoice always, knowing that our joy comes from the Lord and is not dependent on our external situations. Let's commit to a life of unceasing prayer, staying connected to God throughout our day, seeking His guidance, and pouring out our hearts to Him. And in all things, let's give thanks to God, recognizing His goodness and faithfulness in every aspect of our lives.

Prayer: Heavenly Father, thank You for the privilege of approaching You in prayer at any moment, in any circumstance. Help me to cultivate a spirit of joy, prayer, and gratitude in my daily life. Teach me to rejoice always, to pray without ceasing, and to give thanks in all things, knowing that this is Your will for me. May my life be a constant expression of worship and dependence on You. In Jesus' name, Amen.

Meditative Thought: Consider how you can cultivate a lifestyle of joy, prayer, and gratitude today. Reflect on specific areas of your life where you can rejoice, pray, and give thanks more intentionally, and ask God to help you live in alignment with His will.

Scripture: 1 Thessalonians 5:16-18
"Rejoice always, pray without ceasing, in everything give thanks; for this is the will of God in Christ Jesus for you."

Reflection: As the day comes to a close, let's reflect on the exhortation of Paul to rejoice, pray, and give thanks continually. Consider the moments today where you experienced joy, where you turned to God in prayer, and where you expressed gratitude to Him. Take a moment to thank God for His presence with you throughout this day, for His faithfulness, and for the blessings He has bestowed upon you. Let's commit to carrying this spirit of joy, prayer, and gratitude into tomorrow, trusting that it is God's will for our lives.

Prayer: Gracious Father, as I reflect on this day, I am grateful for Your constant presence and provision. Thank You for the moments of joy, the opportunities for prayer, and the reasons to give thanks. Help me to carry this spirit of rejoicing, prayer, and gratitude into the days ahead. May Your will be done in my life as I seek to walk in obedience to You. In Jesus' name, Amen.

Meditative Thought: Think about specific moments from today where you experienced joy, turned to God in prayer, and expressed gratitude. Consider how you can carry this spirit into tomorrow, rejoicing always, praying without ceasing, and giving thanks in all things.

Scripture: 2 Thessalonians 2:16-17

"Now may our Lord Jesus Christ Himself, and our God and Father, who has loved us and given us everlasting consolation and good hope by grace, comfort your hearts and establish you in every good word and work."

Reflection: As we embark on this new day, let's reflect on the profound assurance and encouragement found in these verses. Paul's prayer for the Thessalonian believers serves as a reminder of God's unwavering love and grace towards us. May we find comfort in knowing that our Lord Jesus Christ Himself, along with our heavenly Father, has bestowed upon us everlasting consolation and good hope. Let's allow this truth to permeate our hearts and minds, trusting that God will strengthen and establish us in every good word and work as we walk in His grace.

Prayer: Heavenly Father, I thank You for Your boundless love and grace towards me. May Your everlasting consolation and good hope fill my heart today, bringing comfort and assurance in every circumstance. Lord Jesus, I invite You to be the anchor of my soul, guiding and establishing me in every good word and work. Help me to walk in Your grace and fulfill Your purposes for my life. In Your precious name, Amen.

Meditative Thought: Reflect on God's love and grace towards you, and the assurance of everlasting consolation and good hope that He provides. Consider how you can trust in His guidance and allow Him to establish you in every good word and work today.

Scripture: 2 Thessalonians 2:16-17
"Now may our Lord Jesus Christ Himself, and our God and Father, who has loved us and given us everlasting consolation and good hope by grace, comfort your hearts and establish you in every good word and work."

Reflection: As the day draws to a close, let's revisit the comforting words of Paul's prayer for the Thessalonian believers. Reflect on the ways in which God has shown His love and grace to you throughout this day, providing everlasting consolation and good hope by His unmerited favor. As you prepare for rest, trust in the Lord to comfort your heart and establish you in every good word and work. May His presence bring peace and assurance as you entrust yourself into His care.

Prayer: Gracious God, as I reflect on this day, I am grateful for Your abounding love and grace that sustains me. Comfort my heart, Lord, and grant me assurance in Your promises. Establish me in every good word and work, that I may honor You with my life. Thank You for Your faithfulness, even in the midst of challenges. May Your peace guard my heart and mind as I rest in You tonight. In Jesus' name, Amen.

Meditative Thought: Consider the ways in which God has shown His love and grace to you today, providing everlasting consolation and good hope. Surrender any concerns or worries to Him, trusting in His comfort and guidance as you rest in His care.

MORNING DEVOTION

Scripture: 1 Timothy 2:1-3

"Therefore, I exhort first of all that supplications, prayers, intercessions, and giving of thanks be made for all men, for kings and all who are in authority, that we may lead a quiet and peaceable life in all godliness and reverence. For this is good and acceptable in the sight of God our Savior,"

Reflection: As we begin this day, let's heed Paul's exhortation to prioritize prayer. He encourages us to offer supplications, prayers, intercessions, and thanksgiving for everyone, including those in positions of authority. Through our prayers, we can seek God's wisdom and guidance for leaders, that they may govern with righteousness and justice. As we pray for peace and stability in our world, may we also cultivate lives characterized by godliness and reverence, reflecting the love and grace of our Savior.

Prayer: Heavenly Father, I lift up to You all those in authority, praying for wisdom and discernment to guide them in their decisions. May Your hand be upon them, leading them to govern with righteousness and compassion. Grant us, Lord, the grace to live peaceful and godly lives, honoring You in all we do. Help us to be faithful in prayer, interceding for the needs of others and giving thanks for Your constant provision. In Jesus' name, Amen.

Meditative Thought: Reflect on the importance of prayer in your life, both individually and corporately. Consider how you can cultivate a habit of interceding for others, including those in positions of authority, and how this can contribute to a more peaceful and godly society.

Scripture: 1 Timothy 2:1-3
"Therefore, I exhort first of all that supplications, prayers, intercessions, and giving of thanks be made for all men, for kings and all who are in authority, that we may lead a quiet and peaceable life in all godliness and reverence. For this is good and acceptable in the sight of God our Savior,"

Reflection: As we prepare to rest at the close of this day, let's reflect on the significance of Paul's instructions regarding prayer. Consider the prayers you offered throughout the day, lifting up the needs of others and seeking God's guidance for those in authority. Take a moment to give thanks for the blessings you've experienced and to intercede for those who are in difficult circumstances. Remember that our prayers are pleasing and acceptable to God, and they contribute to His plan for peace and godliness in the world.

Prayer: Lord, as I conclude this day, I thank You for the privilege of prayer. May my petitions, intercessions, and expressions of gratitude be pleasing in Your sight. Strengthen me, Lord, to continue praying for others and seeking Your will in all things. Grant me a peaceful rest, knowing that You are in control and that Your purposes will prevail. In Your mercy, hear my prayer. Amen.

Meditative Thought: Reflect on the prayers you offered today and the impact they may have had on others and on your own spiritual growth. Consider how you can continue to prioritize prayer in your life, seeking God's will and interceding for those in need.

JUNE 3

MORNING DEVOTION

Scripture: Titus 2:13-14
"Looking for the blessed hope and glorious appearing of our great God and Savior Jesus Christ, who gave Himself for us, that He might redeem us from every lawless deed and purify for Himself His own special people, zealous for good works."

Reflection: As we begin this day, let's fix our eyes on the blessed hope of the return of our Lord Jesus Christ. Paul encourages us to eagerly anticipate His glorious appearing, reminding us of the sacrificial love demonstrated through His death on the cross. Jesus gave Himself for us to redeem us from sin and lawlessness, purifying us to be His own special people, devoted to doing good works. Let's live today with a sense of anticipation and purpose, knowing that our Savior has redeemed us and empowered us to live for Him.

Prayer: Heavenly Father, I thank You for the hope we have in Jesus Christ, our Savior. Help me to eagerly await His return and to live each day with purpose and zeal for Your kingdom. Thank You, Jesus, for Your sacrifice on the cross, which has redeemed me from sin and empowered me to live a life devoted to You. Guide me by Your Spirit today, that I may walk in obedience and be zealous for good works. In Your name, Amen.

Meditative Thought: Reflect on the hope we have in Jesus Christ and His promised return. Consider how this hope should impact your perspective and actions today, as you strive to live a life devoted to Him.

Scripture: Titus 2:13-14

"Looking for the blessed hope and glorious appearing of our great God and Savior Jesus Christ, who gave Himself for us, that He might redeem us from every lawless deed and purify for Himself His own special people, zealous for good works."

Reflection: As we close this day, let's reflect on the profound truths found in Titus 2:13-14. Consider the blessed hope we have in the return of our Lord Jesus Christ, and the transformative power of His sacrifice on the cross. Jesus gave Himself to redeem us from sin and lawlessness, purifying us to be His own special people, passionate about doing good works. Let's surrender ourselves afresh to His purposes, seeking to live lives that honor Him and advance His kingdom.

Prayer: Gracious God, as I reflect on Your Word tonight, I am reminded of the hope I have in Jesus Christ. Thank You for His sacrificial love and the redemption He offers. Help me to live as one purified for Your purposes, zealous for good works. Grant me the strength and wisdom to align my life with Your will, bringing glory to Your name. May I rest tonight in the assurance of Your love and the hope of Your promised return. In Jesus' name, Amen.

Meditative Thought: Consider the ways in which you have lived out your faith today, and ask God to continue to empower you to be zealous for good works in His name. Reflect on the hope of Christ's return and how it brings assurance and purpose to your life.

JUNE 4

MORNING DEVOTION

Scripture: Hebrews 2:1
"Therefore, we must give the more earnest heed to the things we have heard, lest we drift away."

Reflection: As we start this day, let's consider the urgency with which the author of Hebrews exhorts us to pay attention to the truths we have heard. Just as a ship can drift off course if not carefully steered, so too can we drift away from the truth if we neglect it. Let's be intentional about grounding ourselves in God's Word, actively listening to His voice, and guarding against spiritual complacency. May we give earnest heed to His teachings, allowing them to shape our thoughts, words, and actions today.

Prayer: Lord, I acknowledge the importance of staying rooted in Your truth. Help me to be vigilant in my pursuit of You, guarding against any tendency to drift away from Your Word and Your will. Open my ears to hear Your voice clearly, and give me the wisdom and strength to apply Your teachings in my life. Lead me today, Lord, and keep me steadfast in Your ways. Amen.

Meditative Thought: Consider the areas in your life where you may have been drifting away from God's truth. Reflect on ways you can refocus your attention on His Word and actively pursue a deeper relationship with Him.

Scripture: Hebrews 2:1
"Therefore, we must give the more earnest heed to the things we have heard, lest we drift away."

Reflection: As we conclude this day, let's reflect on the importance of giving earnest heed to God's Word. Consider the times throughout today when you may have been tempted to drift away from His truth. Reflect on any areas where you may have neglected to pay attention to His teachings or allowed distractions to lead you astray. Take a moment to confess any shortcomings to the Lord and commit to renewing your focus on His Word. May His Spirit strengthen you to remain steadfast in your faith and to diligently pursue His truth.

Prayer: Heavenly Father, as I reflect on this day, I recognize my need for Your guidance and grace. Forgive me for the times when I have allowed distractions or neglect to lead me away from Your truth. Help me, Lord, to give earnest heed to Your Word, remaining steadfast in my commitment to follow You. Renew my passion for Your teachings, and empower me to live faithfully according to Your will. In Jesus' name, Amen.

Meditative Thought: Consider how you can be more intentional about giving earnest heed to God's Word in your daily life. Reflect on practical steps you can take to deepen your understanding of Scripture and to guard against drifting away from His truth.

Scripture: James 5:16b
"The effective, fervent prayer of a righteous man avails much."

Reflection: As we begin this day, let's reflect on the power of prayer high-lighted in James 5:16b. Prayer is not merely a ritual or a religious duty but a dynamic conversation with the Almighty God. When we approach Him with sincerity, righteousness, and fervency, our prayers have a signif-icant impact. Let's remember that our prayers avail much, not because of our own merit, but because of the righteousness granted to us through Christ. May we approach the throne of grace with confidence, knowing that God hears and responds to the prayers of His faithful children.

Prayer: Heavenly Father, I thank You for the privilege of prayer. Help me to approach You with sincerity and fervency, knowing that You hear and answer the prayers of Your people. Grant me the righteousness that comes through faith in Christ, that my prayers may avail much. Teach me to pray according to Your will and to trust in Your perfect timing. In Jesus' name, Amen.

Meditative Thought: Consider the power of your prayers when offered with sincerity and fervency. Reflect on past experiences where God has answered your prayers and reaffirm your trust in His faithfulness.

Scripture: James 5:16b
"The effective, fervent prayer of a righteous man avails much."

Reflection: As we conclude this day, let's reflect on the impact of prayer in our lives. James reminds us that the prayers of the righteous are powerful and effective. Take a moment to consider the prayers you offered today—whether for yourself, your loved ones, or the needs of others. Trust that God has heard each petition and is working according to His perfect will. Even in moments of doubt or uncertainty, hold fast to the truth that your prayers, when offered in faith, avail much in the sight of God.

Prayer: Gracious God, as I come before You in this moment of reflection, I thank You for the privilege of prayer. Thank You for hearing my petitions and for working all things together for good according to Your purpose. Help me to trust in Your faithfulness, even when I do not see immediate answers to my prayers. Grant me a deeper understanding of Your will and a steadfast confidence in Your promises. In Jesus' name, Amen.

Meditative Thought: Reflect on the prayers you offered today and any answers or insights you may have received. Consider how you can continue to grow in your prayer life, trusting in God's faithfulness and seeking His will above all else.

JUNE 6

MORNING DEVOTION

Scripture: Isaiah 42:16
"I will bring the blind by a way they did not know; I will lead them in paths they have not known. I will make darkness light before them, and crooked places straight. These things I will do for them, and not forsake them."

Reflection: As we embark on this new day, let's take comfort in the promise of guidance and illumination found in Isaiah 42:16. God assures us that He will lead us in paths we have not known, making darkness light before us and straightening the crooked places. Even when we feel lost or uncertain, He is there to guide us with His unfailing wisdom and grace. Let's trust in His faithfulness today, knowing that He will never forsake us.

Prayer: Heavenly Father, I thank You for Your promise to guide me and lead me in paths of righteousness. Help me to trust in Your wisdom and to follow Your guidance, even when the way ahead seems uncertain. Illuminate my path with Your light, and straighten the crooked places before me. May Your presence be my constant companion today, guiding me through every challenge and blessing me with Your peace. In Jesus' name, Amen.

Meditative Thought: Reflect on times when God has guided you through unfamiliar paths or difficult circumstances. Consider how His faithfulness in the past strengthens your trust in His guidance for today.

Scripture: Isaiah 42:16
"I will bring the blind by a way they did not know; I will lead them in paths they have not known. I will make darkness light before them, and crooked places straight. These things I will do for them, and not forsake them."

Reflection: As we conclude this day, let's reflect on the faithfulness of God to guide us through every season of life. Even in moments of darkness or confusion, He is there to make our paths straight and to illuminate the way before us. Take a moment to thank Him for His unwavering presence and guidance. Trust that as you rest tonight, He continues to watch over you, working all things together for your good.

Prayer: Gracious God, as I reflect on the events of this day, I am grateful for Your constant presence and guidance in my life. Thank You for leading me in paths of righteousness and for making my way straight. As I rest tonight, I entrust myself into Your care, knowing that You never slumber nor sleep. Grant me peaceful rest and assurance in Your unfailing love. In Jesus' name, Amen.

Meditative Thought: Consider the ways God has guided you through this day, making darkness light before you and straightening your path. Praise Him for His faithfulness and commit to trusting His guidance in the days to come.

MORNING DEVOTION

Scripture: Jeremiah 1:5
"Before I formed you in the womb I knew you; Before you were born I sanctified you; I ordained you a prophet to the nations."

Reflection: As we begin this new day, let's reflect on the profound truth declared in Jeremiah 1:5. God's words to Jeremiah remind us of His intimate knowledge and purpose for each of us even before we were formed in the womb. Just as Jeremiah was sanctified and ordained for a specific calling, so too are we chosen and appointed by God for His divine purposes. Take a moment to ponder the unique calling and gifts that God has bestowed upon you, and let them inspire you to live each moment with purpose and passion.

Prayer: Heavenly Father, I thank You for Your intimate knowledge of me and Your purpose for my life. Help me to embrace the calling You have placed upon me with humility and obedience. Grant me the courage to step boldly into the plans You have for me, trusting in Your guidance and provision every step of the way. May my life bring glory to Your name and bear fruit for Your kingdom. In Jesus' name, Amen.

Meditative Thought: Consider the ways in which God has uniquely equipped and called you for His purposes. Reflect on how you can live out your calling with greater faithfulness and dedication today.

Scripture: Jeremiah 1:5
"Before I formed you in the womb I knew you; Before you were born I sanctified you; I ordained you a prophet to the nations."

Reflection: As we conclude this day, let's meditate on the truth of Jeremiah 1:5 once again. God's declaration to Jeremiah serves as a powerful reminder that His plans for us are established long before we even enter this world. Just as He sanctified and ordained Jeremiah for a specific purpose, so too does He have a divine plan for each of our lives. Take a moment to thank God for His sovereignty and faithfulness in orchestrating every detail of your life. Surrender yourself afresh to His will, trusting in His providence for the days ahead.

Prayer: Gracious God, as I reflect on the events of this day, I am reminded of Your sovereignty and faithfulness in my life. Thank You for Your unwavering love and guidance, even before I was formed in the womb. Help me to walk in obedience to Your calling, trusting in Your provision and direction for each step of the journey. May Your will be done in my life, as it is in heaven. In Jesus' name, Amen.

Meditative Thought: Consider the ways in which God has been at work in your life today, fulfilling His purposes and guiding you according to His plan. Reflect on how you can align your desires and actions more closely with His will in the days to come.

JUNE 8

MORNING DEVOTION

Scripture: John 1:14
"And the Word became flesh and dwelt among us, and we beheld His glory, the glory as of the only begotten of the Father, full of grace and truth."

Reflection: As we begin this new day, let's reflect on the profound truth revealed in John 1:14. This verse encapsulates the essence of the Incarnation—the Word of God, Jesus Christ, taking on human flesh and dwelling among us. The very presence of Jesus among humanity allowed us to witness the glory of God manifested in human form, a glory characterized by grace and truth. Take a moment to ponder the significance of Jesus' earthly ministry and the impact His presence continues to have on your life today.

Prayer: Heavenly Father, I thank You for the incredible gift of Your Son, Jesus Christ, who became flesh and dwelt among us. Thank You for the grace and truth He brought into the world through His life, death, and resurrection. Help me to behold His glory afresh each day and to live in light of His teachings and example. May His presence continue to transform my heart and shape my actions. In Jesus' name, Amen.

Meditative Thought: Consider the ways in which the presence of Jesus in your life brings grace and truth. Reflect on how you can emulate His character and share His love with others today.

Scripture: John 1:14
"And the Word became flesh and dwelt among us, and we beheld His glory, the glory as of the only begotten of the Father, full of grace and truth."

Reflection: As we conclude this day, let's meditate on the truth of John 1:14 once again. The incarnation of Jesus Christ remains one of the most profound mysteries of our faith—God taking on human form to dwell among His creation. Through Jesus, we have beheld the glory of God, a glory marked by boundless grace and unwavering truth. Take a moment to thank God for the revelation of His glory through Jesus Christ and for the ways His grace and truth have impacted your life.

Prayer: Gracious God, as I reflect on the events of this day, I am reminded of Your incredible love demonstrated through the incarnation of Your Son, Jesus Christ. Thank You for revealing Your glory to us and for the grace and truth we find in Him. Help me to abide in Your love and to reflect Your grace and truth to those around me. May Your presence continue to dwell richly in my life. In Jesus' name, Amen.

Meditative Thought: Consider the ways in which you have experienced the grace and truth of Jesus Christ today. Reflect on how you can continue to grow in His likeness and share His love with others in the days ahead.

Scripture: Jude 1:2
"Mercy, peace, and love be multiplied to you."

Reflection: As we begin this new day, let's dwell on the beautiful blessing found in Jude 1:2. These words convey the heartfelt desire for abundant mercy, peace, and love to overflow in our lives. Mercy extends God's compassion and forgiveness, peace brings calmness amid life's storms, and love binds us together in unity. Reflect on the significance of each of these blessings and open your heart to receive them afresh today.

Prayer: Heavenly Father, I thank You for Your abundant mercy, peace, and love that You freely offer to me. May Your mercy soften my heart, Your peace calm my anxieties, and Your love fill me with joy. Multiply these blessings in my life today and help me to extend them to others. In Jesus' name, Amen.

Meditative Thought: Consider how you can actively demonstrate mercy, pursue peace, and show love to those around you today, reflecting the blessings prayed for in Jude 1:2.

Scripture: Jude 1:2
"Mercy, peace, and love be multiplied to you."

Reflection: As we conclude this day, let's reflect on the powerful blessing of Jude 1:2 once again. In the midst of life's challenges and uncertainties, God's desire is for His children to experience multiplied mercy, peace, and love. Take a moment to assess how these blessings have manifested in your life today. Acknowledge God's faithfulness in providing for your needs and sustaining you through the day.

Prayer: Gracious God, I am grateful for the abundance of mercy, peace, and love that You have poured out upon me today. Thank You for Your steadfast presence and provision in every circumstance. As I rest tonight, may Your blessings continue to multiply in my life and may I walk in the fullness of Your grace. In Jesus' name, Amen.

Meditative Thought: Reflect on specific moments throughout the day where you experienced God's mercy, peace, and love. Consider how you can cultivate an attitude of gratitude and trust in God's provision as you prepare for rest tonight.

Scripture: 1 John 5:20
"And we know that the Son of God has come and has given us an understanding, that we may know Him who is true; and we are in Him who is true, in His Son Jesus Christ. This is the true God and eternal life."

Reflection: As we begin this new day, let's meditate on the profound truth revealed in 1 John 5:20. Through the Son of God, we have been given understanding, enabling us to know the true nature of God. Our relationship with Jesus Christ connects us intimately with the truth, anchoring us in the reality of who God is. Reflect on the significance of knowing the true God and the eternal life found in Him, and let this knowledge shape your perspective as you navigate through today's challenges.

Prayer: Gracious Lord, I thank You for the gift of understanding that You have bestowed upon me through Your Son, Jesus Christ. Help me to deepen my knowledge of You and to walk in the truth of Your Word today. May my life be a reflection of Your eternal life, and may I draw nearer to You with each passing moment. In Jesus' name, Amen.

Meditative Thought: Consider how your understanding of God shapes your thoughts, words, and actions. Reflect on how you can cultivate a deeper intimacy with Him throughout the day, drawing closer to the true God who offers eternal life.

Scripture: 1 John 5:20
"And we know that the Son of God has come and has given us an understanding, that we may know Him who is true; and we are in Him who is true, in His Son Jesus Christ. This is the true God and eternal life."

Reflection: As we conclude this day, let's reflect on the profound truth of 1 John 5:20 once again. Through the Son of God, we have been granted the privilege of knowing the true God and experiencing eternal life in Him. Take a moment to assess your day in light of this truth. Consider the ways in which your understanding of God has influenced your thoughts, decisions, and interactions with others.

Prayer: Heavenly Father, I am grateful for the revelation of Your truth through Your Son, Jesus Christ. Thank You for the gift of eternal life that I have in Him. As I reflect on this truth, I pray for a deeper intimacy with You and a greater awareness of Your presence in my life. Renew my spirit as I rest tonight, and may Your truth continue to guide me each day. In Jesus' name, Amen.

Meditative Thought: Reflect on specific moments throughout the day where your understanding of God's truth impacted your attitudes and actions. Consider how you can continue to grow in your knowledge of Him and live out the reality of eternal life in your daily life.

JUNE 11

MORNING DEVOTION

Scripture: Jude 24-25
"Now to Him who is able to keep you from stumbling, and to present you faultless Before the presence of His glory with exceeding joy, To God our Savior, Who alone is wise, Be glory and majesty, Dominion and power, Both now and forever. Amen."

Reflection: As we begin this new day, let's meditate on the powerful doxology found in Jude 24-25. These verses remind us of the unfailing ability of God to keep us from stumbling and to present us faultless before His glorious presence. Reflect on the assurance and confidence that comes from knowing that God, our Savior, is both wise and powerful. Consider the exceeding joy that awaits us as we surrender to His divine will and allow Him to work in and through us.

Prayer: Heavenly Father, I thank You for Your faithfulness and Your power to keep me from stumbling. Help me to trust in Your wisdom and to surrender fully to Your will today. May Your glory and majesty be evident in my life, and may Your name be exalted both now and forever. In Jesus' name, Amen.

Meditative Thought: Consider the ways in which God has kept you from stumbling in the past and give thanks for His faithfulness. Reflect on areas of your life where you need His guidance and ask Him to lead you today.

Scripture: Jude 24-25

"Now to Him who is able to keep you from stumbling, and to present you faultless Before the presence of His glory with exceeding joy, To God our Savior, Who alone is wise, Be glory and majesty, Dominion and power, Both now and forever. Amen."

Reflection: As we conclude this day, let's revisit the profound truth expressed in Jude 24-25. Take a moment to reflect on the assurance that comes from knowing that God is able to keep us from stumbling and to present us faultless before His glorious presence. Ponder the significance of surrendering to His wisdom and acknowledging His dominion and power over all things. Allow these truths to bring you peace and comfort as you prepare for rest tonight.

Prayer: Gracious Lord, I thank You for Your unchanging character and Your unfailing love. As I reflect on Your ability to keep me from stumbling, I am filled with gratitude and awe. Help me to trust in Your wisdom and to surrender to Your will more fully each day. May Your glory and majesty reign in my life, both now and forever. In Jesus' name, Amen.

Meditative Thought: Reflect on the peace and comfort that comes from entrusting yourself to God's care. Meditate on the truth that He is able to keep you from stumbling and present you faultless before His presence with exceeding joy.

Scripture: Matthew 12:47-50

"Then one said to Him, 'Look, Your mother and Your brothers are standing outside, seeking to speak with You.' But He answered and said to the one who told Him, 'Who is My mother and who are My brothers?' And He stretched out His hand toward His disciples and said, 'Here are My mother and My brothers! For whoever does the will of My Father in heaven is My brother and sister and mother.'"

Reflection: As we begin this day, let's reflect on the powerful message Jesus conveyed about the nature of His spiritual family. He wasn't dismissing His biological family but was expanding the concept of family to include all who do the will of His Father in heaven. This is a reminder that our spiritual connections, grounded in our shared faith and obedience to God, are profoundly significant.

Prayer: Heavenly Father, thank You for the gift of being part of Your family. Help me to live in a way that reflects my commitment to Your will. In Jesus name. Amen.

Meditative Thought: Today, I will embrace my spiritual family with love and commitment, knowing that we are united by our shared faith and dedication to God's will.

Scripture: Matthew 12:47-50
"Then one said to Him, 'Look, Your mother and Your brothers are standing outside, seeking to speak with You.' But He answered and said to the one who told Him, 'Who is My mother and who are My brothers?' And He stretched out His hand toward His disciples and said, 'Here are My mother and My brothers! For whoever does the will of My Father in heaven is My brother and sister and mother.'"

Reflection: As the day comes to a close, let's revisit the words of Jesus about true family. Reflect on how you have connected with your spiritual family today. Have you supported and encouraged one another in doing the will of the Father? Consider the ways in which your actions have strengthened these spiritual bonds and how you can continue to nurture them in the future.

Prayer: Lord Jesus, thank You for the reminder of what it means to be part of Your family. Strengthen my relationships with my spiritual family and help us to grow together in faith and love. Amen.

Meditative Thought: Tonight, I rest in the comfort of being part of God's family, resolved to deepen my commitment to His will and to my brothers and sisters in Christ.

JUNE 13

MORNING DEVOTION

Scripture: Isaiah 3:10
"Say to the righteous that it shall be well with them, for they shall eat the fruit of their doings."

Reflection: As the morning sun rises, let us meditate on the assurance given in Isaiah 3:10. God promises that it shall be well with the righteous. This verse reminds us that living a life in alignment with God's will brings peace and rewards. The "fruit of their doings" symbolizes the blessings and positive outcomes that result from living righteously. Start your day with the confidence that when you live according to God's ways, His blessings will follow.

Prayer: Heavenly Father, thank You for the promise that it will be well with the righteous. Help me to live a life that reflects Your righteousness today. Guide my thoughts, words, and actions so that they align with Your will. Let me trust in Your promise and find peace in knowing that You are with me. In Christs' precious name, amen.

Meditative Thought: Today, I will embrace righteousness, trusting that God's blessings will follow, and that it will be well with me as I walk in His ways.

Scripture: Isaiah 3:10
"Say to the righteous that it shall be well with them, For they shall eat the fruit of their doings."

Reflection: As the day draws to a close, reflect on how you have lived out the promise of Isaiah 3:10. Consider the ways in which you have sought to live righteously and the fruits that have come from your actions. Whether through kind words, helpful deeds, or faithful obedience, recognize the peace and assurance that comes from walking in God's ways.

Prayer: Lord, I thank You for guiding me through this day. As I reflect on my actions, I ask for Your continued strength to live righteously. Forgive me for any shortcomings and help me to learn and grow from them. Thank You for the assurance that it will be well with me as I follow You. In Christs' precious name, amen.

Meditative Thought: Tonight, I rest in the assurance that living righteously brings God's peace and blessings. I will continue to seek His guidance and trust in His promises.

JUNE 14

MORNING DEVOTION

Scripture: Revelation 22:16
"I, Jesus, have sent My angel to testify to you these things in the churches. I am the Root and the Offspring of David, the Bright and Morning Star."

Reflection: As the new day begins, consider the powerful declaration of Jesus in Revelation 22:16. Jesus identifies Himself as the "Root and the Offspring of David" and the "Bright and Morning Star." This profound statement reminds us of His eternal nature and His fulfillment of God's promises. He is the source of our faith and the light that guides us through the darkness. As we start our day, let us embrace Jesus as our guide, our hope, and our light.

Prayer: Heavenly Father, thank You for sending Jesus, the Bright and Morning Star, to guide and illuminate our path. Help me to walk in His light today, reflecting His love and truth in all I do. Strengthen my faith and keep me focused on His promises. In Jesus' name, Amen.

Meditative Thought: Today, I will walk in the light of Jesus, the Bright and Morning Star, trusting Him to guide my steps and illuminate my path.

Scripture: Revelation 22:16
"I, Jesus, have sent My angel to testify to you these things in the churches. I am the Root and the Offspring of David, the Bright and Morning Star."

Reflection: As the day comes to an end, let us reflect on the assurance given by Jesus in Revelation 22:16. Jesus is not only our Savior but also our eternal guide and light. Reflect on how His presence has guided you through the day. His light continues to shine, offering hope and peace even as the day ends. Embrace the comfort that comes from knowing Jesus is the Morning Star, always present to guide us through the darkness.

Prayer: Lord Jesus, thank You for being my Bright and Morning Star. As I reflect on this day, I am grateful for Your guidance and presence in my life. Help me to rest in Your light and wake up tomorrow renewed in Your love. Keep my heart focused on You and Your promises. In Jesus' name, Amen.

Meditative Thought: Tonight, I rest in the assurance that Jesus, the Bright and Morning Star, is always with me, guiding and illuminating my path.

Scripture: Genesis 1:27
"So God created man in His own image; in the image of God He created him; male and female He created them."

Reflection: As we begin a new day, let us reflect on the profound truth that we are created in the image of God. This means that each of us carries a unique reflection of God's character and glory. Our worth and identity are rooted in this divine image. As you go through your day, remember that you are fearfully and wonderfully made, with a purpose and a calling that reflect God's nature and love.

Prayer: Heavenly Father, thank You for creating me in Your image. Help me to live today in a way that honors and reflects You. May my thoughts, words, and actions be a testament to Your love and creativity. Fill me with a sense of purpose and guide me in all that I do. In Jesus' name, Amen.

Meditative Thought: Today, I will embrace my identity as one created in God's image, striving to reflect His love, kindness, and creativity in all I do.

Scripture: Genesis 1:27
"So God created man in His own image; in the image of God He created him; male and female He created them."

Reflection: As the day ends, take a moment to reflect on the truth that you are created in the image of God. Consider how this knowledge has influenced your interactions and decisions throughout the day. Recognize the divine worth in yourself and others. Acknowledge the ways you have reflected God's image and areas where you can grow. Rest in the assurance that you are valued and loved by the Creator.

Prayer: Lord, I thank You for creating me in Your image. As I reflect on this day, I ask for Your forgiveness for the times I failed to reflect Your nature. Help me to grow in Your likeness and to see Your image in others. Grant me peace as I rest tonight, and renew my spirit for tomorrow. In Jesus name, Amen.

Meditative Thought: Tonight, I will rest in the peace of knowing that I am created in the image of God, valued and loved by the Creator, and I will seek to reflect His nature more fully each day.

Scripture: Romans 4:7-8
"Blessed are those whose lawless deeds are forgiven, and whose sins are covered; Blessed is the man to whom the Lord shall not impute sin."

Reflection: As we start our day, let us embrace the profound blessing of forgiveness. These verses remind us that through faith in Jesus Christ, our sins are not counted against us. We are blessed because our lawless deeds are forgiven and our sins are covered. This truth should fill our hearts with gratitude and joy, knowing that God's grace has wiped our slate clean. Today, walk in the freedom and peace that comes from being forgiven, and let this assurance guide your interactions and decisions.

Prayer: Heavenly Father, thank You for the incredible blessing of forgiveness. Thank You for covering my sins and not counting them against me. Help me to live in the light of Your grace today, extending the same forgiveness and love to others. May Your forgiveness transform my heart and actions, reflecting Your mercy in all I do. In Jesus name, Amen.

Meditative Thought: Today, I will live in the freedom of God's forgiveness, letting His grace guide my thoughts, words, and actions.

Scripture: Romans 4:7-
"Blessed are those whose lawless deeds are forgiven, And whose sins are covered; Blessed is the man to whom the Lord shall not impute sin."

Reflection: As the day draws to a close, reflect on the blessing of forgiveness that God has granted us. Consider the ways you have experienced His grace today and the peace that comes from knowing your sins are covered. Let this truth bring comfort and rest to your soul. Recognize any areas where you may have fallen short and bring them to God in prayer, confident in His forgiveness and love.

Prayer: Lord, I thank You for Your boundless grace and the forgiveness You have given me. As I reflect on this day, I am grateful for the peace that comes from knowing my sins are covered. Forgive me for any moments when I did not live fully in this truth. Help me to rest in Your grace tonight and wake up renewed and ready to serve You. In Jesus name, Amen.

Meditative Thought: Tonight, I will rest in the assurance of God's forgiveness, allowing His grace to bring peace to my heart and prepare me for a new day.

JUNE 17

MORNING DEVOTION

Scripture: 2 Corinthians 1:3-4
"Blessed be the God and Father of our Lord Jesus Christ, the Father of mercies and God of all comfort, who comforts us in all our tribulation, that we may be able to comfort those who are in any trouble, with the comfort with which we ourselves are comforted by God."

Reflection: As we begin our day, let us bless God, the Father of mercies and the God of all comfort. In every trial and tribulation, He is our source of comfort and strength. Today, remember that the comfort we receive from God is not just for ourselves but to be shared with others. Let His mercy and comfort fill your heart, and be prepared to extend that same comfort to those around you who may be in need.

Prayer: Heavenly Father, I bless Your name this morning and thank You for being the Father of mercies and the God of all comfort. As I go through this day, help me to receive Your comfort in my challenges and be a source of comfort to others. Let Your love and mercy flow through me to those who need it. In Jesus name, Amen.

Meditative Thought: Today, I will be a vessel of God's comfort, sharing His mercy and love with those who are hurting around me.

Scripture: 2 Corinthians 1:3-4
"Blessed be the God and Father of our Lord Jesus Christ, the Father of mercies and God of all comfort, who comforts us in all our tribulation, that we may be able to comfort those who are in any trouble, with the comfort with which we ourselves are comforted by God."

Reflection: As the day ends, take time to reflect on the comfort God has provided you throughout the day. Consider the moments when His mercy and love have carried you through difficult situations. Think about how you have been able to extend that same comfort to others. Rest in the knowledge that God's comfort is always available to you, and let it bring peace to your soul as you prepare for rest.

Prayer: Dear Lord, I thank You for Your constant comfort and mercy throughout this day. As I reflect on the moments of challenge and the peace You provided, I am grateful. Help me to continue being a source of Your comfort to others. As I rest tonight, may Your presence bring me peace and renewal for tomorrow. In Jesus name, Amen.

Meditative Thought: Tonight, I will rest in the comfort of God's presence, reflecting on His mercy and preparing to share His love again tomorrow.

Scripture: 1 Timothy 6:11-12
"But you, O man of God, flee these things and pursue righteousness, godliness, faith, love, patience, gentleness. Fight the good fight of faith, lay hold on eternal life, to which you were also called and have confessed the good confession in the presence of many witnesses."

Reflection: As the day begins, we are reminded of our calling to pursue a life of righteousness, godliness, faith, love, patience, and gentleness. These virtues are essential for living a life that honors God. This morning, let us commit to fleeing from temptations and distractions that hinder our spiritual growth. Embrace the pursuit of these godly qualities, and prepare yourself to fight the good fight of faith. Remember, you are called to eternal life and have made a good confession before many.

Prayer: Heavenly Father, thank You for the new day and the opportunity to pursue righteousness, godliness, faith, love, patience, and gentleness. Help me to flee from anything that draws me away from You. Strengthen me to fight the good fight of faith and to live out my confession before others. May Your Spirit guide me throughout this day. In Jesus name, Amen.

Meditative Thought: Today, I will consciously pursue righteousness and godliness, knowing that I am called to fight the good fight of faith and live out my confession of eternal life.

Scripture: 1 Timothy 6:11-12
"But you, O man of God, flee these things and pursue righteousness, godliness, faith, love, patience, gentleness. Fight the good fight of faith, lay hold on eternal life, to which you were also called and have confessed the good confession in the presence of many witnesses."

Reflection: As the day draws to a close, reflect on how you pursued righteousness, godliness, faith, love, patience, and gentleness today. Consider the battles you faced and how you fought the good fight of faith. Take time to acknowledge the eternal life you have laid hold of and the confession you have made before others. Let these reflections encourage you and strengthen your resolve to continue this pursuit daily.

Prayer: Dear Lord, thank You for guiding me through this day. As I reflect on my actions and decisions, I seek Your forgiveness for the moments I fell short. Strengthen my resolve to pursue righteousness and godliness. Help me to grow in faith, love, patience, and gentleness. As I rest tonight, renew my spirit and prepare me for the challenges of tomorrow. In Jesus name, Amen.

Meditative Thought: Tonight, I rest in the assurance of eternal life, reflecting on the good fight of faith I fought today and seeking to grow in righteousness and godliness each new day.

JUNE 19

MORNING DEVOTION

Scripture: 1 John 3:2
"Beloved, now we are children of God; and it has not yet been revealed what we shall be, but we know that when He is revealed, we shall be like Him, for we shall see Him as He is."

Reflection: This morning, let us reflect on the incredible truth that we are now children of God. Our identity is secure in Him, and our future holds the promise of transformation into His likeness. Although we may not fully understand what we shall become, we have the assurance that when Christ is revealed, we will be like Him. This hope inspires us to live in a way that reflects our heavenly calling, looking forward to the day when we will see Him as He is.

Prayer: Heavenly Father, thank You for the assurance that I am Your child. As I start this day, help me to live in a way that reflects my identity in You. Fill me with hope and joy as I look forward to the day when I will see You as You are and be transformed into Your likeness. Guide my actions, thoughts, and words today so that they honor You. In Jesus' name, Amen.

Meditative Thought: As I begin this day, I embrace my identity as a child of God, looking forward with hope to the day I will be transformed into His likeness when I see Him face to face.

Scripture: 1 John 3:2
"Beloved, now we are children of God; and it has not yet been revealed what we shall be, but we know that when He is revealed, we shall be like Him, for we shall see Him as He is."

Reflection: As the day comes to an end, take a moment to reflect on your identity as a child of God. Despite the uncertainties and challenges you faced today, remember that your future is secure in Him. The promise that you will one day see Christ and be like Him should fill your heart with peace and anticipation. Let this hope shape your thoughts and actions as you prepare to rest.

Prayer: Dear Lord, thank You for carrying me through this day. As I reflect on my identity as Your child, I find peace in the promise of being transformed into Your likeness when I see You. Forgive me for the times I fell short today and help me to rest in Your love and grace. Renew my strength as I sleep, and prepare me for another day of living for You. In Jesus' name, Amen.

Meditative Thought: Tonight, I rest in the comforting truth that I am a child of God, looking forward with anticipation to the day I will see Him and be transformed into His likeness.

JUNE 20

MORNING DEVOTION

Scripture: Psalm 84:11-12
"For the Lord God is a sun and shield; The Lord will give grace and glory; No good thing will He withhold from those who walk uprightly. O Lord of hosts, Blessed is the man who trusts in You!"

Reflection: As you begin this new day, remember that the Lord God is your sun and shield. He illuminates your path and protects you from harm. He is generous, bestowing grace and glory upon those who walk uprightly. Trust in His goodness and His promise that He will not withhold any good thing from you. Embrace the blessing that comes from placing your trust in Him, knowing that He is faithful and just.

Prayer: Heavenly Father, thank You for being my sun and shield. As I start this day, I trust in Your protection and guidance. Fill me with Your grace and glory, and help me to walk uprightly before You. Remind me of Your promises and let Your goodness shine through every aspect of my life. I place my trust in You, knowing that You withhold no good thing from those who seek You. In Jesus' name, Amen.

Meditative Thought: This morning, I trust in the Lord as my sun and shield, embracing His grace and glory, and believing that He will withhold no good thing from me as I walk uprightly.

Scripture: Psalm 84:11-12
"For the Lord God is a sun and shield; The Lord will give grace and glory; No good thing will He withhold from those who walk uprightly. O Lord of hosts, Blessed is the man who trusts in You!"

Reflection: As the day draws to a close, take comfort in the knowledge that the Lord has been your sun and shield. Reflect on His grace and glory evident in your day, and trust in His promise that He withholds no good thing from those who walk uprightly. Your trust in Him brings a blessing that surpasses all understanding. Let this truth bring you peace and rest as you lay down to sleep.

Prayer: Dear Lord, thank You for being my sun and shield throughout this day. Your grace and glory have been my strength. As I reflect on Your goodness, I am grateful for Your promise to withhold no good thing from those who walk uprightly. Help me to continue to trust in You, finding peace and rest in Your presence. Renew my strength as I sleep, and prepare me for another day of walking in Your light. In Jesus' name, Amen.

Meditative Thought: Tonight, I rest in the assurance that the Lord God, my sun and shield, has bestowed His grace and glory upon me, and I am blessed as I trust in Him.

Scripture: Psalm 78:7
"That they may set their hope in God, and not forget the works of God, But keep His commandments."

Reflection: As the new day dawns, set your hope firmly in God. Reflect on the countless works He has done in your life and in the lives of those before you. Let these memories fuel your faith and inspire you to keep His commandments. Starting your day with this mindset brings a sense of purpose and direction, knowing that your hope is rooted in the Creator of all things.

Prayer: Heavenly Father, I thank You for this new day. Help me to set my hope in You and never forget the marvelous works You have done. Guide me to keep Your commandments and walk in Your ways. Let my life be a testament to Your faithfulness and love. Strengthen my resolve to live according to Your word. In Jesus' name, Amen.

Meditative Thought: This morning, I set my hope in God, remembering His mighty works and committing to keep His commandments throughout the day.

Scripture: Psalm 78:7
"That they may set their hope in God, and not forget the works of God, But keep His commandments."

Reflection: As the day comes to an end, take a moment to reflect on how you have placed your hope in God. Recall the ways He has shown His faithfulness and the works He has accomplished in your life today. Consider how you have kept His commandments and where you can grow. Ending the day with this reflection brings peace and a renewed commitment to follow Him more closely.

Prayer: Dear Lord, thank You for Your guidance and presence throughout this day. I set my hope in You and remember Your wonderful works. Forgive me where I have fallen short, and help me to grow in keeping Your commandments. May I rest in the peace that comes from knowing You are in control. Strengthen me for the days ahead, and let my life continually reflect Your love and faithfulness. In Jesus' name, Amen.

Meditative Thought: Tonight, I rest with my hope set in God, recalling His works and committing anew to keep His commandments, trusting in His faithful guidance.

JUNE 22

MORNING DEVOTION

Scripture: Jonah 3:10
"Then God saw their works, that they turned from their evil way; and God relented from the disaster that He had said He would bring upon them, and He did not do it."

Reflection: As we begin this day, let's reflect on the power of repentance and God's boundless mercy. The people of Nineveh turned from their evil ways, and God responded with compassion, sparing them from disaster. This morning, consider areas in your life where you need to turn back to God. His forgiveness and grace are always available, ready to renew and restore us when we genuinely seek Him.

Prayer: Heavenly Father, thank You for Your incredible mercy and willingness to forgive. This morning, I come before You with a heart of repentance, turning away from any wrongdoing. Help me to walk in Your ways and honor You with my actions today. Thank You for Your grace that renews and restores. In Jesus' name, Amen.

Meditative Thought: This morning, I embrace the power of repentance, trusting in God's mercy and grace to guide me throughout the day.

Scripture: Jonah 3:10
"Then God saw their works, that they turned from their evil way; and God relented from the disaster that He had said He would bring upon them, and He did not do it."

Reflection: As the day ends, let us reflect on God's merciful nature. The people of Nineveh were spared because they sincerely repented and changed their ways. Think about your day and the choices you made. Where did you see God's mercy in your life today? How did you turn away from things that didn't honor Him? This reflection helps us understand the importance of repentance and the joy that comes from living in God's forgiveness.

Prayer: Dear Lord, I thank You for Your mercy and for the opportunities to turn back to You throughout this day. Forgive me for any moments where I strayed from Your path. Thank You for Your grace that covers all my shortcomings. As I rest tonight, I pray for a heart that continually seeks to honor You. In Jesus' name, Amen.

Meditative Thought: Tonight, I rest in the assurance of God's mercy, reflecting on His grace and the transformation that repentance brings.

JUNE 23

MORNING DEVOTION

Scripture: Matthew 4:4
"But He answered and said, 'It is written, "Man shall not live by bread alone, but by every word that proceeds from the mouth of God.""'"

Reflection: As we start this new day, let us remember the words of Jesus. In His response to temptation, Jesus emphasized the importance of spiritual nourishment over physical sustenance. Today, make a commitment to prioritize God's Word in your life. Let it guide your thoughts, actions, and decisions. Just as we need food to sustain our bodies, we need God's Word to sustain our spirits.

Prayer: Heavenly Father, thank You for the gift of Your Word that nourishes my soul. As I begin this day, help me to hunger for Your Word and to seek Your guidance in everything I do. Strengthen me to resist temptations and to rely on Your truth. Fill me with Your wisdom and lead me on the path of righteousness. In Jesus' name, Amen.

Meditative Thought: This morning, I choose to feed on the Word of God, letting it nourish my spirit and guide my steps throughout the day.

Scripture: Matthew 4:4
"But He answered and said, 'It is written, "Man shall not live by bread alone, but by every word that proceeds from the mouth of God."'"

Reflection: As the day comes to a close, reflect on how God's Word has guided and sustained you today. Consider the moments when you sought His wisdom and how it influenced your actions and decisions. Jesus taught us that spiritual sustenance is vital for our well-being. Let this be a reminder to end your day by meditating on God's Word and allowing it to renew your mind and spirit.

Prayer: Dear Lord, thank You for the guidance and sustenance of Your Word throughout this day. As I rest tonight, I ask that You continue to speak to me through Your Scriptures. Help me to internalize Your truths and live according to Your will. Thank You for the strength and wisdom that come from Your Word. In Jesus' name, Amen.

Meditative Thought: Tonight, I reflect on the spiritual nourishment provided by God's Word, letting it renew my mind and soul as I rest.

JUNE 24

MORNING DEVOTION

Scripture: Matthew 5:3
"Blessed are the poor in spirit, for theirs is the kingdom of heaven."

Reflection: As we begin this new day, let us contemplate what it means to be "poor in spirit." Jesus teaches us that recognizing our spiritual poverty and our need for God is the pathway to true blessedness. To be "poor in spirit" is to be humble and aware of our dependence on God's grace. Today, embrace humility and open your heart to God's presence and guidance. Acknowledge your need for Him and trust in His provision.

Prayer: Heavenly Father, thank You for the promise that the kingdom of heaven belongs to those who are poor in spirit. Help me to start this day with a humble heart, acknowledging my need for Your grace and guidance. Fill me with Your Spirit and lead me in Your ways. May I find true blessedness in relying on You completely. In Jesus' name, Amen.

Meditative Thought: This morning, I choose to embrace humility and recognize my need for God's presence and guidance in every aspect of my life.

Scripture: Matthew 5:3
"Blessed are the poor in spirit, for theirs is the kingdom of heaven."

Reflection: As the day draws to a close, reflect on how you experienced God's blessings through humility. Consider the moments when you recognized your need for God and how He met you in those times. Jesus' words remind us that true blessedness comes from acknowledging our spiritual poverty and dependence on Him. Let this be a moment of gratitude and reflection on God's grace throughout your day.

Prayer: Dear Lord, thank You for Your faithfulness and the blessings that come from being poor in spirit. As I reflect on this day, I am grateful for the moments when I recognized my need for You and experienced Your grace. Help me to continue living in humility and dependence on You. Strengthen my faith and deepen my relationship with You. In Jesus' name, Amen.

Meditative Thought: Tonight, I reflect on the blessings of humility and the grace that comes from recognizing my need for God's presence and guidance.

Scripture: Matthew 5:4
"Blessed are those who mourn, for they shall be comforted."

Reflection: As we start our day, let us reflect on Jesus' promise that those who mourn will be comforted. Mourning isn't limited to the loss of loved ones; it can also include mourning over our sins, the brokenness in the world, or the suffering of others. This verse reminds us that in our deepest sorrows, God offers His comfort. As you face today, remember that your sorrow is not unnoticed by God. He sees your pain and promises comfort and healing.

Prayer: Heavenly Father, I come to You this morning with a heart open to Your comfort. In my moments of sorrow and mourning, remind me of Your promise to provide comfort. Help me to find solace in Your presence and strength in Your love. May I also be an instrument of Your comfort to others who are mourning. In Jesus' name, Amen.

Meditative Thought: This morning, I trust in God's promise of comfort in my times of sorrow, knowing that He sees my pain and offers His healing embrace.

Scripture: Matthew 5:4
"Blessed are those who mourn, for they shall be comforted."

Reflection: As the day ends, take a moment to reflect on how you experienced God's comfort. Jesus' words assure us that our mourning will lead to divine comfort. Think about the moments of the day when you felt God's presence in your sorrow, or how you were able to comfort others. Acknowledge the ways God has been faithful in fulfilling His promise, and let this reflection bring peace to your heart.

Prayer: Dear Lord, as I end this day, I thank You for Your comfort in times of mourning. Thank You for being present in my sorrows and for the ways You have brought peace to my heart. Help me to continue to trust in Your promise of comfort and to extend that comfort to others in need. In Jesus' name, Amen.

Meditative Thought: Tonight, I find peace in God's promise that my mourning will be met with His comfort, and I am grateful for His faithful presence in my times of sorrow.

Scripture: Matthew 5:5
"Blessed are the meek, for they shall inherit the earth."

Reflection: As the sun rises, let us contemplate the profound truth Jesus shares about meekness. The world often equates meekness with weakness, but in the kingdom of God, meekness is strength under control. It is a humble and gentle attitude that trusts in God's timing and sovereignty. Starting our day with meekness means relying on God's power rather than our own, showing kindness in our interactions, and patiently enduring life's challenges. In this posture, we are promised the inheritance of the earth, symbolizing God's ultimate blessing and provision.

Prayer: Heavenly Father, I come to You this morning seeking the grace to embody meekness. Help me to rely on Your strength and wisdom rather than my own. Grant me a humble and gentle spirit, that I may reflect Your love and patience in all my interactions today. May I trust in Your promise that the meek shall inherit the earth. In Jesus' name, Amen.

Meditative Thought: This morning, I choose meekness, trusting in God's strength and His promise that a humble heart will inherit His blessings.

Scripture: Matthew 5:5
"Blessed are the meek, for they shall inherit the earth."

Reflection: As the day draws to a close, let us reflect on how we lived out meekness. Consider the moments where you showed gentleness, patience, and humility. Were there times when you trusted God's strength over your own? The promise of inheriting the earth reminds us that God rewards those who walk humbly before Him. Let this evening reflection reinforce the value of meekness and inspire us to continue embodying this virtue.

Prayer: Dear Lord, as I end this day, I thank You for teaching me the value of meekness. Forgive me for the moments when I relied on my own strength instead of Yours. Help me to grow in humility and gentleness, trusting in Your promises and Your provision. May I continue to walk in meekness, reflecting Your character to those around me. In Jesus' name, Amen.

Meditative Thought: Tonight, I rest in the assurance that meekness brings God's blessings, and I commit to living humbly and gently, trusting in His promises.

JUNE 27

MORNING DEVOTION

Scripture: Matthew 5:6
"Blessed are those who hunger and thirst for righteousness, for they shall be filled."

Reflection: As we start our day, let's focus on the profound promise Jesus gives in Matthew 5:6. To hunger and thirst for righteousness is to deeply desire to live in accordance with God's will and to seek His presence in every aspect of our lives. This longing is more than a casual wish; it is a passionate pursuit of godliness and justice. When we prioritize righteousness, God promises that we will be filled—our spiritual needs will be met, and we will experience the fullness of His grace and peace. Let this desire for righteousness guide our actions, decisions, and interactions today.

Prayer: Heavenly Father, I come before You this morning with a heart that hungers and thirsts for Your righteousness. Fill me with a deep desire to live according to Your will and to seek Your presence in every part of my life. Help me to make decisions that reflect Your love and justice. Satisfy my soul with Your grace and peace, and guide me in Your paths of righteousness. In Jesus' name, Amen.

Meditative Thought: This morning, I choose to hunger and thirst for righteousness, trusting in God's promise to fill me with His grace and peace.

Scripture: Matthew 5:6
"Blessed are those who hunger and thirst for righteousness, for they shall be filled."

Reflection: As we conclude our day, let's reflect on how we sought righteousness. Did we strive to align our thoughts, words, and actions with God's will? Hungering and thirsting for righteousness means continually seeking God's presence and guidance. Reflecting on our day helps us recognize areas where we succeeded and areas where we can grow. Remember, God's promise is that those who earnestly seek Him will be filled. His grace is abundant, and He meets us where we are, filling us with His love and peace.

Prayer: Dear Lord, as I end this day, I thank You for the promise that those who hunger and thirst for righteousness will be filled. Forgive me for the moments I fell short, and help me to grow in my desire to live according to Your will. Fill me with Your righteousness, and guide me in Your ways. May my life be a reflection of Your love and justice. In Jesus' name, Amen.

Meditative Thought: Tonight, I reflect on my pursuit of righteousness and trust in God's promise to fill me with His grace and peace as I seek Him earnestly.

Scripture: Matthew 5:7
"Blessed are the merciful, for they shall obtain mercy."

Reflection: As we begin our day, let's meditate on the profound truth found in Matthew 5:7. Jesus teaches that those who show mercy will be blessed and will receive mercy in return. Mercy involves compassion, forgiveness, and kindness towards others, even when it is undeserved. This morning, let's commit to being merciful in our interactions. Whether it's forgiving someone who has wronged us, showing kindness to a stranger, or offering help to someone in need, let our actions reflect the mercy that God continually shows us.

Prayer: Heavenly Father, thank You for Your boundless mercy towards me. Help me to be merciful to others as You have been merciful to me. Give me a heart of compassion and forgiveness, and guide my actions today to reflect Your love and grace. Let my life be a testimony of Your mercy. In Jesus' name, Amen.

Meditative Thought: This morning, I will show mercy to others, knowing that as I do, I am reflecting God's love and grace.

Scripture: Matthew 5:7
"Blessed are the merciful, for they shall obtain mercy."

Reflection: As we close the day, let's reflect on how we practiced mercy. Did we extend kindness and forgiveness to those around us? Being merciful means responding to others with the same compassion and grace that God shows us. Reflecting on our day helps us see opportunities where we demonstrated mercy and where we can improve. God's promise is clear: when we are merciful, we will receive mercy. Let this assurance encourage us to continue growing in mercy.

Prayer: Dear Lord, as I end this day, I thank You for the opportunities I had to show mercy. Forgive me for the moments I failed to extend compassion and kindness. Help me to grow in mercy and to reflect Your love more each day. Thank You for Your promise that the merciful will receive mercy. Fill my heart with Your grace and guide me to live a life that honors You. In Jesus' name, Amen.

Meditative Thought: Tonight, I reflect on the mercy I have shown and received, committing to grow in compassion and kindness, following the example of Jesus.

JUNE 29

MORNING DEVOTION

Scripture: Matthew 5:8
"Blessed are the pure in heart, for they shall see God."

Reflection: As we start our day, let us focus on the purity of our hearts. Jesus tells us that the pure in heart are blessed because they will see God. Purity of heart means having a sincere, undivided devotion to God, free from deceit and sin. It involves aligning our thoughts, desires, and actions with God's will. This morning, let us examine our hearts and ask God to cleanse us from anything that separates us from Him. Let our day be guided by a heart that seeks His presence and desires to see Him in every aspect of our lives.

Prayer: Heavenly Father, thank You for the promise that the pure in heart will see You. Cleanse my heart from all impurities and help me to live a life that reflects Your holiness. May my thoughts, words, and actions be pleasing to You today. Give me the strength to resist temptation and to seek Your presence in everything I do. In Jesus' name, Amen.

Meditative Thought: This morning, I commit to having a pure heart, seeking God's presence and guidance in all that I do.

Scripture: Matthew 5:8
"Blessed are the pure in heart, for they shall see God."

Reflection: As we end our day, let us reflect on how we have lived with purity of heart. Did our thoughts, words, and actions reflect a sincere devotion to God? The promise of seeing God is a powerful motivator for maintaining a pure heart. Reflect on the moments when you felt God's presence today and areas where you need His cleansing touch. Ask for His forgiveness for any impurities and thank Him for His grace that purifies our hearts.

Prayer: Dear Lord, as I conclude this day, I thank You for Your grace and mercy. Forgive me for any thoughts, words, or actions that were not pure and pleasing to You. Purify my heart, and help me to live each day with sincerity and devotion to You. Thank You for the promise that the pure in heart will see You. Fill me with Your Spirit and guide me to grow in holiness. In Jesus' name, Amen.

Meditative Thought: Tonight, I reflect on the purity of my heart, seeking God's cleansing and committing to a sincere devotion to Him each day.

JUNE 30

MORNING DEVOTION

Scripture: Matthew 5:9
"Blessed are the peacemakers, for they shall be called sons of God."

Reflection: As we start our day, let us focus on being peacemakers. Jesus calls peacemakers blessed and says they will be called sons of God. Peacemaking involves more than just avoiding conflict; it requires actively promoting reconciliation and harmony in our relationships and communities. This morning, ask God to fill you with His peace so you can extend it to others. Whether at work, home, or in your community, seek ways to build bridges and foster understanding.

Prayer: Heavenly Father, thank You for calling us to be peacemakers and for the promise that we will be called Your children. Fill my heart with Your peace today and help me to bring that peace to others. Show me ways to promote reconciliation and harmony in my relationships. Let my actions reflect Your love and peace. In Jesus' name, Amen.

Meditative Thought: This morning, I commit to being a peacemaker, bringing God's peace and love to every situation I encounter.

EVENING DEVOTION

Scripture: Matthew 5:10
"Blessed are those who are persecuted for righteousness' sake, for theirs is the kingdom of heaven."

Reflection: As we end our day, let us reflect on the challenges we faced in standing up for righteousness. Jesus tells us that those who are persecuted for righteousness' sake are blessed and that the kingdom of heaven belongs to them. Reflect on the times today when you stood up for what is right, even when it was difficult. Remember that enduring persecution for righteousness is a sign of our allegiance to God and His kingdom. Ask for His strength to continue standing firm in your faith.

Prayer: Dear Lord, as I conclude this day, I thank You for the strength to stand up for righteousness. Forgive me for any moments of weakness, and help me to remain steadfast in my faith. Thank You for the promise that those who are persecuted for righteousness' sake are blessed and will inherit the kingdom of heaven. Give me courage to face any opposition and to always seek Your righteousness. In Jesus' name, Amen.

Meditative Thought: Tonight, I reflect on the blessings of standing up for righteousness, remembering that the kingdom of heaven belongs to those who endure persecution for God's sake.

JULY 1

MORNING DEVOTION

Scripture: Matthew 5:11-12

"Blessed are you when they revile and persecute you, and say all kinds of evil against you falsely for My sake. Rejoice and be exceedingly glad, for great is your reward in heaven, for so they persecuted the prophets who were before you."

Reflection: As we begin our day, let's meditate on these words of Jesus. He reminds us that when we face persecution for His sake, we are blessed. It's not easy when people speak ill of us or mistreat us because of our faith, but Jesus encourages us to rejoice in these situations. Why? Because our reward in heaven is great. The prophets faced similar persecution, and we are in good company when we endure for Christ. Let this truth fill you with courage and determination to face whatever challenges come your way today.

Prayer: Lord Jesus, I thank You for the promise that when I face persecution for Your sake, I am blessed. Help me to rejoice even in difficult circumstances, knowing that my reward in heaven is great. Give me the strength to endure and the courage to stand firm in my faith. In Your name, I pray, Amen.

Meditative Thought: Today, I will rejoice in the midst of persecution, knowing that my reward in heaven is great.

JULY 1

EVENING DEVOTION

Scripture: Matthew 5:11-12
"Blessed are you when they revile and persecute you, and say all kinds of evil against you falsely for My sake. Rejoice and be exceedingly glad, for great is your reward in heaven, for so they persecuted the prophets who were before you."

Reflection: As we reflect on the events of the day, let's remember Jesus' words about persecution. When we face opposition or mistreatment because of our faith, it can be disheartening. But Jesus tells us to rejoice and be glad because our reward in heaven is great. Tonight, take comfort in the fact that you are not alone in facing persecution. Many before us, including the prophets, endured similar trials for their faith. Let this knowledge strengthen your resolve to remain faithful to Christ, no matter the cost.

Prayer: Heavenly Father, as I come before You at the close of this day, I thank You for Your presence and strength in the midst of persecution. Help me to hold onto the promise of Your great reward in heaven, especially when I face opposition for Your sake. Give me the courage to continue standing firm in my faith, trusting in Your faithfulness. May Your love and peace fill my heart tonight. In Jesus' name, Amen.

Meditative Thought: Tonight, I find peace and strength in knowing that my reward in heaven is great, even in the face of persecution.

JULY 2

MORNING DEVOTION

Scripture: Romans 8:30
"Moreover whom He predestined, these He also called; whom He called, these He also justified; and whom He justified, these He also glorified."

Reflection: This verse is a powerful reminder of the divine process through which God brings us into His kingdom and perfects us. It speaks of predestination, calling, justification, and glorification—each step demonstrating God's sovereignty and grace in our lives. As we start our day, let's meditate on the assurance that our journey of faith is orchestrated by God. He has a purpose and plan for each of us, and He is faithful to bring it to completion. We are called, justified, and destined for glory through Christ.

Prayer: Dear Lord, thank You for Your divine plan for my life. Thank You for calling me, justifying me, and promising to glorify me. Help me to walk confidently in this assurance today, knowing that You are in control and that Your purposes will be fulfilled in my life. Strengthen my faith and keep my focus on You. Guide my steps and help me to live in a way that honors and glorifies You. In Jesus' name, Amen.

Meditative Thought: Today, I will walk confidently, knowing that I am called, justified, and destined for glory through Christ.

Scripture: Romans 8:30
"Moreover whom He predestined, these He also called; whom He called, these He also justified; and whom He justified, these He also glorified."

Reflection: As we close the day, let us reflect on the incredible journey of faith outlined in this verse. Throughout the day, God has been working in our lives, continuing His divine process of calling, justifying, and preparing us for glory. Despite the challenges or successes we faced today, we can rest in the assurance that God's plan for us is steadfast. He has begun a good work in us and will carry it on to completion. Let this truth bring peace to our hearts as we rest tonight.

Prayer: Heavenly Father, thank You for the assurance that I am part of Your divine plan. As I reflect on the events of this day, I am grateful for Your calling, justification, and the promise of glorification. Help me to trust in Your process and rest in Your sovereignty. As I sleep, may Your peace fill my heart and mind. Strengthen my faith and prepare me for another day of walking in Your purpose. In Jesus' name, Amen.

Meditative Thought: Tonight, I rest in the assurance that God's divine plan is at work in my life, guiding me towards glory through Christ.

Scripture: Psalm 46:10
"Be still, and know that I am God; I will be exalted among the nations, I will be exalted in the earth!"

Reflection: As we start our day, let us take a moment to pause and be still in the presence of God. In the busyness of life, it's easy to become overwhelmed with the tasks and responsibilities ahead of us. However, Psalm 46:10 reminds us of the importance of stillness and the recognition of God's sovereignty. When we take the time to be still, we acknowledge that God is in control and that He is exalted above all our circumstances. This morning, let us commit to starting our day with this truth, trusting that God's presence goes before us and His power sustains us.

Prayer: Heavenly Father, as I begin this day, I come before You with a heart that desires to be still and know that You are God. Help me to quiet my mind and focus on Your presence. Remind me that You are in control of all things and that I can trust You with every aspect of my life. Guide my steps today and help me to bring glory to Your name in all that I do. In Jesus' name, Amen.

Meditative Thought: Take a few moments to sit quietly. Breathe deeply and repeat the phrase, "Be still, and know that I am God." Allow this truth to sink into your heart and mind, bringing peace and clarity as you prepare for the day ahead.

Scripture: Psalm 46:10
"Be still, and know that I am God; I will be exalted among the nations, I will be exalted in the earth!"

Reflection: As the day comes to a close, it's time to reflect on the events that have transpired. In the quiet of the evening, let us once again turn to Psalm 46:10 and be reminded of God's sovereignty. Reflect on how God has been present with you throughout the day, even in the moments when you might not have felt it. His promise to be exalted among the nations and in the earth assures us of His ultimate authority and power. As we prepare for rest, let us surrender our worries and concerns to Him, trusting that He watches over us and will bring us through every situation.

Prayer: Gracious God, as I end this day, I come to You with a heart full of gratitude and reflection. Thank You for being with me through every moment, for guiding my steps and for Your constant presence. I surrender all my worries and concerns to You, knowing that You are in control. Grant me restful sleep and peace as I rest in the assurance of Your sovereignty. May Your name be exalted in my life and in all the earth. In Jesus' name, Amen.

Meditative Thought: In the stillness of the evening, close your eyes and take deep breaths. Repeat the words, "Be still, and know that I am God." Allow this meditation to calm your spirit and prepare you for a peaceful night's rest, enveloped in the love and security of God's presence.

JULY 4

MORNING DEVOTION

Scripture: Proverbs 9:4-6

"Whoever is simple, let him turn in here!" As for him who lacks understanding, she says to him, 'Come, eat of my bread and drink of the wine I have mixed. Forsake foolishness and live, and go in the way of understanding.'"

Reflection: As we begin our day, Proverbs 9:4-6 invites us to seek wisdom and understanding. The passage portrays Wisdom as a gracious host, calling out to those who recognize their need for insight. This morning, let us respond to this invitation by turning away from foolishness and embracing the nourishment that wisdom offers. By choosing to walk in the way of understanding, we set the course for a day filled with purpose and clarity. Let's open our hearts and minds to God's wisdom, allowing it to guide our decisions and interactions throughout the day.

Prayer: Heavenly Father, as I start this day, I ask for Your wisdom and understanding. Help me to forsake foolishness and embrace the guidance You provide. Open my heart to Your teachings and grant me the discernment to make wise choices. May Your wisdom be my guide in every situation I encounter today. In Jesus' name, Amen.

Meditative Thought: Take a few moments to breathe deeply and repeat the phrase, "Come, eat of my bread and drink of the wine I have mixed." Reflect on the nourishment and strength that God's wisdom offers, and invite it to fill your heart and mind as you go about your day.

Scripture: Proverbs 9:4-6
"Whoever is simple, let him turn in here!" As for him who lacks understanding, she says to him, 'Come, eat of my bread and drink of the wine I have mixed. Forsake foolishness and live, and go in the way of understanding.'"

Reflection: As the day draws to a close, we have the opportunity to reflect on how we embraced or perhaps missed the wisdom available to us. Proverbs 9:4-6 offers a gentle reminder that wisdom is always inviting us to come, partake, and live wisely. Consider the moments where you sought understanding and the times you might have acted without it. This evening, let's commit to continually turning towards wisdom, forsaking foolishness, and learning from the experiences of the day. This reflection can prepare our hearts for a peaceful and restorative night.

Prayer: Gracious Lord, as I end this day, I thank You for the wisdom You so freely offer. Forgive me for any moments of foolishness and guide me in understanding and discernment. Help me to learn from today's experiences and to grow in wisdom. Grant me restful sleep and prepare my heart for the day ahead. May I continue to seek Your wisdom and walk in understanding. In Jesus' name, Amen.

Meditative Thought: In the stillness of the evening, close your eyes and take deep, calming breaths. Repeat the words, "Forsake foolishness and live, and go in the way of understanding." Let this meditation bring peace and reflection, allowing you to rest in the knowledge that God's wisdom is with you always.

MORNING DEVOTION

Scripture: Ecclesiastes 12:13-14
"Let us hear the conclusion of the whole matter: Fear God and keep His commandments, For this is man's all. For God will bring every work into judgment, Including every secret thing, Whether good or evil."

Reflection: As we start our day, Ecclesiastes 12:13-14 provides a profound reminder of our purpose and accountability. The essence of life is to fear God and keep His commandments. This morning, let's center our thoughts and actions around this truth. In our daily routines, interactions, and decisions, let us strive to honor God by following His commandments. Recognize that everything we do is seen by God, and He will bring all our actions, even those in secret, into judgment. This awareness should inspire us to live righteously and purposefully, seeking to please God in all things.

Prayer: Heavenly Father, as I begin this new day, I ask for Your guidance and strength to live according to Your commandments. Help me to honor You in all my actions, thoughts, and words. Remind me that my purpose is to fear You and follow Your ways. May my life be a reflection of Your love and righteousness. In Jesus' name, Amen.

Meditative Thought: Take a few moments to sit quietly. Breathe deeply and repeat the phrase, "Fear God and keep His commandments." Let this truth sink into your heart, guiding your intentions and actions throughout the day, with a constant awareness of God's presence and judgment.

JULY 5

EVENING DEVOTION

Scripture: Ecclesiastes 12:13-14
"Let us hear the conclusion of the whole matter: Fear God and keep His commandments, For this is man's all. For God will bring every work into judgment, Including every secret thing, Whether good or evil."

Reflection: As the day comes to a close, reflect on how you have lived in light of Ecclesiastes 12:13-14. Consider whether you have feared God and kept His commandments in your actions and thoughts today. Reflect on both the good and the areas where you fell short. Knowing that God sees and will bring every deed into judgment can encourage us to seek His forgiveness and grace. Use this time to realign your heart with God's purpose for your life, committing to a deeper reverence and obedience to Him.

Prayer: Gracious God, as I reflect on this day, I ask for Your forgiveness for any ways I have fallen short of fearing You and keeping Your commandments. Thank You for Your grace and mercy. Help me to learn from today's experiences and grow in my commitment to live according to Your will. May Your Spirit guide me to make better choices and honor You more fully each day. In Jesus' name, Amen.

Meditative Thought: In the stillness of the evening, close your eyes and take deep breaths. Repeat the words, "For God will bring every work into judgment." Let this meditation bring peace and a sense of accountability, preparing your heart for a restful night's sleep under God's watchful care.

Scripture: Isaiah 44:8

"Do not fear, nor be afraid; Have I not told you from that time, and declared it? You are My witnesses. Is there a God besides Me? Indeed there is no other Rock; I know not one.'"

Reflection: As we begin our day, Isaiah 44:8 provides a powerful reassurance: we are not to fear or be afraid because God is with us. He has declared His sovereignty and faithfulness to us. This morning, let us remember that we are witnesses of God's unfailing love and strength. There is no other rock, no other source of stability and security, besides our God. As we go through our day, let's hold onto this truth and let it shape our perspective and actions. In every challenge and task, let us trust in the unshakeable foundation that is our God.

Prayer: Heavenly Father, as I start this day, I thank You for Your presence and reassurance. Help me to remember that there is no other rock besides You. Guide my steps and give me the courage to face whatever comes my way without fear. May my life be a witness to Your faithfulness and strength. In Jesus' name, Amen.

Meditative Thought: Take a few moments to sit quietly. Breathe deeply and repeat the phrase, "Indeed there is no other Rock." Let this truth settle into your heart, providing strength and confidence as you begin your day, knowing that God is your unshakeable foundation.

Scripture: Isaiah 44:8

"Do not fear, nor be afraid; Have I not told you from that time, and declared it? You are My witnesses. Is there a God besides Me? Indeed there is no other Rock; I know not one.'"

Reflection: As the day comes to an end, Isaiah 44:8 invites us to reflect on God's steadfast presence and the assurance that we need not fear. Throughout the day, God has been our rock, our unchanging foundation. Take time to consider how God's faithfulness has been evident in your life today. Have there been moments when you felt His strength and security? This evening, let us reaffirm our trust in Him, acknowledging that there is no other God, no other rock upon which we can depend. Rest in the knowledge that He is always with us, providing peace and stability.

Prayer: Gracious Lord, as I end this day, I thank You for being my rock and my refuge. Forgive me for any moments of doubt or fear. Help me to rest in Your presence and trust in Your unfailing love. Thank You for guiding me through this day and for the assurance that You are always with me. May I continue to be a witness to Your faithfulness. In Jesus' name, Amen.

Meditative Thought: In the stillness of the evening, close your eyes and take deep, calming breaths. Repeat the words, "Do not fear, nor be afraid." Let this meditation bring peace and a sense of God's steadfast presence, preparing you for a restful night's sleep anchored in His love and security.

Scripture: Daniel 6:11
"Then these men assembled and found Daniel praying and making supplication before his God."

Reflection: As we begin our day, Daniel 6:11 provides a powerful example of dedication and faithfulness in prayer. Despite the threat of persecution, Daniel remained steadfast in his commitment to seek God. This morning, let us be inspired by Daniel's unwavering devotion. In a world filled with distractions and challenges, it's essential to prioritize our time with God. Let Daniel's example encourage us to start our day with prayer and supplication, trusting in God's presence and power. As we face the day's demands, may we remain rooted in our faith, drawing strength and guidance from our time with the Lord.

Prayer: Heavenly Father, as I begin this day, I come before You in prayer, just as Daniel did. Help me to remain steadfast in my faith and commitment to seeking You. Guide my thoughts, words, and actions today, and let Your presence be my strength and refuge. May my life reflect Your love and faithfulness. In Jesus' name, Amen.

Meditative Thought: Take a few moments to sit quietly. Breathe deeply and repeat the phrase, "I will seek You, Lord, in all things." Let this commitment settle into your heart, encouraging you to prioritize prayer and trust in God's guidance throughout your day.

Scripture: Daniel 6:11
"Then these men assembled and found Daniel praying and making supplication before his God."

Reflection: As the day comes to a close, Daniel 6:11 invites us to reflect on our own commitment to prayer and reliance on God. Daniel's faithfulness, even in the face of danger, is a testament to his deep trust in God. This evening, take time to reflect on your day. Have you, like Daniel, made prayer and supplication a priority? Consider how you can strengthen your dedication to seeking God, regardless of the circumstances. As we prepare for rest, let us reaffirm our commitment to be faithful in prayer, trusting that God hears and responds to our supplications.

Prayer: Gracious Lord, as I end this day, I thank You for the example of Daniel's unwavering faithfulness. Forgive me for any moments when I neglected to seek You. Help me to cultivate a heart of prayer and trust in You. Thank You for guiding me through this day and for Your constant presence. May I continue to grow in my commitment to prayer and reliance on Your strength. In Jesus' name, Amen.

Meditative Thought: In the stillness of the evening, close your eyes and take deep, calming breaths. Repeat the words, "I will be faithful in prayer." Let this meditation bring peace and a renewed commitment to seeking God, preparing your heart for a restful night's sleep anchored in His love and faithfulness.

JULY 8

MORNING DEVOTION

Scripture: Matthew 7:6
"Do not give what is holy to the dogs; nor cast your pearls before swine, lest they trample them under their feet, and turn and tear you in pieces."

Reflection: As we begin our day, Matthew 7:6 challenges us to exercise discernment in our interactions and the sharing of our faith and values. Jesus emphasizes the importance of recognizing the preciousness of the truths we hold and the necessity of sharing them wisely. This morning, let us ask God for wisdom to know when and how to share our faith and values, ensuring that they are received with respect and understanding. Let us also seek to discern the right moments and the right audiences for sharing what is sacred to us, so that we can be effective witnesses without facing unnecessary hostility or misunderstanding.

Prayer: Heavenly Father, as I start this day, grant me the wisdom and discernment to know how to share my faith and values appropriately. Help me to recognize when to speak and when to hold back, ensuring that what is holy is treated with the respect it deserves. Guide my interactions today, and let Your Spirit lead me in all that I do. In Jesus' name, Amen.

Meditative Thought: Take a few moments to sit quietly. Breathe deeply and repeat the phrase, "Grant me wisdom and discernment." Let this thought permeate your heart and mind, preparing you to navigate your day with sensitivity and insight.

Scripture: Matthew 7:6
"Do not give what is holy to the dogs; nor cast your pearls before swine, lest they trample them under their feet, and turn and tear you in pieces."

Reflection: As the day comes to a close, Matthew 7:6 invites us to reflect on the interactions and conversations we had today. Did we exercise discernment in sharing our faith and values? Were there moments when we offered what is sacred to those who may not appreciate or respect it? This evening, let us consider how we can improve in wisely stewarding the precious truths we hold. Reflect on how you can better discern when and how to share your faith in a way that honors God and protects the sanctity of what is holy.

Prayer: Gracious Lord, as I end this day, I ask for forgiveness for any times I may have shared what is holy without discernment. Help me to learn from today's experiences and grow in wisdom. Guide me in protecting the sanctity of Your truths and sharing them with those who will receive them with respect. Thank You for Your guidance and presence throughout this day. In Jesus' name, Amen.

Meditative Thought: In the stillness of the evening, close your eyes and take deep, calming breaths. Repeat the words, "Protect what is holy." Let this meditation bring peace and a sense of purpose, preparing your heart for a restful night's sleep anchored in the wisdom and guidance of God.

MORNING DEVOTION

Scripture: Matthew 22:37

"Jesus said to him, 'You shall love the Lord your God with all your heart, with all your soul, and with all your mind.'"

Reflection: As we start our day, Matthew 22:37 reminds us of the greatest commandment: to love the Lord our God with all our heart, soul, and mind. This is a call to total devotion and commitment. This morning, let us reflect on what it means to love God wholeheartedly. Consider how every aspect of our lives—our thoughts, actions, emotions, and desires—can be an expression of our love for God. Let us commit to starting our day with a focus on loving God completely, allowing this love to guide our decisions and interactions throughout the day.

Prayer: Heavenly Father, as I begin this day, help me to love You with all my heart, soul, and mind. May my thoughts, words, and actions reflect my devotion to You. Guide me to live in a way that honors You and demonstrates my love for You in everything I do. Fill me with Your Spirit, so that my love for You will be evident to all those I encounter today. In Jesus' name, Amen.

Meditative Thought: Take a few moments to sit quietly. Breathe deeply and repeat the phrase, "Love the Lord your God with all your heart, soul, and mind." Let this commandment resonate in your heart, setting a foundation of love and devotion as you go through your day.

Scripture: Matthew 22:37
"Jesus said to him, 'You shall love the Lord your God with all your heart, with all your soul, and with all your mind.'"

Reflection: As the day draws to a close, reflect on how you have loved God today. Matthew 22:37 calls us to love God fully and completely. Consider the moments when your thoughts, actions, and emotions reflected this love. Were there times when you fell short? This evening, take time to recommit to this greatest commandment. Seek God's forgiveness for any shortcomings and ask for His strength to love Him more fully. Let this reflection deepen your relationship with God and renew your dedication to living a life that honors Him.

Prayer: Gracious Lord, as I end this day, I reflect on how I have loved You with all my heart, soul, and mind. Forgive me for any moments when I failed to fully devote myself to You. Help me to grow in my love and commitment to You. Thank You for Your unwavering love and grace. Guide me to love You more each day, and may my life be a testament to Your love. In Jesus' name, Amen.

Meditative Thought: In the quiet of the evening, close your eyes and take deep, calming breaths. Repeat the words, "Love the Lord your God with all your heart, soul, and mind." Let this meditation bring peace and a renewed commitment to love God wholeheartedly, preparing your heart for a restful night's sleep in His presence.

JULY 10

MORNING DEVOTION

Scripture: Numbers 6:24-26
"The Lord bless you and keep you; the Lord make His face shine upon you, and be gracious to you; the Lord lift up His countenance upon you, and give you peace."

Reflection: As we begin our day, the blessing from Numbers 6:24-26 offers a profound reminder of God's care and favor. These verses are a declaration of God's protection, grace, and peace over our lives. This morning, let us start by embracing these blessings. Reflect on how God's presence shines upon you, bringing light to your path and grace to your experiences. Consider how His peace, which surpasses all understanding, can guide you throughout the day. As you step into your daily activities, carry this blessing with you, knowing that God's face is shining upon you and He is graciously watching over you.

Prayer: Heavenly Father, as I start this day, I receive Your blessing with a grateful heart. Thank You for Your protection, grace, and peace. May Your face shine upon me and guide my steps today. Help me to be a reflection of Your grace to others, and let Your peace reign in my heart. Thank You for Your constant presence and love. In Jesus' name, Amen.

Meditative Thought: Take a few moments to sit quietly. Breathe deeply and repeat the phrase, "The Lord bless you and keep you." Let this blessing sink into your heart, filling you with a sense of God's love and protection as you begin your day.

Scripture: Numbers 6:24-26
"The Lord bless you and keep you; the Lord make His face shine upon you, and be gracious to you; the Lord lift up His countenance upon you, and give you peace."

Reflection: As the day comes to a close, reflect on the blessings of Numbers 6:24-26. Consider how God has blessed and kept you throughout the day. Reflect on moments where you felt His face shining upon you and His grace in your interactions. Acknowledge the peace that He has provided, even in challenging times. This evening, let us be thankful for God's continuous presence and blessings. As we prepare for rest, may the assurance of His gracious countenance bring us peace and comfort, knowing that we are kept in His loving care.

Prayer: Gracious Lord, as I end this day, I thank You for Your blessings and protection. Thank You for making Your face shine upon me and for Your grace that has carried me through. As I rest tonight, lift up Your countenance upon me and give me peace. May Your presence be with me, bringing comfort and rest. Thank You for Your unfailing love and care. In Jesus' name, Amen.

Meditative Thought: In the stillness of the evening, close your eyes and take deep, calming breaths. Repeat the words, "The Lord give you peace." Let this meditation bring a deep sense of calm and assurance, preparing your heart for a restful night's sleep under the watchful care of God.

Scripture: Proverbs 18:21

"Death and life are in the power of the tongue, and those who love it will eat its fruit."

Reflection: As we begin our day, Proverbs 18:21 reminds us of the immense power our words carry. Each word we speak has the potential to bring life or death, to build up or tear down. This morning, let us be mindful of the impact our words can have on others and ourselves. Consider how you can use your words to encourage, uplift, and bring positivity into the lives of those around you. By choosing words that reflect love, kindness, and truth, we can create an atmosphere of life and growth. Let's start our day with a commitment to speak words that bring life.

Prayer: Heavenly Father, as I begin this day, help me to remember the power of my words. Guide me to speak words of life, encouragement, and truth. May my tongue be an instrument of Your love and grace, bringing positivity and hope to those I encounter. Fill my heart with Your wisdom and let my words reflect Your character. In Jesus' name, Amen.

Meditative Thought: Take a few moments to sit quietly. Breathe deeply and repeat the phrase, "Life and death are in the power of the tongue." Let this truth sink into your heart, guiding you to be intentional with your words throughout the day.

Scripture: Proverbs 18:21
"Death and life are in the power of the tongue, and those who love it will eat its fruit."

Reflection: As the day comes to a close, reflect on the words you have spoken throughout the day. Proverbs 18:21 emphasizes the significance of our words and their ability to impact those around us. Consider moments when your words brought life and encouragement, and times when they may have fallen short. This evening, let us seek forgiveness for any careless words and thank God for the opportunities to speak life. Reflect on how you can continue to use your tongue to build up and bless others, striving to bear the fruit of life-giving words.

Prayer: Gracious Lord, as I end this day, I reflect on the words I have spoken. Forgive me for any words that may have caused harm or discouragement. Thank You for the moments when I could bring life and encouragement to others. Help me to be more mindful of the power of my words and to use them wisely. Fill my heart with Your love and let my speech always reflect Your grace. In Jesus' name, Amen.

Meditative Thought: In the stillness of the evening, close your eyes and take deep, calming breaths. Repeat the words, "The power of the tongue brings life." Let this meditation bring peace and a renewed commitment to speak life-giving words, preparing your heart for a restful night's sleep.

Scripture: Ephesians 2:14-16

"For He Himself is our peace, who has made both one, and has broken down the middle wall of separation, having abolished in His flesh the enmity, that is, the law of commandments contained in ordinances, so as to create in Himself one new man from the two, thus making peace, and that He might reconcile them both to God in one body through the cross, thereby putting to death the enmity."

Reflection: As we begin our day, Ephesians 2:14-16 reminds us of the profound peace and reconciliation that Jesus Christ has brought into our lives. This morning, let us reflect on the peace that Christ has given us and how it can transform our interactions with others. Let us start our day with a heart full of peace, striving to live out this reconciliation in all our relationships.

Prayer: Heavenly Father, as I start this day, I thank You for the peace and reconciliation that Jesus has brought into my life. Help me to live out this peace in my interactions with others. Guide me to be a peacemaker, breaking down walls of division and extending Your love and grace to everyone I meet. May Your peace fill my heart and overflow into all my relationships. In Jesus' name, Amen.

Meditative Thought: Take a few moments to sit quietly. Breathe deeply and repeat the phrase, "He Himself is our peace." Let this truth settle into your heart, filling you with a sense of calm and purpose as you go through your day, committed to living out Christ's reconciliation.

Scripture: Ephesians 2:14-16
"For He Himself is our peace, who has made both one, and has broken down the middle wall of separation, having abolished in His flesh the enmity, that is, the law of commandments contained in ordinances, so as to create in Himself one new man from the two, thus making peace..."

Reflection: As the day comes to a close, Ephesians 2:14-16 invites us to reflect on the peace and reconciliation that Jesus has brought into our lives. Consider how you experienced and shared this peace today. This evening, let us thank God for the reconciliation we have through Jesus and seek His help in extending this peace to others. Let us end our day with a heart full of gratitude and a renewed commitment to live in unity and love.

Prayer: Gracious Lord, as I end this day, I thank You for the peace and reconciliation that Jesus has brought into my life. Forgive me for any moments when I contributed to division or conflict. Help me to be a peacemaker, breaking down walls and extending Your love and grace to others. Guide me to live out this reconciliation in all my relationships. In Jesus' name, Amen.

Meditative Thought: In the stillness of the evening, close your eyes and take deep, calming breaths. Repeat the words, "He has broken down the middle wall of separation." Let this meditation bring peace and a renewed commitment to living out Christ's reconciliation, preparing your heart for a restful night's sleep in His loving presence.

MORNING DEVOTION

Scripture: James 5:18
"And he prayed again, and the heaven gave rain, and the earth produced its fruit."

Reflection: As you begin your day, reflect on the power of persistent prayer as demonstrated by Elijah. His unwavering faith and dedication in seeking God's intervention brought about a miraculous change—rain after a long drought. This serves as a reminder that your prayers have the power to bring about transformation and blessings, no matter how long the wait or how challenging the circumstances.

Prayer: Heavenly Father, As I rise to meet the day, I thank You for Your faithfulness and the power of prayer. Just as Elijah's prayers brought rain and fruitfulness to the earth, I ask that You hear my prayers and bring Your blessings into my life. Guide my actions today so that I may be productive and reflect Your love in all I do. In Jesus' name, I pray. Amen.

Meditative Thought: Imagine the areas of your life that need God's touch and envision His blessings pouring down upon them, bringing growth and renewal. Let this visualization fill you with hope and encouragement for the day ahead.

Scripture: James 5:18
"And he prayed again, and the heaven gave rain, and the earth produced its fruit."

Reflection: As the day draws to a close, take time to reflect on how God has worked in your life today. Consider the moments when you felt His presence and guidance. Think about the ways in which your prayers have been answered, even in small ways, and how God is continually working to bring fruitfulness into your life.

Prayer: Gracious God, Thank You for being with me throughout this day. I am grateful for Your guidance, provision, and the answered prayers I have experienced. As I prepare for rest, I pray that You continue to watch over me and my loved ones. Grant me a peaceful night's sleep and renew my strength for the day ahead. In Jesus' name, I pray. Amen.

Meditative Thought: Spend a few moments in quiet meditation, focusing on the concept of God's provision. Picture the rain falling gently on the earth, symbolizing God's grace and blessings in your life.

MORNING DEVOTION

Scripture: Proverbs 16:1
"The preparations of the heart belong to man, but the answer of the tongue is from the Lord."

Reflection: As you start your day, consider the balance between your plans and God's sovereignty. You make preparations and set goals, but ultimately, it is God who guides your words and actions. Reflect on the idea that while you can plan, true wisdom and direction come from the Lord.

Prayer: Heavenly Father, As I begin this new day, I bring my plans and desires before You. I acknowledge that while I make preparations, it is Your wisdom that truly directs my path. Guide my thoughts, words, and actions today so that they align with Your will. Help me to remain open to Your leading and to trust in Your timing and purpose. Fill me with Your Spirit, that I may speak and act with grace and wisdom. In Jesus' name, I pray. Amen.

Meditative Thought: Take a few moments to meditate on the truth that God is the ultimate source of wisdom and guidance. Visualize handing over your plans and concerns to God, trusting that He will direct your steps. Imagine His presence filling you with peace and clarity, equipping you to face the day with confidence and reliance on His divine wisdom.

Scripture: Proverbs 16:1
"The preparations of the heart belong to man, but the answer of the tongue is from the Lord."

Reflection: As you reflect on your day, consider how your plans unfolded and where you experienced God's guidance. Think about the moments when you felt His presence directing your words and actions. Acknowledge any areas where you relied on your own understanding rather than seeking His wisdom, and bring these before God in prayer.

Prayer: Gracious Lord, Thank You for being with me throughout this day. As I reflect on my plans and the outcomes, I recognize Your hand in guiding my words and actions. Forgive me for the times I relied on my own understanding rather than seeking Your wisdom. I am grateful for Your constant presence and guidance. As I rest tonight, I ask for Your peace to fill my heart and mind. Renew my strength and prepare me for the day ahead. In Jesus' name, I pray. Amen.

Meditative Thought: Close your eyes and take slow, deep breaths. Picture the events of your day, and see God's hand in each moment, guiding and directing you. Let His ongoing presence and care. Allow yourself to rest in the knowledge that God is in control and that He will continue to guide you.

MORNING DEVOTION

Scripture: Ephesians 1:3
"Blessed be the God and Father of our Lord Jesus Christ, who has blessed us with every spiritual blessing in the heavenly places in Christ."

Reflection: As you begin your day, reflect on the abundance of spiritual blessings you have received in Christ. These blessings include God's love, grace, and the promise of eternal life. Consider how these blessings influence your daily life and interactions with others. Think about the ways you can live out these blessings today, showing gratitude to God and sharing His love with those around you.

Prayer: Heavenly Father, I thank You for the countless spiritual blessings You have bestowed upon me through Christ. As I start this new day, help me to remember and appreciate these blessings. Guide my thoughts, words, and actions so that they reflect Your love and grace. Give me the strength to be a blessing to others and to live in a way that honors You. Fill me with Your Spirit and let Your presence be evident in all I do. In Jesus' name, I pray. Amen.

Meditative Thought: Spend a few moments in quiet meditation, focusing on the spiritual blessings you have received. Close your eyes and take deep breaths, allowing yourself to feel God's presence. Visualize these blessings as a radiant light within you, filling you with warmth and peace. As you breathe in, imagine this light growing brighter. As you breathe out, see it extending to those around you, sharing God's love and grace with the world.

JULY 14

EVENING DEVOTION

Scripture: Ephesians 1:3
"Blessed be the God and Father of our Lord Jesus Christ, who has blessed us with every spiritual blessing in the heavenly places in Christ."

Reflection: As the day comes to a close, reflect on how the spiritual blessings you have received in Christ have impacted your day. Think about the moments when you felt God's presence and guidance. Consider how you were able to share His love and grace with others. Acknowledge any challenges you faced and how you can continue to rely on God's blessings in your life.

Prayer: Gracious God, Thank You for the spiritual blessings You have poured into my life through Christ. As I reflect on this day, I am grateful for Your presence and guidance. Forgive me for any moments when I failed to live up to Your calling. Help me to rest in Your grace and renew my spirit for tomorrow. Fill my heart with peace as I sleep, and let Your blessings continue to shape my life. In Jesus' name, I pray. Amen.

Meditative Thought: Take a few moments to meditate on God's blessings. Close your eyes and breathe deeply, allowing yourself to relax and feel God's peace. Picture the blessings you experienced today as a gentle light surrounding you. As you breathe in, feel this light soothing and renewing your spirit. As you breathe out, let go of any stress or worries, trusting in God's continuous provision and care. Rest in the assurance of His love and grace.

JULY 15

MORNING DEVOTION

Scripture: 1 Peter 2:15
"For this is the will of God, that by doing good you may put to silence the ignorance of foolish men."

Reflection: As you begin your day, reflect on the power of doing good. God's will for you includes living a life that demonstrates His love and wisdom. By consistently choosing to do good, you can counteract negativity and ignorance, showing others the reality of God's grace through your actions. Consider how your choices today can reflect God's goodness and serve as a testimony to His love.

Prayer: Heavenly Father, Thank You for the opportunity to start this new day with Your guidance. Help me to understand and follow Your will by doing good in all circumstances. Grant me the strength and wisdom to act in ways that reflect Your love and truth. May my actions today silence any negativity and reveal Your grace to those around me. Fill me with Your Spirit so that I may be a light in the world. In Jesus' name, I pray. Amen.

Meditative Thought: Spend a few moments in quiet meditation, focusing on the concept of doing good. Close your eyes and take deep breaths. Visualize yourself moving through your day, performing acts of kindness and demonstrating integrity. Imagine each good deed as a ripple spreading outwards, impacting others positively. Let this visualization inspire you to act with purpose and love throughout the day.

Scripture: 1 Peter 2:15
"For this is the will of God, that by doing good you may put to silence the ignorance of foolish men."

Reflection: As the day draws to a close, reflect on how you have lived out God's will by doing good. Think about the positive actions you took and how they might have influenced others. Consider any challenges you faced and how you responded to them. Acknowledge areas where you can improve and seek God's guidance to continue growing in goodness.

Prayer: Gracious God, Thank You for being with me throughout this day. I am grateful for the opportunities You provided to do good and reflect Your love. Forgive me for any shortcomings and help me to learn from them. As I rest tonight, renew my strength and prepare me for tomorrow. Guide my heart to continually seek Your will and to silence negativity through acts of kindness and love. In Jesus' name, I pray. Amen.

Meditative Thought: Take a few moments to meditate on your actions today. Close your eyes and breathe deeply, allowing yourself to relax and feel God's peace. Visualize the good you did as lights shining in the darkness, bringing warmth and clarity. As you breathe in, feel God's approval and love filling your heart. As you breathe out, release any stress or regrets, trusting in God's grace and forgiveness. Let this sense of peace and accomplishment guide you into a restful sleep.

JULY 16

MORNING DEVOTION

Scripture: Proverbs 20:27
"The spirit of a man is the lamp of the Lord, searching all the inner depths of his heart."

Reflection: As you start your day, reflect on the idea that your spirit is the lamp of the Lord, illuminating your inner thoughts and intentions. This scripture reminds you that God sees and knows your heart completely. Consider how you can live today with integrity and transparency, allowing God's light to guide your actions and decisions. Reflect on areas where you need God's guidance and wisdom to walk in His ways.

Prayer; Heavenly Father, Thank You for the gift of a new day. I ask that You light my spirit, guiding me to walk in Your truth and wisdom. Search my heart and help me to align my thoughts and actions with Your will. Let Your light shine through me, revealing areas that need growth and change. Grant me the strength to live with integrity and to reflect Your love in all that I do today. In Jesus' name, I pray. Amen.

Meditative Thought: Take a few moments to meditate on the image of your spirit as a lamp illuminated by God's presence. Close your eyes and take deep breaths. Visualize a bright, warm light within you, spreading throughout your entire being. As you breathe in, feel this light filling you with peace and clarity. As you breathe out, imagine it radiating outwards, touching everything you do today. Let this visualization inspire you to live in the light of God's guidance.

Scripture: Proverbs 20:27
"The spirit of a man is the lamp of the Lord, searching all the inner depths of his heart."

Reflection: As the day ends, reflect on how God's light has guided you. Consider the moments when you felt His presence and how it influenced your thoughts and actions. Acknowledge areas where you may have fallen short and need His forgiveness and grace. Think about how your spirit, as the Lord's lamp, has revealed the true intentions of your heart throughout the day.

Prayer: Gracious Lord, Thank You for being with me throughout this day. I am grateful for Your light that searches my heart and guides my spirit. Forgive me for any shortcomings and help me to learn and grow from them. As I prepare for rest, I ask for Your peace to fill my heart and mind. Renew my spirit and grant me the wisdom to follow Your path more closely tomorrow. In Jesus' name, I pray. Amen.

Meditative Thought: Spend a few moments in quiet meditation, focusing on God's light within you. Close your eyes and breathe deeply, allowing yourself to relax. Picture the light of your spirit illuminating the inner depths of your heart. As you breathe in, feel God's peace and forgiveness filling you. As you breathe out, release any worries or regrets from the day. Let this sense of divine light and clarity bring you comfort and prepare you for a restful night's sleep.

MORNING DEVOTION

Scripture: Matthew 7:13-14

"Enter by the narrow gate; for wide is the gate and broad is the way that leads to destruction, and there are many who go in by it. Because narrow is the gate and difficult is the way which leads to life, and there are few who find it."

Reflection: As you begin your day, reflect on the path you choose to follow. Jesus speaks of the narrow gate and the difficult way that leads to life, in contrast to the wide gate and broad way leading to destruction. Consider what it means to choose the narrow path in your daily life. It involves making choices that align with God's will, even when they are challenging or unpopular. Reflect on how you can commit to walking this path today, seeking God's guidance and strength.

Prayer: Heavenly Father, As I start this new day, I seek Your guidance and strength to choose the narrow path that leads to life. Help me to make decisions that honor You, even when they are difficult. Grant me the wisdom to discern Your will and the courage to follow it. Let Your presence be with me, guiding my steps and giving me the strength to stay true to Your path. In Jesus' name, I pray. Amen.

Meditative Thought: Spend a few moments in quiet meditation, focusing on the imagery of the narrow gate and the path that leads to life. Close your eyes and take deep breaths. Visualize yourself standing before the narrow gate, feeling God's presence beside you. As you breathe in, feel a sense of determination and strength filling you. As you breathe out, release any fears or doubts. Let this visualization inspire you to walk the narrow path with confidence and faith throughout your day.

Scripture: Matthew 7:13-14
"Enter by the narrow gate; for wide is the gate and broad is the way that leads to destruction, and there are many who go in by it. Because narrow is the gate and difficult is the way which leads to life, and there are few who find it."

Reflection: As the day comes to a close, reflect on the choices you made and the path you walked today. Consider the moments when you chose the narrow path, and how it felt to align your actions with God's will. Acknowledge any times when you may have strayed towards the broader, easier path, and seek God's forgiveness and guidance to stay true to His way. Reflect on the importance of continuing to seek the narrow gate each day.

Prayer: Gracious Lord, Thank You for being with me throughout this day. I am grateful for the moments when I was able to walk the narrow path and follow Your will. Forgive me for any times I chose the broader, easier way. Help me to learn from these moments and grow in my faith. As I prepare for rest, renew my spirit and strengthen my resolve to seek the narrow gate each day. Fill my heart with Your peace and guide me always. In Jesus' name, I pray. Amen.

Meditative Thought: Spend a few moments in quiet meditation, focusing on the day's journey along the narrow path. Close your eyes and breathe deeply, allowing yourself to relax. Visualize the narrow path you walked today, with its challenges and rewards. As you breathe in, feel a sense of accomplishment and peace. As you breathe out, release any regrets or burdens. Let this meditation bring you a sense of closure and readiness for rest, trusting in God's continued guidance and love.

JULY 18

MORNING DEVOTION

Scripture: Mark 1:22
"And they were astonished at His teaching, for He taught them as one having authority, and not as the scribes."

Reflection: As you start your day, reflect on the authority of Jesus' teachings. Unlike the scribes, Jesus spoke with divine authority, and His words carried power and truth. Consider how His teachings can guide your actions, decisions, and interactions today. Reflect on the areas in your life where you need to embrace His authority and allow His words to transform you.

Prayer: Heavenly Father, Thank You for the gift of this new day and for the teachings of Jesus, which guide and inspire me. Help me to recognize the authority of His words in my life and to follow His teachings with a willing heart. Grant me the wisdom to apply His truths to my daily actions and decisions. Let Your Spirit guide me today, that I may live in a way that reflects Your love and wisdom. In Jesus' name, I pray. Amen.

Meditative Thought: Spend a few moments in quiet meditation, focusing on the authority of Jesus' teachings. Close your eyes and take deep breaths. Visualize Jesus speaking to you, His words filled with power and love. As you breathe in, feel His wisdom filling your heart and mind. As you breathe out, release any resistance to His guidance. Let this visualization inspire you to embrace His teachings fully as you go through your day.

JULY 18

EVENING DEVOTION

Scripture: Mark 1:22
"And they were astonished at His teaching, for He taught them as one having authority, and not as the scribes."

Reflection: As the day comes to a close, reflect on how Jesus' authoritative teachings have influenced your day. Consider the moments when you felt guided by His words and how they impacted your thoughts, actions, and interactions. Acknowledge any areas where you struggled to follow His teachings and seek His forgiveness and strength to do better tomorrow.

Prayer: Gracious Lord, Thank You for being with me throughout this day and for the teachings of Jesus that guide me. I am grateful for the moments when I felt Your presence and followed Your guidance. Forgive me for any times I strayed from Your teachings. As I rest tonight, renew my heart and mind with Your truth. Fill me with Your peace and prepare me for a new day of living under the authority of Jesus' words. In His name, I pray. Amen.

Meditative Thought: Spend a few moments in quiet meditation, focusing on the day's experiences with Jesus' teachings. Close your eyes and breathe deeply, allowing yourself to relax. Visualize the authoritative words of Jesus lighting your path throughout the day. As you breathe in, feel a sense of peace and accomplishment. As you breathe out, release any worries or regrets. Let this meditation bring you comfort and readiness for rest, trusting in God's continuous guidance and love.

Scripture: Acts 8:4
"Therefore those who were scattered went everywhere preaching the word."

Reflection: In this passage, we see the early Christians scattered due to persecution. Despite the hardships, their response was not to hide or despair, but to spread the message of Jesus wherever they went. This teaches us that in times of trial and dispersion, we can turn adversity into an opportunity to share God's love and truth. It challenges us to see every situation, even the difficult ones, as a chance to live out and proclaim our faith. As we start our day, let us consider how we can be a witness to God's goodness in our everyday interactions. Whether we face challenges or smooth sailing, there is always an opportunity to reflect Christ's love and share His word.

Prayer: Heavenly Father, thank You for the example of the early believers who, despite facing great challenges, spread Your word wherever they went. Help us to see opportunities to share Your love in every circumstance. Give us the courage to speak about You and the wisdom to do so with grace. May our actions and words today reflect Your glory. In Jesus' name, Amen.

Meditative Thought: Take a few moments to visualize yourself in various situations you might face today. How can you turn each of these moments into an opportunity to reflect and share God's love? Meditate on the strength and wisdom God provides to be a beacon of His light wherever you go.

Scripture: Acts 8:4
"Therefore those who were scattered went everywhere preaching the word."

Reflection: As we reflect on our day, let's consider the ways we have shared God's word through our actions and conversations. The early Christians' example encourages us to use every circumstance, even the most difficult ones, to witness to others. Think about the interactions you had today – how did you reflect Christ's love? Did you seize opportunities to speak of Him, or let them pass by? Even if we missed some opportunities, God's grace is sufficient. Each day is a new chance to be His witness. Tonight, we can commit to being more mindful of these opportunities tomorrow, trusting that God will guide us and give us the courage we need.

Prayer: Gracious Lord, as we conclude this day, we thank You for Your constant presence and guidance. Forgive us for the times we missed opportunities to share Your love. Help us to be more aware of the chances we have to witness to others. Fill us with Your Spirit so that we may boldly and lovingly proclaim Your word. Refresh us as we rest, and prepare our hearts for a new day to serve You. In Jesus' name, Amen.

Meditative Thought: Spend a few quiet moments reflecting on the day. Where did you see God at work? Where did you feel His prompting to share His word? Consider how you can be more attentive to His leading tomorrow. Let His peace wash over you as you meditate on His faithfulness and your commitment to be His witness.

MORNING DEVOTION

Scripture: Romans 8:28
"And we know that all things work together for good to those who love God, to those who are the called according to His purpose."

Reflection: As we start our day, this verse from Romans reminds us of God's sovereign power and loving purpose in our lives. It's a profound assurance that no matter what we face, God is orchestrating everything for our ultimate good. This doesn't mean that we won't encounter difficulties or suffering, but it reassures us that God can transform every situation to fulfill His divine plan. This morning, reflect on how God has worked in your life so far. Consider the challenges you've faced and how they have shaped you. Trust that today's events, whether good or bad, are being woven into His greater purpose for you.

Prayer: Heavenly Father, thank You for the promise that You work all things together for good for those who love You. Help me to trust in Your plan, even when I don't understand my circumstances. Guide me today to walk in Your purpose and to see Your hand at work in every situation. Fill me with peace and confidence in Your unfailing love. In Jesus' name, Amen.

Meditative Thought: Take a few moments to meditate on the idea that God is working in every aspect of your life. Visualize handing over today's worries and plans to Him, trusting that He will use them for good. Let this assurance bring you peace and focus as you begin your day.

Scripture: Romans 8:28
"And we know that all things work together for good to those who love God, to those who are the called according to His purpose."

Reflection: As the day draws to a close, we can find comfort and reassurance in reflecting on this promise from Romans. Think back on the events of the day—both the moments of joy and the challenges. How can you see God's hand in them? Even if some situations remain unresolved or difficult, trust that God is weaving them into His perfect plan for your life. This verse encourages us to hold onto hope and faith, knowing that God's purposes are always good. As we rest tonight, let's remember that our lives are in His capable hands.

Prayer: Gracious Father, thank You for the assurance that You are working all things together for my good. As I reflect on this day, help me to see Your hand at work in my life. Thank You for Your constant presence and guidance. Give me peace as I rest tonight, and renew my strength for tomorrow. Help me to continue to trust in Your perfect plan. In Jesus' name, Amen.

Meditative Thought: Spend a few quiet moments reflecting on the events of the day. How has God been present in your experiences? Meditate on the promise that He is working everything together for good. Allow this truth to bring you peace and rest, knowing that you are called according to His purpose.

JULY 21

MORNING DEVOTION

Scripture: Philippians 4:6-7
"Be anxious for nothing, but in everything by prayer and supplication, with thanksgiving, let your requests be made known to God; and the peace of God, which surpasses all understanding, will guard your hearts and minds through Christ Jesus."

Reflection: As we begin our day, these verses remind us to approach God with our worries and needs through prayer and supplication, accompanied by thanksgiving. Instead of letting anxiety take hold, we are encouraged to entrust our concerns to God, knowing that He listens and cares deeply for us. This act of faith and trust opens our hearts to the peace of God, a peace that is beyond our understanding and capable of guarding our hearts and minds in Christ Jesus. Starting the day with a heart of gratitude and a spirit of prayer sets a tone of calm and trust. Reflect on what is causing you anxiety today and bring it before God. Trust that His peace will fill you and guide you throughout the day.

Prayer: Heavenly Father, thank You for the assurance that I can bring all my worries and needs to You. Help me to approach today with a heart of thanksgiving and trust in Your perfect peace. Guard my heart and mind through Christ Jesus as I face the challenges and opportunities of this day. May Your peace, which surpasses all understanding, fill me and guide me. In Jesus' name, Amen.

Meditative Thought: Spend a few moments in quiet meditation. Visualize handing over your anxieties to God, one by one, and feel His peace filling your heart and mind. Let this peace remain with you as you move through your day, a constant reminder of God's presence and care.

Scripture: Philippians 4:6-7
"Be anxious for nothing, but in everything by prayer and supplication, with thanksgiving, let your requests be made known to God; and the peace of God, which surpasses all understanding, will guard your hearts and minds through Christ Jesus."

Reflection: As the day comes to an end, reflect on how you handled your worries and stresses. Did you bring your anxieties to God in prayer? Did you thank Him for His blessings? This evening is an opportunity to let go of any lingering anxieties and to rest in God's peace. Remember that God invites you to cast all your cares on Him, and He promises His peace in return. This peace is a gift that guards our hearts and minds, allowing us to rest secure in His love and provision. Reflect on your day, acknowledge your anxieties, and release them to God, trusting in His peace.

Prayer: Gracious Lord, thank You for guiding me through this day. I bring before You any anxieties and worries that remain. Thank You for the many blessings You have given me. Please fill me with Your peace that surpasses all understanding, and guard my heart and mind as I rest tonight. Help me to trust in Your provision and care, and renew my strength for tomorrow. In Jesus' name, Amen.

Meditative Thought: Take a few moments to breathe deeply and slowly. Visualize God's peace as a gentle light that envelops you, calming your mind and heart. Reflect on the blessings of the day and express gratitude to God. As you prepare for sleep, let go of any remaining worries, trusting that God's peace will guard you through the night.

Scripture: 2 Timothy 2:11-12
"This is a faithful saying: For if we died with Him, we shall also live with Him. If we endure, we shall also reign with Him. If we deny Him, He also will deny us."

Reflection: As we begin our day, this passage reminds us of the profound truth of our identity in Christ. The assurance that if we have died with Him, we will also live with Him, gives us a sense of eternal hope and purpose. It calls us to endurance, reminding us that our perseverance in faith leads to reigning with Christ. Conversely, it warns us of the consequences of denying Him. Reflect on the commitment and perseverance in your faith journey. Starting today with this mindset can inspire you to live a life that truly reflects your beliefs. Consider how you can endure in faith through the day's challenges, remembering that our struggles are temporary and that our ultimate reward is eternal life with Christ.

Prayer: Heavenly Father, thank You for the promise of eternal life with You through Christ. Help me to endure through today's challenges with faith and perseverance. Strengthen my commitment to live according to Your will and to reflect Your love in all I do. Keep me mindful of the eternal reward that awaits those who faithfully follow You. In Jesus' name, Amen.

Meditative Thought: Spend a few minutes in quiet meditation, contemplating the meaning of living and reigning with Christ. Visualize the strength and endurance Christ provides, empowering you to face the day. Let this assurance fill you with confidence and peace, knowing that your efforts in faith are not in vain.

Scripture: 2 Timothy 2:11-12
"This is a faithful saying: For if we died with Him, we shall also live with Him. If we endure, we shall also reign with Him. If we deny Him, He also will deny us."

Reflection: As the day draws to a close, take time to reflect on how you lived out your faith today. Did you face challenges with endurance? Were there moments when you felt tempted to deny your faith, or did you stand firm in your beliefs? This passage reminds us of the significance of our daily choices in our walk with Christ. Reflect on the times you felt God's presence and strength helping you to endure. Consider any areas where you may need to seek forgiveness and recommit to living faithfully. Knowing that our faithfulness leads to reigning with Christ gives us hope and encouragement to keep pressing on.

Prayer: Gracious Lord, thank You for guiding me through this day. As I reflect on my actions and choices, I ask for Your forgiveness where I have fallen short. Strengthen my resolve to endure in faith and to live according to Your will. Thank You for the promise of eternal life with You. May Your presence be with me as I rest, renewing my spirit for tomorrow. In Jesus' name, Amen.

Meditative Thought: Take a few moments to sit quietly, breathing slowly and deeply. Reflect on the promise of living and reigning with Christ. Allow this truth to bring you peace and rest. Visualize letting go of any burdens or worries from today, entrusting them to God's care. Let the assurance of His eternal promise fill you with hope and calm as you prepare for sleep.

JULY 23

MORNING DEVOTION

Scripture: 2 Peter 1:5-7
"But also for this very reason, giving all diligence, add to your faith virtue, to virtue knowledge, to knowledge self-control, to self-control perseverance, to perseverance godliness, to godliness brotherly kindness, and to brotherly kindness love."

Reflection: As we start our day, this passage from 2 Peter outlines a beautiful progression of spiritual growth. It begins with faith, the foundation of our relationship with God, and builds upon it with. Each quality is a step towards becoming more like Christ, and we are called to diligently cultivate these attributes in our lives. Reflect on each step mentioned and consider how you can apply them today. How can you demonstrate virtue in your actions? How can you grow in knowledge and exercise self-control? In what ways can you show perseverance, godliness, brotherly kindness, and love? Let this scripture guide you as you strive to grow spiritually throughout the day.

Prayer: Heavenly Father, thank You for providing a path for spiritual growth through Your word. Help me to diligently add to my faith the qualities that reflect Your nature. Guide me in demonstrating virtue, increasing in knowledge, exercising self-control, persevering through challenges, living in godliness, showing brotherly kindness, and loving others. May these attributes shine through me today and bring glory to Your name. In Jesus' name, Amen.

Meditative Thought: Spend a few moments meditating on each attribute listed in the scripture. Visualize how you can incorporate each quality into your actions and interactions today. Allow God's Spirit to inspire and empower you to grow in these areas, bringing you closer to His likeness.

Scripture: 2 Peter 1:5-7
"But also for this very reason, giving all diligence, add to your faith virtue, to virtue knowledge, to knowledge self-control, to self-control perseverance, to perseverance godliness, to godliness brotherly kindness, and to brotherly kindness love."

Reflection: As the day ends, take time to reflect on how you applied these virtues in your life. Did you manage to add to your faith with actions of virtue? Did you seek knowledge and practice self-control? How did you persevere through challenges? Reflect on your demonstration of godliness, brotherly kindness, and love. This passage not only guides us to grow spiritually but also serves as a mirror to evaluate our daily walk with Christ. Acknowledge the areas where you succeeded and those where you need more growth. Remember, spiritual growth is a continuous journey. Celebrate your progress and ask for God's help in areas where you struggle.

Prayer: Gracious Father, thank You for guiding me through this day. As I reflect on my actions, I thank You for the moments where I was able to add to my faith with virtue, knowledge, self-control, perseverance, godliness, brotherly kindness, and love. Forgive me for the times I fell short and help me to grow in these areas. Strengthen my resolve to diligently pursue spiritual growth. May Your Spirit continue to work in me, molding me to be more like Christ. In Jesus' name, Amen.

Meditative Thought: Take a few minutes to quietly reflect on the day. Think about each virtue and how it manifested in your actions. Visualize any moments of struggle and hand them over to God, asking for His guidance and strength. Let His peace fill your heart, knowing that He is at work in you, perfecting your faith and character.

JULY 24

MORNING DEVOTION

Scripture: 1 John 1:7
"But if we walk in the light as He is in the light, we have fellowship with one another, and the blood of Jesus Christ His Son cleanses us from all sin."

Reflection: As we start our day, this verse from 1 John calls us to walk in the light of Christ. Walking in the light means living in truth, righteousness, and transparency before God and others. It promises fellowship with other believers and assures us of the cleansing power of Jesus' blood, which purifies us from all sin. Reflect on what it means to walk in the light today. Consider how you can live honestly and righteously, maintaining fellowship with others and allowing Christ's light to shine through you. Let this scripture guide you in seeking a life that reflects God's purity and grace.

Prayer: Heavenly Father, thank You for calling me to walk in the light as You are in the light. Help me to live today with honesty, integrity, and transparency. Guide me in maintaining fellowship with others and in reflecting Your love and truth in all I do. Thank You for the cleansing power of Jesus' blood that purifies me from all sin. May Your light shine through me today. In Jesus' name, Amen.

Meditative Thought: Spend a few moments in quiet meditation, visualizing yourself walking in the light of Christ. Imagine His light illuminating your path, guiding your actions, and purifying your heart. Let this vision inspire you to live out your day in a way that honors God and strengthens your fellowship with others.

Scripture: 1 John 1:7
"But if we walk in the light as He is in the light, we have fellowship with one another, and the blood of Jesus Christ His Son cleanses us from all sin."

Reflection: As the day comes to an end, reflect on how you walked in the light today. Did you live in truth and righteousness? Did you maintain honest and transparent relationships with others? This verse reassures us that as we strive to walk in the light, we enjoy fellowship with fellow believers and experience the ongoing cleansing power of Jesus' sacrifice. Consider the moments when you felt close to God and others, and acknowledge any times you may have strayed from the light. Seek His forgiveness and thank Him for His grace that continually cleanses and restores you.

Prayer: Gracious Lord, thank You for guiding me through this day. As I reflect on my actions, I ask for Your forgiveness for any moments I did not walk in Your light. Thank You for the fellowship I experienced with others and for the cleansing power of Jesus' blood. Help me to continue growing in truth and righteousness. Renew my spirit as I rest tonight, and prepare me to walk in Your light again tomorrow. In Jesus' name, Amen.

Meditative Thought: Take a few moments to sit quietly and reflect on the day. Visualize the light of Christ surrounding you, cleansing you from all sin and restoring your fellowship with God and others. Let His light bring you peace and rest, knowing that His grace is always sufficient. As you prepare for sleep, commit to walking in His light anew each day.

Scripture: Jude 1:4

"For certain men have crept in unnoticed, who long ago were marked out for this condemnation, ungodly men, who turn the grace of our God into lewdness and deny the only Lord God and our Lord Jesus Christ."

Reflection: As we begin our day, let's reflect on the warning given in Jude 1:4. The passage reminds us of the importance of discernment and vigilance in our faith. It speaks of false teachers who distort the grace of God and lead others astray by denying the Lordship of Jesus Christ. This serves as a reminder to guard ourselves against deception and to hold fast to the truth of the Gospel. Consider the influence of the teachings you encounter today. Are they in line with the truth of God's Word? Are they leading you closer to Jesus or away from Him? Let this passage prompt you to stay rooted in the truth and to be vigilant against false teachings that may lead you astray.

Prayer: Heavenly Father, I thank You for Your Word that guides and instructs me. Grant me wisdom and discernment as I navigate through this day. Help me to recognize and reject any false teachings that distort Your grace and deny the lordship of Jesus Christ. Keep me firmly rooted in the truth of Your Word and strengthen my faith to withstand deception. May Your Holy Spirit lead me into all truth. In Jesus' name, Amen.

Meditative Thought: Take a few moments to meditate on the importance of discernment in your faith journey. Pray for a discerning spirit and ask the Holy Spirit to help you recognize and reject any falsehood that may come your way. Let His peace fill your heart as you commit to staying grounded in the truth throughout the day.

Scripture: Jude 1:4
"For certain men have crept in unnoticed, who long ago were marked out for this condemnation, ungodly men, who turn the grace of our God into lewdness and deny the only Lord God and our Lord Jesus Christ."

Reflection: As the day comes to a close, let's reflect on the warning given in Jude 1:4. The passage reminds us of the subtle dangers of false teachings that can infiltrate our faith community. It warns against those who pervert the grace of God and deny the lordship of Jesus Christ. This serves as a sobering reminder to remain vigilant and discerning in our faith, guarding against influences that may lead us away from the truth. Reflect on how you responded to these influences and whether you remained rooted in the truth.

Prayer: Lord, as I reflect on this day, I am grateful for Your faithfulness and protection. Forgive me for any moments when I may have been swayed by false teachings or influences that distort Your truth. Grant me discernment and wisdom to recognize and reject anything that denies Your lordship and perverts Your grace. Help me to stand firm in Your truth and to remain grounded in Your Word. Guide me as I navigate through each day, keeping my eyes fixed on You. In Jesus' name, Amen.

Meditative Thought: Take a moment to quiet your mind and heart before God. Reflect on the ways you encountered false teachings or influences today. Ask the Holy Spirit to reveal any areas where you may have been led astray and to strengthen your resolve to stand firm in the truth. Surrender any fears or doubts to God, trusting in His faithfulness to protect and guide you. As you prepare for rest, find peace in knowing that He is with you, guarding you against deception and leading you into His truth.

JULY 26

MORNING DEVOTION

Scripture: Revelation 21:5
"Then He who sat on the throne said, 'Behold, I make all things new.' And He said to me, 'Write, for these words are true and faithful.'"

Reflection: As we begin our day, let's meditate on the promise found in Revelation 21:5. In this verse, God declares that He will make all things new. This powerful statement reminds us of God's sovereignty and His ability to bring about transformation and renewal in our lives and in the world around us. It speaks of hope, restoration, and the fulfillment of God's ultimate plan for His creation. Reflect on areas of your life that may be in need of renewal. Perhaps you are facing challenges, struggles, or uncertainties. Take comfort in knowing that God is at work, making all things new according to His perfect will. Allow this promise to fill you with hope and anticipation for the day ahead, trusting in God's faithfulness to fulfill His promises.

Prayer: Heavenly Father, thank You for the promise of renewal and transformation found in Revelation 21:5. Today, I entrust to You all areas of my life that are in need of Your touch. I pray for Your guidance, wisdom, and strength to navigate through challenges and uncertainties. Help me to trust in Your faithfulness and to rest in the assurance that You are making all things new according to Your perfect plan. May Your will be done in my life today. In Jesus' name, Amen.

Meditative Thought: Take a few moments to quiet your heart and mind before God. Visualize His presence surrounding you, bringing renewal and transformation to every aspect of your life. Reflect on the areas where you long for His touch and invite Him to work in those areas today. Surrender your worries and fears to Him, trusting in His promise to make all things new.

Scripture: Revelation 21:5
"Then He who sat on the throne said, 'Behold, I make all things new.'
And He said to me, 'Write, for these words are true and faithful.'"

Reflection: As the day comes to a close, let's reflect on the promise found
in Revelation 21:5. This verse reminds us of God's power and faithfulness to make all things new. It speaks of His ongoing work of renewal
and transformation in our lives and in the world around us. Even in the
midst of challenges and struggles, we can trust in God's promise to bring
about newness and restoration according to His perfect plan. Reflect on
the ways you have experienced God's renewal and transformation today.
Perhaps you have seen glimpses of His work in your life or in the lives
of others. Take a moment to thank God for His faithfulness and for the
ways He is making all things new.

Prayer: Gracious God, as I reflect on this day, I am grateful for Your
promise to make all things new. Thank You for Your ongoing work of
renewal and transformation in my life and in the world around me. Help
me to trust in Your faithfulness, even in the midst of challenges and uncertainties. Give me eyes to see Your hand at work and a heart that is
open to Your leading. May Your will be done in my life, now and always.
In Jesus' name, Amen.

Meditative Thought: Take a few moments to sit in silence before God.
Reflect on the ways you have seen His renewal and transformation at
work in your life today. Thank Him for His faithfulness and for His
promise to make all things new. Surrender any worries or fears to Him,
trusting in His ongoing work of restoration. As you prepare for rest, allow
His peace to fill you and renew your spirit, knowing that He is faithful
to fulfill His promises.

Scripture: Genesis 8:4
"Then the ark rested in the seventh month, the seventeenth day of the month, on the mountains of Ararat."

Reflection: As we begin our day, let's reflect on the significance of this verse from Genesis. After enduring the flood for many days, Noah and his family experienced a moment of rest when the ark finally came to rest on the mountains of Ararat. This moment marked the end of their journey through the storm and the beginning of a new chapter in God's plan for humanity. Consider the storms you may be facing in your own life. Just as Noah found rest in the midst of the floodwaters, may this verse remind you that God is with you in the midst of your trials. Trust in His faithfulness to bring you through the storms and lead you to a place of rest and renewal.

Prayer: Heavenly Father, thank You for Your faithfulness in the midst of life's storms. Like Noah, I trust in Your promise to guide me through difficult times and to bring me to a place of rest and renewal. Help me to anchor my faith in You, knowing that You are with me always. Grant me strength and courage for the day ahead, and may Your peace fill my heart as I face whatever challenges come my way. In Jesus' name, Amen.

Meditative Thought: Take a few moments to meditate on the image of the ark coming to rest on the mountains of Ararat. Imagine the peace and relief Noah and his family must have felt after enduring the storm for so long. Reflect on the storms in your own life and imagine God's presence bringing you peace and rest in the midst of them. Allow His peace to fill you as you start your day, knowing that He is with you always.

Scripture: Genesis 8:4
"Then the ark rested in the seventh month, the seventeenth day of the month, on the mountains of Ararat."

Reflection: As the day draws to a close, let's reflect on the significance of Genesis 8:4. This verse marks a moment of rest and renewal for Noah and his family after enduring the floodwaters for many days. It reminds us of God's faithfulness to bring us through the storms of life and to lead us to places of rest and restoration. Consider the moments of rest and renewal you experienced today, no matter how small they may seem. Give thanks to God for His faithfulness in providing those moments of respite. Reflect on any challenges or trials you faced, knowing that God is with you through them all, just as He was with Noah in the ark.

Prayer: Gracious God, as I reflect on this day, I am grateful for the moments of rest and renewal You provided. Thank You for Your faithfulness in guiding me through life's storms and for Your presence that brings peace in the midst of trials. Help me to trust in Your plan and to find rest in Your presence each day. Grant me a peaceful night's rest and renew my strength for the day ahead. In Jesus' name, Amen.

Meditative Thought: Take a few moments to quiet your mind and heart before God. Reflect on the ways He provided moments of rest and renewal for you today. Give thanks for His faithfulness in guiding you through life's storms. Surrender any worries or fears to Him, trusting in His plan for your life. As you prepare for sleep, allow His peace to fill you and renew your spirit, knowing that He is with you always.

MORNING DEVOTION

Scripture: Psalm 23:1
"The Lord is my shepherd; I shall not want."

Reflection: As we begin our day, let's meditate on the comforting words of Psalm 23:1. In this verse, David declares the Lord as his shepherd, indicating a deep and personal relationship with God. By acknowledging God as our shepherd, we affirm His care, guidance, and provision in our lives. David's declaration that he shall not want reflects a profound trust in God's ability to meet all his needs. Reflect on the ways in which God has shepherded you in the past. Consider the times He has provided for you, protected you, and guided you through difficult circumstances. As you face the challenges of the day ahead, trust in God's provision and guidance, knowing that He is your faithful shepherd who will lead you in paths of righteousness.

Prayer: Heavenly Father, I thank You for being my shepherd, guiding me and providing for me each day. Help me to trust in Your provision and to follow Your lead in all aspects of my life. When I face challenges, remind me of Your faithfulness and reassure me that I shall not want. Grant me wisdom and discernment to recognize Your guidance throughout this day. In Jesus' name, Amen.

Meditative Thought: Take a few moments to quiet your mind and heart before God. Visualize the Lord as your shepherd, leading you beside still waters and restoring your soul. Reflect on His provision and protection in your life, and thank Him for His faithfulness. Surrender any worries or fears to Him, trusting that He will lead you in paths of righteousness. As you go about your day, carry with you the assurance that you shall not want, for the Lord is your shepherd.

Scripture: Psalm 23:1
"The Lord is my shepherd; I shall not want."

Reflection: As the day comes to a close, let's reflect on the comforting truth of Psalm 23:1. David's declaration that the Lord is his shepherd speaks of a deep intimacy and trust in God's care and provision. In acknowledging God as our shepherd, we affirm His presence in our lives, guiding us through both green pastures and dark valleys. Reflect on the ways in which God has shepherded you throughout this day. Consider the moments of provision, guidance, and protection you have experienced. Even in times of challenge or uncertainty, trust in God's faithful care and provision. Let His presence bring you comfort and peace as you rest tonight.

Prayer: Gracious God, as I reflect on this day, I thank You for being my shepherd and guiding me through its challenges and joys. Help me to trust in Your provision and to rest in Your care. Forgive me for the times when I have doubted Your faithfulness. Renew my spirit as I rest tonight, and grant me the assurance that I shall not want, for You are with me always. In Jesus' name, Amen.

Meditative Thought: Reflect on the ways He has shepherded you throughout this day, guiding you in paths of righteousness and providing for your needs. Surrender any worries or fears to Him, trusting in His faithful care. As you prepare for sleep, let His presence bring you comfort and peace, knowing that He is your shepherd who will lead you through every season of life.

Scripture: Corinthians 10:12

"Therefore let him who thinks he stands take heed lest he fall."

Reflection: As we begin our day, let's reflect on the cautionary message of 1 Corinthians 10:12. This verse serves as a reminder that self-assurance can sometimes lead to complacency and spiritual vulnerability. It warns against the danger of pride and encourages us to remain humble and vigilant in our faith journey. Reflect on your own spiritual walk. Are there areas where you have become complacent or overconfident? Take a moment to examine your heart and ask God to reveal any areas of pride or self-reliance. Let this verse prompt you to rely more fully on God's strength and grace, recognizing your need for His guidance and protection.

Prayer: Heavenly Father, I thank You for Your constant presence and guidance in my life. Help me to remain humble and vigilant in my faith journey. Show me any areas where I have become complacent or over-confident, and give me the strength to surrender them to You. May I rely fully on Your grace and guidance, recognizing my need for You in every aspect of my life. In Jesus' name, Amen.

Meditative Thought: Take a few moments to meditate on the warning of 1 Corinthians 10:12. Visualize yourself standing humbly before God, acknowledging your need for His strength and guidance. Reflect on any areas of pride or self-reliance in your life, and surrender them to God in prayer. Allow His Spirit to fill you with humility and dependence on Him as you prepare to face the day ahead.

Scripture: Corinthians 10:12
"Therefore let him who thinks he stands take heed lest he fall."

Reflection: As the day comes to a close, let's reflect on the sobering reminder of 1 Corinthians 10:12. This verse challenges us to examine our spiritual posture and guard against the pitfalls of pride and self-assurance. It serves as a warning to remain humble and vigilant in our walk with God, recognizing our constant need for His strength and guidance. Reflect on the events of the day. Were there moments when you relied too heavily on your own abilities or became complacent in your faith? Take a moment to confess any pride or self-reliance to God and ask for His forgiveness and grace. Let this verse prompt you to renew your commitment to humble dependence on God as you rest tonight.

Prayer: Gracious God, as I reflect on this day, I acknowledge my need for Your grace and guidance in every aspect of my life. Forgive me for the times when I have relied too heavily on my own strength or become complacent in my faith. Help me to remain humble and vigilant, always mindful of my need for You. Thank You for Your constant presence and love. Renew my spirit as I rest tonight, and grant me the grace to walk humbly before You each day. In Jesus' name, Amen.

Meditative Thought: Take a few moments to meditate on the warning of 1 Corinthians 10:12. Visualize yourself surrendering any pride or self-reliance to God, and ask for His grace to keep you humble and dependent on Him. Reflect on His faithfulness and love, and rest in the assurance that He is with you always, guiding and protecting you. As you prepare for sleep, let His peace fill your heart, knowing that He is your strength and refuge.

Scripture: Psalm 119:105
"Your word is a lamp to my feet and a light to my path."

Reflection: As we begin our day, let's reflect on the profound truth of Psalm 119:105. This verse beautifully illustrates the importance of God's word in guiding and illuminating our lives. Just as a lamp provides light to guide our steps in the darkness, so does God's word illuminate our path and provide direction for our journey through life. Reflect on the significance of God's word in your life. How has His word provided guidance, wisdom, and comfort to you in the past? Take a moment to thank God for the gift of His word and ask Him to continue to illuminate your path as you navigate through the day ahead.

Prayer: Heavenly Father, I thank You for Your word, which is a lamp to my feet and a light to my path. Help me to treasure Your word and to meditate on it day and night. Guide me by Your Spirit as I seek to live according to Your will. May Your word continue to provide wisdom, direction, and comfort in every aspect of my life. In Jesus' name, Amen.

Meditative Thought: Take a few moments to meditate on the imagery of Psalm 119:105. Visualize God's word shining brightly before you, illuminating your path and guiding your steps. Reflect on the times when His word has provided clarity and direction in your life. Ask the Holy Spirit to deepen your love for God's word and to help you apply its truths to your daily life. As you prepare to face the day, trust in God's guidance and take comfort in the light of His word.

Scripture: Psalm 119:105
"Your word is a lamp to my feet and a light to my path."

Reflection: As the day comes to a close, let's reflect on the enduring truth of Psalm 119:105. This verse reminds us that God's word is not only a source of guidance and direction but also a source of comfort and assurance. In moments of darkness and uncertainty, His word shines brightly, illuminating our path and leading us to safety. Reflect on the ways in which God's word has guided and comforted you throughout the day. Were there moments when a particular scripture came to mind, providing encouragement or clarity? Take a moment to thank God for His faithfulness in illuminating your path and ask Him to continue to be your guiding light as you rest tonight.

Prayer: Gracious God, as I reflect on this day, I am grateful for the light of Your word that has guided and comforted me. Thank You for Your faithfulness in illuminating my path and leading me in Your ways. As I rest tonight, I pray that Your word would continue to be a lamp to my feet and a light to my path. Renew my spirit as I sleep, and grant me Your peace that surpasses all understanding. In Jesus' name, Amen.

Meditative Thought: Take a few moments to meditate on the truth of Psalm 119:105. Visualize God's word shining brightly before you, guiding and comforting you in every circumstance. Reflect on the ways His word has been a source of strength and encouragement throughout the day. Surrender any worries or fears to Him, trusting in His faithfulness to lead you safely through the night. As you prepare for sleep, take comfort in the light of His word, knowing that He is with you always.

JULY 31

MORNING DEVOTION

Scripture: Hebrews 4:12
"For the word of God is living and powerful, and sharper than any two-edged sword, piercing even to the division of soul and spirit, and of joints and marrow, and is a discerner of the thoughts and intents of the heart."

Reflection: As we begin our day, let's reflect on the profound truth of Hebrews 4:12. This verse describes the Word of God as living and powerful, capable of penetrating to the deepest parts of our being. It reminds us that God's Word is not merely a collection of letters and stories but a living entity that has the power to transform our lives from the inside out. Reflect on the impact of God's Word in your life. How has it brought clarity, conviction, and transformation? Take a moment to thank God for the gift of His Word and ask Him to continue to speak to you through its pages. Allow this verse to inspire you to engage with Scripture daily, allowing it to penetrate your heart and guide your thoughts and actions.

Prayer: Heavenly Father, thank You for the gift of Your Word, which is living and powerful. Help me to approach Your Word with reverence and humility, knowing that it has the power to transform my life. Open my heart and mind to receive Your truth and guidance as I study Scripture today. May Your Word penetrate every aspect of my being and lead me closer to You. In Jesus' name, Amen.

Meditative Thought: Take a few moments to reflect on the areas of your life where you need God's truth and transformation. Surrender those areas to Him, inviting His Word to penetrate and renew you from the inside out.

Scripture: Hebrews 4:12
"For the word of God is living and powerful, and sharper than any two-edged sword, piercing even to the division of soul and spirit, and of joints and marrow, and is a discerner of the thoughts and intents of the heart."

Reflection: As the day comes to a close, let's reflect on the profound truth of Hebrews 4:12. This verse reminds us of the living and powerful nature of God's Word, which has the ability to penetrate to the deepest parts of our being. It serves as a reminder of the transformative power of Scripture in our lives, convicting us of sin, revealing truth, and guiding us in the ways of righteousness. Reflect on the ways in which God's Word has spoken to you throughout the day. Were there moments when a particular verse or passage convicted your heart or brought clarity to a situation? Take a moment to thank God for His Word and ask Him to continue to speak to you through its pages, guiding and transforming you according to His will.

Prayer: Gracious God, thank You for the gift of Your living and powerful Word. As I reflect on this day, I am grateful for the ways in which Your Word has spoken to me, convicting my heart and guiding my steps. Help me to continue to engage with Scripture daily. May Your Word continue to be a lamp to my feet and a light to my path. In Jesus' name, Amen.

Meditative Thought: Take a few moments to reflect on the ways in which God's Word has impacted you throughout the day, convicting you of sin and guiding you in righteousness. Surrender yourself to His transformative power, inviting His Word to continue to penetrate and renew you as you rest tonight.

AUGUST 1

MORNING DEVOTION

Scripture: Psalm 145:3

"Great is the Lord, and greatly to be praised; And His greatness is unsearchable."

Reflection: As we begin our day, let's reflect on the magnitude of Psalm 145:3. The psalmist declares the Lord's greatness, emphasizing that it is beyond our comprehension. This reminder is crucial as we start our day because it shifts our focus from our challenges and uncertainties to the infinite greatness of God. It encourages us to begin our day with praise and gratitude, recognizing that God's greatness encompasses all aspects of our lives, providing us with strength and assurance. Reflect on the greatness of God in your own life. Think about His creation, His providence, and His unwavering love. Let these thoughts fill you with awe and inspire your heart to praise Him throughout the day. Remember that no matter what challenges you face today, the greatness of the Lord is with you, guiding and sustaining you.

Prayer: Heavenly Father, I come before You in awe of Your unsearchable greatness. As I begin this day, I lift my heart in praise and gratitude for Your mighty works and unfailing love. Help me to remember Your greatness in every situation I encounter today. Fill me with Your peace and strength, and let my actions and words reflect Your glory. In Jesus' name, Amen.

Meditative Thought: Take a few moments to meditate on the greatness of God. Imagine His majesty and power encompassing your life, providing guidance and protection. Let this vision of His greatness fill your heart with peace and confidence as you step into the day. Commit to carrying an attitude of praise with you, continually acknowledging His greatness in all you do.

Scripture: Psalm 145:3
"Great is the Lord, and greatly to be praised; And His greatness is unsearchable."

Reflection: As the day draws to a close, let's reflect again on the truth of Psalm 145:3. This verse calls us to end our day with a heart full of praise for God's unsearchable greatness. Throughout the day, we might have experienced moments of joy, challenges, or even sorrow. Yet, in every moment, God's greatness remains constant and His love unwavering. Reflect on how you saw God's greatness in your day. Maybe it was in a moment of answered prayer, a beautiful aspect of creation, or a quiet assurance in a time of need. Let these reflections lead you to praise Him, acknowledging His continuous presence and greatness in your life.

Prayer: Gracious God, as I reflect on this day, I am reminded of Your unsearchable greatness and Your constant presence in my life. Thank You for guiding me, providing for me, and showing Your love in countless ways. Help me to rest in Your greatness tonight, with a heart full of praise and gratitude. May I wake up tomorrow with renewed strength and faith, ready to praise You again. In Jesus' name, Amen.

Meditative Thought: Take a few moments to meditate on God's greatness as you prepare for rest. Reflect on the ways He has shown His greatness to you today. Surrender any remaining worries or burdens to Him, trusting in His infinite power and love. Allow the peace of His presence to fill your heart, and rest in the assurance that His greatness will continue to guide and sustain you.

AUGUST 2

MORNING DEVOTION

Scripture: Proverbs 11:14

"Where there is no counsel, the people fall; But in the multitude of counselors there is safety."

Reflection: As we begin our day, let's reflect on the wisdom found in Proverbs 11:14. This verse underscores the importance of seeking counsel and guidance. It reminds us that relying solely on our own understanding can lead to downfall, but safety and wisdom come from seeking advice from multiple sources. Reflect on the areas in your life where you might need guidance today. Are there decisions or challenges that could benefit from the wisdom of others? Consider the value of seeking counsel from trusted mentors, friends, and God's Word. Embrace the humility required to acknowledge that we do not have all the answers and that collective wisdom can lead to better outcomes.

Prayer: Heavenly Father, thank You for the wisdom found in Your Word. As I start this day, help me to recognize the value of seeking counsel and guidance. Give me the humility to seek advice from others and the discernment to choose wise counselors. Lead me to the right people and resources that will guide me according to Your will. May I make decisions today that honor You and bring safety and wisdom into my life. In Jesus' name, Amen.

Meditative Thought: Take a few moments to meditate on the importance of seeking counsel. Visualize yourself reaching out to trusted advisors and being open to their wisdom. Reflect on past experiences where the counsel of others has led to better decisions and outcomes. As you prepare to face the day, commit to seeking and valuing the guidance of others, knowing that in the multitude of counselors, there is safety.

Scripture: Proverbs 11:14
"Where there is no counsel, the people fall; But in the multitude of counselors there is safety."

Reflection: As the day comes to a close, let's reflect on the wisdom imparted in Proverbs 11:14. This verse highlights the importance of seeking and heeding counsel to avoid pitfalls and ensure safety. As we review the day's events, we can assess how seeking or not seeking advice impacted our decisions and outcomes. Reflect on the moments when you sought or needed guidance today. Did you seek counsel when necessary? How did it affect your decisions? Recognize the value of having wise counselors in your life and the safety that comes from listening to their advice. Consider how you can foster a habit of seeking wisdom regularly.

Prayer: Gracious God, as I reflect on this day, I thank You for the counsel and guidance You provide through Your Word and through others. Forgive me for the times when I relied solely on my own understanding. Help me to continuously seek and value the wisdom of others. Guide me to wise counselors and give me the humility to listen and learn from them. As I rest tonight, fill my heart with peace, knowing that You provide safety through the wisdom You offer. In Jesus' name, Amen.

Meditative Thought: Take a few moments to meditate on the value of seeking counsel. Reflect on the safety and wisdom that come from listening to trusted advisors. Consider the times today when counsel made a difference in your decisions. As you prepare for rest, surrender any lingering anxieties or decisions to God, trusting in His provision of wise counselors. Let the peace of knowing you are not alone in your decisions fill your heart as you sleep.

Scripture: 1 Kings 18:21a
"And Elijah came to all the people, and said, 'How long will you falter between two opinions? If the Lord is God, follow Him; but if Baal, follow him."

Reflection: As we begin our day, let's reflect on the challenging question Elijah posed to the Israelites. This verse calls us to examine our own commitment and faithfulness to God. Are there areas in our lives where we are faltering between two opinions, unsure of whether to fully commit to following God or something else? This morning, let's resolve to follow the Lord wholeheartedly, without wavering. Reflect on your personal walk with God. Are there influences or distractions that cause you to falter in your faith? Consider how you can strengthen your commitment to follow God in all areas of your life. Embrace the clarity and purpose that comes from choosing to follow Him wholeheartedly.

Prayer: Heavenly Father, as I start this day, I am reminded of the importance of wholehearted commitment to You. Help me to examine my heart and identify any areas where I am faltering between two opinions. Give me the strength and resolve to follow You fully, without wavering. Guide my steps today, and help me to make decisions that honor and glorify You. In Jesus' name, Amen.

Meditative Thought: Take a few moments to meditate on Elijah's question. Visualize yourself standing before God, making a firm decision to follow Him without hesitation. Reflect on the areas in your life where you need to commit more fully to Him. As you face the day, let this meditation guide your actions and decisions, ensuring that you are walking in wholehearted devotion to the Lord.

Scripture: 1 Kings 18:21a
"And Elijah came to all the people, and said, 'How long will you falter between two opinions? If the Lord is God, follow Him; but if Baal, follow him.'"

Reflection: As the day comes to a close, let's reflect on Elijah's challenge to the Israelites and consider how it applies to our lives. This evening, let's take the time to evaluate our actions and decisions, and assess whether we followed God wholeheartedly or faltered between different influences. Reflect on the choices you made today. Were there moments when you were tempted to falter between two opinions? How did you respond? Acknowledge any areas where you struggled and seek God's forgiveness and guidance. Reaffirm your commitment to follow Him with all your heart, mind, and soul.

Prayer: Gracious God, as I reflect on this day, I recognize the times when I faltered between following You and being influenced by other things. Forgive me for those moments of wavering. Help me to strengthen my resolve and commitment to You. Fill my heart with a steadfast devotion to follow You in all things. As I rest tonight, grant me peace and a renewed spirit to serve You more faithfully tomorrow. In Jesus' name, Amen.

Meditative Thought: Take a few moments to meditate on the day's events and your responses to various influences. Reflect on the steadfastness of your commitment to God. Visualize letting go of any distractions or influences that caused you to waver, and embrace the peace and clarity that come from a wholehearted commitment to the Lord. As you prepare for rest, trust in God's grace to renew and strengthen you for a new day of following Him faithfully.

AUGUST 4

MORNING DEVOTION

Scripture: Job 42:5
"I have heard of You by the hearing of the ear, but now my eye sees You."

Reflection: As we begin our day, let's reflect on Job's profound declaration in Job 42:5. Job had known about God through what he had heard, but after his intense trials and God's revelation, he experienced a deeper, more intimate understanding—his eyes were opened to truly see God. This morning, let us seek a similar transformation in our own spiritual journey. Move beyond a secondhand knowledge of God, and pursue a personal, firsthand experience of His presence and power. Consider how you have known God up to this point. Have you primarily relied on what you've heard from others, or have you sought a personal encounter with Him? Ask God to reveal Himself to you in new and profound ways today. Let your heart be open to seeing Him more clearly in your life.

Prayer: Heavenly Father, as I start this day, I long to know You more deeply. Like Job, I want to move from simply hearing about You to truly seeing and experiencing Your presence. Open my eyes to see You in every aspect of my life today. Draw me closer to You and deepen my understanding of Your love and grace. Guide my steps and let my life be a reflection of Your glory. In Jesus' name, Amen.

Meditative Thought: Take a few moments to meditate on the transformation from hearing about God to seeing Him. Visualize yourself moving from a place of distant knowledge to one of intimate experience. As you go about your day, remain open and attentive to the ways God reveals Himself to you. Let this meditation guide your interactions and decisions, fostering a deeper connection with the Lord.

Scripture: Job 42:5
"I have heard of You by the hearing of the ear, but now my eye sees You."

Reflection: As the day comes to a close, let's reflect on Job's journey to a deeper understanding of God. Throughout the day, we may have encountered situations and moments that revealed more of God's character and presence. This evening, let's take time to recognize and appreciate those moments where we moved from simply hearing about God to truly seeing Him in our lives. Reflect on the day's experiences. Were there moments when you felt God's presence more profoundly? How did these moments impact your faith and understanding of Him? Thank God for revealing Himself to you and for deepening your relationship with Him.

Prayer: Gracious God, as I reflect on this day, I am grateful for the ways You have revealed Yourself to me. Thank You for moving me from hearing about You to truly seeing and experiencing Your presence. Forgive me for the times I may have overlooked Your work in my life. Help me to continually seek a deeper understanding of You. As I rest tonight, fill my heart with peace and gratitude for Your constant presence and love. In Jesus' name, Amen.

Meditative Thought: Take a few moments to meditate on the experiences of the day. Recall the moments where you sensed God's presence and felt a deeper connection with Him. Allow these reflections to fill your heart with gratitude and awe. As you prepare for rest, surrender any remaining anxieties to God, trusting in His continual presence and care. Let the peace of truly seeing God in your life bring you comfort and rest.

Scripture: Matthew 6:14-15

"For if you forgive men their trespasses, your heavenly Father will also forgive you. But if you do not forgive men their trespasses, neither will your Father forgive your trespasses."

Reflection: As we start our day, let's reflect on the profound teaching of Jesus in Matthew 6:14-15. Forgiveness is a central theme in our faith and daily walk with God. Jesus clearly connects our willingness to forgive others with receiving forgiveness from our heavenly Father. This morning, consider the state of your heart concerning forgiveness. Remember that forgiving others is not only an act of obedience to God but also a path to experiencing His grace and freedom in our own lives. Reflect on any relationships or situations where you need to extend forgiveness. Ask God to help you release any bitterness or resentment and to grant you the strength to forgive as you have been forgiven. Embrace the peace and freedom that come from a forgiving heart.

Prayer: Heavenly Father, thank You for the forgiveness You have extended to me through Jesus Christ. As I begin this day, help me to reflect Your grace by forgiving those who have wronged me. Reveal any areas of unforgiveness in my heart and give me the courage and strength to let go of any bitterness or resentment. May Your love flow through me, bringing healing and reconciliation. In Jesus' name, Amen.

Meditative Thought: Take a few moments to meditate on the power of forgiveness. Visualize yourself releasing any grudges or resentments you may be holding. Imagine the freedom and peace that come with a heart that is free of bitterness. As you go through your day, commit to practicing forgiveness, knowing that it opens the door to experiencing God's grace more fully in your life.

Scripture: Matthew 6:14-15

"For if you forgive men their trespasses, your heavenly Father will also forgive you. But if you do not forgive men their trespasses, neither will your Father forgive your trespasses."

Reflection: As the day comes to a close, let's revisit Jesus' teaching on forgiveness in Matthew 6:14-15. Reflect on the interactions and experiences you had today. Were there moments when you felt wronged or hurt by others? How did you respond? Forgiveness can be challenging, especially when emotions are raw, but Jesus calls us to forgive just as we have been forgiven. Reflect on any instances today where forgiveness was needed. Did you extend forgiveness, or are you holding onto any resentment? Seek God's help to forgive those who may have wronged you, and also to seek forgiveness where you may have wronged others. Let go of any burdens of unforgiveness as you prepare to rest.

Prayer: Gracious God, as I reflect on this day, I am reminded of Your call to forgive others as You have forgiven me. Thank You for Your endless grace and mercy. Help me to forgive those who have wronged me today, and to seek forgiveness where I have fallen short. Cleanse my heart of any bitterness and fill me with Your peace. As I rest tonight, let Your love and forgiveness renew my spirit. In Jesus' name, Amen.

Meditative Thought: Take a few moments visualize yourself releasing any negative feelings and embracing the peace that comes with a forgiving heart. As you prepare for sleep, let go of any lingering anger or resentment, trusting in God's grace to fill you with His peace and love. Rest in the assurance that forgiving others opens the way for you to experience God's forgiveness more deeply.

Scripture: Acts 4:19-20
"But Peter and John answered and said to them, 'Whether it is right in the sight of God to listen to you more than to God, you judge. For we cannot but speak the things which we have seen and heard.'"

Reflection: As we start our day, let's reflect on the boldness and unwavering faith of Peter and John. Despite facing threats and opposition, they stood firm in their commitment to proclaim the truth about Jesus Christ. Their courage and conviction came from their firsthand experiences with Jesus and the transformative power of His message. This morning, consider the depth of your own convictions and your willingness to stand firm in your faith, even when it is challenging or unpopular. Reflect on the ways you can share your faith today. Ask God to give you the courage and conviction to share His truth boldly, regardless of the circumstances or opposition you may face.

Prayer: Heavenly Father, thank You for the example of Peter and John, who boldly proclaimed Your truth despite opposition. As I begin this day, fill me with the same courage and conviction to speak about the things I have seen and heard from You. Help me to stand firm in my faith and to be a witness to Your transformative power in my life. Guide my words and actions today so that they reflect Your love and truth. In Jesus' name, Amen.

Meditative Thought: Take a few moments to meditate on the boldness of Peter and John. Imagine yourself standing firm in your faith, ready to share the things you have seen and heard from God. Visualize opportunities throughout your day where you can be a witness to His love and truth. Let this meditation inspire you to approach each moment with courage and conviction, trusting in God's guidance and strength.

Scripture: Acts 4:19-20

"But Peter and John answered and said to them, 'Whether it is right in the sight of God to listen to you more than to God, you judge. For we cannot but speak the things which we have seen and heard.'"

Reflection: As the day draws to a close, let's revisit the steadfast faith and bold proclamation of Peter and John. Reflect on the interactions and experiences you had today. Were there moments when you had the opportunity to speak about your faith? How did you respond? The example of Peter and John reminds us of the importance of prioritizing God's truth over the opinions of others, standing firm in our convictions despite potential opposition. Reflect on the moments today when you felt challenged in your faith. Seek God's forgiveness and guidance for any missed opportunities, and thank Him for the strength He gave you to stand firm in other moments.

Prayer: Gracious God, as I reflect on this day, I am grateful for the courage and conviction You have given me. Help me to continue growing in boldness and conviction. As I rest tonight, fill me with Your peace and renew my spirit for another day of serving and witnessing for You. In Jesus' name, Amen.

Meditative Thought: Take a few moments to meditate on the events of the day. Recall the moments when you had the opportunity to speak about your faith and how you responded. Visualize releasing any regrets and embracing God's forgiveness and renewal. As you prepare for rest, let the courage and conviction of Peter and John inspire you to stand firm in your faith each day, trusting in God's guidance and strength.

AUGUST 7

MORNING DEVOTION

Scripture: 1 Samuel 18:12
"Now Saul was afraid of David, because the Lord was with him, but had departed from Saul."

Reflection: As we begin our day, the story of Saul and David offers a profound lesson about the presence of God in our lives. Saul's fear of David stemmed from the evident favor of God upon David. Despite being a king, Saul felt insecure and threatened because he knew that God's spirit had departed from him and rested on David instead. This scripture reminds us of the importance of God's presence in our lives. When we walk with God, His presence is a source of strength, courage, and favor. However, when we turn away from God, fear and insecurity can easily take root in our hearts. Saul's life warns us against the dangers of jealousy and disobedience to God's will. As we go about our day, let us seek to remain in God's presence, living in obedience and faith. Let's strive to be like David, who trusted in the Lord wholeheartedly, and avoid the pitfalls of jealousy and fear that ensnared Saul.

Prayer: Heavenly Father, thank You for Your unwavering presence in our lives. Help us to seek You daily and to walk in Your ways. Guard our hearts against jealousy and fear, and fill us with Your peace and courage. As we go through this day, may Your favor and blessings be evident in our lives. In Jesus' name, we pray. Amen.

Meditative Thought: "How can I ensure that God's presence remains with me today? What steps can I take to cultivate a heart like David's, fully trusting in the Lord?"

Scripture: 1 Samuel 18:12
"Now Saul was afraid of David, because the Lord was with him, but had departed from Saul."

Reflection: As the day comes to a close, it's a time for reflection and introspection. The scripture we read this morning about Saul and David can guide us as we review our day. Saul's fear of David serves as a reminder of the importance of staying close to God. Reflecting on Saul's experience, we see how crucial it is to seek God's presence continually. Today, were there moments when fear or insecurity crept into our hearts? Did we face situations where we felt God's presence and strength? Saul's story urges us to rely not on our own understanding or abilities but on God's guidance and support. David's confidence came from knowing that God was with him. As we prepare to rest, let us commit our worries and fears to God, asking Him to fill us with His peace. Let us also seek His forgiveness for any actions or thoughts that may have distanced us from Him today.

Prayer: Gracious Lord, as we end this day, we thank You for Your constant presence and guidance. We confess that there were times when fear and insecurity overshadowed our faith. Please forgive us and help us to trust in You more deeply. May Your peace fill our hearts and minds as we rest tonight. Strengthen us for the days ahead, and help us to live in a manner that reflects Your love and grace. In Jesus' name, we pray. Amen.

Meditative Thought: "In what ways did I experience God's presence today? How can I grow in trusting Him more fully and live without fear and insecurity?"

AUGUST 8

MORNING DEVOTION

Scripture: Psalm 5:11
"But let all those rejoice who put their trust in You; let them ever shout for joy, because You defend them; let those also who love Your name be joyful in You."

Reflection: As we greet the morning, Psalm 5:11 offers a beautiful reminder of the joy and protection found in trusting God. This verse encourages us to rejoice and shout for joy because God defends those who trust in Him. It's a call to begin our day with a heart full of gratitude and confidence, knowing that God is our protector and defender. In our daily lives, we often face uncertainties and challenges that can cause anxiety and fear. However, when we place our trust in God, we can experience a profound sense of peace and joy. This joy is not dependent on our circumstances but is rooted in the assurance of God's steadfast love and faithfulness. Let this verse inspire us to trust in God more deeply today. As we go through our routines and face various tasks, let's remember that God is with us, defending and guiding us. Our joy comes from His presence and the knowledge that we are loved and protected by Him.

Prayer: Heavenly Father, we thank You for this new day and for the promise of Your protection and love. Help us to trust in You wholeheartedly and to find joy in Your presence. As we face the challenges of the day, remind us that You are our defender and that we can find peace and joy in You. Fill our hearts with gratitude and help us to rejoice in Your goodness. In Jesus' name, we pray. Amen.

Meditative Thought: "What specific challenges or anxieties can I entrust to God's care today? How can I cultivate a deeper sense of joy and gratitude in my daily walk with Him?"

Scripture: Psalm 5:11
"But let all those rejoice who put their trust in You; let them ever shout for joy, because You defend them; let those also who love Your name be joyful in You."

Reflection: As the day draws to a close, Psalm 5:11 invites us to reflect on the joy and protection we have experienced by placing our trust in God. This verse calls us to rejoice and be joyful in the Lord, recognizing His defense and care throughout our day. Looking back, we might recall moments when we felt God's guidance and protection. There may have been challenges, but we were not alone. God's presence has been with us, offering peace and reassurance. This evening, we can rest in the confidence that God has been our defender, and His love surrounds us. Reflecting on this scripture, let's examine our hearts: Did we trust God fully today? Did we allow His joy to fill our hearts despite the circumstances? As we prepare for rest, let's commit any lingering worries to Him, knowing He is our faithful defender. Rejoice in His love and find peace in His constant care.

Prayer: Gracious Lord, as we come to the end of this day, we thank You for Your constant protection and love. We rejoice in the joy that comes from trusting in You. Forgive us for the times when we doubted or let fear overshadow our faith. Help us to rest in Your peace tonight, confident in Your defense and care. May we wake up tomorrow with renewed joy and trust in Your unfailing love. In Jesus' name, we pray. Amen.

Meditative Thought: "How did experience God's protection and guidance today? What can I do to deepen my trust in Him and cultivate a more joyful heart, regardless of circumstances?"

AUGUST 9

MORNING DEVOTION

Scripture: Zechariah 12:10
"And I will pour on the house of David and on the inhabitants of Jerusalem the Spirit of grace and supplication; then they will look on Me whom they pierced. Yes, they will mourn for Him as one mourns for his only son, and grieve for Him as one grieves for a firstborn."

Reflection: As we begin our day, let's reflect on the profound message of Zechariah 12:10. This verse speaks of a future outpouring of the Spirit of grace and supplication upon the house of David and the inhabitants of Jerusalem. It foretells a time when they will look upon the one they have pierced and mourn for Him. This scripture points us towards the sacrificial love of Jesus Christ. Through His death and resurrection, He offered salvation to all who believe in Him. As we ponder this verse, let us be reminded of the incredible depth of God's love for us. Despite our sins, He offers us grace and forgiveness through His Son. Let this scripture inspire us to approach the day with hearts filled with gratitude for God's mercy and grace. May we be vessels of His love and grace, sharing the good news with others as we go about our day.

Prayer: Heavenly Father, we thank You for the gift of Your Son, Jesus Christ, who died for our sins and rose again, offering us salvation and eternal life. As we begin this day, fill us anew with Your Spirit of grace and supplication. Help us to be mindful of Your love and to share it with others. May we live today with hearts full of gratitude and a desire to spread Your gospel to those who need it most. In Jesus' name, we pray. Amen.

Meditative Thought: "How can I reflect God's grace and love to those around me today? Who in my life needs to hear about the saving power of Jesus Christ?"

Scripture: Zechariah 12:10
"And I will pour on the house of David and on the inhabitants of Jerusalem the Spirit of grace and supplication; then they will look on Me whom they pierced. Yes, they will mourn for Him as one mourns for his only son, and grieve for Him as one grieves for a firstborn."

Reflection: As we come to the end of the day, let's reflect on the profound message of Zechariah 12:10 once again. This scripture speaks of a future time when the Spirit of grace and supplication will be poured out, leading people to recognize and mourn for the one they pierced. Tonight, let us ponder the sacrificial love of Jesus Christ. He willingly laid down His life for us, bearing the weight of our sins on the cross. In the quiet moments of this evening, let us draw near to God in prayer. Let's express our gratitude for His grace and mercy, and ask Him to help us live as faithful disciples of Jesus Christ. May we be filled with the Spirit's power to share the good news of salvation with others, just as the prophecy in Zechariah foretells.

Prayer: Gracious God, as we end this day, we thank You for the love and mercy You have shown us through Your Son, Jesus Christ. Help us to continually reflect on the significance of His sacrifice and to live our lives in response to Your grace. Fill us with Your Spirit, Lord, and empower us to share Your love and truth with those around us. May Your kingdom come and Your will be done on earth as it is in heaven. In Jesus' name, we pray. Amen.

Meditative Thought: "How can I live out the message of Zechariah 12:10 in my daily life? How can I continue to share the love and grace of Jesus Christ with those around me?"

AUGUST 10

MORNING DEVOTION

Scripture: John 14:21
"He who has My commandments and keeps them, it is he who loves Me. And he who loves Me will be loved by My Father, and I will love him and manifest Myself to him."

Reflection: As we embark on a new day, let's meditate on the profound truth found in John 14:21. Jesus teaches us that loving Him involves more than just words; it requires obedience to His commandments. Those who truly love Him demonstrate their love by keeping His commands. When we love Jesus and keep His commandments, we are loved by the Father, and Jesus promises to love us and reveal Himself to us. This revelation of Jesus in our lives brings about a deeper intimacy and understanding of Him. As we start our day, let's reflect on our obedience to God's commandments. Are we living in a manner that reflects our love for Jesus? Let's ask for His grace to help us align our lives with His teachings so that we may experience the fullness of His love and presence.

Prayer: Lord Jesus, thank You for the privilege of knowing You and experiencing Your love. Help us to love You not only with our words but also through our obedience to Your commandments. Grant us the grace to walk in Your ways today so that we may be recipients of Your love and experience Your presence in our lives. In Your name, we pray. Amen.

Meditative Thought: "What specific areas of my life need alignment with Jesus' commandments? How can I demonstrate my love for Him through my actions today?"

Scripture: John 14:21
"He who has My commandments and keeps them, it is he who loves Me. And he who loves Me will be loved by My Father, and I will love him and manifest Myself to him."

Reflection: As we conclude our day, let's reflect on the promise contained in John 14:21. Jesus assures us that those who love Him by keeping His commandments will be loved by the Father, and He will reveal Himself to them. This manifestation of Jesus in our lives is a testament to the depth of our love for Him and His reciprocal love for us. As we review our day, let's honestly assess our obedience to Jesus' commandments. Were there moments when we faltered or disobeyed? Let's bring these areas before God in repentance, asking for His forgiveness and grace to do better tomorrow. At the same time, let's also celebrate the times when we lived out our love for Jesus through obedience. These moments are evidence of His work in our lives, drawing us closer to Him and allowing us to experience His love and presence more fully.

Prayer: Gracious God, as we close this day, we thank You for Your faithfulness and love towards us. Forgive us for the times when we failed to obey Your commandments. Grant us strength and grace to walk in obedience and love tomorrow. Thank You for the privilege of experiencing Your presence as we seek to follow You. In Jesus' name, we pray. Amen.

Meditative Thought: "How can I build upon today's obedience to Jesus' commandments in the days to come? How can I deepen my love for Him through continued obedience and submission to His will?"

AUGUST 11

MORNING DEVOTION

Scripture: Revelation 4:11
"You are worthy, O Lord, to receive glory and honor and power; for You created all things, and by Your will they exist and were created."

Reflection: As we begin this new day, let us meditate on the profound truth of Revelation 4:11. This verse declares the worthiness of the Lord to receive glory, honor, and power. It reminds us that God is the Creator of all things, and by His will, everything exists. This verse invites us into a posture of worship and awe before our Creator. It calls us to acknowledge God's sovereignty and greatness over all creation. Everything we see around us, every breath we take, is a result of His will and design. As we go about our day, let's keep this truth at the forefront of our minds. Let's approach our tasks and interactions with a heart of gratitude and reverence for the God who created us and sustains us. May our lives reflect the worship that is due to our Creator.

Prayer: Heavenly Father, we praise You for Your greatness and sovereignty over all creation. You alone are worthy to receive glory, honor, and power. As we begin this day, help us to live in constant awareness of Your presence and majesty. May our lives be a reflection of the worship that is due to You, our Creator and Sustainer. In Jesus' name, we pray. Amen.

Meditative Thought: "How can I cultivate a deeper sense of awe and reverence for God's creation in my daily life? How can I reflect His worthiness to receive glory, honor, and power through my actions and attitudes?"

Scripture: Revelation 4:11
"You are worthy, O Lord, to receive glory and honor and power; for You created all things, and by Your will they exist and were created."

Reflection: As the day comes to a close, let's reflect once again on the words of Revelation 4:11. This verse echoes the eternal declaration of worship offered to the Lord, acknowledging His worthiness to receive glory, honor, and power. It reaffirms that everything in creation exists by His will. Tonight, let's take a moment to ponder the magnitude of God's creative power and sovereignty. In light of this truth, let's offer Him our heartfelt worship and adoration. As we prepare for rest, may we carry with us a deep sense of gratitude for the privilege of being created and sustained by our heavenly Father. Let's commit ourselves anew to living lives that honor and glorify Him, recognizing His worthiness in every aspect of our existence.

Prayer: Lord God, as we come to the end of this day, we are in awe of Your greatness and majesty. You alone are worthy of all glory, honor, and power. Thank You for creating us and sustaining us by Your will. Help us to live our lives in constant worship and adoration of You. May Your name be exalted in all the earth. In Jesus' name, we pray. Amen.

Meditative Thought: "How can I carry the attitude of worship and reverence into the night and into tomorrow? How can I live in a way that continually reflects God's worthiness to receive glory, honor, and power?"

Scripture: Psalm 119:37

"Turn away my eyes from looking at worthless things, and revive me in Your way."

Reflection: As we begin this new day, let's reflect on the plea of the psalmist in Psalm 119:37. The psalmist asks God to turn their eyes away from worthless things and to revive them in God's way. This verse reminds us of the importance of guarding our hearts and minds against distractions and temptations that lead us away from God's path. In a world filled with various distractions and influences, it's easy to lose sight of what truly matters. The psalmist's prayer is a recognition of the need for divine guidance and renewal. By turning our focus away from worthless things and aligning our hearts with God's ways, we open ourselves to His transforming power and guidance. As we embark on this day, let's ask God to help us discern what is truly valuable and worthy of our attention. Let's invite Him to redirect our gaze towards His truth and righteousness. May His Spirit revive us and lead us in the path of life and obedience.

Prayer: Gracious God, we come before You this morning, recognizing our need for Your guidance and renewal. Help us to turn our eyes away from worthless things that distract us from Your will. Revive us, Lord, in Your way, and lead us in paths of righteousness. Grant us discernment to recognize what is valuable in Your sight. In Jesus' name, we pray. Amen.

Meditative Thought: "What are the 'worthless things' that often distract me from God's way? How can I intentionally focus my attention on what is truly valuable and align my life with God's purposes today?"

AUGUST 12

EVENING DEVOTION

Scripture: Psalm 119:37
"Turn away my eyes from looking at worthless things, and revive me in Your way."

Reflection: As the day comes to a close, let's reflect on the words of Psalm 119:37 once again. The psalmist's prayer resonates with our own desire to turn away from distractions and be revived in God's way. It's a reminder that true fulfillment and renewal come from aligning our lives with God's purposes. Tonight, let's take a moment to review our day and consider where our focus and attention have been. Have we allowed ourselves to be entangled in worthless pursuits that do not honor God? Or have we consciously sought after His ways and purposes in all that we do? As we bring this day to a close, let's offer a prayer of surrender to God. Let's ask Him to continue turning our eyes away from distractions and to revive us in His way. May His Spirit work in us, guiding us into paths of righteousness and renewing our hearts with His love and truth.

Prayer: Heavenly Father, as we end this day, we confess that we are often drawn to worthless things that distract us from Your will. Please forgive us and turn our eyes towards what is truly valuable in Your sight. Revive us, Lord, in Your way, and lead us in paths of righteousness. Help us to live each moment with a renewed focus on You. In Jesus' name, we pray. Amen.

Meditative Thought: "How can I intentionally seek after God's ways and purposes in my daily life? What steps can I take to guard my heart and mind against distractions that lead me away from Him?"

Scripture: John 6:35

"And Jesus said to them, 'I am the bread of life. He who comes to Me shall never hunger, and he who believes in Me shall never thirst.'"

Reflection: As we embark on a new day, let's meditate on the words of Jesus in John 6:35. Jesus declares Himself as the "bread of life," the ultimate source of nourishment and sustenance for our souls. He promises that those who come to Him will never hunger or thirst spiritually. This verse speaks to the deep longing within each of us for fulfillment and meaning. In a world filled with temporal pleasures and pursuits, Jesus offers Himself as the answer to our deepest needs. He alone can satisfy the hunger and thirst of our souls. As we begin our day, let's consider our spiritual hunger and thirst. Have we been seeking fulfillment in temporary pleasures or material possessions? Let's turn our hearts towards Jesus, the true source of satisfaction and abundant life. May we come to Him in faith, believing that He alone can satisfy the longing of our souls.

Prayer: Heavenly Father, we thank You for the gift of Your Son, Jesus Christ, who is the bread of life. As we start this day, we come to You with our spiritual hunger and thirst. Fill us, Lord, with Your presence and grace. Help us to find our satisfaction in You alone. May we come to Jesus with faith, believing that He is the source of true fulfillment and abundant life. In His name, we pray. Amen.

Meditative Thought: "What are the things in my life that I have been relying on to satisfy my spiritual hunger and thirst? How can I turn my focus towards Jesus as the ultimate source of satisfaction and fulfillment?" I can put my total hope and trust in Him and rest assured in Christ Jesus!

Scripture: John 6:35
"And Jesus said to them, 'I am the bread of life. He who comes to Me shall never hunger, and he who believes in Me shall never thirst.'"

Reflection: As the day draws to a close, let's reflect on the profound truth of John 6:35 once again. Jesus declares Himself as the "bread of life," promising that those who come to Him will never hunger or thirst spiritually. In Him alone, we find true satisfaction and fulfillment. Tonight, let's examine our hearts and consider where we have sought satisfaction apart from Jesus. Have we looked to worldly pursuits, relationships, or possessions to fill the void within us? Let's acknowledge any misplaced priorities and surrender them to Jesus. As we prepare for rest, let's come to Jesus with open hearts, ready to receive His grace and provision. Let's renew our commitment to seek Him above all else, believing that He is the only one who can satisfy the deepest longings of our souls.

Prayer: Gracious Lord, as we conclude this day, we confess that we have often sought satisfaction in things that do not truly fulfill us. Forgive us for looking to the world for fulfillment instead of coming to You, the bread of life. Fill us anew with Your presence and grace. Help us to seek You above all else, knowing that in You alone, we find true satisfaction and abundant life. In Jesus' name, we pray. Amen.

Meditative Thought: "How can I prioritize seeking Jesus as the bread of life in my life tomorrow? What steps can I take to deepen my reliance on Him for spiritual nourishment and fulfillment?"

AUGUST 14

MORNING DEVOTION

Scripture: Mark 8:29

"He said to them, 'But who do you say that I am?' Peter answered and said to Him, 'You are the Christ.'"

Reflection: As we begin this new day, let's reflect on the pivotal question Jesus asked His disciples in Mark 8:29: "But who do you say that I am?" Peter's response, "You are the Christ," encapsulates the profound truth of Jesus' identity as the Messiah, the Son of God. This question is not only for Peter and the disciples but for each one of us as well. Who do we say Jesus is? Our answer to this question shapes our entire lives and perspectives. Jesus is not merely a historical figure or a moral teacher; He is the Savior of the world, the One who came to reconcile us to God. As we meditate on this scripture, let's consider our own response to Jesus' question. Do we truly believe that He is the Christ, the Son of God? Let's reaffirm our faith in Him as our Lord and Savior, acknowledging His authority over our lives and committing to follow Him wholeheartedly today and every day.

Prayer: Heavenly Father, we thank You for the gift of Your Son, Jesus Christ, who is the Messiah, the Savior of the world. As we start this day, help us to acknowledge His lordship in our lives and to follow Him faithfully. Strengthen our faith, Lord, and deepen our understanding of who Jesus is. May our lives reflect His love and truth to those around us. In His name, we pray. Amen.

Meditative Thought: "How does my understanding of Jesus' identity as the Christ influence my daily life and decisions? How can I grow in my relationship with Him today?"

Scripture: Mark 8:29
"He said to them, 'But who do you say that I am?' Peter answered and said to Him, 'You are the Christ.'"

Reflection: As the day comes to a close, let's reflect on the profound question Jesus asked His disciples in Mark 8:29, serves as a reminder of Jesus' true identity as the Savior of the world. Tonight, let's ponder our own response to Jesus' question. Do we truly believe that He is the Christ, the Son of God? Our answer to this question shapes our relationship with Him and our understanding of His role in our lives. As we bring this day to a close, let's reaffirm our faith in Jesus as our Lord and Savior. Let's thank Him for His love, grace, and sacrifice on our behalf. And let's commit to following Him faithfully, trusting in His guidance and provision for our lives.

Prayer: Gracious Lord, as we end this day, we thank You for the revelation of Your Son, Jesus Christ, as the Christ, the Savior of the world. Help us to deepen our faith in Him and to live each moment in light of His lordship. May our lives be a testimony to His love and grace. In Jesus' name, we pray. Amen.

Meditative Thought: "How can I carry the truth of Jesus' identity as the Christ into my interactions and decisions tomorrow? How can I grow in my relationship with Him and share His love with others?"

AUGUST 15

MORNING DEVOTION

Scripture: Matthew 23:11
"But he who is greatest among you shall be your servant."

Reflection: As we begin this new day, let's reflect on the words of Jesus in Matthew 23:11. In this verse, Jesus teaches us about true greatness in the kingdom of God. Contrary to the world's standards, greatness is not measured by power, wealth, or status, but by service. Jesus Himself modeled this principle throughout His ministry. He humbly served others, washing the disciples' feet, healing the sick, and ultimately laying down His life for the salvation of humanity. In God's economy, true greatness is found in selfless service and sacrificial love. As we meditate on this scripture, let's consider how we can emulate Jesus' example of servanthood in our own lives. Let's ask God to give us a heart that is willing to serve others, even in the smallest of ways. May we seek opportunities to demonstrate His love and compassion to those around us today.

Prayer: Heavenly Father, we thank You for the example of Jesus, who showed us that true greatness is found in serving others. As we start this day, help us to cultivate a servant's heart, one that is willing to put the needs of others before our own. Show us how we can love and serve those around us in practical ways. May Your love shine through us today. In Jesus' name, we pray. Amen.

Meditative Thought: "How can I practice servanthood in my daily interactions today? What opportunities has God placed before me to serve others with love and humility?"

Scripture: Matthew 23:11
"But he who is greatest among you shall be your servant."

Reflection: As the day draws to a close, let's reflect on the profound truth of Matthew 23:11 once again. Jesus teaches us that true greatness in the kingdom of God is marked by servanthood. The greatest among us is the one who serves others with love and humility. Tonight, let's examine our own hearts and actions. Have we sought greatness in the eyes of the world, or have we embraced the humility of serving others as Jesus did? Let's ask God to reveal any pride or selfishness within us and to give us a genuine desire to serve others out of love. As we reflect on this scripture, let's commit ourselves anew to the path of servanthood. Let's ask God to empower us to love and serve those around us with humility and compassion. May our lives be a reflection of Jesus' love and may His kingdom come through our acts of service.

Prayer: Gracious God, as we conclude this day, we confess that we often fall short of embodying the humility and love of Jesus. Forgive us for our pride and selfishness. Fill us with Your Spirit and give us a heart that is willing to serve others with humility and love. Help us to follow the example of Jesus in all that we do. In His name, we pray. Amen.

Meditative Thought: "How can I continue to grow in servanthood and humility in my daily life? What steps can I take to serve others with love and compassion tomorrow?"

Scripture: Luke 1:20-21
"But behold, you will be mute and not able to speak until the day these things take place, because you did not believe my words which will be fulfilled in their own time." And the people waited for Zacharias, and marveled that he lingered so long in the temple."

Reflection: In Luke 1:20-21, we see the consequence of Zacharias' disbelief in the angel's message about the birth of John the Baptist. Because of his doubt, he was struck mute until the fulfillment of the prophecy. Despite this setback, the people outside marveled at his delay in the temple, unaware of the divine encounter he had experienced. This passage reminds us of the importance of faith and trust in God's promises. Zacharias' doubt hindered him from speaking, but it did not deter God's plan. Sometimes, our lack of faith may delay the manifestation of God's promises in our lives, but His timing is always perfect. As we begin our day, let's examine our own hearts and attitudes towards God's promises. Are there areas in our lives where doubt has crept in, hindering our faith? Let's pray for the strength to trust in God's timing and the patience to wait for His promises to be fulfilled.

Prayer: Heavenly Father, forgive us for the times when doubt has overshadowed our faith in Your promises. Help us to trust in Your timing and to patiently wait for Your plans to unfold in our lives. Strengthen our faith, Lord, and fill us with confidence in Your faithfulness. May we always believe in Your word and walk in obedience to Your will. In Jesus' name, we pray. Amen.

Meditative Thought: Reflect on a promise of God that you have been struggling to believe in. Ask God to increase your faith and help you trust in His perfect timing.

Scripture: Luke 1:20-21
"But behold, you will be mute and not able to speak until the day these things take place, because you did not believe my words which will be fulfilled in their own time." And the people waited for Zacharias, and marveled that he lingered so long in the temple."

Reflection: As the day comes to a close, let's reflect on the story of Zacharias in Luke 1:20-21. Despite his doubt, God's plan continued to unfold, and Zacharias was left mute until the fulfillment of the angel's prophecy. Zacharias' silence served as a reminder of the consequences of disbelief. Yet, in the waiting, God's faithfulness remained evident. The people outside marveled at his delay, unaware of the divine encounter he had experienced. Tonight, let's ponder the role of faith in our lives. Have there been times when doubt has hindered our trust in God's promises? Let's bring these doubts before God in prayer, asking Him to strengthen our faith and help us wait patiently for His timing.

Prayer: Gracious God, as we conclude this day, we acknowledge our need for greater faith and trust in Your promises. Forgive us for the times when doubt has crept in, hindering our belief in Your word. Help us to patiently wait for Your timing and to trust in Your faithfulness. May we always believe in Your promises and walk in obedience to Your will. In Jesus' name, we pray. Amen.

Meditative Thought: Reflect on how you can actively cultivate a spirit of faith and trust in God's promises in your life. Ask God to help you overcome doubt and wait patiently for His timing.

AUGUST 17

MORNING DEVOTION

Scripture: Galatians 5:1

"Stand fast therefore in the liberty by which Christ has made us free, and do not be entangled again with a yoke of bondage."

Reflection: As we begin this new day, let's reflect on the powerful message of Galatians 5:1. This verse reminds us of the freedom we have in Christ. Through His death and resurrection, Jesus has set us free from the bondage of sin and legalistic rituals. Yet, despite this freedom, it's easy to become entangled once again in the burdens of legalism, self-imposed rules, or worldly desires. The apostle Paul exhorts us to stand firm in the liberty we have received through Christ and to guard against anything that would ensnare us once again. As we meditate on this scripture, let's examine our hearts and lives. Are there areas where we have allowed ourselves to be entangled in bondage? Let's surrender these areas to God and ask Him to help us live in the freedom that He has provided.

Prayer: Heavenly Father, we thank You for the freedom we have in Christ. Help us to stand firm in this liberty and guard against anything that would entangle us once again in bondage. Fill us with Your Spirit, Lord, and empower us to live lives that honor You. May we walk in the freedom and victory that Jesus has secured for us. In His name, we pray. Amen.

Meditative Thought: Reflect on the areas in your life where you may be prone to legalism or bondage. Ask God to help you release these areas to Him and walk in the freedom He has provided through Christ.

AUGUST 17

EVENING DEVOTION

Scripture: Galatians 5:1
"Stand fast therefore in the liberty by which Christ has made us free, and do not be entangled again with a yoke of bondage."

Reflection: As the day comes to a close, let's reflect once again on the words of Galatians 5:1. This verse reminds us to stand firm in the liberty we have received through Christ and to guard against being entangled again in bondage. In the busyness of life, it's easy to lose sight of the freedom we have in Christ and to allow ourselves to be burdened by worldly cares or legalistic expectations. But Jesus has set us free from the power of sin and death, and His desire is for us to live in the fullness of that freedom. As we prepare for rest, let's take a moment to surrender any areas of bondage to God. Let's ask Him to help us walk in the liberty He has provided and to live lives that reflect His grace and love to the world around us.

Prayer: Gracious God, as we conclude this day, we thank You for the freedom we have in Christ. Help us to stand firm in this liberty and to guard against anything that would entangle us in bondage once again. Fill us with Your Spirit, Lord, and empower us to live lives that glorify You. May we walk in the freedom and victory that Jesus has secured for us. In His name, we pray. Amen.

Meditative Thought: Reflect on the ways in which you have experienced God's freedom and grace in your life today. Give thanks for His faithfulness and ask Him to help you continue walking in His liberty.

AUGUST 18

MORNING DEVOTION

Scripture: 1 Thessalonians 5:16-18
"Rejoice always, pray without ceasing, in everything give thanks; for this is the will of God in Christ Jesus for you."

Reflection: As we begin this new day, let's meditate on the exhortation found in 1 Thessalonians 5:16-18. These verses provide us with three powerful instructions for living a life aligned with God's will: to rejoice always, pray without ceasing, and give thanks in everything. "Rejoice always" reminds us that our joy is not dependent on our circumstances but is rooted in our relationship with God. "Pray without ceasing" encourages us to maintain an ongoing dialogue with God, seeking His guidance and presence in every moment. "In everything give thanks" challenges us to cultivate an attitude of gratitude, recognizing God's goodness and sovereignty even in the midst of trials. As we reflect on these instructions, let's ask God to help us embody them in our lives today. May we rejoice in His presence, pray without ceasing, and give thanks in all circumstances, knowing that this is His will for us in Christ Jesus.

Prayer: Heavenly Father, we thank You for the wisdom and guidance of Your word. Help us to rejoice always, to pray without ceasing, and to give thanks in everything. Strengthen us, Lord, to live according to Your will, trusting in Your goodness and sovereignty in every situation. May our lives be a reflection of Your love and grace to those around us. In Jesus' name, we pray. Amen.

Meditative Thought: Reflect on a specific situation or challenge you are facing today. How can you apply the instructions in 1 Thessalonians 5:16-18 to this circumstance? Take a moment to pray and ask God for His guidance and perspective.

Scripture: 1 Thessalonians 5:16-18
"Rejoice always, pray without ceasing, in everything give thanks; for this is the will of God in Christ Jesus for you."

Reflection: As the day comes to a close, let's reflect on the timeless wisdom of 1 Thessalonians 5:16-18. These verses remind us of the importance of maintaining a spirit of joy, prayer, and thanksgiving in our daily lives. "Rejoice always" challenges us to find joy in every circumstance, trusting in God's faithfulness and sovereignty. "Pray without ceasing" encourages us to cultivate a continual posture of dependence on God, seeking His guidance and presence in every moment. "In everything give thanks" reminds us to acknowledge God's goodness and provision, even in the midst of trials and challenges. As we reflect on these instructions, let's take a moment to examine our own lives. Have we approached this day with a spirit of joy, prayer, and thanksgiving? Let's ask God to reveal areas where we may have fallen short and to help us align our hearts with His will.

Prayer: Gracious God, as we conclude this day, we thank You for the wisdom and guidance of Your word. Forgive us for the times when we have failed to rejoice, pray, and give thanks as You have instructed us. Renew our spirits, Lord, and help us to live according to Your will, finding joy, strength, and gratitude in every circumstance. In Jesus' name, we pray. Amen.

Meditative Thought: Think back on the events of today. Where did you see God's presence, provision, or grace? Take a moment to give thanks to Him for these moments, and commit to approaching tomorrow with a spirit of joy, prayer, and thanksgiving.

AUGUST 19

MORNING DEVOTION

Scripture: Titus 2:13

"Looking for the blessed hope and glorious appearing of our great God and Savior Jesus Christ,"

Reflection: As we begin this new day, let's reflect on the encouraging words of Titus 2:13. This verse reminds us to eagerly anticipate the blessed hope and glorious appearing of our great God and Savior, Jesus Christ. In a world filled with uncertainty and challenges, it's easy to become discouraged or distracted. However, as followers of Christ, we are called to fix our eyes on the ultimate hope we have in Him. The promise of Jesus' return gives us hope and assurance, knowing that He will one day come again to make all things new. As we meditate on this scripture, let's renew our focus on the blessed hope of Christ's return. Let's live each moment with a sense of expectancy and readiness, knowing that His coming could be at any time. May the hope of His return fill us with joy, peace, and confidence as we navigate the challenges of this day.

Prayer: Heavenly Father, we thank You for the blessed hope we have in the return of Your Son, Jesus Christ. Help us to eagerly anticipate His glorious appearing and to live each day with faith and expectancy. Fill us with Your peace and joy as we fix our eyes on the ultimate hope we have in Him. In Jesus' name, we pray. Amen.

Meditative Thought: Consider how your perspective on life would change if you lived each day with a constant awareness of Jesus' imminent return. Ask God to help you cultivate a mindset of readiness and anticipation for His coming.

Scripture: Titus 2:13
"Looking for the blessed hope and glorious appearing of our great God and Savior Jesus Christ,"

Reflection: As the day comes to a close, let's reflect once again on the comforting words of Titus 2:13. This verse encourages us to eagerly anticipate the blessed hope and glorious appearing of our great God and Savior, Jesus Christ. In the midst of life's challenges and uncertainties, the promise of Jesus' return serves as an anchor for our souls. It reminds us that this world is not our final home and that one day, Jesus will come again to bring about the fullness of His kingdom. This blessed hope sustains us through difficult times and fills us with anticipation for the future. As we meditate on this scripture, let's take a moment to reaffirm our faith in the promise of Christ's return. Let's entrust our hopes, fears, and dreams to Him, knowing that He is faithful to fulfill all His promises. May the blessed hope of His appearing fill us with peace and assurance as we rest in His love tonight.

Prayer: Gracious God, as we conclude this day, we thank You for the blessed hope we have in the return of Your Son, Jesus Christ. Help us to eagerly anticipate His glorious appearing and to live each moment with faith and expectancy. May the hope of His coming fill us with peace and assurance, knowing that You are faithful to fulfill all Your promises. In Jesus' name, we pray. Amen.

Meditative Thought: Reflect on the ways in which the hope of Jesus' return has impacted your perspective and attitude throughout this day. Give thanks to God for His faithfulness and ask Him to continue filling you with hope and anticipation for the future.

AUGUST 20

MORNING DEVOTION

Scripture: 2 Peter 1:8
"For if these things are yours and abound, you will be neither barren nor unfruitful in the knowledge of our Lord Jesus Christ."

Reflection: As we begin this new day, let's reflect on the promise found in 2 Peter 1:8. This verse speaks of the abundance and fruitfulness that result from possessing and cultivating certain qualities in our lives. Peter outlines a progression of virtues in the preceding verses, including faith, virtue, knowledge, self-control, perseverance, godliness, brotherly kindness, and love. As we actively pursue these qualities and allow them to abound in our lives, we will bear fruit in our knowledge of Jesus Christ. This verse reminds us that our spiritual growth and effectiveness in serving God are not stagnant or passive but require intentional effort and cultivation. As we invest in developing these virtues, we will experience a deepening relationship with Christ and bear fruit that glorifies Him.

Prayer: Heavenly Father, we thank You for the promise of abundance and fruitfulness found in Your word. Help us to cultivate the virtues outlined by Peter in 2 Peter 1:5-7 in our lives. May our faith, virtue, knowledge, self-control, perseverance, godliness, brotherly kindness, and love abound, leading us to a deeper knowledge of Jesus Christ and bearing fruit that honors You. In His name, we pray. Amen.

Meditative Thought: Reflect on the virtues listed in 2 Peter 1:5-7. Consider how you can actively cultivate these qualities in your life today. Ask God to help you grow in these areas and bear fruit that glorifies Him.

Scripture: 2 Peter 1:8
"For if these things are yours and abound, you will be neither barren nor unfruitful in the knowledge of our Lord Jesus Christ."

Reflection: As the day comes to a close, let's reflect once again on the promise of abundance and fruitfulness found in 2 Peter 1:8. This verse assures us that as we possess and abound in certain qualities—faith, virtue, knowledge, self-control, perseverance, godliness, brotherly kindness, and love—we will not be barren or unfruitful in our knowledge of Jesus Christ. Our spiritual growth and effectiveness in serving God are not passive but require intentional effort and cultivation. As we actively pursue these virtues and allow them to abound in our lives, we will experience a deepening relationship with Christ and bear fruit that glorifies Him. Tonight, let's take a moment to examine our hearts and lives. Let's surrender any areas of complacency or neglect to God and ask Him to help us continue growing and bearing fruit for His kingdom.

Prayer: Gracious God, as we conclude this day, we thank You for the promise of abundance and fruitfulness found in Your word. Help us to actively cultivate the virtues outlined by Peter in 2 Peter 1:5-7 in our lives. May our faith, virtue, knowledge, self-control, perseverance, godliness, brotherly kindness, and love abound, leading us to a deeper knowledge of Jesus Christ and bearing fruit that honors You. In His name, we pray. Amen.

Meditative Thought: Reflect on your day and consider where you have seen evidence of growth in the virtues listed in 2 Peter 1:5-7. Give thanks to God for His work in your life and ask Him to continue helping you grow and bear fruit for His glory.

AUGUST 21

MORNING DEVOTION

Scripture: Genesis 3:1
"Now the serpent was more cunning than any beast of the field which the Lord God had made. And he said to the woman, 'Has God indeed said, "You shall not eat of every tree of the garden"?'"

Reflection: As we begin this new day, let's reflect on Genesis 3:1, which introduces the serpent's cunning question to Eve. This moment marks the beginning of temptation and doubt. The serpent's tactic was to question God's word, sowing seeds of doubt and confusion. This passage serves as a reminder of the subtle ways in which temptation can enter our lives. Just as the serpent twisted God's words, we too can encounter moments where we may doubt God's promises or be tempted to stray from His path. It's important to remain vigilant and grounded in the truth of God's word. As we meditate on this scripture, let's commit to starting our day with a firm foundation in God's truth. Let's seek His wisdom and discernment to recognize and resist any attempts to lead us astray.

Prayer: Heavenly Father, we thank You for the truth of Your word. As we begin this day, help us to remain vigilant against temptation and doubt. Grant us wisdom and discernment to recognize the subtle ways in which we may be led astray. Strengthen our faith, Lord, and help us to stand firm in Your promises. In Jesus' name, we pray. Amen.

Meditative Thought: Reflect on the ways in which you can remain vigilant against temptation today. How can you stay grounded in God's truth and resist any doubts or confusion that may come your way?

Scripture: Genesis 3:1
"Now the serpent was more cunning than any beast of the field which the Lord God had made. And he said to the woman, 'Has God indeed said, "You shall not eat of every tree of the garden"?'"

Reflection: As the day comes to a close, let's revisit the subtle yet profound question posed by the serpent in Genesis 3:1. This verse marks the beginning of humanity's struggle with temptation and doubt. The serpent's cunning approach was to create uncertainty about God's command. Throughout the day, we may have encountered moments of doubt or temptation. The enemy often uses subtle questions or situations to lead us away from God's truth. Reflecting on this scripture, we are reminded of the importance of staying rooted in God's word and being aware of the enemy's tactics. As we prepare for rest, let's examine our hearts and minds. Have there been moments today where doubt or temptation crept in? Let's surrender these moments to God, asking for His forgiveness and strength to remain steadfast in His truth.

Prayer: Gracious God, as we conclude this day, we come before You acknowledging our need for Your strength and guidance. Forgive us for any moments of doubt or temptation we may have encountered. Help us to stay rooted in Your word and to recognize the subtle ways the enemy tries to lead us astray. Fill us with Your peace and truth as we rest in Your presence tonight. In Jesus' name, we pray. Amen.

Meditative Thought: Reflect on your day and consider any moments where doubt or temptation may have arisen. How did you respond, and how can you better equip yourself with God's truth to stand firm in the future? Take a moment to pray for strength and discernment.

AUGUST 22

MORNING DEVOTION

Scripture: Job 42:3
"You asked, 'Who is this who hides counsel without knowledge?' Therefore I have uttered what I did not understand, things too wonderful for me, which I did not know."

Reflection: As we begin this new day, let's reflect on the humility and realization found in Job 42:3. Job, after enduring immense suffering and questioning God's justice, comes to a place of deep humility and acknowledgment of God's wisdom and sovereignty. He admits that he has spoken of things beyond his understanding—things too wonderful for him to grasp. This verse reminds us of our limited understanding and the greatness of God's wisdom. Often, we may find ourselves questioning or struggling to understand the circumstances in our lives. However, like Job, we are called to trust in God's infinite wisdom and recognize that His plans are beyond our comprehension. As we meditate on this scripture, let's commit to approaching this day with a heart of humility and trust in God's wisdom. May we seek to understand that while we may not always have the answers, we serve a God who knows all and is in control.

Prayer: Heavenly Father, we thank You for Your infinite wisdom and understanding. As we start this day, help us to approach our lives with humility, trusting in Your plans even when we don't fully understand. Guide our steps and grant us the faith to rely on Your perfect knowledge. In Jesus' name, we pray. Amen.

Meditation Thought: Reflect on a situation in your life where you have struggled to understand God's plan. How can you trust Him more fully today, acknowledging that His ways are higher than yours?

Scripture: Job 42:3
"You asked, 'Who is this who hides counsel without knowledge?' Therefore, I have uttered what I did not understand, things too wonderful for me, which I did not know."

Reflection: As the day comes to a close, let's revisit the profound humility expressed by Job in Job 42:3. After a period of intense questioning and suffering, Job comes to a place of recognition and repentance. He acknowledges that he has spoken of things beyond his understanding and that God's wisdom is far greater than his own. Throughout the day, we may have encountered situations that left us confused or questioning. Job's realization reminds us that it's okay not to have all the answers and that God's plans are often beyond our comprehension. As we prepare for rest, let's examine our hearts for any areas where we may have questioned God's wisdom. Let's surrender our uncertainties to Him and embrace the peace that comes from trusting in His perfect understanding.

Prayer: Gracious God, as we conclude this day, we come before You with hearts full of humility. We acknowledge that Your wisdom and understanding are far beyond our own. Forgive us for any moments of doubt or questioning. Help us to trust in Your perfect plans and rest in the knowledge that You are in control. Fill us with Your peace as we lay down to sleep. In Jesus' name, we pray. Amen.

Meditative Thought: Reflect on the events of today and consider any moments where you questioned or struggled to understand God's plan. Take a moment to thank God for His infinite understanding and care.

Scripture: Psalm 51:1-2

"Have mercy upon me, O God, according to Your lovingkindness; according to the multitude of Your tender mercies, blot out my transgressions. Wash me thoroughly from my iniquity, and cleanse me from my sin."

Reflection: As we begin this new day, let's reflect on the heartfelt plea of David in Psalm 51:1-2. This psalm is a cry for mercy and forgiveness, acknowledging the depth of our need for God's grace. David appeals to God's lovingkindness and tender mercies, asking Him to blot out his transgressions and cleanse him from sin. Starting our day with this scripture reminds us of the importance of repentance and seeking God's forgiveness. It's a call to humility, recognizing our own shortcomings and our deep need for God's cleansing power. His mercy is abundant and His love is unfailing, offering us a fresh start each day. As we meditate on these verses, let's approach God with a repentant heart, asking Him to wash us clean and renew our spirits. May we start the day with a sense of God's grace and the assurance of His forgiveness.

Prayer: Heavenly Father, we come before You this morning with hearts seeking Your mercy. According to Your lovingkindness and tender mercies, blot out our transgressions and cleanse us from our sins. Wash us thoroughly, Lord, and renew our spirits. Help us to walk in Your grace today, reflecting Your love and forgiveness to those around us. In Jesus' name, we pray. Amen.

Meditative Thought: Consider any areas in your life where you need God's forgiveness. Take a moment to confess these to Him, trusting in His mercy and grace to cleanse and renew you. How can you start today with a fresh perspective, grounded in God's forgiveness?

Scripture: Psalm 51:1-2
"Have mercy upon me, O God, according to Your lovingkindness; according to the multitude of Your tender mercies, blot out my transgressions. Wash me thoroughly from my iniquity, and cleanse me from my sin."

Reflection: As the day draws to a close, let's reflect once more on the profound words of Psalm 51:1-2. David's plea for mercy and forgiveness is a powerful reminder of our ongoing need for God's grace. After a day filled with various challenges and encounters, it is fitting to end with a moment of reflection and repentance. Throughout the day, we may have fallen short in our thoughts, words, or actions. This scripture encourages us to bring our shortcomings before God, trusting in His lovingkindness and tender mercies. His desire is to cleanse us and renew our hearts, providing us with peace and restoration as we rest. As we meditate on these verses, let's seek God's forgiveness for any wrongs we have committed today. Let's ask Him to wash us clean and fill us with His peace, preparing us for a new day in His grace.

Prayer: Gracious God, as we conclude this day, we humbly ask for Your mercy. According to Your lovingkindness, blot out our transgressions and cleanse us from our sins. Wash us thoroughly and renew our hearts, Lord. Fill us with Your peace as we rest tonight, and prepare us to wake up renewed in Your grace. Thank You for Your unfailing love and tender mercies. In Jesus' name, we pray. Amen.

Meditative Thought: Reflect on the events of the day and identify any moments where you fell short of God's standards. Confess these to Him, trusting in His mercy and grace to cleanse you. Consider how you can carry the assurance of God's forgiveness and renewal into tomorrow.

AUGUST 24

MORNING DEVOTION

Scripture: Proverbs 12:11
"He who tills his land will be satisfied with bread, but he who follows frivolity is devoid of understanding."

Reflection: As we start this new day, Proverbs 12:11 provides us with valuable insight into the importance of diligent work and wise use of our time. This verse contrasts the outcomes of hard work and frivolity. Tilling the land symbolizes dedication and effort, leading to satisfaction and provision. In contrast, following frivolity—pursuing meaningless activities—leads to a lack of understanding and unfulfilled needs. This verse encourages us to approach our daily tasks with diligence and purpose. Whether in our jobs, studies, or personal responsibilities, putting in consistent effort and focusing on meaningful activities will lead to fruitful outcomes. It's a reminder to prioritize our time and energy wisely, avoiding distractions that do not contribute to our growth or well-being. As we meditate on this scripture, let's commit to working diligently and purposefully today. May we seek God's guidance to help us focus on what truly matters and use our time effectively.

Prayer: Heavenly Father, we thank You for the wisdom found in Your word. Help us to approach our tasks today with diligence and purpose. Guide us to use our time wisely and avoid distractions that lead to unproductive outcomes. May our efforts be fruitful and bring satisfaction, honoring You in all that we do. In Jesus' name, we pray. Amen.

Meditative Thought: Consider the tasks and responsibilities you have today. How can you approach them with a sense of purpose and diligence? Reflect on any areas where you may be prone to distractions, and ask God to help you stay focused and productive.

Scripture: Proverbs 12:11
"He who tills his land will be satisfied with bread, but he who follows frivolity is devoid of understanding."

Reflection: As the day draws to a close, let's reflect on Proverbs 12:11 once more. This verse highlights the importance of diligence and the consequences of pursuing frivolous activities. Reflecting on our day, we can assess how we spent our time and energy. Were we diligent in our work, or did we find ourselves distracted by unproductive pursuits? This verse serves as a reminder that consistent effort and focus lead to satisfaction and provision. It challenges us to evaluate how we allocate our time and encourages us to prioritize meaningful and productive activities. Recognizing where we may have fallen short today can help us adjust our approach for tomorrow. As we meditate on this scripture, let's thank God for the opportunities to work and be productive. Let's also seek His forgiveness for any moments of frivolity and ask for His guidance to use our time wisely in the future.

Prayer: Gracious God, as we end this day, we thank You for the wisdom of Your word. Forgive us for any moments where we allowed distractions to divert our focus from meaningful work. Help us to learn from today's experiences and approach tomorrow with renewed diligence and purpose. May our efforts bring satisfaction and honor to You. In Jesus' name, we pray. Amen.

Meditative Thought: Reflect on your day and consider how you spent your time and energy. Were there moments of distraction or unproductive activities? Take a moment to ask for God's guidance and strength in your efforts.

Scripture: Jeremiah 26:13
"Now therefore, amend your ways and your doings, and obey the voice of the Lord your God; then the Lord will relent concerning the doom that He has pronounced against you."

Reflection: As we begin this new day, Jeremiah 26:13 calls us to reflect on the importance of obedience and repentance. In this verse, Jeremiah urges the people to amend their ways and obey God's voice. The promise is clear: if they turn from their sinful actions and follow God's commands, He will relent from the impending judgment. This verse is a powerful reminder of God's mercy and the transformative power of repentance. It encourages us to evaluate our own lives and consider areas where we need to align our actions with God's will. Starting the day with a heart of repentance and a commitment to obedience sets a foundation for walking in God's favor and blessing. As we meditate on this scripture, let's seek God's guidance to recognize areas in our lives that need change. May we commit to obeying His voice and trust in His mercy and grace to lead us on the right path.

Prayer: Heavenly Father, we thank You for Your mercy and the opportunity to start anew each day. Help us to recognize areas in our lives where we need to amend our ways and obey Your voice. Give us the strength and wisdom to follow Your commands and trust in Your promises. May our actions today reflect our commitment to You and bring glory to Your name. In Jesus' name, we pray. Amen.

Meditative Thought: Consider the areas in your life that need repentance and change. How can you align your actions with God's will today? Ask God for the strength and wisdom to obey His voice and trust in His mercy.

Scripture: Jeremiah 26:13
"Now therefore, amend your ways and your doings, and obey the voice of the Lord your God; then the Lord will relent concerning the doom that He has pronounced against you."

Reflection: As the day comes to a close, let's reflect on the message of Jeremiah 26:13. Throughout the day, we may have faced various challenges and made choices that reflect our commitment to God's commands or reveal areas needing change. This verse reminds us of the importance of ongoing repentance and obedience to God's voice. This scripture reassures us that when we amend our ways and obey God's voice, we open the door to His mercy and the possibility of relenting from judgment. As we meditate on this scripture tonight, let's examine our hearts and actions. Let's seek God's forgiveness for any missteps and commit to making the necessary changes. Trusting in His mercy, we can end the day with a renewed commitment to follow His guidance.

Prayer: Gracious God, as we end this day, we come before You with hearts seeking Your mercy and forgiveness. We acknowledge any areas where we may have strayed from Your will and ask for Your guidance to amend our ways. Help us to obey Your voice and trust in Your promises. Thank You for Your mercy and the opportunity to start anew. In Jesus' name, we pray. Amen.

Meditative Thought: Reflect on your actions throughout the day. Were there moments where you strayed from God's will? How can you make changes to align more closely with His commands? Seek God's forgiveness and guidance as you commit to obeying His voice and amending your ways.

Scripture: Ezekiel 2:7-8
"You shall speak My words to them, whether they hear or whether they refuse, for they are rebellious. But you, son of man, hear what I say to you. Do not be rebellious like that rebellious house; open your mouth and eat what I give you."

Reflection: As we begin this new day, Ezekiel 2:7-8 reminds us of our calling to faithfully deliver God's message, regardless of the response we might receive. God instructs Ezekiel to speak His words to the people, whether they listen or not, emphasizing their rebellious nature. However, God also gives a personal charge to Ezekiel: to listen to Him and to receive His words obediently. This scripture encourages us to remain steadfast in sharing God's truth, even when faced with resistance or indifference. It also highlights the importance of our personal obedience and receptiveness to God's words. As we go about our day, let's commit to being faithful messengers of God's love and truth, while also ensuring that our own hearts remain open and obedient to His guidance.

Prayer: Heavenly Father, we thank You for the privilege of being Your messengers. Help us to speak Your words with boldness and faithfulness, regardless of the response we receive. Grant us the humility and obedience to receive and follow Your guidance. Strengthen us to stand firm in Your truth and to be examples of Your love and grace. In Jesus' name, we pray. Amen.

Meditative Thought: Reflect on your role as a messenger of God's truth. How can you share His love and words with those around you today? Consider your own heart—are you open and obedient to God's guidance? Seek His strength to fulfill both these callings faithfully.

Scripture: Ezekiel 2:7-8
"You shall speak My words to them, whether they hear or whether they refuse, for they are rebellious. But you, son of man, hear what I say to you. Do not be rebellious like that rebellious house; open your mouth and eat what I give you."

Reflection: As the day draws to a close, Ezekiel 2:7-8 invites us to reflect on our faithfulness in delivering God's message and our personal obedience to His word. Today, we may have encountered situations where we were called to share God's truth or live out His commands. Whether our efforts were met with acceptance or resistance, this scripture reassures us that our duty is to be faithful to God's calling. It also prompts us to examine our own hearts. Just as Ezekiel was commanded to eat what God gave him, we too are called to internalize and live out God's words. As we meditate on this scripture tonight, let's seek God's forgiveness for any moments of disobedience or hesitation. Let's also thank Him for His guidance and commit to being faithful messengers and obedient followers.

Prayer: Gracious God, as we end this day, we reflect on our actions and attitudes. Forgive us for any moments of disobedience or hesitation in sharing Your truth. Help us to remain faithful messengers of Your love and grace, regardless of the response we receive. Open our hearts to fully receive and follow Your guidance. Thank You for Your patience and mercy. In Jesus' name, we pray. Amen.

Meditative Thought: Reflect on your actions today. Were there opportunities to share God's truth or live out His commands? How did you respond? Consider your own receptiveness to God's words. Ask for His forgiveness where needed and commit to faithfully following His guidance.

Scripture: Mark 4:39

"Then He arose and rebuked the wind, and said to the sea, 'Peace, be still!' And the wind ceased and there was a great calm."

Reflection: As we start this new day, let's reflect on the power and authority of Jesus as demonstrated in Mark 4:39. In this passage, Jesus calms a raging storm with just a few words, bringing peace and stillness to the tumultuous sea. This miraculous act not only showcases His divine power but also His deep care for His disciples, who were terrified in the face of the storm. This scripture encourages us to remember that no matter the chaos or challenges we may face, Jesus has the power to bring peace and calm to our lives. Just as He spoke to the wind and the sea, He can speak to the storms in our hearts and minds, bringing us tranquility and assurance. As we meditate on this verse, let's start our day with the confidence that Jesus is with us, capable of calming any storm we encounter. Let's invite His peace into our hearts and trust in His sovereign control over our lives.

Prayer: Heavenly Father, we thank You for Your Son, Jesus, who has the power to calm the storms in our lives. As we begin this day, we invite Your peace into our hearts and minds. Help us to trust in Your sovereign control and to face today's challenges with the assurance that You are with us. Speak "Peace, be still" to any anxiety or fear we may have, and guide us with Your calm presence. In Jesus' name, we pray. Amen.

Meditative Thought: Consider any storms or challenges you are currently facing. How can you invite Jesus to bring His peace and calm into these situations? Reflect on His power and authority, trusting that He is able to bring tranquility to your life today.

Scripture: Mark 4:39
"Then He arose and rebuked the wind, and said to the sea, 'Peace, be still!' And the wind ceased and there was a great calm."

Reflection: As the day comes to a close, let's revisit the calming power of Jesus as described in Mark 4:39. After a day filled with various activities, responsibilities, and perhaps some unexpected challenges, this verse reassures us of Jesus' ability to bring peace and calm to our lives. Reflecting on this scripture in the evening allows us to assess how we handled the day's storms. Were there moments of anxiety or unrest? Did we seek Jesus' peace in those moments? This passage reminds us that no matter what we faced today, Jesus is always ready to bring a great calm to our lives. As we meditate on this verse tonight, let's thank Jesus for His presence and power. Let's surrender any lingering worries or stresses to Him, trusting in His ability to calm our hearts and minds. May we rest in His peace, knowing that He is in control.

Prayer: Gracious God, as we end this day, we come before You with hearts grateful for Your calming presence. Thank You, Jesus, for Your power to still the storms in our lives. We surrender any worries or stresses we have encountered today and ask for Your peace to fill our hearts. Help us to rest in the assurance of Your sovereign control and to wake up renewed in Your grace. In Jesus' name, we pray. Amen.

Meditative Thought: Reflect on the events of the day. Were there moments of anxiety or unrest? How did you respond, and how can you invite Jesus' peace into those situations now? Take a moment to surrender any remaining worries to Him, trusting in His power to bring calm and tranquility to your life.

Scripture: Luke 5:31-32

"Jesus answered and said to them, 'Those who are well have no need of a physician, but those who are sick. I have not come to call the righteous, but sinners, to repentance.'"

Reflection: As we begin this new day, Luke 5:31-32 reminds us of Jesus' mission and our place in His heart. Jesus came not for those who perceive themselves as righteous, but for those who recognize their need for a Savior. His ministry was, and is, focused on calling sinners to repentance and offering healing to the spiritually sick. This scripture encourages us to approach Jesus with humility, acknowledging our own shortcomings and need for His grace. It's a reminder that no matter our past or present struggles, Jesus is ready to receive us, heal us, and guide us towards repentance and a renewed life. As we meditate on this verse, let's start our day with a spirit of humility and gratitude. Let's acknowledge our need for Jesus and open our hearts to His transformative power. May we also be inspired to extend His love and message of repentance to others in need.

Prayer: Heavenly Father, we thank You for sending Jesus to call us to repentance and to heal our spiritual wounds. As we begin this day, we acknowledge our need for Your grace and mercy. Help us to walk in humility and openness to Your transformative power. May we be vessels of Your love, sharing the message of repentance and healing with those around us. In Jesus' name, we pray. Amen.

Meditative Thought: Reflect on your own need for Jesus' healing and grace. How can you open your heart more fully to His transformative power today? Consider how you might share His message of repentance and love with others who are in need.

Scripture: Luke 5:31-32
"Jesus answered and said to them, 'Those who are well have no need of a physician, but those who are sick. I have not come to call the righteous, but sinners, to repentance.'"

Reflection: As the day draws to a close, let's reflect once more on the compassionate words of Jesus in Luke 5:31-32. Today, we may have encountered moments where we were reminded of our own need for grace and healing. Jesus' mission to call sinners to repentance and provide healing is a comforting reminder of His love and purpose. Reflecting on this scripture in the evening allows us to assess how we responded to our own and others' needs throughout the day. As we meditate on these verses tonight, let's thank Jesus for His unwavering love and grace. Let's seek His forgiveness for any shortcomings and ask for His continued guidance in our lives. May we rest in the assurance of His healing presence and wake up ready to embrace His mission anew.

Prayer: Gracious God, as we end this day, we come before You with hearts full of gratitude for Jesus' love and grace. Thank You for calling us to repentance and offering healing to our souls. Forgive us for any moments where we fell short today, and guide us to live more fully in Your grace. Help us to extend Your love and message to those in need. In Jesus' name, we pray. Amen.

Meditative Thought: Reflect on the events of the day and consider how you responded to your need for Jesus' healing and grace. Were there moments where you could have extended His love and message more effectively? Seek His forgiveness and guidance as you prepare to rest in His presence.

Scripture: John 6:33
"For the bread of God is He who comes down from heaven and gives life to the world."

Reflection: As we begin this new day, John 6:33 reminds us of the profound truth that Jesus is the bread of God, who came down from heaven to give life to the world. This verse highlights the divine provision and sustenance found in Christ. Just as bread sustains physical life, Jesus sustains our spiritual lives, offering us eternal nourishment and vitality. Reflecting on this verse encourages us to start our day by seeking spiritual nourishment from Jesus. In the same way that we need food to fuel our bodies, we need the presence of Christ to fuel our spirits. By turning to Him first thing in the morning, we invite His life-giving presence into our day, allowing Him to guide, sustain, and strengthen us. As we meditate on this scripture, let's commit to drawing closer to Jesus, the true bread of life, and allowing His presence to fill and sustain us throughout the day.

Prayer: Heavenly Father, we thank You for sending Jesus, the bread of God, who gives life to the world. As we begin this day, we seek Your presence and sustenance in our lives. Nourish our spirits with Your word and guide us in all that we do. May we be filled with Your life-giving presence and reflect Your love to those around us. In Jesus' name, we pray. Amen.

Meditative Thought: Consider how you can seek spiritual nourishment from Jesus today. Reflect on His role as the bread of life and how His presence can sustain you. How can you draw closer to Him and invite His life-giving presence into your daily routine?

Scripture: John 6:33
"For the bread of God is He who comes down from heaven and gives life to the world."

Reflection: As the day draws to a close, John 6:33 invites us to reflect on the life-giving presence of Jesus throughout our day. This verse reminds us that Jesus is the divine bread from heaven, providing spiritual sustenance and vitality. In the quiet of the evening, it's important to acknowledge the ways Jesus has nourished our spirits, whether through moments of prayer, encounters with others, or quiet reflections. Recognizing His life-giving presence helps us to end the day with gratitude and peace, knowing that He has been with us through every moment. As we meditate on this scripture tonight, let's thank Jesus for His sustaining presence and ask for His continued nourishment and guidance. May we rest in the assurance of His love and wake up ready to seek Him anew.

Prayer: Gracious God, as we end this day, we thank You for Jesus, the bread of God who gives life to the world. We are grateful for Your sustaining presence and the spiritual nourishment You provide. Help us to recognize and appreciate Your presence in our lives. As we rest tonight, fill us with Your peace and prepare our hearts to seek You again tomorrow. In Jesus' name, we pray. Amen.

Meditative Thought: Reflect on the ways Jesus has nourished your spirit today. How did you experience His life-giving presence? Consider areas where you may need more of His sustaining power and invite Him to continue guiding and nourishing you as you rest and prepare for a new day.

Scripture: Acts 2:21
"And it shall come to pass that whoever calls on the name of the Lord shall be saved."

Reflection: As we rise to greet this new day, Acts 2:21 offers a powerful reminder of the simplicity and inclusivity of the gospel message. This verse, part of Peter's sermon on the day of Pentecost, emphasizes that salvation is available to all who call on the name of the Lord. There are no prerequisites or exclusions—everyone who seeks the Lord with a sincere heart is welcomed and saved. This scripture invites us to begin our day with the assurance of God's salvation and grace. No matter our circumstances or past mistakes, we have the promise of salvation when we call upon Jesus. It also reminds us of our mission to share this message with others, ensuring that everyone knows they are welcome to call on the Lord. As we meditate on this verse, let's embrace the promise of salvation with gratitude and a renewed commitment to share God's love and grace with those around us.

Prayer: Heavenly Father, we thank You for the promise of salvation for all who call on Your name. As we begin this day, fill our hearts with gratitude for Your grace and assurance of salvation. Help us to live out this truth and share Your love with everyone we encounter. May our lives be a testimony to Your inclusive and transformative love. In Jesus' name, we pray. Amen.

Meditative Thought: Reflect on the inclusivity of God's promise in Acts 2:21. How does this assurance of salvation influence your outlook for the day? Consider how you can share this message of hope and grace with others in your life.

Scripture: Acts 2:21
"And it shall come to pass that whoever calls on the name of the Lord shall be saved."

Reflection: As the day draws to a close, Acts 2:21 serves as a comforting reminder of the accessibility of God's grace and salvation. Reflecting on the events of the day, we can take solace in the fact that regardless of our failures or shortcomings, God's promise of salvation remains steadfast for those who call upon His name. This verse encourages us to reflect on our relationship with God and the ways we've sought His presence today. It also prompts us to consider the opportunities we had to share His message of salvation with others. Knowing that salvation is available to all, we can end our day with a heart full of gratitude and peace, trusting in God's unwavering promise. As we meditate on this scripture tonight, let's thank God for His saving grace and ask for His continued guidance. May we rest in the assurance of His love and wake up ready to live out His promise anew.

Prayer: Gracious God, as we end this day, we thank You for the promise that whoever calls on Your name shall be saved. We are grateful for Your constant presence and saving grace. Forgive us for any moments of doubt or disobedience today, and help us to rest in Your peace. Renew our spirits and prepare our hearts to seek You again tomorrow. In Jesus' name, we pray. Amen.

Meditative Thought: Reflect on how you experienced God's grace and salvation today. Did you call upon His name in moments of need? Consider how you can continue to rely on His promise and share His message of salvation with others. As you prepare for rest, let the assurance of God's love and grace bring you peace.

Scripture: Galatians 5:16

"I say then: Walk in the Spirit, and you shall not fulfill the lust of the flesh."

Reflection: As we embark on a new day, Galatians 5:16 calls us to walk in the Spirit, promising freedom from the desires of the flesh. This verse reminds us of the ongoing battle between our fleshly desires and the leading of the Holy Spirit. When we choose to align our lives with the Spirit, we gain victory over sinful temptations and find true freedom in Christ. Reflecting on this scripture invites us to consider how we can actively walk in the Spirit throughout our day. It's a call to surrender our will to God's guidance, allowing His Spirit to lead us in every thought, word, and action. By walking in the Spirit, we position ourselves to experience the abundant life that Jesus promised. As we meditate on this verse, let's commit to living in obedience to the Holy Spirit's leading, seeking His strength and guidance to overcome the desires of the flesh.

Prayer: Heavenly Father, we thank You for the gift of Your Spirit, who empowers us to walk in victory over sin. As we begin this day, help us to yield to Your Spirit's leading in every area of our lives. Grant us the strength to resist the temptations of the flesh and to live in obedience to Your will. May our lives be a testimony to Your transforming power. In Jesus' name, we pray. Amen.

Meditative Thought: Consider the areas in your life where you struggle with the desires of the flesh. How can you invite the Holy Spirit to help you overcome these temptations? Reflect on practical steps you can take to walk more closely with the Spirit throughout the day.

Scripture: Galatians 5:16
"I say then: Walk in the Spirit, and you shall not fulfill the lust of the flesh."

Reflection: As the day comes to a close, let's reflect on the exhortation in Galatians 5:16 to walk in the Spirit. Throughout the day, we may have faced various temptations and challenges that tested our commitment to following God's leading. This verse reminds us that when we choose to walk in the Spirit, we are empowered to overcome the desires of the flesh. Reflecting on this scripture prompts us to evaluate how we responded to the leading of the Holy Spirit today. Were there moments when we yielded to His guidance, experiencing victory over sinful tendencies? Or were there times when we allowed the desires of the flesh to gain the upper hand? As we meditate on this verse tonight, let's thank God for His Spirit's presence and guidance in our lives. Let's also ask for His forgiveness for any moments of disobedience or weakness, committing to renewed surrender to His leading tomorrow.

Prayer: Gracious God, as we end this day, we thank You for the promise of victory when we walk in the Spirit. Forgive us for any moments of weakness or disobedience today. Strengthen us to yield more fully to Your Spirit's leading and to walk in obedience to Your will. May Your Spirit continue to transform us from within. In Jesus' name, we pray. Amen.

Meditative Thought: Reflect on the moments throughout the day when you experienced victory over the desires of the flesh by walking in the Spirit. Consider any areas where you struggled and ask for God's strength to overcome in the future. Surrender yourself anew to the leading of the Holy Spirit as you prepare for rest.

Scripture: Revelation 3:20

"Behold, I stand at the door and knock. If anyone hears My voice and opens the door, I will come in to him and dine with him, and he with Me."

Reflection: As we begin this new day, Revelation 3:20 offers a beautiful reminder of Jesus' desire for intimate fellowship with us. The image of Jesus standing at the door and knocking signifies His constant presence and willingness to enter our lives. He patiently waits for us to open the door, promising to come in and share a close, personal relationship with us. Starting the day with this verse encourages us to be attentive to Jesus' call. He is ready to guide, comfort, and strengthen us, but we must be willing to invite Him in. This morning, let's commit to opening our hearts and minds to His presence. Let's listen for His voice and welcome Him into every aspect of our lives. As we meditate on this scripture, let's embrace the promise of fellowship with Jesus. Let's invite Him to be part of our day, trusting that His presence will bring peace, guidance, and joy.

Prayer: Heavenly Father, we thank You for Your Son, Jesus, who stands at the door of our hearts and knocks. As we begin this day, we open our hearts to You and invite You in. Guide us, comfort us, and strengthen us through Your presence. Help us to hear Your voice and follow Your leading in all that we do. May our lives reflect the intimate fellowship we have with You. In Jesus' name, we pray. Amen.

Meditative Thought: Consider how you can be more attentive to Jesus' presence and voice today. Reflect on areas of your life where you need His guidance and companionship. How can you open the door of your heart more fully to Him this morning?

SEPTEMBER 1

EVENING DEVOTION

Scripture: Revelation 3:20
"Behold, I stand at the door and knock. If anyone hears My voice and opens the door, I will come in to him and dine with him, and he with Me."

Reflection: As the day draws to a close, Revelation 3:20 provides a comforting reminder of Jesus' desire for a personal relationship with us. Throughout the day, He has been knocking on the door of our hearts, seeking to enter and share His presence with us. Reflecting on this verse in the evening invites us to evaluate how we responded to His call today. Did we hear His voice and open the door to Him? Were there moments when we felt His presence and guidance? Or were there times when we allowed the busyness and distractions of the day to drown out His knock? As we meditate on this scripture tonight, let's thank Jesus for His patience and willingness to be with us. May we rest in the peace of knowing that He is always near, ready to dine with us and share His love.

Prayer: Gracious God, as we end this day, we thank You for Jesus, who stands at the door of our hearts and knocks. Forgive us for any moments today when we failed to hear Your voice or open the door to Your presence. We are grateful for Your patience and love. As we rest tonight, fill our hearts with Your peace and prepare us to be more attentive to You tomorrow. In Jesus' name, we pray. Amen.

Meditative Thought: Reflect on how you responded to Jesus' call today. Were there moments of closeness and guidance? Consider how you can be more receptive to His presence in the future. Surrender any worries or distractions to Him as you prepare for rest, trusting in His constant companionship.

SEPTEMBER 2

MORNING DEVOTION

Scripture: Psalm 46:10
"Be still, and know that I am God; I will be exalted among the nations, I will be exalted in the earth!"

Reflection: As we wake up to a new day, Psalm 46:10 invites us to start with a moment of stillness, recognizing the sovereignty and greatness of God. In a world filled with noise and busyness, it's crucial to take time to be still and reflect on God's presence in our lives. This verse is a call to pause and acknowledge that God is in control, no matter what circumstances we may face. Beginning our day with this mindset helps us to re-align our priorities and focus on what truly matters. It's an opportunity to lay down our anxieties and concerns, trusting that God is exalted and sovereign over all. By starting our day in stillness and acknowledgment of God, we set a foundation of peace and trust for whatever lies ahead. As we meditate on this scripture, let's embrace the stillness and let it shape our hearts and minds. Let's recognize God's power and presence, allowing it to guide us through the day with confidence and tranquility.

Prayer: Heavenly Father, as we begin this day, we come before You in stillness. Help us to quiet our hearts and minds, acknowledging Your sovereignty and presence in our lives. May Your peace fill us and guide us throughout this day. Remind us that You are in control and exalted above all. We trust in Your plans and purposes for our lives. In Jesus' name, we pray. Amen.

Meditative Thought: Take a few moments to sit quietly and focus on God's presence. Reflect on His greatness and sovereignty. Consider ways to create moments of stillness in your daily routine to reconnect with God's presence.

Scripture: Psalm 46:10
"Be still, and know that I am God; I will be exalted among the nations, I will be exalted in the earth!"

Reflection: As the day comes to a close, Psalm 46:10 offers a reminder to end the day in stillness, reflecting on God's power and presence. This verse calls us to cease our striving and remember that God is in control, no matter what challenges or triumphs we experienced today. It's a call to trust in God's sovereignty and to rest in His peace. Reflecting on this scripture in the evening allows us to release any worries or stresses from the day. It's a moment to recognize that God's plans are greater than our own and that He is exalted over all the earth. As we meditate on this verse tonight, let's thank God for His constant presence and control over our lives. Let's surrender our concerns to Him, trusting that He will take care of them as we rest.

Prayer: Gracious God, as we end this day, we come before You in stillness, acknowledging Your sovereignty and power. Thank You for being present with us through every moment of this day. We surrender our worries and concerns to You, trusting in Your perfect plans. Fill our hearts with Your peace as we rest, knowing that You are exalted among the nations and in the earth. In Jesus' name, we pray. Amen.

Meditative Thought: Reflect on your day and identify any moments of stress or anxiety. As you prepare for rest, take a deep breath and release those concerns to God. Acknowledge His control and sovereignty. How can you cultivate a habit of stillness and trust in God's presence in your daily life? Rest in the assurance that He is with you and will watch over you through the night.

SEPTEMBER 3

MORNING DEVOTION

Scripture: Isaiah 40:31

"But those who wait on the Lord shall renew their strength; they shall mount up with wings like eagles, they shall run and not be weary, they shall walk and not faint."

Reflection: As we start our day, Isaiah 40:31 reminds us of the incredible promise of renewed strength for those who wait on the Lord. In our fast-paced world, it's easy to feel overwhelmed and weary. Yet, this verse encourages us to pause, wait on God, and trust in His timing and provision. When we do, we are promised renewal and strength beyond our own capabilities. This morning, let's focus on the imagery of mounting up with wings like eagles. Eagles soar effortlessly, carried by the wind. Similarly, when we rely on God, we can rise above our circumstances, carried by His strength. Running without weariness and walking without fainting speaks to the endurance God provides when we trust Him. As we meditate on this scripture, let's commit to waiting on the Lord today. Let's seek His strength and guidance in every task and decision, trusting that He will renew us and enable us to rise above our challenges.

Prayer: Heavenly Father, as we begin this day, we come to You with hearts open to Your presence. Help us to wait on You and trust in Your perfect timing. Renew our strength, and let us soar above our challenges like eagles. Empower us to run without weariness and walk without fainting. Guide us in every step we take today. In Jesus' name, we pray. Amen.

Meditative Thought: Consider what it means to wait on the Lord in your daily life. Reflect on areas where you need His strength and renewal. How can you cultivate a habit of pausing to seek God's guidance and strength throughout the day?

Scripture: Isaiah 40:31
"But those who wait on the Lord shall renew their strength; they shall mount up with wings like eagles, they shall run and not be weary, they shall walk and not faint."

Reflection: As the day comes to a close, Isaiah 40:31 offers a comforting reminder of God's promise to renew our strength. Reflecting on the events of the day, we may feel tired and weary. This verse reassures us that when we wait on the Lord, He renews our strength, enabling us to continue with resilience and hope. Reflecting on the imagery of mounting up with wings like eagles, we can find peace in knowing that God lifts us above our struggles. Running without weariness and walking without fainting signifies the endurance and perseverance He grants us. No matter what challenges we faced today, God's promise remains true. As we meditate on this scripture tonight, let's thank God for His renewing strength and presence throughout the day. Let's commit to waiting on Him, trusting in His power to sustain us.

Prayer: Gracious God, as we end this day, we thank You for the promise of renewed strength for those who wait on You. We come before You with gratitude for Your presence and guidance today. Renew our strength and lift us up like eagles. Help us to rest in Your peace, knowing that You sustain us. Prepare our hearts to face tomorrow with Your strength and endurance. In Jesus' name, we pray. Amen.

Meditative Thought: Reflect on the moments today when you needed God's strength. How did He provide for you? As you prepare for rest, consider how you can wait on the Lord more intentionally in your daily life. Trust in His promise to renew your strength and sustain you.

SEPTEMBER 4

MORNING DEVOTION

Scripture: Isaiah 43:2
"When you pass through the waters, I will be with you; and through the rivers, they shall not overflow you. When you walk through the fire, you shall not be burned, nor shall the flame scorch you."

Reflection: As we greet this new day, Isaiah 43:2 offers a powerful reminder of God's presence and protection. This verse reassures us that no matter what challenges or trials we face, God is with us. The imagery of passing through waters, rivers, and fire highlights the various difficulties we may encounter. Yet, in all these situations, God promises His unwavering presence and protection. Starting our day with this assurance helps us face the day with confidence and peace. We can trust that God will be with us in every circumstance, guiding and protecting us. This promise encourages us to step out in faith, knowing that we are not alone. As we meditate on this scripture, let's embrace the confidence that comes from knowing God is with us. Let's commit to facing the day with trust in His presence and protection, no matter what challenges may come our way.

Prayer: Heavenly Father, as we begin this day, we thank You for Your promise to be with us through every trial and challenge. Help us to trust in Your presence and protection, no matter what we face. Fill our hearts with confidence and peace, knowing that You are always by our side. Guide us and strengthen us as we walk through this day. In Jesus' name, we pray. Amen.

Meditative Thought: Reflect on the various challenges you may face today. How does knowing that God is with you change your perspective on these challenges? Consider practical ways to remind yourself of His presence and protection throughout the day.

Scripture: Isaiah 43:2
"When you pass through the waters, I will be with you; and through the rivers, they shall not overflow you. When you walk through the fire, you shall not be burned, nor shall the flame scorch you."

Reflection: As the day comes to a close, Isaiah 43:2 reassures us of God's steadfast presence and protection. Reflecting on the day's events, we can find comfort in knowing that God was with us through every moment, whether we faced smooth paths or turbulent waters. This verse reminds us that even in the most challenging times, God's protection is sure and His presence unwavering. Reviewing the day with this promise in mind helps us to see God's hand in every situation. Whether we encountered difficulties or experienced moments of peace, God was there, guiding and protecting us. This reflection can bring us peace and gratitude as we prepare to rest. As we meditate on this scripture tonight, let's thank God for His presence and protection throughout the day. Let's surrender any remaining worries or fears to Him, trusting that He will continue to be with us.

Prayer: Gracious God, as we end this day, we thank You for Your promise to be with us through every trial and challenge. We are grateful for Your presence and protection throughout this day. As we rest tonight, help us to release any worries or fears, trusting in Your continued presence. Fill our hearts with peace and gratitude, and prepare us for the day ahead. In Jesus' name, we pray. Amen.

Meditative Thought: Reflect on the events of the day and identify moments where you experienced God's presence and protection. As you prepare for rest, surrender any remaining concerns to God, trusting in His unwavering presence.

SEPTEMBER 5

MORNING DEVOTION

Scripture: 1 Corinthians 10:13
"No temptation has overtaken you except such as is common to man; but God is faithful, who will not allow you to be tempted beyond what you are able, but with the temptation will also make the way of escape, that you may be able to bear it."

Reflection: As we begin our day, 1 Corinthians 10:13 provides us with a powerful assurance of God's faithfulness. We all face temptations and trials, but this verse reminds us that these challenges are not unique to us; they are common to humanity. Importantly, it reassures us that God is faithful and will not allow us to be tempted beyond our ability to endure. Moreover, He provides a way of escape so that we can bear it. This morning, let's reflect on God's faithfulness and His promise to help us withstand and overcome any temptation or trial. Knowing that He is with us and provides a way out empowers us to face the day with confidence and hope. As we meditate on this scripture, let's commit to seeking God's guidance and strength in moments of temptation. Let's trust in His promise to provide a way of escape and to help us bear all things.

Prayer: Heavenly Father, as we start this day, we thank You for Your faithfulness and the assurance that You will not allow us to be tempted beyond what we can bear. Help us to trust in Your promise and to seek Your guidance and strength in moments of temptation. May we rely on You to provide a way of escape and to empower us to endure and overcome. In Jesus' name, we pray. Amen.

Meditative Thought: Consider the temptations or trials you may face today. How can you remind yourself of God's faithfulness and His promise to help you endure and overcome these challenges? Reflect on practical ways to seek God's guidance and strength throughout the day.

Scripture: 1 Corinthians 10:13
"No temptation has overtaken you except such as is common to man; but God is faithful, who will not allow you to be tempted beyond what you are able, but with the temptation will also make the way of escape, that you may be able to bear it."

Reflection: As the day comes to a close, reflecting on 1 Corinthians 10:13 allows us to review how God has been faithful in helping us navigate temptations and trials. Throughout the day, we may have faced various challenges, but this verse reassures us that God is with us, providing strength and a way of escape. Looking back on the day, we can identify moments where we experienced God's guidance and strength. As we meditate on this scripture tonight, let's thank God for His faithfulness and for providing a way of escape in times of temptation. Let's seek His forgiveness for any moments of weakness and ask for His continued guidance and strength.

Prayer: Gracious God, as we end this day, we thank You for Your faithfulness and for helping us navigate temptations and trials. We are grateful for Your constant presence and guidance. Forgive us for any moments of weakness today, and help us to rely on Your strength and wisdom. As we rest, fill our hearts with peace and prepare us for the day ahead. In Jesus' name, we pray. Amen.

Meditative Thought: Reflect on the moments today where you faced temptations or trials. How did God provide strength and a way of escape? Consider how you can continue to rely on His faithfulness and guidance. Surrender any remaining concerns to Him as you prepare for rest, trusting in His promise to help you endure and overcome.

SEPTEMBER 6

MORNING DEVOTION

Scripture: 2 Corinthians 11:14
"And no wonder! For Satan himself transforms himself into an angel of light."

Reflection: As we begin our day, 2 Corinthians 11:14 serves as a sobering reminder to stay vigilant and discerning. The verse warns us that Satan can disguise himself as an angel of light, which means that not everything that appears good or right is truly from God. This calls us to exercise discernment in our daily lives, ensuring that we seek and follow the true light of Christ. Starting the day with this awareness can help us navigate our interactions, decisions, and thoughts with greater spiritual wisdom. It encourages us to seek God's guidance in all things and to test the spirits to ensure we are following the path God intends for us. As we meditate on this scripture, let's commit to seeking God's truth and wisdom in all we do today. Let's pray for the discernment to distinguish between what merely appears good and what is genuinely of God.

Prayer: Heavenly Father, as we start this day, we ask for Your wisdom and discernment. Help us to see through the deceptions of the enemy and to recognize Your true light. Guide our thoughts, actions, and decisions, so that we may follow Your path. Protect us from the subtle lies that may lead us astray, and help us to stay rooted in Your Word and Your truth. In Jesus' name, we pray. Amen.

Meditative Thought: Consider the various situations and decisions you might face today. Reflect on how you can seek God's wisdom and discernment to ensure you are following His truth and rest assured in Christ Jesus!

Scripture: 2 Corinthians 11:14

"And no wonder! For Satan himself transforms himself into an angel of light."

Reflection: As the day comes to a close, 2 Corinthians 11:14 invites us to reflect on the importance of discernment and vigilance in our spiritual walk. Throughout the day, we may have encountered situations that seemed good or right but were not aligned with God's truth. Reflecting on this scripture in the evening helps us review our day with a discerning eye. Were there moments when something seemed good but didn't align with God's Word? How did we respond to such situations? This reflection encourages us to deepen our reliance on God's wisdom and to remain vigilant against the subtle deceptions of the enemy. As we meditate on this scripture tonight, let's thank God for His guidance and ask for increased discernment. Let's seek His forgiveness for any times we may have been led astray and commit to growing in our understanding and application of His truth.

Prayer: Gracious God, as we end this day, we thank You for Your guidance and protection. Forgive us for any moments when we may have been deceived by appearances and strayed from Your truth. Increase our discernment and help us to recognize the enemy's tactics. Guide us to stay rooted in Your Word and to seek Your wisdom in all things. Fill our hearts with Your light and truth as we rest, and prepare us for the challenges of tomorrow. In Jesus' name, we pray. Amen.

Meditative Thought: Reflect on your day and consider any moments where appearances may have been deceiving. As you prepare for rest, surrender any concerns to God and ask for His wisdom and protection in discerning truth from deception.

Scripture: Psalm 109:26
"Help me, O Lord my God! Oh, save me according to Your mercy,"

Reflection: As we begin our day, Psalm 109:26 offers a heartfelt plea for God's assistance and mercy. This verse reminds us of our dependence on God, highlighting our need for His help and salvation. In our daily lives, we often encounter situations that are beyond our control, moments that require more than our own strength and wisdom. Starting the day by acknowledging our reliance on God sets a tone of humility and trust. When we call out to God for help, we are reminded of His abundant mercy. His help is not based on our merits but on His loving-kindness. This assurance can bring us peace and confidence as we face the day, knowing that God's mercy is always available to us, ready to support and sustain us. As we meditate on this scripture, let's make it our prayer to seek God's help and trust in His mercy. Let's open our hearts to His guidance and strength, allowing His presence to lead us through the day.

Prayer: Heavenly Father, as we begin this day, we cry out to You for help. We recognize our need for Your strength and wisdom in all that we do. Save us according to Your mercy, and guide our steps. Fill our hearts with trust and peace, knowing that Your loving-kindness is ever-present. We rely on You, Lord, and we thank You for Your unending mercy. In Jesus' name, we pray. Amen.

Meditative Thought: Consider the tasks and challenges you may face today. Reflect on how you can seek God's help and rely on His mercy in each situation. How can you cultivate a spirit of humility and trust, acknowledging your dependence on God throughout the day?

Scripture: Psalm 109:26
"Help me, O Lord my God! Oh, save me according to Your mercy,"

Reflection: As the day comes to a close, Psalm 109:26 reminds us to reflect on the many ways we have needed and received God's help and mercy throughout the day. This verse is a call to remember that in all circumstances, our ultimate reliance is on God. As we review the events of the day, we can identify moments where we sought and experienced His help, even in ways we might not have immediately recognized. Ending the day with this scripture allows us to acknowledge God's faithful presence and His merciful interventions. Recognizing His mercy brings comfort and peace, reassuring us that God is always ready to save and support us. As we meditate on this scripture tonight, let's thank God for His help and mercy throughout the day. Let's surrender any remaining concerns to Him, trusting in His continued guidance and care.

Prayer: Gracious God, as we end this day, we thank You for Your help and mercy. We recognize the many ways You have supported and guided us today. Save us according to Your loving-kindness and help us to trust in Your care as we rest. We surrender our worries and concerns to You, knowing that You are always with us. Fill our hearts with peace and gratitude. In Jesus' name, we pray. Amen.

Meditative Thought: Reflect on the day and identify moments where you experienced God's help and mercy. How did His presence guide and support you? As you prepare for rest, consider how you can continue to rely on God's mercy and help in the days to come. Surrender any lingering concerns to Him, trusting in His faithful care.

SEPTEMBER 8

MORNING DEVOTION

Scripture: 2 Samuel 22:3
"The God of my strength, in whom I will trust; My shield and the horn of my salvation, My stronghold and my refuge; My Savior, You save me from violence."

Reflection: As we start our day, 2 Samuel 22:3 offers a powerful declaration of trust and reliance on God. This verse highlights several aspects of God's character and role in our lives: He is our strength, shield, salvation, stronghold, refuge, and Savior. Recognizing God in these ways provides a foundation of confidence and security as we face the day's challenges. Beginning the day with this acknowledgment helps us to remember that we are not alone. Trusting in God means relying on His power and wisdom rather than our own. This morning, let's commit to trusting God fully, knowing that He is our ultimate source of strength and safety. As we meditate on this scripture, let's focus on the specific ways we need God's strength and protection today. Let's open our hearts to His guidance and trust Him to be our refuge and Savior in every situation.

Prayer: Heavenly Father, as we begin this day, we acknowledge You as our strength and our shield. We trust in You, our salvation and stronghold. Guide us and protect us as we navigate the challenges ahead. Help us to rely on Your strength and wisdom rather than our own. Be our refuge and Savior in every moment. Thank You for Your unfailing love and protection. In Jesus' name, we pray. Amen.

Meditative Thought: Reflect on the areas of your life where you need God's strength and protection today. How can you actively trust in Him as your shield and refuge? Consider practical ways to remind yourself of God's presence and power throughout the day.

Scripture: 2 Samuel 22:3
"The God of my strength, in whom I will trust; My shield and the horn of my salvation, My stronghold and my refuge; My Savior, You save me from violence."

Reflection: As the day comes to a close, reflecting on 2 Samuel 22:3 allows us to review the day's events with gratitude and recognition of God's faithfulness. This verse reassures us that God is our strength, shield, salvation, stronghold, refuge, and Savior. Looking back on the day, we can see how He has protected, guided, and sustained us. Ending the day with this acknowledgment helps us to find peace and rest in God's unfailing protection and love. It reminds us that no matter what we faced today, God was with us, providing strength and refuge. As we meditate on this scripture tonight, let's thank God for His strength and protection throughout the day. Let's surrender any remaining fears or anxieties to Him, trusting in His continued care and provision.

Prayer: Gracious God, as we end this day, we thank You for being our strength and shield. We are grateful for Your protection and guidance. Help us to rest in Your presence, trusting in Your unfailing love and salvation. We surrender our fears and anxieties to You, knowing that You are our refuge and stronghold. Thank You for Your constant care and for saving us from harm. In Jesus' name, we pray. Amen.

Meditative Thought: Reflect on the day and identify moments where you experienced God's strength and protection. How did His presence guide and sustain you? As you prepare for rest, consider how you can deepen your trust in God as your refuge and Savior. Surrender any lingering worries to Him, finding peace in His unfailing love and care.

SEPTEMBER 9

MORNING DEVOTION

Scripture: Proverbs 12:1
"Whoever loves instruction loves knowledge, but he who hates correction is stupid."

Reflection: As we begin our day, Proverbs 12:1 challenges us to embrace a spirit of teachability. Loving instruction and knowledge means being open to learning and growing, even when it involves correction. The verse contrasts this positive attitude with the foolishness of rejecting correction. It's a call to humility, encouraging us to value wisdom and learning, even when it comes in the form of constructive criticism. Starting the day with this mindset can set a positive tone for our interactions and decisions. It prepares us to be receptive to feedback and to seek growth in all areas of our lives. As we meditate on this scripture, let's commit to seeking wisdom and being open to correction. Let's ask God to give us a humble heart that values growth and learning.

Prayer: Heavenly Father, as we start this day, we ask for a teachable spirit. Help us to love instruction and to seek knowledge. Give us the humility to accept correction and to learn from it. Guide us in our quest for wisdom and understanding. May we be open to growth in all areas of our lives, reflecting Your love and truth. In Jesus' name, we pray. Amen.

Meditative Thought: Consider how you can be more open to instruction and correction today. Reflect on the benefits of embracing a teachable spirit. How can you apply this attitude in your relationships, work, and spiritual life?

Scripture: Proverbs 12:1
"Whoever loves instruction loves knowledge, but he who hates correction is stupid."

Reflection: As the day comes to a close, Proverbs 12:1 invites us to reflect on our openness to instruction and correction throughout the day. This verse underscores the importance of loving knowledge and being willing to learn from our experiences, including the feedback and correction we receive. It serves as a reminder that rejecting correction is not only unwise but hinders our growth. Reflecting on our reactions helps us to grow in humility and wisdom, preparing us to be better learners in the future. As we meditate on this scripture tonight, let's thank God for the lessons learned today. Let's seek His forgiveness for any moments of resistance to correction and ask for a more receptive heart.

Prayer: Gracious God, as we end this day, we thank You for the opportunities to learn and grow. Forgive us for any times when we resisted correction. Help us to embrace a spirit of humility and to love instruction. Guide us in our pursuit of knowledge and wisdom. May we continue to grow in understanding and reflect Your truth in our lives. In Jesus' name, we pray. Amen.

Meditative Thought: Reflect on your responses to instruction and correction today. How did you embrace or resist these opportunities for growth? Consider how you can cultivate a more teachable spirit in your daily life. As you prepare for rest, ask God for the grace to love knowledge and to welcome correction with an open heart.

Scripture: Romans 12:2 "And do not be conformed to this world, but be transformed by the renewing of your mind, that you may prove what is that good and acceptable and perfect will of God."

Reflection: As we start our day, Romans 12:2 calls us to a life of transformation rather than conformity. The world around us often pressures us to fit in, adopt its values, and follow its ways. However, this verse encourages us to resist that pressure and instead seek transformation through the renewal of our minds. This transformation allows us to understand and live out God's good, acceptable, and perfect will.

Renewing our minds involves immersing ourselves in God's Word, spending time in prayer, and being mindful of the influences we allow into our lives. By focusing on these spiritual disciplines, we align our thoughts with God's thoughts and our ways with His ways. This morning, let's commit to renewing our minds, seeking God's will, and living a life that reflects His truth and love.

Prayer: Heavenly Father, as we begin this day, help us not to conform to the patterns of this world. Transform us by renewing our minds through Your Word and Your Spirit. Guide us to understand and live out Your good, acceptable, and perfect will. Strengthen us to resist the pressures of the world and to live according to Your truth. In Jesus' name, we pray. Amen.

Meditative Thought: Reflect on how you can renew your mind today. What steps can you take to immerse yourself in God's Word and align your thoughts with His? Consider the influences in your life and how you can ensure they are leading you closer to God's will.

Scripture: Romans 12:2 "And do not be conformed to this world, but be transformed by the renewing of your mind, that you may prove what is that good and acceptable and perfect will of God."

Reflection: As the day comes to a close, Romans 12:2 invites us to reflect on how we lived out this call to transformation today. Did we resist the pressures to conform to the world's ways? Did we seek to renew our minds through God's Word and prayer? This verse reminds us that through this renewal, we can discern and demonstrate God's will in our lives.

Reviewing our day with this verse in mind helps us identify moments where we either conformed to worldly patterns or sought transformation through God's truth. It encourages us to continuously seek a deeper understanding of His will and to live it out in our daily actions. This evening, let's reflect on how we allowed God's transforming power to work in us and commit to further renewal.

Prayer: Gracious God, as we end this day, we thank You for Your transforming power in our lives. Forgive us for any moments when we conformed to the ways of this world. Help us to continually renew our minds through Your Word and Spirit. Guide us to discern and live out Your good, acceptable, and perfect will. Strengthen us to resist worldly pressures and to walk in Your truth. In Jesus' name, we pray. Amen.

Meditative Thought: Reflect on your day and consider how you responded to the call to not conform to the world. How did you seek transformation through the renewal of your mind? Identify any areas where you struggled and pray for God's guidance and strength to continue this transformative journey. Surrender your day to God, asking Him to continue to renew and transform you according to His will.

Scripture: Colossians 3:1-2

"If then you were raised with Christ, seek those things which are above, where Christ is, sitting at the right hand of God. Set your mind on things above, not on things on the earth."

Reflection: As we begin our day, Colossians 3:1-2 calls us to focus our hearts and minds on heavenly things. Being raised with Christ means that our lives are now oriented toward His kingdom and values. Instead of being preoccupied with earthly concerns and desires, we are encouraged to seek and prioritize the things that reflect God's eternal kingdom. This shift in focus helps us to live with purpose and direction. By setting our minds on things above, we are reminded of our true identity in Christ and the eternal perspective that should guide our actions and decisions. It brings a sense of peace and purpose, knowing that our lives are aligned with God's will. As we meditate on this scripture, let's commit to starting the day with a heavenly mindset. Let's seek God's presence and guidance in all that we do, allowing His values to shape our thoughts, actions, and priorities.

Prayer: Heavenly Father, as we start this day, we thank You for raising us with Christ. Help us to seek the things which are above and to set our minds on heavenly values. Guide our thoughts and actions so that they reflect Your kingdom. Fill us with Your peace and purpose as we go about our day. May our lives honor and glorify You in all we do. In Jesus' name, we pray. Amen.

Meditative Thought: Consider how you can focus on heavenly things today. What practical steps can you take to set your mind on things above? Reflect on your daily routines and interactions, and think about how you can infuse them with a heavenly perspective.

Scripture: Colossians 3:1-2
"If then you were raised with Christ, seek those things which are above, where Christ is, sitting at the right hand of God. Set your mind on things above, not on things on the earth."

Reflection: As the day comes to a close, Colossians 3:1-2 invites us to reflect on how we sought heavenly things throughout the day. This scripture encourages us to evaluate our thoughts and actions, considering whether they were focused on earthly concerns or aligned with our new life in Christ. Reflecting on this helps us to realign our priorities and renew our commitment to living with an eternal perspective. Reflection brings an opportunity for gratitude for the moments we lived in alignment with God's will and for seeking His forgiveness and guidance where we fell short. As we meditate on this scripture tonight, let's thank God for His presence and guidance today. Let's ask for His continued help in setting our minds on heavenly things and growing in our relationship with Him.

Prayer: Gracious God, as we end this day, we thank You for the opportunity to seek the things above. Forgive us for the times when we were distracted by earthly concerns. Help us to continually set our minds on heavenly values and to live out our identity in Christ. Guide us to grow closer to You and to reflect Your love and truth in our lives. Thank You for Your constant presence and guidance. In Jesus' name, we pray. Amen.

Meditative Thought: Reflect on your day and consider where you focused on heavenly things and where you might have been preoccupied with earthly concerns. How can you continue to set your mind on things above? As you prepare for rest, ask God to help you maintain a heavenly perspective in all aspects of your life.

SEPTEMBER 12

MORNING DEVOTION

Scripture: John 3:18

"He who believes in Him is not condemned; but he who does not believe is condemned already, because he has not believed in the name of the only begotten Son of God."

Reflection: As we begin our day, John 3:18 reminds us of the profound importance of faith in Jesus Christ. This verse presents a clear distinction between those who believe in Him and those who do not. Believing in Jesus means we are not condemned; we are free from judgment because we have accepted the gift of salvation through Christ. Starting our day with this truth encourages us to live in the light of the grace we have received. It challenges us to share the love and truth of Jesus with others, knowing the eternal significance of belief in Him. It also reassures us of our secure position in Christ, allowing us to face the day with confidence and peace. As we meditate on this scripture, let's focus on the gift of salvation through Jesus and commit to living out our faith boldly and compassionately.

Prayer: Heavenly Father, thank You for the gift of salvation through Your Son, Jesus Christ. As we begin this day, help us to live in the light of Your grace, knowing that we are not condemned because of our faith in Him. Give us the courage to share Your love and truth with those around us. Strengthen our faith and help us to reflect Your love in all we do. In Jesus' name, we pray. Amen.

Meditative Thought: Reflect on the assurance of not being condemned because of your faith in Jesus. How can you live out this assurance today? Consider how you can share the message of salvation with someone who has not yet believed.

Scripture: John 3:18
"He who believes in Him is not condemned; but he who does not believe is condemned already, because he has not believed in the name of the only begotten Son of God."

Reflection: As the day comes to a close, John 3:18 invites us to reflect on our faith journey and our witness to others. This verse emphasizes the critical importance of belief in Jesus Christ for salvation and freedom from condemnation. Reflecting on this at the end of the day allows us to evaluate how we lived out our faith and shared the message of Jesus with others. Reviewing our day with this verse in mind helps us to consider whether we have shown the love and truth of Christ in our interactions. As we meditate on this scripture tonight, let's thank God for the assurance of our salvation through faith in Jesus. Let's also pray for opportunities to share this life-saving message with others and for the courage to do so.

Prayer: Gracious God, as we end this day, we thank You for the assurance of salvation through faith in Jesus Christ. Forgive us for any missed opportunities to share Your love and truth with others. Help us to be bold and compassionate witnesses of Your gospel. Strengthen our faith and use us to draw others to believe in the name of Your only begotten Son. Guide us as we rest and prepare for a new day. In Jesus' name, we pray. Amen.

Meditative Thought: Reflect on your interactions today and consider how you lived out your faith. Were there opportunities to share the message of Jesus that you took or missed? As you prepare for rest, ask God for more opportunities to share His love and for the courage to seize them.

Scripture: Revelation 21:4

"And God will wipe away every tear from their eyes; there shall be no more death, nor sorrow, nor crying. There shall be no more pain, for the former things have passed away."

Reflection: As we begin our day, Revelation 21:4 offers a powerful and comforting promise of the future. This verse speaks of a time when God will remove all suffering, pain, and death. It is a vision of the new heaven and new earth where God's presence will bring complete restoration and peace. The assurance that God will wipe away every tear and that sorrow and pain will be no more provides hope and strength for today. Starting our day with this promise can transform our perspective. It reminds us that our current struggles and pains are temporary and that God's ultimate plan is for our eternal joy and peace. This hope empowers us to face our daily challenges with courage and faith, knowing that God's promises are true and that a glorious future awaits us. As we meditate on this scripture, let's hold onto the hope of God's future promises. Let's allow this vision of God's ultimate restoration to inspire and strengthen us throughout the day.

Prayer: Heavenly Father, we thank You for the promise of a future without pain, sorrow, or death. As we start this day, help us to hold onto this hope and allow it to strengthen us in our daily challenges. Remind us that our current sufferings are temporary and that Your plan for us is eternal joy and peace. Fill us with Your peace and courage today. In Jesus' name, we pray. Amen.

Meditative Thought: Reflect on the promise of a future without pain or sorrow. How does this hope impact your perspective on today's challenges? Consider how you can live with this eternal perspective, finding strength and courage in God's promises.

Scripture: Revelation 21:4
"And God will wipe away every tear from their eyes; there shall be no more death, nor sorrow, nor crying. There shall be no more pain, for the former things have passed away."

Reflection: As the day comes to a close, Revelation 21:4 invites us to reflect on God's promise of ultimate restoration and comfort. This verse assures us that there will come a time when God will remove all tears, pain, and sorrow from our lives. Reflecting on this promise at the end of the day can bring deep comfort and peace, especially if we have faced difficulties or pain. This assurance can bring peace to our hearts and help us rest, knowing that God is in control and that His promises are sure. As we meditate on this scripture tonight, let's thank God for His promise of a future without pain and sorrow. Let's seek His comfort for any pain we experienced today and rest in the assurance of His ultimate restoration.

Prayer: Gracious God, as we end this day, we thank You for the promise of a future where there will be no more pain, sorrow, or death. We thank You for the comfort and hope this promise brings. Please comfort us in our current struggles and help us to rest in Your peace tonight. Remind us of Your faithfulness and the eternal joy that awaits us. In Jesus' name, we pray. Amen.

Meditative Thought: Reflect on any pain or sorrow you experienced today. How does the promise of God's ultimate restoration bring comfort to you? As you prepare for rest, consider how this promise of a future free from pain can help you find peace and hope in God's faithfulness.

SEPTEMBER 14

MORNING DEVOTION

Scripture: Psalm 139:23
"Search me, O God, and know my heart; try me, and know my anxieties."

Reflection: As we begin our day, Psalm 139:23 invites us to open our hearts fully to God. This verse is a prayer of vulnerability and trust, asking God to examine our innermost thoughts and feelings. It's a request for God to reveal anything within us that might be causing us distress or leading us away from Him. By inviting God to search our hearts, we acknowledge His intimate knowledge of us and His ability to guide us towards peace and righteousness. Starting our day with this prayer can help us approach our day with a clear and open heart. It sets the tone for self-examination and openness to God's guidance and correction. Trusting God with our anxieties and fears allows us to face the day with a sense of peace, knowing that He is with us and understands us completely. As we meditate on this scripture, let's commit to allowing God to search our hearts and reveal anything that needs His healing touch. Let's begin our day with openness and trust in His perfect knowledge and love.

Prayer: Heavenly Father, as we start this day, we ask You to search our hearts and know our innermost thoughts and anxieties. Reveal to us anything that needs Your healing and guidance. Help us to trust You completely and to walk in Your ways. Fill us with Your peace and lead us throughout this day. In Jesus' name, we pray. Amen.

Meditative Thought: Consider what it means to invite God to search your heart. Reflect on any anxieties or concerns you are carrying and offer them to God. Trust in His ability to bring clarity and peace to your mind and heart.

Scripture: Psalm 139:23

"Search me, O God, and know my heart; try me, and know my anxieties."

Reflection: As the day comes to a close, Psalm 139:23 serves as a powerful prayer for reflection and self-examination. This verse encourages us to invite God into our hearts to reveal our true thoughts and anxieties. It's a moment to pause and reflect on our day, seeking God's insight into our actions, thoughts, and feelings. Reviewing our day with this prayer helps us identify areas where we may have fallen short or where we need God's guidance and healing. It's an opportunity to bring our worries and concerns before God, trusting in His understanding and care. By allowing God to know our hearts, we open ourselves to His transformative power and peace. As we meditate on this scripture tonight, let's seek God's presence and ask Him to search our hearts. Let's find rest in His knowledge and love, trusting Him to guide us and bring peace to our anxieties.

Prayer: Gracious God, as we end this day, we invite You to search our hearts and know our anxieties. Reveal to us anything that needs Your healing and guidance. We bring our worries and concerns before You, trusting in Your understanding and care. Help us to rest in Your peace and to trust in Your loving presence. In Jesus' name, we pray. Amen.

Meditative Thought: Reflect on your day and consider how you responded to various situations and emotions. What anxieties or concerns do you need to bring before God? As you prepare for rest, invite God to search your heart and trust in His ability to bring peace and clarity to your mind and soul.

SEPTEMBER 15

MORNING DEVOTION

Scripture: Isaiah 26:3

"You will keep him in perfect peace, Whose mind is stayed on You, Because he trusts in You."

Reflection: As we begin our day, Isaiah 26:3 offers a powerful promise of God's peace for those who trust in Him wholeheartedly. This verse highlights the connection between maintaining a steadfast focus on God and experiencing His perfect peace. When our minds are fixed on Him, when we trust in His goodness and sovereignty, He guards us with a peace that transcends understanding. Starting our day with this assurance encourages us to intentionally set our minds on God's presence and promises. By trusting in His faithfulness, we can face the challenges of the day with confidence and serenity, knowing that He is with us and that His peace will sustain us. As we meditate on this scripture, let's commit to keeping our minds steadfastly focused on God throughout the day. Let's trust in His promises and allow His peace to reign in our hearts regardless of the circumstances.

Prayer: Heavenly Father, thank You for the promise of perfect peace for those who trust in You. As we start this day, help us to keep our minds steadfastly fixed on You. Grant us the grace to trust in Your goodness and sovereignty, even in the midst of life's challenges. Fill us with Your peace that surpasses all understanding, and guide us in Your ways. In Jesus' name, we pray. Amen.

Meditative Thought: Reflect on times when you have experienced God's peace in the midst of difficulties. Consider how you can intentionally keep your mind stayed on Him throughout the day. As you prepare to face the day, ask God to help you trust in His promises and experience His perfect peace.

Scripture: Isaiah 26:3
"You will keep him in perfect peace, Whose mind is stayed on You, Because he trusts in You."

Reflection: As the day draws to a close, Isaiah 26:3 reminds us of God's promise to keep us in perfect peace when our minds are steadfastly focused on Him. This verse invites us to reflect on how we have experienced God's peace throughout the day and to consider areas where we may have allowed our focus to shift away from Him. Reviewing our day with this scripture in mind helps us to recognize moments when we may have become anxious or stressed due to taking our eyes off of God. As we meditate on this scripture tonight, let's thank God for the moments of peace we experienced today and ask for His forgiveness and guidance in areas where we allowed worry or distraction to take hold.

Prayer: Gracious God, as we end this day, we thank You for the promise of perfect peace for those who trust in You. Forgive us for the times when we allowed our focus to shift away from You, leading to anxiety and stress. Help us to keep our minds steadfastly fixed on You, trusting in Your goodness and sovereignty. Grant us Your peace as we rest tonight, and renew our hearts for the day ahead. In Jesus' name, we pray. Amen.

Meditative Thought: Reflect on the moments of peace you experienced today and thank God for them. Consider areas where you allowed worry or distraction to take hold, and ask God for His forgiveness and guidance. As you prepare for rest, commit to keeping your mind stayed on Him tomorrow, trusting in His promises and experiencing His perfect peace.

Scripture: Romans 8:7
"Because the carnal mind is enmity against God; for it is not subject to the law of God, nor indeed can be."

Reflection: As we begin our day, Romans 8:7 confronts us with the stark reality of the carnal mind's hostility towards God. This verse highlights the inherent opposition between our sinful nature and the righteousness of God. It serves as a sobering reminder of the ongoing battle within us, as our sinful inclinations rebel against God's will and authority. Starting our day with this scripture prompts us to examine our hearts and minds. It challenges us to recognize areas where we may be resisting God's guidance or yielding to the desires of our flesh. As we meditate on this scripture, let's ask God to reveal any areas of enmity towards Him in our hearts. Let's seek His forgiveness and guidance, inviting His Spirit to transform our minds and conform them to His righteousness.

Prayer: Heavenly Father, as we start this day, we acknowledge the enmity of our carnal minds against You. Forgive us for the times when we have rebelled against Your will and yielded to the desires of our flesh. Help us to surrender our hearts and minds to You completely, allowing Your Spirit to renew and transform us. Grant us the grace to walk in alignment with Your truth and righteousness. In Jesus' name, we pray. Amen.

Meditative Thought: Reflect on any areas in your life where you may be resisting God's will or yielding to the desires of the flesh. Ask God to reveal these areas to you and surrender them to His transformative power. Consider how you can actively align your thoughts and actions with His righteousness throughout the day.

SEPTEMBER 16
EVENING DEVOTION

Scripture: Romans 8:7
"Because the carnal mind is enmity against God; for it is not subject to the law of God, nor indeed can be."

Reflection: As the day comes to a close, Romans 8:7 prompts us to reflect on the ongoing battle between our carnal minds and the righteousness of God. This verse reminds us of the inherent enmity within us that rebels against God's law and authority. It calls us to examine our hearts and minds, recognizing any areas where we may have allowed our sinful nature to prevail. Reviewing our day with this scripture in mind helps us to identify moments when we may have yielded to the desires of the flesh or resisted God's guidance. As we meditate on this scripture tonight, let's ask God to continue the work of transformation in our hearts and minds. Let's surrender any areas of enmity towards Him, inviting His Spirit to renew us and conform us to His righteousness.

Prayer: Gracious God, as we end this day, we confess the enmity of our carnal minds against You. Forgive us for the times when we have rebelled against Your law and authority. Renew our hearts and minds, O Lord, and transform us by Your Spirit. Help us to walk in obedience and alignment with Your will. Grant us Your strength and guidance for the day ahead. In Jesus' name, we pray. Amen.

Meditative Thought: Reflect on the moments throughout the day when you may have yielded to the desires of the flesh or resisted God's guidance. Surrender these areas to God and ask for His forgiveness and transformation. Commit to walking in alignment with His righteousness tomorrow, relying on His strength and guidance.

MORNING DEVOTION

Scripture: Hebrews 4:12
"For the word of God is living and powerful, and sharper than any two-edged sword, piercing even to the division of soul and spirit, and of joints and marrow, and is a discerner of the thoughts and intents of the heart."

Reflection: As we begin our day, Hebrews 4:12 reminds us of the profound power and effectiveness of God's Word. This verse portrays the Word of God as a living, dynamic force that penetrates deep into our beings, discerning our thoughts, intentions, and innermost desires. Starting our day with this scripture prompts us to approach God's Word with reverence and expectation. It challenges us to engage with Scripture not merely as a collection of ancient writings but as a living message from God Himself. As we meditate on this scripture, let's commit to immersing ourselves in God's Word each day. Let's open our hearts to its transformative power and allow it to shape our thoughts, intentions, and actions.

Prayer: Heavenly Father, we thank You for the living and powerful Word that You have given us. As we start this day, help us to approach Your Word with reverence and expectation. Open our hearts and minds to its transformative power. Use Your Word to penetrate deep into our beings, discerning our thoughts and intentions, and guiding us into alignment with Your will. May Your Word be a lamp to our feet and a light to our path. In Jesus' name, we pray. Amen.

Meditative Thought: Reflect on your approach to reading and studying God's Word. Are you engaging with it as a living message from God? As you prepare to face the day, ask God to help you approach His Word with reverence and expectation, allowing it to shape your thoughts and actions.

Scripture: Hebrews 4:12

"For the word of God is living and powerful, and sharper than any two-edged sword, piercing even to the division of soul and spirit, and of joints and marrow, and is a discerner of the thoughts and intents of the heart."

Reflection: As the day comes to a close, Hebrews 4:12 invites us to reflect on the transformative power of God's Word in our lives. This verse portrays Scripture as a dynamic force that penetrates deep into our beings, discerning our thoughts, intentions, and innermost desires. Reviewing our day with this scripture in mind helps us recognize moments when we encountered God's Word and the impact it had on us. It serves as a reminder of the ongoing work of transformation that God desires to do in our lives through His Word. As we reflect on our response to Scripture, we can seek God's guidance and ask Him to continue His work in us. As we meditate on this scripture tonight, let's thank God for the gift of His Word and its transformative power.

Prayer: Gracious God, as we end this day, we thank You for the living and powerful Word that You have given us. Forgive us for the times when we have neglected to engage with Your Word or failed to allow it to transform us. Renew our commitment to immersing ourselves in Scripture and opening our hearts to its transformative power. Continue Your work of transformation in us, O Lord, and guide us into alignment with Your will. In Jesus' name, we pray. Amen.

Meditative Thought: Reflect on moments throughout the day when you encountered God's Word. How did it impact you? As you prepare for rest, commit to seeking God's guidance through His Word and allowing it to continue its transformative work in your life.

SEPTEMBER 18

MORNING DEVOTION

Scripture: Philippians 4:8
"Finally, brethren, whatever things are true, whatever things are noble, whatever things are just, whatever things are pure, whatever things are lovely, whatever things are of good report, if there is any virtue and if there is anything praiseworthy—meditate on these things."

Reflection: As we begin our day, Philippians 4:8 provides a blueprint for our thought life. This verse calls us to focus our minds on things that are true, noble, just, pure, lovely, and of good report. It encourages us to fill our thoughts with virtues and things worthy of praise. By aligning our minds with these positive and uplifting qualities, we cultivate a mindset that honors God and brings peace to our souls. As we meditate on this scripture, let's examine our thought patterns and ask God to help us focus on what is good and honorable. Let's commit to cultivating a mindset that reflects His character and brings glory to His name.

Prayer: Heavenly Father, we thank You for the guidance of Your Word in our lives. As we start this day, help us to align our thoughts with what is true, noble, just, pure, lovely, and of good report. Guard our minds from negativity and impurity, and fill us with Your peace as we meditate on Your virtues. May our thoughts honor You and bring glory to Your name. In Jesus' name, we pray. Amen.

Meditative Thought: Reflect on the thoughts that typically occupy your mind. Are they in line with the qualities listed in Philippians 4:8? Ask God to help you redirect your thoughts to what is true, noble, just, pure, lovely, and of good report. Throughout the day, intentionally focus on these positive qualities and notice the difference it makes in your mindset and outlook.

Scripture: Philippians 4:8

"Finally, brethren, whatever things are true, whatever things are noble, whatever things are just, whatever things are pure, whatever things are lovely, whatever things are of good report, if there is any virtue and if there is anything praiseworthy—meditate on these things."

Reflection: As the day comes to a close, Philippians 4:8 reminds us of the importance of guarding our thought life. This verse encourages us to focus our minds on things that reflect God's character and values—things that are true, noble, just, pure, lovely, and of good report. By meditating on these virtues, we cultivate a mindset that honors God and brings peace to our souls. As we reflect on the day, we can seek God's forgiveness for any lapses in our thought life and ask Him to renew our minds. As we meditate on this scripture tonight, let's commit to guarding our thought life diligently. Let's ask God to help us focus on what is true and virtuous, allowing His peace to reign in our hearts and minds.

Prayer: Gracious God, as we end this day, we thank You for the guidance of Your Word. Forgive us for the times when we allowed negativity or impurity to infiltrate our thoughts. Renew our minds, O Lord, and help us to focus on what is true, noble, just, pure, lovely, and of good report. May our thoughts honor You and bring peace to our souls. In Jesus' name, we pray. Amen.

Meditative Thought: Reflect on the thoughts and attitudes you entertained throughout the day. Were they in line with the qualities listed in Philippians 4:8? Ask God to help you guard your thought life diligently and focus on what is true and virtuous. As you prepare for rest, commit to meditating on these positive qualities and allowing God's peace to reign in your heart and mind.

SEPTEMBER 19

MORNING DEVOTION

Scripture: Psalm 105:1
"Oh, give thanks to the Lord! Call upon His name; Make known His deeds among the peoples!"

Reflection: As we begin our day, Psalm 105:1 calls us to a posture of gratitude and praise. This verse exhorts us to give thanks to the Lord, to call upon His name, and to proclaim His mighty deeds among the nations. Starting our day with this scripture invites us to reflect on the countless blessings God has bestowed upon us. It prompts us to acknowledge His sovereignty and grace in our lives and to express our gratitude through prayer and proclamation. By recognizing and sharing God's mighty deeds, we invite others to join us in worship and praise. As we meditate on this scripture, let's take a moment to count our blessings and offer thanks to the Lord for His goodness and faithfulness. Let's commit to calling upon His name and proclaiming His deeds throughout the day, spreading His love and truth to those around us.

Prayer: Heavenly Father, we thank You for Your abundant blessings and unfailing love. As we start this day, help us to cultivate hearts of gratitude and praise. Enable us to call upon Your name and make known Your mighty deeds among the nations. Use us as vessels of Your love and truth, that others may come to know You and worship You. In Jesus' name, we pray. Amen.

Meditative Thought: Reflect on the blessings God has bestowed upon you. Take a moment to thank Him for His goodness and faithfulness in your life. Consider how you can proclaim His deeds among the nations and share His love and truth with those around you throughout the day.

Scripture: Psalm 105:1
"Oh, give thanks to the Lord! Call upon His name; Make known His deeds among the peoples!"

Reflection: As the day comes to a close, Psalm 105:1 reminds us of the importance of continuing in a spirit of thanksgiving and praise. This verse encourages us to give thanks to the Lord, to call upon His name, and to make known His deeds among the nations. As we reflect on the day, we can offer thanks to the Lord for His provision and guidance, and commit to being His ambassadors of love and truth in the world. As we meditate on this scripture tonight, let's take a moment to thank the Lord for His blessings and faithfulness throughout the day. Let's commit to calling upon His name and making known His deeds among the nations, that His name may be glorified and His kingdom may come on earth as it is in heaven.

Prayer: Gracious God, as we end this day, we thank You for Your abundant blessings and unfailing love. Forgive us for the times when we have failed to recognize Your goodness and faithfulness in our lives. Renew our hearts of gratitude and praise, O Lord, and empower us to continue to call upon Your name and make known Your deeds among the nations. May Your name be glorified in all the earth. In Jesus' name, we pray. Amen.

Meditative Thought: Reflect on the blessings and grace you experienced throughout the day. Take a moment to offer thanks to the Lord for His provision and guidance. Consider how you can continue to call upon His name and make known His deeds among the nations, sharing His love and truth with those around you.

Scripture: Colossians 3:15
"And let the peace of God rule in your hearts, to which also you were called in one body; and be thankful."

Reflection: As we begin our day, Colossians 3:15 calls us to allow the peace of God to rule in our hearts. This verse reminds us that as followers of Christ, we are called to live in harmony and unity with one another, grounded in the peace that comes from God. It urges us to cultivate a spirit of gratitude, acknowledging God's goodness and provision in our lives. Starting our day with this scripture invites us to surrender to the peace that surpasses all understanding, which can only come from God. As we meditate on this scripture, let's reflect on the areas of our lives where we may be struggling to find peace. Let's invite God to reign in our hearts and minds, trusting in His provision and guidance. And let's cultivate a spirit of gratitude, acknowledging His goodness and faithfulness in all things.

Prayer: Heavenly Father, we thank You for the peace that You offer to us. As we start this day, help us to let go of anxiety and worry, and to surrender to Your peace that surpasses all understanding. Reign in our hearts, O Lord, and help us to live in harmony and unity with one another. Fill us with a spirit of gratitude, that we may acknowledge Your goodness and provision in our lives. In Jesus' name, we pray. Amen.

Meditative Thought: Reflect on the areas of your life where you may be struggling to find peace. Cultivate a spirit of gratitude by acknowledging God's goodness and provision in your life. As you prepare to face the day, trust in His peace that surpasses all understanding.

Scripture: Colossians 3:15
"And let the peace of God rule in your hearts, to which also you were called in one body; and be thankful."

Reflection: As the day comes to a close, Colossians 3:15 invites us to reflect on the peace that comes from God and to cultivate a spirit of gratitude. This verse reminds us that as members of the body of Christ, we are called to live in unity and harmony, allowing the peace of God to rule in our hearts. As we meditate on this scripture tonight, let's take a moment to reflect on the peace that God has provided throughout the day. Let's surrender any concerns or worries to Him, trusting in His provision and care. And let's cultivate a spirit of gratitude, acknowledging His goodness and faithfulness in our lives.

Prayer: Gracious God, as we end this day, we thank You for the peace that You have provided to us. Forgive us for the times when we have allowed worry or anxiety to overshadow Your peace. Help us to surrender to Your sovereignty and care, trusting in Your provision and guidance. Fill us with a spirit of gratitude, that we may acknowledge Your goodness and faithfulness in all things. In Jesus' name, we pray. Amen.

Meditative Thought: Reflect on the peace that God has provided to you throughout the day. Surrender any concerns or worries to Him and trust in His provision and care. Cultivate a spirit of gratitude by acknowledging His goodness and faithfulness in your life. As you prepare for rest, allow His peace to rule in your heart.

Scripture: 1 Thessalonians 5:16-18

"Rejoice always, pray without ceasing, in everything give thanks; for this is the will of God in Christ Jesus for you."

Reflection: As we begin our day, 1 Thessalonians 5:16-18 offers a powerful reminder of the attitudes and actions that should characterize the life of a believer. These verses exhort us to rejoice always, to pray without ceasing, and to give thanks in all circumstances. They highlight the importance of maintaining a posture of joy, prayer, and gratitude in our daily lives. As we meditate on this scripture, let's reflect on our own practice of rejoicing, prayer, and thanksgiving. Let's ask God to help us cultivate these attitudes and behaviors more fully in our lives, that we may walk in alignment with His will and experience the fullness of His presence and blessing.

Prayer: Heavenly Father, we thank You for the guidance of Your Word in our lives. As we start this day, help us to cultivate a spirit of rejoicing, prayer, and gratitude. Enable us to rejoice always, to pray without ceasing, and to give thanks in all circumstances. May these attitudes and actions be evident in our lives, reflecting Your will for us in Christ Jesus. In His name, we pray. Amen.

Meditative Thought: Reflect on your practice of rejoicing, prayer, and thanksgiving in your daily life. Consider areas where you can grow in cultivating these attitudes and behaviors. Ask God to help you rejoice always, to pray without ceasing, and to give thanks in all circumstances, aligning your life more fully with His will.

Scripture: 1 Thessalonians 5:16-18
"Rejoice always, pray without ceasing, in everything give thanks; for this is the will of God in Christ Jesus for you."

Reflection: As the day comes to a close, 1 Thessalonians 5:16-18 invites us to reflect on the attitudes and actions that should characterize our lives as believers. These verses remind us to rejoice always, to pray without ceasing, and to give thanks in all circumstances. They emphasize the importance of maintaining a posture of joy, prayer, and gratitude in our daily lives. As we meditate on this scripture tonight, let's take a moment to reflect on our day and ask God to help us grow in rejoicing, prayer, and thanksgiving. Let's commit to aligning our lives more fully with His will, that we may experience the fullness of His presence and blessing.

Prayer: Gracious God, as we end this day, we thank You for the reminder of Your will for us in Christ Jesus. Forgive us for the times when we have failed to rejoice, pray, and give thanks as You have commanded. Renew our hearts and minds, O Lord, and help us to cultivate a spirit of rejoicing, prayer, and gratitude in all circumstances. May Your will be done in our lives, to Your glory. In Jesus' name, we pray. Amen.

Meditative Thought: Reflect on your practice of rejoicing, prayer, and thanksgiving throughout the day. Consider moments when you may have fallen short and ask God for forgiveness and guidance. Commit to aligning your life more fully with His will, seeking to cultivate joy, maintain a constant connection with Him through prayer, and express gratitude in all circumstances.

Scripture: 2 Corinthians 5:1

"For we know that if our earthly house, this tent, is destroyed, we have a building from God, a house not made with hands, eternal in the heavens."

Reflection: As we begin our day, 2 Corinthians 5:1 reminds us of the hope we have in Christ beyond the temporary realities of this world. This verse illustrates the contrast between our earthly bodies, described as temporary tents, and the eternal dwelling that awaits us in heaven—a building from God, not made with human hands. As we meditate on this scripture, let's consider how we can live in light of our heavenly citizenship. Let's ask God to help us prioritize eternal values over temporal ones and to invest our time and resources in things that have lasting significance. And let's rejoice in the assurance that, in Christ, we have a secure and eternal dwelling prepared for us in heaven.

Prayer: Heavenly Father, we thank You for the hope we have in Christ beyond the transient realities of this world. As we start this day, help us to fix our eyes on the eternal inheritance that awaits us in heaven. Grant us the wisdom to prioritize eternal values over temporal ones and to live in light of our heavenly citizenship. May our lives reflect the hope we have in Christ to a world in need. In His name, we pray. Amen.

Meditative Thought: Reflect on the contrast between the temporary nature of earthly life and the eternal dwelling that awaits believers in heaven. Consider how you can prioritize eternal values in your daily decisions and actions. Ask God to help you live with a perspective of hope and anticipation for the future glory that awaits you in Christ.

Scripture: 2 Corinthians 5:1
"For we know that if our earthly house, this tent, is destroyed, we have a building from God, a house not made with hands, eternal in the heavens."

Reflection: As the day comes to a close, 2 Corinthians 5:1 invites us to reflect on the eternal hope we have in Christ beyond the transient realities of this world. This verse reminds us that our earthly bodies are temporary. Reviewing our day with this scripture in mind helps us to evaluate how we have lived in light of our heavenly citizenship. It encourages us to rejoice in the assurance of our future glory in Christ, even as we navigate the challenges and uncertainties of this present life. As we meditate on this scripture tonight, let's take a moment to thank God for the hope we have in Christ beyond the transient realities of this world. And let's rest in the assurance that, in Christ, we have a secure and eternal dwelling prepared for us in heaven.

Prayer: Gracious God, as we end this day, we thank You for the hope we have in Christ beyond the transient realities of this world. Forgive us for the times when we have prioritized temporal values over eternal ones and lost sight of our heavenly citizenship. Renew our minds, O Lord, and help us to live with a perspective of eternal significance in all that we do. May our lives bring glory to Your name. In His name, we pray. Amen.

Meditative Thought: Reflect on how you have lived in light of your heavenly citizenship throughout the day. Consider areas where you may need to prioritize eternal values over temporal ones. Ask God to help you live with a perspective of eternal significance and to guide your decisions and actions accordingly. Rest in the assurance of your future glory in Christ.

SEPTEMBER 23

MORNING DEVOTION

Scripture: Philippians 1:21
"For to me, to live is Christ, and to die is gain."

Reflection: As we begin our day, Philippians 1:21 offers a profound perspective on the purpose and meaning of life. This verse encapsulates the essence of the Christian faith, declaring that for the believer, life is found in Christ alone. It reminds us that our ultimate purpose and fulfillment are found in living for Him and His kingdom. As we meditate on this scripture, let's examine our hearts and lives to discern whether we are living with a Christ-centered focus. Let's ask God to help us surrender our ambitions, desires, and fears to Him, trusting in His sovereign plan for our lives. And let's commit to living each moment in light of the truth that to live is Christ.

Prayer: Heavenly Father, we thank You for the gift of life and the privilege of knowing Christ as our Savior and Lord. As we start this day, help us to live with a Christ-centered focus, recognizing that true fulfillment and significance are found in Him alone. Grant us the courage to surrender our ambitions, desires, and fears to You, trusting in Your sovereign plan for our lives. May our lives bring glory to Your name. In Jesus' name, we pray. Amen.

Meditative Thought: Reflect on whether your life is truly centered on Christ. Consider whether your priorities and goals align with His will. Ask God to reveal any areas where you may be living for yourself rather than for Him. Surrender your ambitions, desires, and fears to Him, trusting in His sovereign plan for your life. Commit to living each moment in light of the truth that to live is Christ.

Scripture: Philippians 1:21
"For to me, to live is Christ, and to die is gain."

Reflection: As the day comes to a close, Philippians 1:21 invites us to reflect on the significance of living for Christ. This verse reminds us that true fulfillment and significance are found in Him alone, and that even in death, we gain eternity with Him. It challenges us to evaluate whether we have truly lived with a Christ-centered focus throughout the day. As we meditate on this scripture tonight, let's take a moment to thank God for the gift of life and the privilege of knowing Christ as our Savior and Lord. Let's ask Him to forgive us for any moments when we may have failed to live with a Christ-centered focus and to renew our commitment to His lordship in our lives.

Prayer: Gracious God, as we end this day, we thank You for the gift of life and the privilege of knowing Christ as our Savior and Lord. Forgive us for any moments when we have failed to live with a Christ-centered focus. Renew our hearts and minds, O Lord, and help us to recommit ourselves to His lordship and supremacy. May our lives bring glory to Your name. In Jesus' name, we pray. Amen.

Meditative Thought: Reflect on whether your actions and attitudes throughout the day have reflected your commitment to living for Christ. Confess any areas where you may have fallen short and recommit yourself to His lordship and supremacy. Rest in the assurance that even in death, you gain the ultimate prize of eternity with Him.

SEPTEMBER 24

MORNING DEVOTION

Scripture: Psalm 23:4

"Yea, though I walk through the valley of the shadow of death, I will fear no evil; For You are with me; Your rod and Your staff, they comfort me."

Reflection: As we begin our day, Psalm 23:4 offers comfort and assurance in the midst of life's challenges and uncertainties. This verse depicts the psalmist's unwavering trust in God's presence and protection, even in the darkest and most difficult times. It reminds us that we need not fear, for God is with us, guiding and comforting us with His rod and staff. As we meditate on this scripture, let's consider the challenges we may face today and entrust them to God's care. Let's ask Him to strengthen our faith and give us the courage to walk through the valleys of life without fear, knowing that He is with us. And let's find comfort and reassurance in His presence, knowing that His rod and staff are there to guide and comfort us.

Prayer: Heavenly Father, we thank You for Your faithfulness and presence in our lives. As we start this day, help us to trust in Your provision and protection, even in the midst of life's challenges and uncertainties. Strengthen our faith, O Lord, and give us the courage to walk through the valleys of life without fear, knowing that You are with us. May Your presence comfort and guide us each step of the way. In Jesus' name, we pray. Amen.

Meditative Thought: Reflect on the challenges you may face today and entrust them to God's care. Ask Him to strengthen your faith and give you the courage to walk through the valleys of life without fear. Find comfort and reassurance in His presence, knowing that He is with you, guiding and protecting you each step of the way.

Scripture: Psalm 23:4
"Yea, though I walk through the valley of the shadow of death, I will fear no evil; For You are with me; Your rod and Your staff, they comfort me."

Reflection: As the day comes to a close, Psalm 23:4 continues to offer comfort and reassurance in the midst of life's challenges and uncertainties. This verse reminds us of God's unwavering presence and protection, even in the darkest and most difficult times. It assures us that we need not fear, for He is with us, guiding and comforting us with His rod and staff. As we meditate on this scripture tonight, let's take a moment to thank God for His unwavering presence and protection in our lives. Let's reflect on the ways He has guided and comforted us throughout the day. And let's find peace and rest in His presence, knowing that His rod and staff are there to guide and comfort us each step of the way.

Prayer: Gracious God, as we end this day, we thank You for Your unwavering presence and protection in our lives. Forgive us for the times when we have allowed fear to overshadow Your faithfulness. Renew our hearts and minds, O Lord, and help us to trust in Your provision and protection, even in the darkest valleys of life. May Your presence continue to comfort and guide us each step of the way. In Jesus' name, we pray. Amen.

Meditative Thought: Reflect on the ways God has guided and comforted you throughout the day. Thank Him for His unwavering presence and protection in your life. Find peace and rest in His presence, knowing that His rod and staff are there to guide and comfort you each step of the way.

SEPTEMBER 25

MORNING DEVOTION

Scripture: 1 Peter 5:8-9

"Be sober, be vigilant; because your adversary the devil walks about like a roaring lion, seeking whom he may devour. Resist him, steadfast in the faith, knowing that the same sufferings are experienced by your brotherhood in the world."

Reflection: As we begin our day, 1 Peter 5:8-9 serves as a sobering reminder of the spiritual battle we face as believers. This passage urges us to be vigilant and alert, recognizing that the enemy, Satan, prowls around like a roaring lion, seeking to devour those who are vulnerable. As we meditate on this scripture, let's ask God to strengthen us for the spiritual battle ahead. Let's pray for discernment to recognize the enemy's tactics and wisdom to resist his attacks. And let's draw encouragement from the knowledge that we are not alone in our struggles, but are part of a community of believers who stand together in faith.

Prayer: Heavenly Father, we thank You for the reminder of the spiritual battle we face as believers. As we start this day, we ask for Your strength and protection against the schemes of the devil. Grant us discernment to recognize his tactics and wisdom to resist his attacks. Help us to stand firm in our faith, knowing that we are not alone but are united with our fellow believers who face similar trials. In Jesus' name, we pray. Amen.

Meditative Thought: Reflect on the reality of spiritual warfare and the importance of being spiritually alert. Identify areas in your life where you may be susceptible to the enemy's attacks. Pray for discernment and wisdom to resist the devil's schemes. Draw encouragement from the knowledge that you are part of a community of believers who stand together in faith.

Scripture: 1 Peter 5:8-9
"Be sober, be vigilant; because your adversary the devil walks about like a roaring lion, seeking whom he may devour. Resist him, steadfast in the faith, knowing that the same sufferings are experienced by your brotherhood in the world."

Reflection: As the day comes to a close, 1 Peter 5:8-9 continues to remind us of the ongoing spiritual battle we face as believers. This passage encourages us to remain sober and vigilant, recognizing the constant threat posed by our adversary, the devil. Reviewing our day with this scripture in mind helps us to evaluate how we have responded to the enemy's attacks. As we meditate on this scripture tonight, let's take a moment to reflect on the spiritual battles we have faced throughout the day. Let's confess any moments of weakness or doubt and recommit ourselves to resisting the devil with steadfast faith.

Prayer: Gracious God, as we end this day, we thank You for Your protection and strength in the face of spiritual battle. Forgive us for the times when we have faltered in our faith and succumbed to the enemy's attacks. Renew our hearts and minds, O Lord, and help us to resist the devil with steadfast faith. May we draw strength and encouragement from the solidarity of our fellow believers, knowing that we are not alone in our struggles. In Jesus' name, we pray. Amen.

Meditative Thought: Reflect on the spiritual battles you have faced throughout the day. Confess any moments of weakness or doubt and recommit yourself to resisting the devil with steadfast faith. Draw strength and encouragement from the knowledge that you are part of a community of believers who stand together in faith.

MORNING DEVOTION

Scripture: Hebrews 4:16

"Let us therefore come boldly to the throne of grace, that we may obtain mercy and find grace to help in time of need."

Reflection: As we begin our day, Hebrews 4:16 invites us to approach the throne of grace with boldness and confidence. This verse reminds us that, because of Jesus Christ, we have unrestricted access to God's presence, where we can find mercy and grace to help us in our time of need. As we meditate on this scripture, let's take a moment to consider the areas in our lives where we need God's help and intervention. Let's ask Him to grant us the courage to approach His throne with boldness and confidence, laying our burdens before Him. And let's trust in His promise to provide us with the mercy and grace we need to face the challenges of the day.

Prayer: Heavenly Father, we thank You for the privilege of approaching Your throne of grace with boldness and confidence. As we start this day, grant us the courage to come before You, laying our needs, concerns, and struggles at Your feet. Pour out Your mercy and grace upon us, O Lord, and help us to trust in Your provision and sustenance in every circumstance. In Jesus' name, we pray. Amen.

Meditative Thought: Reflect on the areas in your life where you need God's help and intervention. Ask Him to grant you the courage to approach His throne with boldness and confidence, laying your burdens before Him. Trust in His promise to provide you with the mercy and grace you need to face the challenges of the day.

Scripture: Hebrews 4:16
"Let us therefore come boldly to the throne of grace, that we may obtain mercy and find grace to help in time of need."

Reflection: As the day comes to a close, Hebrews 4:16 continues to remind us of the privilege and power of prayer. This verse encourages us to approach God's throne of grace with boldness and confidence, knowing that He eagerly welcomes us into His presence and offers us mercy and grace to help us in our time of need. Reviewing our day with this scripture in mind helps us to evaluate our prayer life and our reliance on God's provision and sustenance. As we meditate on this scripture tonight, let's take a moment to thank God for His faithfulness in answering our prayers and providing for our needs. Let's reflect on the areas where we may have faltered in our reliance on Him and commit to approaching His throne with boldness and confidence in the days ahead. And let's trust in His promise to continue granting us mercy and grace to help us in our time of need.

Prayer: Gracious God, as we end this day, we thank You for Your faithfulness in answering our prayers and providing for our needs. Forgive us for the times when we have failed to approach Your throne with boldness and confidence. Renew our hearts and minds, O Lord, and help us to rely on Your provision and sustenance in every circumstance. May Your mercy and grace continue to sustain us in our time of need. In Jesus' name, we pray. Amen.

Meditative Thought: Reflect on how you have approached God's throne of grace throughout the day. Thank Him for His faithfulness in answering your prayers and providing for your needs. Commit to approaching His throne with boldness and confidence in the days ahead.

SEPTEMBER 27

MORNING DEVOTION

Scripture: Philippians 4:19
"And my God shall supply all your need according to His riches in glory by Christ Jesus."

Reflection: As we begin our day, Philippians 4:19 reminds us of God's promise to provide for all our needs. This verse assures us that our Heavenly Father, who is infinitely rich in glory, will supply everything we require through Christ Jesus. Starting our day with this scripture prompts us to reflect on the faithfulness of God as our provider. As we meditate on this scripture, let's consider the areas in our lives where we need God's provision today. Let's bring our needs before Him in prayer, trusting that He will supply abundantly and according to His perfect will. And let's approach the day with a heart of gratitude, acknowledging God's faithfulness and provision in all things.

Prayer: Heavenly Father, we thank You for Your promise to supply all our needs according to Your riches in glory by Christ Jesus. As we start this day, help us to trust in Your abundant provision and to rely on Your faithfulness to meet all our needs. Grant us the wisdom to bring our concerns before You in prayer, knowing that You hear and answer according to Your perfect will. May Your provision fill us with confidence and gratitude as we navigate the day ahead. In Jesus' name, we pray. Amen.

Meditative Thought: Reflect on the areas in your life where you need God's provision today. Bring your needs before Him in prayer, trusting that He will supply abundantly and according to His perfect will. Approach the day with a heart of gratitude, acknowledging God's faithfulness and provision in all things.

Scripture: Philippians 4:19
"And my God shall supply all your need according to His riches in glory by Christ Jesus."

Reflection: As the day comes to a close, Philippians 4:19 continues to reassure us of God's faithful provision in our lives. This verse affirms that our Heavenly Father, who is rich in glory, will supply all our needs through Christ Jesus. As we meditate on this scripture tonight, let's take a moment to thank God for His provision throughout the day. Let's reflect on the ways He has met our needs and sustained us in every circumstance. And let's commit to trusting in His ongoing provision, knowing that He will continue to supply all our needs according to His riches in glory.

Prayer: Gracious God, as we end this day, we thank You for Your faithful provision in our lives. Forgive us for the times when we have doubted Your ability to meet our needs. Renew our hearts and minds, O Lord, and help us to trust in Your ongoing faithfulness, even in the face of challenges or uncertainties. May Your provision fill us with gratitude and peace as we rest in Your care tonight. In Jesus' name, we pray. Amen.

Meditation Thought: Reflect on the ways God has provided for you throughout the day. Thank Him for His faithfulness and provision in every circumstance. Commit to trusting in His ongoing provision, knowing that He will continue to supply all your needs according to His riches in glory.

SEPTEMBER 28

MORNING DEVOTION

Scripture: Colossians 3:2
"Set your mind on things above, not on things on the earth."

Reflection: As we begin our day, Colossians 3:2 calls us to shift our focus from earthly concerns to heavenly priorities. This verse reminds us to intentionally direct our thoughts and attention towards things that are eternal and of God, rather than being consumed by the transient and temporal matters of this world. As we meditate on this scripture, let's consider the areas in our lives where our focus may be misplaced or distracted by earthly concerns. Let's ask God to help us set our minds on things above, prioritizing His kingdom and righteousness. And let's commit to intentionally cultivating a mindset that is oriented towards heavenly values and eternal realities.

Prayer: Heavenly Father, we thank You for the reminder to set our minds on things above, not on things of the earth. As we start this day, help us to shift our focus from earthly concerns to heavenly priorities. Grant us the wisdom to discern Your will and the courage to pursue Your kingdom above all else. May our thoughts, words, and actions be guided by Your truth and righteousness. In Jesus' name, we pray. Amen.

Meditative Thought: Reflect on where you invest your thoughts, time, and energy throughout the day. Identify areas where your focus may be misplaced or distracted by earthly concerns. Ask God to help you set your mind on things above, prioritizing His kingdom and righteousness. Commit to cultivating a mindset that is oriented towards heavenly values and eternal realities.

Scripture: Colossians 3:2
"Set your mind on things above, not on things on the earth."

Reflection: As the day comes to a close, Colossians 3:2 continues to remind us of the importance of setting our minds on things above. Reviewing our day with this scripture in mind helps us to evaluate where we have invested our thoughts, time, and energy. It challenges us to consider whether our focus has been aligned with God's kingdom and righteousness or distracted by earthly concerns. As we meditate on this scripture tonight, let's take a moment to reflect on the orientation of our minds and hearts throughout the day. Let's confess any areas where we may have allowed earthly concerns to distract us from God's priorities. And let's commit to intentionally cultivating a mindset that is centered on heavenly values and eternal realities.

Prayer: Gracious God, as we end this day, we confess that our focus has often been consumed by earthly concerns rather than heavenly priorities. Forgive us for allowing distractions to pull us away from Your kingdom and righteousness. Renew our hearts and minds, O Lord, and help us to set our minds on things above. May our thoughts, words, and actions reflect Your truth and glorify Your name. In Jesus' name, we pray. Amen.

Meditative Thought: Reflect on where you invested your thoughts, time, and energy throughout the day. Confess any areas where your focus may have been misplaced or distracted by earthly concerns. Commit to intentionally cultivating a mindset that is centered on heavenly values and eternal realities.

SEPTEMBER 29

MORNING DEVOTION

Scripture: 2 Timothy 1:7
"For God has not given us a spirit of fear, but of power and of love and of a sound mind."

Reflection: As we begin our day, 2 Timothy 1:7 reminds us of the nature of the Spirit that God has given us. This verse reassures us that God has not equipped us with a spirit of fear but rather with a spirit of power, love, and soundness of mind. As we meditate on this scripture, let's consider any areas in our lives where fear may be holding us back. Let's ask God to strengthen us with His Spirit, enabling us to overcome fear and walk in His power, love, and soundness of mind. And let's commit to living each moment of this day with boldness and confidence in the Spirit that God has given us.

Prayer: Heavenly Father, we thank You for the Spirit that You have given us, which is not one of fear but of power, love, and soundness of mind. As we start this day, we ask for Your strength to overcome any fear that may be holding us back. Fill us afresh with Your Spirit, O Lord, empowering us to live boldly and confidently in Your love. May we walk in the power and clarity of mind that come from Your presence within us. In Jesus' name, we pray. Amen.

Meditative Thought: Reflect on any areas in your life where fear may be holding you back. Ask God to strengthen you with His Spirit, enabling you to overcome fear and walk in His power, love, and soundness of mind. Commit to living each moment of this day with boldness and confidence in the Spirit that God has given you.

Scripture: 2 Timothy 1:7
"For God has not given us a spirit of fear, but of power and of love and of a sound mind."

Reflection: As the day comes to a close, 2 Timothy 1:7 continues to remind us of the Spirit that God has given us. This verse affirms that we have not been equipped with a spirit of fear but rather with a spirit of power, love, and soundness of mind. As we meditate on this scripture tonight, let's take a moment to reflect on the ways we have experienced God's Spirit at work in our lives throughout the day. Let's confess any moments when fear may have overshadowed our faith and ask God to renew our minds with His truth and love. And let's commit to living each moment of tomorrow with boldness and confidence in the Spirit that God has given us.

Prayer: Gracious God, as we end this day, we thank You for the Spirit that You have given us, which is one of power, love, and soundness of mind. Forgive us for the times when fear has crept in and hindered our faith and obedience. Renew our minds with Your truth and love, O Lord, and help us to live boldly and confidently in Your Spirit. May we trust in Your guidance and walk in obedience to Your will. In Jesus' name, we pray. Amen.

Meditative Thought: Reflect on the ways you have experienced God's Spirit at work in your life throughout the day. Confess any moments when fear may have overshadowed your faith. Ask God to renew your mind with His truth and love. Commit to living each moment of tomorrow with boldness and confidence in the Spirit that God has given you.

Scripture: Psalm 1:1-2

"Blessed is the man who walks not in the counsel of the ungodly, nor stands in the path of sinners, nor sits in the seat of the scornful; But his delight is in the law of the Lord, and in His law he meditates day and night."

Reflection: As we begin our day, Psalm 1:1-2 sets the tone for a life that is blessed and fruitful. This passage contrasts the blessedness of those who delight in the law of the Lord and meditate on it day and night with the emptiness of those who follow the counsel of the ungodly. As we meditate on this scripture, let's consider the sources of influence in our lives and evaluate whether they align with God's Word. Let's ask God to help us delight in His law and to cultivate a habit of meditating on it day and night. And let's commit to living in a way that reflects the blessedness of those who walk in obedience to God's commands.

Prayer: Heavenly Father, we thank You for Your Word, which guides and sustains us. As we start this day, help us to be discerning in the influences we allow into our lives. Grant us the desire to delight in Your law and to meditate on it continually. May our lives be a reflection of the blessedness that comes from walking in obedience to Your commands. In Jesus' name, we pray. Amen.

Meditative Thought: Reflect on the sources of influence in your life. Ask God to help you delight in His law and to cultivate a habit of meditating on it day and night. Commit to living in a way that reflects the blessedness of those who walk in obedience to God's commands.

Scripture: Psalm 1:1-2
"Blessed is the man who walks not in the counsel of the ungodly, nor stands in the path of sinners, nor sits in the seat of the scornful; But his delight is in the law of the Lord, and in His law he meditates day and night."

Reflection: As the day comes to a close, Psalm 1:1-2 continues to remind us of the path to true blessedness. This passage emphasizes the importance of delighting in the law of the Lord and meditating on it day and night, rather than following the counsel of the ungodly. As we meditate on this scripture tonight, let's take a moment to reflect on the ways we have lived in accordance with God's Word throughout the day. Let's commit to delighting in God's law and meditating on it continually, knowing that true blessedness comes from walking in obedience to Him.

Prayer: Gracious God, as we end this day, we confess any moments when we have strayed from Your commands and followed the counsel of the ungodly. Forgive us, O Lord, and help us to live in accordance with Your Word. Grant us the desire to delight in Your law and to meditate on it continually. May our lives reflect the blessedness that comes from walking in obedience to You. In Jesus' name, we pray. Amen.

Meditative Thought: Reflect on the ways you have lived in accordance with God's Word throughout the day. Confess any moments when you have strayed from His commands. Ask for His forgiveness and guidance. Commit to delighting in God's law and meditating on it continually, knowing that true blessedness comes from walking in obedience to Him.

Scripture: Colossians 3:2-4

"Set your mind on things above, not on things on the earth. For you died, and your life is hidden with Christ in God. When Christ who is our life appears, then you also will appear with Him in glory."

Reflection: As we begin our day, Colossians 3:2-4 urges us to fix our minds on heavenly realities rather than earthly concerns. This passage reminds us that as believers, our true life is found in Christ, and our ultimate destiny is to be revealed in glory with Him. As we meditate on this scripture, let's consider where our minds have been dwelling and whether our priorities align with God's kingdom. Let's ask God to help us set our minds on heavenly things, fixing our gaze on Christ and His eternal glory. And let's commit to living each moment of this day in light of our identity as children of God, hidden with Christ and destined for glory.

Prayer: Heavenly Father, we thank You for the reminder to set our minds on things above, not on things of the earth. As we start this day, help us to redirect our focus from the temporary and fleeting to the eternal and unchanging truths of Your kingdom. Grant us the grace to live in the reality of our union with Christ, knowing that our true life is found in Him alone. May our thoughts, words, and actions reflect the glory of Your name. In Jesus' name, we pray. Amen.

Meditative Thought: Reflect on where your thoughts and priorities have been dwelling. Ask God to help you set your mind on heavenly things, fixing your gaze on Christ and His eternal glory. Commit to living each moment of this day in light of your identity as a child of God, hidden with Christ and destined for glory.

Scripture: Colossians 3:2-4

"Set your mind on things above, not on things on the earth. For you died, and your life is hidden with Christ in God. When Christ who is our life appears, then you also will appear with Him in glory."

Reflection: As the day comes to a close, Colossians 3:2-4 continues to remind us of the importance of setting our minds on heavenly things. This passage emphasizes our union with Christ and our ultimate destiny to be revealed in glory with Him. As we meditate on this scripture tonight, let's take a moment to reflect on the ways we have lived in light of our union with Christ throughout the day. Let's confess any moments when we have allowed earthly concerns to overshadow our focus on heavenly realities. And let's commit to setting our minds on things above, fixing our gaze on Christ and eagerly anticipating the day when we will appear with Him in glory.

Prayer: Gracious God, as we end this day, we confess any moments when we have allowed earthly concerns to overshadow our focus on heavenly realities. Forgive us, O Lord, and help us to live in light of our union with Christ. Grant us the grace to set our minds on things above, fixing our gaze on Him and eagerly anticipating the day when we will appear with Him in glory. May Your name be glorified in all that we do. In Jesus' name, we pray. Amen.

Meditative Thought: Reflect on the ways you have lived in light of your union with Christ throughout the day. Confess any moments when you have allowed earthly concerns to overshadow your focus on heavenly realities. Commit to setting your mind on things above, fixing your gaze on Christ and eagerly anticipating the day when you will appear with Him in glory.

OCTOBER 2

MORNING DEVOTION

Scripture: Luke 12:15
"And He said to them, 'Take heed and beware of covetousness, for one's life does not consist in the abundance of the things he possesses.'"

Reflection: As we begin our day, Luke 12:15 serves as a poignant reminder from Jesus to guard against the trap of covetousness. In a world that often measures success and worth by material possessions, Jesus reminds us that true life is not found in the abundance of things we possess. As we meditate on this scripture, let's consider the areas of our lives where covetousness may be taking root. Let's ask God to help us prioritize the eternal over the temporary, and to find our true identity and value in Him alone. And let's commit to living a life marked by contentment, generosity, and a pursuit of God's kingdom above all else.

Prayer: Heavenly Father, we thank You for the reminder to beware of covetousness and to recognize that true life is found in You alone. As we start this day, help us to guard our hearts against the lure of material possessions and worldly success. Grant us the grace to seek first Your kingdom and Your righteousness, trusting that You will provide all that we need. May our lives be marked by contentment, generosity, and a deepening relationship with You. In Jesus' name, we pray. Amen.

Meditative Thought: Reflect on your attitudes towards wealth and possessions. Ask God to help you prioritize the eternal over the temporary and to find your true identity and value in Him alone. Commit to living a life marked by contentment, generosity, and a pursuit of God's kingdom above all else.

Scripture: Luke 12:15

"And He said to them, 'Take heed and beware of covetousness, for one's life does not consist in the abundance of the things he possesses.'"

Reflection: As the day comes to a close, Luke 12:15 continues to echo in our hearts as a reminder from Jesus to beware of covetousness. This scripture challenges us to reevaluate our priorities and to recognize that true life is not defined by material possessions. As we meditate on this scripture tonight, let's take a moment to examine our hearts and confess any areas where covetousness has taken hold. Let's surrender our desires for material possessions to God and ask Him to fill us with His peace and contentment. And let's commit to living a life that is rich in the things that truly matter: love, joy, peace, and a deepening relationship with our Heavenly Father.

Prayer: Gracious God, as we end this day, we confess any moments when we have been consumed by a desire for more. Forgive us, O Lord, and fill us afresh with Your peace and contentment. Help us to surrender our longing for worldly treasures and to find our satisfaction in You alone. May our lives be marked by love, joy, and a deepening relationship with You. In Jesus' name, we pray. Amen.

Meditative Thought: Examine your heart and confess any areas where covetousness has taken hold. Surrender your desires for material possessions to God and ask Him to fill you with His peace and contentment. Commit to living a life that is rich in the things that truly matter: love, joy, peace, and a deepening relationship with your Heavenly Father.

Scripture: Romans 13:14
"But put on the Lord Jesus Christ, and make no provision for the flesh, to fulfill its lusts."

Reflection: As we begin our day, Romans 13:14 calls us to action: to "put on the Lord Jesus Christ" and to resist the temptations of the flesh. This verse urges us to clothe ourselves with the character and nature of Christ, allowing His presence to permeate every aspect of our lives. As we meditate on this scripture, let's consider the areas of our lives where we may be tempted to gratify the desires of the flesh. Let's ask God to help us recognize and resist those temptations, making no provision for the sinful inclinations of our hearts. And let's commit to daily putting on the Lord Jesus Christ, allowing His transformative power to shape us into His likeness.

Prayer: Heavenly Father, we thank You for the call to put on the Lord Jesus Christ and to resist the temptations of the flesh. As we start this day, help us to actively cultivate the virtues of Christ in our lives. Give us the strength to surrender our desires and impulses to His lordship, allowing His Spirit to guide and empower us. May our thoughts, words, and actions reflect His character and bring glory to Your name. In Jesus' name, we pray. Amen.

Meditative Thought: Reflect on the areas of your life where you may be tempted to gratify the desires of the flesh. Ask God to help you recognize and resist those temptations, making no provision for the sinful inclinations of your heart. Commit to daily putting on the Lord Jesus Christ, allowing His transformative power to shape you into His likeness.

Scripture: Romans 13:14
"But put on the Lord Jesus Christ, and make no provision for the flesh, to fulfill its lusts."

Reflection: As the day comes to a close, Romans 13:14 continues to resonate in our hearts as a reminder of our call to spiritual transformation. This scripture urges us to "put on the Lord Jesus Christ" and to actively resist the temptations of the flesh, making no provision for its lusts. As we meditate on this scripture tonight, let's take a moment to examine our hearts and confess any areas where we have fallen short of reflecting Christ's character. Let's surrender those areas to God and ask Him to renew our minds and strengthen our resolve to resist temptation. And let's commit to continuing the journey of spiritual transformation, trusting in God's grace to sustain us each step of the way.

Prayer: Gracious God, as we end this day, we confess any moments when we have yielded to the desires of the flesh. Forgive us, O Lord, and renew our minds and hearts. Strengthen us to resist temptation and to daily put on the Lord Jesus Christ. May our lives be a reflection of His character and bring glory to Your name. In Jesus' name, we pray. Amen.

Meditative Thought: Examine your heart and confess any areas where you have fallen short of reflecting Christ's character. Surrender those areas to God and ask Him to renew your mind and strengthen your resolve to resist temptation. Commit to continuing the journey of spiritual transformation, trusting in God's grace to sustain you each step of the way.

OCTOBER 4

MORNING DEVOTION

Scripture: Proverbs 28:23
"He who rebukes a man will find more favor afterward than he who flatters with the tongue."

Reflection: As we begin our day, Proverbs 28:23 offers wisdom regarding the power of rebuke and flattery. This verse reminds us that speaking the truth in love, even if it involves rebuke, ultimately leads to greater favor than offering empty praises. As we meditate on this scripture, let's examine our own attitudes and actions towards correction and praise. Let's ask God to give us the courage and wisdom to speak truthfully and lovingly, even when it may be difficult. And let's commit to fostering genuine relationships characterized by mutual respect, honesty, and accountability.

Prayer: Heavenly Father, we thank You for the wisdom found in Your Word. As we start this day, help us to value honesty and integrity in our interactions with others. Give us the courage and wisdom to speak truthfully and lovingly, even when it may be difficult. May our words and actions reflect Your love and grace. In Jesus' name, we pray. Amen.

Meditative Thought: Reflect on your attitudes and actions towards correction and praise. Ask God to give you the courage and wisdom to speak truthfully and lovingly, even when it may be difficult. Commit to fostering genuine relationships characterized by mutual respect, honesty, and accountability.

Scripture: Proverbs 28:23
"He who rebukes a man will find more favor afterward than he who flatters with the tongue."

Reflection: As the day comes to a close, Proverbs 28:23 continues to resonate in our hearts, reminding us of the importance of honesty and integrity in our relationships. This verse emphasizes that speaking the truth in love, even through rebuke, ultimately leads to greater favor than offering empty praises. Reviewing our day with this scripture in mind helps us to reflect on the ways in which we have interacted with others. As we meditate on this scripture tonight, let's take a moment to confess any moments when we have been tempted to flatter with our words rather than speak truthfully and lovingly. Let's ask God to give us the humility to receive correction and the courage to offer it when needed. And let's commit to building relationships characterized by honesty, integrity, and genuine care for one another.

Prayer: Gracious God, as we end this day, we confess any moments when we have prioritized flattery over honesty in our interactions with others. Forgive us, O Lord, and help us to value authenticity and integrity in our relationships. Give us the humility to receive correction and the courage to offer it when needed. May our words and actions reflect Your truth and love. In Jesus' name, we pray. Amen.

Meditative Thought: Confess any moments when you have been tempted to flatter with your words rather than speak truthfully and lovingly. Ask God to give you the humility to receive correction and the courage to offer it when needed. Commit to building relationships characterized by honesty, integrity, and genuine care for one another.

OCTOBER 5

Scripture: 1 Corinthians 15:33
"Do not be deceived: 'Evil company corrupts good habits.'"

Reflection: As we begin our day, 1 Corinthians 15:33 serves as a warning against the influence of bad company. This verse reminds us that the people we surround ourselves with can have a significant impact on our habits and character. Starting our day with this scripture prompts us to reflect on the company we keep and the influence it has on our lives. It challenges us to evaluate whether our relationships are uplifting and edifying, or if they lead us down paths of compromise and moral decline. It invites us to be intentional about cultivating friendships that encourage us to grow in faith and righteousness. As we meditate on this scripture, let's examine the relationships in our lives and consider their influence on our habits and character. And let's commit to surrounding ourselves with people who inspire us to live lives that honor God and reflect His goodness.

Prayer: Heavenly Father, we thank You for the reminder that the company we keep can greatly influence our habits and character. As we start this day, give us discernment in choosing our friends and the strength to stand firm in our convictions. Help us to cultivate relationships that inspire us to grow in faith and righteousness. May our lives be a reflection of Your goodness and grace. In Jesus' name, we pray. Amen.

Meditative Thought: Reflect on the relationships in your life and their influence on your habits and character. Ask God to give you discernment in choosing your friends and the strength to stand firm in your convictions. Commit to surrounding yourself with people who inspire you to grow in faith and righteousness.

Scripture: 1 Corinthians 15:33
"Do not be deceived: 'Evil company corrupts good habits.'"

Reflection: As the day comes to a close, 1 Corinthians 15:33 continues to resonate in our hearts as a reminder of the importance of choosing our company wisely. This verse warns us that associating with the wrong people can lead to the corruption of good habits. Reviewing our day with this scripture in mind helps us to reflect on the relationships we have engaged in and their influence on our thoughts and actions. It challenges us to consider whether we have allowed ourselves to be swayed by negative influences or if we have remained steadfast in our commitment to righteousness. It invites us to reevaluate our friendships and prioritize those that encourage us to live lives that honor God. As we meditate on this scripture tonight, let's take a moment to confess any instances when we have been influenced by the wrong company. Let's commit to surrounding ourselves with people who inspire us to grow in faith and righteousness, so that our lives may continually reflect His goodness and grace.

Prayer: Gracious God, as we end this day, we confess any instances when we have allowed ourselves to be influenced by the wrong company. Forgive us, O Lord, and strengthen us to resist negative influences in the future. Help us to prioritize friendships that encourage us to live lives that honor You. May our lives be a reflection of Your goodness and grace. In Jesus' name, we pray. Amen.

Meditative Thought: Confess any instances when you have been influenced by the wrong company. Ask God to forgive you and to strengthen you to resist negative influences in the future. Commit to surrounding yourself with people who inspire you to grow in faith and righteousness.

Scripture: James 4:4

"Adulterers and adulteresses! Do you not know that friendship with the world is enmity with God? Whoever therefore wants to be a friend of the world makes himself an enemy of God."

Reflection: As we begin our day, James 4:4 delivers a powerful message about the danger of worldly friendship. This verse starkly warns against aligning ourselves too closely with the values and desires of the world, emphasizing that such alliances create enmity with God. Starting our day with this scripture prompts us to examine the nature of our friendships and associations. As we meditate on this scripture, let's reflect on the ways in which we may have been tempted to prioritize the values of the world over those of God. Let's ask God to give us the strength and discernment to resist conformity to the world's ways and to stand firm in our commitment to Him. And let's commit to cultivating friendships and relationships that encourage us to pursue holiness and righteousness in all areas of our lives.

Prayer: Heavenly Father, we thank You for Your Word, which warns us against the danger of worldly friendship. As we start this day, help us to examine the nature of our associations and the influence they have on our lives. May our friendships and relationships be a source of encouragement and edification as we seek to honor You in all that we do. In Jesus' name, we pray. Amen.

Meditative Thought: Reflect on the ways in which you may have been tempted to prioritize the values of the world over those of God. Ask God to give you the strength and discernment to resist conformity to the world's ways and to stand firm in your commitment to Him.

Scripture: James 4:4

"Adulterers and adulteresses! Do you not know that friendship with the world is enmity with God? Whoever therefore wants to be a friend of the world makes himself an enemy of God."

Reflection: As the day draws to a close, James 4:4 continues to echo in our hearts, urging us to reevaluate our allegiances and associations. This verse starkly reminds us that friendship with the world is enmity with God, calling us to prioritize our relationship with Him above all else. Reviewing our day with this scripture in mind prompts us to reflect on the choices we have made and the influences we have allowed into our lives. It challenges us to consider whether we have been more concerned with seeking approval from the world or with pleasing God. As we meditate on this scripture tonight, let's take a moment to confess any instances when we have been tempted to prioritize the values of the world over those of God. Let's commit to cultivating a deep and abiding friendship with God, knowing that true fulfillment and joy are found in Him alone.

Prayer: Gracious God, as we end this day, we confess any instances when we have been tempted to prioritize the values of the world over those of Your kingdom. Help us to cultivate a deep and abiding friendship with You, knowing that true fulfillment and joy are found in You alone. May our lives be a reflection of Your glory and grace. In Jesus' name, we pray. Amen.

Meditative Thought: Confess any instances when you have been tempted to prioritize the values of the world over those of God. Ask God to forgive you and to renew your commitment to living as His faithful disciple. Commit to cultivating a deep and abiding friendship with God, knowing that true fulfillment and joy are found in Him alone.

Scripture: Ephesians 4:29

"Let no corrupt word proceed out of your mouth, but what is good for necessary edification, that it may impart grace to the hearers."

Reflection: As we begin our day, Ephesians 4:29 directs our attention to the power of our words. This verse challenges us to speak words that build up and encourage others, rather than tearing them down with negativity or corruption. Starting our day with this scripture prompts us to reflect on the impact of our speech on those around us. It invites us to cultivate a habit of speaking words that impart grace and bring life to those who hear them. As we meditate on this scripture, let's examine the words we have spoken and the effect they have had on others. Let's ask God to help us guard our tongues and to speak only what is good and beneficial for building others up. And let's commit to using our words to impart grace, encouragement, and love to all whom we encounter.

Prayer: Heavenly Father, we thank You for the reminder to guard our tongues and to speak words that build up and encourage others. As we start this day, help us to be mindful of the impact of our speech on those around us. Give us the grace to speak only what is good and beneficial for edifying others, that Your love and grace may be evident in all that we say. In Jesus' name, we pray. Amen.

Meditative Thought: Reflect on the words you have spoken and the effect they have had on others. Ask God to help you guard your tongue and to speak only what is good and beneficial for building others up. Commit to using your words to impart grace, encouragement, and love to all whom you encounter.

Scripture: Ephesians 4:29

"Let no corrupt word proceed out of your mouth, but what is good for necessary edification, that it may impart grace to the hearers."

Reflection: As the day comes to a close, Ephesians 4:29 continues to resonate in our hearts, reminding us of the importance of our words. This verse urges us to speak words that are good for edification, that they may impart grace to those who hear them. Reviewing our day with this scripture in mind prompts us to reflect on the words we have spoken and their impact on others. It challenges us to consider whether our speech has contributed to the growth and encouragement of those around us or if it has caused harm and division. As we meditate on this scripture tonight, let's take a moment to confess any instances when we have spoken words that were corrupt or harmful. Let's commit to using our words to impart grace, encouragement, and love to all whom we encounter, knowing that in doing so, we reflect the character of our gracious and loving God.

Prayer: Gracious God, as we end this day, we confess any instances when we have spoken words that were corrupt or harmful. Forgive us, O Lord, and help us to guard our tongues, speaking only what is good and beneficial for building others up. May our words always impart grace and encouragement to those who hear them, reflecting Your love and goodness to the world. In Jesus' name, we pray. Amen.

Meditative Thought: Confess any instances when you have spoken words that were corrupt or harmful. Ask God to help you guard your tongue and to speak only what is good and beneficial for building others up. Commit to using your words to impart grace, encouragement, and love to all whom you encounter.

OCTOBER 8

MORNING DEVOTION

Scripture: Proverbs 21:23
"Whoever guards his mouth and tongue Keeps his soul from troubles."

Reflection: As we embark on a new day, Proverbs 21:23 reminds us of the power and importance of guarding our words. This verse highlights the connection between exercising self-control over what we say and experiencing peace and protection in our lives. Starting our day with this scripture prompts us to reflect on the impact of our words on our own well-being and the well-being of others. It invites us to cultivate a habit of speaking with wisdom and restraint, knowing that it leads to greater peace and harmony. As we meditate on this scripture, let's examine the ways in which we have used our words in the past and the consequences they have brought. Let's ask God to help us guard our mouths and tongues, enabling us to speak words that promote peace and build others up. And let's commit to practicing self-control in our speech, knowing that it leads to a life marked by God's favor and protection.

Prayer: Heavenly Father, we thank You for the reminder to guard our mouths and tongues, for they have the power to bring either trouble or peace into our lives. As we start this day, help us to exercise diligence in controlling our speech, speaking words that promote peace and build others up. Grant us the wisdom and self-control to use our words for Your glory and the well-being of those around us. In Jesus' name, we pray. Amen.

Meditative Thought: Reflect on the ways in which you have used your words in the past and the consequences they have brought. Ask God to help you guard your mouth and tongue, enabling you to speak words that promote peace and build others up.

Scripture: Proverbs 21:23
"Whoever guards his mouth and tongue Keeps his soul from troubles."

Reflection: As the day draws to a close, Proverbs 21:23 continues to resonate in our hearts, reminding us of the importance of guarding our words. This verse emphasizes that exercising self-control over what we say leads to protection and peace in our lives. Reviewing our day with this scripture in mind prompts us to reflect on the ways in which we have used our words and the impact they have had. It challenges us to consider whether we have spoken with wisdom and restraint, or if we have allowed careless speech to bring trouble into our lives. As we meditate on this scripture tonight, let's take a moment to confess any instances when we have spoken hastily or carelessly. Let's ask God to forgive us and to help us exercise greater self-control in our speech. And let's commit to speaking words that promote peace and build others up, knowing that in doing so, we experience the abundant life that God desires for us.

Prayer: Gracious God, as we end this day, we confess any instances when we have spoken hastily or carelessly, bringing trouble into our lives. Forgive us, O Lord, and help us to exercise greater self-control in our speech. Grant us the wisdom and discernment to speak words that promote peace and build others up. May our lives be a reflection of Your grace and protection. In Jesus' name, we pray. Amen.

Meditative Thought: Confess any instances when you have spoken hastily or carelessly. Ask God to help you exercise greater self-control in your speech. Commit to speaking words that promote peace and build others up, knowing that in doing so, you experience the abundant life that God desires for you.

OCTOBER 9

MORNING DEVOTION

Scripture: John 8:36
"Therefore if the Son makes you free, you shall be free indeed."

Reflection: As we begin a new day, John 8:36 proclaims the liberating power of Jesus Christ. This verse assures us that when the Son sets us free, we experience true freedom in every aspect of our lives. Starting our day with this scripture prompts us to reflect on the freedom we have received through our relationship with Jesus Christ. It challenges us to consider whether we are living in the fullness of that freedom or if we are still bound by fear, guilt, or sin. It invites us to embrace the truth that in Christ. As we meditate on this scripture, let's take a moment to thank God for the freedom He has given us through His Son, Jesus Christ. Let's surrender any areas of our lives where we still feel entangled or enslaved, trusting in His power to set us free. And let's commit to walking in the freedom that Christ has secured for us, living each day in the joy and confidence of His love and grace.

Prayer: Heavenly Father, we thank You for the freedom we have received through Your Son, Jesus Christ. As we start this day, help us to fully embrace the truth of our freedom in Him. Grant us the strength to let go of anything that holds us captive, knowing that in Christ, we are free indeed. May our lives be a testimony to Your liberating power and grace. In Jesus' name, we pray. Amen.

Meditative Thought: Thank God for the freedom He has given you through His Son, Jesus Christ. Surrender any areas of your life where you still feel entangled or enslaved, trusting in His power to set you free. Commit to walking in the freedom that Christ has secured for you, living each day in the joy and confidence of His love and grace.

Scripture: John 8:36
"Therefore if the Son makes you free, you shall be free indeed."

Reflection: As the day comes to a close, John 8:36 continues to resonate in our hearts, reminding us of the freedom we have in Jesus Christ. This verse affirms that through Him, we are truly free from the bondage of sin and death. Reviewing our day with this scripture in mind prompts us to reflect on the ways in which we have experienced and expressed the freedom found in Christ. It challenges us to consider whether we have lived in the fullness of that freedom or if we have allowed ourselves to be burdened by fear, worry, or sin. As we meditate on this scripture tonight, let's take a moment to surrender any areas of our lives where we still feel enslaved or entangled. Let's ask God to fill us afresh with His Spirit, empowering us to walk in the freedom and victory that Christ has secured for us. And let's rest in the assurance that in Christ, we are truly free indeed, now and for all eternity.

Prayer: Gracious God, as we end this day, we surrender to You any areas of our lives where we still feel enslaved or entangled. Fill us afresh with Your Spirit, empowering us to walk in the freedom and victory that Christ has secured for us. May our lives continually reflect the reality of our freedom in Him. In Jesus' name, we pray. Amen.

Meditative Thought: Surrender any areas of your life where you still feel enslaved or entangled. Ask God to fill you afresh with His Spirit, empowering you to walk in the freedom and victory that Christ has secured for you. Rest in the assurance that in Christ, you are truly free indeed, now and for all eternity.

OCTOBER 10

MORNING DEVOTION

Scripture: Psalm 55:22
"Cast your burden on the Lord, And He shall sustain you; He shall never permit the righteous to be moved."

Reflection: As we begin our day, Psalm 55:22 offers us a comforting reminder of God's faithfulness and provision. This verse encourages us to cast our burdens upon the Lord, knowing that He will sustain us and keep us secure. Starting our day with this scripture prompts us to reflect on the burdens we carry and the tendency to try to manage them on our own. It challenges us to surrender our worries, fears, and anxieties to the Lord, trusting in His care and provision. As we meditate on this scripture, let's take a moment to identify the burdens weighing heavy on our hearts and minds. Let's bring them before the Lord in prayer, releasing them into His capable hands. And let's commit to trusting in His faithfulness and provision, knowing that He is always with us, ready to sustain us through every trial and challenge we face.

Prayer: Heavenly Father, we thank You for Your promise to sustain us and never allow the righteous to be moved. As we start this day, help us to cast our burdens upon You, trusting in Your care and provision. Grant us the peace that comes from placing our trust in You, knowing that You are always with us, ready to sustain us through every trial and challenge we face. In Jesus' name, we pray. Amen.

Meditative Thought: Identify the burdens weighing heavy on your heart and mind. Bring them before the Lord in prayer, releasing them into His capable hands. Commit to trusting in His faithfulness and provision, knowing that He is always with you, ready to sustain you through every trial and challenge you face.

OCTOBER 10

EVENING DEVOTION

Scripture: Psalm 55:22
"Cast your burden on the Lord, And He shall sustain you; He shall never permit the righteous to be moved."

Reflection: As the day comes to a close, Psalm 55:22 continues to resonate in our hearts, reminding us of God's unfailing faithfulness and provision. This verse assures us that when we cast our burdens upon the Lord, He will sustain us and keep us secure. Reviewing our day with this scripture in mind prompts us to reflect on the ways in which we have experienced God's faithfulness in the midst of our trials and challenges. It invites us to recommit to placing our trust in God, knowing that He will never allow the righteous to be shaken. As we meditate on this scripture tonight, let's take a moment to surrender once again any burdens we may still be carrying. Let's bring them before the Lord in prayer, entrusting them into His capable hands. And let's rest in the assurance that He is faithful to sustain us through every trial and challenge we face, never allowing us to be moved.

Prayer: Gracious God, as we end this day, we surrender once again our burdens into Your capable hands. Thank You for Your unfailing faithfulness and provision. Grant us the strength to trust in You completely, knowing that You will sustain us and keep us secure. May Your peace guard our hearts and minds tonight. In Jesus' name, we pray. Amen.

Meditative Thought: Surrender once again any burdens you may still be carrying. Bring them before the Lord in prayer, entrusting them into His capable hands. Rest in the assurance that He is faithful to sustain you through every trial and challenge you face, never allowing you to be moved.

Scripture: Matthew 11:28-29

"Come to Me, all you who labor and are heavy laden, and I will give you rest. Take My yoke upon you and learn from Me, for I am gentle and lowly in heart, and you will find rest for your souls."

Reflection: As we begin our day, Matthew 11:28-29 invites us to find rest in Jesus Christ. These verses extend a gracious invitation to all who are weary and burdened, promising rest and refreshment for our souls. Starting our day with this scripture prompts us to reflect on the weariness and burdens we may be carrying. It challenges us to come to Jesus, laying down our heavy loads at His feet and receiving the rest that He offers. As we meditate on this scripture, let's take a moment to acknowledge our need for rest and refreshment in Jesus Christ. Let's come to Him in prayer, surrendering our burdens and worries, and allowing His peace to fill our hearts. And let's commit to walking closely with Him throughout the day, learning from His example of gentleness and humility, and finding rest for our weary souls.

Prayer: Heavenly Father, we thank You for the invitation to find rest in Jesus Christ. As we start this day, we come to You with our weariness and burdens, laying them at Your feet and receiving the rest that You offer. Fill us with Your peace and refreshment, and help us to walk closely with You throughout this day. May we learn from Your gentle and humble nature, finding true rest for our souls. In Jesus' name, we pray. Amen.

Meditative Thought: Acknowledge your need for rest and refreshment in Jesus Christ. Come to Him in prayer, surrendering your burdens and worries, and allowing His peace to fill your heart.

Scripture: Matthew 11:28-29

"Come to Me, all you who labor and are heavy laden, and I will give you rest. Take My yoke upon you and learn from Me, for I am gentle and lowly in heart, and you will find rest for your souls."

Reflection: As the day draws to a close, Matthew 11:28-29 continues to resonate in our hearts, reminding us of the rest and refreshment found in Jesus Christ. These verses assure us that when we come to Him with our burdens, He provides rest for our weary souls. Reviewing our day with this scripture in mind prompts us to reflect on the ways in which we have experienced the rest and peace of Christ. It challenges us to consider whether we have truly surrendered our burdens to Him or if we have allowed worry and anxiety to consume us. It invites us to recommit to walking closely with Jesus, learning from His gentle and humble nature, and finding rest for our souls. Let's come to Jesus in prayer, laying them at His feet and allowing His peace to fill our hearts. And let's rest in the assurance that He is faithful to provide rest and refreshment for our weary souls, both now and always.

Prayer: Gracious God, as we end this day, we surrender once again our burdens into Your loving hands. Thank You for the rest and refreshment found in Jesus Christ. Fill us with Your peace and renew our souls as we rest in You. Help us to walk closely with Jesus, learning from His gentle and humble nature, and finding true rest for our weary souls. In Jesus' name, we pray. Amen.

Meditative Thought: Surrender once again any burdens you may still be carrying. Come to Jesus in prayer, laying them at His feet and allowing His peace to fill your heart.

Scripture: 2 Corinthians 1:3-4
"Blessed be the God and Father of our Lord Jesus Christ, the Father of mercies and God of all comfort, who comforts us in all our tribulation, that we may be able to comfort those who are in any trouble, with the comfort with which we ourselves are comforted by God."

Reflection: As we begin our day, 2 Corinthians 1:3-4 directs our focus to the source of all comfort and compassion: God Himself. These verses remind us that God, in His infinite mercy, comforts us in all our troubles so that we may in turn offer comfort to others who are in need. Starting our day with this scripture prompts us to reflect on the comfort and consolation we have received from God in times of trouble. It challenges us to consider how we can extend that same comfort to those around us who are facing difficulties. As we meditate on this scripture, let's take a moment to thank God for His comforting presence in our lives. Let's commit to being instruments of God's peace and solace, offering comfort to others in the same way that we have been comforted by Him.

Prayer: Heavenly Father, we praise You as the Father of mercies and the God of all comfort. Thank You for Your loving presence and the comfort You provide in times of trouble. Grant us the wisdom and compassion to extend that same comfort to others who are in need. May we be vessels of Your love and compassion, offering solace and support to those who are hurting. In Jesus' name, we pray. Amen.

Meditative Thought: Thank God for His comforting presence in your life. Pray for discernment and compassion to recognize and reach out to those who are in need of comfort. Commit to being an instrument of God's peace and solace, offering comfort to others in the same way that you have been comforted by Him.

Scripture: 2 Corinthians 1:3-4
"Blessed be the God and Father of our Lord Jesus Christ, the Father of mercies and God of all comfort, who comforts us in all our tribulation, that we may be able to comfort those who are in any trouble, with the comfort with which we ourselves are comforted by God."

Reflection: As the day draws to a close, 2 Corinthians 1:3-4 continues to echo in our hearts, reminding us of the comforting presence of God in our lives. These verses affirm that God comforts us in all our tribulations so that we may in turn comfort others with the same comfort we have received from Him. Reviewing our day with this scripture in mind prompts us to reflect on the ways in which we have experienced God's comfort and compassion. It invites us to continue being channels of God's love and grace, offering comfort to others as we have been comforted by Him. As we meditate on this scripture tonight, let's take a moment to thank God for His faithfulness in comforting us throughout the day. Let's reflect on any missed opportunities to extend comfort to others and ask for forgiveness and guidance to do better tomorrow.

Prayer: Gracious God, as we end this day, we thank You for Your faithful presence and the comfort You provide in times of trouble. Forgive us for any missed opportunities to extend comfort to others. Grant us the courage and compassion to be channels of Your love and grace, and support to those who are hurting. May Your comforting presence be felt in our lives and in the lives of those we encounter. In Jesus' name, we pray. Amen.

Meditative Thought: Thank God for His faithfulness in comforting you throughout the day. Reflect on any missed opportunities to extend comfort to others and ask for forgiveness and guidance to do better tomorrow.

OCTOBER 13

MORNING DEVOTION

Scripture: Galatians 6:1
"Brethren, if a man is overtaken in any trespass, you who are spiritual restore such a one in a spirit of gentleness, considering yourself lest you also be tempted."

Reflection: As we begin our day, Galatians 6:1 calls us to a ministry of restoration and reconciliation within the body of Christ. This verse reminds us of our responsibility to gently and lovingly restore those who have stumbled in their faith, considering our own vulnerabilities in the process. Starting our day with this scripture prompts us to reflect on our attitudes and actions towards those who have fallen into sin or spiritual struggle. It challenges us to resist judgment and condemnation, instead extending a spirit of gentleness and compassion. As we meditate on this scripture, let's take a moment to examine our hearts and attitudes towards those who may be struggling in their faith journey. Let's pray for the wisdom and discernment to offer restoration and support in a spirit of gentleness and humility. And let's commit to being instruments of God's grace and reconciliation, helping to build up and restore our brothers and sisters in Christ.

Prayer: Heavenly Father, we thank You for the reminder to restore those who have stumbled in their faith with a spirit of gentleness and humility. Help us to approach others with empathy and compassion, considering our own vulnerabilities and susceptibility to temptation. May Your grace and love flow through us as we seek to build up and restore our brothers and sisters in Christ. In Jesus' name, we pray. Amen.

Meditative Thought: Examine your heart and attitudes towards those who may be struggling in their faith journey. Pray for wisdom and discernment to offer restoration and support in a spirit of gentleness.

Scripture: Galatians 6:1

"Brethren, if a man is overtaken in any trespass, you who are spiritual restore such a one in a spirit of gentleness, considering yourself lest you also be tempted."

Reflection: As the day draws to a close, Galatians 6:1 continues to challenge us to a ministry of restoration and reconciliation within the body of Christ. This verse reminds us of the importance of approaching those who have stumbled in their faith with gentleness and humility, considering our own vulnerabilities in the process. It challenges us to examine whether we have offered support and restoration in a spirit of gentleness and compassion, or if we have been judgmental or indifferent. Let's pray for the grace to approach others with gentleness and humility, considering our own vulnerabilities. And let's commit to being instruments of God's love and grace, seeking to build up and restore our brothers and sisters in Christ.

Prayer: Gracious God, as we end this day, we confess any attitudes or actions that may have hindered our ministry of restoration and reconciliation. Forgive us for any judgmental or indifferent attitudes towards those who are struggling spiritually. Grant us the grace to approach others with gentleness and humility, considering our own vulnerabilities. May Your love and grace flow through us as we seek to build up and restore our brothers and sisters in Christ. In Jesus' name, we pray. Amen.

Meditative Thought: Confess any attitudes or actions that may have hindered your ministry of restoration and reconciliation. Pray for the grace to approach others with gentleness and humility.

OCTOBER 14

MORNING DEVOTION

Scripture: James 5:19-20

"Brethren, if anyone among you wanders from the truth, and someone turns him back, let him know that he who turns a sinner from the error of his way will save a soul from death and cover a multitude of sins."

Reflection: As we begin our day, James 5:19-20 calls us to a ministry of restoration and reconciliation within the body of Christ. These verses emphasize the importance of reaching out to those who have strayed from the truth, seeking to turn them back to God and save their souls from spiritual death. As we meditate on this scripture, let's take a moment to pray for those who may have wandered from the truth, asking God to guide them back into His loving embrace. Let's commit to being faithful ambassadors of God's love and grace, seeking to turn sinners from the error of their ways and lead them to salvation in Christ.

Prayer: Heavenly Father, we lift up to You those who may have wandered from the truth, asking for Your mercy and grace to guide them back into Your loving embrace. Give us the courage and wisdom to reach out to them with compassion and humility, leading them to repentance and restoration. Help us to be faithful ambassadors of Your love and grace, seeking to turn sinners from the error of their ways and lead them to salvation in Christ. In Jesus' name, we pray. Amen.

Meditative Thought: Pray for those who may have wandered from the truth, asking for God's mercy and grace to guide them back into His loving embrace. Ask for the courage and wisdom to reach out to them with compassion and humility. Commit to being a faithful ambassador of God's love and grace, seeking to turn sinners from the error of their ways and lead them to salvation in Christ.

Scripture: James 5:19-20

"Brethren, if anyone among you wanders from the truth, and someone turns him back, let him know that he who turns a sinner from the error of his way will save a soul from death and cover a multitude of sins."

Reflection: As the day comes to a close, James 5:19-20 continues to resonate in our hearts, reminding us of the importance of our role in restoring those who have strayed from the truth. These verses affirm the profound impact of our actions in leading others back to God and covering a multitude of sins through His grace. As we meditate on this scripture tonight, let's take a moment to pray for those who may be wandering from the truth, asking God to continue His work of transformation in their lives. Let's commit to being vigilant and proactive in our efforts to turn sinners from the error of their ways and lead them to salvation in Christ.

Prayer: Gracious God, as we end this day, we lift up to You those who may be wandering from the truth, asking for Your continued work of transformation in their lives. Forgive us for any missed opportunities to reach out to them with love and compassion. Grant us the courage and wisdom to be faithful in our efforts to turn sinners from the error of their ways and lead them to salvation in Christ. May Your grace abound in our lives and in the lives of those we encounter. In Jesus' name, we pray. Amen.

Meditative Thought: Pray for those who may be wandering from the truth, asking for God's continued work of transformation in their lives. Reflect on your own actions and attitudes, seeking God's forgiveness and guidance to be more faithful in reaching out to those in need of restoration.

OCTOBER 15

MORNING DEVOTION

Scripture: Isaiah 58:8
"Then your light shall break forth like the morning, Your healing shall spring forth speedily, And your righteousness shall go before you; The glory of the Lord shall be your rear guard."

Reflection: As we begin our day, Isaiah 58:8 paints a vivid picture of the blessings that come from living a life of obedience and righteousness before God. This verse speaks of the transformative power of God's presence in our lives, promising light, healing, and protection to those who walk in His ways. Starting our day with this scripture prompts us to reflect on the condition of our hearts and the alignment of our lives with God's will. It invites us to renew our commitment to righteousness and obedience, trusting in God's promise to bless and protect us as we walk in His ways. As we meditate on this scripture, let's take a moment to examine our hearts and confess any areas of sin or disobedience that may be hindering our relationship with God. Let's commit to trusting in God's promise to be our light, our healer, and our protector as we journey through this day and beyond.

Prayer: Heavenly Father, we thank You for Your promise to bless and protect those who walk in Your ways. Forgive us for any areas of sin or disobedience in our lives that have dimmed the light of Your presence within us. Give us the strength and grace to live lives that are pleasing to You, reflecting Your light and righteousness to the world around us. May Your presence go before us and be our rear guard, guiding us and protecting us each step of the way. In Jesus' name, we pray. Amen.

Meditative Thought: Examine your heart and confess any areas of sin or disobedience that may be hindering your relationship with God. Pray for the strength and grace to live a life that honors and glorifies Him.

Scripture: Isaiah 58:8
"Then your light shall break forth like the morning, Your healing shall spring forth speedily, And your righteousness shall go before you; The glory of the Lord shall be your rear guard."

Reflection: As the day draws to a close, Isaiah 58:8 continues to remind us of the transformative power of living in alignment with God's will. This verse speaks of the blessings and protection that come from walking in righteousness before Him, promising light, healing, and the presence of His glory. Reviewing our day it challenges us to consider whether we have fully embraced His call to righteousness and obedience, or if we have allowed distractions and temptations to lead us astray. As we meditate on this scripture tonight, let's take a moment to thank God for His faithfulness in blessing and protecting us throughout the day. Let's reflect on any areas where we may have fallen short of His standards and ask for His forgiveness and guidance.

Prayer: Gracious God, as we end this day, we thank You for Your faithfulness in blessing and protecting us. Forgive us for any areas where we have fallen short of Your standards and guide us in the paths of righteousness. Help us to fully embrace Your call to obedience and trust in Your promise to be our healer and protector. May Your presence go before us and be our rear guard as we rest in You tonight. In Jesus' name, we pray. Amen.

Meditative Thought: Thank God for His faithfulness in blessing and protecting you throughout the day. Reflect on any areas where you may have fallen short of His standards and ask for His forgiveness and guidance. Commit to continuing to walk in righteousness and obedience.

OCTOBER 16

MORNING DEVOTION

Scripture: Lamentations 3:58
"O Lord, You have pleaded the case for my soul; You have redeemed my life."

Reflection: As we begin our day, Lamentations 3:58 directs our focus to the faithfulness and redemption of God. This verse serves as a reminder of God's continuous advocacy for our souls and His ultimate redemption of our lives through His grace and mercy. Starting our day with this scripture prompts us to reflect on the depth of God's love and commitment to us. It challenges us to consider the ways in which He has intervened on our behalf, pleading our case and redeeming us from sin and death. It invites us to respond with gratitude and praise for His unending faithfulness and redemption. Let's offer Him our heartfelt thanks for His faithfulness and mercy. And let's commit to living each moment in light of His redemption, allowing His grace to transform us from the inside out.

Prayer: Heavenly Father, we thank You for Your unending love and faithfulness towards us. Thank You for pleading the case for our souls and redeeming our lives through Your grace and mercy. Help us to live each moment in light of Your redemption, allowing Your grace to transform us and make us more like You. May our lives be a reflection of Your love and mercy to the world around us. In Jesus' name, we pray. Amen.

Meditative Thought: Reflect on the ways in which God has intervened in your life, pleading your case and redeeming you from sin. Offer heartfelt thanks for His faithfulness and mercy. Commit to living each moment in light of His redemption, allowing His grace to transform you from the inside out.

Scripture: Lamentations 3:58
"O Lord, You have pleaded the case for my soul; You have redeemed my life."

Reflection: As the day draws to a close, Lamentations 3:58 continues to echo in our hearts, reminding us of the faithfulness and redemption of God. This verse affirms His continuous advocacy for our souls and His ultimate redemption of our lives through His grace and mercy. Reviewing our day with this scripture in mind prompts us to reflect on the ways in which God's intervention has been evident in our lives throughout the day. As we meditate on this scripture tonight, let's take a moment to thank God for His continual advocacy and redemption in our lives. Let's reflect on any missed opportunities to respond to His grace with obedience and trust. And let's commit to living each moment with a renewed awareness of His presence and redemption, allowing His love to shape and guide us in all that we do.

Prayer: Gracious God, as we end this day, we thank You for Your continual advocacy and redemption in our lives. Forgive us for any missed opportunities to respond to Your grace with obedience and trust. Help us to live each moment with a renewed awareness of Your presence and redemption, allowing Your love to shape and guide us in all that we do. May our lives be a testament to Your faithfulness and mercy. In Jesus' name, we pray. Amen.

Meditative Thought: Thank God for His continual advocacy and redemption in your life. Reflect on any missed opportunities to respond to His grace with obedience and trust. Commit to living each moment with a renewed awareness of His presence and redemption, allowing His love to shape and guide you in all that you do.

OCTOBER 17

MORNING DEVOTION

Scripture: Joel 2:25a
"So I will restore to you the years that the swarming locust has eaten."

Reflection: As we begin our day, Joel 2:25a speaks of God's promise to restore what has been lost or destroyed. This verse serves as a reminder of His faithfulness and power to bring renewal and redemption to our lives, even in the face of devastation and loss. Starting our day with this scripture prompts us to reflect on the areas of our lives where we may have experienced loss or devastation. It challenges us to consider the ways in which God is able to bring restoration and healing to those areas, turning mourning into joy and ashes into beauty. As we meditate on this scripture, let's take a moment to surrender our losses and disappointments to God, trusting in His ability to bring beauty from ashes. Let's commit to living each moment with hope and expectancy, knowing that God is able to turn our trials into triumphs for His glory.

Prayer: Heavenly Father, we thank You for Your promise to restore what has been lost or destroyed in our lives. Help us to surrender our losses and disappointments to You, trusting in Your ability to bring beauty from ashes. Give us the faith to believe in Your promise of restoration and renewal, even in the midst of difficult circumstances. May Your purposes be fulfilled in our lives, and may Your name be glorified through it all. In Jesus' name, we pray. Amen.

Meditative Thought: Surrender your losses and disappointments to God, trusting in His ability to bring beauty from ashes. Pray for the faith to believe in His promise of restoration and renewal, even in the midst of difficult circumstances. Commit to living each moment with hope and expectancy, knowing that God is able to turn your trials into triumphs for His glory.

Scripture: Joel 2:25a
"So I will restore to you the years that the swarming locust has eaten."

Reflection: As the day draws to a close, Joel 2:25a continues to echo in our hearts, reminding us of God's promise to restore what has been lost or destroyed. This verse affirms His faithfulness and power to bring renewal and redemption to our lives, even in the face of devastation and loss. It challenges us to consider the moments when He has brought healing and renewal to areas of brokenness and loss. It invites us to respond with gratitude and praise for His faithfulness and mercy. As we meditate on this scripture tonight, let's take a moment to thank God for His continual work of restoration and renewal in our lives. Let's reflect on any missed opportunities to respond to His grace with trust and obedience. And let's commit to living each moment with a renewed sense of hope and expectancy, knowing that God is able to turn our trials into triumphs for His glory.

Prayer: Gracious God, as we end this day, we thank You for Your continual work of restoration and renewal in our lives. Forgive us for any missed opportunities to respond to Your grace with trust and obedience. Help us to live each moment with a renewed sense of hope and expectancy, knowing that You are able to turn our trials into triumphs for Your glory. May Your name be glorified in all that we do. In Jesus' name, we pray. Amen.

Meditative Thought: Thank God for His continual work of restoration and renewal in your life. Reflect on any missed opportunities to respond to His grace with trust and obedience. Commit to living each moment with a renewed sense of hope and expectancy, knowing that God is able to turn your trials into triumphs for His glory.

OCTOBER 18

MORNING DEVOTION

Scripture: 1 John 4:4

"You are of God, little children, and have overcome them, because He who is in you is greater than he who is in the world."

Reflection: As we begin our day, 1 John 4:4 reminds us of our identity as children of God and our victory over the forces of darkness. This verse assures us that the indwelling presence of God within us is greater than any opposition we may face in the world. Starting our day with this scripture prompts us to reflect on the power and authority we have as believers in Christ. It challenges us to remember that we are not alone in our battles, but that the Almighty God resides within us, empowering us to overcome every obstacle and challenge that comes our way. As we meditate on this scripture, let's take a moment to reaffirm our identity in Christ and thank God for His presence and power within us. Let's pray for the wisdom and discernment to recognize His leading and guidance in our lives. And let's commit to walking in faith and obedience, trusting in the strength and victory.

Prayer: Heavenly Father, we thank You for the assurance of victory that we have in Christ. Help us to remember our identity as Your children and to walk in the authority and power that You have given us. Give us the wisdom and discernment to recognize Your leading and guidance in our lives. May we walk in faith and obedience, trusting in Your strength and victory in every situation. In Jesus' name, we pray. Amen.

Meditative Thought: Reaffirm your identity in Christ and thank God for His presence and power within you. Pray for wisdom and discernment to recognize His leading and guidance in your life. Commit to walking in faith and obedience, trusting in His strength and victory in every situation.

Scripture: 1 John 4:4
"You are of God, little children, and have overcome them, because He who is in you is greater than he who is in the world."

Reflection: As the day draws to a close, 1 John 4:4 continues to resonate in our hearts, reminding us of our identity as children of God and our victory over the forces of darkness. This verse assures us that the One who dwells within us is greater than anything in the world. Reviewing our day with this scripture in mind prompts us to reflect on the ways in which God's presence and power have been evident in our lives throughout the day. It challenges us to consider the moments when we have experienced victory over temptation, doubt, or fear, knowing that it is the indwelling Spirit of God that enables us to overcome. It invites us to respond with gratitude and praise for His faithfulness and strength. As we meditate on this scripture tonight, let's take a moment to thank God for His continual presence and power within us. And let's commit to surrendering ourselves fully to His will, trusting in His greater purposes and plans for our lives.

Prayer: Gracious God, as we end this day, we thank You for Your continual presence and power within us. Forgive us for any missed opportunities to rely on Your strength and guidance in our daily lives. Help us to surrender ourselves fully to Your will, trusting in Your greater purposes and plans for our lives. May Your name be glorified in all that we do. In Jesus' name, we pray. Amen.

Meditative Thought: Thank God for His continual presence and power within you. Reflect on any missed opportunities to rely on His strength and guidance in your daily life. Commit to surrendering yourself fully to His will, trusting in His greater purposes and plans for your life.

Scripture: Proverbs 10:12

"Hatred stirs up strife, But love covers all sins."

Reflection: As we begin our day, Proverbs 10:12 brings to light the contrast between hatred and love. This verse teaches us that while hatred breeds conflict and division, love has the power to cover and overcome sin. Starting our day with this scripture prompts us to reflect on the attitudes and actions we choose to cultivate in our interactions with others. It challenges us to consider whether our words and deeds are motivated by hatred, which only leads to strife and discord, or by love, which has the power to heal and restore relationships. As we meditate on this scripture, let's take a moment to examine our hearts and ask God to reveal any areas where hatred may be lurking. Let's commit to living lives characterized by the transformative power of love, knowing that it has the ability to cover all sins and bring healing to broken relationships.

Prayer: Heavenly Father, we confess that at times we have allowed hatred to creep into our hearts and dictate our words and actions. Forgive us for the times when we have contributed to strife and discord instead of choosing love. Grant us the grace to choose love in every situation, seeking reconciliation and forgiveness instead of conflict and division. Help us to live lives characterized by the transformative power of Your love, knowing that it has the ability to cover all sins and bring healing to broken relationships. In Jesus' name, we pray. Amen.

Meditative Thought: Examine your heart and ask God to reveal any areas where hatred may be lurking. Pray for the grace to choose love in every situation, seeking reconciliation and forgiveness instead of conflict and division. Commit to living a life characterized by the transformative power of love.

Scripture: Proverbs 10:12
"Hatred stirs up strife, But love covers all sins."

Reflection: As the day draws to a close, Proverbs 10:12 continues to resonate in our hearts, reminding us of the power of love to overcome sin and strife. This verse challenges us to choose love as the guiding principle in all our interactions, knowing that it has the power to heal and restore relationships. Reviewing our day with this scripture in mind prompts us to reflect on the ways in which our words and actions have impacted those around us. It challenges us to consider whether we have contributed to strife and discord through harboring hatred in our hearts, or whether we have chosen love, seeking reconciliation and forgiveness. As we meditate on this scripture tonight, let's take a moment to confess any instances where we have allowed hatred to influence our words or actions. Let's pray for God's grace to choose love in every situation, seeking reconciliation and forgiveness instead of conflict and division.

Prayer: Gracious God, as we end this day, we confess that at times we have allowed hatred to influence our words and actions, contributing to strife and discord instead of choosing love. Forgive us for these moments of failure, and grant us Your grace to choose love in every situation. Help us to seek reconciliation and forgiveness, knowing that Your love has the power to cover all sins and bring healing to broken relationships. In Jesus' name, we pray. Amen.

Meditative Thought: Confess any instances where you have allowed hatred to influence your words or actions. Pray for God's grace to choose love in every situation. Commit yourself anew to living a life characterized by the transformative power of His love."

Scripture: John 8:11b
"...Neither do I condemn you; go and sin no more."

Reflection: As we begin our day, John 8:11b brings to light the compassion and grace of Jesus towards the woman caught in adultery. This part of the verse emphasizes Jesus's words of forgiveness and His call to a life free from sin. Starting our day with this scripture prompts us to reflect on the mercy and forgiveness that Jesus offers to each of us. It challenges us to consider the weight of condemnation that we may carry and to embrace the freedom that comes from His forgiveness. It invites us to respond to His grace by turning away from sin and living a life of obedience and righteousness. As we meditate on this scripture, let's take a moment to thank Jesus for His mercy and forgiveness in our lives. Let's pray for the strength to resist temptation and to live in accordance with His will. And let's commit to walking in the freedom that comes from His grace, knowing that He has called us to a life of holiness and purity.

Prayer: Gracious Lord, we thank You for Your boundless mercy and forgiveness towards us. Forgive us for the times when we have fallen short and help us to embrace the freedom that comes from Your grace. Grant us the strength to resist temptation and to live in obedience to Your will. May we walk in the light of Your love, free from condemnation and empowered to live a life of holiness and purity. In Your name, we pray. Amen.

Meditative Thought: Thank Jesus for His mercy and forgiveness in your life. Pray for the strength to resist temptation and to live in accordance with His will. Commit to walking in the freedom that comes from His grace.

Scripture: John 8:11b
"...Neither do I condemn you; go and sin no more."

Reflection: As the day draws to a close, John 8:11b continues to echo in our hearts, reminding us of the mercy and forgiveness that Jesus offers to each of us. This part of the verse emphasizes His call to a life free from sin. Reviewing our day with this scripture in mind prompts us to reflect on the choices we have made and the ways in which we have responded to Jesus's call to live in obedience and righteousness. As we meditate on this scripture tonight, let's take a moment to confess any sins or failures from the day and to ask for Jesus's forgiveness and cleansing. Let's pray for His grace to empower us to live in obedience to His will and to resist temptation. And let's rest in the assurance that His mercy is greater than our sin and that He is faithful to forgive and restore us when we turn to Him in repentance.

Prayer: Merciful Savior, as we end this day, we confess our sins and failures before You. We ask for Your forgiveness and cleansing, knowing that Your mercy is greater than our sin. Grant us Your grace to live in obedience to Your will and to resist temptation. May we walk in the light of Your love, free from condemnation and empowered to live a life of holiness and purity. In Your name, we pray. Amen.

Meditative Thought: Confess any sins or failures from the day and ask for Jesus's forgiveness and cleansing. Pray for His grace to empower you to live in obedience to His will and to resist temptation. Rest in the assurance that His mercy is greater than your sin and that He is faithful to forgive and restore you when you turn to Him in repentance.

OCTOBER 21

MORNING DEVOTION

Scripture: John 14:27

"Peace I leave with you, My peace I give to you; not as the world gives do I give to you. Let not your heart be troubled, neither let it be afraid."

Reflection: As we begin our day, John 14:27 reminds us of the profound peace that Jesus offers to His disciples. This peace is not fleeting or temporary, like the peace that the world offers, but it is a deep and abiding peace that comes from knowing and trusting in Him. Starting our day with this scripture prompts us to reflect on the source of true peace in our lives. It challenges us to examine the areas of our lives where we may be experiencing anxiety, fear, or turmoil, and to surrender them to Jesus, who alone can bring peace to our hearts. As we meditate on this scripture, let's take a moment to release our worries and concerns to Jesus and to receive His peace afresh.

Prayer: Heavenly Father, we thank You for the peace that Jesus offers to us, a peace that surpasses all understanding. We confess that at times we allow fear and anxiety to grip our hearts, instead of trusting in Your promises. Grant us the strength to surrender our worries and concerns to Jesus and to receive His peace afresh. Help us to trust in Him completely and to let go of our fears and anxieties. May we live each moment with hearts filled with His peace, knowing that He is with us always, guiding and sustaining us through every trial and tribulation. In Jesus' name, we pray. Amen.

Meditative Thought: Release your worries and concerns to Jesus and receive His peace afresh. Pray for the strength to trust in Him completely and to let go of fears and anxieties. Commit to living each moment with a heart filled with His peace.

Scripture: John 14:27
"Peace I leave with you, My peace I give to you; not as the world gives do I give to you. Let not your heart be troubled, neither let it be afraid."

Reflection: As the day draws to a close, John 14:27 continues to echo in our hearts, reminding us of the peace that Jesus offers to His disciples. This peace is not like the peace that the world offers, which is often fleeting and temporary, but it is a deep and abiding peace that comes from knowing and trusting in Him. Reviewing our day with this scripture in mind prompts us to reflect on the ways in which we have experienced Jesus's peace in the midst of life's challenges and trials. It challenges us to consider the moments when we have allowed fear and anxiety to grip our hearts, instead of trusting in His promises. It invites us to surrender our worries and concerns to Jesus once again, and to rest in the assurance of His presence and power to calm the storms of life.

Prayer: Gracious Lord, as we end this day, we thank You for the peace that Jesus offers to us, a peace that surpasses all understanding. Forgive us for the times when we have allowed fear and anxiety to overshadow His peace in our lives. Help us to surrender our worries and concerns to Jesus once again, and to rest in the assurance of His presence and power to calm the storms of life. In Jesus' name, we pray. Amen.

Meditative Thought: Thank Jesus for the peace He offers, which surpasses all understanding. Confess any moments when fear and anxiety overshadowed His peace in your life. Commit yourself anew to trusting in Him completely, knowing that His peace is with you always, guiding and sustaining you through every trial and tribulation.

OCTOBER 22

MORNING DEVOTION

Scripture: Revelation 22:20-21
"He who testifies to these things says, 'Surely I am coming quickly.' Amen. Even so, come, Lord Jesus! The grace of our Lord Jesus Christ be with you all. Amen."

Reflection: As we begin our day, Revelation 22:20-21 reminds us of the promise of Jesus's return and the grace that He offers to all who believe in Him. These verses conclude the book of Revelation with a powerful declaration of hope and blessing. Starting our day with this scripture prompts us to reflect on our anticipation of Jesus's return and our readiness to meet Him. It challenges us to consider the state of our hearts and lives in light of His imminent coming. It invites us to live each day with a sense of urgency and expectancy, eagerly awaiting the fulfillment of His promises. As we meditate on this scripture, let's take a moment to renew our commitment to live faithfully for Christ in anticipation of His return. Let's pray for the grace to live with hearts filled with hope and expectancy, knowing that He is coming quickly.

Prayer: Heavenly Father, we thank You for the promise of Jesus's return and the grace that He offers to all who believe in Him. Help us to live each day with hearts filled with hope and expectancy, eagerly awaiting His coming. Grant us the grace to live faithfully for Christ in anticipation of His return. And empower us to share the message of His grace and salvation with others, so that all may be ready to meet Him when He comes again. In Jesus' name, we pray. Amen.

Meditative Thought: Renew your commitment to live faithfully for Christ in anticipation of His return. Pray for the grace to live with hearts filled with hope and expectancy. Commit yourself to sharing the message of His grace and salvation with others.

EVENING DEVOTION

Scripture: Revelation 22:20-21
"He who testifies to these things says, 'Surely I am coming quickly.' Amen. Even so, come, Lord Jesus! The grace of our Lord Jesus Christ be with you all. Amen."

Reflection: As the day draws to a close, Revelation 22:20-21 continues to echo in our hearts, reminding us of the promise of Jesus's return and the grace that He offers to all who believe in Him. These verses serve as a fitting conclusion to the book of Revelation, leaving us with a sense of hope and expectation. Reviewing our day with this scripture in mind prompts us to reflect on our readiness to meet Jesus when He comes again. It challenges us to consider whether we are living in a way that is pleasing to Him and whether we are sharing the message of His grace and salvation with others. As we meditate on this scripture tonight, let's take a moment to thank God for His promise of Jesus's return and the grace that He offers to us.

Prayer: Gracious Lord, as we end this day, we thank You for the promise of Jesus's return and the grace that He offers to us. Forgive us for any ways in which we have fallen short in living faithfully for Him. Grant us Your grace to be with us always, guiding and sustaining us until the day of His return. May we live each day with hearts filled with hope and expectancy, eagerly awaiting the fulfillment of Your promises. In Jesus' name, we pray. Amen.

Meditative Thought: Thank God for His promise of Jesus's return and the grace that He offers to us. Confess any areas where you have fallen short in living faithfully for Him. Commit yourself anew to living each day with hearts filled with hope and expectancy, eagerly awaiting the fulfillment of His promises.

OCTOBER 23

MORNING DEVOTION

Scripture: Matthew 16:24
"Then Jesus said to His disciples, 'If anyone desires to come after Me, let him deny himself, and take up his cross, and follow Me.'"

Reflection: As we begin our day, Matthew 16:24 calls us to a life of discipleship and self-denial. Jesus's words challenge us to consider the cost of following Him and the commitment required to be His disciple. Starting our day with this scripture prompts us to reflect on the demands of discipleship and the call to wholeheartedly follow Jesus. It challenges us to examine our hearts and lives, and to surrender our own desires and ambitions to His will. It invites us to take up our cross daily and to follow Him, no matter the sacrifices or challenges we may face along the way. As we meditate on this scripture, let's take a moment to examine our priorities and ask ourselves if we are truly living as disciples of Jesus. Let's pray for the grace to deny ourselves, take up our cross, and follow Him faithfully each day. And let's commit ourselves anew to living lives that reflect His love, grace, and truth to the world around us.

Prayer: Heavenly Father, we thank You for the call to discipleship and the invitation to follow Jesus. Help us to examine our hearts and lives, and to surrender our own desires and ambitions to His will. Grant us the grace to deny ourselves, take up our cross, and follow Him faithfully each day. May our lives be a reflection of His love, grace, and truth to the world around us. In Jesus' name, we pray. Amen.

Meditative Thought: Examine your priorities and ask yourself if you are truly living as a disciple of Jesus. Pray for the grace to deny yourself, take up your cross, and follow Him faithfully each day. Commit yourself anew to living a life that reflects His love, grace, and truth to the world around you.

Scripture: Matthew 16:24
"Then Jesus said to His disciples, 'If anyone desires to come after Me, let him deny himself, and take up his cross, and follow Me.'"

Reflection: As the day draws to a close, Matthew 16:24 continues to resonate in our hearts, reminding us of the call to discipleship and self-denial that Jesus extends to each of us. His words challenge us to consider the cost of following Him and the commitment required to be His disciple. Reviewing our day with this scripture in mind prompts us to reflect on the ways in which we have lived out our commitment to follow Jesus. It challenges us to examine if we have truly denied ourselves, taken up our cross, and followed Him faithfully. It invites us to confess any areas where we have fallen short and to recommit ourselves to living as His disciples. As we meditate on this scripture tonight, let's take a moment to confess any moments when we have prioritized our own desires over following Jesus. Let's pray for His forgiveness and grace to help us live as His disciples in every aspect of our lives.

Prayer: Gracious Lord, as we end this day, we confess any moments when we have prioritized our own desires over following Jesus. Forgive us for our shortcomings, and grant us Your grace to help us live as His disciples in every aspect of our lives. Help us to deny ourselves, take up our cross, and follow Him faithfully, knowing that He is with us always, guiding and empowering us along the way. In Jesus' name, we pray. Amen.

Meditative Thought: Confess any moments when you prioritized your own desires over following Jesus. Pray for His forgiveness and grace to help you live as His disciple. Commit yourself anew to denying yourself, taking up your cross, and following Him faithfully.

OCTOBER 24

MORNING DEVOTION

Scripture: Ephesians 2:4-5

"But God, who is rich in mercy, because of His great love with which He loved us, even when we were dead in trespasses, made us alive together with Christ (by grace you have been saved)."

Reflection: As we begin our day, Ephesians 2:4-5 reminds us of the incredible mercy and love of God towards us. These verses highlight the richness of God's mercy and the depth of His love, which He demonstrated by making us alive in Christ even when we were dead in our sins. Starting our day with this scripture prompts us to reflect on the immeasurable grace and love that God has shown us through Jesus Christ. It challenges us to consider the depth of our own unworthiness and the magnitude of His forgiveness and salvation. It invites us to respond to His love with gratitude, humility, and a renewed commitment to live for Him. As we meditate on this scripture, let's take a moment to thank God for His mercy and love towards us. Let's commit ourselves anew to living lives that reflect His love and grace to the world around us, knowing that we have been made alive together with Christ by His amazing grace.

Prayer: Heavenly Father, we thank You for Your incredible mercy and love towards us. Forgive us for the times when we have failed to live up to Your perfect standard, and cleanse us from all unrighteousness. Help us to respond to Your love with gratitude, humility, and a renewed commitment to live for You. May our lives be a reflection of Your love and grace to the world around us. In Jesus' name, we pray. Amen.

Meditative Thought: Thank God for His mercy and love towards you. Confess any areas where you have fallen short of His perfect standard and ask for His forgiveness and cleansing. Commit yourself anew to living a life that reflects His love and grace to the world around you.

Scripture: Ephesians 2:4-5
"But God, who is rich in mercy, because of His great love with which He loved us, even when we were dead in trespasses, made us alive together with Christ (by grace you have been saved)."

Reflection: As the day draws to a close, Ephesians 2:4-5 continues to resonate in our hearts, reminding us of the incredible mercy and love of God towards us. These verses speak of God's richness in mercy and His great love, which He demonstrated by making us alive in Christ even when we were dead in our sins. Reviewing our day with this scripture in mind prompts us to reflect on the ways in which we have experienced God's mercy and love throughout the day. It challenges us to consider how His grace has been at work in our lives, bringing us forgiveness, healing, and transformation. As we meditate on this scripture tonight, let's take a moment to thank God for His mercy and love towards us. Let's reflect on the ways in which His grace has been evident in our lives today.

Prayer: Gracious Lord, as we end this day, we thank You for Your incredible mercy and love towards us. Thank You for the ways in which Your grace has been evident in our lives today, bringing us forgiveness, healing, and transformation. Help us to respond to Your love with gratitude and praise, acknowledging Your goodness and faithfulness. May our lives be a reflection of Your love and grace to the world around us. In Jesus' name, we pray. Amen.

Meditative Thought: Thank God for His mercy and love towards you. Reflect on the ways in which His grace has been evident in your life today. Commit yourself anew to living a life that reflects His love and grace to the world around you.

OCTOBER 25

MORNING DEVOTION

Scripture: Revelation 19:14
"And the armies in heaven, clothed in fine linen, white and clean, followed Him on white horses."

Reflection: As we begin our day, Revelation 19:14 paints a vivid picture of the triumphant return of Jesus Christ, accompanied by the heavenly armies clothed in fine linen, white and clean, riding on white horses. This scene depicts the ultimate victory of Christ over sin, death, and evil. Starting our day with this scripture prompts us to reflect on the glorious return of Jesus and the fulfillment of God's promises. It challenges us to consider the hope and assurance we have as believers in His victorious reign. It invites us to live each day with a sense of anticipation and readiness for His return. As we meditate on this scripture, let's take a moment to rejoice in the victory that Jesus has already won on our behalf. Let's renew our commitment to live faithfully for Him, knowing that He is coming again to reign in power and glory.

Prayer: Heavenly Father, we thank You for the glorious return of Jesus Christ, accompanied by the heavenly armies, clothed in fine linen, white and clean. We rejoice in the victory that He has won on our behalf and the hope and assurance we have as believers in His victorious reign. Help us to live each day with a sense of anticipation and readiness for His return, knowing that He is coming again to establish His kingdom of righteousness and peace. Give us the strength and courage to stand firm in our faith, even in the midst of trials and tribulations, knowing that our ultimate victory is assured in Him. In Jesus' name, we pray. Amen.

Meditative Thought: Rejoice in the victory that Jesus has won on your behalf. Renew your commitment to live faithfully for Him, knowing that He is coming again to reign in power and glory.

Scripture: Revelation 19:14
"And the armies in heaven, clothed in fine linen, white and clean, followed Him on white horses."

Reflection: As the day draws to a close, Revelation 19:14 continues to resonate in our hearts, reminding us of the triumphant return of Jesus Christ and the victory that He has won on our behalf. This scene fills us with hope and anticipation as we look forward to the fulfillment of God's promises. Reviewing our day with this scripture in mind prompts us to reflect on the ways in which we have lived in light of the hope of Christ's return. It challenges us to consider if our lives have reflected the reality of His victory over sin and death. As we meditate on this scripture tonight, let's take a moment to thank God for the hope and assurance we have in Jesus Christ. Let's reflect on the ways in which we have lived out our faith today and ask for His forgiveness and guidance where we have fallen short. And let's commit ourselves anew to living lives that reflect His victory and glory, knowing that our ultimate victory is assured in Him.

Prayer:nGracious Lord, as we end this day, we thank You for the hope and assurance we have in Jesus Christ and the victory that He has won on our behalf. Forgive us for the times when we have failed to live in light of His victory over sin and death. Guide us in the days ahead to live faithfully for Him, knowing that He is coming again to establish His kingdom of righteousness and peace. May our lives reflect His victory and glory, bringing honor and praise to Your name. In Jesus' name, we pray. Amen.

Meditative Thought: Reflect on the ways in which you have lived out your faith today. Commit yourself anew to living a life that reflects His victory and glory, bringing honor and praise to His name.

OCTOBER 26

MORNING DEVOTION

Scripture: John 14:23
"Jesus answered and said to him, 'If anyone loves Me, he will keep My word; and My Father will love him, and We will come to him and make Our home with him.'"

Reflection: As we begin our day, John 14:23 reminds us of the intimate relationship that Jesus desires to have with those who love Him and keep His word. This verse speaks of the Father's love for those who obey Jesus's teachings and the promise of His presence in their lives. Starting our day with this scripture prompts us to reflect on the nature of our relationship with Jesus and the importance of obedience to His word. It challenges us to consider if our love for Him is evidenced by our willingness to follow His commands. As we meditate on this scripture, let's take a moment to examine the state of our hearts and lives in relation to Jesus's teachings. Let's pray for the grace to love Him more deeply and to obey His word more faithfully.

Prayer: Heavenly Father, we thank You for the promise of Your presence in our lives as we love and obey Your Son, Jesus Christ. Help us to examine the state of our hearts and lives in relation to His teachings. Grant us the grace to love Him more deeply and to obey His word more faithfully each day. May Your presence fill us, guiding us in all that we do, and may we continually abide in Your love. In Jesus' name, we pray. Amen.

Meditative Thought: Examine the state of your heart and life in relation to Jesus's teachings. Pray for the grace to love Him more deeply and obey His word more faithfully. Invite the Father and the Son to make their home in your heart, filling you with their presence and guiding you in all that you do.

OCTOBER 26

EVENING DEVOTION

Scripture: John 14:23

"Jesus answered and said to him, 'If anyone loves Me, he will keep My word; and My Father will love him, and We will come to him and make Our home with him.'"

Reflection: As the day draws to a close, John 14:23 continues to resonate in our hearts, reminding us of the promise of God's presence in the lives of those who love and obey Jesus. This verse speaks of the Father's love for His children and the intimate relationship He desires to have with them. Reviewing our day with this scripture in mind prompts us to reflect on the ways in which we have loved and obeyed Jesus's teachings. It challenges us to consider if our actions and attitudes have reflected our love for Him. As we meditate on this scripture tonight, let's take a moment to thank God for His promise of presence in our lives. Let's reflect on the ways in which we have lived out our love for Jesus today and ask for His forgiveness and guidance where we have fallen short. And let's invite the Father and the Son to dwell in our hearts, filling us with their presence and empowering us to live lives that honor and glorify them.

Prayer: Gracious Lord, as we end this day, we thank You for the promise of Your presence in our lives as we love and obey Your Son, Jesus Christ. Forgive us for the times when we have failed to love Him as we should and to obey His word faithfully. Fill us anew with Your presence, guiding us in all that we do, and may we continually abide in Your love. In Jesus' name, we pray. Amen.

Meditative Thought: Thank God for His promise of presence in your life. Reflect on the ways in which you have lived out your love for Jesus today. Invite the Father and the Son to dwell in your heart.

Scripture: Psalm 119:40

"Behold, I long for Your precepts; revive me in Your righteousness."

Reflection: As we begin our day, Psalm 119:40 expresses a deep longing for God's commandments and a plea for revival in His righteousness. This verse captures the psalmist's earnest desire to live according to God's ways and to experience spiritual renewal. Starting our day with this scripture prompts us to reflect on our own longing for God's guidance and righteousness in our lives. It challenges us to examine the depth of our hunger for His word and our need for spiritual revival. It invites us to surrender ourselves to His righteousness, knowing that only He can truly satisfy the longing of our souls. As we meditate on this scripture, let's take a moment to evaluate our relationship with God's commandments. Let's surrender ourselves afresh to His guidance and direction, trusting that He will lead us in paths of righteousness for His name's sake.

Prayer: Heavenly Father, we long for Your precepts and Your righteousness. Revive us, we pray, with a hunger for Your word and a longing for Your ways. Renew our hearts and minds, and lead us in paths of righteousness for Your name's sake. May our lives be a testimony to Your goodness and grace. In Jesus' name, we pray. Amen.

Meditative Thought: Evaluate your relationship with God's commandments. Pray for a renewed hunger for His word and a revival of His righteousness in your heart. Surrender yourself afresh to His guidance and direction.

Scripture: Psalm 119:40
"Behold, I long for Your precepts; revive me in Your righteousness."

Reflection: As the day draws to a close, Psalm 119:40 continues to resonate in our hearts, expressing a deep longing for God's commandments and a plea for revival in His righteousness. This verse reminds us of our ongoing need for spiritual renewal and our dependence on God's guidance in our lives. Reviewing our day with this scripture in mind prompts us to reflect on the ways in which we have pursued God's precepts and righteousness. It challenges us to consider if we have truly longed for His word and sought after His ways. It invites us to acknowledge any areas where we have fallen short and to renew our commitment to follow Him wholeheartedly. As we meditate on this scripture tonight, let's take a moment to confess any shortcomings and ask for God's forgiveness and renewal. Let's pray for a deeper hunger for His word and a greater desire to live according to His ways.

Prayer: Gracious Lord, as we end this day, we confess our need for Your guidance and renewal. Forgive us for the times when we have failed to long for Your precepts and to seek after Your righteousness. Revive us, we pray, with a deeper hunger for Your word and a greater desire to live according to Your ways. Lead us in paths of righteousness for Your name's sake. In Jesus' name, we pray. Amen.

Meditative Thought: Confess any shortcomings in pursuing God's precepts and righteousness. Pray for a deeper hunger for His word and a greater desire to live according to His ways. Surrender yourself once again to His righteousness, trusting that He will revive you and lead you in paths of righteousness for His name's sake.

OCTOBER 28

MORNING DEVOTION

Scripture: Isaiah 53:5

"But He was wounded for our transgressions, He was bruised for our iniquities; the chastisement for our peace was upon Him, and by His stripes we are healed."

Reflection: As we begin our day, Isaiah 53:5 offers a profound reflection on the sacrifice of Jesus Christ for humanity's redemption. This verse vividly portrays the suffering and atoning work of the Messiah, emphasizing that His wounds and bruises were borne for the sins of all. Starting our day with this scripture prompts us to reflect on the depth of God's love demonstrated through Christ's sacrifice. It challenges us to contemplate the extent of His suffering on our behalf and the peace and healing that His sacrifice brings. It invites us to respond with gratitude and awe to the incredible gift of salvation. As we meditate on this scripture, let's take a moment to thank God for the sacrificial love of Jesus Christ. Let's commit ourselves anew to living lives that honor His sacrifice, walking in the peace and healing that He has provided.

Prayer: Gracious Father, we thank You for the immeasurable love demonstrated through the sacrifice of Your Son, Jesus Christ. Help us to comprehend the depth of His suffering on our behalf and the peace and healing that His sacrifice brings. May our lives be a reflection of gratitude and honor for His sacrifice, as we walk in the freedom and healing He has provided. In Jesus' name, we pray. Amen.

Meditative Thought: Thank God for the sacrificial love of Jesus Christ. Reflect on the significance of His wounds and bruises, recognizing that they were endured for your sake. Commit yourself anew to living a life that honors His sacrifice, walking in the peace and healing He has provided.

Scripture: Isaiah 53:5
"But He was wounded for our transgressions, He was bruised for our iniquities; the chastisement for our peace was upon Him, and by His stripes we are healed."

Reflection: As the day draws to a close, Isaiah 53:5 continues to resonate in our hearts, reminding us of the sacrificial love of Jesus Christ. This verse invites us to contemplate the depth of His suffering and the peace and healing that His sacrifice offers to all who believe. Reviewing our day with this scripture in mind prompts us to reflect on the ways in which we have experienced the peace and healing that Christ provides. It challenges us to consider if we have fully embraced His sacrifice and allowed it to transform our lives. It invites us to surrender ourselves anew to His love and grace. As we meditate on this scripture tonight, let's take a moment to thank God for the peace and healing that Christ's sacrifice brings. Let's commit ourselves afresh to living lives that honor His sacrifice, walking in the freedom and healing that He has provided.

Prayer: Heavenly Father, we thank You for the sacrificial love of Jesus Christ and the peace and healing that His sacrifice brings. Touch our hearts tonight with Your healing grace, and help us to fully embrace the freedom that He offers. May our lives be a testimony to Your love and grace, as we walk in the peace and healing that He has provided. In Jesus' name, we pray. Amen.

Meditative Thought: Thank God for the peace and healing that Christ's sacrifice brings. Reflect on the areas of your life where you need His healing touch. Commit yourself afresh to living a life that honors His sacrifice, walking in the freedom and healing He has provided.

Scripture: Matthew 25:6

"And at midnight a cry was heard: 'Behold, the bridegroom is coming; go out to meet him!'"

Reflection: As we begin our day, Matthew 25:6 paints a vivid picture of anticipation and readiness for the arrival of the bridegroom. This verse signifies the urgency and excitement surrounding the return of Jesus Christ, urging believers to be prepared to meet Him. Starting our day with this scripture prompts us to reflect on our own readiness for the second coming of Christ. It challenges us to consider if we are living in eager anticipation of His return or if we have become complacent in our faith. It invites us to examine our hearts and actions, ensuring that we are actively seeking to live according to His will. As we meditate on this scripture, let's take a moment to evaluate our spiritual readiness for the return of Jesus. Let's commit ourselves anew to living lives that honor and glorify Him, eagerly awaiting His arrival.

Prayer: Heavenly Father, as we begin this day, we are reminded of the urgency and excitement surrounding the return of Jesus Christ. Grant us the grace to live each day with eager anticipation of His coming. Help us to examine our hearts and actions, ensuring that we are ready to meet Him when He returns. May our lives be a testimony to Your grace and glory, as we eagerly await the arrival of our bridegroom. In Jesus' name, we pray. Amen.

Meditative Thought: Evaluate your spiritual readiness for the return of Jesus. Pray for the grace to live each day with eagerness and anticipation of His coming. Commit yourself anew to living a life that honors and glorifies Him, eagerly awaiting His arrival.

Scripture: Matthew 25:6
"And at midnight a cry was heard: 'Behold, the bridegroom is coming; go out to meet him!'"

Reflection: As the day draws to a close, Matthew 25:6 continues to resonate in our hearts, reminding us of the urgency and excitement surrounding the return of Jesus Christ. This verse challenges us to be prepared and ready to meet Him when He comes. Reviewing our day with this scripture in mind prompts us to reflect on our spiritual readiness for the return of Jesus. It challenges us to consider if we have lived each day with eager anticipation of His coming or if we have allowed the cares and distractions of this world to dim our longing for His return. It invites us to recommit ourselves to living lives that reflect His love and grace, eagerly awaiting His arrival. As we meditate on this scripture tonight, let's take a moment to confess any areas where we have fallen short in our readiness for the return of Jesus.

Prayer: Gracious Lord, as we end this day, we confess any areas where we have fallen short in our readiness for Your return. Grant us the grace to live each day with eager anticipation of Your coming. Help us to surrender ourselves anew to Your will, eagerly awaiting Your arrival and the fulfillment of Your promises. May our lives be a reflection of Your love and grace, as we eagerly await the arrival of our bridegroom. In Jesus' name, we pray. Amen.

Meditative Thought: Confess any areas where you have fallen short in your readiness for the return of Jesus. Pray for the grace to live each day with eagerness and anticipation of His coming. Surrender yourself anew to His will, eagerly awaiting His arrival and the fulfillment of His promises.

Scripture: 1 Peter 5:14

"Greet one another with a kiss of love. Peace to you all who are in Christ Jesus. Amen."

Reflection: As we begin our day, 1 Peter 5:14 offers a beautiful reminder of the importance of love and peace within the Christian community. This verse encourages believers to greet one another with a kiss of love, symbolizing the deep bonds of fellowship and unity that exist among those who are in Christ Jesus. Starting our day with this scripture prompts us to reflect on the quality of our relationships within the body of Christ. It challenges us to consider if we are actively demonstrating love and affection towards our brothers and sisters in Christ, fostering an atmosphere of peace and unity. It invites us to prioritize building and maintaining strong, supportive relationships within our Christian community. As we meditate on this scripture, let's take a moment to evaluate the state of our relationships with our fellow believers. Let's commit ourselves anew to fostering an environment of peace and unity within the body of Christ, reflecting the love and grace of our Lord Jesus Christ.

Prayer: Heavenly Father, we thank You for the gift of Christian fellowship and the unity that we share in Christ Jesus. Help us to greet one another with genuine love and affection, fostering an atmosphere of peace and unity within our Christian community. Grant us the grace to build strong, supportive relationships with our brothers and sisters in Christ, reflecting Your love and grace to the world around us. In Jesus' name, we pray. Amen.

Meditative Thought: Evaluate the state of your relationships within the body of Christ. Pray for the grace to extend love and kindness to others.

Scripture: 1 Peter 5:14
"Greet one another with a kiss of love. Peace to you all who are in Christ Jesus. Amen."

Reflection: As the day draws to a close, 1 Peter 5:14 continues to resonate in our hearts, reminding us of the importance of love and peace within the Christian community. This verse encourages believers to extend greetings of love and affection to one another, fostering an environment of unity and harmony. As we meditate on this scripture tonight, let's take a moment to reflect on the ways in which we have lived out the principles of love and peace within the body of Christ. Let's commit ourselves anew to fostering an environment of love, peace, and unity within the body of Christ, reflecting the love and grace of our Lord Jesus Christ.

Prayer: Gracious Lord, as we end this day, we confess any areas where we have failed to demonstrate love and kindness towards our fellow believers. Forgive us for any words or actions that have caused division or discord within Your body. Grant us the grace to prioritize reconciliation and forgiveness, seeking to promote peace and unity among Your people. May our lives be a reflection of Your love and grace, as we strive to build strong, supportive relationships within the body of Christ. In Jesus' name, we pray. Amen.

Meditative Thought: Reflect on the ways in which you have lived out the principles of love and peace within the body of Christ. Confess any areas where you have fallen short. Commit yourself anew to fostering an environment of love, peace, and unity, reflecting the love and grace of Jesus Christ.

Scripture: 1 John 1:5
"This is the message which we have heard from Him and declare to you, that God is light and in Him is no darkness at all."

Reflection: As we begin our day, 1 John 1:5 reminds us of the fundamental truth about God's nature - He is light, and in Him, there is no darkness at all. This verse encapsulates the essence of God's character, emphasizing His holiness, purity, and righteousness. Starting our day with this scripture prompts us to reflect on the implications of God being light. It challenges us to consider the contrast between light and darkness and the transformative power of God's light in our lives. It invites us to examine our own hearts and actions, ensuring that we are walking in the light of His truth and righteousness. As we meditate on this scripture, let's take a moment to thank God for His light that shines in our lives, dispelling the darkness of sin and ignorance. Let's commit ourselves anew to embracing the truth of God's Word and allowing His light to illuminate every area of our lives.

Prayer: Heavenly Father, we thank You for being the light in our lives, dispelling the darkness of sin and ignorance. Grant us the grace to walk in Your light each day, seeking to live lives that reflect Your holiness and purity. Help us to embrace the truth of Your Word and to allow Your light to illuminate every area of our lives. In Jesus' name, we pray. Amen.

Meditative Thought: Thank God for His light that shines in your life, dispelling the darkness of sin and ignorance. Pray for the grace to walk in His light each day. Commit yourself anew to embracing the truth of God's Word and allowing His light to illuminate every area of your life.

Scripture: 1 John 1:5
"This is the message which we have heard from Him and declare to you, that God is light and in Him is no darkness at all."

Reflection: As the day draws to a close, 1 John 1:5 continues to resonate in our hearts, reminding us of the fundamental truth about God's nature - He is light, and in Him, there is no darkness at all. Reviewing our day with this scripture in mind prompts us to examine our response to God's light shining in our lives. It challenges us to consider if we have embraced His truth and allowed His light to illuminate every area of our lives, or if we have allowed darkness to creep in through sin and disobedience. As we meditate on this scripture tonight, let's take a moment to confess any areas where we have allowed darkness to take hold in our lives. Let's surrender ourselves anew to the transforming power of His light, allowing it to illuminate every corner of our hearts and minds.

Prayer: Gracious Lord, as we end this day, we confess any areas where we have allowed darkness to take hold in our lives. Forgive us for our sins and disobedience, and cleanse us from all unrighteousness. Grant us the grace to walk in Your light each day, seeking Your truth and righteousness above all else. May Your light illuminate every corner of our hearts and minds, transforming us into vessels of Your glory. In Jesus' name, we pray. Amen.

Meditative Thought: Confess any areas where you have allowed darkness to take hold in your life. Pray for God's forgiveness and grace to walk in His light each day. Surrender yourself anew to the transforming power of His light, allowing it to illuminate every corner of your heart and mind.

NOVEMBER 1

MORNING DEVOTION

Scripture: Jude 1:20-21
"But you, beloved, building yourselves up on your most holy faith, praying in the Holy Spirit, keep yourselves in the love of God, looking for the mercy of our Lord Jesus Christ unto eternal life."

Reflection: As we begin our day, Jude 1:20-21 provides us with essential guidance on nurturing our spiritual lives. These verses urge believers to actively engage in building themselves up in their most holy faith, praying in the Holy Spirit, and keeping themselves in the love of God. Starting our day with this scripture prompts us to reflect on the importance of spiritual growth and communion with God. It challenges us to prioritize our relationship with Him, investing time and effort in deepening our faith through prayer and study of His Word. It invites us to guard our hearts and minds against the distractions and temptations of the world, remaining steadfast in His love. As we meditate on this scripture, let's take a moment to evaluate the state of our spiritual lives. Let's look forward with hope and anticipation to the mercy of our Lord Jesus Christ, which leads to eternal life.

Prayer: Heavenly Father, we thank You for the guidance and encouragement found in Your Word. Grant us the grace to build ourselves up in our most holy faith, rooted in Your love. Help us to cultivate a life of prayerful dependence on the Holy Spirit, seeking His guidance and strength in all that we do. Keep us steadfast in Your love, and help us to look forward with hope to the mercy of our Lord Jesus Christ unto eternal life. In His name, we pray. Amen.

Meditative Thought: Evaluate the state of your spiritual life. Pray for the grace to deepen your faith and cultivate a life of prayerful dependence on the Holy Spirit.

Scripture: Jude 1:20-21

"But you, beloved, building yourselves up on your most holy faith, praying in the Holy Spirit, keep yourselves in the love of God, looking for the mercy of our Lord Jesus Christ unto eternal life."

Reflection: As the day draws to a close, Jude 1:20-21 continues to resonate in our hearts, reminding us of the importance of nurturing our spiritual lives. These verses encourage believers to actively engage in building themselves up in their most holy faith, praying in the Holy Spirit, and keeping themselves in the love of God. Reviewing our day with this scripture in mind prompts us to reflect on how we have prioritized our relationship with God. It challenges us to consider if we have invested time and effort in deepening our faith through prayer and study of His Word, or if we have allowed the busyness of life to distract us from what truly matters. Let's pray for God's forgiveness and grace to renew our commitment to Him. And let's surrender ourselves anew to His love and mercy, trusting in His faithfulness to sustain us and lead us into eternal life.

Prayer: Gracious Lord, as we end this day, we confess any areas where we have neglected to prioritize our relationship with You. Forgive us for our distractions and busyness, and renew our commitment to building ourselves up in our most holy faith. Grant us the grace to remain steadfast in Your love, looking forward with hope to the mercy of our Lord Jesus Christ unto eternal life. In His name, we pray. Amen.

Meditative Thought: Confess any areas where you have fallen short in nurturing your spiritual life. Pray for God's forgiveness and grace to renew your commitment to Him. Surrender yourself anew to His love and mercy, trusting in His faithfulness to lead you into eternal life.

Scripture: 1 John 4:7

"Beloved, let us love one another, for love is of God; and everyone who loves is born of God and knows God."

Reflection: As we begin our day, 1 John 4:7 calls us to a fundamental truth: love originates from God Himself. This verse reminds us that our ability to love others is rooted in our relationship with God, for He is the source of all love. Starting our day with this scripture prompts us to reflect on the significance of love in our lives. It challenges us to examine our relationships and interactions with others, considering whether our words and actions are motivated by genuine love. It invites us to deepen our understanding of God's love for us and to allow that love to overflow into the lives of those around us. As we meditate on this scripture, let's take a moment to thank God for His love that has been poured out into our hearts. Let's commit ourselves anew to cultivating a spirit of love in all that we do, reflecting the love of God to a world in need.

Prayer: Heavenly Father, we thank You for the gift of Your love that has been poured out into our hearts. Help us to love one another as You have loved us, sacrificially and unconditionally. Grant us the grace to reflect Your love in all that we do, showing kindness, compassion, and forgiveness to those around us. May Your love shine brightly through us, drawing others into relationship with You. In Jesus' name, we pray. Amen.

Meditative Thought: Thank God for His love that has been poured out into your heart. Pray for the grace to love others as He has loved you. Commit yourself anew to reflecting God's love in all that you do, showing kindness, compassion, and forgiveness to those around you.

Scripture: 1 John 4:7
"Beloved, let us love one another, for love is of God; and everyone who loves is born of God and knows God."

Reflection: As the day draws to a close, 1 John 4:7 continues to resonate in our hearts, reminding us of the central importance of love in the Christian life. This verse urges us to love one another, for love originates from God Himself, and those who love are born of God and know Him. Reviewing our day with this scripture in mind prompts us to reflect on the ways in which we have lived out the command to love others. It challenges us to consider whether our words and actions have been motivated by genuine love, or if we have allowed selfishness and pride to hinder our relationships. As we meditate on this scripture tonight, let's take a moment to confess any areas where we have fallen short in loving others. Let's pray for God's forgiveness and grace to empower us to love more deeply and selflessly. And let's surrender ourselves anew to His love, allowing it to transform our hearts and minds, so that we may truly reflect His love to a world in need.

Prayer: Gracious Lord, as we end this day, we confess any areas where we have failed to love others as You have commanded. Forgive us for our selfishness and pride, and renew within us a spirit of genuine love. Grant us the grace to love more deeply and selflessly, reflecting Your love to a world in need. May Your love shine brightly through us, drawing others into relationship with You. In Jesus' name, we pray. Amen.

Meditative Thought: Confess any areas where you have fallen short in loving others. Pray for God's forgiveness and grace to empower you to love more deeply and selflessly. Surrender yourself anew to His love.

Scripture: Matthew 11:4-5

"Jesus answered and said to them, 'Go and tell John the things which you hear and see: The blind see and the lame walk; the lepers are cleansed and the deaf hear; the dead are raised up and the poor have the gospel preached to them.'"

Reflection: As we begin our day, Matthew 11:4-5 presents us with a powerful testimony to the miracles performed by Jesus. When John the Baptist sent his disciples to inquire if Jesus was the Messiah, Jesus responded by pointing to the evidence of His ministry: the blind seeing, the lame walking, the lepers being cleansed, the deaf hearing, the dead being raised, and the poor receiving the gospel. Starting our day with this scripture prompts us to reflect on the transformative power of Jesus' ministry. It challenges us to consider the miraculous works that Jesus continues to perform in our lives and in the lives of those around us. It invites us to recognize Jesus as the source of true healing and salvation, and to share His message of hope and redemption with others. As we meditate on this scripture, let's take a moment to thank Jesus for His ongoing work in our lives.

Prayer: Heavenly Father, we thank You for the miraculous works performed by Jesus during His ministry on earth. Open our eyes to see Your ongoing work in our lives and in the lives of those around us. Grant us the grace to trust in Jesus as the source of true healing and salvation, and empower us to share His message of hope and redemption with others. In Jesus name, we pray. Amen.

Meditative Thought: Thank Jesus for His ongoing work in your life. Pray for the grace to recognize His presence and power at work. Commit yourself anew to sharing the good news of Jesus' love and salvation with others.

Scripture: Matthew 11:4-5

"Jesus answered and said to them, 'Go and tell John the things which you hear and see: The blind see and the lame walk; the lepers are cleansed and the deaf hear; the dead are raised up and the poor have the gospel preached to them.'"

Reflection: As the day draws to a close, Matthew 11:4-5 continues to resonate in our hearts, reminding us of the miraculous works performed by Jesus during His ministry on earth. This scripture challenges us to recognize Jesus as the source of true healing and salvation, and to share His message of hope and redemption with others. Reviewing our day with this scripture in mind prompts us to reflect on the ways in which we have witnessed God's ongoing work in our lives and in the lives of those around us. It challenges us to consider if we have been attentive to His presence and power at work, or if we have allowed doubt and distraction to cloud our vision. It invites us to renew our commitment to sharing the good news of Jesus' love and salvation with those who need to hear it.

Prayer: Gracious Lord, as we end this day, we thank You for Your ongoing work in our lives and in the world around us. Open our eyes to see Your presence and power at work, even in the midst of challenges and difficulties. Grant us the grace to trust in You as the source of true healing and salvation, and empower us to share Your message of hope and redemption with everyone we encounter. In Jesus' name, we pray. Amen.

Meditative Thought: Thank Jesus for His ongoing work in your life and in the world around you. Pray for the grace to recognize His presence and power at work.

NOVEMBER 4

MORNING DEVOTION

Scripture: Mark 1:17-18

"Then Jesus said to them, 'Follow Me, and I will make you become fishers of men.' They immediately left their nets and followed Him."

Reflection: As we begin our day, Mark 1:17-18 invites us into the transformative encounter between Jesus and His first disciples. When Jesus called Simon (Peter) and Andrew, He didn't just invite them to follow Him; He promised to transform them into "fishers of men." In response to His call, they immediately left their livelihoods and followed Him. Starting our day with this scripture prompts us to reflect on our own response to Jesus' call to follow Him. It challenges us to consider whether we have fully surrendered ourselves to His transformative work in our lives, allowing Him to shape us into His disciples and to use us for His kingdom purposes. It invites us to examine what nets we may need to leave behind – whether they be material possessions, habits, or attitudes – in order to follow Jesus wholeheartedly. As we meditate on this scripture, let's take a moment to recommit ourselves to following Jesus wherever He may lead. Let's pray for the grace to surrender everything to Him, trusting that He will transform us and use us for His glory.

Prayer: Heavenly Father, we thank You for the invitation to follow Jesus and to be transformed into His disciples. Give us the courage to leave behind anything that hinders us from fully surrendering to Him. Grant us the grace to trust in His transformative work in our lives, and empower us to join Him in His mission of making disciples and bringing others into relationship with Him. In His name, we pray. Amen.

Meditative Thought: Recommit yourself to following Jesus wherever He may lead. Pray for the grace to surrender everything to Him.

Scripture: Mark 1:17-18

"Then Jesus said to them, 'Follow Me, and I will make you become fishers of men.' They immediately left their nets and followed Him."

Reflection: As the day draws to a close, Mark 1:17-18 continues to resonate in our hearts, reminding us of the radical response of Simon (Peter) and Andrew to Jesus' call. In response to His invitation to follow Him and become fishers of men, they immediately left their nets and followed Him. Reviewing our day with this scripture in mind prompts us to reflect on our own response to Jesus' call to follow Him. It challenges us to consider if we have fully surrendered ourselves to His transformative work in our lives, or if we have hesitated or held back out of fear or self-interest. As we meditate on this scripture tonight, let's take a moment to examine our hearts and confess any areas where we have hesitated to follow Jesus fully. Let's pray for the grace to surrender everything to Him, trusting that He will transform us and use us for His glory. And let's rest in His love and faithfulness, knowing that He is always with us, guiding us and empowering us to fulfill His purposes.

Prayer: Gracious Lord, as we end this day, we confess any areas where we have hesitated to follow You fully. Forgive us for our fear and self-interest, and renew within us a spirit of wholehearted commitment to You. Grant us the grace to surrender everything to You, trusting in Your transformative work in our lives. May Your kingdom come and Your will be done in us and through us. In Jesus' name, we pray. Amen.

Meditative Thought: Examine your heart and confess any areas where you have hesitated to follow Jesus fully. Pray for the grace to surrender everything to Him. Rest in His love and faithfulness, knowing that He is always with you, guiding you and empowering you to fulfill His purposes.

NOVEMBER 5

MORNING DEVOTION

Scripture: Psalm 66:20
"Blessed be God, Who has not turned away my prayer, nor His mercy from me!"

Reflection: As we begin our day, Psalm 66:20 reminds us of the steadfast faithfulness of God. The psalmist expresses profound gratitude, recognizing that God has neither ignored his prayers nor withheld His mercy. This verse invites us to start our day with thanksgiving, acknowledging that God hears our prayers and continually extends His mercy towards us. Reflecting on this verse in the morning encourages us to trust in God's responsiveness to our needs and His enduring compassion. It challenges us to approach our day with a heart full of gratitude, confident in the knowledge that God is attentive to our cries and generous with His grace. This assurance can transform our outlook, enabling us to face challenges with hope and joy. As we meditate on this scripture, let's take a moment to thank God for His faithfulness. Let us remember times when He has answered our prayers and shown us His mercy. Let's carry this gratitude throughout the day, letting it shape our interactions and decisions.

Prayer: Heavenly Father, we bless Your name this morning, thanking You for Your faithfulness in hearing our prayers and extending Your mercy. Help us to begin this day with a heart full of gratitude, trusting in Your responsiveness and compassion. May Your assurance of grace and mercy guide us through every moment, filling us with hope and joy. In Jesus' name, we pray. Amen.

Meditative Thought: Spend a few moments in gratitude, recalling specific instances when God has answered your prayers and shown you mercy. Let this gratitude shape your outlook for the day.

Scripture: Psalm 66:20
"Blessed be God, Who has not turned away my prayer, nor His mercy from me!"

Reflection: As the day comes to a close, Psalm 66:20 offers a beautiful reminder of God's faithfulness throughout our day. Reflecting on this verse in the evening invites us to review our day with a grateful heart, recognizing the ways God has heard our prayers and shown us His mercy. This verse encourages us to end our day with thanksgiving, acknowledging God's constant presence and care. It challenges us to see the day's events through the lens of God's mercy, even if it has been a difficult day. Recognizing His faithfulness helps us to cultivate a heart of gratitude and peace, trusting that He will continue to guide and support us. As we meditate on this scripture tonight, let's thank God for the specific ways He has been present in our day. Let's reflect on the moments He has answered our prayers or shown us mercy and allow this reflection to bring us peace as we rest.

Prayer: Gracious Lord, we bless Your name as we close this day, thanking You for Your faithfulness in hearing our prayers and showing us mercy. Help us to review our day with a heart of gratitude, recognizing Your constant presence and care. Fill us with peace as we rest, confident in Your enduring compassion and grace. In Jesus' name, we pray. Amen.

Meditative Thought: Reflect on your day, identifying moments when you experienced God's mercy or saw His hand at work. Let this reflection bring you peace and gratitude as you prepare to rest.

Scripture: Lamentations 3:24

"The Lord is my portion," says my soul, "Therefore I hope in Him!"

Reflection: As we begin our day, Lamentations 3:24 offers a profound declaration of faith and hope. The prophet Jeremiah, in the midst of great sorrow and suffering, proclaims that the Lord is his portion. This means that God is his everything, his inheritance, and his sufficiency. Despite the circumstances, Jeremiah's soul finds hope in the Lord because of this truth. Starting our day with this verse encourages us to center our lives around God, recognizing that He is our ultimate source of satisfaction and security. It invites us to place our hope not in the fleeting things of this world but in the eternal and unchanging nature of God. By doing so, we can face the day's challenges with confidence and peace, knowing that our portion is secure in Him. As we meditate on this scripture, let's take a moment to affirm that God is our portion. Let us remind ourselves that no matter what the day holds, our hope is firmly anchored in Him. This assurance can transform our outlook, filling us with peace and confidence as we step into the day.

Prayer: Heavenly Father, as we begin this day, we declare that You are our portion. Thank You for being our source of satisfaction, security, and hope. Help us to keep our focus on You throughout the day, trusting in Your sufficiency. Fill us with Your peace and confidence as we face whatever lies ahead. In Jesus' name, we pray. Amen.

Meditative Thought: Spend a few moments affirming that God is your portion. Reflect on how this truth changes your perspective on the day ahead and fills you with hope.

Scripture: Lamentations 3:24
"The Lord is my portion," says my soul, "Therefore I hope in Him!"

Reflection: As the day draws to a close, Lamentations 3:24 invites us to reflect on the steadfast hope we have in God. Jeremiah's proclamation that the Lord is his portion serves as a reminder that no matter what has transpired throughout the day, God remains our ultimate source of hope and fulfillment. Reviewing our day with this scripture in mind helps us to refocus on the truth that our circumstances do not define our hope. Instead, our hope is rooted in the character and faithfulness of God. This perspective allows us to find peace and rest, even if the day has been filled with challenges or disappointments. We are reminded that God is enough and that His presence sustains us. As we meditate on this scripture tonight, let's take a moment to thank God for being our portion. Let's reflect on the day and recognize how He has been present with us. Let this recognition fill us with gratitude and hope as we prepare to rest.

Prayer: Gracious Lord, as we end this day, we declare that You are our portion. Thank You for being our constant source of hope and fulfillment. Help us to rest in the knowledge of Your sufficiency and faithfulness. Fill our hearts with gratitude and peace as we reflect on Your presence throughout this day. In Jesus' name, we pray. Amen.

Meditative Thought: Reflect on your day, identifying moments where you experienced God's presence and sufficiency. Let this reflection bring you peace and gratitude as you prepare to rest, knowing that the Lord is your portion.

NOVEMBER 7

MORNING DEVOTION

Scripture: Galatians 6:7
"Do not be deceived, God is not mocked; for whatever a man sows, that he will also reap."

Reflection: As we begin our day, Galatians 6:7 offers a sobering yet empowering reminder of the principle of sowing and reaping. This verse tells us that our actions have consequences and that we cannot deceive God. Whatever we invest our time, energy, and resources into will yield corresponding results. Reflecting on this scripture in the morning encourages us to consider the seeds we are planting in our lives and the lives of others. Are we sowing seeds of kindness, love, and faith, or are we planting seeds of negativity, selfishness, and sin? Understanding that we will reap what we sow motivates us to make conscious, positive choices today. Starting the day with this mindset sets a tone of intentionality and purpose. It challenges us to be mindful of our actions and their potential outcomes. As we meditate on this verse, let's commit to sowing seeds that honor God and bless others, trusting that in due time, we will reap a bountiful harvest of goodness.

Prayer: Heavenly Father, as we start this day, help us to remember the principle of sowing and reaping. Guide us to plant seeds of kindness, love, and faith in all that we do. Keep us mindful of our actions and their consequences, so we may live in a way that honors You. Strengthen us to make positive choices that will yield a harvest of blessings. In Jesus' name, we pray. Amen.

Meditative Thought: Spend a few moments contemplating the seeds you are sowing in your life. Reflect on how you can intentionally plant seeds of goodness and righteousness throughout your day.

Scripture: Galatians 6:7
"Do not be deceived, God is not mocked; for whatever a man sows, that he will also reap."

Reflection: As the day comes to an end, Galatians 6:7 invites us to reflect on the seeds we have sown throughout the day. This verse serves as a reminder that our actions are significant and that they contribute to the future we are creating. In the quiet of the evening, we can assess our day and consider the nature of the seeds we have planted. Did we act with kindness and love, or were there moments of negativity and selfishness? Acknowledging our actions allows us to learn and grow, understanding that God sees all and that our efforts, good or bad, will bear fruit in time. This reflection encourages us to seek forgiveness for any negative seeds we may have sown and to thank God for the opportunities to plant seeds of goodness. It reassures us that tomorrow is another chance to sow righteously. As we prepare for rest, let's commit our actions to God, trusting that He will help us to cultivate a life that honors Him.

Prayer: Gracious Lord, as we conclude this day, we reflect on the seeds we have sown. Forgive us for any actions that did not honor You, and help us to learn from our mistakes. Thank You for the opportunities to plant seeds of kindness, love, and faith. Guide us to be mindful of our actions and their consequences. May we rest in the assurance of Your grace and look forward to a new day of sowing righteously. In Jesus' name, we pray. Amen.

Meditative Thought: Reflect on your day and the seeds you have sown. Seek God's forgiveness for any missteps and His guidance to continue planting seeds of righteousness. Let this reflection bring you peace and prepare you for a restful night.

NOVEMBER 8

MORNING DEVOTION

Scripture: Matthew 28:6
"He is not here; for He is risen, as He said. Come, see the place where the Lord lay."

Reflection: As we start our day, Matthew 28:6 reminds us of the cornerstone of our faith: the resurrection of Jesus Christ. The angel's proclamation to the women at the tomb, "He is not here; for He is risen," echoes through the ages, affirming that Jesus has conquered death. This powerful truth gives us hope and assurance every morning. Reflecting on the resurrection as we begin our day encourages us to live in the victory that Jesus has secured for us. It's a reminder that no matter what challenges we face, we serve a risen Savior who has overcome the greatest obstacle. This perspective can transform our attitude and actions, filling us with joy, courage, and purpose. As we meditate on this verse, let's allow the reality of the resurrection to infuse our day with hope and strength. Let it remind us that we are not defined by our struggles but by the victory of our risen Lord.

Prayer: Heavenly Father, we thank You for the incredible gift of Your Son's resurrection. As we start this day, let the truth that Jesus is risen fill our hearts with hope and joy. Help us to live in the victory and freedom that He has won for us. Guide our actions and thoughts today so that they reflect the power of the resurrection. In Jesus' name, we pray. Amen.

Meditative Thought: Spend a few moments reflecting on the significance of the resurrection. Consider how this truth impacts your perspective on today's challenges and opportunities. Let it fill you with hope and courage.

Scripture: Matthew 28:6
"He is not here; for He is risen, as He said. Come, see the place where the Lord lay."

Reflection: As the day draws to a close, Matthew 28:6 offers a profound reminder of God's faithfulness and power. The angel's message at the empty tomb reassures us that Jesus' words are true and His promises are reliable. Reflecting on the resurrection in the evening helps us to see the day's events through the lens of Christ's victory over death. Reviewing our day with this scripture in mind allows us to put our challenges and successes in perspective. No matter what we encountered, the risen Christ is our anchor and hope. This reflection can bring peace and gratitude, knowing that our faith rests on the solid foundation of the resurrection. As we meditate on this verse tonight, let's thank God for His faithfulness and the hope we have in Jesus. Let's allow the reality of the resurrection to give us peace as we rest, confident that our Savior lives and reigns.

Prayer: Gracious Lord, we thank You for the assurance that Jesus is risen. As we end this day, let the truth of the resurrection bring us peace and rest. Thank You for Your faithfulness and the hope we have in Christ. Help us to reflect on the ways You have been present with us today. May we rest in Your victory and wake up ready to serve You anew. In Jesus' name, we pray. Amen.

Meditative Thought: Reflect on your day in light of the resurrection. Consider how the risen Christ has been with you through today's experiences. Let this reflection bring you peace and gratitude as you prepare for rest.

NOVEMBER 9

MORNING DEVOTION

Scripture: 2 Timothy 3:16-17

"All Scripture is given by inspiration of God, and is profitable for doctrine, for reproof, for correction, for instruction in righteousness, that the man of God may be complete, thoroughly equipped for every good work."

Reflection: As we begin our day, 2 Timothy 3:16-17 reminds us of the power and purpose of God's Word. The Bible is not just a historical document or a collection of stories; it is the inspired Word of God, given to us for our growth and guidance. It is profitable for teaching us the truth, rebuking us when we go astray, correcting our mistakes, and training us in righteousness. Reflecting on these verses in the morning sets a tone of reverence and eagerness to engage with Scripture. It encourages us to approach our Bible reading with the expectation that God will speak to us and equip us for the day ahead. Understanding that the Scriptures are meant to make us complete and thoroughly equipped for every good work helps us see the importance of starting our day rooted in God's Word.

Prayer: Heavenly Father, thank You for the gift of Your inspired Word. As we start this day, help us to engage with the Scriptures deeply and sincerely. Teach us, correct us, and guide us through Your Word so that we may be thoroughly equipped for every good work. May Your truths dwell in us richly and guide our steps today. In Jesus' name, we pray. Amen.

Meditative Thought: Spend a few moments reflecting on the significance of the Bible in your life. Consider how you can make time for Scripture reading and meditation today. Allow its truths to sink into your heart and mind, preparing you for the day ahead.

Scripture: 2 Timothy 3:16-17

"All Scripture is given by inspiration of God, and is profitable for doctrine, for reproof, for correction, for instruction in righteousness, that the man of God may be complete, thoroughly equipped for every good work."

Reflection: As the day comes to an end, 2 Timothy 3:16-17 encourages us to reflect on how God's Word has guided us today. The Scriptures are not just for morning devotions; they are our constant companion, providing wisdom and direction throughout the day. In the evening, we can look back and see how the Bible's teachings have influenced our actions, decisions, and interactions. Reviewing our day in light of these verses helps us recognize areas where we have followed God's guidance and areas where we need His correction. As we meditate on this passage tonight, let's express gratitude for God's Word and its role in our daily lives. Let's also commit to continued growth and learning, allowing Scripture to shape us into the people God wants us to be.

Prayer: Gracious Lord, we thank You for the gift of Your inspired Word. As we conclude this day, we reflect on how Your Scriptures have guided and instructed us. Forgive us for any moments where we have strayed from Your teachings, and help us to learn and grow. Thank You for equipping us for every good work. May Your Word continue to dwell richly in us and guide us in the days to come. In Jesus' name, we pray. Amen.

Meditative Thought: Reflect on your day and how God's Word has influenced you. Consider areas where you have experienced growth and areas where you need further correction and instruction. Let this reflection deepen your appreciation for the Bible and its role in your life.

NOVEMBER 10

MORNING DEVOTION

Scripture: Hebrews 13:6
"So we may boldly say: 'The Lord is my helper; I will not fear. What can man do to me?'"

Reflection: As we rise to greet the new day, Hebrews 13:6 offers a powerful reminder of God's unwavering support. This verse invites us to boldly declare that the Lord is our helper, casting out all fear. The knowledge that God is with us in every moment gives us courage and confidence. We can face the day's challenges, uncertainties, and tasks with a calm assurance that we are not alone. By starting our day with this truth, we set our minds and hearts on a foundation of divine support. This confidence allows us to approach our interactions and responsibilities with a sense of peace and strength. The world's pressures and stresses lose their power when we remember that the Almighty is our helper.

Prayer: Heavenly Father, thank You for Your constant presence and support. As we begin this day, we boldly declare that You are our helper. Help us to walk without fear, knowing that You are with us. Fill us with Your peace and courage, and guide our steps today. In Jesus' name, we pray. Amen.

Meditative Thought: Take a few moments to visualize God walking alongside you throughout your day. Picture His support in each task and interaction. Let this image strengthen your resolve and bring you peace as you face the day's challenges.

Scripture: Hebrews 13:6
"So we may boldly say: 'The Lord is my helper; I will not fear. What can man do to me?'"

Reflection: As the day draws to a close, Hebrews 13:6 reminds us to reflect on God's faithfulness throughout our experiences. Whether we faced triumphs or trials, this verse reassures us that the Lord was our constant helper. We can look back and see His hand in the support, guidance, and protection we received. Reflecting on this verse in the evening encourages us to release any remaining fears or worries. We can rest in the assurance that nothing can ultimately harm us because God is with us. This understanding allows us to find peace and gratitude as we prepare for rest, trusting that God will continue to be our helper in all circumstances.

Prayer: Gracious Lord, as we end this day, we thank You for being our helper. We reflect on Your faithfulness and the strength You provided in every situation. Help us to release our fears and rest in Your peace tonight. Continue to guide and protect us in the days to come. In Jesus' name, we pray. Amen.

Meditative Thought: Spend a few moments in quiet reflection on how God helped you today. Acknowledge His presence in your life and let go of any lingering anxieties. Embrace the peace that comes from knowing that the Lord is your constant helper, now and always.

NOVEMBER 11

MORNING DEVOTION

Scripture: 1 Corinthians 11:25-26
"In the same manner He also took the cup after supper, saying, 'This cup is the new covenant in My blood. This do, as often as you drink it, in remembrance of Me.' For as often as you eat this bread and drink this cup, you proclaim the Lord's death till He comes."

Reflection: As we begin our day, we reflect on the profound significance of the Lord's Supper. These verses remind us of the new covenant established through Jesus' sacrifice. Each time we partake in communion, we remember His death and the immense love that led Him to the cross. This act of remembrance is not only a reflection on the past but a proclamation of our faith and hope in His return. Starting our day with this understanding grounds us in gratitude and reverence. It reminds us that our lives are intertwined with Christ's sacrifice and His promise of eternal life. As we go about our daily tasks, let us carry this sense of remembrance and proclamation, living in a way that honors His sacrifice and eagerly anticipates His return.

Prayer: Lord Jesus, thank You for Your sacrifice and the new covenant established through Your blood. As we begin this day, help us to live in remembrance of You, proclaiming Your death and resurrection in all that we do. Fill our hearts with gratitude and reverence, and guide us to reflect Your love and grace to others. In Your precious name, we pray. Amen.

Meditative Thought: Take a moment to meditate on the sacrifice of Jesus and the new covenant in His blood. Visualize the act of communion and the deep connection it creates with Christ. Let this reflection fill you with gratitude and purpose as you start your day.

Scripture: 1 Corinthians 11:25-26
"In the same manner He also took the cup after supper, saying, 'This cup is the new covenant in My blood. This do, as often as you drink it, in remembrance of Me.' For as often as you eat this bread and drink this cup, you proclaim the Lord's death till He comes."

Reflection: As we end our day, these verses call us to reflect on the significance of the Lord's Supper and our continual proclamation of His death. Each act of communion is a powerful reminder of the sacrifice Jesus made for us, the new covenant He established, and the hope of His return. This remembrance brings us into a deeper relationship with Him and reaffirms our faith. Reflecting on this at the close of the day helps us to remember the foundation of our faith and the eternal hope we hold. It encourages us to examine how we lived out our faith today and how we can continue to honor Christ in our lives. Ending the day with this reflection brings a sense of peace and purpose, knowing that our lives are a testament to His sacrifice and love.

Prayer: Heavenly Father, as we conclude this day, we thank You for the new covenant in Jesus' blood. Help us to continually remember His sacrifice and live in a way that proclaims His death and resurrection. As we rest tonight, fill us with peace and hope, and prepare us to continue living out our faith tomorrow. In Jesus' name, we pray. Amen.

Meditative Thought: Spend a few moments in quiet reflection, contemplating the sacrifice of Jesus and the new covenant. Think about how you have remembered and proclaimed His death today. Allow this reflection to bring you peace and resolve as you prepare for rest, trusting in the promise of His return.

NOVEMBER 12

MORNING DEVOTION

Scripture: Romans 10:12

"For there is no distinction between Jew and Greek, for the same Lord over all is rich to all who call upon Him."

Reflection: As we wake to a new day, Romans 10:12 reminds us of the inclusivity and generosity of God's love. There is no distinction in God's eyes between people of different backgrounds, ethnicities, or cultures. The same Lord is Lord over all, and His riches—His mercy, grace, and blessings—are available to everyone who calls upon Him. This truth is a powerful reminder of the unity we share in Christ. Starting our day with this scripture encourages us to see others through the lens of God's love and equality. It challenges us to break down barriers and extend kindness and grace to everyone we encounter. It also reassures us that regardless of our own background or situation, God's love and blessings are available to us as we call upon Him.

Prayer: Dear Lord, thank You for Your boundless love and the truth that there is no distinction in Your eyes. Help us to see others with the same love and compassion that You do. As we go through this day, may we call upon You in all circumstances, knowing that You are rich in mercy and grace to all who seek You. Guide our hearts to be inclusive and generous, reflecting Your love to everyone we meet. In Jesus' name, we pray. Amen.

Meditative Thought: Take a moment to meditate on the unity and inclusivity of God's love. Imagine His blessings flowing equally to all who call upon Him, regardless of their background. Let this vision shape your interactions and attitudes throughout the day.

Scripture: Romans 10:12
"For there is no distinction between Jew and Greek, for the same Lord over all is rich to all who call upon Him."

Reflection: As we end our day, Romans 10:12 calls us to reflect on the universality of God's love and the richness of His grace. Throughout the day, we may have encountered different people and faced various situations. This verse reminds us that God's love and blessings are not limited by human distinctions or differences. Reflecting on this, we can see how we have experienced and shared God's inclusive love today. This reflection helps us to evaluate how well we have embraced and extended God's love to others, regardless of their background. It also invites us to be grateful for the ways God has been rich in His blessings toward us. Ending the day with this thought fosters a sense of unity and peace, knowing that we are all equally loved and valued by our Lord.

Prayer: Heavenly Father, as we conclude this day, we thank You for Your universal love and the riches of Your grace. Forgive us if we have made distinctions that You do not make. Help us to embrace Your love more fully and to extend it to others without bias or judgment. We are grateful for the ways You have blessed us today. As we rest tonight, fill our hearts with peace and unity, knowing that we are all cherished by You. In Jesus' name, we pray. Amen.

Meditative Thought: Spend a few moments in quiet reflection, considering the ways you have seen and shared God's love today. Think about how His grace has been rich to you and to those around you. Let this reflection bring you peace and a deeper understanding of God's inclusive love as you prepare for rest.

NOVEMBER 13

MORNING DEVOTION

Scripture: John 20:29

"Jesus said to him, 'Thomas, because you have seen Me, you have believed. Blessed are those who have not seen and yet have believed.'"

Reflection: As we begin a new day, John 20:29 reminds us of the blessedness of faith. Thomas, one of Jesus' disciples, struggled to believe in the resurrection until he saw Jesus with his own eyes. Jesus acknowledged Thomas's belief but also highlighted the special blessing for those who have not seen Him physically yet still believe. Starting our day with this scripture challenges us to reflect on the nature of our faith. Like Thomas, we may sometimes struggle to believe without tangible evidence. However, Jesus assures us that there is a unique blessing for those whose faith transcends what they can see. Our faith in Christ brings us into a relationship with Him, even though we cannot physically see Him, and this relationship is deeply blessed.

Prayer: Lord Jesus, we thank You for the gift of faith and the assurance that comes from believing in You. Strengthen our faith today, especially in times of doubt or uncertainty. Help us to trust in You wholeheartedly, even when we cannot see You physically. May our faith be a source of blessing and strength as we navigate this day. In Your name, we pray. Amen.

Meditative Thought: Take a moment to meditate on the nature of your faith. Consider the ways in which you have seen God's faithfulness in your life, even without physical evidence. Reflect on the blessings that come from trusting in Him, even when you cannot see Him. Allow this reflection to deepen your faith and reliance on God as you start your day.

Scripture: John 20:29
"Jesus said to him, 'Thomas, because you have seen Me, you have believed. Blessed are those who have not seen and yet have believed.'"

Reflection: As we conclude this day, John 20:29 invites us to reflect on the blessing of faith. Jesus' words to Thomas affirm the reality of Thomas's belief upon seeing Him after the resurrection. However, Jesus also highlights the special blessing for those who believe without seeing Him physically. Reflecting on this scripture in the evening prompts us to examine our own faith journey. We may have experienced moments of doubt or uncertainty, longing for tangible evidence of God's presence. Yet, Jesus reminds us that there is a unique blessing for those whose faith transcends the need for physical proof. Our belief in Christ, even in the absence of visible evidence, deepens our relationship with Him and brings us spiritual blessings.

Prayer: Gracious God, as we end this day, we thank You for the blessing of faith. Forgive us for the times when we have doubted Your presence or questioned Your work in our lives. Help us to trust in You more deeply, even when we cannot see You physically. May our faith bring us closer to You and enrich our lives with Your blessings. In Jesus' name, we pray. Amen.

Meditative Thought: Take a few moments to meditate on the blessings of faith in your life. Reflect on the ways in which your belief in Christ has brought you closer to Him and enriched your spiritual journey. Allow gratitude to fill your heart as you acknowledge the blessings that come from trusting in God, even without seeing Him physically.

NOVEMBER 14

MORNING DEVOTION

Scripture: Psalm 1:1-2

"Blessed is the man who walks not in the counsel of the ungodly, nor stands in the path of sinners, nor sits in the seat of the scornful; But his delight is in the law of the Lord, and in His law he meditates day and night."

Reflection: As we begin this new day, Psalm 1:1-2 sets the tone for a life of blessing and fulfillment. It contrasts the path of the righteous with that of the ungodly. The blessed individual avoids the counsel of the ungodly, the path of sinners, and the seat of the scornful. Instead, their delight is in the law of the Lord, and they meditate on it day and night. Starting our day with this scripture prompts us to reflect on the choices we make and the influences we allow into our lives. It challenges us to seek wisdom from God's Word rather than the advice of those who do not follow Him. Delighting in God's law and meditating on it continuously lead to a life of depth, purpose, and blessing.

Prayer: Gracious God, we thank You for Your Word, which guides and sustains us. Help us to be discerning in the influences we allow into our lives, choosing Your wisdom over the counsel of the ungodly. May our delight be in Your law, and may we meditate on it day and night. Guide our steps today, Lord, and lead us in the path of righteousness. In Jesus' name, we pray. Amen.

Meditative Thought: Take a moment to meditate on the significance of delighting in God's law and meditating on it day and night. Consider how you can incorporate more time for reflection on Scripture into your daily routine. Allow God's Word to shape your thoughts and actions as you begin your day. And rest assured in Christ Jesus!

Scripture: Psalm 1:1-2
"Blessed is the man who walks not in the counsel of the ungodly, nor stands in the path of sinners, nor sits in the seat of the scornful; But his delight is in the law of the Lord, and in His law he meditates day and night."

Reflection: As we close this day, Psalm 1:1-2 reminds us of the importance of our choices and priorities. It contrasts the blessed life of those who delight in God's law with the empty pursuits of the ungodly. The blessed individual avoids negative influences and finds joy in meditating on God's Word day and night. Reflecting on this scripture in the evening invites us to evaluate the influences that shaped our day and the extent to which we prioritized God's Word. It challenges us to realign our priorities and commit ourselves afresh to delighting in God's law and meditating on it continually. This commitment leads to a life of blessing, purpose, and fulfillment.

Prayer: Heavenly Father, as we conclude this day, we thank You for Your guidance and presence with us. Forgive us for the times when we allowed negative influences to shape our thoughts and actions. Help us to delight in Your law and meditate on it day and night, finding joy and fulfillment in Your Word. Strengthen us to walk in Your ways and live a life that honors You. In Jesus' name, we pray. Amen.

Meditative Thought: Take a few moments to meditate on the choices you made today and the influences that shaped your thoughts and actions. Ask God to reveal areas where you can prioritize His Word more fully in your life. Surrender your desires and intentions to Him, committing to delight in His law and meditate on it continually as you rest tonight.

NOVEMBER 15

MORNING DEVOTION

Scripture: Isaiah 55:8-9

"'For My thoughts are not your thoughts, nor are your ways My ways,' says the Lord. 'For as the heavens are higher than the earth, so are My ways higher than your ways, and My thoughts than your thoughts.'"

Reflection: As we begin this new day, Isaiah 55:8-9 reminds us of the incomprehensible nature of God's thoughts and ways. His wisdom and understanding far surpass our own limited understanding. This scripture invites us to humbly acknowledge that God's perspective is infinitely higher and more profound than ours. Starting our day with this scripture prompts us to reflect on our tendency to rely on our own understanding and plans. It challenges us to surrender our will to God and trust in His wisdom and guidance. Acknowledging the vast difference between God's ways and our own leads to a deeper reliance on Him and a willingness to submit to His will.

Prayer: Heavenly Father, we humbly acknowledge that Your thoughts and ways are far above our own. Forgive us for the times when we have relied solely on our own understanding. Help us to trust in Your wisdom and guidance, even when we cannot comprehend Your ways. Guide us today, Lord, and lead us according to Your perfect plan. In Jesus' name, we pray. Amen.

Meditation Thought: Take a moment to meditate on the vast difference between God's ways and your own. Surrender any plans or thoughts that you have been holding onto and ask God to lead you according to His perfect will. Allow His wisdom to guide you as you begin your day.

Scripture: Isaiah 55:8-9

"'For My thoughts are not your thoughts, nor are your ways My ways,' says the Lord. 'For as the heavens are higher than the earth, so are My ways higher than your ways, and My thoughts than your thoughts.'"

Reflection: As we conclude this day, Isaiah 55:8-9 continues to remind us of the vast difference between God's ways and our own. His thoughts and understanding far surpass our limited perspective. This scripture prompts us to reflect on our need to trust in God's wisdom, even when we cannot fully comprehend His ways. Reflecting on this scripture in the evening invites us to evaluate the ways in which we have relied on our own understanding throughout the day. It challenges us to surrender our plans and desires to God, trusting that His ways are higher and better than our own. Embracing this truth leads to a deeper sense of peace and assurance, knowing that God's wisdom guides our steps.

Prayer: Lord God, as we end this day, we thank You for Your incomprehensible wisdom and understanding. Forgive us for the times when we have relied solely on our own understanding. Help us to trust in Your ways, even when we cannot comprehend them. Lead us according to Your perfect plan, and grant us peace as we rest tonight. In Jesus' name, we pray. Amen.

Meditative Thought: Take a few moments to meditate on the vast difference between God's ways and your own. Surrender any lingering doubts or questions to Him and ask for His peace to fill your heart as you prepare for rest. Trust that His wisdom guides your life, even when you cannot fully understand His ways.

NOVEMBER 16

MORNING DEVOTION

Scripture: Philippians 4:8
"Finally, brethren, whatever things are true, whatever things are noble, whatever things are just, whatever things are pure, whatever things are lovely, whatever things are of good report, if there is any virtue and if there is anything praiseworthy—meditate on these things."

Reflection: As we begin this new day, Philippians 4:8 provides a roadmap for our thoughts and attitudes. It encourages us to focus on things that are true, noble, just, pure, lovely, and of good report. This scripture reminds us that our thought life has a profound impact on our overall well-being and spiritual growth. Starting our day with this scripture prompts us to reflect on the content of our thoughts. Are we dwelling on negative or unproductive thoughts, or are we intentionally filling our minds with things that are uplifting and edifying? Philippians 4:8 challenges us to choose the latter, cultivating a mindset that reflects God's truth and goodness.

Prayer: Heavenly Father, we thank You for Your Word, which guides and shapes our thoughts. Help us to focus our minds on things that are true, noble, just, pure, lovely, and of good report. Guard us from negative and unproductive thoughts, and fill our hearts with Your peace and joy. May our thoughts honor You and lead us closer to Your presence. In Jesus' name, we pray. Amen.

Meditative Thought: Take a moment to meditate on each of the qualities mentioned in Philippians 4:8. Reflect on examples of these qualities in your life and in the world around you. Consider how you can intentionally cultivate a mindset that aligns with God's truth and goodness as you start your day.

Scripture: Philippians 4:8
"Finally, brethren, whatever things are true, whatever things are noble, whatever things are just, whatever things are pure, whatever things are lovely, whatever things are of good report, if there is any virtue and if there is anything praiseworthy—meditate on these things."

Reflection: As we conclude this day, Philippians 4:8 continues to guide our thoughts and attitudes. It reminds us to focus on things that are true, noble, just, pure, lovely, and of good report. This scripture encourages us to intentionally cultivate a positive and God-honoring mindset, even in the midst of life's challenges. Reflecting on this scripture in the evening prompts us to evaluate the content of our thoughts throughout the day. Were our thoughts aligned with the qualities outlined in Philippians 4:8, or did we allow negativity and pessimism to cloud our minds? This scripture challenges us to choose to meditate on things that reflect God's truth and goodness, even as we prepare for rest.

Prayer: Lord God, as we end this day, we thank You for Your guidance and presence with us. Forgive us for the times when our thoughts strayed from what is true, noble, and pure. Help us to cultivate a mindset that honors You in all things. Fill our hearts with Your peace and joy as we rest tonight, knowing that You are with us. In Jesus' name, we pray. Amen.

Meditative Thought: Take a few moments to reflect on the content of your thoughts throughout the day. Ask God to reveal any areas where your thoughts may have strayed from what is true and good. Surrender any negative or unproductive thoughts to Him, and ask for His grace to fill your mind with His truth and goodness as you prepare for rest.

Scripture: Luke 15:7

"I say to you that likewise there will be more joy in heaven over one sinner who repents than over ninety-nine just persons who need no repentance."

Reflection: As we begin this new day, Luke 15:7 reminds us of the immense joy that comes from repentance and reconciliation with God. In this parable, Jesus teaches about the joy in heaven when even one sinner turns from their ways and embraces God's forgiveness. This scripture underscores the depth of God's love and His desire for all to come to repentance. Starting our day with this scripture prompts us to reflect on the incredible grace and mercy of God. It challenges us to consider our own response to repentance and reconciliation. Are we quick to extend forgiveness and grace to others, just as God has done for us? Luke 15:7 invites us to align our hearts with God's heart for the lost and to rejoice in the redemption of sinners.

Prayer: Heavenly Father, we thank You for Your boundless love and mercy. Help us to rejoice in the repentance of sinners, just as You do in heaven. Give us hearts that are quick to extend forgiveness and grace to others, knowing the depth of Your forgiveness towards us. May our lives reflect Your love and mercy to those around us. In Jesus' name, we pray. Amen.

Meditative Thought: Take a moment to meditate on the joy in heaven when a sinner repents. Reflect on the depth of God's love and His desire for reconciliation with each person. Consider how you can align your heart with God's heart for the lost and extend forgiveness and grace to those in need of repentance.

Scripture: Luke 15:7

"I say to you that likewise there will be more joy in heaven over one sinner who repents than over ninety-nine just persons who need no repentance."

Reflection: As we conclude this day, Luke 15:7 continues to remind us of the joy in heaven when a sinner repents. This scripture underscores the depth of God's love and His desire for reconciliation with each person. It challenges us to rejoice in the redemption of sinners and to extend forgiveness and grace to those in need of repentance. Reflecting on this scripture in the evening prompts us to evaluate our response to repentance and reconciliation throughout the day. Have we rejoiced in the forgiveness and restoration of others, or have we been slow to extend grace? Luke 15:7 invites us to align our hearts with God's heart for the lost and to reflect His love and mercy to those around us.

Prayer: Lord God, as we end this day, we thank You for Your boundless love and mercy. Forgive us for the times when we have been slow to extend forgiveness and grace to others. Help us to rejoice in the repentance of sinners and to reflect Your love and mercy in all that we do. May our lives bring glory to Your name. In Jesus' name, we pray. Amen.

Meditation Thought: Take a few moments to reflect on your response to repentance and reconciliation throughout the day. Ask God to reveal any areas where you may need to extend forgiveness and grace to others. Surrender any reluctance or hesitation to Him, and ask for His strength to reflect His love and mercy in all that you do.

Scripture: John 5:24

"Most assuredly, I say to you, he who hears My word and believes in Him who sent Me has everlasting life, and shall not come into judgment, but has passed from death into life."

Reflection: As we begin this new day, John 5:24 offers a profound promise from Jesus Himself. He assures us that those who hear His word and believe in God who sent Him have everlasting life. This scripture brings hope and assurance to believers, knowing that through faith in Christ, they have been granted eternal life and are freed from the fear of judgment. Starting our day with this scripture prompts us to reflect on the incredible gift of salvation that Jesus offers to all who believe in Him. It challenges us to examine our own faith and commitment to Christ. Are we truly living in the reality of our salvation, or do we still harbor doubts and fears about our eternal destiny? John 5:24 encourages us to anchor our faith firmly in Christ and to live each day with confidence in His promise of everlasting life.

Prayer: Gracious Lord, we thank You for the assurance of salvation that You offer to all who believe in You. Help us to anchor our faith firmly in Your promises and to live each day with confidence in Your gift of everlasting life. May our lives reflect the reality of our salvation as we walk in faith and obedience to Your word. In Jesus' name, we pray. Amen.

Meditative Thought: Take a moment to meditate on the promise of eternal life. Reflect on the assurance that comes from believing in Jesus Christ as your Savior. Consider any doubts or fears you may have about your salvation and surrender them to God in prayer. Allow His truth to fill your heart with peace and confidence as you begin your day.

Scripture: John 5:24
"Most assuredly, I say to you, he who hears My word and believes in Him who sent Me has everlasting life, and shall not come into judgment, but has passed from death into life."

Reflection: As we conclude this day, John 5:24 continues to echo in our hearts, reminding us of the assurance of salvation that Jesus offers to all who believe in Him. This scripture affirms that believers have passed from death to life, freed from the fear of judgment and granted eternal life through faith in Christ. Reflecting on this scripture in the evening prompts us to evaluate the depth of our faith and the reality of our salvation. Have we lived this day with confidence in God's promises, or have we allowed doubts and fears to overshadow our faith? John 5:24 encourages us to rest in the assurance of our salvation and to trust in God's faithfulness to fulfill His promises.

Prayer: Heavenly Father, we thank You for the assurance of salvation that You offer through Jesus Christ. As we end this day, we surrender any doubts or fears about our eternal destiny to You. Help us to rest in the assurance of Your promises and to live each day with confidence in Your faithfulness. May Your peace fill our hearts as we rest tonight. In Jesus' name, we pray. Amen.

Meditative Thought: Take a few moments to reflect on the assurance of salvation found in John 5:24. Thank God for His faithfulness in fulfilling His promises. Surrender any doubts or fears about your salvation to Him in prayer, and ask Him to fill your heart with His peace and assurance as you prepare for rest.

Scripture: Acts 4:12
"Nor is there salvation in any other, for there is no other name under heaven given among men by which we must be saved."

Reflection: As we begin this new day, Acts 4:12 directs our focus to the exclusive nature of salvation through Jesus Christ. This scripture boldly declares that salvation is found in no one else and in no other name but Jesus. It emphasizes the uniqueness and sufficiency of Christ as the only way to eternal life. Starting our day with this scripture prompts us to reflect on the exclusivity of salvation through Jesus Christ. It challenges us to examine our beliefs and convictions about the nature of salvation. Do we truly believe that Jesus is the only way to God, or do we entertain the idea of multiple paths to salvation? Acts 4:12 calls us to anchor our faith firmly in Christ and to proclaim His name as the only hope for humanity.

Prayer: Gracious Father, we thank You for the gift of salvation through Your Son, Jesus Christ. Help us to boldly proclaim His name as the only way to eternal life. Strengthen our faith in the exclusivity of salvation through Christ alone, and empower us to share this truth with others. May Your Holy Spirit guide us as we seek to live out our faith in obedience to Your word. In Jesus' name, we pray. Amen.

Meditative Thought: Take a moment to meditate on the exclusivity of salvation through Jesus Christ as declared in Acts 4:12. Reflect on the significance of His name and the sufficiency of His sacrifice for our salvation. Consider any areas in your life where you may have wavered in your belief in Christ as the only way to God, and ask God to strengthen your faith in His exclusive role as Savior and Lord.

Scripture: Acts 4:12
"Nor is there salvation in any other, for there is no other name under heaven given among men by which we must be saved."

Reflection: As we conclude this day, Acts 4:12 continues to resonate in our hearts, reminding us of the exclusive nature of salvation through Jesus Christ. This scripture reaffirms that there is no other name under heaven by which humanity can be saved, emphasizing the unique role of Jesus as Savior and Redeemer. Reflecting on this scripture in the evening prompts us to evaluate our response to the exclusivity of salvation through Christ. Have we embraced this truth wholeheartedly, or have we allowed doubts or alternative beliefs to cloud our understanding? Acts 4:12 challenges us to anchor our faith firmly in Christ and to share His message of salvation with boldness and conviction.

Prayer: Heavenly Father, as we end this day, we thank You for the truth of salvation through Your Son, Jesus Christ. Help us to remain steadfast in our belief in His exclusive role as Savior and Lord. Fill us with boldness and courage to proclaim His name to a world in need of salvation. May Your Holy Spirit continue to work in our hearts, drawing others to faith in Christ. In Jesus' name, we pray. Amen.

Meditative Thought: Take a few moments to reflect on the exclusivity of salvation through Jesus Christ as declared in Acts 4:12. Consider any ways in which you may have hesitated to fully embrace this truth, and ask God to strengthen your faith in His Son as the only way to eternal life. Surrender any doubts or alternative beliefs to Him, and commit to boldly proclaiming the name of Jesus to those around you.

Scripture: 2 Peter 3:9

"The Lord is not slack concerning His promise, as some count slackness, but is longsuffering toward us, not willing that any should perish but that all should come to repentance."

Reflection: In 2 Peter 3:9, we are reminded of the unfathomable patience and love of our Lord. Despite the passing of time and the seeming delay of His promises, God remains faithful. His timing is perfect, and His patience is boundless. This verse assures us that God's apparent delay in fulfilling His promises is not a sign of forgetfulness or negligence on His part. Instead, it is a demonstration of His mercy and grace, giving us ample opportunity to turn to Him in repentance. As we start our day, let us ponder on the depth of God's love and His desire for all to come to repentance. Let us not be discouraged by delays or setbacks but instead trust in His perfect timing. May we use each moment of waiting as an opportunity to draw closer to Him, knowing that He is patiently waiting for us to turn to Him in repentance and faith.

Prayer: Dear Heavenly Father, thank You for Your unfailing love and patience towards us. Help us to trust in Your perfect timing and to use each moment of waiting as an opportunity to draw closer to You. Give us the grace to repent of our sins and to turn to You wholeheartedly. May Your will be done in our lives, and may Your love and mercy shine through us to others. In Jesus' name, we pray, Amen.

Meditative Thought: Take a few moments to meditate on the patience and love of God. Reflect on any areas of your life where you need to repent and turn to Him. Ask Him to help you trust in His perfect timing and to use each moment of waiting for His glory.

Scripture: 2 Peter 3:9
"The Lord is not slack concerning His promise, as some count slackness, but is longsuffering toward us, not willing that any should perish but that all should come to repentance."

Reflection: As we come to the end of another day, let us once again reflect on the truth of 2 Peter 3:9. God's patience and longsuffering toward us are beyond comprehension. He is not slow in fulfilling His promises, but rather, He is patient, desiring that all should come to repentance and salvation. In our busy lives, it's easy to become impatient with God's timing. We may question why He hasn't answered our prayers or fulfilled His promises yet. However, let us remember that His ways are higher than ours, and His timing is always perfect. As we close our eyes tonight, let us surrender our impatience and doubts to Him, trusting that He is working all things together for our good.

Prayer: Heavenly Father, as we end this day, we thank You for Your patience and longsuffering toward us. Forgive us for the times when we have become impatient and doubted Your promises. Help us to trust in Your perfect timing and to rest in Your unfailing love. May Your will be done in our lives, and may we always be open to Your leading and guidance. In Jesus' name, we pray, Amen.

Meditative Thought: Take a few moments to meditate on the patience of God. Reflect on the ways He has shown His love and faithfulness to you throughout this day. Surrender any doubts or impatience to Him, trusting that He is working all things together for your good.

Scripture: 1 Timothy 2:8

"I desire therefore that the men pray everywhere, lifting up holy hands, without wrath and doubting."

Reflection: In 1 Timothy 2:8, Paul emphasizes the importance of prayer for men, urging them to pray everywhere with holy hands, free from anger and doubt. Prayer is not merely a religious duty but a vital connection with God, a privilege granted to us by His grace. As we begin our day, let us ponder the significance of prayer in our lives. It is through prayer that we communicate with the Almighty, pouring out our hearts, seeking His guidance, and expressing our gratitude. Paul's instruction to pray without wrath and doubting reminds us to approach God with reverence and faith. Anger and doubt can hinder our prayers, blocking the flow of God's blessings into our lives. Therefore, let us strive to cultivate hearts of humility, forgiveness, and unwavering trust in God's goodness and faithfulness.

Prayer: Heavenly Father, we come before You in prayer, acknowledging Your sovereignty and goodness. Teach us to pray without wrath and doubting, lifting up holy hands in reverence and faith. Help us to cultivate a heart of humility and forgiveness, free from anger and doubt. May our prayers be pleasing to You and bring glory to Your name. In Jesus' name, we pray, Amen.

Meditative Thought: Take a few moments to meditate on the importance of prayer in your life. Reflect on any areas where anger or doubt may hinder your prayers. Surrender them to God, asking Him to help you approach Him with holy hands and unwavering faith.

Scripture: 1 Timothy 2:8
"I desire therefore that the men pray everywhere, lifting up holy hands, without wrath and doubting."

Reflection: As we conclude another day, let us reflect on the instruction given in 1 Timothy 2:8 regarding prayer. Prayer is not limited to specific times or places but is meant to be a continual conversation with God, lifting up holy hands in reverence and faith. It is through prayer that we commune with our Heavenly Father, seeking His guidance, expressing our gratitude, and laying our burdens at His feet. Paul's admonition to pray without wrath and doubting serves as a reminder of the importance of cultivating a heart of humility and faith. Anger and doubt can cloud our minds and hinder our relationship with God. Therefore, let us examine our hearts this evening, confessing any feelings of anger or doubt to God and asking Him to replace them with peace and trust in His providence.

Prayer: Gracious God, as we come to the end of this day, we thank You for the privilege of prayer. Help us to lift up holy hands in reverence and faith, free from anger and doubt. Grant us the grace to cultivate hearts of humility and trust in Your goodness and faithfulness. May our prayers be a sweet aroma to You, bringing glory to Your name. In Jesus' name, we pray, Amen.

Meditative Thought: Take a few moments to meditate on your prayer life. Reflect on the times when anger or doubt may have hindered your prayers. Surrender them to God, asking Him to fill you with His peace and unwavering faith.

Scripture: Galatians 5:25
"If we live in the Spirit, let us also walk in the Spirit."

Reflection: Galatians 5:25 urges us to live in the Spirit and walk in the Spirit. As believers, we are indwelt by the Holy Spirit, who empowers and guides us in our Christian journey. Living in the Spirit means allowing the Holy Spirit to influence every aspect of our lives, surrendering our will to His leading and allowing His fruit to be manifested in us. Walking in the Spirit involves daily obedience and alignment with the will of God. It requires a deliberate choice to crucify the flesh and follow the promptings of the Spirit. As we embark on this new day, let us reflect on our commitment to living and walking in the Spirit. May we be sensitive to His voice, yielding to His guidance in all that we do.

Prayer: Heavenly Father, we thank You for the gift of Your Holy Spirit, who dwells within us. Help us to live in the Spirit, allowing Your presence to permeate every area of our lives. Give us the strength and courage to walk in the Spirit, obedient to Your will and surrendered to Your leading. May Your fruit be evident in our lives as we seek to glorify You in all that we do. In Jesus' name, we pray, Amen.

Meditation Thought: Take a few moments to meditate on the presence of the Holy Spirit in your life. Reflect on areas where you may have resisted His leading and ask for His forgiveness and guidance. Surrender afresh to His will, committing to live and walk in the Spirit throughout this day.

Scripture: Galatians 5:25

"If we live in the Spirit, let us also walk in the Spirit."

Reflection: As we come to the close of another day, let us reflect on the admonition found in Galatians 5:25 to live and walk in the Spirit. Living in the Spirit involves being continually aware of the presence of God within us, allowing His love, joy, peace, patience, kindness, goodness, faithfulness, gentleness, and self-control to manifest in our lives. Walking in the Spirit requires conscious effort and intentional obedience to His leading. It means denying the desires of the flesh and aligning ourselves with the will of God. As we reflect on the events of this day, let us examine whether our thoughts, words, and actions have been in accordance with the Spirit. Where we have fallen short, let us humbly seek forgiveness and recommit ourselves to walking in step with the Spirit.

Prayer: Gracious God, as we conclude this day, we thank You for the privilege of living and walking in the Spirit. Forgive us for the times when we have yielded to the desires of the flesh and neglected Your leading. Renew within us a steadfast commitment to live in accordance with Your will, empowered by Your Holy Spirit. May we continually surrender to Your guidance and be transformed into vessels of Your love and grace. In Jesus' name, we pray, Amen.

Meditative Thought: Take a few moments to meditate on your day in light of Galatians 5:25. Reflect on instances where you have lived and walked in the Spirit, as well as areas where you may have fallen short. Surrender any shortcomings to God, asking for His forgiveness and guidance as you seek to live and walk in the Spirit each day.

Scripture: Mark 9:35

"And He sat down, called the twelve, and said to them, 'If anyone desires to be first, he shall be last of all and servant of all.'"

Reflection: In Mark 9:35, Jesus teaches us a profound lesson about servant leadership. Contrary to the world's standards, where greatness is often measured by power, prestige, and prominence, Jesus reveals that true greatness is found in servanthood. He, the Son of God, exemplified this by His life of humility and service, ultimately sacrificing Himself for the salvation of humanity. As we begin this day, let us reflect on our attitudes towards leadership and greatness. Jesus calls us to follow His example, to prioritize the needs of others above our own, and to serve with love and compassion.

Prayer: Heavenly Father, teach us the true meaning of greatness as demonstrated by Your Son, Jesus Christ. Help us to cultivate hearts of humility and servanthood, following His example in our daily lives. May we seek opportunities to serve others selflessly, reflecting Your love and compassion to those around us. Empower us by Your Spirit to lead with grace and humility. In Jesus' name, we pray, Amen.

Meditative Thought: Take a few moments to meditate on the example of Jesus Christ as the ultimate servant leader. Reflect on ways you can emulate His humility and servanthood in your interactions today.

Scripture: Mark 9:35
"And He sat down, called the twelve, and said to them, 'If anyone desires to be first, he shall be last of all and servant of all.'"

Reflection: As we come to the close of another day, let us reflect on the words of Jesus in Mark 9:35 regarding servant leadership. In a world that often values self-promotion and ambition, Jesus challenges us to adopt a different mindset—one of humility and service. True greatness, He tells us, is found in being the servant of all. Consider your interactions and actions throughout this day. Have you sought to elevate yourself above others, or have you humbly served those around you? Take a moment to examine your heart and motives, asking God to reveal any areas where you may have fallen short of His example.

Prayer: Lord Jesus, as we reflect on the events of this day, we confess our tendency to seek recognition and status. Forgive us for our pride and self-centeredness. Help us to embrace the way of servanthood, following Your example of humility and love. May Your Spirit empower us to serve others selflessly, putting their needs above our own. Thank You for the privilege of serving You by serving others. In Your name, we pray, Amen.

Meditative Thought: Take a few moments to meditate on your day in light of Mark 9:35. Reflect on moments where you may have missed opportunities to serve others with humility and love. Surrender any feelings of pride or self-centeredness to God, asking Him to help you embrace the way of servanthood in all areas of your life.

NOVEMBER 24

MORNING DEVOTION

Scripture: Matthew 25:13
"Watch therefore, for you know neither the day nor the hour in which the Son of Man is coming."

Reflection: Matthew 25:13 serves as a reminder of the importance of vigilance and readiness for the return of Christ. Just as a wise servant remains alert for the arrival of his master, so too must we be vigilant and prepared for the coming of our Lord. The exact timing of His return remains unknown to us, underscoring the need for constant readiness and spiritual watchfulness. As we embark on this new day, let us reflect on our readiness for the return of Christ. Are we living in anticipation of His coming, faithfully stewarding the time, resources, and talents entrusted to us? Let us not become complacent or distracted by the cares of this world but remain steadfast in our devotion to Christ, eagerly awaiting His return.

Prayer: Heavenly Father, we thank You for the promise of the return of Your Son, Jesus Christ. Grant us the grace to be vigilant and prepared for His coming. Help us to live each day with a sense of urgency, faithfully stewarding the time, resources, and talents You have entrusted to us. May we be found ready and watching when He returns. In Jesus' name, we pray, Amen.

Meditative Thought: Take a few moments to meditate on the return of Christ. Reflect on your readiness and vigilance in light of His imminent return. Ask God to reveal any areas of your life where you may need to refocus your priorities and renew your commitment to living in anticipation of His coming.

Scripture: Matthew 25:13
"Watch therefore, for you know neither the day nor the hour in which the Son of Man is coming."

Reflection: As we conclude this day, let us reflect on the exhortation found in Matthew 25:13 to watch and be prepared for the return of Christ. The uncertainty of the timing of His coming serves as a sobering reminder of the need for continual readiness and spiritual watchfulness. Each passing moment brings us closer to the fulfillment of His promise to return and establish His kingdom on earth. Consider the events of this day and how well you have lived in anticipation of Christ's return. Have you been vigilant and prepared, faithfully serving Him and others with urgency and purpose? Take a moment to examine your heart and motives, asking God to reveal any areas where you may need to repent and refocus your priorities.

Prayer: Gracious God, as we come to the close of this day, we confess our need for Your grace to remain vigilant and prepared for the return of Your Son, Jesus Christ. Forgive us for the times when we have become complacent or distracted by the cares of this world. Renew within us a sense of urgency and purpose in our daily walk with You. May we eagerly anticipate the coming of Your kingdom and faithfully serve You until that day. In Jesus' name, we pray, Amen.

Meditative Thought: Take a few moments to meditate on your readiness for the return of Christ. Reflect on any areas where you may have become complacent or distracted. Surrender them to God, asking Him to renew your sense of urgency and purpose in living for Him each day.

Scripture: Ephesians 1:7-8
"In Him we have redemption through His blood, the forgiveness of sins, according to the riches of His grace which He made to abound toward us in all wisdom and prudence."

Reflection: Ephesians 1:7-8 reminds us of the incredible riches of God's grace poured out upon us through Jesus Christ. Through His sacrifice on the cross, we have been redeemed and forgiven of our sins. God's grace knows no bounds, and He has lavished it upon us with wisdom and prudence. This grace is not something we can earn or merit but is freely given to us out of His great love for us. As we begin this day, let us reflect on the magnitude of God's grace towards us. It is a grace that exceeds our understanding and covers our sins completely. Let us respond to this grace with gratitude and humility, recognizing that we are unworthy of such a gift yet deeply loved and cherished by our Heavenly Father.

Prayer: Heavenly Father, we thank You for the immeasurable riches of Your grace poured out upon us through Jesus Christ. Thank You for the redemption and forgiveness we have received through His sacrifice on the cross. Help us to live each day in gratitude for Your grace, walking in wisdom and prudence. May Your grace abound in us and overflow to those around us, that others may come to know the richness of Your love. In Jesus' name, we pray, Amen.

Meditative Thought: Take a few moments to meditate on the grace of God revealed in Ephesians 1:7-8. Reflect on the depth of His love for you and the extent to which He has forgiven your sins. Consider how you can respond to His grace with gratitude and humility throughout this day.

Scripture: Ephesians 1:7-8
"In Him we have redemption through His blood, the forgiveness of sins, according to the riches of His grace which He made to abound toward us in all wisdom and prudence."

Reflection: As we conclude this day, let us once again reflect on the profound truth of Ephesians 1:7-8. In Jesus Christ, we have been redeemed and forgiven of our sins through His sacrificial death on the cross. God's grace towards us is boundless, overflowing with wisdom and prudence. It is a grace that knows no limits and covers all our shortcomings. Take a moment to ponder on the depth of God's grace in your life. Consider the ways in which He has forgiven you and showered you with His love and mercy. Let His grace humble you and fill you with awe and wonder. And as you rest tonight, may you find peace and comfort in the assurance of His unfailing love for you.

Prayer: Gracious God, as we come to the end of this day, we thank You for the immeasurable riches of Your grace poured out upon us through Jesus Christ. Thank You for the redemption and forgiveness we have received through His precious blood. May Your grace continue to abound in us, filling us with wisdom and prudence. Grant us rest tonight, knowing that we are loved and forgiven by You. In Jesus' name, we pray, Amen.

Meditative Thought: Take a few moments to meditate on the grace of God revealed in Ephesians 1:7-8. Reflect on the ways His grace has been evident in your life today. Surrender any burdens or worries to Him, trusting in His unfailing love and forgiveness.

NOVEMBER 26

MORNING DEVOTION

Scripture: John 5:39
"You search the Scriptures, for in them you think you have eternal life; and these are they which testify of Me."

Reflection: In John 5:39, Jesus addresses those who diligently study the Scriptures, reminding them that the Scriptures themselves point to Him. The Pharisees and religious leaders of His time prided themselves on their knowledge of the Scriptures, believing that in them they found eternal life. However, Jesus reveals that the true purpose of the Scriptures is to testify about Him, the Messiah, through whom eternal life is found. As we begin this day, let us reflect on our approach to Scripture. Do we view it merely as a book of rules and regulations, or do we see it as a testimony to the person and work of Jesus Christ? The Scriptures are meant to lead us to a deeper relationship with God through His Son. Let us approach the Word of God with hearts open to the revelation of Christ and His redemptive work.

Prayer: Heavenly Father, we thank You for the gift of Your Word, which testifies about Your Son, Jesus Christ. Help us to approach Scripture with open hearts and minds, seeking to encounter Jesus in its pages. May Your Spirit enlighten our understanding as we study Your Word, revealing the truth about Your Son and His redemptive work. May we find eternal life in Him alone. In Jesus' name, we pray, Amen.

Meditative Thought: Take a few moments to meditate on John 5:39. Reflect on your attitude towards Scripture. Are you seeking Jesus within its pages, or are you focused solely on its rules and regulations? Ask God to open your heart to the revelation of His Son as you study His Word today.

Scripture: John 5:39
"You search the Scriptures, for in them you think you have eternal life; and these are they which testify of Me."

Reflection: As we come to the end of this day, let us once again reflect on the words of Jesus in John 5:39. The Scriptures are not merely a collection of religious texts but a testimony to the person and work of Jesus Christ. They point us to Him as the source of eternal life and salvation. Consider your interactions with Scripture throughout this day. Have you approached it with a desire to encounter Jesus and His redemptive work, or have you viewed it merely as a set of moral guidelines? Take a moment to examine your heart and ask God to deepen your understanding of His Word, revealing more of His Son to you.

Prayer: Gracious God, as we conclude this day, we thank You for the Scriptures, which testify about Your Son, Jesus Christ. Forgive us for the times when we have approached Your Word with a shallow understanding, focusing solely on its surface meanings. Open our hearts and minds to receive the revelation of Your Son as we study Your Word. May we find our hope and eternal life in Him alone. In Jesus' name, we pray, Amen.

Meditative Thought: Take a few moments to meditate on John 5:39. Reflect on your approach to Scripture throughout this day. Ask God to deepen your understanding of His Word and to reveal more of His Son to you as you study and meditate on His Word.

NOVEMBER 27

MORNING DEVOTION

Scripture: Revelation 21:5
"Then He who sat on the throne said, 'Behold, I make all things new.' And He said to me, 'Write, for these words are true and faithful.'"

Reflection: Revelation 21:5 offers a glimpse of the glorious future that awaits those who belong to Christ. In this verse, God Himself declares His intention to make all things new. It is a promise of restoration, renewal, and transformation beyond our wildest imaginations. The brokenness and suffering of this present world will be replaced with everlasting joy and peace in the presence of God. As we begin this day, let us reflect on the hope and assurance found in God's promise to make all things new. Despite the trials and tribulations we may face, we can take comfort in knowing that God is in control and that He is working all things together for our good. Let us fix our eyes on the promise of the new heaven and new earth, eagerly anticipating the day when we will dwell in His presence forever.

Prayer: Heavenly Father, we thank You for the promise of a new heaven and new earth, where You will make all things new. Help us to hold fast to this hope, especially during times of difficulty and uncertainty. Strengthen our faith and fill us with anticipation for the glorious future You have prepared for Your people. May we live each day in light of this promise, seeking to bring glory to Your name. In Jesus' name, we pray, Amen.

Meditative Thought: Take a few moments to meditate on Revelation 21:5. Reflect on the promise of God to make all things new. Consider how this promise gives you hope and assurance, even in the midst of challenges and struggles. Ask God to deepen your faith and fill you with anticipation for the future He has prepared for you.

Scripture: Revelation 21:5
"Then He who sat on the throne said, 'Behold, I make all things new.' And He said to me, 'Write, for these words are true and faithful.'"

Reflection: As we come to the end of this day, let us once again reflect on the truth and faithfulness of God's promise in Revelation 21:5. In a world filled with brokenness and decay, God offers us the hope of a new beginning—a future where pain and suffering will be no more. His promise to make all things new is not based on wishful thinking but on His unwavering faithfulness and power to fulfill His word. Take a moment to consider the ways in which you have experienced God's faithfulness in your life. Reflect on the times when He has brought beauty out of ashes and turned your mourning into joy. As you rest tonight, may you find peace and comfort in the assurance that God is making all things new, both in this present age and in the age to come.

Prayer: Gracious God, as we conclude this day, we thank You for Your faithfulness and the promise of a new heaven and new earth. Help us to trust in Your word and to live each day with hope and anticipation for the future You have prepared for us. May Your promise to make all things new fill us with peace and joy, even in the midst of trials and challenges. In Jesus' name, we pray, Amen.

Meditative Thought: Take a few moments to meditate on Revelation 21:5. Reflect on the faithfulness of God and His promise to make all things new. Surrender any worries or fears to Him, trusting that He is working all things together for your good.

Scripture: Isaiah 49:16

"See, I have inscribed you on the palms of My hands; Your walls are continually before Me."

Reflection: Isaiah 49:16 beautifully depicts the intimate and personal care of God for His people. The imagery of inscribing His children on the palms of His hands speaks of God's constant awareness and remembrance of us. It signifies His unfailing love, protection, and provision for His beloved ones. Furthermore, the mention of our walls being continually before Him highlights His attentiveness to every detail of our lives, including our circumstances and challenges. As we embark on this new day, let us meditate on the profound truth of Isaiah 49:16. Regardless of the trials or uncertainties we may face, we can take comfort in knowing that we are securely held in the hands of our loving Heavenly Father. His watchful gaze is upon us, and He is actively working on our behalf, guiding us through every season of life.

Prayer: Heavenly Father, we thank You for the assurance that we are inscribed on the palms of Your hands. Help us to grasp the depth of Your love and care for us, especially during times of difficulty and uncertainty. Grant us the faith to trust in Your providence and the confidence to face each day knowing that You are continually watching over us. May Your presence bring peace and comfort to our hearts. In Jesus' name, we pray, Amen.

Meditative Thought: Take a few moments to meditate on Isaiah 49:16. Reflect on the imagery of being inscribed on the palms of God's hands. Consider the implications of His constant awareness and remembrance of you. Allow His love and care to permeate your heart and fill you with confidence and peace as you begin this day.

Scripture: Isaiah 49:16
"See, I have inscribed you on the palms of My hands; Your walls are continually before Me."

Reflection: As we conclude this day, let us once again reflect on the comforting words of Isaiah 49:16. In times of weariness or doubt, it is reassuring to know that we are engraved on the palms of God's hands. His unwavering love and attentive care are constant reminders of His faithfulness to His children. The imagery of our walls being continually before Him serves as a reminder that God is intimately acquainted with every aspect of our lives. Take a moment to consider the events of this day in light of Isaiah 49:16. Reflect on the ways in which you have experienced God's presence and provision. Even in moments of struggle or adversity, may you find solace in the knowledge that God is ever-present and actively working on your behalf.

Prayer: Gracious God, as we come to the end of this day, we thank You for the assurance that we are inscribed on the palms of Your hands. Thank You for Your unwavering love and attentive care for us. Help us to rest in Your presence tonight, knowing that You are continually watching over us. Grant us peaceful sleep and renewed strength for the day ahead. In Jesus' name, we pray, Amen.

Meditative Thought: Take a few moments to meditate on Isaiah 49:16. Reflect on the ways in which you have experienced God's presence and provision throughout this day. Surrender any worries or burdens to Him, trusting in His faithful care for you.

Scripture: Proverbs 3:5-6

"Trust in the Lord with all your heart, And lean not on your own understanding; In all your ways acknowledge Him, And He shall direct your paths."

Reflection: Proverbs 3:5-6 offers timeless wisdom on the importance of trusting in the Lord wholeheartedly and surrendering our understanding to Him. It reminds us that our own understanding is limited and fallible, but God's wisdom and guidance are infinite and perfect. When we acknowledge Him in all our ways, entrusting every aspect of our lives to His care, He promises to direct our paths and lead us in the way we should go. As we begin this day, let us reflect on the significance of trusting in the Lord with all our hearts. Are we relying on our own understanding and wisdom, or are we surrendering to His guidance and wisdom? Let us commit to acknowledging Him in all our ways, seeking His direction and guidance in every decision we make.

Prayer: Heavenly Father, we thank You for the wisdom and guidance found in Your Word. Help us to trust in You with all our hearts and to lean not on our own understanding. May we acknowledge You in all our ways, seeking Your direction and guidance in every aspect of our lives. Lead us on the path of righteousness and grant us the grace to follow You faithfully. In Jesus' name, we pray, Amen.

Meditative Thought: Take a few moments to meditate on Proverbs 3:5-6. Reflect on your level of trust in the Lord and your reliance on His guidance. Surrender any areas where you may be leaning on your own understanding, and ask God to help you trust Him more fully as you navigate through this day.

Scripture: Proverbs 3:5-6
"Trust in the Lord with all your heart, And lean not on your own understanding; In all your ways acknowledge Him, And He shall direct your paths."

Reflection: As we come to the end of this day, let us once again reflect on the wisdom found in Proverbs 3:5-6. Trusting in the Lord with all our hearts requires a daily surrender of our own understanding and wisdom. It involves acknowledging His sovereignty and seeking His guidance in every aspect of our lives. When we commit our ways to Him, He promises to direct our paths and lead us in the way we should go. Take a moment to review the events of this day. Were there moments when you leaned on your own understanding rather than trusting in the Lord? Reflect on any areas where you may have failed to acknowledge Him and seek His guidance. As you prepare to rest tonight, surrender these concerns to God and trust in His promise to direct your paths.

Prayer: Gracious God, as we conclude this day, we thank You for Your faithfulness and guidance. Forgive us for the times when we relied on our own understanding rather than trusting in You wholeheartedly. Help us to acknowledge You in all our ways and to seek Your guidance in every decision we make. Grant us peaceful rest tonight, knowing that You are directing our paths. In Jesus' name, we pray, Amen.

Meditative Thought: Take a few moments to meditate on Proverbs 3:5-6. Reflect on your reliance on your own understanding versus your trust in the Lord. Surrender any worries or concerns to Him, trusting in His promise to direct your paths.

Scripture: Psalm 16:7-8

"I will bless the Lord who has given me counsel; My heart also instructs me in the night seasons. I have set the Lord always before me; Because He is at my right hand I shall not be moved."

Reflection: Psalm 16:7-8 expresses profound trust and confidence in the Lord's guidance and presence. The psalmist acknowledges the Lord's counsel and guidance, even in the darkest of times. By setting the Lord always before him, the psalmist finds stability and assurance, knowing that God is ever-present and steadfast. As we begin this day, let us reflect on the wisdom found in Psalm 16:7-8. Are we seeking the counsel of the Lord in all our decisions, both big and small? Do we set Him always before us, keeping His presence at the forefront of our minds? Let us strive to cultivate a heart that trusts in the Lord completely, finding strength and stability in His unfailing presence.

Prayer: Heavenly Father, we thank You for Your guidance and counsel that leads us through the challenges of life. Help us to seek Your wisdom in all our decisions and to set You always before us. May Your presence bring stability and assurance to our hearts, knowing that You are ever-present and faithful. Grant us the strength to trust in You completely, even in the darkest of times. In Jesus' name, we pray, Amen.

Meditation Thought: Take a few moments to meditate on Psalm 16:7-8. Reflect on the counsel and guidance of the Lord in your life. Consider ways you can set Him always before you, keeping His presence at the forefront of your thoughts throughout this day.

Scripture: Psalm 16:7-8
"I will bless the Lord who has given me counsel; My heart also instructs me in the night seasons. I have set the Lord always before me; Because He is at my right hand I shall not be moved."

Reflection: As we come to the end of this day, let us once again reflect on the wisdom and assurance found in Psalm 16:7-8. The psalmist's declaration of trust in the Lord's counsel and presence serves as a reminder of the faithfulness of our Heavenly Father. In times of darkness and uncertainty, He is our constant guide and support, leading us with His wisdom and grace. Take a moment to review the events of this day. Were there moments when you sought the counsel of the Lord, and did you set Him always before you? Reflect on any areas where you may have faltered in trusting His guidance or acknowledging His presence. As you prepare for rest tonight, surrender these concerns to God and trust in His unfailing faithfulness.

Prayer: Gracious God, as we conclude this day, we thank You for Your guidance and presence in our lives. Forgive us for the times when we failed to seek Your counsel or acknowledge Your presence. Help us to trust in You completely, knowing that You are always with us, guiding and sustaining us. Grant us peaceful rest tonight, knowing that You are at our right hand, and we shall not be moved. In Jesus' name, we pray, Amen.

Meditative Thought: Take a few moments to meditate on the text. Reflect on the faithfulness of God's counsel and presence in your life. Surrender any worries or concerns to Him, trusting in His unfailing guidance and support as you rest tonight.

DECEMBER 1

MORNING DEVOTION

Scripture: Psalm 121:1-2
"I will lift up my eyes to the hills— From whence comes my help? My help comes from the Lord, Who made heaven and earth."

Reflection: Psalm 121:1-2 beautifully captures the essence of trust and dependence on the Lord. The psalmist acknowledges the source of his help, lifting his eyes to the hills with a sense of expectation. In a moment of uncertainty, he confidently declares that his help comes from the Lord, the Creator of heaven and earth. This acknowledgment reflects a deep-seated trust in God's sovereignty and ability to provide assistance in every situation. As we begin this day, let us reflect on the truth of Psalm 121:1-2. Are we lifting our eyes to the Lord, the ultimate source of our help and strength? In times of need or difficulty, do we turn to Him with confidence, knowing that He is the Creator and sustainer of all things? Let us cultivate a heart of trust and dependence on God, recognizing His power and faithfulness to come to our aid.

Prayer: Heavenly Father, we thank You for being our ever-present help in times of trouble. Help us to lift our eyes to You, knowing that our help comes from You alone. Strengthen our faith and trust in Your sovereignty and provision. May we rely on You completely in every situation, confident in Your power to sustain us. In Jesus' name, we pray, Amen.

Meditative Thought: Take a few moments to meditate on the text. Reflect on the source of your help and strength. Consider ways you can lift your eyes to the Lord and depend on Him more fully throughout this day.

Scripture: Psalm 121:1-2
"I will lift up my eyes to the hills— From whence comes my help? My help comes from the Lord, Who made heaven and earth."

Reflection: As we come to the close of this day, let us once again reflect on the comforting words of Psalm 121:1-2. The imagery of lifting our eyes to the hills symbolizes an act of seeking and expecting help from above. The psalmist's declaration that his help comes from the Lord underscores the assurance of God's faithful provision and care. Take a moment to review the events of this day. Were there moments when you turned to the Lord for help and strength? Reflect on the ways in which He came to your aid and sustained you. As you prepare for rest tonight, may you find peace and comfort in the knowledge that your help comes from the Lord, the Maker of heaven and earth.

Prayer: Gracious God, as we conclude this day, we thank You for Your constant help and provision in our lives. Forgive us for the times when we relied on our own strength instead of turning to You. Help us to trust in Your unfailing care and provision. Grant us peaceful rest tonight, knowing that our help comes from You, the Creator of heaven and earth. In Jesus' name, we pray, Amen.

Meditative Thought: Take a few moments to meditate on Psalm 121:1-2. Reflect on the ways God has been your help and strength throughout this day. Surrender any worries or concerns to Him, trusting in His faithful provision as you rest tonight.

Scripture: Joshua 24:15
"And if it seems evil to you to serve the Lord, choose for yourselves this day whom you will serve, whether the gods which your fathers served that were on the other side of the River, or the gods of the Amorites, in whose land you dwell. But as for me and my house, we will serve the Lord."

Reflection: Joshua 24:15 is a powerful declaration of commitment to serve the Lord. Joshua challenges the Israelites to make a choice: to serve the gods of their ancestors or the false gods of the land they inhabit. But in the midst of this challenge, Joshua firmly declares his allegiance to the Lord, declaring, "As for me and my house, we will serve the Lord." This statement reflects Joshua's unwavering faith and determination to prioritize God's commands above all else. As we begin this day, let us reflect on the example of Joshua and his commitment to serve the Lord wholeheartedly. In a world filled with competing demands and distractions, let us resolve to prioritize our relationship with God above all else, choosing to serve Him faithfully in every aspect of our lives.

Prayer: Heavenly Father, we thank You for the example of Joshua and his unwavering commitment to serve You. Help us to make a similar declaration of faith and commitment in our lives today. Give us the strength and courage to choose You above all else, even when faced with challenges and temptations. May our lives be a testimony to Your faithfulness and goodness. In Jesus' name, we pray, Amen.

Meditative Thought: Take a few moments to meditate on Joshua 24:15. Reflect on your own commitment to serve the Lord. Consider any areas of your life where you may need to reaffirm your allegiance to Him.

Scripture: Joshua 24:15
"And if it seems evil to you to serve the Lord, choose for yourselves this day whom you will serve, whether the gods which your fathers served that were on the other side of the River, or the gods of the Amorites, in whose land you dwell. But as for me and my house, we will serve the Lord."

Reflection: As we come to the end of this day, let us reflect once again on the profound words of Joshua 24:15. Joshua's declaration to serve the Lord stands as a timeless reminder of the importance of making a deliberate choice to prioritize our relationship with God. In a world filled with distractions and competing demands, Joshua's resolve serves as an inspiration for us to remain steadfast in our commitment to serve the Lord faithfully. Take a moment to review the events of this day. Were there moments when you were tempted to prioritize something other than your relationship with God? Reflect on any areas where you may have faltered in your commitment to serve Him wholeheartedly.

Prayer: Gracious God, as we conclude this day, we thank You for the example of Joshua and his unwavering commitment to serve You. Forgive us for the times when we have been tempted to prioritize something other than our relationship with You. Renew our resolve to serve You faithfully, even in the face of challenges and temptations. May our lives bring glory to Your name. In Jesus' name, we pray, Amen.

Meditative Thought: Take a few moments to meditate on Joshua 24:15. Reflect on your commitment to serve the Lord. Surrender any areas of weakness or temptation to Him, asking for His strength to help you remain steadfast in your faithfulness to Him.

Scripture: Psalm 100:1-2
"Make a joyful shout to the Lord, all you lands! Serve the Lord with gladness; Come before His presence with singing."

Reflection: Psalm 100:1-2 calls us to approach God with joyful praise and gladness in our hearts. It is an invitation to worship Him with exuberant shouts and songs of thanksgiving. This psalm reminds us that our worship is not merely an obligation but a joyful response to the goodness and faithfulness of God. When we come before His presence with singing, we acknowledge His sovereignty and express our gratitude for His abundant blessings in our lives. As we begin this day, let us reflect on the significance of worship in our lives. Are we approaching God with joy and gladness, eager to lift our voices in praise? Let us cultivate a heart of worship that rejoices in the presence of the Lord, acknowledging His goodness and faithfulness in all circumstances.

Prayer: Heavenly Father, we thank You for the privilege of worshiping You with joyful hearts. Help us to approach You with gladness and thanksgiving, recognizing Your sovereignty and faithfulness in our lives. May our worship be a pleasing offering to You, bringing glory and honor to Your name. In Jesus' name, we pray, Amen.

Meditative Thought: Take a few moments to meditate on Psalm 100:1-2. Reflect on the joy and gladness with which you approach God in worship. Consider ways you can cultivate a heart of worship throughout this day, expressing gratitude for His goodness and faithfulness in your life.

Scripture: Psalm 100:1-2
"Make a joyful shout to the Lord, all you lands! Serve the Lord with gladness; Come before His presence with singing."

Reflection: As we come to the end of this day, let us once again reflect on the call to worship found in Psalm 100:1-2. This psalm reminds us of the importance of serving the Lord with gladness and coming before His presence with singing. Even in the midst of challenges and difficulties, our worship is an expression of our trust and gratitude towards God. Take a moment to review the events of this day. Were there moments when you approached God with joy and gladness, offering Him heartfelt worship? Reflect on the ways in which you have acknowledged His presence and faithfulness throughout this day. As you prepare for rest tonight, may you find peace and contentment in the presence of the Lord, knowing that He is worthy of all our praise.

Prayer: Gracious God, as we conclude this day, we thank You for the privilege of worshiping You with gladness and joy. Forgive us for the times when we have approached You with indifference or complacency. Renew our hearts to worship You with sincerity and gratitude, acknowledging Your presence and faithfulness in our lives. May our worship bring delight to Your heart and honor to Your name. In Jesus' name, we pray, Amen.

Meditative Thought: Take a few moments to meditate on Psalm 100:1-2. Reflect on your worship throughout this day. Surrender any distractions or burdens to the Lord, and offer Him heartfelt praise and thanksgiving as you prepare for rest tonight.

DECEMBER 4

MORNING DEVOTION

Scripture: Ezekiel 36:28
"Then you shall dwell in the land that I gave to your fathers; you shall be My people, and I will be your God."

Reflection: Ezekiel 36:28 speaks of God's promise to restore His people and establish a new covenant with them. Despite their disobedience and exile, God assures His people that He will bring them back to the land He promised to their ancestors. This covenant relationship entails a deep bond between God and His people, with Him as their God and them as His chosen people. As we begin this day, let us reflect on the faithfulness of God in fulfilling His promises. Just as He remained faithful to His covenant with the Israelites, He remains faithful to us today. Through Jesus Christ, God has established a new covenant with all who believe in Him, offering forgiveness, redemption, and eternal life.

Prayer: Gracious God, we thank You for Your faithfulness and the promises You have made to Your people. Help us to trust in Your provision and guidance, knowing that You are always true to Your word. May we live as Your people, walking in obedience and faithfulness to You. Thank You for the new covenant established through Jesus Christ, in whose name we pray, Amen.

Meditative Thought: Take a few moments to meditate on Ezekiel 36:28. Reflect on God's faithfulness in fulfilling His promises. Consider the new covenant established through Jesus Christ and the blessings it brings to those who believe. Allow gratitude to fill your heart as you contemplate the depth of God's love and faithfulness towards His people.

Scripture: Ezekiel 36:28
"Then you shall dwell in the land that I gave to your fathers; you shall be My people, and I will be your God."

Reflection: As we come to the end of this day, let us once again reflect on the promise of restoration and covenant relationship found in Ezekiel 36:28. God's desire is for His people to dwell securely in the land He has provided, experiencing the fullness of His presence and blessings. This promise extends beyond physical boundaries to encompass a spiritual relationship between God and His people. Take a moment to review the events of this day. Reflect on the ways in which you have experienced God's presence and provision. Consider the depth of your relationship with Him and your response to His faithfulness. As you prepare for rest tonight, may you find peace and assurance in the knowledge that you belong to God, and He is faithful to His promises.

Prayer: Heavenly Father, we thank You for the promise of restoration and covenant relationship found in Your word. Help us to dwell securely in Your presence, experiencing the fullness of Your blessings in our lives. Strengthen our faith and commitment to You, knowing that You are faithful to Your promises. May we rest tonight in the assurance of Your love and faithfulness. In Jesus' name, we pray, Amen.

Meditative Thought: Take a few moments to meditate on Ezekiel 36:28. Reflect on the promise of restoration and covenant relationship with God. Surrender any worries or concerns to Him, trusting in His faithfulness to fulfill His promises in your life.

Scripture: Matthew 8:27

"So the men marveled, saying, 'Who can this be, that even the winds and the sea obey Him?'"

Reflection: Matthew 8:27 captures the awe and wonder of the disciples as they witness Jesus's authority over nature. In the midst of a raging storm, Jesus commands the winds and the sea to be still, and they obey Him instantly. This demonstration of power prompts the disciples to marvel at the identity of Jesus, recognizing Him as more than just a mere man but as one who possesses divine authority. As we begin this day, let us reflect on the sovereignty of Jesus Christ over all creation. Just as He calmed the storm with a word, He has the power to calm the storms in our lives—whether they be physical, emotional, or spiritual. Let us marvel at the greatness of our God, who is able to do far more abundantly than all we ask or think.

Prayer: Heavenly Father, we thank You for the reminder of Your sovereign power and authority over all creation. Help us to trust in Your ability to calm the storms in our lives, knowing that nothing is too difficult for You. May we marvel at Your greatness and seek Your guidance and protection each day. In Jesus' name, we pray, Amen.

Meditative Thought: Take a moment to meditate on Matthew 8:27. Reflect on the awe and wonder of the disciples as they witness Jesus's authority over nature. Consider areas in your life where you need Jesus's calming presence and ask Him to bring peace and tranquility to those situations.

Scripture: Matthew 8:27
"So the men marveled, saying, 'Who can this be, that even the winds and the sea obey Him?'"

Reflection: As we come to the end of this day, let us once again reflect on the awe-inspiring power of Jesus Christ, as demonstrated in Matthew 8:27. The disciples' marvel at Jesus's authority over the elements serves as a reminder of His divine nature and sovereignty. In moments of fear and uncertainty, we can take comfort in knowing that Jesus has power over every storm we face. Take a moment to review the events of this day. Reflect on any storms or challenges you encountered and how you responded to them. Consider how Jesus's authority can bring peace and calmness to even the most tumultuous situations. As you prepare for rest tonight, may you find solace in the knowledge that Jesus is Lord over all, and He is able to bring peace to your soul.

Prayer: Gracious God, we thank You for the reminder of Your sovereign power and authority over all creation. Help us to trust in Your ability to calm the storms in our lives and bring peace to our troubled hearts. May we rest tonight in the assurance of Your presence and protection. In Jesus' name, we pray, Amen.

Meditative Thought: Take a few moments to meditate on Matthew 8:27. Reflect on Jesus's authority over the winds and the sea. Surrender any fears or anxieties to Him, trusting in His power to bring peace and tranquility to your soul as you rest tonight.

Scripture: Jeremiah 33:3

"Call to Me, and I will answer you, and show you great and mighty things, which you do not know."

Reflection: Jeremiah 33:3 is a powerful invitation from God to His people to call upon Him in prayer. God promises to answer those who seek Him earnestly and to reveal great and mighty things that are beyond human understanding. This verse reminds us of the importance of prayer in our relationship with God and the limitless possibilities that are available to us when we come before Him with open hearts and minds. As we begin this day, let us reflect on the significance of calling upon the Lord in prayer. Are we approaching God with boldness and expectancy, trusting in His promise to answer us? Let us not underestimate the power of prayer to bring about transformation and revelation in our lives. May we be diligent in seeking God's guidance and wisdom through prayer, knowing that He is faithful to respond to those who call upon Him.

Prayer: Heavenly Father, we thank You for the invitation to call upon You in prayer. Help us to approach You with faith and expectancy, trusting in Your promise to answer us. Grant us the wisdom to seek Your guidance and the humility to accept Your will for our lives. May our prayers be a source of strength and comfort, knowing that You are always attentive to the cries of Your children. In Jesus' name, we pray, Amen.

Meditative Thought: Take a moment to meditate on Jeremiah 33:3. Reflect on the promise of God to answer those who call upon Him. Consider the areas in your life where you need His guidance and wisdom. Spend time in prayer, calling upon the Lord and trusting in His faithfulness to respond.

DECEMBER 6

EVENING DEVOTION

Scripture: Jeremiah 33:3
"Call to Me, and I will answer you, and show you great and mighty things, which you do not know."

Reflection: As we come to the close of this day, let us once again reflect on the promise found in Jeremiah 33:3. God invites us to call upon Him in prayer, promising to answer us and reveal great and mighty things that are beyond our comprehension. This verse reminds us of the boundless love and wisdom of our Heavenly Father, who delights in revealing His purposes to those who seek Him earnestly. Take a moment to review the events of this day. Reflect on the ways in which you have called upon the Lord in prayer and the ways He has answered you. Consider the great and mighty things that God has revealed to you, both in His Word and through His Spirit. As you prepare for rest tonight, may you find peace and assurance in the knowledge that God is always ready to respond to the prayers of His children.

Prayer: Gracious God, we thank You for the assurance that You hear and answer our prayers. Help us to call upon You with confidence, trusting in Your faithfulness to reveal Your purposes to us. Grant us wisdom and discernment as we seek Your guidance in every area of our lives. May Your presence bring peace and comfort to our hearts as we rest tonight. In Jesus' name, we pray, Amen.

Meditative Thought: Take a few moments to meditate on Jeremiah 33:3. Reflect on the ways in which God has answered your prayers and revealed His purposes to you. Surrender any worries or concerns to Him, trusting in His faithfulness to guide and protect you as you rest tonight.

Scripture: 1 Corinthians 6:19
"Or do you not know that your body is the temple of the Holy Spirit who is in you, whom you have from God, and you are not your own?"

Reflection: In 1 Corinthians 6:19, Paul reminds believers that their bodies are temples of the Holy Spirit. This profound truth underscores the sanctity and importance of our physical bodies in God's eyes. As temples of the Holy Spirit, our bodies are not our own; they belong to God. This reality calls us to honor God with our bodies, treating them with respect and using them to glorify Him in all that we do. As we begin this day, let us reflect on the significance of our bodies being temples of the Holy Spirit. Are we stewarding our bodies well, honoring God in our thoughts, actions, and behaviors? Let us commit to living in a way that reflects the presence of the Holy Spirit within us, seeking to glorify God in every aspect of our lives.

Prayer: Heavenly Father, we thank You for the gift of the Holy Spirit who dwells within us, making our bodies temples of Your presence. Help us to honor You with our bodies, treating them with reverence and using them to bring glory to Your name. May Your Spirit guide us in living lives that are pleasing to You in thought, word, and deed. In Jesus' name, we pray, Amen.

Meditative Thought: Take a moment to meditate on 1 Corinthians 6:19. Reflect on the reality that your body is a temple of the Holy Spirit. Consider ways you can honor God with your body today, whether through acts of service, kindness, or obedience to His word. Invite the Holy Spirit to guide you in living a life that glorifies God in all that you do.

Scripture: 1 Corinthians 6:19
"Or do you not know that your body is the temple of the Holy Spirit who is in you, whom you have from God, and you are not your own?"

Reflection: As we come to the close of this day, let us once again reflect on the truth of 1 Corinthians 6:19. Our bodies are temples of the Holy Spirit, a dwelling place for God's presence. This reality should shape how we live our lives, reminding us of the responsibility we have to honor God with our bodies in all that we do. Take a moment to review the events of this day. Reflect on the ways in which you have honored God with your body and the areas where you may have fallen short. Consider how you can live more intentionally as a temple of the Holy Spirit, seeking to glorify God in every aspect of your life.

Prayer: Gracious God, we thank You for the privilege of being temples of the Holy Spirit, vessels of Your presence in this world. Forgive us for the times when we have dishonored You with our bodies through our thoughts, words, or actions. Renew our commitment to living lives that reflect Your presence within us, bringing glory to Your name. In Jesus' name, we pray, Amen.

Meditative Thought: Take a few moments to meditate on 1 Corinthians 6:19. Reflect on the responsibility you have to honor God with your body. Surrender any areas of your life where you may have fallen short, and invite the Holy Spirit to empower you to live a life that brings glory to God in all that you do.

DECEMBER 8

MORNING DEVOTION

Scripture: Exodus 34:14
"For you shall worship no other god, for the Lord, whose name is Jealous, is a jealous God."

Reflection: Exodus 34:14 emphasizes the exclusive worship of the Lord and highlights His jealousy for His people's devotion. God's jealousy is not rooted in insecurity but in His desire for an intimate and exclusive relationship with His people. He wants them to worship Him alone, recognizing His supremacy and sovereignty over all other gods. As we begin this day, let us reflect on the significance of worshiping the Lord as the one true God. Are there any other gods or idols competing for our devotion and affection? Let us examine our hearts and ensure that we are giving God the reverence and worship He deserves. May our devotion be singular and wholehearted, acknowledging the Lord as the only God worthy of our worship.

Prayer: Heavenly Father, we acknowledge You as the one true God, worthy of all honor and worship. Forgive us for the times when we have allowed other gods to take precedence in our lives. Help us to worship You alone, giving You the reverence and devotion You deserve. May our hearts be fully devoted to You this day and always. In Jesus' name, we pray, Amen.

Meditative Thought: Take a moment to meditate on Exodus 34:14. Reflect on the exclusive worship of the Lord and His jealousy for His people's devotion. Consider any areas of your life where other gods or idols may be vying for your attention. Surrender those idols to God and recommit yourself to worshiping Him alone.

Scripture: Exodus 34:14
"For you shall worship no other god, for the Lord, whose name is Jealous, is a jealous God."

Reflection: As we come to the end of this day, let us once again reflect on the importance of worshiping the Lord alone, as emphasized in Exodus 34:14. God's jealousy for His people's devotion underscores the exclusivity of our relationship with Him. He desires our wholehearted worship and allegiance, not divided among other gods or idols. Take a moment to review the events of this day. Reflect on any moments when other gods or idols may have competed for your devotion. Consider how you can further align your heart with God's desire for exclusive worship. As you prepare for rest tonight, may you renew your commitment to worshiping the Lord alone, giving Him the honor and reverence He deserves.

Prayer: Gracious God, we thank You for Your jealousy for our devotion and allegiance. Help us to worship You alone, giving You the honor and reverence You deserve. Forgive us for the times when we have allowed other gods or idols to take precedence in our lives. Renew our commitment to wholehearted worship of You, our one true God. In Jesus' name, we pray, Amen.

Meditative Thought: Take a few moments to meditate on Exodus 34:14. Reflect on God's jealousy for your devotion and allegiance. Surrender any idols or distractions to Him, and recommit yourself to worshiping Him alone with all your heart, soul, and strength.

Scripture: Genesis 6:8
"But Noah found grace in the eyes of the Lord."

Reflection: Genesis 6:8 highlights Noah's exceptional character in the midst of a corrupt and sinful world. Despite the prevailing wickedness, Noah stood out as a righteous man who found favor, or grace, in the eyes of the Lord. God's grace toward Noah was not based on his own merit but on God's mercy and love for him. As we begin this day, let us reflect on the significance of finding grace in the eyes of the Lord. Like Noah, we are recipients of God's grace, undeserved favor lavished upon us by His mercy and love. Let us be grateful for the grace that God extends to us each day, empowering us to live righteous and obedient lives in a world filled with sin and darkness.

Prayer: Heavenly Father, we thank You for Your abundant grace that sustains us each day. Like Noah, we are grateful for the favor You have shown us despite our shortcomings. Help us to walk in righteousness and obedience, relying on Your grace to guide and strengthen us. May we be vessels of Your grace in a world in need of Your mercy and love. In Jesus' name, we pray, Amen.

Meditative Thought: Take a moment to meditate on Genesis 6:8. Reflect on the grace that God extended to Noah in the midst of a sinful world. Consider how God's grace has impacted your own life and how you can extend that grace to others today. Spend time in gratitude for God's mercy and love toward you.

Scripture: Genesis 6:8
"But Noah found grace in the eyes of the Lord."

Reflection: As we come to the end of this day, let us once again reflect on the profound truth of Genesis 6:8. Noah's experience of finding grace in the eyes of the Lord serves as a reminder of God's unfailing love and mercy toward His people. In a world characterized by sin and wickedness, God's grace shines forth as a beacon of hope and redemption. Take a moment to review the events of this day. Reflect on the ways in which you have experienced God's grace and favor in your life. Consider the ways in which you have extended grace to others, reflecting God's love and mercy. As you prepare for rest tonight, may you find comfort and peace in the assurance of God's grace, knowing that His love never fails.

Prayer: Gracious God, we thank You for Your unending grace that sustains us each day. Help us to rest in the assurance of Your love and mercy, knowing that Your grace is sufficient for us. May we extend grace to others as You have graciously extended it to us. Grant us peaceful rest tonight, knowing that Your love surrounds us always. In Jesus' name, we pray, Amen.

Meditative Thought: Take a few moments to meditate on Genesis 6:8. Reflect on the grace that God extended to Noah and how it parallels His grace in your own life. Consider ways you can extend grace to others, reflecting God's love and mercy. Surrender any worries or burdens to God, resting in His grace and love tonight.

DECEMBER 10

MORNING DEVOTION

Scripture: Revelation 19:9

"Then he said to me, 'Write: Blessed are those who are called to the marriage supper of the Lamb!' And he said to me, 'These are the true sayings of God.'"

Reflection: Revelation 19:9 unveils a glorious scene of the marriage supper of the Lamb, symbolizing the ultimate union between Christ, the Lamb of God, and His bride, the Church. This divine banquet represents the culmination of God's redemptive plan, where believers are blessed to partake in eternal fellowship and celebration with the Lord. As we begin this day, let us reflect on the profound blessing of being called to the marriage supper of the Lamb. It is a reminder of God's lavish love and grace toward His people, inviting them to share in the joy of His eternal kingdom. Let us eagerly anticipate the fulfillment of this promise and live each day in readiness for the glorious return of Christ.

Prayer: Heavenly Father, we thank You for the blessed hope of being called to the marriage supper of the Lamb. Help us to live each day in anticipation of the glorious day when we will celebrate with You for all eternity. May our lives be a testimony to Your love and grace, as we eagerly await the return of Christ. In Jesus' name, we pray, Amen.

Meditative Thought: Take a moment to meditate on Revelation 19:9. Reflect on the joy and anticipation of being called to the marriage supper of the Lamb. Consider how this blessed hope shapes your perspective and priorities in life. Spend time in gratitude for the promise of eternal fellowship and celebration with the Lord.

DECEMBER 10

EVENING DEVOTION

Scripture: Revelation 19:9
"Then he said to me, 'Write: Blessed are those who are called to the marriage supper of the Lamb!' And he said to me, 'These are the true sayings of God.'"

Reflection: As we come to the close of this day, let us once again reflect on the profound blessing of being called to the marriage supper of the Lamb, as described in Revelation 19:9. This divine banquet represents the culmination of God's redemptive plan, where believers are invited to share in the joy of eternal fellowship and celebration with the Lord. Take a moment to review the events of this day. Reflect on the ways in which you have lived in anticipation of the marriage supper of the Lamb. Consider any areas where you may need to realign your priorities and focus on the eternal promises of God. As you prepare for rest tonight, may you find peace and assurance in the blessed hope of being called to share in the joy of God's eternal kingdom.

Prayer: Gracious God, we thank You for the blessed hope of being called to the marriage supper of the Lamb. Help us to live each day in anticipation of the glorious day when we will celebrate with You for all eternity. May our lives be a reflection of Your love and grace, as we eagerly await the return of Christ. In Jesus' name, we pray, Amen.

Meditative Thought: Take a few moments to meditate on Revelation 19:9. Reflect on the joy and anticipation of being called to the marriage supper of the Lamb. Surrender any worries or burdens to God, trusting in His faithfulness to fulfill His promises. Rest in the blessed hope of eternal fellowship and celebration with the Lord.

Scripture: Job 37:14
"Listen to this, O Job; Stand still and consider the wondrous works of God."

Reflection: In Job 37:14, Elihu urges Job to pause and contemplate the magnificent works of God. Amidst life's trials and uncertainties, Elihu reminds Job of the greatness and majesty of God's creation. This verse invites us to adopt a posture of awe and reverence, recognizing God's sovereignty and wisdom displayed in the world around us. As we begin this day, let us heed Elihu's exhortation to stand still and consider the wondrous works of God. Take a moment to reflect on the beauty of creation, the intricacy of life, and the providence of God in all things. May we cultivate a heart of gratitude and wonder, acknowledging God's greatness and trusting in His unfailing love and care for us.

Prayer: Heavenly Father, we thank You for the wondrous works of Your hands displayed in creation. Help us to stand still and contemplate Your greatness, even amidst life's challenges and uncertainties. May we be filled with awe and reverence for You, recognizing Your sovereignty and wisdom in all things. In Jesus' name, we pray, Amen.

Meditative Thought: Take a moment to meditate on Job 37:14. Reflect on the wondrous works of God displayed in creation. Consider the beauty and intricacy of the world around you, and how it reflects God's greatness. Spend time in silent contemplation, allowing God's presence to fill you with awe and reverence.

Scripture: Job 37:14
"Listen to this, O Job; Stand still and consider the wondrous works of God."

Reflection: As we come to the close of this day, let us once again reflect on the exhortation found in Job 37:14. Elihu's words to Job serve as a reminder for us to pause and reflect on the wondrous works of God. In the midst of life's busyness and distractions, it is essential to stand still and contemplate the greatness and majesty of our Creator. Take a moment to review the events of this day. Reflect on the ways in which you have witnessed God's wondrous works in your life and in the world around you. Consider the blessings and challenges you have experienced, and how they have shaped your faith and perspective. As you prepare for rest tonight, may you find peace and comfort in knowing that God's works are wondrous, and His love for you is unfailing.

Prayer: Gracious God, we thank You for the wondrous works displayed in creation and in our lives. Help us to stand still and consider Your greatness, even in the midst of life's challenges. May we find peace and comfort in knowing that Your love for us is unfailing, and Your works are wondrous. In Jesus' name, we pray, Amen.

Meditative Thought: Take a few moments to meditate on Job 37:14. Reflect on the wondrous works of God displayed in creation and in your life. Consider the ways in which God has shown His love and faithfulness to you. Surrender any worries or burdens to Him, and rest in the assurance of His presence and care for you.

Scripture: Philippians 4:6
"Be anxious for nothing, but in everything by prayer and supplication, with thanksgiving, let your requests be made known to God."

Reflection: Philippians 4:6 offers a powerful reminder to relinquish anxiety and worry, instead, turning to God in prayer with thanksgiving. Rather than allowing anxiety to consume us, we are encouraged to bring our concerns before God, trusting in His provision and care. This verse highlights the importance of prayer as a means of finding peace amidst life's challenges. As we begin this day, let us reflect on the significance of casting our anxieties upon the Lord in prayer. Are there areas of your life where anxiety has taken hold? Take a moment to surrender those worries to God, trusting in His faithfulness to provide and sustain you. May prayer become your refuge and source of peace, knowing that God hears and answers the prayers of His children.

Prayer: Heavenly Father, we thank You for the invitation to bring our anxieties to You in prayer. Help us to release our worries and concerns, trusting in Your provision and care. May prayer be our refuge and source of peace in the midst of life's challenges. Teach us to approach You with thanksgiving, knowing that You hear and answer our prayers according to Your will. In Jesus' name, we pray, Amen.

Meditative Thought: Take a moment to meditate on Philippians 4:6. Reflect on the areas of your life where anxiety may be present. Surrender those worries to God in prayer, allowing His peace to fill your heart and mind. Spend time in thanksgiving, acknowledging God's faithfulness and provision in your life.

Scripture: Philippians 4:6
"Be anxious for nothing, but in everything by prayer and supplication, with thanksgiving, let your requests be made known to God."

Reflection: As we come to the close of this day, let us once again reflect on the wisdom of Philippians 4:6. This verse encourages us to be anxious for nothing but to bring everything to God in prayer with thanksgiving. In the busyness and uncertainties of life, prayer becomes our lifeline, offering us peace and assurance in God's faithfulness. Take a moment to review the events of this day. Were there moments when anxiety crept in, stealing your peace? Reflect on how you responded to those moments and whether you turned to God in prayer. As you prepare for rest tonight, may you commit to entrusting your worries to God, knowing that He cares for you and hears your prayers.

Prayer: Gracious God, we thank You for the gift of prayer, which allows us to bring our anxieties to You with thanksgiving. Forgive us for the times when we have allowed worry to overshadow our trust in You. Help us to cultivate a heart of prayer, turning to You in every circumstance. May Your peace guard our hearts and minds as we rest tonight. In Jesus' name, we pray, Amen.

Meditative Thought: Take a few moments to meditate on Philippians 4:6. Reflect on the significance of prayer as a means of finding peace amidst anxiety. Surrender any worries or concerns to God, trusting in His faithfulness to provide and sustain you. Rest in the assurance that God hears and answers your prayers according to His perfect will.

Scripture: Isaiah 49:16

"See, I have inscribed you on the palms of My hands; Your walls are continually before Me."

Reflection: Isaiah 49:16 portrays the tender care and intimate knowledge that God has for His people. The imagery of inscribing His people on the palms of His hands signifies the everlasting love and constant remembrance that God has for His children. This verse assures us that we are never forgotten or abandoned by God; He holds us close to His heart, and our well-being is always before Him. As we begin this day, let us reflect on the profound truth of Isaiah 49:16. Are you aware of God's unwavering love and care for you? Take comfort in knowing that you are engraved on the palms of His hands, and He is intimately acquainted with every detail of your life. May this assurance strengthen your faith and fill you with confidence as you face the challenges of this day.

Prayer: Heavenly Father, we thank You for Your steadfast love and faithfulness toward us. Help us to grasp the depth of Your care and concern for our well-being. May we find comfort and assurance in knowing that we are engraved on the palms of Your hands, and You are always mindful of us. Guide and protect us throughout this day, knowing that You are with us every step of the way. In Jesus' name, we pray, Amen.

Meditative Thought: Take a moment to meditate on Isaiah 49:16. Reflect on the imagery of being inscribed on the palms of God's hands. Consider the significance of this imagery in your life and how it shapes your understanding of God's love for you. Spend time in silent contemplation, allowing God's presence to reassure and comfort you.

Scripture: Isaiah 49:16
"See, I have inscribed you on the palms of My hands; Your walls are continually before Me."

Reflection: As we come to the close of this day, let us once again reflect on the comforting truth of Isaiah 49:16. This verse reminds us of God's unwavering love and constant presence in our lives. The imagery of being inscribed on the palms of God's hands speaks of His intimate knowledge and steadfast commitment to His people. Take a moment to review the events of this day. Reflect on the ways in which you have experienced God's love and care throughout the day. Consider any moments when you felt His presence guiding and comforting you. As you prepare for rest tonight, may you find peace and assurance in the knowledge that you are engraved on the palms of God's hands, and He is always mindful of you.

Prayer: Gracious God, we thank You for Your abiding presence and steadfast love in our lives. As we come to the close of this day, we rest in the assurance that we are engraved on the palms of Your hands. May Your love and protection surround us as we sleep, and may we awaken refreshed and renewed to serve You anew. In Jesus' name, we pray, Amen.

Meditative Thought: Take a few moments to meditate on Isaiah 49:16. Reflect on the significance of being inscribed on the palms of God's hands. Surrender any worries or burdens to Him, trusting in His faithfulness to care for you. Rest in the assurance of God's love and presence as you prepare for sleep tonight.

Scripture: Psalm 1:6
"For the Lord knows the way of the righteous, But the way of the ungodly shall perish."

Reflection: Psalm 1:6 contrasts the destinies of the righteous and the ungodly. The Lord intimately knows the way of the righteous, guiding and sustaining them along the path of righteousness. In contrast, the way of the ungodly leads to destruction and ultimately perishes. This verse underscores the importance of choosing to walk in alignment with God's will and seeking righteousness in all aspects of life. As we begin this day, let us reflect on the significance of aligning our lives with God's will. Are we actively seeking righteousness and walking in obedience to His commands? Let us commit to cultivating a life that is pleasing to God, knowing that He intimately knows and cares for those who walk in righteousness.

Prayer: Heavenly Father, we thank You for Your guidance and provision along the path of righteousness. Help us to walk in obedience to Your commands and seek Your will in all aspects of our lives. May we trust in Your intimate knowledge of us and find comfort in Your presence as we journey through this day. Lead us in the way of righteousness, that we may honor and glorify You in all that we do. In Jesus' name, we pray, Amen.

Meditative Thought: Take a moment to meditate on Psalm 1:6. Reflect on the contrast between the destinies of the righteous and the ungodly. Consider the significance of aligning your life with God's will and seeking righteousness in all aspects of life. Spend time in silent contemplation, inviting God to guide and sustain you along the path of righteousness throughout this day.

Scripture: Psalm 1:6
"For the Lord knows the way of the righteous, But the way of the ungodly shall perish."

Reflection: As we come to the close of this day, let us once again reflect on the truth of Psalm 1:6. This verse reminds us of the intimate knowledge and care that God has for the righteous, guiding and sustaining them along the path of righteousness. In contrast, the way of the ungodly leads to destruction and perishes. Take a moment to review the events of this day. Reflect on the choices you have made and the ways in which you have aligned your life with God's will. Consider any areas where you may have strayed from righteousness and seek God's forgiveness and guidance. As you prepare for rest tonight, may you find peace and assurance in the knowledge that God intimately knows and cares for those who walk in righteousness.

Prayer: Gracious God, we thank You for Your guidance and provision along the path of righteousness. Forgive us for the times when we have strayed from Your will and walked in unrighteousness. Help us to align our lives with Your truth and seek Your will in all that we do. May we find comfort in Your intimate knowledge of us and trust in Your guidance as we rest tonight. In Jesus' name, we pray, Amen.

Meditative Thought: Take a few moments to meditate on Psalm 1:6. Reflect on the contrast between the destinies of the righteous and the ungodly. Surrender any areas of your life where you may have strayed from righteousness to God, seeking His forgiveness and guidance. Rest in the assurance of God's care and provision as you prepare for sleep tonight.

Scripture: Psalm 116:1-2

"I love the Lord, because He has heard My voice and my supplications. Because He has inclined His ear to me, Therefore I will call upon Him as long as I live."

Reflection: Psalm 116:1-2 expresses the psalmist's deep gratitude and love for the Lord because of His attentive care and responsiveness to prayer. The psalmist acknowledges God's faithfulness in hearing and answering their cries, prompting a lifelong commitment to calling upon Him. This passage reminds us of the privilege and power of prayer, as well as the unfailing love and compassion of our Heavenly Father. As we begin this day, let us reflect on the psalmist's heartfelt response to God's faithfulness. Are we cultivating a deep love for the Lord in response to His attentive care and responsiveness to our prayers? Let us commit to a life of continual prayer, trusting in God's unfailing love and faithfulness to hear and answer us.

Prayer: Gracious God, we thank You for Your attentive care and responsiveness to our prayers. Help us to cultivate a deep love for You in response to Your unfailing love and faithfulness. May we approach You with confidence, knowing that You hear and answer our cries. Guide us in a life of continual prayer, calling upon You as long as we live. In Jesus' name, we pray, Amen.

Meditative Thought: Take a moment to meditate on Psalm 116:1-2. Reflect on the psalmist's deep gratitude and love for the Lord because of His attentive care and responsiveness to prayer. Consider the ways in which God has heard and answered your prayers in the past. Spend time in silent contemplation, expressing your love and gratitude to God for His faithfulness.

Scripture: Psalm 116:1-2
"I love the Lord, because He has heard My voice and my supplications. Because He has inclined His ear to me, Therefore I will call upon Him as long as I live."

Reflection: As we come to the close of this day, let us once again reflect on the psalmist's heartfelt response to God's faithfulness in Psalm 116:1-2. The psalmist's love for the Lord is deeply rooted in God's attentive care and responsiveness to their prayers. This passage reminds us of the enduring love and faithfulness of our Heavenly Father, prompting a lifelong commitment to calling upon Him in prayer. Take a moment to review the events of this day. Reflect on the ways in which God has heard and answered your prayers. Consider the moments when you experienced God's attentive care and responsiveness to your cries. As you prepare for rest tonight, may you be filled with gratitude and love for the Lord, committing to a life of continual prayer and dependence on Him.

Prayer: Heavenly Father, we thank You for Your attentive care and responsiveness to our prayers. Help us to cultivate a deep love for You in response to Your unfailing love and faithfulness. May we approach You with confidence, knowing that You hear and answer our cries. Guide us in a life of continual prayer, calling upon You as long as we live. In Jesus' name, we pray, Amen.

Meditative Thought: Take a few moments to meditate on Psalm 116:1-2. Reflect on the psalmist's deep gratitude and love for the Lord because of His attentive care and responsiveness to prayer. Surrender any worries or burdens to God, trusting in His unfailing love and faithfulness. Rest in the assurance that God hears and answers your prayers, and commit to calling upon Him as long as you live.

DECEMBER 16

MORNING DEVOTION

Scripture: Proverbs 5:7
"Therefore hear me now, my children, And do not depart from the words of my mouth."

Reflection: Our text urges us to heed wisdom's call and not stray from its teachings. The speaker implores their listeners to listen attentively and adhere to the guidance provided. This verse serves as a reminder of the importance of listening to wise counsel and following the path of righteousness. As we begin this day, let us reflect on the significance of heeding wisdom's call. Are we attentive to the counsel and guidance provided by those who seek our well-being? Let us commit to listening with an open heart and mind, allowing wisdom to guide our thoughts, words, and actions throughout this day.

Prayer: Heavenly Father, we thank You for the wisdom and guidance You provide through Your Word and those You place in our lives. Help us to listen attentively to wise counsel and adhere to the teachings of righteousness. May Your wisdom guide our thoughts, words, and actions today and every day. In Jesus' name, we pray, Amen.

Meditative Thought: Take a moment to meditate on Proverbs 5:7. Reflect on the importance of heeding wisdom's call and adhering to its teachings. Consider any areas of your life where you may need to be more attentive to wise counsel. Spend time in silent reflection, allowing God to speak to your heart and guide you in the path of righteousness.

Scripture: Proverbs 5:7
"Therefore hear me now, my children, And do not depart from the words of my mouth."

Reflection: As we come to the close of this day, let us once again reflect on the wisdom found in Proverbs 5:7. The speaker urges their listeners to heed wise counsel and not stray from its teachings. This verse serves as a reminder of the importance of remaining attentive to wisdom's call and following the path of righteousness. Take a moment to review the events of this day. Reflect on the ways in which you have listened to wise counsel and adhered to the teachings of righteousness. Consider any moments when you may have strayed from wisdom's path and seek God's forgiveness and guidance. As you prepare for rest tonight, may you commit to listening attentively to wisdom's call and allowing it to guide your thoughts, words, and actions.

Prayer: Gracious God, we thank You for the wisdom and guidance You provide through Your Word and those You place in our lives. Forgive us for the times when we have strayed from wisdom's path and failed to heed wise counsel. Help us to listen attentively to Your voice and adhere to Your teachings of righteousness. May Your wisdom guide our steps as we rest tonight. In Jesus' name, we pray, Amen.

Meditative Thought: Take a few moments to meditate on Proverbs 5:7. Reflect on the importance of heeding wise counsel and adhering to its teachings. Surrender any areas of your life where you may have strayed from wisdom's path to God, seeking His forgiveness and guidance. Rest in the assurance that God's wisdom is available to guide you in every aspect of your life.

Scripture: Isaiah 46:9-10

"Remember the former things of old, For I am God, and there is no other; I am God, and there is none like Me, Declaring the end from the beginning, And from ancient times things that are not yet done, Saying, 'My counsel shall stand, And I will do all My pleasure,'"

Reflection: Isaiah 46:9-10 emphasizes the sovereignty and omniscience of God. He declares Himself as the one and only God, unmatched in His power and knowledge. From ancient times, God has been declaring the end from the beginning, demonstrating His authority over all things. His plans and purposes will always come to pass, and His will shall be accomplished. As we begin this day, let us reflect on the greatness and sovereignty of God. Are we acknowledging His unmatched power and wisdom in our lives? Let us trust in His divine plan, knowing that He holds the future in His hands. May we find comfort and assurance in His unchanging nature, confident that His counsel will stand, and His will shall be done.

Prayer: Heavenly Father, we thank You for Your sovereignty and wisdom. Help us to trust in Your plans and purposes, knowing that You are in control of all things. May we find peace and assurance in Your unchanging nature, confident that Your will shall be accomplished. Guide us through this day, and help us to honor You in all that we do. In Jesus' name, we pray, Amen.

Meditative Thought: Take a moment to meditate on Isaiah 46:9-10. Reflect on the sovereignty and omniscience of God. Consider the ways in which you can trust in His plans and purposes for your life. Spend time in silent contemplation, surrendering any worries or fears to God, and resting in His unchanging nature and perfect will.

Scripture: Isaiah 46:9-10
"Remember the former things of old, For I am God, and there is no other; I am God, and there is none like Me, Declaring the end from the beginning, And from ancient times things that are not yet done, Saying, 'My counsel shall stand, And I will do all My pleasure,'"

Reflection: As we come to the close of this day, let us once again reflect on the truth found in Isaiah 46:9-10. God declares Himself as the one and only God, unmatched in His power and wisdom. He has been declaring the end from the beginning, demonstrating His authority over all things. His plans and purposes will always come to pass, and His will shall be accomplished. Take a moment to review the events of this day. Reflect on the ways in which you have witnessed God's sovereignty and wisdom at work. Consider any moments when you may have doubted His plans or felt uncertain about the future. As you prepare for rest tonight, may you find peace and assurance in the unchanging nature of God, confident that His counsel will stand, and His will shall be done.

Prayer: Gracious God, we thank You for Your sovereignty and wisdom. Help us to trust in Your plans and purposes, knowing that You are in control of all things. May we find peace and assurance in Your unchanging nature, confident that Your will shall be accomplished. Grant us rest tonight, knowing that You are always working for our good. In Jesus' name, we pray, Amen.

Meditative Thought: Take a few moments to meditate on Isaiah 46:9-10. Reflect on the sovereignty and omniscience of God. Surrender any doubts or fears about the future to Him, trusting in His perfect plan. Rest in the assurance that His counsel will stand, and His will shall be done.

Scripture: Matthew 5:44
"But I say to you, love your enemies, bless those who curse you, do good to those who hate you, and pray for those who spitefully use you and persecute you,"

Reflection: Matthew 5:44 presents a challenging command from Jesus: to love our enemies and pray for those who mistreat us. This goes against our natural inclinations, but it reflects the radical love and grace of God. By loving our enemies and praying for them, we demonstrate the transformative power of God's love in our lives and extend His grace to others. As we begin this day, let us reflect on the command to love our enemies. Are there individuals in our lives whom we find difficult to love? Let us ask God to soften our hearts and fill us with His love so that we may respond to our enemies with kindness, blessing, and prayer.

Prayer: Loving Father, Your command to love our enemies challenges us, but we know that Your love knows no bounds. Fill us with Your love so that we may extend grace and kindness even to those who mistreat us. Help us to bless and pray for our enemies, reflecting Your love and grace in all that we do. In Jesus' name, we pray, Amen.

Meditative Thought: Take a moment to meditate on Matthew 5:44. Reflect on the command to love your enemies, bless those who curse you, and pray for those who mistreat you. Consider any individuals in your life whom you find difficult to love. Surrender those feelings to God and ask Him to fill you with His love so that you may respond to them with grace and kindness.

Scripture: Matthew 5:44
"But I say to you, love your enemies, bless those who curse you, do good to those who hate you, and pray for those who spitefully use you and persecute you,"

Reflection: As we come to the close of this day, let us once again reflect on the command of Jesus in Matthew 5:44. Loving our enemies, blessing those who curse us, and praying for those who mistreat us may seem difficult, but it is a reflection of God's radical love and grace. When we respond to hatred with love and pray for those who persecute us, we demonstrate the transformative power of God's love in our lives. Take a moment to review the events of this day. Reflect on any interactions you had with individuals whom you may consider enemies or difficult to love. Did you respond to them with grace and kindness? As you prepare for rest tonight, ask God to continue to fill you with His love so that you may extend grace and kindness to all, even to those who mistreat you.

Prayer: Gracious God, Your command to love our enemies challenges us, but we know that Your love knows no bounds. Fill us with Your love so that we may extend grace and kindness even to those who mistreat us. Help us to bless and pray for our enemies, reflecting Your love and grace in all that we do. Grant us rest tonight, knowing that Your love surrounds us always. In Jesus' name, we pray, Amen.

Meditative Thought: Take a few moments to meditate on Matthew 5:44. Reflect on the command to love your enemies, bless those who curse you, and pray for those who mistreat you. Consider any interactions you had today with individuals whom you find difficult to love. Surrender any feelings of resentment or anger to God.

Scripture: Luke 1:46-47
"And Mary said: 'My soul magnifies the Lord, and my spirit has rejoiced in God my Savior.'"

Reflection: In Luke 1:46-47, Mary, upon receiving the news of her miraculous pregnancy, bursts into a beautiful song of praise known as the Magnificat. She exalts God for His greatness and rejoices in Him as her Savior. Mary's response demonstrates profound faith, humility, and gratitude in the face of unexpected circumstances. Her words inspire us to magnify the Lord and rejoice in His salvation, regardless of our circumstances. As we begin this day, let us reflect on Mary's song of praise. Are we magnifying the Lord in our lives, regardless of our circumstances? Let us cultivate a spirit of gratitude and rejoicing in God our Savior, knowing that He is faithful and worthy of all praise.

Prayer: Heavenly Father, we thank You for Your greatness and faithfulness. Help us to magnify You in our lives, regardless of our circumstances. May we rejoice in You as our Savior, knowing that You are worthy of all praise and adoration. Guide us through this day, and fill our hearts with gratitude and joy. In Jesus' name, we pray, Amen.

Meditative Thought: Take a moment to meditate on Luke 1:46-47. Reflect on Mary's song of praise and her rejoicing in God her Savior. Consider the ways in which you can magnify the Lord in your life today. Spend time in silent contemplation, allowing God's presence to fill you with gratitude and joy.

Scripture: Luke 1:46-47
"And Mary said: 'My soul magnifies the Lord, and my spirit has rejoiced in God my Savior.'"

Reflection: As we come to the close of this day, let us once again reflect on Mary's song of praise in Luke 1:46-47. Despite the unexpected circumstances she faced, Mary exalted God for His greatness and rejoiced in Him as her Savior. Her response serves as a reminder to us to magnify the Lord and find joy in His salvation, regardless of our circumstances. Take a moment to review the events of this day. Reflect on the ways in which you have magnified the Lord and rejoiced in His salvation. Consider any moments when you may have allowed circumstances to overshadow your joy in the Lord. As you prepare for rest tonight, may you find peace and contentment in magnifying the Lord and rejoicing in His salvation.

Prayer: Gracious God, we thank You for the example of Mary's faith and rejoicing in Your salvation. Help us to magnify You in our lives and find joy in Your salvation, regardless of our circumstances. May Your presence fill us with peace and contentment as we rest tonight. In Jesus' name, we pray, Amen.

Meditative Thought: Take a few moments to meditate on Luke 1:46-47. Reflect on Mary's song of praise and her rejoicing in God her Savior. Surrender any worries or concerns to God, and allow His peace to fill your heart. Rest in the assurance of His faithfulness and salvation as you prepare for sleep tonight.

Scripture: John 13:8

"Peter said to Him, 'You shall never wash my feet!' Jesus answered him, 'If I do not wash you, you have no part with Me.'"

Reflection: In John 13:8, we witness Peter's initial resistance to Jesus washing his feet. Peter, out of reverence for Jesus, felt unworthy to have his feet washed by the Lord. However, Jesus gently corrects Peter, explaining that without this act of service, Peter cannot share in the relationship and blessings that Jesus offers. This interaction illustrates Jesus' humility, love, and the necessity of receiving His cleansing grace. As we begin this day, let us reflect on Peter's response and Jesus' gentle correction. Are there areas in our lives where we resist receiving God's grace and service? Let us humble ourselves before the Lord, acknowledging our need for His cleansing and transformative grace. May we embrace His love and allow Him to minister to us in whatever ways He deems necessary.

Prayer: Gracious Lord, we thank You for Your humility and love demonstrated through the act of washing the disciples' feet. Help us to humbly receive Your cleansing grace in our lives. Remove any resistance or pride that hinders us from fully embracing Your love and service. May we surrender ourselves to Your care and allow You to minister to us as You see fit. In Jesus' name, we pray, Amen.

Meditative Thought: Take a moment to meditate on John 13:8. Reflect on Peter's initial resistance and Jesus' gentle correction. Consider any areas in your life where you may be resistant to receiving God's grace and service. Surrender those areas to Him in prayer, asking for humility and openness to His work in your life. Spend time in silent contemplation, allowing God to minister to you as He sees fit.

Scripture: John 13:8
"Peter said to Him, 'You shall never wash my feet!' Jesus answered him, 'If I do not wash you, you have no part with Me.'"

Reflection: As we come to the close of this day, let us once again reflect on the interaction between Jesus and Peter in John 13:8. Peter's initial resistance to Jesus washing his feet highlights our human tendency to resist receiving God's grace and service. However, Jesus' gentle correction reminds us of the necessity of humbly receiving His cleansing and transformative grace in our lives. Take a moment to review the events of this day. Reflect on any moments when you may have resisted receiving God's grace and service. Consider the areas in your life where you need His cleansing and transformative work. As you prepare for rest tonight, may you surrender yourself to God's care, allowing Him to minister to you and lead you into deeper intimacy with Him.

Prayer: Loving Father, we confess our tendency to resist receiving Your grace and service in our lives. Forgive us for our pride and stubbornness. Help us to humbly surrender ourselves to Your care, allowing You to minister to us as You see fit. May Your cleansing and transformative grace work in us, leading us into deeper intimacy with You. In Jesus' name, we pray, Amen.

Meditative Thought: Take a few moments to meditate on John 13:8. Reflect on Peter's initial resistance and Jesus' gentle correction. Surrender any areas in your life where you may be resistant to receiving God's grace and service. Allow His cleansing and transformative grace to work in you as you prepare for sleep tonight.

Scripture: Romans 1:16
"For I am not ashamed of the gospel of Christ, for it is the power of God to salvation for everyone who believes, for the Jew first and also for the Greek."

Reflection: Romans 1:16 expresses Paul's unwavering confidence in the gospel of Christ. He declares boldly that he is not ashamed of the gospel because it holds the power of God for salvation. This verse reminds us that the gospel is not merely a message but a divine power that transforms lives. It is inclusive, offering salvation to all who believe, regardless of their background or ethnicity. As we begin this day, let us reflect on our attitude toward the gospel. Are we embracing it with confidence and boldness, or do we shrink back in fear or shame? Let us be encouraged by Paul's example to stand firm in our faith and proclaim the gospel with conviction, knowing that it has the power to bring salvation to all who believe.

Prayer: Heavenly Father, we thank You for the gospel of Christ, which holds the power of salvation for all who believe. Give us boldness and confidence to proclaim Your truth to the world around us. Help us to overcome any fear or shame and to embrace the gospel with joy and conviction. May Your message of salvation reach the hearts of many today. In Jesus' name, we pray, Amen.

Meditative Thought: Take a moment to meditate on Romans 1:16. Reflect on Paul's confidence in the gospel and his refusal to be ashamed of it. Consider any areas in your life where you may struggle with fear or shame in sharing your faith. Surrender those feelings to God, asking Him to fill you with boldness and confidence to proclaim His truth. Spend time in silent contemplation, allowing God to strengthen your faith and resolve.

DECEMBER 21

EVENING DEVOTION

Scripture: Romans 1:16
"For I am not ashamed of the gospel of Christ, for it is the power of God to salvation for everyone who believes, for the Jew first and also for the Greek."

Reflection: As we come to the close of this day, let us reflect once again on the powerful declaration of Paul in Romans 1:16. He boldly proclaims his lack of shame in the gospel of Christ, recognizing it as the divine power of God for salvation to all who believe. This verse serves as a reminder of the inclusive nature of the gospel, offering salvation to everyone, regardless of their background or ethnicity. Take a moment to review the events of this day. Reflect on any opportunities you had to share the gospel or live out your faith in front of others. Consider whether you approached those opportunities with confidence and boldness or with fear and hesitation. As you prepare for rest tonight, may you be encouraged by Paul's example to stand firm in your faith and boldly proclaim the gospel to those around you.

Prayer: Gracious God, we thank You for the gospel of Christ, which holds the power of salvation for all who believe. Forgive us for any times when we have hesitated to share Your truth with others. Give us boldness and confidence to proclaim Your gospel to the world around us. May Your message of salvation reach the hearts of many tonight. In Jesus' name, we pray, Amen.

Meditative Thought: Take a few moments to meditate on Romans 1:16. Reflect on Paul's confidence in the gospel and his refusal to be ashamed of it. Surrender any feelings of fear or hesitation to God, asking Him to fill you with boldness and confidence to proclaim His truth. Rest in the assurance that the gospel holds the power of salvation for all who believe.

Scripture: Galatians 6:2

"Bear one another's burdens, and so fulfill the law of Christ."

Reflection: In Galatians 6:2, Paul encourages believers to bear one another's burdens, highlighting the importance of community and mutual support. This command reflects the heart of Christ's teachings, which emphasize love, compassion, and service to others. By helping each other with our struggles and challenges, we not only provide practical assistance but also embody the love of Christ. As we start this day, let us reflect on how we can bear the burdens of those around us. Are there friends, family members, or colleagues who need our support and encouragement? Let us be attentive to their needs and ready to offer a helping hand, knowing that in doing so, we are fulfilling the law of Christ and demonstrating His love in action.

Prayer: Heavenly Father, we thank You for the community of believers You have placed us in. Help us to be mindful of the needs of those around us and to bear one another's burdens with love and compassion. Give us the strength and wisdom to offer support and encouragement, reflecting Your love in all that we do. Guide us today as we seek to fulfill the law of Christ by serving others. In Jesus' name, we pray, Amen.

Meditative Thought: Take a moment to meditate on Galatians 6:2. Reflect on the command to bear one another's burdens and consider how you can apply this in your daily life. Think of specific individuals who might need your support today. Spend time in silent contemplation, asking God to give you the strength and compassion to help carry the burdens of others.

Scripture: Galatians 6:2
"Bear one another's burdens, and so fulfill the law of Christ."

Reflection: As we come to the close of this day, let us once again reflect on Paul's exhortation in Galatians 6:2. Bearing one another's burdens is a practical expression of Christ's love and compassion. It reminds us of the importance of community and the role we play in supporting each other through life's challenges. Reflecting on our day, we can evaluate how we have responded to the needs of those around us. Take a moment to review the interactions and opportunities you had today. Did you notice someone in need of support? Were you able to offer encouragement or assistance? As you prepare for rest tonight, let us commit to being more attentive and responsive to the needs of others, continually seeking to fulfill the law of Christ by bearing one another's burdens.

Prayer: Gracious God, we thank You for the opportunities we had today to serve and support those around us. Forgive us for any moments we may have missed or ignored the needs of others. Help us to be more attentive and compassionate, ready to bear one another's burdens. Fill us with Your love and wisdom as we seek to fulfill the law of Christ in our daily lives. Grant us rest tonight, and renew our strength for the coming day. In Jesus' name, we pray, Amen.

Meditative Thought: Take a few moments to meditate on Galatians 6:2. Reflect on the interactions and opportunities you had today to bear one another's burdens. Consider any moments you may have missed and ask God for guidance and compassion to be more responsive in the future. Rest in the assurance that by fulfilling the law of Christ, you are participating in His work of love and service.

DECEMBER 23

MORNING DEVOTION

Scripture: 1 Corinthians 15:58
"Therefore, my beloved brethren, be steadfast, immovable, always abounding in the work of the Lord, knowing that your labor is not in vain in the Lord."

Reflection: 1 Corinthians 15:58 is a powerful encouragement from Paul to the believers. He exhorts them to be steadfast and immovable, always giving themselves fully to the work of the Lord. This verse reminds us that our efforts in serving God are not in vain; they have eternal significance. The foundation of this steadfastness is the assurance of the resurrection and the victory over death that Jesus Christ has secured for us. As we begin this day, let us reflect on our commitment to the work of the Lord. Are we steadfast and immovable in our faith and service? Are we abounding in the work of the Lord, confident that our labor has eternal value? Let us dedicate ourselves anew to serving God with perseverance and joy, knowing that our efforts are never in vain.

Prayer: Heavenly Father, we thank You for the assurance that our labor in the Lord is not in vain. Help us to be steadfast and immovable in our faith and service to You. Fill us with the strength and perseverance to abound in Your work today. May our efforts bring glory to Your name and bear eternal fruit. In Jesus' name, we pray, Amen.

Meditative Thought: Take a moment to meditate on 1 Corinthians 15:58. Reflect on the call to be steadfast and immovable in your faith. Consider how you can abound in the work of the Lord today. Spend time in silent contemplation, asking God to fill you with the strength and perseverance to serve Him faithfully.

Scripture: 1 Corinthians 15:58
"Therefore, my beloved brethren, be steadfast, immovable, always abounding in the work of the Lord, knowing that your labor is not in vain in the Lord."

Reflection: As we come to the close of this day, let us once again reflect on Paul's encouragement in 1 Corinthians 15:58. Throughout the day, we may have faced challenges and obstacles in our efforts to serve God. This verse reassures us that our labor in the Lord is not in vain. Our steadfastness and commitment to God's work have eternal significance and impact. Take a moment to review the events of this day. Reflect on how you have been steadfast and immovable in your faith and service. Consider the ways in which you have abounded in the work of the Lord. As you prepare for rest tonight, find comfort in the assurance that your efforts have not been in vain, and commit to continuing steadfastly in your service to God.

Prayer: Gracious God, we thank You for the assurance that our labor in You is not in vain. Forgive us for any moments of wavering or discouragement today. Help us to remain steadfast and immovable in our faith and service. Renew our strength and resolve to abound in Your work, knowing that our efforts have eternal significance. Grant us rest tonight, and prepare us for another day of faithful service. In Jesus' name, we pray, Amen.

Meditative Thought: Take a few moments to meditate on 1 Corinthians 15:58. Reflect on the ways you have been steadfast and immovable in your faith and service today. Surrender any feelings of discouragement or weariness to God. Rest in the assurance that your labor is not in vain, and ask God for renewed strength and perseverance for the days ahead.

DECEMBER 24

MORNING DEVOTION

Scripture: Lamentations 3:22-23

"Through the Lord's mercies we are not consumed, because His compassions fail not. They are new every morning; great is Your faithfulness."

Reflection: As we wake up to a new day, Lamentations 3:22-23 reminds us of God's unending mercies and steadfast love. Each morning brings a fresh start, a new opportunity to experience God's compassion and faithfulness. No matter the challenges or struggles of yesterday, today is a new day filled with the promise of God's grace and love. This scripture encourages us to begin our day with gratitude and hope, trusting in the Lord's faithful care.

Prayer: Heavenly Father, we thank You for Your mercies that are new every morning. As we begin this day, help us to be mindful of Your great faithfulness. Fill our hearts with gratitude and hope, knowing that Your compassion never fails. Guide us through this day with Your wisdom and love, and help us to reflect Your grace in all that we do. In Jesus' name, we pray, Amen.

Meditative Thought: Take a moment to meditate on Lamentations 3:22-23. Reflect on the newness of God's mercies every morning. Consider how His faithfulness has sustained you through past challenges and how it will continue to do so today. Spend time in silent contemplation, allowing God's presence to fill you with peace and hope for the day ahead.

Scripture: Lamentations 3:22-23
"Through the Lord's mercies we are not consumed, because His compassions fail not. They are new every morning; great is Your faithfulness."

Reflection: As the day comes to a close, we are reminded once again of God's unfailing mercy and compassion. Reflecting on Lamentations 3:22-23, we can look back on the events of the day with gratitude, knowing that it was God's faithfulness that carried us through. Even if the day brought challenges or disappointments, we can rest in the assurance that tomorrow brings new mercies. This verse invites us to end our day with a heart of thankfulness and a spirit of trust in God's continual care.

Prayer: Gracious God, we thank You for Your mercies that sustained us throughout this day. As we prepare for rest, we reflect on Your great faithfulness and unfailing compassion. Help us to release any worries or burdens from today, trusting that Your mercies will be new again in the morning. Grant us a peaceful night's rest, and renew our strength for the day ahead. In Jesus' name, we pray, Amen.

Meditative Thought: Take a few moments to meditate on Lamentations 3:22-23. Reflect on how God's mercies were evident in your day. Consider any challenges you faced and how His compassion helped you through. Surrender your anxieties and concerns to God, and rest in the promise that His faithfulness and mercy will greet you anew tomorrow. Allow this assurance to bring you peace as you prepare for sleep.

DECEMBER 25

MORNING DEVOTION

Scripture: Luke 2:10-11
"Then the angel said to them, 'Do not be afraid, for behold, I bring you good tidings of great joy which will be to all people. For there is born to you this day in the city of David a Savior, who is Christ the Lord.'"

Reflection: As we begin this day, let us remember the angel's proclamation to the shepherds, a message that has echoed through the ages: "Do not be afraid." This powerful assurance is followed by the announcement of "good tidings of great joy" for all people—the birth of Jesus Christ, our Savior. This message reminds us of God's incredible love for humanity and the hope we have in Christ. No matter what challenges or fears we may face today, we can hold on to the joy and peace that comes from knowing Jesus as our Savior.

Prayer: Heavenly Father, we thank You for the good news of great joy that the angel proclaimed. As we start this day, help us to remember that Jesus, our Savior, has come to bring hope and peace to our lives. Fill our hearts with joy and courage, knowing that we do not need to be afraid because You are with us. Guide us today to share this good news with others through our words and actions. In Jesus' name, we pray, Amen.

Meditative Thought: Take a moment to meditate on Luke 2:10-11. Reflect on the angel's message of "good tidings of great joy" and how this applies to your life today. Consider how you can live out the joy and peace that comes from knowing Jesus. Spend time in silent contemplation, asking God to fill you with His joy and to guide you in sharing His love with others throughout the day.

Scripture: Luke 2:10-11
"Then the angel said to them, 'Do not be afraid, for behold, I bring you good tidings of great joy which will be to all people. For there is born to you this day in the city of David a Savior, who is Christ the Lord.'"

Reflection: As we end this day, let us revisit the angel's message to the shepherds. The announcement of Jesus' birth is a timeless reminder of God's love and the joy that Jesus brings into our lives. Reflect on how this "good tidings of great joy" has influenced your day. Consider the moments when you felt God's presence and the ways in which you experienced His peace. This evening, let us thank God for the gift of His Son and the joy that fills our hearts because of Him.

Prayer: Gracious God, we thank You for the good news of great joy that the birth of Jesus brings to all people. As we prepare to rest tonight, we are grateful for the moments today where we felt Your presence and experienced Your peace. Help us to carry this joy and hope into our lives continually. May we rest securely in the knowledge that our Savior, Christ the Lord, is with us always. Grant us a peaceful night's rest and renew our strength for tomorrow. In Jesus' name, we pray, Amen.

Meditative Thought: Take a few moments to meditate on Luke 2:10-11. Reflect on how the announcement of Jesus' birth has impacted your day. Think about the joy and peace that come from knowing Christ as your Savior. As you prepare for sleep, let go of any worries or fears, resting in the assurance of God's love and the presence of Jesus in your life. Allow this truth to bring you peace and comfort as you end your day.

Scripture: John 14:1
"Let not your heart be troubled; you believe in God, believe also in Me."

Reflection: As we greet this new day, we are met with the comforting words of Jesus from John 14:1. He encourages us not to let our hearts be troubled, but to trust in God and in Him. This assurance from Jesus is a reminder that, no matter what uncertainties or challenges we may face today, we can have peace knowing that He is with us. Believing in Jesus means trusting His promises, His guidance, and His love. It means resting in the knowledge that He is in control, and we are secure in His hands.

Prayer: Heavenly Father, we thank You for the promise of peace and assurance in Your Word. As we start this day, help us to let go of our worries and place our trust in You and in Jesus. Fill our hearts with peace and confidence, knowing that You are with us and that You care for us. Guide us through this day with Your wisdom and love, and help us to reflect Your peace to those around us. In Jesus' name, we pray, Amen.

Meditative Thought: Take a moment to meditate on John 14:1. Reflect on Jesus' command to let not your heart be troubled. Consider what it means to believe in God and in Jesus in your daily life. Spend time in silent contemplation, allowing the peace of Christ to fill your heart and mind, and carry that peace with you throughout the day.

Scripture: John 14:1
"Let not your heart be troubled; you believe in God, believe also in Me."

Reflection: As the day comes to a close, we return to Jesus' comforting words in John 14:1. Reflect on the events of the day and how you responded to challenges or moments of anxiety. Jesus' invitation to not let our hearts be troubled is a powerful reminder of the peace that comes from trusting in Him. No matter what happened today, we can find rest and reassurance in His presence. Believing in Jesus means surrendering our fears and embracing His peace.

Prayer: Gracious God, we thank You for being with us throughout this day. As we prepare for rest, we reflect on Jesus' words and ask for Your peace to fill our hearts. Help us to let go of any anxieties or troubles and to trust fully in You. Thank You for Your constant presence and care. Grant us a restful night's sleep, and renew our strength for tomorrow. In Jesus' name, we pray, Amen.

Meditative Thought: Take a few moments to meditate on John 14:1. Reflect on how you have experienced or struggled with Jesus' command to not let your heart be troubled today. Surrender any remaining worries to Him, and rest in His promise of peace. Allow this time of quiet meditation to bring calm and reassurance to your heart as you prepare for sleep.

Scripture: Ephesians 6:4
"And you, fathers, do not provoke your children to wrath, but bring them up in the training and admonition of the Lord."

Reflection: As we start this new day, Ephesians 6:4 calls parents, especially fathers, to a high standard of nurturing their children. This verse emphasizes the importance of raising children with love, patience, and guidance rooted in the Lord's teachings. It's a reminder to focus on creating a positive, loving environment where children can grow in their faith and character. Rather than provoking anger or frustration, we are encouraged to model Christ-like behavior and provide godly instruction and encouragement. Whether you are a parent, grandparent, or someone who influences young lives, consider how you can positively impact the next generation today. Reflect on ways to nurture, guide, and teach with the heart and wisdom of Christ.

Prayer: Heavenly Father, we thank You for the privilege and responsibility of raising and influencing children. Help us to nurture them with love, patience, and godly wisdom. May we model Christ-like behavior and provide guidance that leads them closer to You. Fill us with Your Spirit, so we may not provoke to anger but train and admonish with Your grace and truth. In Jesus' name, we pray, Amen.

Meditative Thought: Take a moment to meditate on Ephesians 6:4. Reflect on how you can embody the nurturing and instructive role this verse describes. Consider specific actions or words that can positively influence the children in your life today. Spend time in silent contemplation, asking God to give you the wisdom and love needed to fulfill this important role.

Scripture: Ephesians 6:4
"And you, fathers, do not provoke your children to wrath, but bring them up in the training and admonition of the Lord."

Reflection: As the day draws to a close, let us revisit Ephesians 6:4 and reflect on our interactions with children and young people today. This verse challenges us to avoid behaviors that might provoke anger and instead focus on nurturing through godly instruction. Reflect on how you have guided and influenced the children in your life today. Were there moments of frustration or anger? How did you handle those situations? Did you provide the love, patience, and godly instruction this verse calls for? Reflect on your successes and areas for growth. Remember, raising children in the Lord is a daily journey requiring grace and patience, both for the children and for ourselves.

Prayer: Gracious God, we thank You for the guidance and strength You provide in raising and nurturing children. As we reflect on this day, we ask for forgiveness for any moments we may have provoked frustration or anger. Help us to grow in patience, love, and godly wisdom. Guide us in bringing up children in Your training and admonition. Renew our strength and fill us with Your Spirit as we continue this important work. In Jesus' name, we pray, Amen.

Meditative Thought: Take a few moments to meditate on Ephesians 6:4. Reflect on your interactions with children today and how you can improve in nurturing and guiding them according to the Lord's teachings. Surrender any feelings of guilt or frustration to God, and ask for His peace and guidance. Rest in the assurance that God's grace is sufficient for you and that He will continue to equip you for this vital role.

DECEMBER 28

MORNING DEVOTION

Scripture: Deuteronomy 6:6-7
"And these words which I command you today shall be in your heart. You shall teach them diligently to your children, and shall talk of them when you sit in your house, when you walk by the way, when you lie down, and when you rise up."

Reflection: As we begin this new day, we are reminded of the importance of keeping God's commandments in our hearts and teaching them diligently to the next generation. Deuteronomy 6:6-7 emphasizes the continuous and intentional effort required to instill God's Word in our lives and in the lives of our children. This passage encourages us to integrate God's teachings into every aspect of our daily routine—whether we are at home, traveling, resting, or starting our day. Starting today, let us be mindful of how we can incorporate God's Word into our daily activities. Let us seek to embody His commandments and share His truths with those around us, especially our children. throughout our lives.

Prayer: Heavenly Father, thank You for Your Word and the guidance it provides. As we start this day, help us to keep Your commandments in our hearts and diligently teach them to our children and those around us. Give us the wisdom and strength to integrate Your teachings into every aspect of our daily lives. May our actions and words reflect Your love and truth. In Jesus' name, we pray, Amen.

Meditative Thought: Take a moment to meditate on Deuteronomy 6:6-7. Reflect on how you can make God's Word a central part of your day. Consider specific moments—whether at home, on the go, or during quiet times—when you can focus on His teachings and share them with others.

Scripture: Deuteronomy 6:6-7
"And these words which I command you today shall be in your heart. You shall teach them diligently to your children, and shall talk of them when you sit in your house, when you walk by the way, when you lie down, and when you rise up."

Reflection: As the day draws to a close, we reflect on the words of Deuteronomy 6:6-7 and how we have integrated God's commandments into our lives today. This passage encourages us to keep God's Word at the forefront of our minds and to teach it diligently to our children. Reflect on the conversations and actions of your day—did you make an effort to incorporate God's teachings into your routine? Did you find opportunities to share His Word with others, especially with your children. As we wind down, let us commit to making God's Word an integral part of our lives, not just today, but every day. Let us seek ways to instill His teachings in our hearts and in the hearts of those we influence.

Prayer: Gracious God, we thank You for Your Word and the guidance it provides. As we reflect on this day, we ask for Your forgiveness for any moments we missed to share Your teachings. Help us to be more diligent in keeping Your commandments in our hearts and in teaching them to our children and those around us. As we prepare for rest, fill us with Your peace and renew our commitment to live according to Your Word. In Jesus' name, we pray, Amen.

Meditative Thought: Take a few moments to and reflect on the ways you have incorporated God's Word into your day and how you can do so more intentionally in the future. Think about specific times and places where you can discuss and teach His commandments with those around you. As you prepare for sleep, ask God to help you carry His Word in your heart and live it out each day.

Scripture: Luke 24:31a
"Then their eyes were opened and they knew Him;"

Reflection: As we rise to a new day, Luke 24:31a reminds us of the moment when the disciples' eyes were opened, and they recognized the risen Jesus. This verse invites us to begin our day with a desire for spiritual awakening and a deeper recognition of Jesus in our lives. Each morning is an opportunity to seek a fresh revelation of Christ, to see Him in the everyday moments, and to recognize His presence with us. Starting today, let us pray for open eyes and hearts that are attuned to Jesus. Let us look for Him in our interactions, in nature, in the quiet moments, and in the hustle and bustle of daily life. May we be attentive to His guidance and His love throughout the day.

Prayer: Heavenly Father, as we begin this day, we pray that You open our eyes to see Jesus in all aspects of our lives. Help us to recognize His presence and to be aware of His guidance and love. May we be attentive to Your voice and responsive to Your leading. Fill our hearts with the joy of knowing that You are with us always. In Jesus' name, we pray, Amen.

Meditative Thought: Take a moment to meditate on Luke 24:31a. Imagine the joy and surprise of the disciples when they recognized Jesus. Reflect on how you can be more aware of Jesus' presence in your daily life. Spend a few minutes in silent contemplation, asking God to open your eyes and heart to His presence today.

Scripture: Luke 24:31a
"Then their eyes were opened and they knew Him;"

Reflection: As the day comes to an end, we reflect on the ways we have encountered Jesus today. Luke 24:31a speaks of a profound moment of recognition and awareness. Reflect on your day—were there moments when you felt particularly aware of Jesus' presence? Did you see His hand at work in your life and the lives of those around you? This evening, let us give thanks for the moments when our eyes were opened to recognize Jesus. Let us also seek forgiveness for any missed opportunities to see Him. As we prepare for rest, we can ask God to continue opening our eyes and deepening our understanding of His presence.

Prayer: Gracious God, we thank You for the moments today when our eyes were opened, and we recognized Your presence. Forgive us for any times we were too distracted to see You. As we rest tonight, we ask that You continue to open our eyes and hearts to Your presence. Help us to carry the awareness of Your love and guidance into tomorrow. In Jesus' name, we pray, Amen.

Meditative Thought: Take a few moments to meditate on Luke 24:31a. Reflect on the moments of your day when you felt Jesus' presence. Consider how you can cultivate a deeper awareness of Him in your daily life. As you prepare for sleep, ask God to reveal Himself to you in new and profound ways, and rest in the assurance of His constant presence.

DECEMBER 30

MORNING DEVOTION

Scripture: Revelation 21:5
"Then He who sat on the throne said, 'Behold, I make all things new.' And He said to me, 'Write, for these words are true and faithful.'"

Reflection: As we begin this new day, let us reflect on the profound promise of renewal found in Revelation 21:5. God declares, "Behold, I make all things new." This verse reminds us that God is continually at work, transforming and renewing all aspects of our lives and the world around us. Each morning is an opportunity to experience His newness—new mercies, new beginnings, and new possibilities. Let this truth fill our hearts with hope and expectancy as we go about our day, knowing that God's faithful and true words assure us of His ongoing work in our lives.

Prayer: Heavenly Father, thank You for the promise of making all things new. As we start this day, we invite You to renew our hearts and minds. Help us to see the new opportunities and blessings that You have prepared for us today. Fill us with Your hope and joy, and guide us to live in the light of Your faithful and true words. In Jesus' name, we pray, Amen.

Meditative Thought: Take a moment to meditate on Revelation 21:5. Imagine the transformative power of God's promise to make all things new. Consider areas in your life where you need renewal and invite God to bring His newness into those areas. Spend a few minutes in silent contemplation, allowing the hope of God's promise to fill your heart and mind as you prepare for the day.

Scripture: Revelation 21:5

"Then He who sat on the throne said, 'Behold, I make all things new.' And He said to me, 'Write, for these words are true and faithful.'"

Reflection: As the day draws to a close, we return to the comforting words of Revelation 21:5. Reflect on how God's promise of making all things new has been evident in your life today. Consider the moments of renewal, transformation, or new beginnings you experienced. This verse reassures us that God's work in our lives is ongoing and that His words are trustworthy and true. As we reflect on the day, let us give thanks for His faithfulness and look forward to the newness He will bring tomorrow.

Prayer: Gracious God, thank You for Your promise to make all things new. As we reflect on this day, we are grateful for the moments of renewal and transformation we experienced. Forgive us for any missed opportunities to embrace Your newness. As we prepare for rest, we trust in Your faithful and true words, knowing that You are continually at work in our lives. Renew our strength and fill us with hope for tomorrow. In Jesus' name, we pray, Amen.

Meditative Thought: Take a few moments to meditate on Revelation 21:5. Reflect on how you witnessed God's promise of making things new in your life today. Think about the areas where you need God's renewing touch and invite Him to continue His work in those areas. As you prepare for sleep, rest in the assurance of God's faithful and true promise, and let His peace fill your heart.

DECEMBER 31

MORNING DEVOTION

Scripture: Revelation 22:20-21

"He who testifies to these things says, 'Surely I am coming quickly.' Amen. Even so, come, Lord Jesus! The grace of our Lord Jesus Christ be with you all. Amen."

Reflection: As we begin this new day, let us reflect on the words of Revelation 22:20-21. This passage concludes the book of Revelation with a powerful declaration of Jesus' imminent return. The phrase "Surely I am coming quickly" echoes with a sense of urgency and anticipation. It reminds us to live with expectant hearts, eagerly awaiting the glorious return of our Lord Jesus Christ. As we go about our day, let us remember the hope of His coming and the assurance of His grace. May our hearts be filled with longing for His presence, and may His grace empower us to live faithfully until He comes again.

Prayer: Heavenly Father, we thank You for the promise of Jesus' swift return. Help us to live each day with eager anticipation of His coming. Fill our hearts with hope and excitement as we await the fulfillment of Your kingdom. May Your grace sustain us and empower us to live faithfully until that glorious day. In Jesus' name, we pray, Amen.

Meditative Thought: Take a moment to meditate on Revelation 22:20-21. Reflect on the promise of Jesus' return and what it means for your life. Consider how you can live with a sense of expectancy and readiness for His coming. Spend a few moments in silent contemplation, inviting the Holy Spirit to fill you with hope and grace as you begin your day.

Scripture: Revelation 22:20-21
"He who testifies to these things says, 'Surely I am coming quickly.'
Amen. Even so, come, Lord Jesus! The grace of our Lord Jesus Christ
be with you all. Amen."

Reflection: As the day comes to a close, let us return to the words of
Revelation 22:20-21. This passage concludes the book of Revelation with
a fervent prayer for the Lord Jesus to come quickly. It serves as a reminder
to end each day with a longing for His return and a desire for His grace
to be with us. As we prepare for rest, let us echo the prayer of "Even so,
come, Lord Jesus!" with sincerity and anticipation. May His grace continue to sustain us through the night, and may we awake with renewed
hope and expectancy for the day when He will return in glory.

Prayer: Gracious God, as we close this day, we pray for the swift return
of Your Son, our Lord Jesus Christ. Come quickly, Lord Jesus, and bring
Your kingdom of peace and righteousness. May Your grace continue to
abide with us through the night, comforting us and strengthening us for
the days ahead. In Jesus' name, we pray, Amen.

Meditative Thought: Take a few moments to meditate on Revelation
22:20-21. Reflect on your longing for Jesus' return and the grace that
sustains you each day. Surrender any worries or burdens to Him, and
rest in the assurance of His faithful promise to come again. Allow His
peace to fill your heart as you prepare for sleep.

Made in the USA
Columbia, SC
03 November 2024

45553203R00443